The Handbook of Continuing Professional Development for the Health Informatics Professional

Second Edition

The Handbook of Continuing Professional Development for the Health Informatics Professional

Second Edition

JoAnn Klinedinst,

M.ED., CPHIMS, PMP, DES, CPTD, FHIMSS, FACHE, FCAHME

Foreword by Hal Wolf, FHIMSS, President & CEO, HIMSS

Routledge
Taylor & Francis Group

A PRODUCTIVITY PRESS BOOK

First edition published 2017
Second edition published 2021

by Routledge
600 Broken Sound Parkway #300, Boca Raton FL, 33487

and by Routledge
2 Park Square, Milton Park, Abingdon, Oxon, OX14 4RN

Routledge is an imprint of the Taylor & Francis Group, an informa business.

ISBN: 978-0-367-02685-1 (hbk)
ISBN: 978-0-367-02678-3 (pbk)
ISBN: 978-0-429-39837-7 (ebk)

DOI: 10.4324/9780429398377

Typeset in Times
by MPS Limited, Dehradun

Contents

SECTION I   Positioning The Health IT Professional For Lifelong CPD

SECTION II   Establishing and Nurturing Your Career

SECTION III   Learning From Others

SECTION IV   The Aspiring Leader

Foreword

Today, seismic change is constant in both our professional and personal lives. We have been forced to embrace uncertainty and ambiguity like never before—and we must prepare ourselves for inevitable continued change in the global health ecosystem. During this period of disruption, it is essential that health informatics professionals have professional development plans that provide a pathway for the future and that can be updated as the healthcare landscape evolves.

The Handbook of Continuing Professional Development for the Health Informatics Professional, Second Edition offers tools and resources to prepare emerging health informatics leaders for the challenges of today and tomorrow. It includes five new sections encompassing 27 essential career topics, as well as a new section focused on issues and trends that have taken on critical importance during the COVID-19 pandemic—such as digital health transformation, accelerating innovation, caring for the underserved, ethical standards, the workforce of the future, and the clinically integrated supply chain.

Whether you want to develop a career road map, differentiate yourself with professional certification, learn from others through mentoring, understand the multi-generational workplace, or expand your knowledge in myriad other ways, this handbook is an invaluable resource on your health informatics career journey.

As you embrace healthcare's ongoing challenges and opportunities with remarkable dedication and passion, I wish you continued success. Thank you for all you do, every day, to transform health and wellness for all.

Hal Wolf, FHIMSS
President and CEO, HIMSS

Accelerate: A Digital Ecosystem Designed for Health IT Professionals

Engaging in professional development and networking activities are critical for anyone in the healthcare information and technology industry. But with rapid change occurring at unparalleled speed, not to mention the pressures of delivering care during the COVID-19 pandemic, it's even more important for health information and technology professionals to have access to tools and resources that are easy to use and fulfill the specific needs of a healthcare audience. HIMSS has responded to these challenges.

Debuting in July 2021, Accelerate (youraccelerate.com) was created to drive 365 healthcare digital transformation by connecting health professionals to insights from peers and thought leaders, professional development tools, networking opportunities and curated content—anytime, anywhere. Designed as a natural extension of HIMSS's origins and foundation as a member-driven society, Accelerate is the first digital transformation platform built solely for the global health ecosystem that enables connecting, collaborating, learning, engaging all in one place

With Accelerate, professionals can collaborate directly with peers and thought leaders, utilize professional development tools, participate in networking opportunities, and access curated content – all specifically designed for a healthcare audience. Organizations benefit from radically improved ways of managing, supporting, and developing their staff and members.

While over three dozen chapters in *The Handbook of Continuing Professional Development for the Health Informatics Professional, 2nd edition* that will help you grow and nurture your career, Accelerate supplements your goals by combining professional networking and professional development, digitally, to drive your career in any direction you desire.

Dennis Upah
Managing Director, Accelerate,
HIMSS Solution

Reflections on My Career

Maybe I am one of those rare people who worked their entire career – 46 years – in some part of the healthcare field. I had humble beginnings in an Upstate New York nursing home washing dishes and later moved to Strong Memorial Hospital working their cafeteria tray line for the patients. Then throughout college I worked at other Rochester healthcare facilities designing a new, automated purchasing system. When I graduated from college, I continued to have increased roles in healthcare.

I outline this because I have learned that there are two factors that can greatly influence your career development. The first is your education. I perceive this as the foundation for everything that you will develop and build on throughout your career. The second are your experiences. When I say experiences, I encompass everything—not just work experience. While it is true that work experience will be specifically outlined on your resume, it is the other life experiences that shape you and the decisions you will make. As you move through your life, those experiences will greatly influence your career.

Starting with education, it is certainly different today than it was when I was in school. Of note: I obtained an Associate's degree in Optical Engineering, a Bachelor's in Computer Science, and then a Master's in Public Administration. However, degrees today are much more specialized. It can be a daunting decision to make, when faced with many options at the start of your educational journey. Rest assured, that during my tenure I have hired many people that did not have a specific degree in an area that I was hiring for, but they had the experiences along the way that made them the best candidate for the job.

Experience is where you will develop the "house above the foundation" of your education. Early in my career, I took on as many roles as I could for each position I accepted. For example, in addition to creating and running the IT department for a facility (aging myself here!), I took on the work associated with for-profit housing and established a formal set of procedures and policies for the procurement department. What is key to understand here is that these experiences not only add to your toolbox of skills and make you a more well-rounded resource, but more importantly, they expose you to other smart people that you can network with and learn from.

Similar to gaining experience through paid employment opportunities, volunteering is another excellent way of increasing your personal and professional network as well as learning more about the other opportunities that abound from people who live those experiences every day. I chose to volunteer in three different ways. The first was doing something that would benefit the community in which I live. I became a Board member for a group that helped people stay out of nursing homes by providing services so they could remain independent. The second was volunteering for something specific in my field of expertise that would help improve operations for healthcare while expanding my technical skills. My example is helping to develop the first automated resource utilization Groups (RUGS) for New York State.

Lastly, but certainly very important, was volunteering for HIMSS. I have been a HIMSS member for over 15 years and during this time I have volunteered on several committees, helped with many white papers, developed tools for our constituency, and served as Board member for local chapters.

HIMSS can be your ultimate networking experience. There are so many ways you can volunteer and help improve healthcare while gaining strong, relative experience that will not only guide you as you move through your healthcare career but also enable you to meet so many intelligent career-oriented people with differing experiences that can help shape your future goals. For example, today I am the Chair of the HIMSS Professional Development Committee. Our goal is to develop methodologies in many forms to help people both new in their career or looking to do something a bit different. Our Committee is focused on providing education in many forms to help the current and future leaders of healthcare.

In closing, I'd be remiss in not recognizing all of the authors of this second edition, and the first edition too, for their contribution to all of us in sharing their experiences on the important topics delivered in these chapters. I would also like to recognize all of the members of the HIMSS Team that I have worked with over the years, especially JoAnn Klinedinst whose dedication to this effort has been phenomenal. In addition, I'd like to thank Mari Greenberger, a recently departed HIMSS employee, who worked closely with me throughout the years on Interoperability committees. Mari was always there to help with her great knowledge not only in the field, but her vast experience with the key players as well.

Joseph J. Wagner
MPA, FHIMSS

My Career Journey

Professional development is a lifelong journey. Fortunately, I learned about the importance of professional development from a faculty advisor during my undergraduate college experience. The two key components I learned early in my career were joining a professional organization and obtaining continuing education. You are fortunate to have at your fingertips the advice of many experts on a diverse set of topics all related to professional development. *The Handbook of Continuing Professional Development for the Health Informatics Professional, Second Edition* can get you started on your lifelong journey in professional development. There are suggestions on a variety of topics and you are certain to find many of interest.

My personal journey in professional development started right out of college as I joined the American Nurses Association and registered for a licensure exam review course in preparation to become a registered nurse. I knew early in my nursing career that I was interested in leadership roles, so over time I further enrolled in continuing education on a variety of management topics. As I was considering applying for admittance to a university for an advanced degree, I took an undergraduate-level course entitled "Introduction to Computers." This course really marks the start of my transition into the informatics space within healthcare. I had an informatics leadership mentor who recommended I join and actively participate in the North Carolina Nurses Association Council on Nursing Informatics. This group offered excellent learning and networking opportunities with a group of open and welcoming members. Around the same time, I became a member of HIMSS and later started volunteering within the organization. Professional organizations have offered me the opportunity to be mentored, take on leadership roles, mentor others, achieve certification, and obtain professional advancement.

While I was fortunate to obtain good advice at the start of my journey, I want to acknowledge how much easier my journey could have been having the advice in this handbook readily available. Some key items for me would have been the chapters on "Creating a Personal Brand" and "Developing a Career Roadmap," along with the sections on "Learning from Others" and "The Aspiring Leader". This second edition offers a new section on "Industry Influences Critical to Your Career" with key chapters on a number of timely topics. Readers, I hope you find many chapters of interest whether your style is to pick and choose or read from cover to cover.

Anyone working in health informatics knows the pace of change has always been high. A global pandemic has pushed the pace of change to an even higher level with technology changes being a core component. Having a handbook and guide to assist you in putting your best foot forward and maintaining a competitive edge is a timely and welcome addition.

Thanks to all my peers, mentors, faculty, and leaders along the way who listened, coached, and advised me to become a better health informatics professional, and helped shape who I am today. I could not have done it without you! I hope each of you reading finds a spark within that helps you become your better self.

Kay S. Lytle,
DNP, RN-BC, NEA-BC, CPHIMS, FHMISS

Editor

JoAnn Klinedinst, M.Ed., CPHIMS, PMP, DES, CPTD, LFHIMSS, FCAHME, FACHE, is vice president of professional development for HIMSS, based in Chicago, IL, U.S. She defines strategies that attribute to the lifelong learning, continuing engagement, and professional development for 108,000+ (2021) health information and technology professionals globally. Prior to her position with HIMSS, Ms. Klinedinst held various management positions spanning 18 years in the applications and development and support discipline at Doylestown Hospital, Doylestown, Pennsylvania. During this time, she also served as an engaged volunteer with HIMSS, having been a HIMSS Board-appointed chair to the Annual Conference Education Committee, a member of the Public Policy Committee, and served on number task forces. A lifelong learner, Ms. Klinedinst holds a Master's in Adult Education from The Pennsylvania State University as well as various industry certifications. She is Board Certified in healthcare management by the American College of Healthcare Executives and she is a Life Fellow of HIMSS. Additionally, Ms. Klinedinst volunteers her time by serving on various national boards that promote the transformation of healthcare information and technology initiatives.

Contributors

Kerry Amato, CAE, is the Executive Director of Health Innovation for HIMSS, where she leads healthcare innovation strategy and business unit operations for HIMSS that includes two global membership organizations; Health 2.0 and the Personal Connected Health Alliance (PCHA) as well as the HIMSS Innovation Brand, Accelerate Health. In her dynamic role her and her team execute on robust product portfolio aimed at accelerating the development and adoption of health technologies through market research, events, policy efforts, networking and global membership activities. Mrs. Amato is a proud graduate of the University of Iowa and received her CAE in 2014 and in 2016 was named one of *Connect Association Magazine's* "Top 40 Under 40" award winners. Most recently, she received Association Forum's 40 Under 40 Award in 2018 for her work to expand HIMSS' product offerings for the venture and startup audiences. She currently resides in Chicago, IL, and when she is not wearing one of her multiple hats (mom, podcast host, boss lady, volunteer, thought leader), you will find her seeking a little "room to breathe."

Fran Ayalasomayajula is an executive healthcare strategist and technologist with over 20 years of leadership experience. She is dedicated to serving the health needs of populations around the world, and is presently the Head of Digital Health, Worldwide at HP Inc. Prior to HP, Fran worked for major health and life science institutions, including the Pan American Health Organization, Bristol Myers Squibb, and UnitedHealth Group. Fran is a devoted volunteer serving as the President of Reach, a global non-profit social impact organization, and a board member of multiple industry leading organizations, including the Consumer Technology Association Health and Fitness Division and NHA of San Diego. Fran is also the author of several publications on a variety of healthcare topics, including best practices for the successful adoption of virtual reality in the clinical setting, scaling global connected health programs, clinical empathy, technology adoption for aging well, and the deployment of digital technology for the prevention of maternal mortality and morbidity.

Jason Bickford is an award-winning health information technology leader focused on maximizing outcomes by developing trusting relationships, analyzing business processes, and enabling technology adoption. A highly-skilled technology strategist who acts as a change champion in converting technology plans into workable solutions while benchmarking performance against key operational metrics. Serves as a bold, creative, and forward-thinking collaborator that is adept at bridging the gap between people, process, and technology & between IT and Business\Clinic departments.

As the 2015 HIMSS Founders Leadership Award recipient, he has a proven track record in promoting, supporting and being an advocate for Healthcare Information Technology education, networking, and process change. As an industry thought leader, he is aimed to align stakeholders for improved patient outcomes and in lowering operating costs.

Richard E. Biehl teaches quality and systems engineering in the Healthcare Systems Engineering master's program in the College of Engineering & Computer Science at the University of Central Florida. He served as a Black Belt in industry, mostly at Honeywell from 1995 to 2006, before shifting exclusively into healthcare in 2007. He specializes in using informatics to improve healthcare systems, publishing a book on Data Warehousing for Biomedical Informatics through CRC Press in 2016.

Dr. Anthony Blash received his Bachelor's in Computer Science from Kean University, his Bachelor's in Pharmacy from Long Island University, and his Doctor of Pharmacy degree from Creighton University. Dr. Blash also completed his Pharmacy Informatics residency at Creighton and is currently responsible for the Healthcare Informatics concentration of the Pharm. D. Curriculum at the Belmont University College of Pharmacy in Nashville, TN. As a result of meeting the Healthcare Information and Management Systems Society's (HIMSS) rigorous standards for quality healthcare education, The College of Pharmacy at Belmont University was named the society's inaugural HIMSS Approved Education Partner (AEP).

Dr. Tiffany Champagne-Langabeer is an assistant professor at the UTHealth School of Biomedical Informatics where she teaches health informatics, telehealth, and technology management. Prior to working at UT Health, she served as the founding vice president of Healthconnect, the ONC-funded health information exchange for Southeast Texas. Dr. Champagne-Langabeer is also a registered dietitian with a passion for preventive healthcare. She received her PhD in Healthcare Management from UTHSC. Dr. Champagne-Langabeer is a member of HIMSS, AMIA, ACHE, and the Academy of Nutrition and Dietetics. She co-authored several articles in peer-reviewed journals, including *JHIM*.

Michelle Cotton is the CFO and Privacy Officer for the Clinical Operations Group (COG) at HCA Healthcare. Michelle began her career in HCA Internal Audit in 2002 and held numerous positions within Internal Audit before joining COG. Michelle holds a BS in Accounting and MBA from Western Kentucky University and is a Certified Public Accountant (CPA), Certified Fraud Examiner (CFE), Certified Internal Auditor (CIA), Certified Construction Auditor (CCA), and Certified Professional in Health Information and Management Systems (CPHIMS).

Dr. Selena Davis has more than 25 years of combined experience in the Canadian healthcare and health informatics industries, research, and academia. She is an Adjunct Professor at University of British Columbia Faculty of Medicine, Department of Family Practice, and a Director of an independent consulting firm, providing strategic and operational executive leadership to organizations in health informatics and data science. Selena completed her PhD in Health Informatics at the University of Victoria, Canada. She has authored numerous publications including peer-reviewed journals, white-papers, conference papers, and book chapters. Selena holds both PMP and CPHIMS-CA certifications. Her research interests are integrated patient-provider digital health systems, implementation science and implementation practice, and patient engagement.

Avni Doshi, PharmD Candidate currently serves as the domestic HISMM TIGER™ Scholars Informatics intern. She is pursuing a Doctorate in Pharmacy at the University of Texas College of Pharmacy in Austin, Texas. Avni's previously spent time working as a project manager at a technology-based start-up focused on the execution of successful enterprise solutions. She received her Bachelor of Science in Health Policy from the University of Alabama at Birmingham.

Dr. Anne L. Drabczyk is an Associate Professor and Chair of the Healthcare Management Department at Indian River State College on Florida's Treasure Coast. Anne is an international research partner with University of Limerick, Ireland on their Public and Patient Involvement Grant, funded by the Irish Health Research Board. Anne earned Fulbright Specialist designation through the U.S. Department of State, Bureau of Educational and Cultural Affairs. In previous positions, Anne served as Director of the Advanced Practice Center at the National Association of County and City Health Officials in Washington D.C. She was the principal investigator for The Ohio State University College of Public Health, where she liaised with the Ohio Department of Health on preparedness initiatives for community readiness, resilience, and recovery. She has consulted for several clients in the public health enterprise, and was interim CEO, directing reorganization of a national healthcare organization. Anne earned a Doctor of Philosophy degree in public health from Walden University, Minneapolis, MN. She retains a Master of Arts degree in health administration and a Bachelor of Science degree in community health education and psychology from Central Michigan University, Mount Pleasant, MI. She is certified in the Appreciative Inquiry protocol from the Weatherhead School of Management at Case Western Reserve University, Cleveland, OH. Dr. Drabczyk is a sought-after conference presenter and keynote speaker, and has led international workshops in Scotland, Ireland, Nepal, and Canada. She is the author of several peer-reviewed journal articles and books, and most recently published *Healthcare Workforce Transitioning: Competency Conversations through World Café*.

John Eckmann is an accomplished health information technology professional with vision and proven successes navigating complex initiatives from feasibility to reality. His experiences as an health IT professional include numerous care settings: clinical, acute, post-acute, etc. As an executive who leverages best practices to achieve results, he is recognized as a leader who contributes value. Additionally, he is aware of the industry's trending reports indicating careers in information security and privacy are much needed and one of the top ten fastest growing professions. He has recently completed a postgraduate certificate in Information Assurance, Security and Privacy at the University of North Carolina at Greensboro. Since 2006, he is a CPHIMS. He served on the HIMSS Enterprise Information Systems Steering Committee in 2006.

Vic Eilenfield served as the Nation's Interim Deputy National Coordinator for Health Information Technology at the Department of Health and Human Services. He is now President and CEO of a health information technology firm focusing principally on health information exchange at national and regional levels, including those between the Departments of Defense (DoD) and Veterans Affairs (VA). During his military career, he managed the military EHR program as well as data warehousing and analytical resources programs. Consulting in the private sector, he informs corporations' responses to national rule-making processes in the area of health information technology.

Leslie Evans is passionate about mission driven innovation which impacts the lives of diverse people through education, healthcare, technology, and workforce development. Leslie is the Director, Social Impact, HIMSS Institute, leading efforts to engage new audiences and nurture an environment which accelerates the growth of new ideas to advance innovation and transform health and healthcare for all people. Her pathway into health IT started with her entrepreneurial experience and love of education. While working as the Director of Strategic Programs, charged with developing alternate sources of revenue for an all-girls K-12 independent school, Leslie launched "Music with a Mission" which grew to become the largest music festival in Northeast Ohio, LaurelLive. She also encountered bootstrapped entrepreneurs whose lack of coding skills were constraining growth. She heard very clearly: "These girls need to learn to CODE!" As a result, Leslie spearheaded the development of a suite of educational programs to engage more girls in STEM. Working with Laurel School's Center for Research on Girls helped her to further understand the barriers to engaging more girls in STEM, such as stereotype threat and imposter syndrome. As she recognized how far educational institutions needed to go to fill the gap to engage more girls in computer science, she transitioned to her next role as President of a coding bootcamp focused upon bridging the diversity divide in tech. Leslie represented coding bootcamps at The White House Summit on Inclusion in Tech (2016) and partnered with Fortune 500 companies to help fill their tech talent pipeline with diverse developers. She also serves on a regional, collaborative board seeking to attract more talent into health IT careers. At HIMSS, a global non-profit at the intersection of healthcare and technology, Leslie has served as the Director of the HIMSS Innovation Center and the primary architect of the HIMSS Global Health

Equity Network. Leslie sees the intersection of innovation and health equity as crucial as we seek to design solutions which improve health outcomes for our most vulnerable populations. Leslie's leadership roles have crossed industry sectors all the while building upon a consistent theme and ability to help businesses align strategy and mission to grow, drive new market opportunities, and identify innovative pathways to enhance the lives of underrepresented communities.

Nanne M. Finis, RN, MS, is the chief nurse executive for UKG (Ultimate Kronos Group), a global provider of HCM, payroll, HR service delivery, and workforce management solutions. At UKG, Finis applies her strong foundational knowledge of the global healthcare system to advance the application of innovative technology to create more meaningful and connected work experiences for all healthcare employees. A 40-year industry executive consistently focused on nursing and patient care delivery, Finis is passionate about building and leading a culture of innovation and collaboration across clinical, operational, and administrative environments, and has committed her career to driving improvements in the healthcare system. Since joining UKG, Finis has expanded the company's influence and impact within the healthcare industry through inspired initiatives. Most recently, Finis established the UKG Chief Nurse Executive Advisory Board, a group of recognized leaders from healthcare organizations across the continuum of care, whose ideas, insights, and feedback help shape the future of UKG strategies and solutions. She also launched a bimonthly speaker series in which healthcare leaders share their perspective on industry issues and challenges with UKG employees. Finis additionally serves on the advisory board of The Workforce Institute at UKG, a global think tank that empowers organizations with education, research, and practical ideas for optimizing the 21st century workplace. Before joining UKG, Finis was nurse executive for TeleTracking Technologies, where she formed and led an advisory service optimizing patient flow processes and technology adoption at hospitals nationwide. Earlier in her career, Finis spent more than two decades at Northwestern Memorial Hospital in both clinical and progressive management roles. She then transitioned to Joint Commission Resources (JCR), the knowledge transfer subsidiary of The Joint Commission, where she designed and led the U.S. patient safety and quality consulting practice and operationalized the industry alliance strategy. Finis earned her master's degree in nursing from the University of Illinois at Chicago and earned her bachelor's degree in nursing from Saint Mary's College in South Bend, Indiana. She also spent five years in Tokyo, Japan, attending the International School of the Sacred Heart (ISSH). Currently, Finis serves on the American Organization of Nurse Leaders (AONL) Foundation Corporate Advisory Council.

Mari Greenberger, MPPA, was most recently the Senior Director of Informatics for HIMSS, a global, cause-based, not-for-profit organization focused on realizing the full health potential of every human, everywhere. In this role she executed and directed all Health Information Exchange (HIE), standards, and interoperability initiatives including HIMSS Global Interoperability Showcases. This included all related thought leadership and programming activities and public policy efforts. The area's content scope includes health information exchange, blockchain, public health, and interoperability initiatives. She informed and oversaw the development of strategic goals and related budgets. Greenberger began working for HIMSS in 2006, where she served as a member of the Government Relations team in Washington D.C., where she worked with the Advocacy & Public Policy Community and Congressional Affairs. Greenberger then transitioned to the Professional Development team where she worked with subject matter experts to develop programming for the HIMSS Global Conference & Exhibition. In 2019, Greenberger was promoted to senior director of the Informatics team, which is a part of the Technology & Innovation business unit of HIMSS. Prior to rejoining HIMSS in 2014 as a member of the Informatics team, Greenberger was a part of the initial planning, launching and implementation for the MetroChicago Health Information Exchange, where she served as principal liaison and relationship manager between metropolitan Chicago stakeholders and leadership, the State of Illinois, regional HIE leadership, Illinois Regional Extension Centers (RECs) and other stakeholders. Greenberger has experience contributing to the strategic direction of program development and implementation for large-scale national improvement projects preventing healthcare associated infections while working for the Health Research and Educational Trust at the American Hospital Association. In 2017, Greenberger received the honor of being named one of Association Forum and USAE's Forty Under 40®. This prestigious program recognizes 40 accomplished association or non-profit professionals who are under the age of 40, demonstrate high potential for continued success in leadership roles and exhibit a strong passion for—and commitment to—the association management and nonprofit industries.

Christopher B. Harris has 21 years' experience in healthcare. He spent more than 8 years as an accomplished Information Services (IS) leader within academic medical center organizations with broad understanding of the IS role, including governance, planning, project management/delivery, aligning change sponsorship for success, and developing staff." He has demonstrated success over 13 years in top-tier consulting organizations and has a proven track record of large technology-enabled change in complex academic multiple entity healthcare institutions.

Robert Havasy is Senior Director of Connected Health at HIMSS and the Managing Director of the Personal Connected Health Alliance. In this role he focuses on issues around connected health, including remote patient monitoring, telemedicine, patient engagement, shared decision-making, and interoperability. In 2018, he also served on the Office of the National Coordinator for Health IT's US Core Data for Interoperability Task Force. Prior to joining HIMSS, Mr. Havasy was the Corporate Team Lead for Product and Technology Development at the Center for Connected Health (CCH), part of the Mass General Brigham System in Boston, Massachusetts. At CCH Mr. Havasy lead the team that integrated the Center's technology with Mass General Brigham's enterprise clinical systems. Major achievements of the Center include connecting remote patient monitoring data to Mass General Brigham's electronic medical record (EMR) system, the integration of consumer activity monitoring data with the EMR, and a new platform for acquiring and integrating Patient Reported Outcome Measures data into clinical practice. Prior to joining CCH, Mr. Havasy held a variety of positions over 10 years in Sales, Marketing, and Services with Enterasys Networks (now part of Extreme Networks), culminating as Service Operations Manager where he had responsibility for Maintenance and Professional Services offerings and for driving global service revenues of over $100 million annually. Mr. Havasy holds a B.S. in Environmental Science from Keene State College and an M.S. in Health and Medical Informatics from Brandeis University. When not geeking out with some new tech gadget, Rob can be found hiking the woods and mountains of New England or at home perfecting his barbeque skills. He spends time as a volunteer for the Trustees of Reservations, where he helps maintain a 196 acre open-space preserve in Central Massachusetts and other properties around the state. He's also a motorcycle rider, a welder, a gardener, and amateur maple syrup maker.

John P. Hoyt, FACHE, FHIMSS, is Executive Vice President Emeritus, HIMSS Analytics at the Healthcare Information and Management Systems Society, the largest U.S. not-for-profit healthcare caused-based organization focused on providing global leadership for the optimal use of information technology. While a full-time Executive Vice President, Mr. Hoyt was responsible for providing executive leadership and direction to HIMSS Analytics worldwide, where he also provided direction for all Stage 6 and Stage 7 validations and derivative research. Now as EVP Emeritus, Mr. Hoyt continues to conduct Stage 6 and Stage 7 validations, conduct consulting engagements globally and is the principle architect and interpreter of the revised acute care EMRAM standards which were announced at HIMSS 2016 in Las Vegas for use in 2017.

Throughout his healthcare career, Hoyt has been instrumental in defining business and IT strategy as well as selecting, implementing, and integrating mission-critical healthcare information systems across the enterprise. Before joining HIMSS, Hoyt served as a hospital Chief Operating Officer and twice as a Chief Information Officer with various healthcare organizations, accumulating in over 22 years of hospital executive committee leadership experience. Mr. Hoyt served in consultancy practices, including IBM Healthlink Services and First Data Health Systems Group.

Hoyt holds a BSBA in Economics from Xavier University in Cincinnati, Ohio, and an MHA from St. Louis University in Missouri. He is an HIMSS Fellow and a Fellow of the American College of Healthcare Executives (ACHE).

Dr. Christine A. Hudak is Professor and Director of the Health Informatics program at Kent State University, School of Library & Information Science. She is also a Contributing Interdisciplinary Faculty Member in the School of Digital Sciences. She has more than 30 years of experience in Health Care Informatics, including teaching, instructional development, systems analysis, systems implementation, and data analysis. Her professional affiliations include the AMIA, ANIA ASHIM, HIMSS, and the National Institutes of Health Informatics in Canada. She is a member of the Health Informatics Society of Ireland and is a United Kingdom Certified Health Information Professional. She received her BSN from Case Western University. Her MEd in postsecondary education and her PhD in Urban Education Administration were both earned from Cleveland State University (CSU), focusing on adult learning, curriculum development, instructional design, educational administration, and computer uses in education. Her dissertation title was: "Organizational Factors in the Implementation of End User Computing Systems in Ohio Hospitals."

Amir Ismail is a Senior Research Executive at IPSOS, working in healthcare research for two years. He holds a master's degree in Pharmacy and also has experience working in a community pharmacy. Amir currently works on a number of quantitative and qualitative projects, across numerous therapy areas including HIV, cardiology, and diabetes mellitus, where his specialty lies. With a passion for connected health himself, Amir is a proud member of the connected health center of excellence at IPSOS and works across a variety of connected health projects bringing innovative ideas to the project team to make an impact and pioneer developments in big data, wearable technology, and artificial intelligence. In addition to this, Amir is the Program Manager of Reach—Thought Leadership, where he seeks and influences the design of new innovations and approaches to help Key Opinion Leaders facilitate and address industry challenges. Amir brings members of the industry together to participate in open dialogues on ways to address these industry challenges.

Valayia Jones-Smith is a Healthcare Management consultant and a Professional Coach. Valayia is a dynamic, highly experienced healthcare management consultant with more than 20 years of healthcare experience. Her coaching focuses on the future vision of her clients and how they can achieve those visions as quickly and efficiently as possible. Valayia is board certified in Healthcare Management from the American College of Healthcare Executives, a 360 Reach Master Personal Branding Strategist, and a Five O'Clock Club Certified Career Coach. Valayia also holds several other professional certifications in both healthcare and professional coaching.

Craig M. Klugman, Ph.D., is a professor of bioethics and health humanities at DePaul University. He also serves on the ethics committee of Northwestern Memorial Hospital, consults with health care organizations, and is a voting member of the U.S. Department of Health & Human Services' National Biodefense Science Board. He holds a PhD in medical humanities from the University of Texas Medical Branch, a MA in Medical Anthropology and a MA in Bioethics from Case Western Reserve

University, and a BA in Human Biology from Stanford University. Dr. Klugman is the editor of several books, including *Research Methods in the Health Humanities* (Oxford 2019), *Medical Ethics* (Gale Cengage 2016), and *Ethical Issues in Rural Health* (Hopkins 2013; 2008). He is the author of over 600 scholarly articles, book chapters, OpEds, and blog posts on such topics as digital medicine, crisis and disaster ethics, professionalism, end-of-life issues, education, health/medical humanities, ethics of execution, and health policy. Dr. Klugman has been interviewed for *The New York Times*, *LA Times*, ABC News, HBO Vice, New Republic, *National Geographic*, *Men's Health*, *The Daily Beast*, Sinclair Broadcasting, Scripps News Service, and NPR. Besides numerous academic journals, his writing has appeared in *Pacific Standard Magazine, Huffington Post, Chicago Tribune, Medium, Cato Unbound, The Hill, San Francisco Chronicle,* and *the Houston Chronicle.*

David Lafferty is a senior technology executive with a unique mix of business acumen and technical expertise. He possesses a strong background of diverse industry experience, spanning the consulting, Fortune 100 distribution, healthcare, and manufacturing industries. Currently the Chief Information Officer for Tidewell Hospice, he is responsible for information technology as well as building and property management. David previously served as the Corporate Director of Information Technology with Plexus Corp., a global EMS provider, where he was responsible for worldwide IT infrastructure, support, and operations. Prior to this role, David led IT for a $150 million division of McKesson Medical-Surgical in Hartford, CT. He has also held various senior-level technology roles with Tech Data Corporation; Reptron; Metamor Worldwide, an information technology consulting firm; and CNA Insurance. David has co-authored a number of SQL Server training guides and was a contributing editor for leading technology trade publications, including Network Magazine and Windows Magazine. He obtained his Bachelor of Science degree from DeVry University in Chicago, and has further studied various executive courses at MIT/Sloan School of Business and Florida State University. David holds a CPHIMS and is a certified health care CIO (CH-CIO). He is currently seeking his MBA from Webster University.

Dr. Jean Ann Larson is the Chief Leadership Development Officer for the University of Alabama-Birmingham (UAB) Health System and the Senior Associate Dean of Leadership Development in the UAB School of Medicine. She has over 30 years' experience as a senior leader, organizational and leadership development expert and process improvement consultant. During her career she's served as an assistant hospital director, a Chief Learning Officer, VP of Patient Safety and Quality and as a leadership and strategic change consultant. Previously she led her own boutique leadership and organizational development consultancy while serving on the executive education program faculty for Southern Methodist University's Cox School of Business. She serves as an executive advisor and adjunct faculty for the University of Alabama at Birmingham's award winning Master's Program in Health Administration where she lectures on change, personal productivity and effectiveness and managing conflict. She is a sought after facilitator and speaker who enjoys bringing out the very best in leaders and teams. She has several certifications as a facilitator and executive coach as well as several leadership assessments; she is a Certified Lean Black Belt and an ASQ certified Six Sigma Green Belt.

Larson holds a doctorate in organizational change from Pepperdine University and an MBA in international management from Thunderbird, the Garvin School of International Management and a bachelor's degree in industrial engineering from Wichita State University. She is a graduate of Momentum's Executive Women's Leadership Program in Birmingham, AL. Her dissertation topic deals with the timely issue of professional transitions and explores ways that we can move through the inevitable changes in our lives more effectively. She is a past board member and industry award winner in both the Healthcare Information and Management Systems Society (HIMSS) and the Society for Health Systems of the Institute for Industrial Engineering. She is a Fellow in the American College of Healthcare Executives, a Life Fellow in HIMSS and a Fellow in the Institute for Industrial and Systems Engineers. She has edited and authored several books and published many articles. Her most recent book is *Organizational and Process Reengineering Approaches for Health Care Transformation,* Published August 2015, CRC Press, and a Winner of the 2015 HIMSS Book of the Year Award.

She and her husband of 32 years, Robert Jaramillo live in the Forest Park neighborhood of Birmingham, Alabama. They have two grown daughters, Danielle of Auburn Hills, Michigan, and Natalie of Austin, Texas.

Tom Lawry. After spending more than 20 years in healthcare, Tom Lawry believes that merely making the current system more efficient is akin to building a super-highway by paving over old cow paths. As National Director for Artificial Intelligence in Health and Life Sciences, and a former Director of Worldwide Health, at Microsoft, he works with innovative clinicians and health leaders who are leveraging the world's data and ever-expanding computational powers to rethink approaches to improve outcomes, quality, and satisfaction, He's a passionate advocate for harnessing the power of Artificial Intelligence to empower knowledge workers and drive meaningful reform of health systems around the world. Tom lives in Seattle, WA. When not working, he can be found hiking the trails of the Pacific Northwest, traveling the world to find his next favorite place, or exploring the beaches near his home on the Oregon Coast.

Man Qing Liang, Pharm D, MSc Student currently serves as the international HIMSS TIGER™ Scholars Informatics Intern. She is pursuing a Master of Health Services Administration program at the Université de Montréal School of Public Health (Montréal, Canada). Her research focuses on leveraging innovative methods and technologies to optimize medication use, such as computerized provider order entry systems and electronic health records. Man Qing obtained her Doctorate of Pharmacy (Pharm D) from the Université de Montréal and practices as a community pharmacist.

Dr. Kay S. Lytle is the CNIO with Duke University Health System and a Clinical Associate for Duke University School of Nursing. She is a CPHIMS and recognized as a FHIMSS by HIMSS. She is also certified as an Informatics Nurse and as a Nurse Executive Advanced (NEA-BC) by the American Nurses Credentialing Center (ANCC). Dr. Lytle has spent the last 28 years working with a wide variety of clinical information systems. Her primary focus has been on implementation and maintenance. Her research interests include evaluating process and clinical outcomes associated with electronic health records.

John A. Mandujano, CPHIMS, PMP, CSM, was the first American of Hispanic heritage to be named Top Freshman Debater of Boston College, New England Novice Debate Champion, alternate to the U.S. International Discussion and Debate Team, and third-place speaker in the Leonard Persuasive Speaking Contest. As a Distinguished Toastmaster, he spoke at two Toastmasters International Conventions as part of the Accredited Speaker Program. John was an employee of Adventist Health Systems from 2007 to 2013. As a technical advisor, he has consulted at Fidelity Investments, Gillette, Northeastern University, Empire Blue Cross Blue Shield, and Blue Cross Blue Shield of Massachusetts. He has been a Project Management Consultant at Blue Cross Blue Shield of Michigan, PharMerica, and Humana.

Dr. Laura Marks graduated from the University of Nebraska Medical Center with a Doctor in Pharmacy in 1993. Laura has extensive experience in clinical care, leadership, and healthcare technology. Laura now applies these experiences to the Nebraska Prescription Medication Monitoring Program (PDMP) as the Pharmacy Services Program Manager for CyncHealth. The PDMP is a part of the overall efforts to democratize healthcare information and to provide effective tools to help clinicians provide the best care possible.

Pamela V. Matthews is an accomplished Information Technology executive leader with over 25 years of experience focused on health information technology, strategic planning, IT operations and management, and clinical informatics. She has worked in management consulting, served as a CIO of a nationwide healthcare provider and worked for several healthcare provider systems leading clinical IT initiatives and operations including a major academic medical university. She has served on several boards and advisory councils as well as participated on federal grant endeavors and state specific initiatives. Under Collie Group Consulting, Ms. Matthews served in positions including Executive Operations Officer for a state wide Health Information Exchange organization, Executive Director of a non profit professional society and adjunct professor for graduate level university Informatics program. She continues to participate in grants and provides consulting and advisory services in the area of HIT/HIE, strategic planning, clinical informatics, and HIE operations. Ms. Matthews served as the Vice President of Education and Business Development at the College of Healthcare Information Management Executives (CHIME). Prior to CHIME, Ms Matthews worked at HIMSS in various capacities and launched the HIE and Financial Systems content area. Ms. Matthews is a Registered Nurse with a bachelor in Industrial Engineering and a Master's in Business Administration. Ms. Matthews makes numerous presentations and has published articles on health information technology, strategic planning, clinical informatics, quality outcomes and healthcare information exchange. Currently, she serves as the Vice Chair on the eHealth Exchange Board of Directors and participates in several industry HIE/HIT workgroups.

Kristin Myers is an Executive IT Leader with extensive experience in IT Management, Change Management and Program Management. She has a proven record of significant accomplishments leading strategic planning, selection processes, process improvement and health care technology initiatives for multi-year Epic EMR and Revenue Cycle implementations, Accountable Care and Population Health, Meaningful Use, Interoperability and Health care reform programs such as DSRIP. Reputation for developing a strategic plan, collaborating with clinical and operational stakeholders, building a cohesive, dedicated team, and implementing systems that are on time, on budget, and on target in generating business value and operational efficiencies.

Deborah Newman, MBA, FHIMSS, FACHE, is the President of RJA Consulting International which is a consulting company that specializes in ISO and regulatory standards related to medical devices, quality management, information security, and anti-bribery. Industry experience encompasses the fields of manufacturing, service organizations, product design, healthcare and business operations. Ms. Newman has over 25 years of progressive leadership experience in healthcare operations which encompasses responsibility for: risk management, compliance, high reliability and patient safety, quality improvement, accreditation, process improvement, management engineering, biostatistics, and auditing.

Ms. Newman received her MBA from The Ohio State University, and holds Lead Auditor Certifications in ISO 9001 Standards, and ISO 13485 Medical Device Standards. Additionally, she is a Fellow in the American College of Healthcare Executives, Fellow in the Health Information Management Systems Society, and Senior in the American Society of Quality.

Kathryn Owen is a seasoned clinical and informatics specialist with more than 38 years of healthcare experience. For the past five years, Ms. Owen has leveraged her technical expertise as a lead consultant for UKG (Ultimate Kronos Group), a global provider of HR and workforce management solutions powering breakthrough outcomes for organizations across all care settings. Ms. Owen has been an active member in HIMSS for 16 years and is currently co-chair of the

HIMSS Nursing Informatics Education Workgroup focused on providing quality informatics education webinars within HIMSS and the HIMSS Nursing Informatics Committee. After receiving her Bachelor of Science in Nursing (BSN) degree from Northern Illinois University, Ms. Owen began her career in pediatric intensive care at Children's Memorial Hospital (now Ann & Robert H. Lurie Children's Hospital of Chicago) and worked in various roles over her 30 years at the organization. She received her master's degree from DePaul University in nursing with a focus on education. In her spare time, Ms. Owen has taught for both DePaul University and Chamberlain College of Nursing. She also has her American Nurses Credentialing Center (ANCC) board certification in Nursing Informatics and has been instrumental in promoting nursing informatics through her work with HIMSS and the American Nursing Informatics Association (ANIA).

Rod Piechowski, MA, MS, CPHIMS, CFP, is Vice President, Thought Advisory at HIMSS. In this role, he leads a team responsible for the HIMSS Davies Award program and a range of member committees including Privacy, Security, and Cybersecurity; Innovation, Long Term and Post-Acute Care; and Clinical & Business Intelligence. Rod holds a BS in English Literature from Northern Michigan University; an MA in Bioethics and Health Policy from Loyola University; and an MS in Information and Communications Technology Security from the University of Denver. Rod also holds CPHIMS and Certified Foresight Practitioner certifications. He is passionate about futurism and the implications of technology and ethics.

Kevin P. Seeley, Colonel, USAF, MSC, MBA, CPHIMS, FHIMSS, is the Military Health System (MHS) Deputy Chief Information Officer (Deputy CIO) and Deputy Director, Health Information Technology (HIT) J-6 Directorate, Defense Health Agency (DHA). He leads and provides executive oversight of U.S. Armed Forces health technology and is responsible for planning, budgeting and execution of HIT operations, cyber security, technology transformation, infrastructure, health data, and its clinical and business application portfolio supporting 699 military clinics and hospitals worldwide. He develops policies, deploys new capabilities, and ensures Electronic Health Record (EHR) functional integration across Federal Agencies and private sector care. He serves as a principal military advisor to the Assistant Secretary of Defense for Health Affairs, DHA Director, Department of Defense (DoD) and senior healthcare leaders on HIT matters. His previous positions include Chief, DHA Infrastructure and Operations Division, Chief Technology Officer (CTO), HQ USAF Office of the Surgeon General; CIO, Air Force Medical Operations Agency; Chief Operating Officer (COO), DHA HIT Infrastructure Support Branch; Commander, 7th Medical Support Squadron; Acting Commander and Administrator, 7th Medical Group; and Chief Enterprise Architect (EA), Air Force Medical Service. He holds a Technology Innovation Management MBA, University of Colorado, Boulder, B.S.CIS, Park University, Missouri, Healthcare Executive Leader certificate, University of California, San Diego; membership with American College of Healthcare Executives (ACHE); and is a Certified Professional (CPHIMS) and Fellow (FHIMSS) with the Health Information & Management Systems Society (HIMSS). He helped pioneer early work on the Office of the National Coordinator for HIT's "Meaningful Use" rulemaking, and was recipient of the 2018 HIMSS Federal HIT Leadership award.

Toria (Tori) Shaw Morawski, MSW, currently serves as the Senior Manager of Professional Development (formerly of Clinical Informatics) and HIMSS TIGER™ Staff Liaison for the Healthcare Information and Management Systems Society (HIMSS) since 2014. In this role, she directs all programs, activities, resources, volunteer efforts, and research for the advancement of health informatics and workforce development efforts aligned with the HIMSS TIGER™ (*Technology Informatics Guiding Education Reform*) Initiative and HIMSS TIGER's™ Virtual Learning Environment (VLE). She also executed the EU*US eHealth Work Project's scope of work and project deliverables on behalf of the HIMSS Foundation with project fulfillment by HIMSS TIGER™.

Prior to HIMSS, Toria spent 12 years working in countries throughout Africa, the Caribbean, and Europe focused on global health and international development initiatives and in academia. In 2009, she co-created Global Implementation Solutions (GIS), a non-profit organization with a mission to provide customized sustainable solutions that support the strengthening of healthcare systems worldwide. Tori obtained her Master of Social Work (MSW) from University of Illinois at Chicago's Jane Addams College of Social Work in 2012 with a mental health concentration. There, she trained to become a clinical therapist focused on vulnerable, at-risk, and marginalized populations impacted by addiction, Hepatitis C, HIV/AIDS, and PTSD. Today, Tori proudly serves as the President of the GIS Board of Directors and is working on the 5th edition of the *Nursing Informatics: An Interprofessional and Global Perspective* textbook anticipated to be published by Springer Nature in summer 2021.

Bonnie Siegel is an Independent Career Consultant in the health IT and higher education IT industries. She most recently was a Consultant at Witt Kieffer in Oak Brook, Illinois, a preeminent healthcare and higher education executive search firm. She specialized in recruiting CIOs, CTOs, Clinical IT leaders, and other health IT senior leadership positions. Bonnie formerly held executive search leadership roles at Sanford Rose Associates, Cejka Search, and Hersher Associates. She began her healthcare IT career at Dorenfest & Associates, where she was a consultant and led health IT market research studies. Bonnie presents at national health IT conferences and writes a CIO career management blog for www.healthsystemcio.com. She was an adjunct professor at the University of Illinois at Chicago for their Masters of Health Informatics program, is a fellow member of Healthcare Information and Management Systems Society (HIMSS) and a member of the American Nursing Informatics Association (ANIA). Bonnie has a Bachelor's degree in Biology Education from the University of Illinois, Champaign-Urbana, Illinois. Bonnie Siegel may be reached at https://www.linkedin.com/in/bonniesiegel.

Detlev H. (Herb) Smaltz, PhD, is the Founder, President & CEO of CIO Consult, LLC. He works with healthcare provider and vendor organizations to provide CIO-level professional services to include IT strategic planning, BI/analytics strategic planning, analytics competency center planning and implementation, IT and data governance, IT product market placement advice, RFI/RFP planning and oversight, IT executive & staff coaching and mentoring, IT departmental assessments, IT PMO planning and evaluation and a number of other services designed to maximize IT organizational performance and business value creation. Herb has over 30 years of experience in healthcare management primarily as CIO at various sized organizations including CIO of International Operations at the Cleveland Clinic as well as CIO at the Ohio State University Wexner Medical Center. He also founded and led, as CEO and Co-Chairman of the Board of Directors, a healthcare analytics company, Health Care DataWorks. Herb is a Life Fellow of the Healthcare Information & Management Systems Society (LFHIMSS) and has served on the HIMSS Board of Directors (BOD) from 2002–2005 and as the HIMSS 2004–2005 BOD Vice Chair. In addition he is a Life Fellow in the American College of Healthcare Executives (LFACHE) and a two-time CIO-100 award recipient from CIO Magazine.

Anne Snowdon, RN, PhD, FAAN, is a Professor of Strategy and Entrepreneurship at the University of Windsor's Odette School of Business. Currently, Dr. Snowdon is leading research initiatives focused on digital health and system transformation, as well as accelerating supply chain infrastructure across global health systems to strengthen quality, safety and sustainability outcomes for global health systems. She is the currently the Vice Chair of the Board of the Directors for Alberta Innovates, a member for the Health Futures Council at Arizona State University and has recently been appointed to be the Chief Scientific Research Officer at HIMSS. She is also an Adjunct Faculty at the Department of Computer Science at the University of Windsor, Adjunct Faculty at the School of Nursing at Dalhousie University and most recently appointed as Adjunct

Professor of Clinical Supply Chain Innovation at the Centre for Innovative Medical Technology, University of Southern Denmark.

Joseph J. Wagner, as the Vice President of TELUS Health, has been responsible for the U.S. professional services team for the past 9 years. Prior to that he was the VP & CIO of Broward Health in Fort Lauderdale Florida. He served as HIMSS Chapter President for South Florida and New York and is currently the Treasurer of Central Florida HIMSS. He is also currently the HIMSS Chair for the Integration and HIE committee. Prior to this, he served on several other HIE committees that were responsible for white papers or other deliverables. He has presented to Columbia University MSH candidates (multiple times) on what it is like to work as a Provider, Consultant or with a healthcare applications firm, assisting them with their decisions on where in healthcare they fit best.

Dennis Winsten has over 30 years in the application of computer systems to healthcare as an entrepreneur with his own healthcare systems consulting corporation. He has published extensively in books and professional journals and has spoken at numerous national and regional professional meetings. Affiliations include: Fellow, HIMSS; Fellow, Clinical Laboratory Management Association and Board of Directors, 2011–2013 and 1990–1993; Association for Pathology Informatics; Clinical and Laboratory Standards Institute-Committee on Automation and Informatics. He has served as Clinical Systems Editor for Healthcare Informatics and Clinical Laboratory Management Review and is on the editorial board for Advance for Laboratory Administrators.

Dr. John R. Zaleski is Head of Clinical Informatics for Capsule Technologies, Inc., a leader in real-time medical device data integration and enterprise patient safety surveillance. He has been awarded nine U.S. Patents in the field, has written four seminal books and two book chapters on medical device integration & analytics, and is a contributing author to the *Dictionary of Computer Science, Engineering and Technology* by CRC Press. He has authored journal articles, conference symposia presentations, and continuing medical education training sessions. Dr. Zaleski has 30+ years of professional experience, has led IRB-approved clinical trials and the development of three clinical product lines including achieving Class II FDA approval on each. He is also a pre-hospital clinician, first responder and fire fighter.

Joyce Zerkich has been a CPHIMS for over 12 years, earned an Information Technology/Business Masters degree, MBA, Project Management Master's Certificate, PMP certification (pmi.org), and ACC Coaching certification (ICF). She was a speaker at HIMSS 2019 and 2016, the Michigan PMI Huron Valley and Great Lakes Chapters, Michigan Hospital Association, American Hospital Association, and published an article in PSQH. In addition, she helped author HIMSS *Implementing Business Intelligence in Your Healthcare Organization.* She works at Trinity Health as a Program Manager in the Enterprise Project Management Office. She has led implementations of Electronic Medical Record system, Buildings, IT, clinical process changes, HR changes, accounting changes at hospitals, physician offices, home health, senior living, PACE, and global business (Ford Motor Company) for IT divisions, finance, accounting, insurance, HR in the global auto, global IT, and United States Healthcare industries serving in main roles as a Scrum master, program manager, project manager, website manager, SIxSigma Champion, risk manager, strategic planning, futuring manager, and coach.

Introduction

Although I have the privlidge of serving as editor of the second edition of *The Handbook of Continuing Professional Development for the Health Informatics Professional,* this resource would not be possible without the continued generosity of health informatics professionals who volunteered their time and talent to produce updated and original content. The insights, experiences, and examples of our contributing authors continue to serve as excellent resources for anyone interested in developing, maintaining, or enriching a continuing professional development (CPD) plan.

While the impact of COVID-19 on health informatics professionals, both personally and professionally, continues to be catastrophic, I stand in awe of healthcare heros globally who place their lives on the line, unselfishly, each and every day to care for patients, regardless of the diagnosis. We are experiencing profound and sesmic change: our "new normal" will never return. And with this, the resilience and innovation of health informatics professionals will dominate health and healthcare globally.

New to the second edition, we have updated content across 13 chapters to reflect the many changes we've seen since the first edition was published in 2017. In addition, we have added 14 new chapters in a new section entitled "Industry Influences Critical to Your Career." These chapters focus on topics like innovation, health disparities, workforce, and so much more. And to help you leverage all the incredible content contained within these pages, we have added a checklist in the Appendix that leverages each chapter to help you build your career development priorities.

The environment of a health informatics professional continues to be one which is fast-paced, dynamic, ever-changing, and global. And because of this, professionals should recognize that "change and uncertainty require lifelong learning," as suggested by Edwards and Usher (2006) in Dzubinski et al. (2012, p. 103). And, as health informaticists engaged in helping to positively affect patients and the care that is delivered, "Professional development is a part of [one's] professional responsibility and accountability and [is] essential to organisational [sic] and professional success" (Cleary et al., 2011, p. 3562).

Continuing to develop professionally is critical for not only health informatics professionals but also others who strive to maintain personal competency in one's chosen profession. I trust that this Handbook will be valuable to you in your pursuit of your professional (and personal) goals.

REFERENCES

Cleary, M., Horsfall, J., O'Hara-Aarons, M., Jackson, D., & Hunt, G. E. (2011). The views of mental health nurses on continuing professional development. *Journal of Clinical Nursing, 20*(23–24), 3561–3566.

Edwards, R., & Usher, R. (2006). A troubled space of possibilities: Lifelong learning and the postmodern. In P. Sutherland & J. Crowther (Eds.), *Lifelong Learning: Concepts and Contexts.* New York, NY: Routledge.

Advocating for Change: Becoming Involved

The Age of Digital Healthcare is upon us. We are experiencing a transformative shift in how care is being delivered. The COVID-19 pandemic created a greater sense of urgency on policy change to ensure laws and regulations meet the needs and requirements of healthcare staff across the globe. As you advance in your career, you will benefit from paying close attention to the current policy landscape, and whether you are asked OR more importantly, you foresee an unintended consequence of pending policy change, you should develop the interest and skills in informing your local policy makers on the potential impact of new policy requirements.

Healthcare transformation requires nimble legislative and regulatory change. Regardless of where you live, the cost of healthcare and the policy decisions to advance value-based care to control cost and ensure greater use of information and technology. We need to switch the narrative from policy change that happens to healthcare to one where everyone influences policy, especially those with a specific expertise.

As we have weathered the storm of the COVID-19 pandemic, HIMSS and our members have identified a series of changes that should occur to help countries, states and provinces, communities, healthcare systems, and individual providers deliver higher quality care. Keeping such observations as our Call to Action to governments "hidden" did nothing to serve our members or the communities they serve.

In the summer of 2020, as the global pandemic continued to escalate, HIMSS public policy members and staff responded to a request on "what to do before the next pandemic" that was published by the U.S. Senate's Health Education Labor and Pensions Committee. Our response anticipated that certain categories, such as disease surveillance, just-in-time data collection, improvements to public health infrastructure, advancements in telehealth and remote patient monitoring, and data ownership and privacy all needed to evolve beyond the current state.

At the core of our recommendations is the concept that timely data is most impactful when it is converted to actionable information that influences policy formation. For example, data from hospitals treating COVID-19 patients points to a growing disparity on the quality and timeliness of care between white people and people of color. Population-level data collection and analysis are essential to improving policy and care delivery. HIMSS strongly supports robust data collection and information analysis to achieve equitable care delivery.

Our other major observations included the following:

- **Public Health Capacity**: Great resilience in the healthcare system is necessary to improve our pandemic preparation. Temporary regulatory change in the areas of telehealth and remote patient monitoring improved the healthcare delivered to patients without creating unnecessary burden. Following the pandemic, advocates will have the opportunity to demonstrate why the changes need to be made permanent.
- **Contact Tracing**: Governments at all levels should engage and deploy standards-based mobile digital contact tracing applications that can help expedite outbreak management and response.
- **Data Modernization**: Public Health Infrastructure platforms are woefully behind the technology curve. Strategic investments in technology modernization and workforce development efforts will equip the federal government, states, territories, local, and tribal public health officials with the ability to capture and assess complete data points and information necessary to address 21st Century public health concerns.

- **Privacy Protections**: Government policies must ensure pandemic response technologies and accompanying technologies go beyond what is offered by HIPAA-covered entities with a particular focus on alignment between federal, state, and local privacy laws. Any location data and all other personally identifiable inforatmoin should be appropriately safeguarded to include strong encryption management practices.
- **Stockpiles, Distribution, and Surges**: Governments should incorporate data-linkage tools to provide organizations with a strategic pathway to track processes and products used in care by mobilizing data to create real-world evidence of impact and outcome for patient populations.

My challenge to you as you advance through this book and your career is to be an active participant in public policy development. If you are always on the sidelines complaining about changes in public policy rather than actively educating policymakers, you will always be complaining. By getting involved and being informed, you will truly grow as a leader in your community.

Section I

Positioning the Health IT Professional for Lifelong CPD

1 Identifying Your Professional Potential

Bonnie Siegel
FHIMSS

CONTENTS

THE DEMAND

It is a great time to be a health information technology (IT) professional. The good news is that there is an increased demand for qualified talent. The reasons are many:

- Marketplace competitiveness
- IT security needs
- Enterprise data analytics and optimization of the electronic health record
- Patient safety and clinical quality
- Baby boomers retiring
- Value-based healthcare and quality-driven metrics
- Expansion of IT services with mergers, acquisitions, connections to community, physicians, and new facilities
- Project management needs in all areas

DOI: 10.4324/9780429398377-2

Whether you are looking internally at your current employer for your next career move or making the big move to another organization, you need to identify your own skills, attributes, strengths, and weaknesses and match them to the right job, culture, and organization. Hiring managers are looking for talented IT professionals. Do you have the skills, attributes, experiences, and background to match this demand? This chapter will help you identify your career potential and suggest tools and ideas to create a successful roadmap or plan for your health IT career.

WHERE ARE THE HEALTH IT JOBS?

The options for health IT jobs are vast. Here are some of the organizations that you should consider:

* Hospitals/health systems
* Academic medical centers
* Physician organizations/medical groups
* Consulting firms
* Software vendors
* Biotechnology/research companies
* Pharmaceutical companies
* Associations
* Government/military
* Academia/education
* Start-ups

If you currently work in a health organization and want to move into an IT career, consider becoming a "super-user" of your electronic health record system, volunteering to be on an implementation project, or applying for an IT opening. This is a common pathway for many successful IT careers. A super-user is described as a non-technical person who has mastered the use of the installed computer system and has the ability to communicate to others how to best utilize the system. Super-users can be nurses or other clinicians as well as financial, administrative, or departmental staff. Their ability to learn a computer system and train others makes them valuable liaisons between the IT department and their own areas. If you are drawn to data, love working with people, and can communicate effectively with others, a super-user position can be a great stepping stone to a health IT career. If you do not have an opportunity at your current employer or you are new to health IT, follow the steps in this chapter to make an IT career roadmap.

WHAT ARE THE HEALTH IT POSITIONS?

Health organizations seek all levels of IT talent from entry level to VP level and C-Suite. Hiring managers and recruiters want to fill new or replacement positions with the most qualified individuals that meet their specific criteria. The "ideal" health IT background for the management level includes:

* Five-plus years of health IT management experience
* Bachelor's degree from an accredited college or university, master's preferred
* Successful track record implementing clinical, financial, and administrative systems
* Excellent communication, people and project management skills, and customer service savvy

Here is a list of frequently used health IT titles at many different levels:

Sample Health Information Technology Positions

Senior Vice President, Chief Information Officer
   Vice President, Chief Information Officer
   Vice President of Technology
   Vice President, Clinical Systems
   Vice President, Information Technology
   Vice President, Enterprise Analytics
   Vice President, Project Management
   Chief Applications Officer
   Chief Advanced Analytics
   Chief Clinical Information/Informatics Officer
   Chief Health Information Officer
   Chief Information Officer
   Chief Information Security Officer
   Chief Medical Information/Informatics Officer
   Chief Technology Officer
   Deputy Chief Information Officer
   Associate Vice President, Clinical Applications
   Associate Vice President, Program Director
   Regional Information Technology Director
   Senior Director of Information Technology
   Enterprise Technology Architect
   Director, Clinical Informatics
   Director, Clinical Information System
   Director, Analytics
   Director, Electronic Health Record
   Director, Applications
   Director, Telecommunications
   Director, Web Development
   Director, Technology Operations
   Director, Technology and Information Services
   Director, Information Security
   Manager, Ambulatory Electronic Health Record
   Manager, Information Technology
   Network Manager
   Project Leader or Manager
   Application or Systems Analyst
   Application or Project Coordinator

EVALUATE YOURSELF

Whether you are beginning a health IT career or preparing to advance your career, you need to assess your skills and abilities. Do you have the proper education and training? Can you communicate detailed processes effectively? Do you listen more than you talk? Are you open minded, able to see several ways to accomplish the same tasks? Do you have an experienced mentor to guide you? Have you taken the time to learn the healthcare business and learn the clinical side? Have you cultivated your interpersonal and customer service skills? The following activity is an excellent way to evaluate your skills, qualifications, and abilities and pull together material to help develop your resume. The material you need to gather to be organized will include: older versions of your resumes, accurate names of previous organizations and their demographics, correct titles and dates of positions, number of staff and descriptions of key accomplishments for each position, all degree and certification information, and names of professional affiliations and memberships. Review your past projects, and write down key facts to include in your resume. Hiring managers and recruiters will ask you for details on your work and life history, and this activity will help you prepare.

HEALTH IT CAREER PLANNING ACTIVITY

1. List all previous positions with:
   a. Employer names and descriptions
   b. Dates
   c. Responsibilities, number of staff
   d. Titles reported to
   e. Accomplishments
   f. Reasons for leaving
   g. What you liked and disliked about each job

2. List all other pertinent experience.
   a. Education, degrees, certifications, licenses
   b. Professional organizations
   c. Public speaking
   d. Volunteer activities
   e. Sports
   f. Government
   g. Interests and hobbies

3. Which positions have you enjoyed the most? Why?
4. Which projects did you find the most enjoyable? Why?
5. Which projects would you never be willing to do again? Why?
6. What type of environment is most comfortable for you (entrepreneurial, for-profit, not-for profit, large, small, etc.)? What work environment do you like the best?
7. How would you rate your people management skills?
   a. Excellent
   b. Good
   c. Average
   d. Fair
   e. Poor

8. How would you rate your project management skills?
   a. Excellent
   b. Good
   c. Average
   d. Fair
   e. Poor

9. Do you enjoy managing projects? Why or why not?
10. What kind of projects do you enjoy?
11. What vendor systems and products do you know well?
12. Identify your greatest challenges. How have you handled these situations? What have you learned?
13. Have you presented to senior executives, and did you feel comfortable?
14. What are your long-term career goals?
15. Can you relocate? Yes_____No_____If yes, what is your geographic preference?

16. Based on your ratings and evaluation, what skills do you need to acquire or improve in the short term?
17. Develop a plan to acquire those important skills through:
    a. Education and training
    b. Experience
    c. Working with a mentor
    d. Professional associations

THE RESUME

Your resume is your most important career document. It represents your career narrative in reverse chronological order, not a curriculum vitae format. The reader of your resume, whether a hiring manager or recruiter, will expect it to be coherent and attractive. Your resume and career narrative will be assessed and consumed across many platforms, databases, mobile apps, and devices, and your look and tone have to be excellent. Career advisors have many approaches to formatting resumes, but for the health IT industry, stick with a conservative style.

TIPS FOR CRAFTING YOUR RESUME

- Prepare your resume like an executive summary of your work history and why you are qualified.
- Utilize easily readable fonts like Calibri, Tahoma, or Cambria in size 11 or 12.
- Write out your entire work history, not just the last 10 years; do not restrict yourself to one or two pages.
- Place contact information on top: name, address, city, state, email, and cell phone.
- Write a career summary paragraph with specific key words and phrases that make your health IT experiences stand out.
- Include key demographic facts about your employers; they add credibility to your background and aid the reader in his or her understanding of your experiences.
- Craft your professional experiences in reverse chronological order with brief descriptions of your employers before your job titles.
- Include all job titles under each employer separately with separate accomplishments.
- Bullet point key accomplishments in a list for each job title, and begin each bullet with an action verb (Developed, Managed, Implemented, Planned, Led, etc.).
- List your key projects, describing your management experience and time and money saved.
- Name vendors and products you have worked with, since they can be unique in health IT.
- End your resume with education, including degrees and dates, memberships, awards, publications, presentations.
- Spell and grammar check your resume.
- Ask others to critique your resume.

AVOID THESE RESUME WRITING PROBLEMS

1. *Boring:* Do not list your responsibilities with no mention of accomplishments. Do not include generic phrases not related to health IT or current trends.
2. *Brief:* Less than two pages is unwise if you have been a professional for more than two years.
3. *Wordy:* Do not place multiple sentences in bullets or use long, wordy paragraphs. Make sure to include white space to rest the reader's eye. Your resume should not look too crowded and busy.

4. *Gaps:* Do not leave off the first 10 years of employment or have holes in your history. If you are unemployed, add "independent consultant" as your current role; explain any gaps in employment during your work history.
5. *Slick/Salesy:* Do not overuse bolding, underlining, shading, columns, or fonts and sizes. Never use pictures or decorative graphics.
6. *Acronyms:* Avoid acronyms or unusual abbreviations not known to health IT or the general public.
7. *Humble:* Make sure to include key accomplishments that set you apart in health IT. Always include employer descriptions.
8. *Egotistical:* Do not use first person, exaggerated titles, and egocentric language or opinions.
9. *Personal:* Do not include anything personal, your salary, or your references (Figure 1.1).

COVER LETTER

Your cover letter can be written directly in an email addressed to a specific person or attached as a separate document. It should be one to two paragraphs and include all of your contact information. Verify the name, title, and address of the person receiving the cover letter. State your reasons for your interest in the position and why you are uniquely qualified. Ask for confidentiality.

Resume/cover letter writing is an ongoing task, and you may have several versions when applying for different positions. To help you prepare different versions, read the job description carefully and include key words that show you fit the required criteria. Your resume and your cover letter can help you open the door to an interview.

CONTACTS AND NETWORKING

To land a job in health IT or to advance your current health IT role, you need to expand and grow your network. Your colleagues, associates, friends, family, and recruiters are a wealth of connections and knowledge to help you. Reach out to them with calls or emails, and send them your resume. You can invite them to lunch and remind them of your experiences. Follow up with them, and send thank-you notes.

REFERENCE

Choose your references wisely, and stay in touch with them. Make sure they will be your champions. Never put their names and contact information on your resume, but have a separate list avatilable upon request. You will need to have three to five business references such as previous managers, peers, or subordinates. They will need to know your leadership skills and be able to give an example of what you have done. Be sure to prepare them ahead of time, and let them know that they may receive a call from a prospective employer.

SOCIAL MEDIA

Utilize LinkedIn to your best advantage; it is your professional branding tool. It is a great way to market yourself in a very competitive world. Refresh your online presence frequently. Here are some key factors in conveying the "best" professional profile:

- *Professional photo:* Use one in business attire, ideally taken by a professional photographer.
- *Connections:* Build up your connections to 500+; reach out to many health IT leaders in the industry.
- *Career summary:* Write one or two paragraphs describing your career; include key words important to health IT.

(a)

To help you visualize a well-crafted health IT resume, here is an example.

Your Name

12 Your Street
Your City, Your State XXX11

XXX-555-1212
sampleresume@XXXX.com

SUMMARY

A proven business director who specializes in driving excellence via continuous process improvement within healthcare organizations capitalizing on proven skills in clinical informatics, data analysis and health information management. Over eleven years' experience in fast-paced, entrepreneurial and intellectually stimulating environments, an effective leader who works well with others or alone and relentlessly drives toward optimizing efficiency and maximizing effectiveness. Key areas of expertise:

PROFESSIONAL EXPERIENCE

LARGEST HEALTH SYSTEM City, State   2008–present
The largest health system in the Big City region with $5.8 billion of annual revenues comprised of eight hospitals and 35,000 employees that provide quality healthcare services annually to more than 150,000 inpatients and over 500,000 outpatients.

Assistant Vice President of Clinical Applications   2011–present
Responsible for the enterprise clinical systems and reporting to the Vice President, Chief Information Officer. Lead a team of 75 IT professionals and contractors.

- Develop the clinical systems strategic roadmap for the health system and the eight hospitals
- Serve in the Office of the CIO and attend executive and Board meetings as needed
- Recruit and build a high performing clinical applications team and work within the established budget
- Partner with all key stakeholders including senior executive leaders, physicians and clinical department heads for all clinical implementation projects and ongoing systems maintenance
- Developed a strategic "roadmap" which was published to the repository enabling successful bulk testing of more than 10,000 product items contained on formulary across seven hospitals

Director of Clinical Information Systems   2009–2011
Recruited to the IT department after a successful clinical and electronic health record information system implementation from the Leading Clinical Systems vendor. Reported to the Assistant Vice President of Clinical Applications.

- Built the department to 30 by recruiting other clinical IT leaders to help design and maintain the new system
- Established customer service and strategic plans to help build credibility with department heads and physicians
- Provided timely implementations and optimizations of systems for all clinical areas

Project Manager – Pharmacy Information Systems   2008–2009
Recruited to the new computer system project team to lead the enterprise wide deployment of the Big System pharmacy's solution and corresponding data conversion "cut over" responsibilities. Challenged with implementing in a fast paced environment with limited resources, stringent timelines and budgetary constraints reported to the Assistant Vice President of Clinical Applications.

- Established credibility by partnering with pharmacists, consultants and senior executive leadership during the first week of tenure to quickly evaluate and understand current/future state processes, design decisions and stakeholder influence to regain project accountability
- Developed a strategic "roadmap" which was published to the repository enabling successful bulk testing of more than 10,000 product items contained on formulary across seven hospitals
- Rolled out Pharmacy's order entry and barcode medication scanning, EMAR validation, mobile device viewing, and CPM charge code validation to ensure integrity with the bill dropping process

LEADING RETIREMENT COMMUNITY Mid-size City, State   2005–2008
A leading company which has developed and manages more than full service retirement communities nationwide offering its 22,000 residents ownership in maintenance free living accommodations. Recently recognized in FORTUNE Magazine as one of the top "100 Companies to Work For" in 2008 and 2009.

(b)

Director of Business Process Improvement   2006–2008
Identified by the Vice President of Operations as a high potential Director to join an elite start up team of internal Six Sigma consultants. Challenged with executing projects, establishing a Six Sigma/disciplined process improvement program within the corporate Operations department, developing a metrics reporting system with Key Performance Indicators, influencing change management at the senior leadership level and recruiting and training both resources to execute projects.

- Executed president satisfaction scores from 73% to 87% in one year by targeting during process variability, eliminating bottlenecks through cycle time reductions, standardizing processes and implementing control plans necessary for sustainability
- Established a project pipeline which defined approximately $1.75 million of potential cost saving opportunities
- Added more robust quality assurance capabilities throughout the organization by introducing the Balanced Scorecard approach to the quarterly review process and geared agendas to consistently embrace the concept of continuous improvement
- Established "critical mass" and momentum within three weeks of initial project engagement by leading a cross functional mix of Operations team members through the design and implementation phases necessary in creating an infrastructure of excellence.

Director of Project Management – Operations   2005–2006
Recruited to take over and turn around a failed asset management software implementation, halt escalating costs associated with the original deployment, identify root cause and establish a best practice model. Reported to the Vice President of Operations.

- Formulated a reimplementation plan renewing a sense of urgency within 35 days of initial start by conducting a gap analysis and identifying and prioritizing shortfalls to senior leadership to influence change.
- Launched the Rapid Design process reengineering methodology responsible for eliminating over 200 unnecessary processes and standardizing work flow across 23 retirement communities.

LEADING CLINICAL SYSTEMS CORPORATION, Big City, State   2000–2005
A global healthcare information technology corporation with $1.3 billion of annual revenue that offers its 6,000 health organization clients information solutions to optimize and improve their healthcare processes.

Senior Solutions Delivery Consultant   (2003–2005)
Promoted to manage complex project implementations "highly visible" to executive management at two large health care delivery systems. Challenged with strengthening client/vendor relationships, identifying client strategies, imperatives and influencing decisions associated with their capital request/purchasing process. Projects involved automating healthcare processes via transforming highly paper intensive business to electronic data management.

- Re-established credibility with strategic accounts by identifying project deviations, renegotiating contracts, facilitating contract change orders and maintaining overall project overhead and profit margins.
- Increased project team's productivity within by 38% by reallocating resources, shuffling roles and responsibilities, reducing travel, and reengineering the remote support process.

Application Specialist   2000–2003
Spearheaded efforts as a consultative role to implement entire suite of software solutions to include into acute care facilities throughout North America. Led notable client engagements and project successes.

- Played a key role in client leadership's successful initiative to reduce costs in excess of $1.5 million associated with the off site storage of paper medical records by orchestrating the application of technical data storage strategies and the digitizing of "paper based" health information.
- Empowered client teams to improve data quality specifically reducing the number of scheduling and registration errors per day to a level below 1% by creating systemized workflow and instructing on data quality best practices.

HEALTHCARE CONSULTING PRACTICE, Big City, State   1999–2000
A global services firm that offers healthcare solutions via consulting, technology and outsourcing services that drive improvements to their client's business performance.

(c)

Application Consultant – Sales and Marketing   1999–2000
Promoted to build strategic relationships with new and existing clients, increase customer base and maximize existing account sales. Challenged with creating marketing and sales forecasting plans, developing an updated pricing model, and reducing RFP response time.

- Instrumental in generating approximately $65,000 in new revenue within 6 months of promotion by broadening the business line from selling software to also providing professional consulting services.

Application Consultant – Implementations (1999)
Hired to implement clinical and patient accounting information systems throughout the long term care industry in North America. Executed software implementations including requirements gathering, process design, development of data conversion, communication procedures and user acceptance testing.

- Eliminated project backlog by 50% from 12 to 6 in a month duration by averaging one project completion per month contributing to the company's ability to head "Wall Street's" 4th quarter earnings projection for fiscal year 1999.

REGIONAL MEDICAL CENTER *Big City, State*   1997–1999
A 790-bed Joint Commission accredited academic medical center nationally recognized for its geriatric center, neonatal intensive care unit and burn center.

Health Information Systems Administrator
Hired into a newly created role to act as the liaison between the Medical Records and Information Technology departments.

- Raised worker productivity levels on all reportable metrics by automating Health Information Management processes to optimize workflow and reassigning departmental roles and responsibilities
- Played a key role in the hospital's ability to recoup approximately $750,000 in accounts receivable by analyzing and presenting data illustrations which influenced senior leadership's decision to execute on their collection strategy.

EDUCATION AND PROFESSIONAL CERTIFICATIONS

College of State, City, State
- Bachelor of Science – Health Information Management   May 1997

American Health Information Management Association, Chicago, IL
- Registered Health Information Administrator (RHIA)   January 1998

Breakthrough Management Group, City, State
- BMG Certified Six Sigma Black Belt – Process Improvement Methodology   January 2008
- Lean for Transactional Processes – Lean SCORE Methodology   February 2008

PROFESSIONAL AFFILIATIONS

- American Health Information Management Association (AHIMA)
- Healthcare Information and Management Systems Society (HIMSS)
- International Society of Six Sigma Professionals (ISSP)

FIGURE 1.1   Sample resume.

- *Experience:* List all of your key positions, employers, and years of experience; this is not a duplicate of your resume or as lengthy.
- *Groups:* Be active on LinkedIn, and join health IT groups; follow their discussions.
- *Publications, presentations, projects:* Add your unique events, and increase your exposure.
- *Recommendations, skills:* Note any recommendations and acknowledgment of skills.

A well-written LinkedIn profile is an excellent part of your career narrative and can be a stepping stone to a new position. Use other social media with caution; Twitter, Facebook, and personal blogs can appear to be harmless, but personal photos, strong opinions, and comments are easily retrieved by hiring managers and recruiters while doing candidate background and media checks. Research your online presence on a regular basis by doing a Google search. Be upfront with potential employers on any less-than-flattering public reports like bankruptcy, DUIs, or other items that they may find.

INTERVIEWING/NEGOTIATING

There are several different methods used to interview health IT candidates. Internal candidates as well as external candidates may follow the same process. You may be involved in one or more of these methods:

- Phone interviews (can take an hour or longer)
- In-person interviews (one-on-one, group or panel, meal interview)
- Video conference interview (desktop, laptop, or video conference center)

Each of these methods will have different approaches. With a phone interview, speak clearly and slowly with confidence and enthusiasm. With an in-person interview, wear formal business attire, arrive early, use a firm handshake, make eye contact, sit up straight, listen more, and talk less. A video interview is similar to an in-person interview but requires that you provide good lighting and neutral surroundings behind you to avoid distracting elements. Be realistic, candid, and truthful with your answers. This is your chance to show your interpersonal skills and style.

MAJOR GAFFES TO AVOID AT IN-PERSON INTERVIEWS

1. Getting lost and arriving late.
2. Being discourteous to administrative staff and receptionists.
3. Carrying a briefcase in one hand and a glass of water in the other, so as not to be able to shake hands when you meet someone.
4. Dressing too casually—such as an open polo shirt underneath a jacket or no tie for a man, or a casual dress or slacks outfit for a woman—for a formal selection committee meeting.
5. Wearing excessive amounts of cologne or perfume.
6. Using slang or profanity during the interview.
7. Looking down or not making eye contact with anyone.
8. Over-selling one's abilities, being pompous, and talking too much.
9. Bringing unsolicited presentations or handouts.
10. Not listening, not taking notes, and not answering questions directly.

Be prepared to answer situational questions like *STAR* behavioral-based questions:

- **S**ituation or **T**ask you faced
- **A**ction you took: What was done and how it was done
- **R**esult of your actions

CURRENT SITUATION/JOB HISTORY
- Tell me about your current situation.
- Describe your current environment/position.
- What title do you report to?
- What aspects of your current position do you like most?
- What aspects of your current position do you like least?
- How many staff do you manage, directly or indirectly? What is the largest number of staff that you have managed? When?
- Describe your computer systems experience in healthcare, applications, and electronic medical record systems, etc.
- Describe your management style. How do people perceive you as a manager, leader?
- Do you attend meetings or present to senior executives? Please explain.
- Describe your strengths and any weaknesses.

WHY CONSIDERING A CHANGE
- Why are you looking for a new opportunity now?
- What don't you like about your current job? What else? What else?
- Is your organization aware that you are looking for something else?

DESIRED POSITION, LOCATION, TOWN SIZE
- What is your ideal next job?
- What would be most important to you? Why is this important to you?

OTHER OPPORTUNITIES
- Have you had the chance to look at other opportunities?
- Have you received any other serious interests?
- Have you scheduled any interviews yet? Have you attended them?
- What did you like/dislike about what you have already seen?

TIMEFRAME FOR DECISION
- What timeframe do you need to part with your current situation?
- Are there any obligations you have that may affect your decision to make a move at this time (house, children in school)?

FAMILY SITUATION AND PRIORITIES (these are optional but may come up)
- Is there another person we need to consider?
- Will someone else be relocating with you?
- What else should I know about you that I haven't already asked?

OUTSIDE INTERESTS/NEEDS/HOBBIES
- What are your hobbies/outside interests?
- What do you enjoy doing most?

CURRENT INCOME AND MINIMUM TO RELOCATE
- What is your current salary and bonus?
- Is there anything else in the way of benefits and compensation that is important to you?

FIGURE 1.2   Sample interview questions.

To be skillful at interviewing, you need to practice and be prepared. That is why it is important to know everything about yourself and the hiring organizations. Spend extra time doing research on the organization and the executives. Know your accomplishments and achievements, and be able to articulate why you believe you are qualified for the position (Figure 1.2).

Let's review the best way to answer these questions. Recall your experiences, and write them down with as much specific detail as you can remember. Vary your stories, and be concise. Reread the job description, because the employer will want to match their needs, not your desired job. Practice and rehearse your answers, and be honest.

After the interview, follow up with thank-you emails or even a handwritten note. It is an honor to be interviewed. View it as a life achievement and the next step on your career ladder. Stay in close contact during the active phase of interviewing. Whether chosen to move forward or not selected, ask for feedback.

NEGOTIATING

Congratulations, you are a finalist for a health IT position and may receive an offer. What do you need to do? You want to come out a winner in the negotiation process and leave no bad feelings behind. Be ready to discuss your needs and know which ones are deal breakers if not met. Here is an outline of suggested items you need to have clarified during negotiations of an offer.

1. Title
2. Base salary/performance yearly bonus percentage, sign-on bonus
3. Reporting relationship(s)
4. Benefits
5. Basic health insurance: major medical, dental, vision, life, disability
6. Retirement: 401(k), 403(b), SERP, deferred compensation, other benefit packages
7. Perks: mobile and handheld devices, PC/laptop, vehicle allowance or travel expense, allowance, data lines, memberships, paid tuition for self or family members
8. Health and drug screen
9. Psychometric screening
10. Paid time off/vacation: Current number of weeks, paid holidays, sick days
11. Office support/location
12. Relocation: Temporary housing, moving of household goods, realtor visits, rent stipend
13. Unusual or rare relocation items: Sale of house, down payments, housing stipend, boats, horse, etc.
14. Upcoming events already scheduled
15. Start date/availability date

Here are some examples of negotiation scenarios to be aware of:

Surprise Verbal Offers

Be prepared in case a hiring manager extends an offer to you verbally. This is not the best scenario, but it can happen, so review the list of suggested items even before the first interview, and do your best with the negotiations. If you are working with a recruiter, they can handle the negotiations if they are aware of your needs.

Counteroffers

Your current organization may find out that you are actively looking for another opportunity. This is a hazardous situation. They may decide to let you go or, in an effort to keep you, offer you a counteroffer. It can include a promotion, a title change, more money, and/or increased benefits. This is tempting but remember, a counteroffer benefits the organization, not you. Step away wisely from these types of offers. You will be considered disloyal for thinking of leaving, and accepting a counteroffer almost always leads to regret.

Serious Multiple Offers

You are lucky if you ever experience multiple job offers at once. These are rare occurrences, but they do happen. Be prepared to do your due diligence on all the pros and cons of each organization and their offers.

Deal Breakers

Be realistic about your demands and needs, and include items that are important to your family. Relocation issues are at the top of the deal-breaker list. Try to solve them before a job offer. Research the new area completely—housing, schools, taxes, quality of life, etc.

In conclusion, it is best if your recruiter can handle negotiations for you. Share your complete salary, benefit and housing needs, as well as other demands with the recruiter. Be careful not to accept counteroffers from your current employer. Know what your "true" deal breakers are, and be realistic in your demands.

CONCLUSION

To best identify your health IT professional potential, you need to develop a health IT Career Action Plan. This chapter includes action steps to help guide you. Review the health IT opportunities, and be realistic about your abilities. Target and research health IT organizations, and learn the industry vendors and products. Complete the Health Information Technology Career Planning Activity to help you learn about your skills and abilities. Consider moving forward with an advanced degree and certifications. Develop your managerial skills, and seek out ways to lead IT projects or become a super-user. Prepare an outstanding resume and cover letter, and use key words unique to the health IT industry. Identify internal/external mentors, and build your connections on LinkedIn. Take care of your references, and treat them like gold. Don't forget to have a work-life balance. Practice your interviewing skills, and be prepared. Good luck with your career in health IT!

2 Creating a Personal Brand

Valayia Jones-Smith
FACHE, CPHIMS, PCMH, CCE, PMI-PBA, CCP

CONTENTS

INTRODUCTION

When you hear the word *branding,* what are the first thoughts that come to mind? For most, the word *branding* is associated with a business or products. Very few of us would think of ourselves as a brand. However, each one of us is the most unique brand that exists: there is no other brand just like you!

Personal branding is fast becoming the primary method to be influential, indispensable, and incredibly happy at work.

Following is a three-step process that will help you uncover and express your brand in a way that will help you reach your goals.

First we will start with defining "what is a brand?" as it applies to personal branding. William Arruda's definition of a brand is "YOUR unique promise of value" (http://williamarruda.com). Picture your brand as being at the intersection of three connecting circles, and at each of the three circles are the words "promise," "unique," and "value": what is unique to you, what is the promise you commit to delivering, and what has value to the people who are making decisions about you?

When you think of some of the world's strongest brands such as Apple, Google, or McDonald's, not only are you able to immediately recognize these brands by their logos, but also each brand illicits words, feelings, and associations. What makes these strong brands is that the words, feelings, and associations that each person has tied to the brands are consistent. When you think of the Apple brand, what are some of the words that come to mind? One of those words may be innovative. Why? Because almost everything Apple does is innovative! Apple distributes innovative products that consumers don't even realize they want or need. Apple's innovation extends past their products: you can see it in their packaging and in their stores, which have "Genius Bars" instead of check-out lines. Why is this important? Well, there are two reasons. One is branding is based on authenticity. Branding is not about creating a fake image for the outside world or convincing people about something that isn't true. It is based on what is true, genuine, and real. Ann Morrow Lindbergh stated, "The most exhausting thing you can be is insincere" (http://www.

DOI: 10.4324/9780429398377-3

brainyquote.com/quotes/authors/a/ anne_morrow_lindbergh.html). The second reason Apple is a strong brand is that they are known for some "thing" and not a hundred "things." Take a moment to think of what words would be used when your name is said.

The goal is to think about what your brand is and how you can use your brand to deliver value for yourself, for your career, for your team, and for your organization. You may be asking yourself, "Why do I need to think of myself as a brand?" Simply because the world of work has changed forever! There was a time when an organization managed its employees' careers since things were static. Today, it isn't uncommon for most individuals to have worked at least ten jobs by the age of 40. Based on a study by the U.S. Bureau of Labor Statistics, those born in the years of 1957–1964 held, on average, 11.7 jobs from ages 18 to 48, with 27% holding 15 or more jobs (http://www.bls.gov/nls/nlsfaqs.htm#anch41). Companies are aware of this and expect the best from you while you are there. To succeed in this new world of work, you need to be your best self and integrate what makes you exceptional for everything you do to prove your value to your organization.

THE DITCH FRAMEWORK

Based on the research of Arruda and Dib, there are three actions that are critical to successful branding: DITCH, DARE, DO.

DITCH

A "ditch" is something you need to eliminate. It could be a success strategy that got you where you are today but won't take you further, or it could be a mindset or habit that will get in the way of your success. You need to be willing to ditch it, and you need to actively search for what these things are so that you can get them out of the way and be successful.

DARE

A "dare" is a risk you need to take. By doing so, you need to step outside your comfort zone. You need to be able to take calculated risks to get noticed and move your career forward.

DO

A "do" is an action you take every single day to build and nurture your personal brand. You can't expect your brand to be built for you. You need to deliberately work on your brand daily.

REACH 1–2-3 SUCCESS ™!

Reach 1–2-3 Success™! is a personal branding process. It is composed of three steps:

1. *Extract:* Unearth/uncover your brand by digging deep into who you are to figure out what your brand is about.
2. *Express:* Communicate your brand to your target audience.
3. *Exude:* Align your brand environment with everything that surrounds you. This is the easiest part as you are now crystal clear about your brand and have a communication plan for your brand to make it visible to others.

Notice that each word of the Reach 1–2-3 Success™! phases begins with the letters "EX." The reason is because your brand, although based in authenticity, is held in the hearts and minds of those around you—"EX" = external. Actually, it is what others think that counts.

Before examining each phase of the branding process, let me take a moment to discuss the benefits and what is in it for you to unearth and live your brand.

You:

- Do a lot of introspection so you can increase your self-awareness.
- Increase your visibility and presence.
- Stand out from others who do what you do and share your job title.
- Put yourself in control of your career.
- Increase your wealth, since strong brands are paid more than commodities.
- (Most importantly) Increase your achievement and professional fulfillment because you are aligning who you are with what you do and how you do it.

These are the benefits to you. But why would an organization want its people to build their brands? Some organizations are concerned about personal branding. They worry about having thousands of individual brands in the industry. Organizations need to deliver a consistent experience to their stakeholders. It is true that organizations need their employees to deliver on the brand promise consistently. And there is an important distinction between consistency and conformity: conformity may come across as fake or inauthentic, but it isn't transparent. Consistency is the key.

One great example of consistency is the Nordstrom brand. In the Nordstrom employee manual it states, "deliver the finest customer service." Nordstrom does not dictate how an employee should "deliver the finest customer service." This allows each employee to deliver on the brand promise in a way that is authentic to them. The employees will be engaged and motivated and will deliver their best in support of the company's objectives. At this point, you should have a better understanding of the benefits of personal branding for both yourself and your organization.

EXTRACT

By further examining the Extract phase of the Reach 1–2–3 Success! model, we identify three separate components. The first component starts with the "promise" of the brand definition, which is "your unique promise of value." Promise relates to your authenticity. In uncovering your brand, take a look at yourself introspectively as well as getting feedback from those around you. What types of things do you need to know? Do you know your vision, purpose, values, and passions? These are referred to as your VPs for your personal brand.

Your vision is what you see as possible/desirable for the world; something you could not accomplish yourself.

Your purpose is your role in turning your vision into reality.

Your values are your operating principles; you carry them with you every day. They impact how you behave, how you feel.

Your passions are those things that get you out of bed early on a Saturday morning. When you can connect your passions with your work, you are unstoppable!

Another important element of your brand is goals. Goals give your brand direction. They help you identify what things you want to do, what things you don't want to do, and how you can eliminate things because they are not connected to those goals. You need to think about where you want to go and how your brand will get you there. When it comes to goals, you will want to document your goals and read them every day. Why? Because you are resetting a part of your brain called the RAS (Reticular Activating System). It's the part of your brain that decides what makes it into your conscious mind and what doesn't. Every day, a person is bombarded with over 700 billion stimuli, and only a tiny, tiny fraction make it into their conscious mind. You want to make sure what makes its way into your conscious mind is that which is self-serving. This is why reading your goals every morning is important. The act of reading them resets your RAS and says "this is important to me" and "be on the lookout for anything that will help me reach these goals." What you see that day will be different from what you will see if you do not read your goals. All of us have experienced our RAS in action. Perhaps you have decided what color, make, and model you are going to buy for your next vehicle. Maybe a red BMW? As soon as you make that decision, you suddenly start to notice all the red BMWs on the road. That is your RAS at work. Your "DO" here is to document your goals and read them regularly.

Up until now we have been discussing your brand from the inside out: who you are, your vision, your purpose, your values, your passion, your goals. You also need to get feedback from the outside in. The question is "what do people think about you?" What words would they use to describe you? Are they the same words you would use to describe yourself? Would they all use the same words to describe you or would they use different words depending on who you talk to? To help understand your brand and your reputation from the outside in, it is helpful to use a tool called the 360Reach personal branding assessment, available at www.360Reach.me. This tool gives you a good understanding of your brand attributes, which are the adjectives people use to describe you. The DARE is to seek and be open to feedback. All strong brands seek feedback and take action as a result of what they learn.

The last thing you need to remember when uncovering your brand is to eliminate the word "FINE!" Nobody gets excited in life about things that are fine. When you hear the word *fine,* you also think of average, adequate, OK, and acceptable. Do you want people describing your work that way? Probably not! Yet, we accept one's mindset that the way to succeed is to fix our weaknesses. When you fix your weaknesses, you become "fine" at a lot of things. That is the opposite of branding. What strong brands do is take the things they are great at and become exceptional at them. They maximize it, and they maximize the visibility of it.

Regarding your weaknesses, think about the following. For any weakness identified, you should ask yourself, "Will this weakness get in the way of my success?" If the answer is yes, then you absolutely need to work on it. If the answer is no, then you need to ignore it and focus on your strengths. Identify which ones will be most helpful to you and will enable you to deliver on superlatives. The goal is to have people using words such as *best, outstanding,* or *exceptional* when they think of you.

The DITCH is to stop fixing weaknesses and start working on strengths. The question you need to be thinking about is "what do you want to be known for?" How do you instill everything you have learned about yourself in the Extract phase and use it as a way to define the brand called you?

The second area of "unique promise of value" is the "unique" piece. Branding is about differentiation. What do you have in common with your peers, but most importantly what sets you apart from others? What is your brand differentiation? An example to think about is MasterCard, Visa, and American Express. What is the difference between a Visa card or a MasterCard versus an American Express card? What makes someone choose to pay an annual membership fee of $450 to carry an American Express card versus carrying a card with no fee like MasterCard or Visa, when they all have the same function of letting you make purchases? When you dig deeper into the practice of maintaining a membership with a credit card, is there something available from American Express that isn't available from the others? When you think about what you do and your ability to do that job, you are in a sense functioning as the MasterCard or Visa. If you think of yourself as your job title, you are interchangeable with anyone else who shares that job title. But when you start thinking about that unique experience that you deliver such as those things that you deliver, in addition to the competence of being able to do your job, that's when you are thinking about yourself as a brand. When you think about your brand, you need to think about what you have to offer and who your audience may be. Then, make sure you are always relevant and compelling to them. That's the lesson for a strong brand. The DARE here is to know that differentiation and flaunt your quirks. Take those things that make you YOU and make them visible. And, as William Aruda says, "What makes you unique, makes you successful."

The third element of "unique promise of value" has to do with the "value." The value is not determined by you but rather by your target audience, by the people making decisions about you, and those that influence them. That includes people both internal and external to your organization. You need to know who this group is so you may build your brand and increase your visibility in front of them. Personal branding is not about being famous; rather, it is about being selectively famous.

After you learn about yourself introspectively and through external feedback, you will distill these leanings into what is called your personal brand statement (PBS). This statement is for you. It is NOT your elevator pitch that you share with people you meet. It is an internal statement that you use to remind yourself to be on-brand every day in everything that you do. You need to place your PBS somewhere so that you will see it every day.

Once you are clear about your brand, including what is authentic to you, what is differentiating you from your peers, and what is relevant and compelling to your target audience, you are ready for the Express phase of the personal branding process.

EXPRESS

In the Express phase, the focus is on the "ilities":

- *Visibility:* Making sure your target audience sees you
- *Credibility:* Demonstrating your unique promise of value in everything you do

Visibility and credibility is a combination of show and tell. In this phase, you will use your communication wheel, which shows which communication vehicle(s) you are going to use. At the center of the wheel is your message—your thought leadership—what you want people to know. You apply that message to all communications. When choosing the tools/methods to use for your communication wheel, be sure it is something you enjoy doing and that it reaches your target audience. Some of the tools/methods to consider using to develop your communication wheel are social media, public speaking, or volunteering. If you don't enjoy public speaking, then it is not a tool that should appear on your communication wheel.

There is certain branded content that we all need, like your 3D brand bio, your headshot, and your thought-leadership content. Your 3D brand bio is much more than a list of accomplishments: it expresses who you are, what makes you great, and why people should care. The 3D brand bio makes your target audience want to get to know you. It has your personality, your values, your passions, and the things that you want other people to know about you. And your headshot is a way for people to be able to connect a face with some information and content.

Thought-leadership content is what you want to be known for by others. It might have to do with your area of expertise, for example, like patient engagement or population health. Or it could have to do with your thoughts on leadership or building relationships. This can come in the form of interviews, blog posts/comments, articles, presentations, or videos.

In the Express phase of the process, we deliver on the 3 C's of branding:

- *Clarity:* Being clear about who you are and who you are not.
- *Consistency:* Always being that.
- *Constancy:* Always being visible to the people who need to know you.

If you don't show up in Google, do you exist? Have you have ever googled yourself? Have you ever googled someone else? If so, then following logic if you are googling others, then they are googling you. Many will make decisions about you based on what Google reveals. DO google yourself regularly. Your Google results can change as quickly as the weather in Texas—so google yourself regularly.

There is a phenomenon that is making Google more important in your personal branding. That phenomenon is called Digital First. Digital First describes how we more often form first impressions online before we connect with people in the real world. The term was described in Mitch Joel's book *Ctrl Alt Del: Reboot Your Business. Reboot Your Life. Your Future Depends on It.* Two concepts are really important to the Digital First phenomenon. The first is primacy. Primacy relates to the fact that we believe the first thing we learn, and we remember it. This is important because if someone is learning about you first on the Web, then what they learn becomes permanent. That becomes who you are. When primacy is combined with another concept called anchoring, this is why you need to focus on building your brand in bits and bytes. Anchoring means that once you have formed an opinion of something, even if you receive new data that contradicts that opinion, you make the new data fit with the initial belief. This is why it is imperative that you make sure the virtual world "you" is consistent with the real world "you."

Without even realizing it, when someone googles you they are looking at five measures of online ID. They are evaluating you based on value, relevance, validation, purity, and diversity. To increase volume and relevance, use social networking sites, your own web site, web portals, or thought-leadership sites. Thought-leadership sites are those sites specific to your area of expertise where you can post content or comments and include blogs, publications, etc. Key social networking sites to focus on include LinkedIn, Google+, Twitter, and Facebook.

When people google your name, they have become very skilled at using the appropriate filter words to achieve the desired search results. Part of your personal branding process is determining what filter words are associated with you and being sure that everything you post on the Web contains those words. This contributes to purity. One possible way to determine the filter words associated with your name is by looking at your top skills and endorsements on LinkedIn.

Diversity speaks to having different types of content. You do not want to convey your brand just in text on the Web. You want to make sure you are using videos, images, images of yourself, and real-time content so people can get a truer, richer experience. Having a professional headshot is absolutely critical and is a worthwhile investment while building your brand. The DARE is to get a professional headshot and use it.

Video is the new frontier when it comes to personal branding. Thanks to high-speed Internet, video, or video-sharing sites like YouTube, it is easy to create, view, and share video content. Go to www.personalbranding.tv and learn how to build your brand in both the real and virtual world. DARE to produce your first video.

The last of the five measures, validation, is becoming more and more important. Validation is less about what you say and more about what other people say about you. Do other people back up what you say about yourself with recommendations and testimonials? People make decisions about each other based on the feedback of others. Get comfortable sharing what others think about you, and make a plan to get testimonials, endorsements, references, and recommendations.

EXUDE

In the third phase, Exude, you align your brand environment. That means you make sure everything that surrounds you sends the same on-brand message. Your brand environment consists of:

- Your personal appearance
- Your office environment
- Your personal brand ID system
- Most importantly, your professional network

Your appearance and office environment (and every decision you make in fact) says something about your brand. You want to ensure that you are reinforcing your brand message instead of detracting from it. The technique used to determine what is on—or off—brand is called "living in the inquiry." Ask yourself, "Is this on-brand for me?" and if the answer is no, make a plan to make it on-brand. The DARE is to brand your office. Even in organizations with very strict rules there are things you can do to make sure your brand is reflected in the items in your office. When you are communicating on behalf of your organization you are going to use their branding system. When you are communicating on behalf of yourself, use your own personal brand ID system.

Your personal brand identity system is a critical component of your brand. It is made up of a signature color, a standard font, images, textures, a personal logo, and a tagline. One of the most important elements of your brand identity system is your brand color. What color best represents your brand, and how can you use it consistently to create recognition? Access the video at bit.ly/ brandcolor to help you determine which color best represents your brand. Use your brand color consistently to reflect your brand. When you communicate on behalf of your organization, use its brand color!

The most important part of your brand environment is your professional network or brand community. These are the people who can help extend your brand. You can look at it as a series of concentric rings. The ring closest to you has the people who know you best; the stronger your brand, the clearer the message to the people in the outer rings. The DITCH is to drop the go-it-alone attitude. You need a network of resources to be successful.

Remember that your personal brand is your unique promise of value. It is authentic to you, differentiating you from your peers and making you relevant and compelling to your target audience. It is the key to your professional success and fulfillment. Use the Reach 1-2-3 Success! process to unearth your brand, express it to your target audience, and align everything that surrounds you so you exude a consistent, on-brand message.

CONCLUSION

Your personal brand is:

- Authentic
- Differentiated
- Compelling

The steps to Reach 1–2-3- Success™ are”:

- Extract
- Express
- Exude

Remember to Ditch, Dare and DO!

We all need to think of ourselves as brands if we want to be successful. What you think you are portraying is usually not the same as how people are perceiving you. People's perception will win out every time. If you are thinking like a brand, that will translate into acting like a brand. A brand is a unique promise of value. Your brand is your unique promise of value. It is unique because it sets you apart from your peers. It's a promise because it is authentic to you and you commit to delivering it every day with everything you do. It has value to your target audience, the people who need to know you so you can be successful.

DO you leave your mark on everything you do? Every email you write, every meeting you attend, every teleconference you lead? And if not, how can you?

DARE to be your best self. Personal branding is about giving yourself the mandate to be your best self—ALWAYS!

REFERENCE

Arruda, W. and Dib, D. *Ditch, Dare, Do: 3D Personal Branding for Executives.* Hachette Book Group, NY, 2013.

3 Diversifying Your Skillset

Vic Eilenfield
MS, MHA, FACHE, CPHIMS

CONTENTS

INTRODUCTION

Remember when you were talking to your parents or other personal or academic mentors about applying for college? They often said, "You need a well-rounded application. It can't just contain academics or sports. You need academics *and* sports *and* a record of community or civic involvement." That doesn't really change much when you move into the workplace environment. You need to be diversified in the workplace as well.

DIVERSIFICATION IN THE HEALTH IT WORKPLACE

Let's begin to explore diversification that would be helpful in the health information technology (IT) workspace by looking at the complexity of our healthcare system. The healthcare system is a surprisingly complex ecosystem filled with many subspecialty niches that do not have good parallels in other industries. In a physician's practice alone, there are over 150 specialties and subspecialties. Add to this the specialization of the nursing profession; ancillary service providers (laboratory, pharmacy, etc.); and hospital administrative, information systems, and logistical operations and we see a vastly complex ecosystem that has few parallels. We've all heard the one about automated teller machines (ATMs), right? It goes something like this: "If bankers can figure out how to do secure transactions between thousands of competing banks around the world, then why can't the health IT community figure out how to share my health information?" It seems simple, doesn't it? People who make such statements are completely unaware of the tremendous complexity of our healthcare system and the systems that support it.

As an example, in the niche of the health IT coding space there is great nuance in determining diagnostic codes far transcending the simple concept of "is this a withdrawal or a deposit?" The specificity of these concepts has greatly increased in recent years, such that a provider may not simply record that a patient has asthma; they must record whether the asthma is mild/intermittent,

DOI: 10.4324/9780429398377-4

mild/persistent, moderate/persistent, severe/persistent, or other/unspecified and select from three subcategories to more finely qualify the diagnosis, resulting in 18 potential diagnostic codes for the presumably simple diagnosis of asthma. And these 18 codes are only a tiny fragment of the 69,000 codes in the 10th revision of the International Classification of Diseases (ICD-10), now required for use in the United States to support billing and multiple other clinical documentation-related activities. This is not your average ATM withdrawal! This example only begins to open the Pandora's box of health IT.

So what does this have to do with skill diversification in health IT? The number of diverse niches in which you could play a vital role in improving performance of your healthcare organization is huge. This example of the complexity of the workspace and the opportunities to fill multiple roles in one scenario just scratches the surface. Who helps the IT developers with determining how to expose clinical code pick lists for providers to appropriately code their clinical encounters? Who ensures clinical practice supports not only effective coding but optimizes accounts receivable? Who trains the providers to optimize their documentation while not adversely impacting the efficiency of their clinical activities? Who ensures clinical quality measures derived from the codes are reviewed and reported to the Centers for Medicare and Medicaid Services (CMS)? These questions begin to reveal the plethora of sub-specialties or experiential bases of health IT staff trying to optimize these complicated business practices in healthcare settings. Does your level of diversity help you fill one or more valued roles in this space?

TOTAL QUALITY MANAGEMENT (TQM) AND HEALTHCARE

Most students of health IT and others with business backgrounds have a reasonable understanding of quality management processes. Many of these quality assessment models, dating back to Total Quality Management (TQM) and healthcare, evolved from Deming and Juran and strongly suggest that problem solving in high-performing organizations be supported by robust, multi-disciplinary teams [1]. The value of such a tenet cannot be understated. In complex systems, it is quite implausible that upper management will routinely be able to discern what the root cause of a problem is or define the best solution to that problem. Approaches similar to and evolving from TQM very frequently emphasize the power of using cross-functional teams in improving system processes to enhance performance and outcomes.

An analogy frequently used in the quality management or quality improvement space is that of the infection control challenge in clinical environments. When a hospital encounters an increase in hospital-acquired infections, can this problem be solved only by nurses? No! The entire patient care environment must be examined by everyone who enters it, from provider hand-washing practices, to sterile supply, house-keeping services, ventilation system maintenance, nursing care, and beyond. Are you serving as clinic staff with experience in hospital infrastructure (heating, ventilation and air conditioning systems) or perhaps a health IT person with a good background in quality management practices? The broader your diversity in such situations, the greater your value as a team member in these settings! Do you just bring one skill to the table, or do you have a breadth of skills from which to assess challenges and improve organizational or system performance?

SKILLS DIVERSITY AND PROFESSIONAL CERTIFICATION

Another way to view the diversity of skills necessary to make healthcare enterprises function effectively and efficiently is to look at the tremendous range of job roles and professional certifications in this space. Another chapter discusses certification programs in more detail, but as an example of diversity here are just a few adapted from a substantially more robust listing from Toms IT Pro:

DATABASE JOB ROLES

- Database Administrator (DBA)
- Database Developer
- Database Designer/Database Architect
- Data Analyst/Data Scientist
- Data Mining/Business Intelligence (BI) Specialist
- Data Warehousing Specialist

HEALTH IT CERTIFICATIONS

- CAHIMS: Certified Associate in Healthcare Information Management and Systems
- CPHIMS: Certified Professional in Healthcare Information and Management Systems
- RHIA: Registered Health Information Administrator
- HCISPP: HealthCare Information Security and Privacy Practitioner
- CompTIA Healthcare IT Technician
- CPHIT: Certified Professional in Health Information Technology

INFORMATION SECURITY CERTIFICATIONS

- CISSP: Certified Information Systems Security Professional
- CISM: Certified Information Security Manager
- CompTIA Security +
- CEH: Certified Ethical Hacker
- GSEC: SANS GIAC Security Essentials

PROJECT MANAGEMENT CERTIFICATIONS

- PMP: Project Management Professional
- CAPM: Certified Associate in Project Management
- CSM: Certified ScrumMaster
- CompTIA Project+
- CPM: Certified Project Manager Certification

This list of 20 roles and certifications barely scratches the surface of the specialties in a hospital setting, and this is just a slice of the IT space! Taking a more clinical focus, you may find your contribution in such clinical and administrative areas, including:

- *Clinical provider:* Physician, nurse, physicians' assistant, nurse practitioner, laboratory or radiology technician, pharmacist or pharmacy technician, etc.
- *Clinical administration:* Hospital or clinic administrator, finance officer or specialist, hospital facilities engineer or specialist, human resources, etc.

Developing your skills through on-the-job experience and acquiring additional training or certifications helps build a strong resume and contribution to the healthcare team. As an example of both experiential and academic maturation over a career, I will use myself to illustrate how skillsets can build on each other and make you a more valuable asset to your organization (Figure 3.1).

Looking back, I know that my opportunities were uncharacteristic and remarkably fortuitous, but it does provide an illustration of how one skillset builds upon another to offer an ever-

Case Study: Starting with a couple degrees in psychology, my first Army healthcare assignment was as a Company Commander of a brick and mortar hospital where I tended to the training and professional development of our healthcare team as well as their rewards and discipline [**human resource** skill set]. After a couple years, I was accepted to patient administration school and, upon completion of training, became the administrator of the medical records division of a small hospital [**medical records** skillset and first exposure to **health IT**]. Going back to school for my Master of Healthcare Administration years later, I completed a residency in health policy in the Pentagon [**health governance and policy** skillset]. I was selected to teach post-graduate education in patient administration and managed care to Army healthcare officers when health IT systems were evolving rapidly [**teaching/training skillset**]. This exposure and my professional network kept me in constant contact with IT staff causing my subsequent placement to be as Chief Health Informatics Officer in the Office of the Army Surgeon General [Major cross-over into **health informatics** – a strong link between IT and the clinical processes of care]. Working at this corporate level and with my background in health IT, I was recruited to serve as program manager for an enterprise data warehouse program supporting the Military Health System [**project management & data warehousing** skillsets]. Success with this program led to formal acquisition training and program management of the military electronic health record (EHR) program [**EHR & acquisition** skillsets]. And so on...

FIGURE 3.1 Example of experiential and academic maturation over one's career: Vic Eilenfield's Personal Journey.

increasing range of opportunities to diversify and contribute as a valued member of your organization.

ASSESSING YOUR SKILLS DIVERSIFICATION

If you have been in the health IT field for a few years, take a look at your diversity of knowledge, skills, abilities, and certifications. Consider building a storyboard or narrative as in the case study above. Even using a graphical storyboarding technique may be helpful. How do you picture yourself in the "story" of the healthcare environment? I've built a simple storyboard for illustration (Figure 3.2).

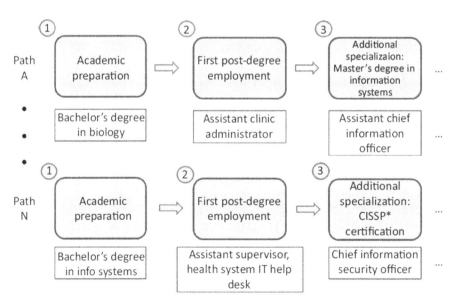

FIGURE 3.2 Storyboard technique (many alternative paths).

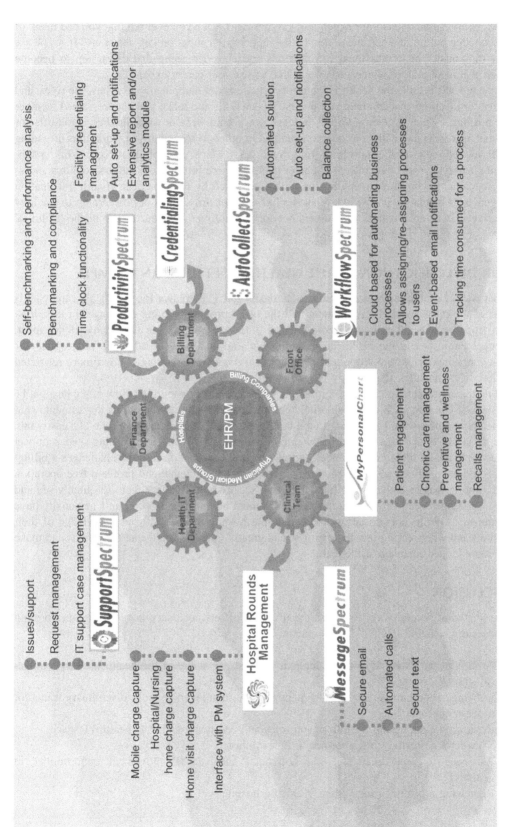

FIGURE 3.3 Diversification of problems occurring in a health IT setting. (Reprinted with permission from the Health IT Blog Network: http://www.healthcarescene.com.)

Does your resume reflect your experiential knowledge? Have you ever felt that you had much of the knowledge but not the certification to better support your input on key decisions? If so, please review the chapter on professional certifications and consider going that extra step to become certified if it is an area in which you would like to see your career expand.

If you haven't been in the health IT field for long, consider mapping out skillsets, job roles, and possibly certifications that can help you diversify your skills and make you a more valued member of the healthcare team over time. In this process, you would write down a number of job titles or skills that are associated with your position and that of others with whom you work, thus providing a multi-layered view of alternatives in job growth upon which you could proceed. While a subsequent chapter develops the concept of career mapping more fully, an exceptional tool that shows both vertical and horizontal diversification is that produced by the American Health Information Management Association (AHIMA). Visit the link at https://my.ahima.org/careermap to see how interactive it is as an illustration of diversification possibilities for your career in the health IT space!

WORK DIVERSIFICATION IN THE HEALTH IT SETTING: AN EXAMPLE

Another way of examining how diversification makes you a key player for your healthcare team is to look at a typical hospital environment and the usual problem-solving challenge. In this illustration from www.healthitoutcomes.com (Figure 3.3), you quickly see that many, if not most, challenges addressed in the healthcare environment impact a very broad range of hospital—or clinic—functions. While the scope and diversity of the outpatient setting is often more restricted than that of the hospital, the analogy is easy to follow.

While this representation has a lot of moving parts, it is a very simplified view of the hospital IT ecosystem. If you find yourself with a problem or process challenge in the billing department, what other team members would you bring to the table? Are you that team member who can easily talk across these soft boundaries in your healthcare organization? How does the billing system impact the electronic health record data sources and vice-versa? Can you discern the challenges a billing issue would have on provider credentialing? Both hospital efficiency and problem-free operation rely greatly on team members who have a diverse set of skills enabling them to quickly see and resolve challenges occurring across intra-organizational boundaries. If you don't personally have the requisite skills to operate across these multiple hospital divisions, your knowledge of their operations and who to bring into the dialogue can greatly improve healthcare operations and make you a more valued member of the team!

CONCLUSION

We've looked at several ways to assess the diverse skillsets necessary to run a high-performing healthcare organization (HCO). These include:

- Examining an example of the complexity in just one niche of the healthcare environment (diagnostic coding).
- Looking at common quality management practices that leverage multi-disciplinary teams for process improvement.
- Reviewing a surprising breadth of job roles and certifications in the health IT space.
- Viewing a case study in career health IT evolution.
- Assessing a career map showing horizontal and vertical movement opportunities in health IT.
- Reviewing a health IT ecosystem view of a hospital.

Ensuring high-quality products and processes is often dependent on having a diverse group of subject matter experts review and provide input on their part of the process. But who identifies all the various experts that might own a piece of the current process or the future improved process? Possessing a more diverse skillset enables you to identify the many contributing players to a process and perhaps play more than one role in the process resolution, making you a much more valued member of the healthcare team!

REFERENCE

1. Total Quality Management (TQM), Inc.com, http://www.inc.com/encyclopedia/total-quality-management-tqm.html

4 Developing a Career Roadmap

Detlev H. (Herb) Smaltz
PhD, LFACHE, LFHIMSS

CONTENTS

INTRODUCTION

It seems like such a simple edict—plan ahead. Most of us that toil daily in the field of healthcare informatics certainly apply that edict to the myriad of initiatives that we lead or participate in over the years. Yet, some of us tend to neglect that same edict when it comes to our own professional career development. One of my favorite childhood books was Lewis Carroll's *Alice's Adventures in Wonderland.* Recall the exchange between the Cheshire cat and Alice:

> *One day, Alice came to a fork in the road and saw a Cheshire cat in a tree. "Would you tell me, please, which way I ought to go from here?" she asked. "That depends a good deal on where you want to get to." was his response. "I don't much care where." Alice answered. "Then it doesn't matter which way you go" said the cat.*

Brilliant in its simplicity, yet it has such a deep and profound message.

I was recently going through my high school yearbook, which I haven't looked at in about five years. I wasn't going through it nostalgically to relive my high school years, which were uneventful to say the least, but rather to retrieve a doodling that I put together on a piece of butcher block paper some 36 years ago. I had just enlisted in the U.S. Air Force earlier that year to both fulfill a patriotic desire to serve (I grew up a military brat so that runs deep in me) as well as a means to an end—specifically to complete my baccalaureate education. I was just completing my technical training as a biomedical equipment repair technician (BMET) and was about to be transferred to my first assignment to MacDill Air Force Base in Tampa, Florida. I apologize for the handwriting (mine was never very good)—this is my original handwritten career roadmap (Figure 4.1).

What I continue to this day to find amazing is that, 33 years later, I'm actually on one of those career paths that I laid out in my own personal roadmap many years ago. At the time, I didn't think much of it—I'm analytical by nature. So laying out a decision tree with all of the possible career paths that I could envision from the starting point I was currently at was just a simple way for me to visualize my career options. Yet, that simple act of writing down, not just the end-state goals, but the intermediate steps I might have to take in order to move to the next step on that roadmap,

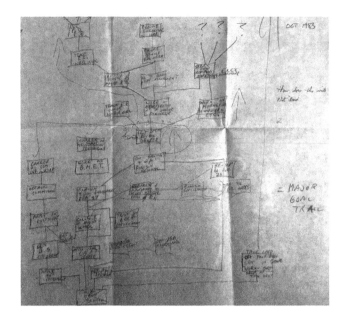

FIGURE 4.1 My own career roadmap—circa 1983.

was empowering. If I wanted to move forward on the roadmap, I needed to take the next step, which in my case was enrolling in night school and completing my bachelor's degree. Thereafter, it's a matter of taking the next incremental step on your roadmap.

The roadmap in Figure 4.1 above was completed by my inexperienced self, without benefit of a mentor at the time, and without benefit of help from any professional societies, like HIMSS (at the time I was not involved in IT so I wasn't a member yet). If I could redo it today, the figure below outlines the elements of an effective career roadmap (Figure 4.2).

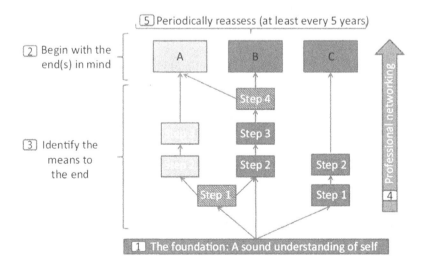

FIGURE 4.2 Components of a career roadmap.

CAREER ROADMAP: THE FOUNDATION—SELF-UNDERSTANDING

Prior to embarking on laying out a career roadmap, introspection is an important foundational step. And in being introspective, it's very important to be honest with yourself. It's not uncommon for some to fall into the trap of pursuing career paths that others have chosen for them, whether through the influence of parents, friends, or other well-intentioned people in their life.

It's a good thing to discuss and gain insight with others you know and trust about what they believe, but in the end, you, and you alone, will ultimately have to live your career path every day. So it's important to think about what you like to do, what you don't like to do, and what are your strengths and weaknesses. While a web search will provide a wealth of career-related self-assessment resources, the goal is to help you be truly introspective and gain a better understanding of your true self. A good example is the self-assessment survey provided by Claremont Graduate University [1], a link to which is provided in the "Web Resources" section at the end of this chapter. Armed with an honest self-assessment, you are ready to move on to the next step in creating a career roadmap.

CAREER ROADMAP: BEGIN WITH THE END IN MIND

Stephen Covey in his seminal work *The Seven Habits of Highly Effective People* [2] suggests that successful people tend to focus on the end goal that they are trying to achieve in all of their dealings in life. This is particularly true when embarking on drafting your own career roadmap. My own belief is that it's not as important to reconcile yourself to a single "achieve-it-or-bust" end goal. That, particularly in today's economy, is setting yourself up for frustration. Rather, conceive of a number of potential end goals that align with your self-assessment as outlined in Figure 4.2. For instance, for someone with a background as a pharmacy technician that has just graduated with a bachelor's degree in healthcare informatics, after an honest self-assessment that suggests an affinity for managing people and leading teams, the following might be plausible roadmap goals:

A. Director, Pharmacy Information Systems
B. Director, Clinical Information Systems
C. Deputy CIO/CIO

The important thing is to leave plausible alternatives and not lock yourself into a single "be-all" end goal, recognizing that there are lots of forces potentially at work (e.g., the economy, a growing family, changes in your own desires) that will have an impact on how your career roadmap actually evolves. In essence, you are planning ahead for end goals that are all plausible and acceptable to you at the point in time that you are creating your roadmap.

CAREER ROADMAP: IDENTIFY THE MEANS TO THE END

Next, think through what steps you might need to take to achieve each of your stated end goals. For instance, the healthcare informatics graduate pharmacy technician could conceivable envision the following for her "B" path above to Director, Clinical Information Systems. As you can see in Figure 4.3 below, the pharmacy technician in our example envisioned a distinct path that she believes will help her achieve her goal. It has concrete intermediate goals/steps that she can take to help prepare her to move toward her ultimate goals as opportunities within her own or other organizations present themselves.

Of course, a career path for someone working in the healthcare IT vendor space or as a healthcare IT consultant will have a different set of steps to achieve their respective desired end goal. Nevertheless, the methodology laid out in Figure 4.2 will be the same.

FIGURE 4.3   Designing a path to achieve your goals: A potential approach.

CAREER ROADMAP: PROFESSIONAL NETWORKING

Professional networking is an important component of a career roadmap for a number of reasons. First, by continuing to expand your network of professional friends and colleagues you are expanding the pool of people that might serve as references for new positions that you may want to compete for as you move through your career. Second, developing a strong and growing professional network gives you greater visibility into how others are moving through their own careers; this will help you gain validation for intermediate steps you believed you needed to take when you first built your career roadmap. Alternatively, the interaction with others in your professional network may suggest changes you may want to make to your career roadmap. Third, a professional network can be a great source of mentors who can help you continue to refine your career roadmap over time. Later in this book, Joseph J. Wagner (Section III: Learning from Others; Chapter 11: The Mentoring Process) is going to cover the mentoring process, and Dr. Joyce A. Zerkich (Section III: Learning from Others; Chapter 15: Professional Coaching) will cover professional coaching, so I won't go into depth here. I will say, however, that seeking out and maintaining a long-time professional mentoring relationship with someone whom you admire is a huge plus in helping you think through a career roadmap and also in evaluating career roadmap course changes from time to time. When I was a young healthcare administrator, I was leery about approaching senior leaders in my organization or professional society. I worried that they didn't want to be bothered with me, that they were too busy to care about me, etc. Nothing could be further from the truth. Almost all senior leaders love to give back—they love to mentor and relish the opportunity to work with young up-and-coming healthcare leaders, like you, to develop or evaluate your career roadmap, to serve as sounding boards when new opportunities present themselves, and to share lessons learned and give advice from their own experiences of navigating the same waters you are now trying to navigate. So take note—put your fears aside, and simply ask! You'll be pleasantly surprised by the positive response.

If you haven't been able to get much traction in developing your professional network, I strongly urge you to consider greater participation in health IT professional societies like HIMSS. Not only do they offer career development services, but by participating in annual and state conferences and events, you naturally will begin to grow your network of colleagues, which you will benefit from for a lifetime. A web resource to the HIMSS site has been provided at the end of this chapter [3].

CAREER ROADMAP: PERIODIC REASSESSMENT

Finally, it's important to recognize that people change, industries change, and economies change. It only makes sense to periodically take stock of your career roadmap and yourself to see if it still holds true or if changes are warranted. At the very least, pull your roadmap out every five years and assess not only the end goals that you originally listed but also the intermediate steps you thought you needed to take to achieve the goals and update your roadmap accordingly. Just like hospitals and health systems don't build a strategic plan one time and never update it, so, too, should you expect to periodically update your own career roadmap.

CONCLUSION

Know yourself. A good friend, Jaime Parent , Associate CIO, Vice President, IT Operations, and Assistant Professor, College of Health Sciences, Rush University, once told me, "Do what you love, and love what you do." Like Lewis Carroll's Cheshire cat, Jaime's words are brilliantly simple yet deeply profound. Seek out things you enjoy doing, and love doing those, whatever level in the organization those may be. Don't let naysayers dissuade you from what you professionally gravitate toward. But above all, commit to creating your own career roadmap.

KEY TAKEAWAYS

Commit to drafting a career roadmap with the following components:

1. Conduct an honest self-assessment to identify your strengths, weaknesses, likes and dislikes, etc.
2. Begin with the end in mind: Identify at least two to three plausible future career goals.
3. Identify the steps you believe you need to take or you believe will be useful in helping you move toward that desired end goal.
4. Develop and nurture your professional network throughout your career.
5. Reassess at least every five years to update your career roadmap.

REFERENCES

1. How to Build a Career Roadmap, Claremont Graduate University. https://my.cgu.edu/career-development/wp-content/uploads/sites/8/2020/07/CareerRoadmap-2018-fillable.pdf
2. Covey, Stephen. *The Seven Habits of Highly Effective People*. Simon & Schuster, New York, NY, 1989.
3. Healthcare Information & Management Systems Society, Resource Center.https://www.himss.org/resources-all

5 Work-Life Balance: Does It Exist? Can You Achieve It?

Jean Ann Larson
EdD, MBA, BSIE, FACHE, LFHIMSS, FIISE

CONTENTS

INTRODUCTION

The ability to traverse the struggles and challenges of life is critical to our health and our lives. Workplace stress has long been cited as a major cause of rising healthcare costs and lower workplace productivity (Ganster and Schaubroeck 1991). We sense that if we could achieve work-life balance (WLB), it would help make workplace stress more manageable and we could live more satisfying, healthy, and productive lives. The concept of WLB has existed for decades. As each generation gets busier and busier, often even before they enter the workforce, it seems that WLB becomes more of an elusive goal. And with the impact of technology that aims to simplify our lives, the everyday distractions and stress become worse. This chapter will answer several questions such as: What is WLB, and should we pursue it? What does WLB mean to different individuals at different stages of their lives? Who is responsible for helping us achieve it? What are strategies that we can employ to achieve it through the various roles and challenges of our lives?

WLB is defined as "being able to properly prioritize activities related to job, family, community, and self-development" (Wu et al. 2016). Though the definition seems fairly straightforward, WLB happens differently for each individual. Our own understanding of WLB also changes throughout our lives as we take on different roles professionally and personally, and as those roles evolve over time. For example, for the role of parent, the demands, priorities, and rewards of that role change as you first become a parent, as your children grow up, and then as they leave and live independent lives. At all these different times, what WLB means to us and how we achieve WLB with this particular role changes. Also, how this role and our other roles intersect and overlap will change. Thus, how we "achieve WLB" will be very different at different stages of our lives and present very unique challenges. I have found that just when I feel I am successfully creating WLB in my life, a role changes significantly or I take on a new role. The truth is that at any given moment, I am not achieving WLB. However, it is much like piloting a plane or a ship. At any given time, the plane is not headed directly toward its destination. In fact, 99% of the time it may be technically "off course." If this is true, how do planes or ships ever arrive at their destinations? Just as the pilot continuously makes very small changes to keep the plane on its intended flight path, we must make choices, big and small, throughout the day, the week, the month, and ultimately our life to make sure that we are achieving the things that are important to us and that we are maintaining key relationships with ourselves and others.

Creating WLB in your life, whatever that means to you at this point in your life, is critical to your health and productivity. But there is good news and bad news. First of all, though your organization or employer can help support—or at least not get in the way of WLB—it is ultimately up to you and the choices you make that will allow you to create it. Why? Because it looks different for everyone. What helps create balance in one person's life may actually create stress for another. We all have different values and objectives, as well as different priorities that may change over time. Thus, you never achieve or arrive at WLB; you must constantly create and reconnect with it!

A particular challenge that IT professionals have is that they are under tough deadlines amidst constantly changing technologies and organizational priorities. It is also not infrequent that the IT team finds itself in an intense system implementation and go-live process that becomes all-consuming. For hopefully short periods of time, WLB will be difficult to impossible to achieve. If we allow ourselves to get caught up in the frenetic pull of multiple stakeholders with different priorities and different levels of appreciation and understanding of the complexities of our industry, we can end up in a downward spiral that makes us ineffective both personally and professionally, while making the concept of WLB seemingly out of reach and just another frustrating and impossible goal.

However, there are ways we can step off this hamster wheel, identify what is important to us and what we want to achieve, and create balance in our lives. And as critical change agents for our organizations, we can show the way and model WLB. As we modify our reactions and the choices that we make throughout the day, we can demonstrate to our peers, teams, and clients that there is a better way to deal with change in our organizations. Even during times of non-stop deadlines, such as the go-live mentioned above, there are small things we can choose to do that give us a moment of self-care.

So what can we do? First, recognize that *you alone* are responsible for creating WLB in your life, minute by minute. No one can or will ever create it for you. Plus, if you wait, the right time will never come. But, you always have choices. The challenge is to be aware of when to make those choices and then to have the courage to make them and live by them! Even though you may be busy and stressed out, take the time to sit down to *thoughtfully and intentionally* identify what matters most to you. Specifically, you must discover your governing values—those enduring, passionate, and distinctive core beliefs that do not change; your roles, which are key relationships and responsibilities; and ultimately your mission, which is your unique purpose in life. I realize that if you've never done this before, it can seem a very daunting task. It can also seem intimidating if you feel you have removed yourself far from who you are and who you want to be.

DEVELOPING VALUES

The important first step is to spend time developing and reflecting upon your values. To make it easier, walk yourself through a series of questions and journal your answers to them. Understand that they will evolve and become clearer as you refer back to them and as you begin to use them in your life to make choices and decisions around where you want to spend your time and energy. Ask yourself the following questions:

- What is really important to me?
- Why is it important?
- Throughout my life, what remains important to me?
- What would others say are my signature traits and strengths? (You may want to ask trusted colleagues and friends what they would say.)
- Where do my talents and passions lie?
- What gives me energy?
- What and who causes my eyes to light up?

Some sample values might include:

- To be balanced in hand, heart, mind, and soul to bring out the best in myself and others.
- In all my dealings with others, I choose to assume that they are creative, capable, and complete.
- To be tolerant and compassionate toward all.
- To be grateful.
- To be continuously learning.
- To be curious and engage myself and those around me in lifelong learning and discovery—values of curiosity, learning, sense of adventure, open-mindedness.
- To be fit and healthy.
- To be financially secure.
- To cherish family, friends, and loved ones.
- To be creative.
- To embrace all of life's changes.

Make sure that these values really are yours and not those of someone else. Later, as you identify key roles and your goals and objectives, you will get more specific around what these values mean to you. Record your values in a small notebook, journal, or on your phone or computer where you can refer back to them and reconnect with them annually, monthly, and weekly. To help you, see Appendix 5.1 for a values exercise that can help you with this process.

DEVELOPING YOUR MISSION STATEMENT

A mission statement is a powerful document that expresses your personal sense of purpose and meaning in life. It acts as a governing constitution by which you evaluate decisions and choose behaviors and the ways you engage with others personally and professionally. The process of writing a mission statement involves answering a series of questions:

- What am I about?
- What are my values? (You have already identified these!)
- What are the qualities of character I would like to emulate?
- What is important to me?
- What are my roles?
- What things do I want to have that I feel are important?
- What legacy do I want to leave?

Again, spend some time reflecting on these questions and recording your answers in your notebook or journal. For me, this step was challenging because I kept thinking that there should be a formula or process that would help me do this. Unfortunately, there is not. The good news is that this mission statement may be kept private and confidential. Also, I had to live with what I wrote down, grow into it, and get comfortable with it. Even though I was teaching workshops on WLB, it took some time and courage for me to become vulnerable enough to share small parts of it. Since then, and through several professional and personal transitions, my mission statement has changed very little, and it has helped me reinvent myself and accept new opportunities over most of my life. For more help and inspiration go to http://msb.franklincovey.com/inspired/mission_statement_ examples for examples and some ideas to help you write your unique mission statement.

YOUR KEY ROLES AND RELATIONSHIPS

Most of us live multi-faceted lives. In fact, we may relish the multiple roles that we take on. However, this can make WLB even harder to achieve. Incorporating your values and mission around your key roles and relationships can not only lead to a more satisfying life, but it can also serve as a compass to keep you in balance. Some roles you might wish to think about as you develop your values and your mission include:

- Professional roles you assume at work. For example, are you a leader of a team? Are you the boss? What about a colleague to your peers? You are also an employee of your organization. This might be your formal title or description of what you do. For example, my current title is Leadership Development Officer. Key relationships I have include those with my two bosses as well as the leaders across the organization who I serve.
- You may be a spouse or partner.
- You may be a parent, a child, or both.
- You are a community member.
- You may have a relationship with a higher power and be a member or leader of a place of worship.
- You may be a member of a professional or recreational organization that is important to you.

I offer these examples and suggest you consider all of them and select the four to six most important ones in your life right now. Make sure that your values and mission are aligned around them and include them. This will ensure that you can create balance around all of your key relationships and roles. Often we find it hard to reconcile our work and personal lives because all of our goals are centered on just one or two roles, ignoring other parts of our lives that help define who we are.

In addition to identifying those key four to six roles that you play in your life, you should also intentionally identify the key relationships or people that these roles serve or relate to. For example, one of my roles is that of being a "mother." In that role, I have two key relationships that are important to me—the one with each of my two daughters. I am also a daughter, and that key relationship is with my elderly mother. As I mentioned earlier, in my place of employment I am the chief leadership development officer, and I have key roles with the CEO and the Chief of the Medical School to whom I report. As a relatively new employee, it is critical that I develop a healthy, trusting relationship with each of them. As an author, my relationship is to my readers, and I must do my best to communicate to them and relate to their challenges.

There is also one key and sometimes neglected relationship that we all have in common. That is the relationship we have to ourselves. Similar to the safety message we hear on the airlines, before we help others with their oxygen masks during a time of emergency, we should first secure and put on our own. If we don't take care of ourselves, we cannot help others. Stephen R. Covey used the metaphor of "sharpening the saw." If the saw is dull, the wood cutter is unable to work at full capacity and cut down the number of trees he needs to cut down. Once he sharpens that saw, he can go back to working full speed ahead.

This metaphor is true of our lives. The key lesson here is that in order to be effective in all of our roles, we must take time to take care of ourselves, refresh and recharge, and "sharpen our saw" in order to be at full capacity. To achieve WLB, it is vital that we manage not only our time, but also our energy. In fact, some researchers now suggest that managing our energy is more important than managing our time (Loehr and Schwartz 2005). In order to manage both our energy and time, we need to care for ourselves on four dimensions: the physical, the emotional/social, the intellectual, and the spiritual.

On the physical side, we need to care for our physical health and spend time and attention on exercising, eating healthy, hydration, and adequate rest and sleep. One physician executive shared with me that without exercise, his sleep was impacted. Without exercise and sleep, he could not think as creatively or be as productive in his role. On the social and emotional side, we need to spend time connecting with our family, friends, and community. Intellectually, we should ask ourselves if we're challenging our minds. Are we learning new things? Are we reading? Are we finding new solutions and approaches to problems? Spiritually, are we connecting to a higher power or source however we choose to worship and acknowledge the divine? There is no one way to sharpen the saw for any one person—and the ways in which we sharpen the saw may change over time as our circumstances change.

Remember, you do not have to address every dimension every day. However, you should work on each of the four dimensions at least once a week—though some of you will prefer to do some of them on a daily basis. Here are some examples I've heard from friends and colleagues of how they sharpen the saw in each of the four dimensions. To sharpen the saw in the physical dimension, we often select some sort of regular exercise and eating "healthy." Physical exercise for you may be anything from 30 minutes of daily walking to training for a race, marathon, or triathlon. The key is to do what makes sense for you. Depending on your circumstances and what is most important for you to be doing to improve your physical health, you may also select getting seven to nine hours of sleep each night, drinking 64 oz. of water per day, not skipping meals, or scheduling an important preventive checkup. Think about one or two physical activities that if you incorporated them into your day-to-day life would help you improve or maintain good health.

For good emotional health, are you maintaining good relationships with family, friends and loved ones? Can you think of one thing you can do to nurture an important relationship in your life? It might be a date night with your partner or spouse or a call to parents or grandparents in another city. Maybe you'll spend some focused one-on-one time with one of your children. As both of my children are living in different states than I am, I make sure to text them every morning to say "good morning" and let them know I am thinking of them. These are simple things, but they help me stay connected daily to those who I love.

To keep your intellect sharp, are you reading, studying, taking classes, or learning? Do you have a reading list you're working your way through every day? Maybe you want to brush up on a foreign language or musical instrument. Maybe you have an interest or hobby you've always wanted to learn more about such as cooking, gardening, painting, dance, yoga, or crafting. Find a good friend or family member to join you, and you may be able to sharpen your saw intellectually, socially, and even physically.

What about your spiritual side? Similar to the other three aspects, how you engage and recharge spiritually is very personal and unique to each individual. For some, it is traditional worship in a church, synagogue, temple, mosque, or other faith-based community. Others connect to their spirituality through reading inspirational literature, meditation, journaling, reflective writing, or even walking in nature. Some experience spirituality within like-minded groups, and others are engaged in a more solitary journey.

Now that you've previously identified your values, mission statement, and key roles and relationships, it is time to write down your goals and objectives. Many people do this at least annually. Depending on how quickly your roles change, or if you are in a time of personal or professional transition, you may need to set or at least review your goals more frequently. For example, when I first started my business, I reviewed, assessed, and often reset my goals every 12 weeks. I had to do this because I was learning so much so quickly that some goals became obsolete or irrelevant within a few months. A resource I found helpful for developing and considering my goals and objectives at that time was a book entitled *The Twelve Week Year: Get More Done in 12 Weeks Than Others Do in 12 Months* (Moran and Lennington 2013). The authors' premise is that you ideally focus on only three goals or major objectives every 12 weeks. For each goal or objective, you list tactics that will help you achieve the highly specific and measurable goal. If at the end of the 12 weeks, you have not achieved that goal, you ask yourself the following questions:

1. Did you achieve the goal? If not, ask the following:
2. Did you successfully complete all the tactics for that goal?
3. If you made some progress but you still did not achieve the goal, you will need to investigate and employ new tactics that will allow you to achieve the goal. This approach is helpful if you have stretch goals where many of the tactics to achieve those goals might be determined by trial and error and in areas that are very new to you. A simple example of how this approach might work is to use losing ten pounds as one of your key goals within the 12-week timeframe. If at the end of the 12 weeks, you have not lost the weight, you need to determine if you have a discipline problem or a problem with your tactics. If you've nailed all of your tactics but the weight still didn't come off, you'll have to investigate and try different tactics.

WEEKLY PLANNING: PUT THE BIG ROCKS IN FIRST

Every week, review your goals, objectives, and roles. For each goal, ask what one to two action items you can take *that week* to help move you toward achievement of that goal. Also for each key role in your life, ask what one to two things you can do to build on and strengthen the relationship. Once you have your weekly list of action items for each of your goals, objectives, and roles, schedule them into your day. Also include your "sharpen the saw" activities. Be realistic about your schedule. By scheduling these into your calendar as a commitment, you are putting the big rocks or most important activities in first. To keep me on track, I use the Franklin Covey weekly compass based upon Stephen R. Covey's book *The Seven Habits of Highly Effective People* (1989) and *First Things First* (Covey et al. 1994) in order to record the two to three important tasks for each of my roles and goals. It reminds me at a glance and every day of my important roles and goals as well as the ways in which I choose to "sharpen my saw" physically, intellectually, socially, and spiritually. Please see Appendix 5.2 for an example. In the example, the individual selected four key roles: that of boyfriend, team leader, friend, and volunteer. For each role, he recorded one or two important tasks he wanted to accomplish that week. He also filled out all four dimensions for sharpening the saw.

DAILY PLANNING

Once you've identified your roles, set your goals, and done your weekly planning, daily planning becomes very easy. However, there are a couple of tips that I've learned along the way. First, as much as possible, schedule those key activities or big rocks for a specific date and time on your calendar by making it an appointment or commitment you make to yourself to accomplish the task. Second, allow a certain percentage of "unscheduled" time on your calendar to take care of urgent activities and other things that you must handle immediately. When I didn't do this, I got frustrated when I couldn't get everything I had planned done. What I discovered was that I was over-scheduling myself. As a healthcare professional and leader, it was unrealistic and undesirable to try to schedule and control every minute of my day. Depending upon your role and situation, you'll need to leave more or less unscheduled time on your calendar to handle the necessary urgent and important tasks that make up your day. Also, if you attend a lot of meetings as many of us do, make sure you allow ample travel time, preparation time, and time to follow up on action items. If you don't do this, you will make your day more hectic and rushed than it needs to be. Last but not least, be flexible. Some days you may feel that your priorities are changing almost hourly, so your

	Urgent	Not urgent
Important	Quadrant #1 "Necessity" ——————— Your key action: "Manage" ——————— *Common activities* – Crises – Deadline-driven activities – Medical emergencies – Other "true" emergencies – Pressing problems. – Last-minute preparations	Quadrant #2 "Quality and personal leadership" ——————— Your key action: "Focus" ——————— *Common activities* – Preparation and planning – Values clarification – Empowerment – Relationship-building – True recreation
Not important	Quadrant #3 "Deception" ——————— Your key action: "Use caution or avoid" ——————— *Common activities* – Meeting other people's priorities and expectations – Frequent interruptions: – Most emails, some calls – Urgency masquerading as importance	Quadrant #4 "Waste" ——————— Your key action: "Avoid" ——————— *Common activities* – Escapist activities – Mindless tv-watching – Busywork – Just mail – Some emails – Some calls

FIGURE 5.1 Covey's four quadrants for time management. (Adapted from Stephen Covey's "First Things First," Covey Leadership, Inc. ©2003.)

schedule will need to flex accordingly. Most important, don't be too hard on yourself. By focusing on the one or two things you want to do around your key roles and goals, no matter how crazy the week gets, you'll be able to engage (most of the time) in those activities that speak to who you are and your deepest held beliefs.

COVEY'S FOUR QUADRANTS FOR TIME MANAGEMENT

A model that will help you assess how you currently spend your days versus how you'd like to spend them is Covey's four quadrant time management construct as illustrated in Figure 5.1. Think about the types of activities that keep you running all day and where you spend your time. Begin to think about the *importance* versus the *urgency* of your daily tasks.

QUADRANT 1

It is very easy to get caught in the urgency trap. Some people I've worked with seemed at times to be addicted to urgency. As you can see from the graphic, quadrant 1 is comprised of activities that are both urgent AND important. Examples are deadlines, medical emergencies, and family emergencies. These are truly items that cannot be deferred and must be handled now. However, they can be *managed*. A very simple example is a project deadline. Assuming that you weren't just assigned the project, you usually have time to work on the project and complete it before it becomes a crisis. However, if you routinely leave everything to the last minute, you spend more time in quadrant 1 than is necessary.

QUADRANT 3

Another way to get trapped in the urgency trap with even more negative implications is to spend time in quadrant 3. This quadrant is called the quadrant of deception because these are tasks that seem to be *urgent* but are not at all important. They demand our immediate attention but do not require it. Most of them can be deferred or even ignored in some cases. What are examples? Looking at your phone every time you get a ping for a social media update, ill-defined meetings, some emails, and frequent interruptions. You want to avoid this quadrant as much as possible.

QUADRANT 4

Quadrant 4 activities, which are defined as not urgent and unimportant, need to be avoided as much as possible. This is the quadrant of waste. These activities include any kind of escapist-type activities such as mindless TV watching, Internet surfing, games, and busywork. So why would we go there? After too much urgency and stress, we end up in this quadrant to escape the pressure. Better to go into quadrant 2 for rest, recovery, and rejuvenation. But be careful that these activities don't morph back into quadrant 4. We may also go into quadrant 4 to procrastinate and avoid undesirable or seemingly overwhelming tasks. Understand why you are procrastinating. Are you lacking information or resources, or are you overwhelmed or afraid of tackling the task? Some of my favorite remedies for my own procrastination include:

- Start the day with the task I've been procrastinating.
- Work on the task for just 10–15 minutes.
- At the end of each major step, start the next step so that it is easier to jump back in where I left off.
- Brainstorm what information I need, who I need to talk to, or what resources I need to take the next step.

What are your ways to avoid procrastination? How can you employ them more frequently?

QUADRANT 2

Quadrant 2 activities do not occur if we do not focus on them and take time to do them. Why? Because they are not urgent, and they do not pull on our attention the way urgent tasks do. It is critical to work-life and personal life leadership to focus our efforts in this quadrant. We must take time to prepare for the week and the important tasks and roles in our lives. It is the time that we spend clarifying our values, mission statements, and goals and connecting with who we are. These are the tasks we do in order to build relationships that matter to us. And quadrant 2 is where we take time for true recreation and sharpening of the saw.

CONCLUSION

Most people live half their lives "below the line" of Covey's time quadrant on the unimportant tasks and activities. This leads to frustration, a sense of being out of control, and lots of stress. The critical skill is to learn to live above the horizontal line and focus on doing the important things as much as possible. Otherwise, we'll find ourselves reacting to every urgent stimulus.

So what's the secret of WLB? First, it doesn't just happen. You have to create it. Year by year, month by month, week by week, and day by day as your life changes and as you evolve and grow. Like the earlier mentioned airplane crossing the country, you're 99% off course or not in balance at any given time. Just like the adjustments that the pilot makes that allows the plane to travel from point A to point B, for you, it is the constant adjustments and decisions that you make during your day that allows you to do what matters most and feel a sense of balance. When you feel that you are making the right choices and navigating your life's journey, stress decreases and you can have some sense of peace and accomplishment. The bad news is that sometimes making the right decisions can be difficult as we are distracted and pulled in many different directions. The good news is that when you frequently connect to who you are—your mission, vision, and values—it makes it easier to make the hard decisions.

In the words of Mahatma Gandhi:

Your beliefs become your thoughts,
Your thoughts become your words,
Your words become your actions,
Your actions become your habits,
Your habits become your values,
Your values become your destiny.

REFERENCES

Covey, S. R. 1989. *The Seven Habits of Highly Effective People*. New York: Simon & Schuster.

Covey, S. R., A. R. Merrill, and R. R. Merrill. 1994. *First Things First*. New York: Fireside.

Ganster, D. C., and J. Schaubroeck. 1991. Work stress and employee health. *Journal of Management* 17 (2): 235–271.

Loehr, J., and T. Schwartz. 2005. *The Power of Full Engagement: Managing Energy, Not Time, Is the Key to High Performance and Personal Renewal*. New York: Simon and Schuster.

Moran, B. P., and M. Lennington. 2013. *The 12 Week Year: Get More Done in 12 Weeks than Others Do in 12 Months*. Hoboken, NJ: Wiley.

Wu, S., X. Nhengzheng, F. Li, W. Xiao, X. Fu, P. JIang, J. Chen et al. 2016. Work-recreation balance, health-promoting lifestyle and suboptimal health status in southern China: A cross-sectional study. *International Journal of Environmental Research and Public Health* 13 (339): 1–16.

APPENDIX 5.1 VALUES EXERCISE

Identifying and prioritizing one's values can be a challenge. It may take time. Be uncomfortable, and highlight areas where your current life is not congruent with what you value most.

First, look at the list of potential values as brainstormed by others and circle or highlight up to 50% that might be your values. **Second,** in the column on the right, add any values that you don't see.

Being kind	Serving the less well-off	Financial independence
Being involved in politics	Health and energy	
Doing something worthwhile	Having loving relationships	
A strong marriage or partnership	Intellectual growth	
Integrity	Being a good listener	
Religious beliefs	Being a good leader	
Professional success	Personal excellence	
Credibility in my profession	A balanced life	
Peace of mind	Discipline	
Self-sufficiency	Ability to influence	
Law and order	Ability to make things happen	
Open-mindedness	Compassion	
Individual freedom	Being a risk-taker	
Success and achievement	Preparing children for adulthood	
Family happiness and well-being	Being a good team player	
Social issues and causes	Being funny	
Love	Trust in God	
Creativity	Tolerance of others	
Musical excellence	A wide range of friends	
Art and beauty	Standing firm on principles	
Financial excellence	Being decisive	
Fairness and justice	Patriotism	

Third, pick out the top ten values that are closest to your heart *(Highlight or underline each one)*. **Fourth,** rank in order of importance one that you feel is number one, then number two, and so on.

Sometimes short words and phrases do not quite catch the overall impact of a value. Write what these values mean to you in your life using "to" statements.

My core values are: *1ˢᵗ Draft*

To

To

To

To

To

To

To

To

To

To

To

To

To

APPENDIX 5.2 WEEKLY COMPASS EXAMPLE

WEEKLY COMPASS

*What is the most important thing
I can do in this role this week?*

Date:

ROLES AND BIG ROCKS'

Role: Sharpen the Saw'

Physical Yoga 3 times

Social/Emotional Dinner with Josh and Marie

Mental Read professional journal

Spiritual Spend time at river

Role: Boyfriend

Big rocks • Plan weekend date

Role: Team Leader

Big rocks • Hold team meeting
about communication plan
• Recognize team contributions

Role: Volunteer

Big rocks • Research adult literacy
program

Role: Friend

Big rocks • Call Renee and set up lunch

Role:

Big rocks:

Section II

Establishing and Nurturing Your Career

6 The Role of the Professional Association

Anthony Blash
Pharm.D. BCompSc, CPHIMS

JoAnn Klinedinst
MEd, CPHIMS, PMP, DES, CPTD, LFHIMSS, FCAHME, FACHE

CONTENTS

INTRODUCTION

Professional associations (also called professional bodies, professional organizations, or professional societies) are generally defined as a group of individuals with a general field of interest or expertise that comes together to advocate, set standards, and speak for the respective profession in local, regional, national, and international discussions with other legislative or professional bodies.[1,2] The association may also provide support, educate, certify, and facilitate meetings for members, individuals interested in the profession, and the public. Table 6.1 lists a representative sample of health information technology (IT) professional associations.

DOI: 10.4324/9780429398377-8

TABLE 6.1

Health Information Technology (Health IT) Professional Associations

Acronym	Association Name	Focus	Individual Annual Membership Cost	Website
	AcademyHealth Health Information Technology (HIT) Interest Group	Health care delivery and management, U.S.	$45.00–$200.00	http://www.academyhealth.org/index.cfm
ADA	American Dental Association Center for Informatics and Standards	Dental, U.S.	$0.00–$552.00	http://www.ada.org/en/member-center/member-benefits/practice-resources/dental-informatics
AATP	American Association for Technology in Psychiatry	Psychiatric informatics, U.S.	$45.00–$75.00	http://www.techpsych.org
ACHE	American College of Healthcare Executives	Healthcare executives, U.S.	$150.00–$325.00	http://www.ache.org/
AHIMA	American Health Information Management Association	Many aspects of healthcare, U.S.	$175.00–$185.00	http://www.ahima.org/
AMIA	American Medical Informatics Association	Many aspects of healthcare, U.S. and international	$45.00–$350.00	https://www.amia.org/
ANIA	American Nursing Informatics Association	Nursing, U.S.	$79.00	https://www.ania.org/
ASHP	American Society of Health-System Pharmacists	Pharmacy, U.S.	$49.00–$305.00	http://www.ashp.org/
AAIM	Argentine Association of Medical Informatics	Medical and bio-informatics, Argentina	N/A	N/A – Email contact: info@aaim.com.ar
ACDM	Association for Clinical Data Management	Clinical data management, U.S.	$60.00	https://acdmglobal.org/
AHIN	Association for Health Informatics of Nigeria	Medical and bio-informatics, Nigeria	N/A	https://ahin.wordpress.com
AS IS	Association for Information Science and Technology Health Informatics (HLTH)	Various disciplines, U.S.	$40.00–$140.00	https://www.asist.org/sig/sighlth/
AMBIS	Association for Medical and Bio-Informatics, Singapore	Medical and bio-informatics, Singapore	$15.00–$1,500.00 (SGD)	http://www.ambis.org.sg/
API	Association for Pathology Informatics	Pathology, U.S.	$0.00–$225.00	http://pathologyinformatics.org/
AVI	Association for Veterinary Informatics	Veterinary, U.S.	$0.00–$35.00	https://avinformatics.wildapricot.org/
AMDIS	Association of Medical Directors of Information Systems	Medical directors, U.S.	$185.00–$385.00	http://www.amdis.org
ACHI	Australasian College of Health Informatics	Healthcare, international	$0.00–$60.00	http://www.achi.org.au/

ATHS	Australasian Telehealth Society	Telehealth, international	$25.00–$50.00	http://aths.org.au/
ÖGBMT	Austrian Society for Biomedical Engineering	Medical and bio-informatics, Austria	N/A	http://iig.umit.at/akmi/akmi.htm
OCG	Austrian Working Group Medical Informatics and eHealth of the Austrian Computer Society	Medical and bio-informatics, Austria	N/A	N/A – Email contact: guenter.schreier[at]ait.ac.at
MIM	Belgian Society for Medical Informatics ("MIM")	Medical informatics, Belgium	$30.00–$200.00 Euros	https://www.bmia.be/en/home/
SBIS	Brazilian Society of Informatics in Health	Promote the development of all aspects of IT applied to health	$75.00–$1425.00 Brazilian Real	http://www.sbis.org.br/
BCSHIF	British Computer Society Health Informatics Forum	Healthcare informatics, U.K.	£20–£199	https://www.bcs.org/
ACHISA	Chilean Health Informatics Society	Healthcare informatics, Chile	5,000–20,000 pesos	https://www.achisa.cl/
CMIA	China Medical Informatics Association	Academic community, health IT in China	N/A	http://www.cmia.info/
CHIME	College of Healthcare Information Management Executives	Healthcare information management executives, U.S.	$375.00	https://chimecentral.org/
ACIESA	Colombian Association of Health Informatics	Healthcare informatics, Colombia	N/A	N/A - Email: carteta@gmail.com
CSMI	Croatian Society for Medical Informatics	Healthcare informatics, Croatia	Free	https://www.hdmi.hr/
ČLS JEP, zs	Czech Society for Biomedical Engineering and Medical Informatics	Medical informatics, Czech Republic	N/A	http://www.csbmili.cz/en/about
DSDS	Danish Society for Digital Health	Healthcare informatics, Denmark	N/A	https://www.dsds-dk.dk/
N/A	Digital Health Canada	Healthcare informatics, Canada	$35.00–$225.00	https://digitalhealthcanada.com/
eHAP	eHealth Association of Pakistan	Healthcare informatics, Pakistan	Rs. 500–Rs. 30,000	http://ehap.net.pk/
eHDA	eHealth Development Association	Healthcare informatics, Jordan	N/A	http://ehda.org.jo
EHIS	Emirates Health Informatics Society	Medical, dental informatics, United Arab Emirates	N/A	http://www.ehis.ae
FinnSHIA	Finnish Social and Health Informatics Association	Healthcare informatics, Finland	N/A	https://www.stty.org/
AIM	French Medical Informatics Association	Healthcare informatics, France	N/A	http://france-aim.org
GMDS	German Association for Medical Informatics, Biometry and Epidemiology	Medical informatics, Germany	€ 0–€ 600	http://www.gmds.de

(Continued)

TABLE 6.1 (Continued)
Health Information Technology (Health IT) Professional Associations

Acronym	Association Name	Focus	Individual Annual Membership Cost	Website
N/A	Ghana Health Informatics Association	Healthcare informatics, Ghana	N/A	N/A - Email address: wk.atiwoto@gmail.com
GBHIA	Greek Biomedical and Health Informatics Association	Healthcare informatics, Greece	N/A	http://www.gbhia.com
HiNZ	Health Informatics New Zealand	Healthcare informatics, New Zealand	$0.00–$198.00	http://www.hinz.org.nz
HiNZ	Health Informatics New Zealand	Healthcare, New Zealand	$20.00–$189.00	http://www.hinz.org.nz/
HISA	Health Informatics Society of Australia Ltd.	Healthcare informatics, New Australia	$87.50–$350.00	https://www.hisa.org.au
HISI	Health Informatics Society of Ireland	Healthcare, Ireland	$0.00–$55.00	https://www.hisi.ie/
HISSL	Health Informatics Society of Sri Lanka	Healthcare informatics, Sri Lanka	N/A	https://hissl.lk/
HIMAA	Health Information Management Association of Australia Limited	Health information management, Australia	$0.00–$385.00	http://www.himaa2.org.au/
HFMA	Healthcare Financial Management Association	Healthcare financial management executives, U.S.	$315.00	https://www.hfma.org/
HISI	Healthcare Informatics Society of Ireland	Healthcare informatics, Ireland	€0.00–€50.00	http://www.hisi.ie
HIMSS	Healthcare Information and Management Systems Society	Many aspects of healthcare, U.S. and international	$30.00–$199.00	http://www.himss.org/
	Hong Kong Society for Medical Informatics	Healthcare informatics, Hong Kong	$50.00	http://www.hksmi.org
IAMI	Indian Association for Medical Informatics	Medical informatics, India	INR 150–INR 15,000	https://imia-medinfo.org/wp/imia-member-societies/
IAMI	Indian Association for Medical Informatics	Healthcare, India	$100.00	https://www.iami.org.in/
IAHSS	International Association of Healthcare Security and Safety	Healthcare security, international	$50.00–$150.00	http://www.iahss.org
IHTSDO	International Health Terminology Standards Development Organisation	Data standardization, international	Free	https://www.snomed.org/
IMIA	International Medical Informatics Association	Physicians, international	$0.00–$100.00	http://www.imia-medinfo.org/wp
IrMIA	Iranian Medical Informatics Association	Healthcare informatics, Iran	N/A	https://imia-medinfo.org/wp/iranian-medical-informatics-association/

Abbreviation	Association	Scope	Fee	URL
ISBHI	Ivorian Society of Biosciences and Health Informatics	Healthcare informatics, Ivory Coast	N/A	N/A - Email: fsehua@yahoo.fr
JAMI	Japan Association for Medical Informatics	Medical informatics, Japan	¥3,000–¥100,000	http://www.jami.jp/english/
NJSZT	John von Neumann Computer Society (Hungary)	Healthcare informatics, Hungary	00.-HUF–2400.-HUF	http://www.njszt.hu
KeHIA	Kenya Health Informatics Association	Healthcare informatics, Kenya	N/A	http://www.kehia.org
KOSMI	Korean Society of Medical Informatics	Healthcare informatics, Korea	30,000 won–500,000 won	http://www.kosmi.org/
MIAM	Medical Informatics Association of Malawi	Medical enformatics, Malawi	N/A	N/A - Email: info@miam.org.mw
MLA	Medical Library Association, Medical Informatics Section	Medical librarians, health professionals, information sciences professionals, U.S.	$50.00–$130.00	http://www.mlanet.org/p/cm/ld/fid=532
SMIMS	Moroccan Society of Medical Informatics and Health	Medical enformatics, Morocco	N/A	http://smims.ma/
NASCIO	National Association of State Chief Information Officers	State Chief Information Officers, U.S.	$0.00–$500.00	http://www.nascio.org/
NCHICA	North Carolina Healthcare Information and Communications Alliance	Healthcare data exchange, U.S.	$25.00–$300.00	http://nchica.org/
NorHIT	Norwegian Society for Medical Informatics	Medical informatics, Norway	N/A	https://imia-medinfo.org/wp/norwegian-society-for-medical-informatics/
PMIS	Philippine Medical Informatics Society	Medical informatics, Philippines	Php 100–Php 7,500	https://imia-medinfo.org/wp/philippine-medical-informatics-society/
RSMI	Romanian Society of Medical Informatics	Medical informatics, Romania	5 RON–100 RON	http://medinfo.umft.ro/rsmi/
SHINE	Scottish Health Information Network	Healthcare, Scotland		https://shinelib.org/
SIMIA	Slovenian Medical Informatics Association	Medical informatics, Slovenia	N/A	http://www.sdmi.si/
VMBI	Society for Healthcare Informatics (The Netherlands)	Healthcare informatics, The Netherlands	€35–€65	http://www.vmbi.nl/
SIIM	Society for Imaging Informatics in Medicine	Biomedical imaging, U.S.	$0.00–$200.00	http://siim.org/
BHSMI	Society for Medical Informatics of Bosnia and Herzegovina	Medical informatics, Bosnia and Herzegovina	N/A	https://imia-medinfo.org/wp/society-for-medical-informatics-of-bosnia-and-herzegovina/
SAHIA	South African Health Informatics Association	Healthcare informatics, South Africa	R 0–R 8000	http://www.sahia.org.za/
SEIS	Spanish Society of Health Informatics	Healthcare informatics, Spain	N/A	https://seis.es/

(Continued)

TABLE 6.1 (Continued)
Health Information Technology (Health IT) Professional Associations

Acronym	Association Name	Focus	Individual Annual Membership Cost	Website
SFMI	Swedish Association of Medical Informatics	Medical informatics, Sweden	SEK 0–SEK 2000	http://www.sfmi.se/
SGMI	Swiss Society for Medical Informatics	Medical informatics, Switzerland	Fr. 60.- –Fr. 800.-	http://www.sgmi-ssim.ch/
TAMI	Taiwan Association for Medical Informatics	Medical informatics, Taiwan	600 yuan–20,000 yuan	http://www.medinfo.org.tw/
TMI	Thai Medical Informatics Association	Healthcare informatics, Thailand	N/A	http://www.tmi.or.th/
CSMI	The Cyprus Society of Medical Informatics	Physicians, Cyprus	$22.00	https://efmi.org/countries/cyprus/
ILAMI	The Israeli Association for Medical informatics	Medical informatics, Israel	N/A	N/A - Email: sadanba@netvision.net.il
SOMIBS	The Mali Society of Biomedical and Health Information	Healthcare informatics, Mali	N/A	https://imia-medinfo.org/
SAHI	The Saudi Association for Health Informatics	Healthcare informatics, Saudi Arabia	SR 100–SR 200	http://www.sahi.org.sa/
ATIM-TELEMED	Togolese Association of Medical Informatics and Telemedicine	Healthcare informatics, Togo	N/A	N/A - Email: atim.telemed@gmail.com
TURKMIA	Turkish Medical Informatics Association	Medical informatics, Turkey	20 TL	http://www.turkmia.net/
UACM	Ukrainian Association for Computer Medicine	Healthcare informatics, Ukraine	N/A	http://www.uacm.kharkov.ua/
AVIS	Venezuelan Association of Computer Science in Health	Healthcare informatics, Venezuela	N/A	https://imia-medinfo.org/wp/venezuelan-association-of-computer-science-in-health-avis/
WEDI	Workgroup for Electronic Data Interchange	Healthcare information exchange, U.S.	$0.00–$300.00	http://www.wedi.org/

PROFESSIONAL ASSOCIATIONS

As Table 6.1 shows, the cost of one-year active membership varies between organizations. Even if you're a cash-strapped new hire, joining a professional association will likely be one of the best investments you'll ever make. Most associations will offer different types of membership:

Active student: This member is a full- or part-time student on the pathway to a certification or degree that may or may not reflect the profession represented by the association. The student member's dues are usually the lowest of the membership categories.

General members: General members make up the body of the association. These are professionals in the workplace, working within the profession.

Corporate members: Corporate membership allows a company to enjoy benefits similar to an individual in terms of being in a position to network, advocate, set standards, and represent the respective profession in local, regional, national, and international discussions with other legislative or professional bodies. A company with a number of employees who would benefit from joining the association may choose to join as a group.

Affiliate members: An affiliate member is characterized as a person engaged in a commercial enterprise doing business with or providing goods or services to members.

Other: Additional membership types may be available, but these represent the most common.[2-4]

WHY JOIN A HEALTH IT PROFESSIONAL ASSOCIATION?

Joining a professional association is a great way to meet people. Membership grants you access to health IT professionals at the state, regional, and national levels. It gives you a structured opportunity to meet other health IT professionals—those with equivalent experience, leaders in the field, and people just entering the profession. You will be exposed to new ways of thinking about the world of health IT, meet potential employers, and make friends. Health IT professional association members may contribute professionally through engagement at meetings and conferences.

Membership may also provide other benefits, such as a subscription to the association's journal, swift communication on key issues that may affect the health IT professional, attendance at meetings for reduced rates, and the opportunity to experience and participate in Special Interest Groups (also known as SIGs) designed for your subspecialty.[1,5]

MEMBER BENEFITS

PERSONAL AND PROFESSIONAL GROWTH

On a resume, membership in a health IT professional association shows an understanding of the importance of professional networking. Current and future employers value a person dedicated to staying current and connected to their profession. Employers also want to know that a person's skill extends beyond the classroom. Opportunities to obtain knowledge and experience are available through the many volunteer opportunities offered in professional associations.

The association can assist in skills development by offering classes and presentations in your field. There may be opportunities to earn and maintain professional certifications or other credentials. Being recognized in this way validates your skills and demonstrates a high level of competence in your chosen profession.

Opportunities to volunteer also bring value to the member. Members who volunteer experience benefits far beyond the actual act of volunteering. Associations need the time and talent of volunteers to help shape and support key projects affecting the profession. Volunteering on a service project or committee you are passionate about will motivate you, which in turn will motivate others. As a volunteer, you may have opportunities to organize people and resources while participating in professional service projects. You may also gain valuable field experience by volunteering.

Association members also have the opportunity to mentor and be mentored. Most associations offer mentoring programs. Within the professional association your area of expertise may be nurtured and shared with members of greater and/or lesser experience. If your passion has not yet been promoted by the association, you may be given ample space, support, and opportunity to turn your ideas into action.[4–7]

ROLE IN SHAPING THE PROFESSION

In the association's policy-making body, sometimes called the House of Delegates, recommendations concerning the profession and its members are made. Usually any member may submit proposals for consideration by the House of Delegates. Accepted proposals are then used to position health IT as an influencer in the area of legislative and political decision making. Your association's actions assist in ensuring that health IT is actively supported in influencing and shaping health and healthcare policy.

VOICE IN WASHINGTON

Your professional association monitors legislative activity on issues that may affect the future of its members, such as the Health Information Technology for Economic and Clinical Health (HITECH) Act and Meaningful Use progress. Professional associations may also represent health IT interests before the U.S. Congress and federal regulatory agencies. The association is your partner and advocate in efforts to identify and offer guidance on critical issues regarding technology in the U.S. healthcare system.

LEADERSHIP OPPORTUNITIES

Participation in the governance of the professional association offers a service to the profession and to the members while providing a sense of satisfaction to the member serving in this capacity. Association members may serve as local, regional or national committee chairpersons, chapter officers, or members of the House of Delegates. There will be ample opportunity to develop or exercise leadership skills that may also be used in community or professional capacities.[3,6,8–11]

CHAPTER ACTIVITIES

In most professional associations, local association members are also recognized as members at the national level. Your local or regional chapter may offer many opportunities for involvement. Usually there are chapter meetings, conferences, community service projects, socials, fundraisers, elections, and membership drives to name a few. Members may also have the opportunity to develop and present on topics of importance to the profession or the community.[3,4,10]

ASSOCIATION ACTIVITIES

Continuing professional education and community outreach are important components of health IT association activities. Members will be able to learn while earning or maintaining professional licensure or other credentials. Many programs and activities are sponsored by professional associations to assist and support the credentialing efforts of their members. Nonmembers may also be able to participate in professional development activities sponsored by the association, but usually at a significantly higher enrollment cost.

Because of the number of individuals involved, associations are able to effect change faster and have a much greater impact than just one person. Some notable efforts are described below.

AMIA: EHR-2020 TASK FORCE

Our nation's healthcare system is in the midst of an unprecedented transformation that is designed to improve the safety, efficiency, and quality of patient care. The HITECH Act instituted incentive programs for the meaningful use of certified electronic health record (EHR) technology. EHRs can help advance care in ways that paper records cannot. EHRs can improve patient and provider access to data and also improve the quality of care that patients receive by helping healthcare providers identify potential safety issues and better follow up with patients on long-term care goals. However, turning paper health records into EHRs is not enough. The EHR will provide the most benefit when the information is standardized, structured, and stored in uniform ways.[8,12–15]

Meaningful use of EHR technology has the potential to prevent medical errors, decrease unnecessary healthcare costs, reduce paperwork, and improve the quality of healthcare. This task force creates recommendations and advises the American Medical Informatics Association Board on Electronic Health Record (EHR) functionality, integration with workflow, and safety and efficiency of care.[6,16]

HIMSS: INTEROPERABILITY AND HEALTH INFORMATION EXCHANGE COMMITTEE

Because the health information exchange landscape continues to evolve, interoperability becomes a key driver toward achieving secure, lower cost, and higher quality patient care. Interoperability is the foundation for a learning healthcare system where the best evidence is generated, shared, and applied for collaborative patient care.

The Interoperability & Health Information Exchange Committee focuses on the advancement of interoperability and standards that help drive health information exchange.[13,16,17]

CAREER DEVELOPMENT

Professional associations provide many opportunities for members to explore their career options. Career fairs are traditionally held during annual meetings and give members the opportunity to interview with companies from all over the country and possibly the world. Regional and local conference meetings may also feature career fairs, which gives attendees the opportunity to interact with representatives from the health IT industry while staying closer to home.[5,18]

INTERNATIONAL MEMBERSHIP

Some associations are global in scope or are members of international federations. This allows the member to collaborate with chapters or similar associations outside of the United States. The member then has the opportunity to participate in global initiatives, exchanges, or conferences.[8,13,19–23]

SPECIAL INTEREST GROUP MEMBERSHIP

The term *health IT* encompasses a large number of subgroups, and all health IT association members are not the same. Your individual areas of expertise and research are likely represented in a SIG by the professional association. A SIG is defined as a subgroup within a larger group where members share information or research in specialized fields. Joining a SIG within the association allows members to discuss and research items of importance related to the member's specific subspecialty with professionals of similar interests.[13,21,23,24]

ANNUAL CONFERENCES/MEETINGS

Annual meetings are meetings of the general membership of an association. These meetings are held annually in various cities across the country and provide information on career options and legislative issues affecting health IT. The annual meeting also provides many opportunities for interactions with companies and products focused on health IT. These meetings may also serve as a location for health IT-related certification examinations and continuing education seminars. The presenters and presentations at the annual meeting represent the best the industry has to offer. Topics are contemporary and can set the tone for the national or global health IT conversation for the year. Local chapter representatives may elect regional officers at this time and propose topics for resolution. The annual meeting may also host elections for national association officers. Members have the opportunity to meet with colleagues from across the nation and around the world.[7–9,19] The annual meeting is also a platform for bestowing awards. The association may recognize a Book of the Year, exceptional leadership, innovative practices, scholarship recipients, or other professional developments. Table 6.1 lists select association annual meeting details for the next three years, where available.

SUBSCRIPTION TO ASSOCIATION PUBLICATIONS

A few health IT associations sponsor their own journal, while others recognize an independently published work as the official journal of the association.

The *Journal of the American Medical Informatics Association* (JAMIA), the American Medical Informatics Association's (AMIA) official peer-reviewed journal, has articles on health IT-related studies, legislature affecting the profession, analytics and big data, and original research. Information is presented in a clinical practice-oriented format.[25]

Methods of Information in Medicine is the official journal of the International Medical Informatics Association (IMIA) and of the European Federation for Medical Informatics. It is also the official international journal of the German Association for Medical Informatics, Biometry and Epidemiology. The journal covers articles in health information technology, statistical analyses of medical data, and epidemiology.[26]

The Online Journal of Nursing Informatics (OJNI) is an official journal of the Healthcare Information and Management Systems Society (HIMSS) Foundation. Articles published in the peer-reviewed journal address the theoretical and practical aspects of nursing informatics as it relates to the field of nursing.[27]

Telemedicine and e-Health, an official journal of the American Telemedicine Association, is a peer-reviewed journal covering telemedicine and management of EHRs. The journal has articles on telemedicine in home healthcare, remote patient monitoring, and disease management in rural health battlefield care, nursing home, assisted living facilities, maritime, and aviation settings. Association members will usually receive discounted subscriptions to their association's journal.[28,29]

OTHER BENEFITS AVAILABLE TO MEMBERS OF SOME ASSOCIATIONS INCLUDE

- Professional liability insurance, which may be provided for free or reduced prices for association members.
- Life insurance, home insurance, and auto insurance.

- Financial services such as scholarships, association credit cards, loans, credit unions, or money market accounts with partner financial institutions.
- Discounts in the community on car rentals.[2]

MEMBERSHIP CASE STUDY

Why do members get involved with associations? What do they get from volunteering? Here, a member shares her story.

JoAnn Klinedinst, M.Ed., CPHIMS, PMP, DES, CPTD, FHIMSS, FACHE Vice President, Professional Development, HIMSS

My involvement with professional associations has been pivotal in my development as a health IT professional. While working in the Management Information Systems (MIS) Department of a local hospital in Southeastern Pennsylvania, in the United States, I realized that healthcare was the place for me. At the time (early 1990s), a career in health IT was not viewed as positive since the industry lacked advanced technology and offered lower pay than the IT industry in general. However, I welcomed the family-like atmosphere among many of the departments in this small community hospital setting.

After being hired in the MIS Department for my knowledge of PC-based applications for word processing, database, and spreadsheet applications, I started getting more involved in the technical aspects of implementing MEDITECH through report writing, dictionary building, and other activities. While my degree was in business management, I had little knowledge of the hospital setting. As a result, I began exploring various professional associations that could provide additional education and training to supplement my healthcare knowledge.

After a search of many different types of organizations, I joined HIMSS in 1991. I did so because of the thought leadership that was available through peer-reviewed themed journals which allowed me to expand my knowledge in the areas of telehealth, clinical systems applications, the computer-based patient record, and many others. Further, HIMSS held an annual conference that combined education, exhibition, and networking. For me, this was a great start on my journey to begin my understanding of health IT. (And that journey still exists today.)

Much to my surprise, my involvement in HIMSS was not only accessing thought-leadership journals but much more. I attended my first conference in 1995 (San Antonio, TX) and was immediately captivated. After a few years, I decided that I, too, had experiences to contribute and responded to my first call for proposal on a poster session entitled "Critical Success Factors of Application Upgrades." I was accepted and actually earned recognition for the best poster session overall. And I was hooked!

In addition to speaking at a HIMSS annual conference three times over ten years for HIMSS, I also served as a paper reviewer for many years. Through this experience, I decided that I wanted to serve on the Annual Conference Education Committee, so I also applied for an appointment by the HIMSS Board of Directors. There were no guarantees that I would get appointed, but I wanted to try. Much to my surprise, I was selected for a two-year term (1999–2000) and served as chair in 2000. This was such an honor. To think that someone from a small community hospital could be recognized for her skillsets and abilities was just amazing to me. And this is true today as well: HIMSS welcomes the involvement of individuals from all different types of stakeholders. The only differentiating factors are a willingness to serve the health IT sector.

As my appointment came to an end on the Annual Conference Education Committee, I applied for an appointment to the Advocacy Committee. I too was accepted for a two-year term. By this point, I was very engaged in my local DVHIMSS (Delaware Valley) chapter and served on the State Advocacy Committee. My responsibilities included setting up the appointments for attendees to meet with their legislative representatives: all 110 attendees. While advocacy was a different area for me, I learned quite a lot, which helped me to become even more well-rounded as a health IT professional.

As I progressed in my volunteer efforts with HIMSS, I realized that I may not always want to work in health IT, so I diversified my professional association involvement and joined the Project Management Institute (PMI). Because so much of what I did in health IT was project-focused, I decided that PMI was a good fit for me as well. I served in a variety of capacities for the PMI Healthcare SIG. While I wanted to diversify, I kept coming back to health IT. At the same time, I became involved in various Special Interest Groups (SIGs) with HIMSS: the Supply Chain Management SIG, Long-Term Care SIG, and the Project Management SIG. All provided an opportunity to engage but without the commitment of a HIMSS Board appointment. And to this day, I have continued focusing on my professional development by earning two additional credentials since the first edition of *The Handbook for Continuing Professional Development for Health IT Professionals* was published: the FACHE (Fellows of ACHE) and the CPTD (Certified Professional in Talent Development offered by ATD).

One advantage to becoming involved with a professional society as an active volunteer is that one can earn points for advancement. HIMSS has advancement opportunities for Senior Member and Fellow. Many of these activities contributed to my overall advancement score, and I became a Fellow in 2000. Based on the longevity of my membership at HIMSS, I also earned the Life Fellow of HIMSS (LFHIMSS) designation, recognizing 30 continuous years of membership.

And another advantage to becoming an engaged volunteer is earning points for certification. After I earned the FHIMSS, a new certification was being launched by HIMSS called the Certified Professional in Healthcare Information and Management Systems (CPHIMS). I decided to study and then sit for that exam. Again, my involvement in HIMSS definitely prepared me to understand the vast body of health IT knowledge. So, with 200 of my closest friends on a Sunday morning at HIMSS02 Atlanta, we were the first to be seated to take the exam. I passed and now was both an FHIMSS and a CPHIMS.

As an engaged volunteer, one has the opportunity to work with peers both nationally and internationally. And this recognition sometimes results in an industry or service award nomination, as it did for me. I was nominated and selected for the HIMSS Leadership Award based on my many years of involvement with HIMSS. While I never expected anything like this, professional associations do recognize their well-deserving members. I happened to be one who was recognized—a moment I still remember to this day.

While still involved with PMI and HIMSS jointly, I decided to earn the Project Management Professional (PMP) certification. I had the experience needed to apply and had also enrolled in Villanova University's Master's Certificate in IS/IT Project Management (which is still available today). Based on three modules, the third was devoted to preparing for the PMP exam. I completed the certificate and then sat for the exam. Although I failed the first time, I decided to try again. This exam was (and still is) highly rigorous, but I felt I had the competencies to succeed. I passed on my second try.

With my time approaching an end on the HIMSS Advocacy Committee, I decided that I would apply to sit on the Ambulatory Information Systems Committee. Since I had moved from the acute setting to the ambulatory setting in my workplace, this made sense to me. At the same time, HIMSS was hiring subject matter experts like myself and others. I interviewed for and was selected as the Director of Enterprise Information Systems. Fortunately for me I was hired; however, my volunteer involvement with HIMSS came to an end as a paid employee.

While my experience may be atypical, one never knows where an engagement with a professional association may lead. To this day, I see vendors that I worked with at my community hospital who also exhibit at the HIMSS Global Health Conference and Exhibition. While some may have retired, I still seem to find a person or two who I worked with some 20 years previously.

CONCLUSION

Our best advice to those interested in joining a professional association is to not only join but also to get involved. There are many ways to become involved with professional associations, and some require a minimal commitment while others require longer terms. Based on your level of commitment, your rewards may be immediate or long term. Regardless, your experience with professional association involvement will be as priceless as ours has been. While JoAnn's role has changed from a practicing health IT professional to one who serves the professional development needs of the health IT professional, she searched and found the Association for Talent Development (ATD) that helps her learn and grow as an education professional. Please consider not only joining a professional association or two of your choice but also getting involved. Both you and your career will benefit immensely.

REFERENCES

1. Hovekamp TM. Professional associations or unions? A comparative look. *Library Trends.* 1997;46(2):232–245.
2. Graner B. Membership in a professional organization. *The Prairie Rose.* 2010;79(4):10.
3. Ayres EJ, Hoggle LB. 2011 Nutrition informatics member survey. *Journal of the Academy of Nutrition and Dietetics.* 2012;112(3):360–367.
4. Adler-Milstein J, McAfee AP, Bates DW, Jha AK. The state of regional health information organizations: Current activities and financing. *Health Affairs.* 2008;27(1):w60–w69.
5. Anderson BL. Nursing informatics: Career opportunities inside and out. *Computers in Nursing.* 1992;10(4):165–170.
6. Greenes RA. Strategic planning activities of the American Medical Informatics Association. *Journal of the American Medical Informatics Association: JAMIA.* 1994;1(3):263–271.
7. Honey M, Newbold S. Initiatives to support the emergence of nursing informatics. *Studies in Health Technology and Informatics.* 2009;146:107–111.
8. Special issue: APAMI 94. Asia Pacific Association of Medical Informatics conference. Singapore, November 10, 1994. *International Journal of Bio-Medical Computing.* 1995;40(2):77–163.
9. Proceedings of the 1st TTUHSC Radiology Informatics Conference on Advanced Technologies for Radiology Operations. *Journal of Digital Imaging.* 1998;11(4 Suppl 2):1–47.
10. Ayres EJ, Hoggle LB. ADA nutrition informatics member survey: Results and future steps. *Journal of the American Dietetic Association.* 2008;108(11):1822–1826.
11. Greenwood K, Murphy J, Sensmeier J, Westra B. Nursing profession reengineered for leadership in landmark report: Special report for the alliance for nursing informatics member organizations. *CIN: Computers, Informatics, Nursing.* 2011;29(1):66–67.
12. Osheroff JA, Teich JM, Middleton B, Steen EB, Wright A, Detmer DE. A roadmap for national action on clinical decision support. *Journal of the American Medical Informatics Association.* 2007;14(2):141–145.
13. Peltonen L-M, Topaz M, Ronquillo C, et al. Nursing informatics research priorities for the future: Recommendations from an international survey. *Studies in Health Technology and Informatics.* 2016;225:222–226.

14. Embi PJ, Payne PR. Clinical research informatics: Challenges, opportunities and definition for an emerging domain. *Journal of the American Medical Informatics Association*. 2009;16(3):316–327.
15. Petrakaki D, Barber N, Waring J. The possibilities of technology in shaping healthcare professionals: (Re/ De-) Professionalisation of pharmacists in England. *Social Science and Medicine*. 2012;75(2):429–437.
16. Payne TH, Corley S, Cullen TA, et al. Report of the AMIA EHR 2020 Task Force on the status and future direction of EHRs. *Journal of the American Medical Informatics Association*. 2015;22(5):1102–1110.
17. Committee H-IHIE. Improving Patient Care through an HIE. http://www.himss.org/library/health-information-exchange/improving-patient-care?ItemNumber=47235
18. Staggers N, Lasome CEM. RN, CIO: An executive informatics career. *Computers, Informatics, Nursing:* CIN. 2005;23(4):201–206.
19. Berleur J, Nurminen MI, Impagliazzo J. *Social Informatics: An Information Society for All?* In *Remembrance of Rob Kling: Proceedings of the Seventh International ConferenceHuman Choice and Computers'(HCC7), IFIP TC9, Maribor, Slovenia*, September 21–23, 2006. Vol 223: Springer; 2007.
20. Mantas J, Ammenwerth E, Demiris G, et al. Recommendations of the International Medical Informatics Association (IMIA) on education in biomedical and health informatics. First revision. *Methods of Information in Medicine*. 2010;49(2):105–120.
21. De Lusignan S. International informatics research, communication, episodes of care, evaluation and measuring outcomes. *Informatics in Primary Care*. 2012;20(1):1–2.
22. Dowding DW, Currie LM, Borycki E, et al. International priorities for research in nursing informatics for patient care. *Studies in Health Technology and Informatics*. 2013;192:372–376.
23. Alexander GL, Abbott P, Fossum M, Shaw RJ, Yu P, Alexander MM. The future of informatics in aged care: An international perspective. *Studies in Health Technology and Informatics*. 2016;225:780–782.
24. Bahri P, Dodoo AN, Edwards BD, et al. The ISoP CommSIG for Improving Medicinal Product Risk Communication: A New Special Interest Group of the International Society of Pharmacovigilance. *Drug Safety*. 2015;38(7):621–627.
25. Association AMI. *Journal of the American Medical Informatics Association*, About. 2016, Retrieved August 19, 2021, from http://jamia.oxfordjournals.org/about
26. Methods of Information in Medicine, About. 2016. http://methods.schattauer.de/about/description.html
27. Online Journal of Nursing Informatics. 2016. Retrieved August 19, 2021, from https://www.himss.org/resources/online-journal-nursing-informatics
28. Telemedicine and e-Health, About this journal. *Telemedicine and e-Health* https://home.liebertpub.com/publications/telemedicine-and-e-health/54/overview
29. Bashshur RL, Goldberg MA. The origins of telemedicine and e-Health. *Telemedicine Journal and E-Health: The Official Journal of the American Telemedicine Association*. 2014;20(3):190–191.

7 The Importance of Volunteering

Pamela V. Matthews
RN, MBA, FHIMSS, CPHIMS

CONTENTS

INTRODUCTION

Volunteerism is part of the fabric of society, with a wide variety of opportunities, such as participation in professional societies, civic organizations, and nonprofit entities. One can focus volunteer activities on personal interests such as environmental conservation, animal welfare, or helping with local food pantries and building homes for those less fortunate. One may volunteer without a conscious thought or need of recognition, such as working with little league baseball; coaching a fellow colleague; giving monetary donations; or assisting with a local hospital, church, or community group. Many Fortune 500 companies provide Employee Volunteering Programs or Employer Supported Volunteering, which allow employees to volunteer during work hours. There are many benefits to companies that support these types of corporate citizenship programs, including corporate image enhancement and improved employee retention. Regardless of company benefits, the most important benefit is the positive impact made from their employee volunteer activities [1].

April is National Volunteer Month in the United States, which began with Presidential Proclamation 4288 signed by President Richard Nixon in 1974 [2]. Since the holiday's inception, a new proclamation has been issued each year by the sitting president designating a week in April as National Volunteer Week to honor volunteers. Celebrations and news stories across the country focus on volunteers and emphasize their value. The President's Volunteer Service Award (PVSA) is the premier volunteer awards program, encouraging citizens to live a life of service through presidential gratitude and national recognition [3].

Volunteers provide a significant economic impact on America's economy. In 2018, 30.3% of the population, about 77.3 million people, volunteered according to the Corporation for National and Community Service, which equates to an estimated value of $167 billion [4]. The estimated national value of each volunteer hour is $25.43 [5]. Volunteering is for all ages. The U.S. Bureau of Labor Statistics reported in 2015 the median annual hours spent on volunteer activities ranged from a high of 94 hours for those age 65 and over to a low of 36 hours for those under 35 years old [6].

Clearly, volunteerism has a significant impact on today's society.

VOLUNTEERISM

According to the Meriam-Webster dictionary, a *volunteer* is a person who does work without getting paid to do something or is a person who voluntarily undertakes or expresses a willingness to undertake service [7]. In broader terms, *volunteering* is generally considered an altruistic activity where services are provided with no financial gain. Volunteering is also renowned for skill development and is often intended to promote goodness or improve human quality of life.

We do not know for sure when the volunteer phenomenon begin. *Voluntaire,* originally from middle French, was used as early as the 1600s to describe one who volunteers for military service. The non-military use of *volunteer* was first recorded as early as the 1630s. Also, the word *volunteer* has roots in Latin as *voluntaries,* meaning "voluntary of one's free will" [8]. The word *volunteerism* was first officially noted in use as of 1844 to describe the act or practice of doing volunteer work in community service [9].

HEALTHCARE AND VOLUNTEERISM

Volunteerism intersected with health and medical care throughout history and played a significant role in forming today's healthcare industry. While this chapter is not intended to provide an historical account of healthcare, it is of interest to review a few examples where volunteerism in America helped to shape today's industry.

The earliest origins of hospitals were primarily religious and charitable institutions caring for the sick rather than medical institutions for their cure. Those who worked in these institutions, mostly as volunteers, were typically bound with a common identity and strong communal character. The history of hospitals is distinctive for first primarily being for the poor and only later gaining a significant role in the scientific medical treatment of patients. The Pennsylvania Hospital became the first permanent general hospital in America in 1752. The New York Hospital was chartered in 1771, and Massachusetts General Hospital opened in 1821. These specific hospitals were called "voluntary" hospitals because they were financed by voluntary donations rather than taxes.

Physicians' practice of medicine in America dates back to the early 1600s. Physicians were formally trained, often through apprenticeships, and may have held a university degree. The New Jersey Medical Society, chartered in 1766, was the first medical professional organization in the colonies, which "form[ed] a program embracing all professional matters: the practice, apprentice educational standards, fee schedules and a code of ethics." These physician professional societies began regulating medical practice using examination and licensure as early as the 1760s. By the early 1800s, medical societies were charged with establishing physician practice standards and certification [10]. The turning point occurred on May 5, 1847, when nearly 200 delegates, representing 40 medical societies and 28 colleges from 22 states and the District of Columbia, met in Philadelphia, Pennsylvania. Out of this came the first session of the newly formed American Medical Association (AMA), where delegates adopted the first code of medical ethics and established the first national standard for preliminary medical education and the degree of Medical Doctor (MD) [11].

Hospitals, clinics, and other provider entities sprung up across America, due in part to local communities, religious institutions, and various forms of volunteerism. Only a few hundred hospitals were located across America as of the 1870s, which had closer connections to charity than to medicine [12]. While Florence Nightingale had reformed England's military hospitals, trained nurses before the 1870s across America were generally not known or not organized. During the American Civil War (1861–1865), the U.S. Sanitary Commission handled most medical and nursing care of the Union armies. Dorothea Dix, who volunteered as the Commission's Superintendent of Army Nurses, convinced the medical corps of the value of women working in 350 Commission or Army hospitals. As a result, over 20,000 women were volunteers working in hospitals throughout the North and South during the Civil War.

America's driving need for highly skilled nurses paved the path for today's nursing profession, which came largely from volunteers—those who formed groups, charities, and concerned citizens focused on monitoring and developing the nursing profession [13]. Fast forward to the 20th century: the American Society of Superintendents of Training Schools for Nurses and the Nurses' Associated Alumnae of the United States, founded in 1896, merged in 1901 to form the American Federation of Nurses. This federation then joined the National Council of Women and the International Council of Nurses, which led to the formation of the American Nurses Association (ANA) in 1911 [14].

Clara Barton, who gained fame for her work in nursing, led efforts with her circle of acquaintances to establish the American Red Cross in Washington, D.C., on May 21, 1881. Barton first heard of the Swiss-inspired global Red Cross network while visiting Europe. Returning home, she campaigned for an American Red Cross. From the beginning, the American Red Cross's activities included mobilizing volunteers for disaster relief operations, which can still be seen today. One of the first activities of the American Red Cross was providing disaster relief to the victims of the 1889 Johnstown Flood [15].

These are just a few examples where volunteers and the roots of volunteerism provided the platform for dedicated people to advance the betterment of healthcare and the public's well-being that helped shape today's healthcare industry.

HEALTHCARE ASSOCIATIONS AND SOCIETIES

Today's healthcare industry, like other industries, enjoys the benefits provided by many professional societies, associations, and other nonprofit organizations. Professional associations and professional societies are used interchangeability for the most part and are typically nonprofit. Societies represent individuals of a specific profession focused on a common goal of advancing their profession and their individual knowledge through a common identity and strong community character [16]. These societies provide their membership with tools, resources, information, and opportunities that their members may not otherwise have. They provide the environment for members to engage, stay connected, advocate with others, share experiences, and celebrate triumphs. Also, professional society engagement is a foundation for individual career growth and advancement. The result of active volunteerism in these types of organizations benefits the employer and the advancement of the industry at large, resulting in a "win-win" for all.

Individuals may even elect to participate in more than one professional society based on their job and career. When evaluating the benefits of a particular professional society, the following question should be asked: How will participation in the society support immediate job needs and assist in long-term career growth and development?

For more information on professional associations, see Chapter 6 of this book, Dr. Anthony Blash and JoAnn Klinedinst's "The Role of the Professional Association."

BENEFITS OF VOLUNTEERISM

Volunteering in professional societies can be rewarding and beneficial regardless of where one may be in their career. It not only supports building and maintaining a current resume, but it also sends a signal to employers, colleagues, and other associates that one is dedicated to the profession and the industry while seeking career growth opportunities. Society members may even have a competitive advantage over others in the industry and stand out as a job candidate. A student who has volunteer activities, even community-based activities, on their resume demonstrates their ability to handle commitments and achieve results while being actively engaged. Benefits from participation or volunteerism in a professional society are many [17]. Society membership provides access to:

- Unique opportunities to learn new skills and knowledge.
- Educational opportunities leveraging a wide variety of platforms, ranging from onsite programs to online and interactive vehicles.
- Latest news and developments while providing a broad perspective of the industry.
- Federal and state policy advocacy activities that drive industry legislation, regulation, and compliance activities.
- Networking events at the national, regional, local, and affiliated chapter level.
- Colleagues and peers that energize and diminish the feeling of individual aloneness.
- National and influential industry leaders.
- Opportunities to serve on volunteer workgroups that sharpen team-building and management skills.
- Opportunities to "fill in professional gaps" with specific skills and leadership development that inadvertently may not be available with specific job positions.
- Job and career opportunities which may be exclusive to only society members.
- Opportunities that may lead to another career or profession.

The 2015 Healthcare Information and Management Systems Society (HIMSS) Individual Membership Satisfaction Survey results identified the top four motivating factors for professionals joining HIMSS as professional development, chapter involvement, annual conference discounted pricing, and availability of volunteer opportunities. Survey results identified the top four motivating factors for existing members to renew HIMSS membership as professional development, discounted conference pricing, volunteer opportunities, and educational opportunities.

These driving motives can be drilled down into several services offered by societies that members find to be of great importance to volunteering their time and effort, including networking, education, mentoring, and career development.

NETWORKING

Volunteerism, regardless if it is community based or professional, can expose one to a broad range of people with diverse backgrounds from many walks of life. One's circle of professional friends and colleagues can greatly expand through professional networking activities. Professional societies can offer unparalleled networking opportunities for members to connect with peers, mentors, and industry leaders. Meeting with others who are like-minded can be equally beneficial and rewarding through building a trusted community of those with similar interests. Professional societies provide this trusted environment for member networking opportunities to compare experiences, discuss best practices, brainstorm ideas, explore innovative ideas, and develop collaborations—all of which is pushing the profession and industry forward. Many societies support formal special interest groups and access to various social media and virtual platforms for members to stay connected. Volunteer work group opportunities are another option for members to engage for networking purposes as well as skill development. Members may attend society-sponsored conventions, conferences, regional events, and workshops where collaboration discussions can begin and continue to be nurtured after the event. In addition, networking is an excellent way to sharpen interpersonal and communication skills with a diverse group of colleagues. There is limited evidence that people who actively volunteer tend to make more money due to their efforts with developing their professional network [18]. Above all, the ultimate benefit of networking is development of lifelong professional colleagues and friends that are forged only through active participation in professional societies throughout a career.

EDUCATION

Professional societies offer many opportunities that allow members to grow and develop through writing, presentation, and communication skills. Activities which support a volunteer's continuing professional development can be done through participation in educational events at the national, state, or regional level as well as with local affiliated chapters. These events may also provide opportunities for members to participate as speakers, honing their presentation skills. Volunteers may participate in planning groups whose purpose is identifying educational program topics and speakers or by reviewing submitted speaker proposals. A volunteer member may learn new skills and expand their use of communication and interactive tools with society-sponsored education delivered through virtual platforms and social media. In addition, volunteer members may sharpen their writing skills by developing articles or case studies to share with others in exclusive society publications or web-based content, including journals, podcasts, newsletters, DVDs, and online forums. The 2015 HIMSS Individual Membership Satisfaction Survey revealed the top three program and service opportunities that members participated in over the year were accessing information and content from the website, attending in-person conferences and events, and participating in virtual conferences.

MENTORING

Giving back to a profession—or paying it forward—is a key volunteer motivation factor for many experienced professionals. Mentoring programs, both formal and informal, provide an avenue for experienced professionals to share with those who are early in their career or with those who do not have extensive experience in a particular area. Likewise, those seeking mentors benefit from a mentor's experience that can be leveraged both immediately with current job positions and long term with careers. Mentors may share their experiences, assist with problem solving, make industry introductions, as well as provide coaching with job interviewing, career planning, and skill development. This benefits not only the emerging professional but the industry at large. Volunteer mentoring is also a great opportunity for retirees to assist others through sharing their vast knowledge and expertise while staying engaged in the industry.

CAREER DEVELOPMENT

Professional societies provide many volunteer opportunities focused on career development like professional certifications, where volunteers may be used in developing certification examinations and training materials as well as serving as training instructors. This helps the volunteer stay current in their profession and industry while advancing their writing and presentation skills. Volunteers who become certified demonstrate that a standard level of industry proficiency and knowledge beyond academic degrees and work experience enhances career growth opportunities. Many societies offer advanced membership status, such as fellowships, fellow member status, or lifetime member status. These status designations are based on active participation of a member in long-term volunteer service within the society and the industry. These are only a few examples of voluntary credentials that assist members in demonstrating their dedication to a profession while benefiting from continuous industry education and career development.

Societies may offer volunteer opportunities for members to participate in formal career planning services such as sharing guidance to members in job search strategies, resume writing, effective interview techniques, or salary negotiations. Volunteers not only hone their career planning efforts in helping the society provide these services, but they also can gain new insights and guidance for the future. Volunteers who utilize exclusive job posting services offered through a society can benefit through finding new employment opportunities or determining their next position for career advancement. Likewise, a member seeking new staff may employ the society's job posting services to quickly seek out qualified candidates, leading to faster fulfillment of open positions. This can leave a positive impression on the member with their peers and employer leadership.

Professional development (including certification, career services, and advancement) was the number one motivating factor in both joining HIMSS as a new member and renewal as an existing HIMSS membership according to the 2015 HIMSS Individual Membership Satisfaction Survey.

In addition to the benefits derived from volunteering in professional societies, there are many benefits from volunteering based on personal hobbies, interests, and community services.

PERSONAL HOBBIES AND INTERESTS

Volunteerism can lead to new interests and may provide an outlet for pursuing hobbies and expanding one's horizons. One may have personal ties or experiences that lead to volunteerism, such as volunteering for a hospice organization after a loved one experienced cancer. Hobbies and interests can be an outlet for maintaining a work-life balance and may improve overall motivation. The sense of fulfillment and satisfaction that come from hobbies or interests may spill into the work life and minimize work-related tension. Pursuing these interests may open doors to learning new skills that can be leveraged professionally and even lead to a new career.

COMMUNITY SERVICE: GIVE BACK/PAY IT FORWARD!

The community one lives in can easily be taken for granted with daily pressures and balancing work with personal life. Also, communities can suffer from budget cuts and lack of skilled employees just like corporate organizations. Many mission-driven and community nonprofit organizations rely on volunteers to supplement paid staff in order to achieve their goals and mission. Examples range from libraries, museums, religious institutions, healthcare providers, and even government services such as local fire departments, as well as national organizations providing local community services. One's professional experience and skills can be of great need by these organizations and leveraged through volunteerism. Likewise, community service may benefit the volunteer by opening doors for a new job or assist in changing career paths.

Community volunteerism is another way of giving back where individuals see the direct impact of their efforts in their community and with local residents. It also provides a great opportunity to stay informed and engaged with the local community. Most importantly, community volunteerism provides the opportunity to build one's network of friends and colleagues.

HEALTH

Over the past two decades, there is a growing body of research that indicates that volunteering provides individual health benefits in addition to social ones. The Corporation for National and Community Service (CNCS) presented the report, entitled "The Health Benefits of Volunteering," which established a strong correlation between volunteerism and individual health. This research shows that individuals who volunteer benefit from both psychological and physical benefits such as improved sense of belonging, lower blood pressure, greater sense functional ability, and lower rates of depression [19]. This is most likely due to the fact that volunteering may take the focus off one's problems and creates a greater appreciation for work, family, and personal life. Volunteering may give one a greater perspective, increase positive self-awareness, and enhance overall life fulfillment. Early involvement with volunteering tends to create a more meaningful and purposeful volunteer in later years that continues after career retirement [20].

CONCLUSION

Volunteerism supports communities as well as promotes the advancement of professions and industries while providing significant contribution toward the well-being of the volunteer and the general public.

Volunteerism can reflect the picture of the whole person—ranging from personal interests and community engagement to professional and industry achievements. Volunteerism demonstrates dedication and commitment as well as serving as an inspiration to others to get involved.

Why volunteer? Regardless of the motivation, everyone can volunteer to "pay it forward" (or pay back) in some capacity to individuals, communities, professions, industries, and society at large. Most important of all, the volunteer will equally be rewarded!

The year 2020 saw the inability of volunteers to provide their services due to the COVID-19 pandemic, which is extending into 2021. Undoubtedly, all volunteer statistics will dramatically decrease due to this unprecedented event. Regardless, American ingenuity will prevail, where volunteers will identify new ways to safely provide services and volunteer their time, which can be leveraged for years to come.

REFERENCES

1. Boston College, Center for Corporate Citizenship, Carroll School of Management. Corporate Volunteerism. Retrieved August 28, 2021, from http://ccc.bc.edu/corporate-volunteerism.html
2. The American President Project, 1974 Presidential Proclamation 4288 National Volunteer Week, 1974. https://www.presidency.ucsb.edu/documents/proclamation-4288-national-volunteer-week-1974
3. Americorps. The President's Volunteer Service Award. Retrieved August 28, 2021, from https://www.presidentialserviceawards.gov/
4. Rankings. Corporation for National and Community Service. https://www.nationalservice.gov/serve/via/rankings
5. Value of Volunteer Time. Independent Sector. https://independentsector.org/value-of-volunteer-time-2018/
6. U.S. Bureau of Labor Statistics. 2015 Volunteering in the United States. Retrieved August 28, 2021, from http://www.bls.gov/news.release/volun.nr0.htm
7. Merriam-Webster (n.d.) Merriam-Webster online dictionary. Retrieved August 27, 2021, from http://www.merriam-webster.com/dictionary/volunteer
8. Online Etymology Dictionary. (n.d.)Onlineetymologydictionary.com dictionary. Retrieved August 27, 2021, from https://www.etymonline.com/search?q=volunteer
9. Merriam-Webster (n.d.)Merriam-Webster online dictionary. Retrieved August 27, 2021, from http://www.merriam-webster.com/dictionary/volunteerism
10. National Library of Medicine. (n.d.).. Doctor of Medical Profession. Retrieved on August 27, 2021, from https://www.nlm.nih.gov/medlineplus/ency/article/001936.htm
11. American Medical Association. AMA History Timeline. http://www.ama-assn.org/ama/pub/about-ama/our-history/ama-history-timeline.page?
12. Starr, P. 1982. *The Social Transformation of American Medicine*. New York: Basic Books, The Perseus Books Group, 25.
13. Starr, P. 1982. *The Social Transformation of American Medicine*. New York: Basic Books, The Perseus Books Group, 155.
14. American Nurses Association. ANA History. Retrieved August 27, 2021, from http://www.nursingworld.org/history
15. American Red Cross. Our history. Retrieved August 27, 2021, from http://www.redcross.org/about-us/who-we-are/history
16. Analytic Quality online Glossary. Professional Body. Retrieved August 28, 2021, from http://www.qualityresearchinternational.com/glossary/professionalbody.htm
17. Positive Force Consulting, 12 reasons why people volunteer Retrieved August 27, 2021, from https://positiveforce.com/12-reasons-people-volunteer/
18. Grow Ensemble. 2021.Why Volunteer? 7 Benefits of Volunteering that Will Inspire You to Take Action 2020. https://growensemble.com/why-volunteer/

19. The Health Benefits of Volunteering: A Review of Recent Research. The Corporation for National and Community Service. http://www.nationalservice.gov/serve-your-community/benefits-volunteering

20. Carr, DC. 2014. Five reasons why you should volunteer. *Psychology Today*. https://www.psychology today.com/us/blog/the-third-age/201403/5-reasons-why-you-should-volunteer

ADDITIONAL RESOURCES

Association for Healthcare Volunteer Resource Professions: www.ahvrp.org

Association of Leaders in Volunteer Engagement: www.volunteeralive.org

Corporation for National and Community Service/AmeriCorps: www.nationalservice.gov

International Association for Volunteer Effort: https://www.iave.org/about-iave/

National Volunteer Week: https://www.pointsoflight.org/nvw/

The President's Volunteer Service Award: https://www.presidentialserviceawards.gov

8 Earning a Certificate to Demonstrate Competency

John Eckmann
MPH, CPHIMS, CIPM

CONTENTS

INTRODUCTION

Many factors motivate health informatics professionals to demonstrate competency by earning a professional certificate, like seeking gainful employment or enhancing one's skillsets. Health informatics professionals generally rely on a combination of experience and education to demonstrate competency. The broader field of information technology (IT) finds "practitioners" with mixed experiences and academic credentials. There are numerous examples of individuals demonstrating competency with four-year college degrees; others have careers based on experience alone; or a combination of both. Earning a professional certificate has merit, too, and this chapter will explore why. Very often, individuals explore university-level certificate programs as a powerful alternative to professional certification.

A prerequisite to understanding the compelling dynamics of health IT certificates necessitates defining the term *health information and technology*, as well as differentiating between professional *certificate* and professional *certification*. Many definitions of *health information and technology* exist. Generally, it describes the management and resources needed for exchanging data among providers, payers, patients, etc. The health informatics professional or "practitioner" is primarily concerned about obtaining, storing, and using data for the purposes of healthcare delivery. Subsequently, due to the dynamic nature of healthcare combined with the complexity of IT, health IT certificates often focus not only on the technical aspects of a healthcare setting, like managing computer networks, managing projects, fostering change through change management techniques, disaster recovery, and cybersecurity, but also on clinical topics relevant to informatics. This chapter will broadly consider a few factors that converge on how the health IT professional can embrace health IT certificates as a viable career enhancement.

TERMS AND DEFINITIONS

The definitions of the terms *certificate* and *certification* are unique when applied to demonstrating competency. The online Oxford Dictionaries provides the following definitions (https:// en.oxforddictionaries.com):

DOI: 10.4324/9780429398377-10

- *Certificate:* (noun) An official document attesting a certain fact.
- *Certification:* (noun) The action or process of providing someone or something with an official document attesting to a status or level of achievement.

While there are similarities between the two definitions, because of the distinct influences a certificate versus a certification might have to a health informatics practitioner's competency, it is important to more fully understand and appreciate the uniqueness of earning a professional certificate. The definitions supplied by the Institute for Credentialing Excellence (ICE) will be used to further clarify *certificate* and *certification,* because the audience of interest is *health* IT. This chapter explores why earning a certificate to demonstrate competency is important to health IT practitioners, and ICE's sentinel background is in healthcare credentialing. ("ICE began in 1977, when in cooperation with the federal government, the National Commission for Health Certifying Agencies (NCHCA) was formed to develop standards of excellence for voluntary certification programs in healthcare."[1]) Understanding the differentiating aspects of a certificate will help the health informatics professional when considering an assessment-based certificate as an alternative method for demonstrating their competency.

1. A *certification* program is designed to test the knowledge, skills, and abilities required to perform a particular job, and, upon successfully passing a certification exam, to represent a declaration of a particular individual's professional competence. In some professions, certification is a requirement for employment or practice.
2. In contrast to certification and licensure, an *assessment-based certificate* program is an educational or training program that is used to teach learning objectives and assess whether those objectives were achieved by the student.

FACTORS INFLUENCING EARNING A HEALTH IT CERTIFICATE

One obvious reason to earn a certificate may be money: finding new employment, staying employed, being promoted, learning a new skill, etc. Health informatics professionals who enhance their skillsets are more attractive to prospective employers. Employers, when looking for health IT talent, are constrained by budgets and therefore attempt to "strike gold" with experienced and certificate-proven professionals.

Another factor to consider is "time in career." Reasons vary for earning a certificate when contrasting entry-level individuals with mid-level or senior health informatics professionals. Before proceeding, it is worth noting there are limited data available to conclude whether a certificate results in competency.[2] The presumed benefit of a certificate is questionably observed elsewhere in healthcare, too. It is safe to say, however, that health informatics professionals who earn a professional certificate are adding to their "professional toolbox" by demonstrating competency, since a healthcare certificate is prescribed and understood as a "good dose of medicine."

Many colleges and universities offer certificate programs which deliver knowledge and skills anticipated to fill jobs for projected areas of economic growth. Certificate programs are a way of attending to students whether they are traditional full-time or part-time students. Often the certificate programs are available online to capture attention from students with a preference for this method of instruction delivery. The goals of certificate programs are to enhance an understanding of a body of knowledge that can serve students intending entry into the job market or to continue their education. The academic courses assembled for a certificate program, while fewer and focused, have equivalent learning objectives when the same courses are applicable for matriculating college degrees. Moreover, while the certificate programs are a fraction of the cost of pursuing a college degree, there is always the option of applying the investment into pursuing a college degree.

An example of an area where institutions of higher education have developed certificate programs is information security. Because information security has been identified by the U.S.

Department of Labor as one of the fastest growing professions, certificate programs are widely offered. Some of these programs are designed to address their learning objectives in as little as two semesters. The successful conclusion of a certificate program has merit for students wanting to enter a job sector, continue their education, advance their career, change careers, or simply demonstrate their competency.

Admission requirements into certificate programs may have both business-centric and academic entry requirements: cover letter or statement of purpose highlighting goals, resume, letters of recommendation, and official transcripts from an accredited college or university. Almost without exception, certificate programs follow their host institution's academic calendar in as much as relevant start and stop deadlines apply. Because of the higher educational institution's influence on their certificate programs, most often the roster of courses comprising a certificate program is recognizable and transferable. An example of a *Graduate Certificate in Health Information Technology,* offered by a university, is shown below and illustrates a familiar collegiate classification of a certificate offering.

Required Core Courses (12 credit hours)

* Foundation in Health
* Healthcare Data Analysis
* Decision Analysis in Healthcare
* Introduction to Health Informatics
* Elective Courses (3 credit hours from a list of approved courses)

The health information and technology industry is fortunate to have numerous online certificate opportunities (see Table 8.1) where the certificate programs are valued both in the health care industry as well as related areas in higher education.

Certificates are often recognized and considered trusted, reliable, and consistent with the healthcare industry's standards of practice. The visibility of earning a certificate demonstrates a higher education accomplishment which further supports and contributes to best practice.

There is comfort in being "certified," too. It is worth noting that in 2013, the Office of the National Coordinator for Health Information Technology (ONC) unveiled their "mark" for Electronic Health Records (EHR) and other health IT products. ONC's certification mark was to serve as visual proof of an EHR's functionality, interoperability, and security. An ONC news release at that time suggested ONC's branding was a positive for providers: "The use of the ONC

TABLE 8.1

Sample of Health Information Technology (IT) and Related Graduate Certificates

George Mason University	The Department of Health Administration and Policy	Health Informatics and Data Analytics	In-person, or Online	https://hap.gmu.edu/program/view/19933
University of Wisconsin	Graduate School School	Clinical and Health Informatics, Capstone Certificate	In-person or Online	https://guide.wisc.edu/nondegree/capstone/clinical-health-informatics-capstone-certificate/
Boston University	Graduate College	Health Informatics	Online	https://www.bu.edu/online/programs/certificate-programs/health-informatics/
The University of North Carolina at Charlotte	The School of Data Science	Health Informatics & Analytics	Online	https://hia.uncc.edu/about-us/program-overview/graduate-certificate

Certified HIT mark will help to assure them that the EHR they have purchased will support them in meeting the Meaningful Use requirements." Although ONC's Certified health IT mark is about systems, similarly comforting, competent assurance is the purpose applied to certificate programs that are celebrated.

ONC Certified HIT   2014 EDITION

Patient safety has also been offered as a foundational reason health informatics professional must demonstrate their competency. Health IT professionals are "electronic field medics" when considering the digital evolution in healthcare has generated a greater reliance on electronics and an expectation for real-time access to digital information. Because of their direct involvement when introducing technical innovation and subsequently supporting technology's evolution into the mainstream patient care settings, there exists legitimate concern as to whether health informatics practitioners might affect patient safety.[2] The Institute of Medicine observed: "It is widely believed that, when designed and used appropriately, health information and technology can help create an ecosystem of safer care... "

Another factor influencing the decision of health informatics professionals to earn a certificate to demonstrate competency is to remain relevant by refreshing their understanding of a body of knowledge. This motivator is more common among mid-level and seasoned professionals. Similarly, because certificate programs are often offered by reputable academic centers, prestige can influence health informatics professionals with extensive experience.

As key stakeholders, organizations rely upon health informatics professionals for their innovation to not only construct the digital solutions necessary but also to supply the subsequent maintenance to sustain the technologies when they are implemented and operational to healthcare. According to a study by International Data Corporation (IDC), thriving organizations will have the "ability to adjust to the speed and needs demanded by digitally empowered business transformation." (*Thriving* is categorically familiar to healthcare, as a patient who is at risk has a *failure to thrive*.) In the IDC study, the IT organizations characterized as "thrivers" (% of respondents):

- Are highly responsive and collaborate in real time across the enterprise (53%)
- Have an IT culture that excels at experimentation in every part of the business (58%)
- Have a hyper focus on user experience as a differentiator from competitors (51%)

On October 9, 2016, *60 Minutes*, the CBS news show, televised a segment stating, "It might not be long before machines begin thinking for themselves—creatively, independently and with judgment sometimes better than ours." Perhaps for good reason—Will Rogers said, "Good judgment comes from experience, and a lot of that comes from bad judgment."

During this 1-hour television show there was compelling information about artificial intelligence supplying benefit to healthcare. For years, health IT professionals have relied on academic programs and/or technical certificate programs to demonstrate their competency as technical experts—participating and contributing to the highly technical and digitized transformation the world of healthcare has experienced by supplying their expert judgment. Health IT professionals rely on learning to stay informed, and earning a technical certificate demonstrates both a commitment and understanding of the challenge.

TIMING IS IMPORTANT, TOO!

When should health informatics professionals actively seek to earn a certificate? The short answer is constantly. As was previously discussed, some professionals are attempting to enter the field and find employment in health information and technology, and others are trying to advance their health information and technology careers. As a career, health information and technology is sufficiently complex and dynamic: earning a certificate is a reliable way to demonstrate understanding of a body of knowledge that is continually evolving.

Individuals who are seeking to enter the profession often explore earning certificates to enhance their marketability and expedite their entry into the field of work. For individuals already employed as health informatics professionals, their interest in earning a certificate may be to demonstrate their competency in a specialized technical area to enhance or broaden their skillset. Because the evolution of technology is fast-paced and ever changing, many times health IT professionals will seek technical certificates to reinforce and refine their skills. By doing so, they position themselves as someone with a better understanding of contemporary and/or "cutting-edge" technologies. Health informatics professionals recognize their investment in a certificate program has benefit to their career both in the short term and long term.

Equally interesting are government programs that influence the popularity of seeking a professional certificate by creating jobs. For several years, the U.S. Bureau of Labor Statistics has characterized the health information and technology "landscape" as needing additional skilled professionals capable of supplying technical skills. The Health Information Technology for Economic and Clinical Health (HITECH) Act, enacted as part of the American Recovery and Reinvestment Act of 2009, was signed into law on February 17, 2009 to promote the adoption and meaningful use of health IT. At that time, CMS established requirements for eligible professionals and eligible hospitals for the electronic capture of clinical data, including providing patients with electronic copies of health information in return for incentive payments. Due to the health IT talent shortage generated by the stimulus program, in 2010, there were government awards approximating $84 million to universities and community colleges to help support the training and development of more than 50,000 new healthcare IT professionals. In the article, Gwen Darling, CEO, Health IT Central, went on to say: "Those of us who are involved with workforce development were pretty excited about this allocation of resources, as were the thousands of students who enrolled in the programs who believed a lucrative career in HIT [health IT] would be waiting for them upon graduation."

SUMMARY

Health informatics professionals often demonstrate their professional competency by earning a certificate. The health informatics certificate programs, widely available at universities and community colleges, teach to learning objectives and assess whether those objectives were achieved by the student. This type of learning is an attractive alternate to technical professional certification for several reasons: (1) The economy of supply and demand for trained health informatics professionals is clearly a factor contributing to the viability of certificate programs; (2) The value perceived by prospective students and employers is a known motivator for training pursuits; and (3) The element of time is a consistent factor that contributes to motivating entry into certificate programs. Not surprising, patient safety is offered as a reason for demonstrating competency—health informatics professionals should do no harm.

One of the appealing reasons for demonstrating competency by earning a certificate via an assessment-based certificate program is its "shelf life." A common criticism of technical certifications is they usually have an "expiration date" and will expire if the individual does not maintain the certification. Maintenance of Certification (MOC) is an important consideration for health IT professionals when choosing between technical professional certification versus an academic professional certificate program. MOC must be factored into the overall cost and time commitment when making choices about demonstrating competency.

OBSERVATIONS AND CONCLUSIONS

Although it is not an exhaustive list, the reasons why health informatics professionals earn certificates to demonstrate their competency include: patient safety, prestige, improvement in earnings, and career longevity. A more difficult conclusion, without further analysis, is discerning which of these is a primary motivator and which is secondary, etc. Money is an apparent primary motivator because, in theory, earning a health IT certificate to demonstrate competency has both macro and micro economic benefit. It is widely accepted that being more competent is a valued attribute to both employees and employers who are optimistic about career longevity. Certificates are observed to have positive effects on job entry and career mobility (changing jobs or promotion), too.

Health informatics professionals may find themselves in careers with expectations to be generalists or highly specialized. Specialization, or the competency of understanding a body of knowledge about a specialized area, is the objective of certificate programs.

REFERENCES

1. Institute for Credentialing Excellence Website, About Us. http://www.credentialingexcellence.org/p/cm/ld/fid=32
2. Institute of Medicine (IOM). *Health IT and Patient Safety: Building Safer Systems for Better Care.* Washington, DC: National Academy Press, 2012.

9 Differentiating Yourself with a Professional Certification

Kay S. Lytle
DNP, RN-BC, NEA-BC, CPHIMS, FHIMSS, FAMIA

CONTENTS

INTRODUCTION

Professional certification indicates an individual has voluntarily met a level of requirements or standards within a defined area (National Library of Medicine, 2016). Certification is specific to a defined role, area of practice, or body of knowledge. This chapter covers the benefits of certification, selecting a certification, preparing for certification, applying for certification, displaying your credential, and maintaining your certification.

BENEFITS OF CERTIFICATION

Individuals pursue professional certification for a variety of reasons. Sometimes professional certifications are an entry-level requirement for a job or a preferred qualification. Professional certification may be an organizational requirement for career advancement along a career ladder. Getting a certification can boost your career options and can result in salary increases. Some organizations provide certification bonus payment to staff on achievement of the certification. Other individuals set certification as a professional goal and plan to meet for their own personal sense of accomplishment. Achieving certification can provide a professional challenge, offer professional growth, determine competence, validate knowledge, provide a source of professionalism, increase satisfaction, provide recognition, and increase one's professional credibility (Kaplow, 2011; McLaughlin and Fetzer, 2015.)

Employers vary in their support for professional certification. Some may offer financial support for review classes, provide free access to online modules for review, provide time for certification preparation, and/or pay the certification examination fees. Other organizations may defer reimbursement based on successful completion of the examination, provide a salary increase, or compensate with a separate bonus payment. Unfortunately some organizations provide no financial support directly for certification-related activities. Your supervisor or human resources representative can answer questions as you investigate. For many individuals, the personal and professional gains of certification outweigh the costs.

SELECTING A CERTIFICATION

There are a wide variety of professional certifications available for the health information technology (IT) professional. Determine your personal goals, and review the options available to you. The choice may vary based on your current and intended career path. Most certification materials are available online. Start with a thorough review of the certification qualifications. Qualifications will vary by the specific certification and can include things such as education level, years of experience, and a specific type of experience (health IT, project management, leadership, etc.). Review the certification handbook that will provide details to you about the qualifications, cost, credential earned, and renewal process. While it may seem early to review the renewal process, it is important to be informed about the ongoing requirements so you can determine if you will be able to meet them (more on renewal later). Some certifying bodies offer an entry-level certification and a more advanced certification, usually distinguished with required education and/or experience. You may select a preferred professional certification that requires you to complete further education, get more years of experience, or have more targeted experience. Depending on the time involved, you can begin your certification review in parallel with meeting these basic requirements.

A variety of certifications exist based on your current or future desired health IT focus. Consider speaking with peers outside your organization by engaging with those in a professional organization (see Section II Establishing and Nurturing Your Career, Chapter 6: The Role of the Professional Association). A brief overview of a subset of the certifications is provided here, including those offered by Healthcare Information and Management Systems Society (HIMSS), Project Management Institute (PMI), American Health Information Management Association (AHIMA), College of Healthcare Information Management Executives (CHIME), as well as those geared toward healthcare clinicians.

HIMSS offers two professional certifications, the Certified Associate in Healthcare Information and Management Systems (CAHIMS) and the Certified Professional in Healthcare Information and Management Systems (CPHIMS) (HIMSS, 2016a) (A third professional certification, the Certified Professional in Digital Health Transformation, is currently under development and about to be released into a beta form by HIMSS. The expected final release timeframe is July 2022.). The CAHIMS is the entry-level certification, requiring a high school diploma or equivalent, and has no practice requirement. The CPHIMS is for experienced professionals and includes education and experience requirements. CPHMIS professionals include roles such as CIOs, VPs or directors of IT/IS, consultants, managers, system analysts, and project managers; and they represent a variety of work sites such as hospitals, health systems, consulting firms, vendors, and governments (HIMSS, 2016b).

PMI offers a variety of certifications; the most well known is the Project Management Professional (PMP) for the experienced project manager (PMI, 2016a). PMI also offers the Certified Associate in Project Management (CAPM) for the entry-level professional, in addition to other specialty-focused certifications (PMI, 2016a). AHIMA offers a variety of certifications through the Commission on Certification for Health Informatics and Information Management (CCHIIM), including a Certified Healthcare Technology Specialist (CHTS) as well as certifications for coding, health information management, and privacy and security (AHIMA, 2016b). CHIME offers a Certified Healthcare CIO (CHCIO) program for chief information officers and IT executives (CHIME, 2016).

The American Nurses Credentialing Center (ANCC) offers an Informatics Nursing certification using the RN-BC credential that requires a registered nurse hold a bachelor's degree and meet one of several practice requirements (ANCC, 2016b). ANCC reported 2,979 certified informatics nurses as of the end of 2020 (ANCC, 2016a). The certification is based on the scope and standards

TABLE 9.1

List of Certifications, Credentials, and Websites

Certification	Credential	Website
Advanced Health Informatics Certification (in development)	AHIC	https://www.amia.org/advanced-health-informatics-certification
Certification of Competency in Business Analysis	Certification of Capability in Business Analysis*	https://www.iiba.org/business-analysis-certifications/ccba
Certified Associate in Healthcare Information and Management Systems	CAHIMS	http://www.himss.org/health-it-certification/cahims
Certified Associate in Project Management	CAPM*	http://www.pmi.org/certification/certified-associate-project-management-capm.aspx
Certified Business Analysis Professional	CBAP*	https://www.iiba.org/business-analysis-certifications/cbap/
Certified Coding Associate	CCA*	http://www.ahima.org/certification/CCA
Certified Coding Specialist	CCS*	http://www.ahima.org/certification/CCS
Certified Coding Specialist—Physician-based	CCS-P*	http://www.ahima.org/certification/ccsp
Certified Documentation Improvement Practitioner	CDIP*	http://www.ahima.org/certification/cdip
Certified Healthcare Chief Information Officer	CHCIO	https://chimecentral.org/chcio/
Certified Health Data Analyst	CHDA*	http://www.ahima.org/certification/chda
Certified Health Informatics Systems Professional	CHISP*	http://www.ashim.com/health-it-certification/
Certified Healthcare Privacy and Security	CHPS*	http://www.ahima.org/certification/chps
Certified Healthcare Technology Specialist	CHTS	
Certified Professional in Healthcare Information and Management Systems	CPHIMS	http://www.himss.org/health-it-certification/cphims
Certified Professional in Learning & Performance	CPLP*	https://www.td.org/Certification
Certified Professional in Operating Rules Administration	CPORA	http://www.healthitcertification.com/overview.html
Certified Technical Trainer	CTT+	https://certification.comptia.org/certifications/ctt
Clinical Informatics Subspecialty	BC	https://www.amia.org/clinical-informatics-board-review-course/board-exam
HealthCare Information Security and Privacy Practitioner	HCISPP*	https://www.isc2.org/hcispp/default.aspx
Healthcare IT Technician (Retired February 28, 2017)	–	
Informatics Nursing	RN-BC	https://www.nursingworld.org/our-certifications/informatics-nurse/
PMI Agile Certified Practitioner	PMI-ACP*	http://www.pmi.org/certification/agile-management-acp.aspx
PMI Professional in Business Analysis	PMI-PBA*	http://www.pmi.org/certification/business-analysis-pba.aspx
PMI Risk Management Professional	PMI-RMP*	http://www.pmi.org/certification/risk-management-professional-rmp.aspx

(Continued)

TABLE 9.1 (Continued)
List of Certifications, Credentials, and Websites

Certification	Credential	Website
PMI Scheduling Professional	PMI-SP*	http://www.pmi.org/certification/scheduling-professional-sp.aspx
Portfolio Management Professional	PfMP*	http://www.pmi.org/certification/portfolio-management-professional-pfmp.aspx
Program Management Professional	PgMP*	http://www.pmi.org/certification/program-management-professional-pgmp.aspx
Project Management Professional	PMP*	http://www.pmi.org/certification/project-management-professional-pmp.aspx
Registered Health Information Administrator	RHIA*	http://www.ahima.org/certification/RHIA
Registered Health Information Technician	RHIT*	http://www.ahima.org/certification/RHIT

of practice for nursing informatics (American Nurses Association, 2015). Board-certified physicians may certify in the subspecialty of Clinical Informatics and take the examination through either the American Board of Preventive Medicine (ABPM) or the American Board of Pathology (ABP) based on their core certification (Detmer and Shortliffe, 2014). The Clinical Informatics subspecialty was first offered in 2013. The American Medical Informatics Association (AMIA) has recently released the AMIA Health Informatics Certification (AHIC) (www.amia.org/careers-certifications). It is based on the same core content as clinical informatics with a phased approach to eligibility requirements for non-physicians (Gadd et al., 2016a, 2016b; Gardner et al., 2009).

There are many other certification options available based on your career focus such as advanced IT or computer certifications, training, business analyst, and others. See Table 9.1 for a partial listing of available certifications that may be pertinent to health IT professionals. You may easily identify a preferred certification to meet your goals. Others may need to select among several and weigh the career advancement and other benefits against the cost and renewal requirements. You can always talk with peers, seek out those already in the roles you desire, or work with a mentor (see Section III, Learning from Others; Chapter 11, The Mentoring Process). Select a certification that aligns with your personal and career goals.

PREPARING FOR CERTIFICATION

Once you have selected a certification that meets your professional needs, it is time to start preparing. Start by reviewing the test content outline provided by the certifying body. This will include the subjects and topics on the examination and may indicate the percentage of each on the examination. Most certifying bodies complete a role delineation study to determine the knowledge, skills, and activities that inform the test content outline (ANCC, 2013; HIMSS, 2015; PMI, 2016b). Take the practice or sample test provided; most certifying bodies offer a short set of questions for free. Some certifying bodies may also offer a more detailed practice exam for purchase. Identify your areas of strength and weakness. Identify gaps in your personal knowledge. Develop a plan to remediate the gaps.

A certification study plan may include a variety of activities, such as self-study, online review courses, or instructor-led review courses. Review the list of references; these are used to develop the exam questions. Select one or two items that, based on the table of contents, provide the best coverage in your identified areas of weakness. Identify materials available in your personal library or available to you on loan from your local library, organizational library, or your manager (as an alternative to purchase). You may want to pursue more formal review options such as certification prep courses; many are offered in person and online. Study options are often an extension of your personal learning preferences. Some individuals prefer self-study, and others prefer study buddies or a study group. Plan time on your calendar, and allow yourself a reasonable amount of time based on your areas of weakness; it may be six months or more. Set a goal for yourself, and plan to meet it.

Once you have completed your initial review and preparation, plan to retake the provided sample exam questions. Most examinations have a standard format for their questions, including a stem sentence and multiple-choice answers with one right answer, one close but incorrect answer, and two distractors. Typically, certification exams will not use multiple-choice answers or include stem sentences that state *all, not,* or *except.* Read each question slowly so you are clear on what the question is asking. If you have improved and feel satisfied with your performance and preparation, then it is time to apply for certification.

APPLYING FOR CERTIFICATION

The certification handbook will provide you with details needed to submit your application and contain additional information about the certification examination process. Timing will be important in relation to completion of your personal preparation, as most require scheduling of the examination within a defined time period, such as 90 days. Many certification exams are offered locally or within a short drive at regional testing centers that administer many different exams. If the location is not familiar, you may want to get directions and consider a dry run, especially if this will help you feel prepared and reduce your anxiety. The certification handbook should have included the number of test questions and overall time allotted to take the examination. Consider the location logistics and your personal preferences for best performance as you schedule an examination date and time in the morning or afternoon.

Prepare yourself to be on your best performance by getting a good night's sleep, eating a healthy meal, dressing comfortably, and taking a few deep breaths. Allow for extra time, and plan to arrive early; most examination centers do not allow for late starts. Be clear on the entrance requirements such as your candidate number and driver's license or other required identification documentation. Some testing sites provide onsite lockers, and you may not enter the testing area with cell phones, keys, sweaters, or other personal items. Some certification bodies allow testing centers to provide your results at the end of the testing session, and others send notification via mail.

In the event you do not pass, give yourself some time before reconsidering. Based on your results, you may want to plan for additional study and review time and then retake the examination. Many examination scores will be broken down by areas of focus, so it may be clear that you need additional study in one or two areas. Some certification bodies provide for a shortened application process if you retake the exam within a defined time period such as 90 days. Other certification bodies limit the time period before you can retake the exam, such as 60 days, and limit the total number allowed within a year. The reexamination information is located in the candidate handbook.

DISPLAYING YOUR CREDENTIAL

Celebrate your success! Once you earn your credential, you can display it with pride such as including it on your email signature line, business card, and on business letters or other formal communications. Each certifying body will identify the appropriate credential to use based on the certification achieved. The standard format for the order of credentials is your highest degree (if desired) followed by the certification credential. Some examples are:

- John Brown, CPHIMS
- Mary Jones, BA, CPHIMS
- Bill Smith, MS, CPHIMS

You may want to announce your certification accomplishment. The certifying body may provide you with a letter or announcement format that can be used with your employer, the local newspaper, or your professional organization. If your organization offers reimbursement, bonus payment, or career advancement, there may be additional documentation and paperwork required. Take pride in your accomplishment!

MAINTAINING YOUR CERTIFICATION

Maintaining your certification becomes the next step in the process. It is important to review the renewal requirements early. Certifications are normally renewed on a three- or five-year cycle, depending on the certifying body. Most renewals will have similar requirements as in the initial certification around ongoing experience or practice requirement, commonly in the specific area of the certification. There are frequently requirements for continuing education with a minimum number of hours to complete, and many provide alternative options for some of the hours such as professional presentations, publications, academic credit, student mentoring, and the like. Be clear on the exact requirements; presentations may require a certain number of presentations, excluding those provided as part of your work, and may not allow for a repeat of the same content. Some options may include activities offering further professional development through services such as item writing for the examination. For continuing education, investigate any requirements for topics related to the test content outline or a percentage of the hours being by certain approved providers. Identify what materials you will need to submit at the time of renewal to validate that you attended, the material presented, and the continuing education provider. A continuing education certificate may be sufficient, but sometimes additional material such as the education outline from the session may also be necessary. Several months before the expiration of your certification, the certifying body will notify you via mail and/or email. At this time you can verify you have met the renewal requirements and prepare to submit the renewal application. Some provide online sites to track your continuing education in an ongoing basis, so it is easier to provide information about meeting the renewal requirements. For additional information on continuing education, see Section V, The Importance of Lifelong Learning; Chapter 24, The Many Facets of Continuing Education.

Check with your employer to see if recertification fees will be paid or reimbursed. Some organizations offer a recertification bonus payment, often lower than the initial certification bonus, to help defray the costs. Review the certification renewal requirements early so you can be prepared with all necessary requirements.

CONCLUSION

Certification provides validation that an individual meets a set of standards and provides one with a sense of professional accomplishment. Certification can help advance your career. Chose a certification that aligns with your personal and professional goals. Review the certification materials to verify that you meet the necessary qualifications. Review the test content outline to determine your strengths and weaknesses and develop an action plan for your gaps. Develop a plan to meet the gaps. Complete the application for certification, schedule your examination, and prepare for the exam day. Celebrate your certification success, and proudly display your earned credential. Turn your eye to maintaining your certificate, and review the ongoing requirements. Certification can foster your career success.

REFERENCES

American Health Information Management Association (2016b). *Types of certification.* http://www.ahima.org/certification/exams?tabid=specialty

American Nurses Association (2015). *Nursing informatics: Scope and standards of practice* (2nd ed.). Silver Spring, MD: Nursesbooks.org.

American Nurses Credentialing Center [ANCC] (2013). *2013 nursing informatics role delineation study: National survey results.* https://www.nursingworld.org/~4ace6c/globalassets/certification/certification-specialty-pages/resources/role-delineation-studies/nursingcasemanagement-rds.pdf

American Nurses Credentialing Center [ANCC] (2016a). *2015 ANCC certification data.* https://www.nursingworld.org/~49930b/globalassets/docs/ancc/ancc-cert-data-website.pdf

American Nurses Credentialing Center [ANCC] (2016b). *Informatics nursing.* https://www.nursingworld.org/our-certifications/informatics-nurse/

College of Healthcare Information Management Executives [CHIME] (2016). CHCIO certification & CEUs. https://chimecentral.org/chcio/

Detmer, D. E., and Shortliffe, E. H. (2014). Clinical informatics: Prospects for a new medical subspecialty. *JAMA*, 311, no. 20: 2067–2068.

Gadd, C. S., Williamson, J. J., Steen, E. B., Andriole, K. P., Delaney, C., Gumpper, K., LaVenture, M., Rosendale, D., Sittig, D. F., Thyvalikakath, T., Turner, P., and Fridsma, D. B. (2016a). Eligibility requirements for advanced health informatics certification. *J Am Med Inform Assoc*, 23: 851–854.

Gadd, C. S., Williamson, J. J., Steen, E. B., and Fridsma, D. B. (2016b). Creating advanced health informatics certification. *J Am Med Inform Assoc*, 23: 848–850.

Gardner, R. M., Overhage, J. M., Steen, E. B., Munger, B. S., Holmes, J. H., Williamson, J. J., and Detmer, D. E. (2009). Core content for the subspecialty of clinical informatics. *J Am Med Inform Assoc*, 16: 153–157.

HIMSS (2015). *HIMSS CPHIMS Certified professional in healthcare information & management systems: Candidate handbook and application.* Retrieved August 23, 2021, from http://www.himss.org/health-it-certification/cphims/handbook

HIMSS (2016a). *Health IT certifications.* http://www.himss.org/health-it-certification

HIMSS (2016b). *Who is CPHIMS certified?* http://www.himss.org/health-it-certification/cphims/who-cphims-certified

Kaplow, R. (2011). The value of certification. *AACN Advance Critical Care*, 22, no. 1: 25–32.

McLaughlin, A., and Fetzer, S. J. (2015). The perceived value of certification by Magnet® and non-Magnet nurses. *JONA*, 45, no. 4: 194–199.

National Library of Medicine (2016). *Medical subject headings.* https://meshb-prev.nlm.nih.gov/#/record/ui?ui=D002568

Project Management Institute [PMI] (2016a). *Certifications.* http://www.pmi.org/certification.aspx

Project Management Institute [PMI] (2016b). *Project management professional (PMP) handbook.* http://www.pmi.org/-/media/pmi/documents/public/pdf/certifications/project-management-professional-handbook.pdf

10 Seeking an Advanced Professional Designation

Selena Davis
PhD, PMP, CPHIMS-CA

CONTENTS

INTRODUCTION

An increasing number of people are looking to establish, advance, or nurture their career, and as such, many more people today are earning professional designations than ever before. While changes to the way healthcare is delivered continues to evolve and will be forever changed due to pandemics like COVID-19, having advanced knowledge and skills is likely to offer leadership opportunities and active and expert contribution to the conversations. Simply put, for employers, a professional designation brings comfort, and for employment seekers, it brings confidence. Such qualifications identify an individual as: (1) having reached the highest standard of professional knowledge and skills; (2) actively participating in a professional practice which is guided and informed by ethical standards, and the norms and global language of the related domain; (3) belonging to a community of highly educated and skilled professionals, organizations, and experts worldwide; and (4) committing to continuing professional development.

The idea of cultivating one's career and voluntarily seeking further qualification often arises from a desire for personal recognition, increased income, inherent drive for lifelong learning, and/or to perform a job to the best of one's ability. The process of seeking an advanced professional designation in and of itself offers numerous informal possibilities to nurture one's career and expand one's network by way of exploring and investigating continuing learning opportunities, both virtually and face-to-face with experts in the profession. More formally, seeking an advanced qualification is most associated with certificate programs, professional certifications, and professional designations. Formal online learning programs have exploded in popularity in the past couple decades (ThoughtCo, 2019), and global plagues such as COVID-19 have radically transformed how we do things, including achieving advanced professional and academic education online (Kalantzis and Cope, 2020).

The literature and the industry tend to describe certificate programs easily but blur the terms *professional certification* and *professional designation,* perhaps because by definition a *certificate program* may be simpler to characterize than the other two. A certificate program is distinguished as a set of course work or curriculum completed within a set period of time for a specific field of study that results in a certificate of completion. Such programs are often prerequisite education requirements for licensure or for a specific industry's professional certification or designation.

The terms *certification* and *designation* are usually used interchangeably, and while there are many similarities among the terms, such as formal training, specific body of knowledge, examinations, membership and fees, and code of ethics and professional conduct, it may be reasoned that the difference is that an advanced professional designation associates with a professional governing body, which establishes a nationally or internationally accepted level of knowledge and skill that must be regularly demonstrated through maintenance requirements to represent ongoing competency. In this way, the maintenance requirements of a professional designation support a reduction in the risk of professional obsolescence—i.e., the discrepancy between a professional's level of proficiency and the current state-of-the-art standards in the field required for successful performance (Setor et al., 2015). A professional certification (e.g., PMP, CPHIMS) is typically defined as a formal recognition of professional or technical *competence* (Lysaght and Altschuld, 2000). It validates that an individual has attained the knowledge and skills necessary for competent practice in a particular profession. A professional designation (e.g., CRNBC, FRCPC) conveys a *continuing competency* as measured by the issuing national or international professional governing body and as managed by the individual on a regular basis.

PROFESSIONAL COMPETENCE

The term *competence* has been described in the literature in numerous ways with no generally accepted definition. Further, and in many cases, the terms *competence* and *competency* are not necessarily synonymous. That is, competence has been referred to as a potential ability and/or a capability to function in a given situation, whereas competency focuses on one's actual performance in a situation. According to Schroeter (2008), this means that competence is required before one can expect to achieve competency. Other authors have described competence as involving the implementation of combined knowledge, know-how, and behavior (Bennour and Crestani, 2007) or as a cross-functional integration and coordination of one's ability to exploit the resources or building blocks of competence (Torkkeli and Tuominen, 2002). Still other authors have described competence as the habitual and judicious use of communication, knowledge, technical skills, clinical reasoning, emotions, values, and reflection in daily practice for the benefit of the individual and community (Epstein and Hundert, 2002).

The nature of professional competence is multi-dimensional. To simplify, a list of the key components of competence are synthesized into a conceptual framework (Table 10.1) and described based on the work of several authors (Capece and Bazzica, 2013; Epstein and Hundert, 2002; Lysaght and Altschuld, 2000).

CHARACTERISTICS OF COMPETENCY

Competency, too, has been defined in a few different ways. For example, competency has been described as a set of characteristics (knowledge, skills, and abilities), which are relatively stable across different situations (Ley and Albert, 2003), or as the degree to which individuals can apply the skills and knowledge associated with the profession to the full range of situations that fall within the domain of that particular profession (Lysaght and Altschuld, 2000). Irrespective of the differences in definition, and fundamental to the understanding of the close relationship between ability and the "work" of the profession, the key characteristics of competency have been summarized in the literature as an individual's ability to

- Combine various resources where their value arises from more than the simple possession of these resources.

TABLE 10.1

List of Components in Competence Conceptual Framework

Competence Dimension	What Is It?	How Is It Achieved?
Know	Theoretical knowledge, judgment, and reasoning	Formal and on-the-job training and continuing professional development
Can	Ability to perform a task in a structured setting under observation	Application of theoretical knowledge to a task
Do	Ability to perform a task in daily practice unobserved	Practical experience
Share	Ability to communicate knowledge and build competence in others	Distribution of knowledge, mentoring others, and peer review contributions

- Support the way the activity is performed by way of a cognitive structure that organizes the way the activity is performed and is relatively stable across a full range of situations.
- Construct an action such that each time it is called upon, it may be improved, enriched, and developed in order to be adapted to the changing features of the situation (Capece and Bazzica, 2013).

The literature holds that one's competence can become a competency once it has been built over time and not easily exceeded. That is, one's capability to integrate knowledge, skills, and experience in a given situation may become, over time, a proficient application of such characteristics in the full range of situations that fall within a given profession. Ultimately, the collection of one's competencies that are widespread become one's core competency (Torkkeli and Tuominen, 2002). For example, as a health information technology (IT) professional certified in healthcare information and management systems (CPHIMS), numerous competencies are required to collectively hold a core competency in the profession. For example, some key competencies include information management and IT, project management, system analysis, system evaluation, clinical health services, and leadership and organizational management.

Giving shape to the work of various authors (Capece and Bazzica, 2013; Lysaght and Altschuld, 2000), a professional competency model (Figure 10.1) illustrates how the continuous collection of theoretical knowledge ("Know"); application of skill in a structured setting ("Can"); performance in daily practice over a wide range of situations ("Do"); and sharing of information, skill, and wisdom with others ("Share") leads to competency. With the continued development and application of knowledge and skills, a reduction in the risk of professional obsolescence is supported.

It may be argued that the highest level of competence relates to the "Do" and "Share" dimensions as they are dependent upon the proficiency at the "Know" and "Can" levels. In this way, knowledge and skills performed in a structured setting are a necessity but insufficient condition of competency (Lysaght and Altschuld, 2000). Subsequently, it may be rationalized that the professional designation may be distinguished and valued from the professional certification through well-structured, up-to-date maintenance requirements established by a related national or international professional governing body, which includes the demonstration of the "Do" and "Share" dimensions of professional competence and results in a reduction of the probability of a discrepancy between a professional's level of proficiency and the current standards in the field required for successful performance.

FIGURE 10.1   Professional competency model.

BENEFITS AND BARRIERS

Many professional designations are used as "post-nominal letters," meaning that they are included after the person's name (e.g., Janet Smith, ABC). Top-level professionals across a broad spectrum of sectors have unequivocally agreed that a few letters after a name can make a difference in one's career (Schonfeld, 2010). Simply stated, possessing a professional designation proves beneficial both personally and professionally, as well as with the public (Foubister, 2003; Williams and Counts, 2013).

BENEFITS

For the individual, a professional designation provides personal recognition, opportunities to increase one's professional network, access to emerging tools and continuing professional development courses both in-person and online, increased job satisfaction, and often an increase in income and career advancement (Kaplow, 2011). In practice, retaining a professional designation leads to empowerment by way of an increased confidence for the effective execution of domain knowledge and skills, as well as enhancing collaboration (Wade, 2009; Fritter and Shimp, 2016). It also is associated with positive in-practice peer assessments (Wenghofer et al., 2014).

For the organization that employs experts with a professional designation, it leads to higher retention rates, a sense of pride and achievement, and a higher level of professional service (Fritter and Shimp, 2016; Kaplow, 2011). It also has benefits to other stakeholders. While empirical evidence of outcomes is limited for the customer, studies in healthcare of providers who retain their professional designation have identified an increased adherence to evidence-based best practices (Kaplow, 2011). For the profession itself, an increased confidence in the service provided by its professionals is most celebrated.

INTRINSIC AND EXTRINSIC MOTIVATING FACTORS

Different factors motivate different professionals to pursue and maintain advanced qualifications like professional designations or certifications. Two distinct groupings, described as intrinsic and extrinsic factors in the literature, offer insight into the motivators for an individual to personally

TABLE 10.2
Internal and External Motivators

Internal Motivators	External Motivators
Enhances feeling of personal accomplishment	Promotes recognition from peers
Provides personal satisfaction	Promotes recognition from other professionals
Validates specialized knowledge	Increases marketability
Indicates professional growth	Promotes recognition from employers
Provides professional challenge	Increases public confidence
Enhances professional credibility	Increases salary
Provides evidence of professional commitment	
Indicates attainment of a practice standard	
Enhances personal confidence in abilities	
Provides evidence of accountability	
Indicates level of professional competence	
Enhances professional autonomy	

and professionally grow. The intrinsic factors, or rewards, relate to the internal motivators while the extrinsic rewards are typically motivators supported externally. Table 10.2 lists the main internal and external motivators associated with the value of an advanced qualification (Niebuhr and Biel, 2007).

CHALLENGES AND ISSUES

For many professions, despite the evidence that there are benefits and intrinsic rewards for obtaining and maintaining advanced qualifications, the lack of strength of the extrinsic value makes it challenging and less attractive to seek or keep the professional designation. Considerations to address barriers by organizations, administrators, and employers in general should be made to increase such things as opportunities for recognition and greater compensation (Wade, 2009). In fact, financial concerns over the cost of the examination and the costs to maintain the designation are frequently reported in studies as two of the most significant barriers (Fritter and Shimp, 2016; Williams and Counts, 2013). Table 10.3 lists the barriers, identified in the literature, to obtaining an advanced qualification in order of strongest barrier (Niebuhr and Biel, 2007).

BEGINNING YOUR SEARCH

Whether you are just establishing your career or are a seasoned professional, the best place to begin your search for the right professional designation is with your professional association or governing body. When it comes to the health IT professional, the best place to start is with the Healthcare Information and Management Systems Society (HIMSS), an international professional governing body (http://www.himss.org/ProfessionalDevelopment).

The key for those seeking an advanced professional designation is to look for a(n)

- Requirement of a specific level of knowledge and experience as a prerequisite.
- Academically rigorous and comprehensive credentialing process.
- Program to support continuing professional development.
- Requirement of adherence to a professional and ethical code of conduct.

TABLE 10.3
Barriers to Certification

Cost of examination
Lack of institutional reward
Lack of institutional support
Lack of access to preparation courses or materials
Discomfort with test-taking process
It costs too much to maintain the credential
Lack of access to examination site
Lack of access to or availability of continuing education
I did not pass the examination when I took it
No desire/interest in certification
Not relevant to my practice

- Necessity for maintenance of professional competency—i.e., "Know-Can-Do-Share"—to a prescribed standard.
- Condition for removal of the credential if professionals are not compliant with the outlined standards.

MAINTAINING YOUR PROFESSIONAL DESIGNATION

Given the rate of change in most fields, many would argue that the legitimacy of a professional governing body—and by extension, the professional designations it confers—rests in its commitment to: (i) test the knowledge of an individual before granting the designation; (ii) require a regular demonstration of professional competency; and (iii) be willing and able to discipline, and even revoke the designation of, those who break rules or fail to meet stringent standards on an ongoing basis.

Competence planning, monitoring, and maintenance activities play an important role in building a professional competitive advantage. In reality, competencies are considered resources which need to be identified, measured, and managed, and in fact, studies indicate a significant positive relationship between competency and one's ability to create and sustain a competitive advantage (Capece and Bazzica, 2013). Maintaining and renewing an advanced qualification with the governing organization supports professional competency and the notion of competitive advantage. It is contingent on one's commitment to undertake continuous professional development so as to maintain and advance one's ability to apply the current knowledge and skills of the profession.

Before and once a professional designation is obtained, an individual should review the national or international governing body's maintenance requirements. Many governing organizations now have online systems for tracking and managing credentialing of their professionals who hold an advanced qualification. It is strongly recommended that the online system be utilized to document the fulfillment of requirements on an ongoing basis. At the very minimum, engaging with the system well in advance of the renewal date of the designation is prudent.

To maintain a professional designation, and in addition to the annual membership dues, professionals commonly must:

- Submit details of their activities which maintain competency according to the prescribed standards of the professional governing body.
- Submit fees for renewal of the designation.
- Commit to the code of ethics and standard professional conduct.

CONCLUSION

In the fast-paced field of health informatics, many health IT professionals may seek a professional designation as an aspect of lifelong learning to ensure they have the professional competency to advance initiatives that positively impact patient care. This worthwhile endeavor must be considered carefully to ensure that the benefits resonate and there exists an ongoing commitment to oneself and the profession. Ultimately and once obtained, the more you use your professional designation, the more its meaning will be recognized as a symbol of highest professionalism.

REFERENCES

Bennour, M., and Crestani, D. (2007). Using competencies in performance estimation: From the activity to the process. *Computers in Industry*, 58(2), 151–163.

Capece, G., and Bazzica, P. (2013). A practical proposal for a "competence plan fulfillment" key performance indicator. *Knowledge and Process Management*, 20(1), 40–49.

Epstein, R. M., and Hundert, E. M. (2002). Defining and assessing professional competence. *JAMA*, 287(2), 226–235.

Foubister, V. (2003). Tales of success. Certification proves beneficial, both personally and professionally. *Materials Management in Health Care*, 12(6), 33–36. Retrieved from http://www.ncbi.nlm.nih.gov/pubmed/12854208

Fritter, E., and Shimp, K. (2016). What does certification in professional nursing practice mean?. *Med-Surg Matters*, 25(2), 8–10.

Kalantzis, M., and Cope, B. (2020). After the COVID-19 crisis: Why higher education may (and perhaps should) never be the same. *ACCESS: Contemporary Issues in Education*, 40(1), 51–55. https://doi.org/10.46786/ac20.9496

Kaplow, R. (2011). The value of certification. *AACN Advanced Critical Care*, 22(1), 25–32.

Ley, T., and Albert, D. (2003). Identifying employee competencies in dynamic work domains: Methodological considerations and a case study. *Journal of Universal Computer Science*, 9(12), 1500–1518.

Lysaght, R. M., and Altschuld, J. W. (2000). Beyond initial certification: The assessment and maintenance of competency in professions. *Evaluation and Program Planning*, 23(1), 95–104.

Niebuhr, B., and Biel, M. (2007). The value of specialty nursing certification. *Nursing Outlook*, 55(4), 176–181.

Peterson, D. (2019). How Professional Certificates Can Help Jump-Start Your Career. A publication of ThoughtCo. Retrieved October 18, 2020, from https://www.thoughtco.com/what-is-professional-certification-31527

Schonfeld, G. R. (2010). Privilege of peerage: The value of professional designations. A publication of the New York Society of Security Analysts.. Retrieved June 26, 2016, from http://post.nyssa.org/nyssa-news/2010/04/privilege-of-peerage-the-value-of-professional-designations.html

Schroeter, K. (2008). Competence literature review, Competency & Credentialing Institute. Retrieved d October 18, 2020 from https://www.innovationlabs.com/research/pre/reading_materials /competence_lit_review.pdf

Setor, T., Joseph, D., and Srivastava, S. C. (2015). Professional obsolescence in IT: The relationships between the threat of professional obsolescence, coping and psychological strain. In *Proceedings of the 2015 ACM SIGMIS Conference on Computers and People Research* (pp. 117–122).

ThoughtCo. (2019). How professional certificates can help jump-start your career. Retrieved October 18, 2020, from https://www.thoughtco.com/what-is-professional-certification-31527

Torkkeli, M., and Tuominen, M. (2002). The contribution of technology selection to core competencies. *International Journal of Production Economics*, 77(3), 271–284.

Wade, C. H. (2009). Perceived effects of specialty nurse certification: A review of the literature. *AORN Journal*, 89(1), 183–192.

Wenghofer, E. F., Marlow, B., Campbell, C., Carter, L., Kam, S., McCauley, W., and Hill, L. (2014). The relationship between physician participation in continuing professional development programs and physician in-practice peer assessments. *Academic Medicine*, 89(6), 920–927.

Williams, H. F., and Counts, C. S. (2013). Certification 101: The pathway to excellence. *Nephrology Nursing Journal: Journal of the American Nephrology Nurses' Association*, 40(3), 197–209, 253. Retrieved from http://www.ncbi.nlm.nih.gov/pubmed/23923799

Section III

Learning From Others

11 The Mentoring Process

Joseph J. Wagner
MPA, FHIMSS

CONTENTS

INTRODUCTION

Mentoring—just what is mentoring? Well, it is defined by Webster's as:

> To teach or give advice or guidance to (someone, such as a less experienced person or a child): to act as a mentor for (someone)[1]

We acquired "mentor" from the literature of ancient Greece. In Homer's epic *The Odyssey,* Odysseus was away from home fighting and journeying for 20 years. During that time, Telemachus, the son he left as a babe in arms, grew up under the supervision of Mentor, an old and trusted friend. When the goddess Athena decided it was time to complete the education of young Telemachus, she visited him disguised as Mentor, and they set out together to learn about his father. Today, we use the word mentor for anyone who is a positive, guiding influence in another (usually younger) person's life.[IBID]

In this chapter, we discuss what it means to be a mentor or a mentee, the value of both, and some effective methods to employ as the mentor or mentee.

THE MENTOR

Being a mentor is an important responsibility and one that can be very rewarding. The mentor role is similar to being a teacher in that you provide instruction to someone who is less knowledgeable than yourself. Yet, mentoring goes further than that because as a mentor you also provide your work and personal life experiences, things that can only be learned through daily interactions with others. A perfect example is the real-time knowledge that is gained through actual experiences of a seasoned project manager. For example, a project manager will lead a team of resources from many different departments comprised of staff from all levels within an organization. The project manager and this group of individuals are formed to deliver some type of solution. Initially, the project manager may start out with a small project and over time be given more complex projects. Learning how to deal with multifaceted issues that involve multiple stakeholders comes with the experiences gained by working on increasingly challenging projects over time.

DOI: 10.4324/9780429398377-14

The role of the mentor is to educate or pass on the knowledge that was gained from working on these more complex projects. Describing the "gotchas," sharing best practices, and explaining how to deal with difficult human resource issues are experiences that cannot be fully learned from books. The seasoned project manager should consider himself or herself an important mentor.

As a mentor, you should focus on the development of your mentee by coaching them and providing counseling on their projects and the issues they may encounter. When you meet with your mentee, your initial discussion should be a time for introductions. What is the mentee looking for in terms of guidance? What are their aspirational goals? What are their career plans? During this meeting you will explore these details, which will determine if you have the correct background and experiences to be a good mentor to them.

With this information, you can then focus on the areas where the mentee is deficient in certain skills or experiences. You should always be looking for places that you can push the mentee beyond their current skillset so that there is ongoing, continuous development.

When deciding to be a mentor, you must be sure that you have the time and energy necessary to work with your mentee. Make sure that you can commit to the time it takes to be a good mentor.

THE MENTEE

A mentee is often thought of as a younger person; however, this is not always true. Throughout your career you will have many opportunities to meet well-educated and highly experienced people. Your work may span several different technologies, skillsets, and required experience. Take technology as an example. With so much new technology being introduced into the healthcare environments today, many times the younger person has been exposed to the technical requirements in early learning situations, training sessions, or actual work. Regardless of age, the mentee is the person that will be learning form the mentor.

The role of a mentee is to gain as much knowledge as possible from their selected mentor. Meetings should be scheduled and dedicated to time for the mentor and the mentee to share experiences and discuss how they were handled so that they can be analyzed to determine if there is room for improvement. The mentee should take note of issues that arise that are difficult or unusual so that they can be discussed with their mentor. It is important to have regularly scheduled meetings so that your progression in skills is continuous and relative to your time with the organization.

It should be mentioned that throughout your career you will probably have several mentors. As you progress in your career and become more knowledgeable and experienced, your mentors will change. It is also common for someone to have more than one mentor due to the diversity of their role with the organization. Some people will require education from mentors who have human resource skills, technical skills, and specific skills related to their chosen course of study.

SELECTING YOUR MENTOR

The mentor is someone who has more experience, education, or training than other people in the organization with similar or more novice roles. The concept of mentorship is to have the mentor teach, train, or share the wisdom they have gained from the additional experience, education, or training. This is done to help the more amateur person to learn from the mentor. This helps the person to become proficient in their role faster, by assimilating this knowledge without having to experience it independently through more formal methods or having to wait to have similar experiences that may come much later in their life.

It is important when selecting a mentor that you choose someone who has the prerequisite skills and experience that you are seeking. One way to get this information is to check with your human resources department. Representatives should have an understanding of the requirements and roles that each potential mentor possesses. You can also use the Internet as well. One particularly popular site that is frequently used to gather information on people is LinkedIn.[2] Many professionals use LinkedIn to create their professional profile. By reviewing the professional profiles for individuals in your company or city you can create a list of potential mentors.

When beginning your career in health IT, there will be many areas where only real-life experiences will give you the depth and breadth of knowledge that is required to become a truly successful employee. Some roles in health IT may require that you become a subject matter expert—an example being when you work with clinical application systems (e.g., lab, pharmacy, radiology). Large-scale hospital clinical information systems have many supporting ancillary systems, each requiring a different set of skills. The same is true for integration applications that are used in hospitals and Health Information Exchanges (HIE). Programming, development skills, project management, support services, and strategy development are just a few of the areas you may be considering. It will be important for you to find a mentor who has experience in the specific area you are considering for yourself.

If you are not quite sure of what you wish to pursue, then you should select a mentor who has managed or supported several different areas you are interested in or select more than one mentor so that you can better understand each of the various areas. In addition to the methods described above you can check with local career counseling agencies, like the Career Counselling Consortium (www.careercc.org), as they may have local mentorship programs available for you to solicit. Most states have several counseling centers that can be easily found on the Internet.

The one area that is typically universal in every healthcare field is human resource management. Working with people from all different departments and levels of an organization takes solid resource management skills. As you progress in your career, you will undoubtedly be required to manage your own resources as well. The human resource management department typically has clearly written policies and procedures; however, managing people cannot always be governed by what is written. It is important to consider having a strong mentor who you can turn to for advice when a situation arises. This can be a human resources person, or someone who is managing a large group of people.

There are two different scenarios when it comes to healthcare organizations and mentorship. Some organizations have a formal mentorship program while others have not embraced these programs and you will have to structure a mentorship program on your own.

FORMAL MENTORSHIP PROGRAMS

Formal mentorship programs are becoming more common in the workplace. The formal program ensures that there is some type of process to set up people who wish to be mentors. Typically the mentors will have their mentoring skillsets listed so that selecting your mentor is made by simply identifying the person(s) who have the experience you are looking for. Most programs have published policies and procedures that are to be followed by the mentor/mentee. These programs typically limit the number of mentees a mentor can accept so that the mentor has the proper amount of time for their mentees. Policies set up guidelines for meeting schedules, roles of the mentee and mentor, and an evaluation process.

Even if you work for an organization that has a formal program with a list of potential mentors, it is still important that you speak to several possible mentor candidates to be sure that you are selecting the best resource. You should treat your first meeting with a potential mentor as an interview. Spend time interviewing them to be sure that they have the skills and experience that you wish to gain. Have the mentor speak of their previous experiences mentoring and how those people are now doing. Be sure to ask how much time per month they have available for your sessions. During these interviews you will probably find that you feel more comfortable with a particular person. You should take this into consideration because the mentoring process should be comfortable and engaging with honest and open conversations.

Once you have decided on your mentor, be sure to create an outline or list of goals and expectations. Review this with your mentor so that they have input into your mentorship. You want to be sure that you both agree on what will be accomplished during your mentorship to ensure that you have the best possible experience.

INFORMAL MENTORSHIP PROGRAMS

Organizations that do not have a formal program for assigning mentors will require you to search out and select a mentor on your own. Not having a list of mentors and their skillsets will require you to do some research on your organization's leaders. This should not discourage you from proceeding. There are several simple methods to use to gain the required information you need to get the right person for you.

Start with your human resources department. Obtain an organizational chart for the company; sit down with your human resources representative; and discuss the levels in the organization, positions, and job responsibilities. Remember that your mentor may come from a department that is not closely related to your own.

Set up meetings with the potential mentor candidates, and discuss with them your desire to have a mentor. Clearly define what you would expect from them using the details provided in this chapter. Be sure that the person understands and is ready to commit to the time and effort it takes to make the mentorship a valuable use of time for both of you.

OTHER CONSIDERATIONS WHEN SELECTING A MENTOR

As mentioned, it is not cast in stone that you have just a single mentor. Different people offer varying experiences that can provide a significant benefit to you. It may seem most appropriate to select a mentor from your current place of employment; however, there are many other places you should also consider. You can break down your development goals into many different categories. Here are just a few to illustrate where you may consider seeking a mentor:

Human resources: Human resource management is a very important part of your education. Learning the policies and procedures of the organization is important, but their experiences when dealing with resource issues will be invaluable.

Project managers: Large, complex project leaders possess significant work experiences and may have relative industry-accepted certifications you may wish to consider, such as Project Management Professional (PMP), Agile, or Black Belt.

Technical skills: If your work is technical in nature, it will be helpful to identify a System Matter Expert (SME) that has the technical skills you will need to acquire. Look within your organization, check with vendors, and search the Internet for relative user-support blogs.

Future educational considerations: Undergraduate school, graduate school, and PhDs should all be considered when mapping out your development plan. Higher education is quickly becoming the norm for many healthcare careers. Seek out managers within your organization who have graduate or doctoral degrees for their advice. Set up a meeting or attend an orientation with local colleges and universities to better understand what your opportunities may be.

Volunteering: Volunteering should also be part of your career plan as it offers a great way to network and "give back" at the same time. Speak to your managers and directors about possible volunteer opportunities in the healthcare field.

CONCLUSION

Finding a strong mentor should be part of everyone's development plan. The process will provide you with many benefits. Over the course of your relationship with your mentor(s), you have the opportunity to increase your understanding and skills related to human resources, technical skills, managing complex projects, handling change management, and increasing your professional network.

Sun Microsystems compiled the following metrics associated with mentoring[3]:

- Both mentors and mentees were approximately 20% more likely to get a raise than people who did not participate in the mentoring program.
- 25% of mentees and 28% of mentors received a raise—versus only 5% of managers who were not mentors.
- Employees who received mentoring were promoted FIVE times more often than people who didn't have mentors.
- Mentors were SIX times more likely to have been promoted to a bigger job.

The statistics speak for themselves. As you progress in the development of your skills and gain experience, you should consider being a mentor. The mentoring experience can be a rich and rewarding way of giving something back to the healthcare community. Bestowing your life experiences and skills on a mentee ought to be part of your own career plan.

NOTES

1 Merriam-Webster, Online Dictionary, www.merriam-webster.com
2 LinkedIn is a business-oriented social networking service which can be accessed at: https://www.linkedin.com
3 Quest, Lisa Forbes, October 31, 2011, How becoming a Mentor Can Boost Your Career, http://www.forbes.com/sites/lisaquast/2011/10/31/how-becoming-a-mentor-can-boost-your-career/#735fee75662a

12 Managing by Walking Around

Jason Bickford
MCSE

CONTENTS

INTRODUCTION

Healthcare professionals are confronted with trying to find a balance in improving the quality of care while decreasing medical errors. This ongoing challenge and tightrope that is being walked also includes reducing costs with fewer resources. The role of a health information technology (IT) professional is not only to provide support to providers, nurses, and ancillary departments so they can provide exceptional patient care, but also to support systems and technologies that do so too. The pinnacle of a health IT professional is to contribute to improving patient care outcomes and/or enabling the business to provide exceptional patient care through the use of technology. One style of business management that can foster a productive workplace culture and help you reach pinnacle career success is Managing by Walking Around (MBWA).

> Whether you are rounding for bedside clinical care, or simply to gain a better perspective of your customer, the opportunities to recognize where a small change can have a large impact may never be realized if you are restricted to the confines of an office or desk. Jason's personal adoption of the MBWA strategy enabled him to quickly recognize an opportunity to transform direct access to electrocardiographic tracings within the electronic medical record from a poor-quality reference image to a high-value addition for physicians with near diagnostic quality results!
>
> Joel McAlduff, M.D.
> Vice President and CMIO, MedStar Health (former CMIO at Banner Health)

THE CONCEPT

The concept of MBWA, also known as management by wandering around, has been around for decades and can be traced back to management practices that were deployed by Hewlett-Packard back in the 1970s (https://www.mindtools.com/pages/article/newTMM_72.htm). MBWA involves leaders stepping away from their offices or desks in order to roam around the workplace to solicit

DOI: 10.4324/9780429398377-15

staff feedback, observe processes and workflows, build relationships, and show visibility and appreciation for the work that is being done.

THE BENEFITS

The benefits of MBWA for a healthcare IT professional can be very rewarding as well as enlightening. William Edwards Deming, who was an American engineer, statistician, professor, author, lecturer, and management consultant, once shared that "If you wait for people to come to you, you"ll only get small problems. You must go and find them. The big problems are where people don't realize they have one in the first place" (http://itmanagersinbox.com/1687/management-by-walking-around-mbwa/).

MBWA, when used consistently, can make you more approachable and helps build trust so that everyone is empowered to share their ideas and problems with you. The additional healthcare process and business knowledge that can be gained will help to connect the dots and see the big picture as well as the finer details. This process can also accelerate decision making and information sharing. MBWA can also create accountability and lessen that perception that when you're out of sight, you're out of mind. MBWA may improve employee morale by increasing employee productivity, engagement, and job satisfaction, which may also impact the retention of talented employees. Organization morale or workplace culture can be an influence when an employee's voice is being heard and their trust is earned. It can also help foster a collaborative workplace culture through the sharing and exchange of ideas that could improve productivity and creativity, and create cost-saving measures.

STRATEGIES AND SUGGESTIONS

There are numerous MBWA strategies and suggestions, offered in the upcoming paragraphs, that can help you achieve many desired outcomes, but the most important for sustained achievement is that your walking around excursions must have results that matter. There must be follow through on action items, commitments, and communication. MBWA can be a consistent part of your routine for general rounding, for a one-on-one discussion, as part of project planning, or event solution brainstorming. *MBWA is less about having the right answers and more about having the right questions.* You need to be able to listen to feedback that is shared and then, in turn, provide timely follow-through or your credibility will be lost. MBWA should be a process of active listening, soliciting feedback, prompting suggestions, and developing ideas that create an opportunity to identify and resolve issues. The process must enable active problem solving, increasing the ability for health IT professionals to act on improvement suggestions, but with a balance between gathering more suggestions and prioritizing them, versus implementing existing ones that have already been identified. A lack of balance and not allowing enough time for reflection will create challenges for yourself and those you are leading. MBWA is also an opportunity to be social and share communications on current opportunities as well as giving updates on upcoming changes. A health IT professional can become the bridge between business and clinical teams and help create dialogue across leadership lines, resulting in an improved workplace culture. If an in-person MBWA format is not possible, then try a virtual means by connecting through video, chat, or a phone call.

IMPLEMENTING MBWA

As a health IT professional, you may be wondering how you can implement your own MBWA routine. I offer you a few tips to get started, but first, you must have your own goal or purpose defined. Whether it's to discover process improvements, create new ideas, or build upon lessons learned, it is valuable to have a cause.

1. *Reserve time:* Block your calendar for 1–2 hours either bi-weekly or monthly.
2. *Create an identity:* You should be yourself, be curious, be genuine, and be transparent.
3. *Relax:* Keep it informal, but bring something along to take notes.
4. *Inquire*: Listen, observe, ask open-ended questions, and solicit feedback.
5. *Praise:* Recognize those who are making positive changes and contributions.
6. *Actualize:* If you say you're going to do something, find an answer or ask a question; make sure you respond within a few days or be ready to answer the next time you walk around.
7. *Build:* Make sure to build relationships, business knowledge, and process improvements.

In today's healthcare landscape many organizations are challenged with managing rapid change. A regular MBWA routine can transform health IT professionals by helping them become more approachable. This routine will encourage staff to speak up and share. If the purpose is aligned with improving outcomes and is a collaborative process aimed at uncovering gaps in policies, procedures, and technology usage, the results should yield the creation of best practices and development or refinement of standard operating procedures.

As a health IT professional, you can be respected and sought after for your technical skills and subject matter expertise and habits formed through MBWA. You can also avoid becoming too distant and disconnected. The more connected you are and the more relationships you build, the better you can anticipate your customer needs.

MBWA MAJOR CONSIDERATIONS

There are three major components that you should consider when using MBWA in a health IT setting. They are getting to know (1) the people, (2) the process, and (3) the technology that is involved. Peter Fine, President and CEO of Banner Health, often shares with his staff that "visibility breeds credibility, credibility breeds trust; so if you want to be trusted, you have to be visible." This quote and message that Peter shares from one of his mentors is a great reminder that inspires my own MBWA excursions.

IMPROVING PATIENT CARE DELIVERY WITH MBWA: AN EXAMPLE

There are many examples and stories that can be shared about the benefits of MBWA and also having a mindset that everything takes people, process, and technology. I would like to share one that is personal to me. Dr. Joel McAlduff, former CMIO at Banner Health, shared with me that physicians were frustrated with interpreting EKGs that were being scanned into the electronic medical record due to image degradation after being scanned. As an ambitious health IT professional, I made it my mission to make the process better. My approach was to first understand the entire process, the people involved, and the current technologies in place. I contacted the Head of Radiology and asked for permission to observe an EKG technician while the technician was conducting an EKG test with a patient. The patient was accommodating while I observed the technician connecting wires to the patient from a mobile cart. The technician conducted the test and then rolled the cart into a room where it was connected to the network for transmitting to the EKG server for later printing of the EKG on specialized paper. Using a desktop scanner, a preliminary report was scanned into a Document Imaging solution that indexed and released the EKG report to the patient's chart but, of course, with less-than-desirable quality. I attempted to improve everything I could with the scanner and scanning software, but it only resulted in marginal improvements to the image quality. I consulted an external vendor resource that supported the Document Imaging solutions to see if there were other possibilities. He suggested a computer output to laser disk (COLD) feed process using technology that we owned but had not yet implemented. A COLD feed is an older term that refers to the scanning or importing of documents and making the images available in another source system. I researched the software and started exploring its capabilities in order to feel comfortable with its potential before moving on to the next steps. One requirement of the software was importing the EKG output as an XML or PDF document. This required me to engage the EKG application owner, who was an individual who worked in Technology Management, since that was a clinical system. I shared the complaint from the Chief Medical Officer (CMO) and the potential of the COLD feed software that could possibly unalter the EKG report and deliver an exceptional provider-viewing experience. The Technology Management leader was receptive to converting the EKG to a PDF, but it required an upgrade and some configuration as well as report formatting standardization in order to populate required fields such as patient Medical Record and Encounter numbers, which were necessary for routing to the correct patient's chart. These formatting changes required us to present them to a steering committee, and once approved, we were able to move forward with non-production testing. We engaged a Healthcare Informatics Leader to help us in coordinating the change process and procedures as well as getting hospital leadership support. Once we were satisfied with our testing efforts, we scheduled an implementation date and time. I arrived onsite in the Radiology department and waited patiently for the first EKG report to be generated and then exported as a PDF for the COLD feed software to pick up and route to the patient's chart. It was truly an exciting and rewarding experience to visualize the results and then share them with CMO. The result was an improvement in the patient care process, and the clinician's voice was heard. In this accomplishment, I knew that the people that I learned and worked with, such as the Radiology Department Head, EKG Technician, Technology Management and Informatics Leaders, and the CMO, all contributed to the success. The CMO, sharing his frustrations with a poor process, and myself, observing the process from beginning to the end, helped inspire me to find a better process and to learn about a technology that significantly improved workflow and cost savings since expensive EKG paper was no longer required. The new process not only resulted in a better image for clinicians to view, but the time it took to post the chart was reduced by hours, thereby improving patient care.

SUMMARY

MBWA was not a concept I was familiar with during the EKG project, but I somehow knew it was going to be essential for me to go beyond my office cubicle in order to facilitate necessary change, as well as earn stakeholder support. The visibility I created did indeed earn credibility and, in turn, trust with peers. MBWA was created for management, but there are clear benefits for health IT professionals who are leading projects or providing technology support. There have been many advancements in technology that have allowed teams to meet virtually, but truly effective meetings—with planning, collaboration, and most importantly engagement—in my opinion, are typically done in person. That is the spirit of MBWA.

CONCLUSION

One of your most important commodities, besides your health, is how you spend your time. I believe that MBWA is worthy of adopting, but only if you are clear with purpose and intent and can invest the necessary time, effort, and consistency. MBWA-related communications and managing expectations will also need to be carefully balanced between daily duties and trying to please everyone. Engage and build relationships with people. Ask questions to clarify the process and determine why specific things are done a certain way. Understand the function of technology and to expand its benefits in reaching a maximum outcome. As part of your MBWA initiative, if you're always mindful of the people, process, and technology components and diligent about creating consistency in delivering purpose, value, and outcomes you'll be on your way to becoming a health IT professional rock star! MBWA can create an opportunity for you to develop your own personal brand and style for delivering organizational value, influencing workplace culture, and aligning yourself with strategic initiatives that can signify you as a subject matter expert, rising star, or future leader, or help you be considered for a promotional leadership opportunity.

13 Experiencing a Job Exchange

Deborah Newman
MBA, FACHE, FHIMSS

CONTENTS

INTRODUCTION

How do you describe a job exchange? And how do you have an understanding of what a job exchange is? It is not as uncommon as you might think. There are benefits from a job exchange that are not always evident with the initial thoughts of this job growth activity.

The key components of the job exchange process create a structure that takes the initial idea through to ensuring a successful experience (Figure 13.1). The beginning of the process involves identifying the potential job that would be part of the job exchange. A job exchange has many benefits to both parties, so there must be a commitment and understanding of the benefits for all interested parties. The next key step is to document the proposal, including risks and benefits to each participant as well as the organization.

Multiple levels of approval must be obtained for the job exchange to occur. The hierarchy of approvals follow the natural approval process beginning with the immediate supervisor through executive approval. After support is obtained for the job exchange, Human Resources (HR) must be involved to ensure all labor laws and competencies are aligned prior to the experience.

After the job exchange, documentation of the experience will ensure appropriate communication to all interested parties as to the benefits and lessons learned. This documentation should be communicated to all interested parties, including management and HR. This documentation also forms the basis to "pay it forward" and creates a path for others to experience this rewarding and career-enhancing activity.

DOI: 10.4324/9780429398377-16

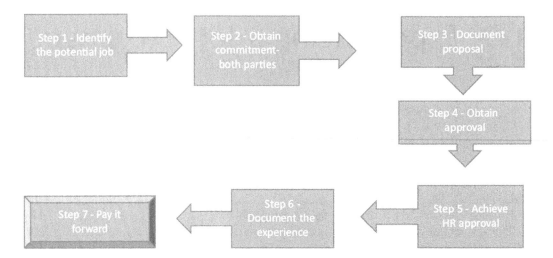

FIGURE 13.1   Job exchange process flow.

JOB EXCHANGE PROCESS STEP 1: IDENTIFY THE POTENTIAL JOB

When determining the job that you would like to experience with a job exchange, it is important to ensure it is aligned with your current job or is aligned with a position for which you are obtaining (or considering) additional education. One way to identify the job exchange role is to look at your supervisor's scope of responsibilities. If you are obtaining additional education or professional certification, the job exchange position can be aligned with the new opportunity. In healthcare, departments are typically categorized under top leadership in four basic areas: Clinical Care, Clinical Professional, Clinical Support, and Administration.

CLINICAL CARE LEADERSHIP AREA

The first employee category is Clinical Care, which includes physicians, nursing, clinical departments (e.g., the emergency department, surgery, acute care nursing) and clinical care support staff such as CNAs (certified nursing aide) and clinical area secretaries. This category of employees has the most interaction with patients and documentation in the medical record. Many of these employees are required to have a certain degree (RN, CNA, MD, or CNP), which is a constraint on which roles would be available for a job exchange. A job exchange in this category is usually between one department and another (e.g., the Emergency Department [E] or Intensive Care Unit [I]) or one location and another (e.g., Surgical Center or Urgent Care Center).

CLINICAL CARE JOB EXCHANGE EXAMPLES

- A CNA who just received his CNA degree experiences a three-week job exchange as a Unit Secretary to achieve an understanding of the work flow and the role of the CNA in the patient care process.
- An ICU RN experiences a one-month rotation in the Oncology Clinic to better understand the cancer disease process from the onset of diagnosis.
- The Unit Secretary in the Orthopedic Office experiences a two-week job exchange as a Unit Secretary in the Surgical Center and another two-week experience in the Orthopedic Inpatient Unit to better understand the course of a patient's surgical experience.

CLINICAL PROFESSIONAL LEADERSHIP AREA

The second job classification category is Clinical Professional, which includes departments such as physical therapy, respiratory, rehabilitation, radiology, pharmacy, and laboratory. Clinical Professional employees also have interaction with patients, but may also have other administrative responsibilities to ensure the care received by the patient is the most appropriate. For example, a Clinical Dietitian may make rounds in the mornings and interview patients, but then has a portion of their day monitoring test results and patient diagnoses which affect the diet for the next day. These employees have a key role in documenting in the medical record and also tend to document in specific areas of the medical record that require specific training prior to working in their role. This specific documentation requirement can be a constraint on which roles would be available for a job exchange and may require additional medical record training prior to the job exchange. With this employee category, a job exchange would typically occur between different locations but in a similar job role.

CLINICAL PROFESSIONAL JOB EXCHANGE EXAMPLES

- A Clinical Dietitian in the nursing home experiences a one-month job exchange with a Clinical Dietitian at the acute care hospital to better understand the patient transfer process between the two settings.
- The Physical Therapy (PT) Department Director has a program in place to have a two-week job exchange for all PT Technicians between the outpatient clinic, the acute care hospital, and the nursing home.
- An Orthopedic Office Radiology Technologist experiences a one-month rotation at the acute care hospital to obtain educational experience toward an advanced certification.

CLINICAL SUPPORT LEADERSHIP AREA

The Clinical Support area is the third job category section that includes departments focused on the patient indirectly such as patient accounting, quality management, risk management, social work, discharge planning, and health information management. Employees in this category may interact with patients, but it is not an interaction that is key to the delivery of care. Some of these employees may have a degree or professional certification, such as a Registered Health Information Administrator in Medical Records or Certified Social Worker in Case Management, but these certifications may not be required prior to performing the job. Healthcare organization's HR policies often allow these employees to gain experience in their role in anticipation of an upcoming certification exam. Employees in these positions have a greater flexibility in choosing a job exchange position without the constraints of having a certification or degree prior to the exchange. The medical record documentation required in these positions is not always in the medical record and can be in a separate software specifically designated for the process they are responsible for. These could be separate modules within the medical record (Patient Complaint Module, Quality Management Module, and Patient Accounting Module) or separate software that may or may not be interfaced with the medical record (Patient Billing Software, Care Management & Discharge Planning Software, and Surgical Quality Software).

CLINICAL SUPPORT JOB EXCHANGE EXAMPLES

- A Quality Management Specialist experiences a one-month job exchange with a Risk Management Specialist to better understand the overlap between the two functions.
- The Patient Accounting Representative dedicated to Outpatient Clinic billing gains a better understanding of the revenue cycle process by shadowing the Outpatient Clinic Coding Specialist for one week and then participating in a job exchange for two weeks.
- The Director of Health Information Management obtains approval for a one-month job exchange with the Director of Risk Management to explore a potential career change.

ADMINISTRATION LEADERSHIP AREA

The remaining departments constitute the Administrative areas that are not focused directly on the patient such as accounting, marketing, administration, facility engineering, and HR. These departments tend to have a very focused set of skills specifically geared to the job that is performed, and although there are some required degrees and certifications, much of the job expertise is obtained on the job and through continuous training and education. These employees have the flexibility to experience a job exchange without extensive prior preparation. The work instructions tend to be robust in these categories, making them ideal for a job exchange. The work balance in Administrative areas does depend on some computer software systems, but also has a manual or hands-on component such as filing, painting, interviewing, preparing press announcements, and auditing. These are excellent departments for a job exchange when a person is interested in a career change in the future and can experience the job prior to an educational commitment.

ADMINISTRATIVE JOB EXCHANGE EXAMPLES

- The Executive Secretary to the President experiences a job exchange with the Nursing Home Secretary prior to going to school for her Certified Nursing Aide degree.
- An HR Specialist is interested in Public Relations and arranges a two-week job exchange with a Marketing Specialist to better understand the overlap in their customers.
- An Accounting Secretary experiences a job exchange with the Patient Accounting Secretary to understand the differences between the two financial processes.

Once you determine the general leadership category, review the requirements of each department within that category. Some departments require a clinical certificate such as an RN license or a certified respiratory technician. Other departments require a certain level of education such as a master's degree, or a certain number of years in a field. Evaluating the job requirements will be important to ensure you are identifying a reasonable potential job to exchange with. With this analysis, you will determine if you will be qualified for the job exchange. Job requirements can be found on the job description located in HR for the role or job of interest. Documentation of the job requirements will include the physical requirements, degree or certification requirements, years of experience, required business environments, and supervisory responsibilities of the position.

Another approach for a job exchange is to assume the responsibilities of the job that you would like to exchange with and have the job owner sign off or approve the work or tasks that you perform. This is an effective way to experience a job exchange that you may not be qualified for, but are able to perform some of the duties to experience the job. This is a good job exchange option when you are investigating if you are interested in the other job as a viable new job but would need to obtain additional education or experience in order to advance to the desired new position.

JOB EXCHANGE PROCESS STEP 2: OBTAIN COMMITMENT FROM BOTH PARTIES

A job exchange process is dependent on two parties essentially agreeing to the process and benefits of the job exchange. The person interested in the job exchange will typically have the innate commitment from a personal and professional perspective. This person initiating the job exchange will have already processed their personal pros and cons related to the job exchange. The person who is receiving the request for a job exchange may not have yet had a chance to think through the pros and cons of the job exchange. Often, the person initiating the job exchange will have multiple conversations with the person receiving the job exchange request to deliberate and discuss the benefits to ensure the activity will benefit both parties.

This is a key time to collaborate with the job exchange parties to organize a trial period where there is a limited time of a few days to see if a longer time period job exchange will work out for both parties. During this trial period, both parties can determine what activities are appropriate for the job exchange and what the extent of the job exchange proposal will be. This is an ideal situation in which both parties can determine the content of the job exchange proposal and the contents of that activity.

A trial period for a limited amount of time can also be accomplished virtually, utilizing information and computer technology. In this situation, the parties enter a virtual platform where they can talk through the job tasks with video and audio assistance. Computer screens can be shared to show how a person does documentation, reviews information, or enters data required for the position. A mobile device can also be utilized in video mode to show different aspects of the job, such as how to operate a wheelchair or visually see the patient alarm system outside patient rooms.

As a result of this commitment from both parties, it is important to ensure there is a documented commitment statement from both parties prior to working on the job exchange proposal. The healthcare organization may permit certain job exchanges, while denying others, for various reasons. Despite the benefits, the current workloads of the departments and/or organization may be too much to allow for the learning curve during the job exchange. If the job exchange is with the same position, but in different areas, these are typically easier to obtain approval for. The commitment statement does not need to be formal, but should be documented in a fashion such as an letter or memo to administration indicating the commitment by both parties to the job exchange experience and the positive benefits that are desired from the activity. This documentation is important for the next step of documenting the job exchange proposal.

JOB EXCHANGE PROCESS STEP 3: DOCUMENT THE JOB EXCHANGE PROPOSAL

There will be benefits and challenges, for both parties, with a job exchange arrangement. The proposal should outline the benefits in addition to the potential challenges and the actions or plans to address the challenges. One benefit for the organization is that the job exchange will empower the parties to understand the specific requirements of the other role. For example, if a Quality Professional in a rural area has a job exchange with a Quality Professional in an urban area, they will be able to achieve a better understanding of the factors associated with a different population environment. Another benefit for the organization is related to cross training of team members and the ability to assume the other person's job with minimal orientation. One good example is where a medical unit nurse participates in a job exchange with a critical care nurse. This nurse may now be able to cover both settings depending on the staffing needs after an effective job exchange arrangement and appropriate HR approval.

The job exchange proposal will also have the benefit of fostering a positive collaboration and relationship between colleagues. When there is a structured job exchange, there are intangible benefits for both parties which manifest themselves in a mutual respect for the other person's job tasks and challenges. For example, in an urban neighborhood, it may be more common to have patients arrive at the hospital with guns and knives on their person. In a rural neighborhood, it may be a rare experience to have a gun or knife in the facility. Those two arrival methods may require different policies and procedures, and the job exchange can enlighten one person as to inherent risks that may not have been evident in current policies.

A series of responsibilities should be present in the proposal, and those responsibilities need to be well documented. If the job exchange is a full exchange where one person is doing the activities of another person, that expectation should be outlined in detail, so all parties understand the scope of the job exchange. If only a selected set of duties are encompassed in the job exchange, those need to be documented with explicit areas of responsibilities assigned. If the job exchange includes record documentation responsibilities, those requirements and approvals will need to be in place since there are guidelines regarding appropriate and authorized documentation in the medical record and other formats.

The job exchange proposal should encompass the disadvantages of the interaction, such as the productivity of both parties and the salary of cross training. The more important part of the proposal needs to focus on the positive aspects of the job exchange, which should include achieving a job freshness, appreciation of associated colleagues, and a level of awareness of other colleagues' tasks. Another advantage is to understand the perspective of another industry, such as a nursing home RN working as a hospital intensive care RN. A personal satisfaction perspective is also achievable through a job exchange as the individuals are learning, growing, and exploring an enjoyable and fulfilling personal experience. The experience is likely to be extremely satisfying and personally fulfilling, and any personal thoughts and perceptions to include in the proposal would be helpful for ensuring a complete and comprehensive job exchange proposal. Employee satisfaction can be greatly enhanced with an opportunity for a job exchange experience.

JOB EXCHANGE PROCESS STEP 4: OBTAIN INITIAL APPROVAL

When a person is interested in a job exchange experience, it is important that the request is supported by the direct supervisor. The job exchange proposal should describe the scope of the job exchange, the length of the experience, the benefits for the individual, and the benefits for the organization. A Job Exchange Proposal Sample Template is provided in Appendix 13.1. This approval should be obtained with a tiered approach, beginning with an initial verbal exchange of the idea and ending with a job exchange proposal document that solidifies the discussions with your supervisor about the experience. If an organization has a formal job exchange program through the HR Department, this document and process may be further defined in a policy or form.

During the initial approval process, the work reassignment details will need to be addressed. This is related to the work reassignment of both parties. The person who wishes to have a job exchange experience must document the plans for coverage of current work duties while they are experiencing the job exchange. This could entail a temporary reassignment to others on the team, or procurement of a temporary position to cover the assigned tasks. Thought also has to occur for the person that is sharing the job exchange and if that person will serve as a mentor or will be temporarily reassigned to other tasks. It is ideal if the person will serve as a mentor to ensure the job exchange tasks are well understood and communicated.

A job exchange experience is considered a temporary opportunity to experience another position in the organization and should have a specific time limit assigned to the experience. A typical experience is one to two months in length and requires a formal report to the direct supervisor as to the information or experiences accomplished during the experience.

When initial approval is achieved, it is imperative to document this approval in a formal fashion. See Appendix 13.1 for an example of formal approval. Evidence of approval could be documented as a cosigned document agreeing to the specifics of the job exchange, and should be officially documented versus obtaining verbal approval.

JOB EXCHANGE PROCESS STEP 5: ACHIEVE HUMAN RESOURCES APPROVAL

After initial approval is received from the direct supervisors, the next step is to have HR review and approve the job exchange proposal. The Fair Labor Standards Act and other employment laws govern how an organization can manage employee work accommodations and payment. The HR Department will review the job exchange proposal and ensure all legal regulations are satisfied and that the pay rate for the time spent during the job exchange is appropriate. Depending on the local market (rural, urban, inner city, country, etc.) there can be a difference in the pay that is appropriate for time spent. Reimbursement can be affected by different countries, states, etc., and these items need to be negotiated and included in the agreement. This information should also include travel expenses incurred in the provision of services, including international considerations such as passport or other travel considerations. Approval from HR is important to ensure there is compliance with all appropriate employment laws.

JOB EXCHANGE PROCESS STEP 6: DOCUMENT THE EXPERIENCE

When a job exchange experience concludes, it is important to document the experience. A Job Exchange Summary and Report Sample Template can be found in Appendix 13.2.

Documentation of the experience should include the dates, time spent, and the activities. If there is a virtual component to the experience, this format should also be noted in the report. The report should also include information related to general comments, positive observations, and opportunities for improvement. The dates and time spent will justify and document the length of the experience, and you should also indicate when your current job responsibilities were covered by others. General comments should include information such as the people who were involved in the activity (e.g., a mentor, a supervisor, or a committee) and other details about the specific interaction (e.g., attending a committee, a planning session, or a meeting). Positive observations should include thoughts on how the process worked well, how feedback was delivered, or how a task seemed effective. This information is subjective and should be worded in a professional manner indicating it was a brief observation of a complex process. Opportunities for improvement are typically a result of conversations with the job exchange team member about significant ideas that could affect the job process in a positive fashion that is actionable and agreed upon. It is advisable to document a daily log of time spent with participants, including executives and other participants whom you interacted with. This log should include the participant, the essence of the interaction, time spent with each activity, the setting of the interaction (meeting, virtual, training, etc.), and action items or follow-up items. Interactions with patients or other stakeholders should also be documented as a part of the job exchange to ensure the time spend with the other job is effective and efficient and satisfies the qualifications of the job exchange proposal. The report, though, should not include any Patient Health Information or medical information that is considered protected and confidential information.

JOB EXCHANGE PROCESS STEP 7: PAY IT FORWARD

A job exchange experience is one that can be very valuable for the job exchange personnel. Many job exchange personnel ensure that job proposal information is well documented so that another person will be able to have the same valuable experience. If you are effective in documenting the proposal and the benefits of the job exchange, you can set up the situation for another person to experience a similar set of events. Documentation will also further the quality and positive aspects of the job that you are witnessing—and your current job. Excellent documentation of a job exchange experience will ensure another person will be able to have a job exchange experience that will further their career and job experiences.

CONCLUSION

A job exchange is an excellent way to experience other positions in a variety of settings. It is important that HR policies are followed when setting up job exchanges. Participants can gain valuable insights into positions of interest without leaving their current position. Experiencing a job exchange can be a rewarding exercise that benefits both participants and is a vehicle to appreciate both one's current position and a colleague's position.

APPENDIX 13.1 JOB EXCHANGE PROPOSAL SAMPLE TEMPLATE

[YOUR ORGANIZATION]
JOB EXCHANGE PROPOSAL
[Select Date]

OVERVIEW

1. Job Exchange Background and Description

2. Job Exchange Scope

3. Advantages & Disadvantages

4. Deliverables

5. Affected Parties

6. Affected Business Processes or Systems

7. Implementation Plan

8. High-Level Timeline/Schedule

APPROVAL AND AUTHORITY TO PROCEED

We approve the job exchange proposal as described above, and authorize the team to proceed.

Name	Title	Date

Approved By _____   Date _____   Approved By _____   Date _____

APPENDIX 13.2 JOB EXCHANGE SUMMARY & REPORT SAMPLE TEMPLATE

[YOUR ORGANIZATION]
JOB EXCHANGE SUMMARY & REPORT
[Select Date]

OVERVIEW

1. Job Exchange Background and Description

2. Job Exchange Scope

3. Deliverables – Summary of Achievement
   - Activities
   - Time Spent
   - Observations

4. Affected Business Processes or Systems-Observed Effect

5. Timeline/Schedule Analysis

6. Positive Observations

7. Opportunities for Improvement

8. General Comments

_____   _____   _____   _____
Report Author   Date   Report Author   Date
Approval   Approval

14 The 360-Degree Assessment

David Lafferty
ACHE, CHCIO, CPHIMS

CONTENTS

I am not a product of my circumstances. I am a product of my decisions.

—Steven R. Covey

INTRODUCTION

The Center for Creative Leadership describes the 360-degree assessment as a method of systematically collecting opinions about an individual's performance from a wide range of coworkers. This could include peers, direct reports, the boss, and the boss's peers—along with people outside the organization, such as customers. This form of assessment has grown in popularity due to its ability to help individuals discern differences between their own perception of their performance (self-perception) and the perception of others whom they work with. Often, the disparity in these two viewpoints is vastly different, something that psychologists refer to as "fundamental attribution error." But before we get into the particulars of the finer points of perception disparity, let's first understand a bit about where this feedback approach originated and how it can have a transformational impact on the career of today's health information technology (IT) professional.

WHERE DID IT COME FROM?

One of the fundamental ideas of the 360-degree assessment, to understand and contrast self-perception with how others perceive you, is rooted in the studies of Kurt Lewin, an American-born

DOI: 10.4324/9780429398377-17

social psychologist[1]. Lewin proposed that human behavior is influenced largely by its environment, with variations in the norm being a function of tensions between the self and the environment. Later on in his research, Lewin developed his theories of group dynamics, that groups alter the individual behavior of their constituents.

Looking through the lens of Lewin's theories today, it's easy to view a number of examples in today's healthcare environment. Certainly you're familiar with the phrase "The leaders set the tone." This concept memorializes the fact that a team, department, or even an entire organization's attitude and work performance are directly influenced by the behaviors and attitudes of the senior-most leaders in that organization. In fact, the same holds true when considering the behaviors and attitudes of peers in the organization as well. Quite simply, it's an example of modeling behaviors. Now, let's look at just one practical example illustrating the effects of behavior modeling in a healthcare setting.

In 2014, a study was conducted to determine whether or not peer influence had any effect on hand hygiene in the hospital setting. The study focused on observations of a 20-bed medical intensive care unit at a large university study. This study found that when a worker was alone, meaning no recent contact with other healthcare workers, the observed adherence rate to hygiene protocols was 20.85%. In contrast, when other healthcare workers were present, the observed adherence rate increased to 27.9%. The study found that this increase was statistically significant and was measurable at various times of the day and in a variety of social context settings. As a result, the study concluded that the presence and proximity of other healthcare workers can be associated with higher hand hygiene rates (Monsalve et al., 2014).

FUNDAMENTAL ATTRIBUTION ERROR

So we've established that the behavior of others can influence one's own behavior, exactly as Lewin had theorized. However, the example of the hygiene study clearly shows how one reacts to the situation. It doesn't really give us any insight into how or why individuals reacted the way they did. Did the sole healthcare workers make a conscience decision to change their hygiene habits on their own? Or did they worry about how others might perceive the quality of their hygiene habits, endeavoring to make their hand hygiene more visible to their peers?

Now, put yourself in the shoes of one of the sole worker's peers—do you automatically assume that the sole worker has substandard hygiene adherence, or do you consider the very real possibility that their hygiene adherence is more compliant than your own? Maybe it's simply a matter of you not observing your peer as frequently as they are practicing their hygiene behind the closed doors of a patient room.

Often we make assumptions that the problem is the person and not that the situation or environment may be contributing to the problem. This very human response illustrates the basic concept of fundamental attribution error, or cognitive bias. Fundamental attribution error suggests that people often attribute the behavior of others to dispositional causes rather than situational ones (Reeder, 2015).

Now, let's look at how cognitive bias factors into the situation of the sole healthcare worker's hand hygiene. As a peer, do you assume that that this person just doesn't wash their hands because you never observe it? Do you consider that this person doesn't wash their hands because there are not sufficient hygiene stations placed throughout the hospital? Or, as suggested earlier, do you even consider the possibility that this person's hygiene is exceptional?

By now, it's easy to establish that one's environment, the observations of others, and one's own perception of what others will think have a clear and measurable impact on job performance.

TRADITIONAL FEEDBACK METHODS

So it's clear that one's environment has a direct influence on job performance. In addition, it's also clear that fundamental human nature often causes us to assume that the person is the problem. Lastly, simple human nature predisposes us to react differently—either consciously or unconsciously—when we are being observed by others.

One of the primary benefits of the 360-degree assessment is that it provides a mechanism to capture the impact of fundamental attribution error on an individual's job performance. It effectively contrasts the various differences in how others perceive the person's performance with how that individual perceives their own performance. Moreover, the 360-degree assessment also presents an individual with performance-related feedback derived from the observations of others. To better understand the differentiating benefits of the 360-degree assessment, it helps to contrast this with what is typically evaluated in the traditional performance review process.

RESEARCH

Probably one of the most fundamental challenges with the traditional performance review is that it has historically employed a top-down approach, with feedback flowing from manager to subordinate. This method is really an artifact from the days when managers were tasked with force-ranking individual employees from best to worst performance, the intent being that the lowest performers would be managed out of an organization. However, this feedback method poses at least three questions which, it can be argued, are more effectively addressed using the collaborative and peer-based approach of the 360-degree assessment:

1. Is that manager directly involved at the daily task or assignment level with the employee, or is the manager too far removed from the day-to-day operations that their assessment of performance lacks true evidence?
2. Does the manager perhaps rate the employee that they hired as a better performer than the employee they did not hire—otherwise known as rater bias? (Sutton, 2006)
3. While the traditional top-down performance review might assess individual performance, what does it do in the context of evaluating (or improving) team performance?

In today's health IT climate, the need for instant feedback, solid collaboration, and effective interdisciplinary teamwork are tantamount to quality patient care. Yet, traditional performance/feedback mechanisms don't address team performance and, more likely than not, are not conducted with the necessary frequency so that an individual's performance can be coached and improved on a regular basis. Dare we say that the "annual performance review" leaves many gaps and opportunities on the table for both individual and team performance improvements?

ADMINISTERING THE ASSESSMENT: WHO SHOULD PARTICIPATE?

So how can we begin to close these gaps and utilize a mechanism more reflective of today's team-based goals and one which surfaces very real observations and perceptions of one's performance? To start, it's essential to determine who will participate in the 360-degree assessment process. With the many models that are available today, it's important to know that there is not just one answer. In fact, organizations may even employ a model where the stakeholders participating in the assessment may change as the employee travels higher up the organizational chart (Figure 14.1).

The most common methods of 360-degree assessment include a component of review from a supervisor(s), peer, and subordinate. However, many models also include a review component from an individual outside of the organization. This may be comprised of a customer, vendor, service provider, or similar party. This suggests that a minimum number of reviewers (feedback sources) might begin with three to four individuals. However, larger organizations might select multiple representatives for each of these roles and may end up with seven, ten, or more.

According to the U.S. Office of Personnel Management, studies have shown that feedback results are more accurate and credible when multiple feedback sources are utilized (U.S. Office of

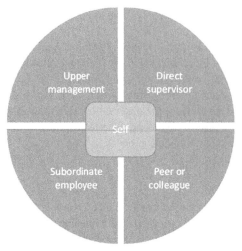

FIGURE 14.1 Possible feedback sources for a middle-management employee.

Personnel Management, 1997). However, it's also important to consider feedback sources (individuals) that are within the sphere of influence of the employee who is being assessed. So while there is no magic number of feedback sources, selecting the right feedback sources—those that the employee influences—is a critical aspect of achieving a good 360-degree assessment. Failure to do this effectively yields the same poor feedback result as when the high-level manager administers the top-down annual performance review to a lower level employee.

ADMINISTERING THE ASSESSMENT: RATING CRITERIA

To implement a 360-degree assessment does not necessarily equate to having to completely re-design and develop new performance criteria. While we've already discussed some of the gaps presented by a traditional performance review process, what's important is that an organization has a mature and consistent process of some sort. Job performance criteria should be clearly spelled out and be related to the job description and duties of the employee being rated.

To design a 360-degree assessment from the ground up is truly beyond the scope of this chapter. There are a number of performance management companies and performance management toolsets that can be employed to build a comprehensive performance review tool. But again, if the organization already has a performance tool, often this existing tool can be adapted from the traditional approach and become the basis for a highly effective 360-degree assessment.

Let's look at an example of a traditional, top-down, annual performance review. Figures 14.2 and 14.4 depict a portion of the annual performance review for a nurse at a large nonprofit post-acute care provider.

This portion of the review deals with specific criteria related to the regular job duties of a nurse in the organization. Performance in each area (goal) is weighted as each item contributes to an overall score for the employee's review. The reviewer scores each item using a Likert (Jamieson, 2016) scale rating of 1–5, with 5 being exceptional and 1 indicating that improvement is needed.

Now, consider how this review might be adapted for use in a 360-degree assessment. Consider how the nurse's case manager might evaluate their performance of how well they perform patient assessment and develop effective care plans. In an interdisciplinary setting, consider for a moment how various members of the patient care team (i.e., physician, social worker, LPN, CNA, ARNP) might view the nurse's performance. In certain care settings, patient/family satisfaction surveys are required in order to satisfy regulatory quality requirements. How might the patient or family members perceive the performance of the individual nurse? When these various viewpoints are considered as a whole, it begins to portray a much more comprehensive picture of an individual's

Performance Objectives
Performance Period: July 1, 2015 thru September 30, 2016

Competency/Core Value	Results Achieved	Rating	Weighted Rating
Compassion Understanding the emotional state of another; sympathetic consciousness of others' distress, together with desire to alleviate it.			**5.00%**
Respect An assumption of good faith and competence in another person or in the whole of oneself; a high special regard, the quality or state of being esteemed.			**5.00%**
Integrity Firm adherence to a code of moral values; honesty; basing of one's actions on an internally consistent framework of principles.			**5.00%**
Teamwork People working together to accomplish a common goal.			**5.00%**
Communication A process by which information is exchanged between individuals through a common system.			**5.00%**
Development The process of growth; to make active or promote the growth of another person or oneself.			**5.00%**
Stewardship The careful and responsible managing of something one does not own such as property or financial affairs.			**5.00%**

FIGURE 14.2   Example of a Performance Objectives Worksheet.

performance. Again, we have to remember that a key benefit of the 360-degree assessment is that it provides not only a means to rate the individual, but also can improve team performance dynamics as well.

So in the case of our example review document, two minor changes could be effected which would easily adapt this conventional top-down review into our desired 360-degree review. First, it is helpful to understand the role of the reviewer. In this case, adding a section for the reviewer to indicate their level of participation with the individual being reviewed (peer, subordinate, manager, other) is helpful. This becomes a determinate factor in how closely the reviewer interacts with the individual being reviewed. This is illustrated in Figure 14.5.

Lastly, it is likely helpful to look at the rating scale choices to ensure that they are better reflective of the individual performance. Remember, earlier we discussed rater bias. Providing a rating scale with choices ranging from "Unacceptable" to "Successful," or "Meets Criteria," may not offer a suitable choice for a peer reviewer, especially one who is not a capable manager. The unintended result is rater bias, as the peer reviewer chooses a rating that is nonconfrontational or overly positive. So it's important to select rating criteria that lend themselves to the varied participants in the 360-degree review process; for example:

- Consistently demonstrates behavior or skill
- Sometimes demonstrates behavior or skill

Performance Goals
Performance Period: July 1, 2015 thru June 30, 2016

Performance Goal #1	Performance Goal and Due Dates	Results Achieved	Rating	Weighted Rating
Assessment and care planning, essential job requirements	1. Assesses the impact of the terminal diagnosis on the patient's physical, functional, psychosocial, spiritual and environmental needs. 2. Develops an individualized plan of care specific to the identified needs, reevaluates the plan, updates the plan of care when the need arises. 3. Demonstrates the ability to assess the need for symptom management and communicates with the physician and other team members in an effort to alleviate the distressing symptoms. 4. Completes ongoing assessments of the patient's terminal diagnosis and accurately evaluates eligibility for recertification using the local coverage determination (LCD) criteria. 5. Assesses for the need to change the level of hospice care as appropriate. **Measurement:** CD chart audit, discussion at IDG meeting, interaction with and feedback from CD and other team members.			35.00%

Performance Goal #2	Performance Goal and Due Dates	Results Achieved	Rating	Weighted Rating
Compliance	1. Follows standards of practice of hospice nursing as well as legal, and regulatory requirements. 2. Utilizes point of service for documentation to ensure accuracy and timeliness. 3. Determines and meets appropriate frequency with scope of services. 4. Adheres to company policy and procedures and follows these in all work work-related activities. **Measurement:** EMR documentation and missed visit report; Clinical director chart audits; service recovery reports.			15.00%

Performance Goal #3	Performance Goal and Due Dates	Results Achieved	Rating	Weighted Rating
Communication and teamwork	1. Coordinates the needs of the patient and family with other interdisciplinary team members using the case management approach to meet the changing needs of the patient and family. 2. Exhibits flexibility, time management skills, and dependability as it relates to all internal and external customers. 3. Consistently demonstrates all core values **Measurement:** IDG meeting and team member discussion, EMR scheduler and time log, feedback from internal and external customers, facilities, patients, and family members.			15.00%

FIGURE 14.3   Example of performance tactics to achieve performance goals.

Performance Goals
Performance Period: July 1, 2015 thru June 30, 2016

Competency/Core Value	Results Achieved	Rating	Weighted Rating
Compassion Understanding the emotional state of another; sympathetic consciousness of others' distress, together with desire to alleviate it.			**5.00%**
Respect An assumption of good faith and competence in another person or in the whole of oneself; a high special regard, the quality or state of being esteemed.			**5.00%**
Integrity Firm adherence to a code of moral values; honesty; basing of one's actions on an internally consistent framework of principles.			**5.00%**
Teamwork People working together to accomplish a common goal.			**5.00%**
Communication A process by which information is exchanged between individuals through a common system.			**5.00%**
Development The process of growth; to make active or promote the growth of another person or oneself.			**5.00%**
Stewardship The careful and responsible managing of something one does not own such as property or financial affairs.			**5.00%**

FIGURE 14.4   Example of a form to document performance goal achievements.

Time spent	Every day	A few times a week	A few times a month	Every few months	NA (Never)
Your interaction with employee					

Role	Supervisor/ manager	Peer	Subordinate	Patient	Family member
What is your relationship with the employee?					

FIGURE 14.5   Example of documenting time spent and role of interaction with employee.

- Rarely demonstrates behavior or skill
- Almost never demonstrates behavior or skill

In this way, the reviewer can select more accurate ratings that provide a more realistic picture of the individual performance.

PRACTICAL APPLICATIONS

Evidence has shown that an effective 360-degree survey, combined with employee coaching, does have a marked effect on patient satisfaction measures (Hageman et al. 2015). While it may be feasible to easily adapt an existing, traditional review tool for use in a 360-degree approach, a larger, more complex organization may require a much more formalized and structured approach that takes into account the many complex relationships and factors of physician–patient interaction in a large healthcare setting.

The Pulse360 survey tool (Physician's Universal Leadership-Teamwork Skills Education), was developed by the U.S. Department of Health and Human Services to serve as the benchmark for quality healthcare. It serves as a tool to provide for patient feedback based on their experience with staff and clinicians. With Medicare-based compensation becoming closely tied to patient satisfaction measures, survey tools like this will become more critical to gauge and assess employee performance across the episodic healthcare experience.

CONDUCTING A 360-DEGREE ASSESSMENT

In an outpatient setting, the value of including patient and family member evaluations in the 360-degree process becomes even more insightful. In this case, the vastly different perceptions of performance between the healthcare professional and the patient or family member becomes even more pronounced. In 2010, a study was conducted comprised of over 800, 360-degree evaluations for pediatric residents over a five-week period (Chandler et al. 2010). This study concluded that while overall performance of the medical residents was rated very highly from the healthcare team, the ratings were consistently much lower when viewed from the standpoint of the patient and family members. Had the input of the patients not been considered, it would seem that the overall performance of these residents was considered very positive, perhaps not requiring any further coaching or development. However, with the patient feedback included, now more specific and meaningful aspects of performance are brought to light, aspects that may have a much greater bearing on patient quality measures and overall satisfaction. This is just one example which truly illustrates the benefits of the 360-degree approach. A conventional top-down performance review not only would have excluded any feedback from the patient, but very likely may not have even rated the residents as good performers compared to the feedback that was received by the other members of the healthcare team.

NO SYSTEM IS PERFECT: WHAT THE 360 DOES NOT DO

Despite the numerous benefits found in the 360-degree assessment, it is clear that there is no perfect performance-rating system. Any attempt to apply a precise measure of performance against the imprecise and complex concept of job performance can never yield a perfect result.

While it's highly insightful to gain a complete view of performance for the individual, oftentimes poor performance in one area might garner more attention and concern compared with the broad context of performance from the various raters. Conversely, overly positive feedback from many raters may hide or minimize the impact of perceived poor performance in one particular area. While these issues can be mitigated, the possibility should always be considered when evaluating the complete performance picture.

For example, an employee who does not frequently deal with patients certainly should not have a patient or family member participate in the 360-degree process. Similarly, a senior-level executive should not participate if he or she does not have the benefit of some degree of close interaction with the individual being rated.

One of the other significant risks in the 360-degree assessment is the potential for the emotional or political motives of the rating participants to affect evaluations. Consider a peer reviewer who stands to make personal or professional gain, creating a quid-pro-quo[2] situation. "You scratch my back, and I'll scratch yours" or "I'll rate you highly if you do the same for me." Similarly, consider the disgruntled employee: "I'm going to get back at so-and-so, so I'll give them a bad review." The distinct possibility of these very real issues makes it even more important to effectively select the appropriate rating sources for the employee.

In order to ensure that the assessment process is used effectively, it's important that these factors are considered within the context of the overall review. Managers (reviewers) must strive to understand the underlying causes of individual, and perhaps incongruent, areas of performance, and work to either evidence or discount that particular behavior. Similar to the well-known concept in statistical analysis where the top and bottom measures are discounted, the manager should be versed enough in the inner workings of the various departments and reviewer roles to effectively factor in (or out) these potential outliers in performance.

CONCLUSION

A 360-degree assessment can have a dramatic and transformational effect on employee performance. Understanding how others perceive an individual's performance can often cause a level of introspective improvement that is more powerful than a manager simply discussing an issue with the individual. In today's highly collaborative and complex healthcare environment, adapting performance tools to positively shape individual and team performance can positively affect patient outcomes and quality of care. In this way, the individual can become a product of their decisions and not their environment.

NOTES

1 Kurt Lewin, September 9, 1890–February 12, 1947 (brittanica.com).
2 *Quid pro quo:* something that is given or taken in return for something else; substitute (dictionary.com).

REFERENCES

Chandler, N., Henderson, G., Park, B., Byerley, J., Brown, W. D., and Steiner, M. J. (2010). Use of a 360-degree evaluation in the outpatient setting: The usefulness of nurse, faculty, patient/family, and resident self-evaluation. *Journal of Graduate Medical Education*, 2(3), 430–434. https://doi.org/10.4300/JGME-D-10-00013.1

Hagemen, M. G. J. S., Ring, D. C., Gregory, P. J., Rubash, H. E., and Harmon, L. (2015). Do 360-degree feedback survey results relate to patient satisfaction measures? *Clinical Orthopaedics and Related Research*, 473(5), 1590–1597. https://doi.org/10.1007/s11999-014-3981-3

Jamieson, S. (2016, May 10). *Encyclopedia Brittanica*. Retrieved August 27, 2021, from https://www.britannica.com/topic/Likert-Scale

Monsalve, M. N., Pemmaraju, S. V., Thomas, G. W., Herman, T., Segre, A. M., and Polgreen, P. M. (2014, October). Do peer effects improve hand hygiene adherance among healthcare workers? *Infection Control and Hospital Epidemiology*, 35(10), 1277–1285.

Reeder, G. D. (2015, May 8). *Fundamental attribution error/correspondance bias*. Retrieved from Oxford Bibliographies: oxfordbibliographies.com/view/document/obo-9780199828340/obo-9780199828340-0114.xml

Sutton, J. P. (2006). *Hard facts, dangerous half-truths & total nonsense*. Boston: Harvard Business School Publishing.

U.S. Office of Personnel Management. (1997). *360-Degree assessment: An overview*. Washington, DC: Performance Management and Incentive Awards Division.

15 Professional Coaching

Joyce Zerkich
PMP, CPHIMS, ACC, MBA, MSBIT

CONTENTS

INTRODUCTION

So you've decided you want to take more responsibility for your career, but are not sure what to do next.

A professional coach enables one (referred to as a "client") to more clearly define their desired future, take an honest view of their current situation, analyze the gap between both, and define a plan to move toward their desired future. The coach asks key questions which enable the client to gain insight into what the client really wants as well as plan next steps.

Some companies offer coaching to their employees. MetrixGlobal published results of coaching in a Fortune 500 company with participants from the United States and Mexico. Merrill C. Anderson reports that the results were positive, with 77% of the 30 respondents indicating that coaching had significant or very significant impact on at least one of nine business measures: "Coaching sessions were rich learning environments that enabled the learning to be applied to a variety of business situations." Other results yielded increases in employee satisfaction and productivity: "Employee satisfaction was viewed both in terms of the respondents being personally more satisfied as a result of the coaching as well as the being able to increase the employee satisfaction of their team members" [1].

The bottom line is that coaching benefits the client both personally and professionally, which in turn increases the effectiveness of the client's employer.

WHY WORK WITH A COACH

Among many reasons to use a coach for professional insight, those planning their career path can explore self-awareness, current job performance, long-term career planning, and professional relationship enhancement. Coaching also helps a client work on personal effectiveness such as

DOI: 10.4324/9780429398377-18

skillful communication, listening, social and emotional intelligence, mindfulness, trust building, time management, and mental models.

At times our own mental models hold us back because there is a gap between reality and our understanding of reality [2]. In the fable about the little girl who was frightened away by a spider, her mental model was to be afraid of spiders. In contrast, the reality is that spiders do help decrease the fly population and not all spiders are poisonous. In business terms, one may have developed a mental model to keep quiet at meetings which may have been reinforced by a previous boss or employer. So now when their boss asks them to speak up in meetings, they do not speak up, which causes their boss to question their performance. Their mental model is that the spider may bite them, but in reality the spider is not harmful. A coach can ask questions to help them look at their mental model and determine the gap between it and reality: It helps them to look at the spider differently. In a constantly changing business environment, coaching helps clients explore their connection to the world today.

A great example of a coach is the sport coaches in the United States. A baseball player's coach learns the player's aspirations (become the best pitcher in the country), strengths (fast ball pitch), and weaknesses (pitching to left-handed batters) by working with them. It is through understanding the baseball player that the coach can provide feedback to enable the ball player to plan the next steps to reach their aspirations. Similarly, a career coach looks to understand the client's aspirations (e.g., an improved resume, confidently speaking up in meetings), strengths (dependability, education, personality), and perceived weaknesses (patience with staff, making presentations, interviewing for a job, making a career move). Just like the baseball player, a career coach can work with the client to help them focus on moving toward their ambitions. Both the sports and career coaches provide honest insight to help the ball player/client ground themselves in reality, yet see how to remove barriers themselves to reach their goal.

WHAT TO EXPECT IN A COACHING JOURNEY

A baseball player and a coach are successful if both the ball player and coach are dedicated. During each session, the coach must be fully present and attentive to the player, and the player must actively listen, examine their performance, clearly articulate their desired result, and understand the gap between their performance and desired result. The ball player must take responsibility after the coaching sessions to follow through with the planned next steps because they encompass the player's journey to greatness ("greatness" is defined as whatever the ball player's aspiration is) just as the coaching sessions. Excellent ball players practice hours to skillfully master a technique they have been coached on. If a client is committed to making a change, one of the first steps can be working with a coach; however, it is not the only step. It is one of the many steps in the journey to reach one's aspirations. Commitment to a plan as well as taking the responsibility to follow through is essential for the client undergoing career coaching.

Engage a career coach if you have time for homework in between coaching sessions. The coach will usually ask questions that require the client to spend some time reflecting, writing, or even researching ideas. The homework is intended to help the client dig deeper to reveal the client's truth. Some busy clients schedule monthly coaching because they want time to absorb the information as well as do the homework. Others are anxious for a change and dive right into weekly appointments. Either way, the level of client satisfaction is dependent upon the effort the clients puts into the sessions and homework. For example, one client of a professional coach was very well-educated and detail-oriented. He was looking for a job change. He used the coaching time to help him define his "perfect" job. Part of his first set of homework was to list what he did and did not want in his next position. This required undisturbed time for him to reflect on what was most important to him (which ended up being autonomy in an information technology position requiring deep thinking), what would be nice to have (work in the healthcare industry), and what he could not tolerate in a job (sales, a lot of phone calls, a lot of interruptions, supervising staff). After several coaching sessions, he found that becoming a data scientist would meet his goals and aspirations. He could leverage his experience and education only needing one or two college classes to move into that position.

Summary: Work with a coach when you are committed to taking active responsibility for your future.

WHAT TO EXPECT IN A COACHING SESSION

Coaching usually encompasses several sessions. Each coaching session lasts about 50–60 minutes. The purpose of the sessions is to solely focus on the client's need. If the client wants the session to be effective, the client cannot multi-task during the coaching sessions. It is time set aside in one's schedule to stop all other stimuli and focus purely on the topic at hand: the client's agenda.

The coach will begin by asking the client to sign a confidentiality contract, meaning that the coach will reveal none of the discussion to anyone else unless the client provides written permission. Trust is important in a client–coach relationship, so this document lays the trust foundation. Without trust, the client cannot feel free to explore and reveal their truth—which is what the coach needs to understand in order to help the client.

During the session, the coach asks exploratory questions with the intent to better understand the client's truth: Who they are, what is important to them, and what is keeping them from moving ahead. These types of questions can help the client see what is standing in their way of reaching success as well as the steps needed to move ahead. Good coaches are skilled at asking powerful questions which inspire a new awareness in the client: about their life, job, relationship, or anything they want to work on. Questions such as "What is important to you?" "What does that help you with?" "What is it costing you to continue to hold back?" "What will happen if you do nothing?" or "Why is this true for you?" are among the many questions that help the client obtain clarity. A person can ask themselves these questions, but it takes a coach to listen to the client and ask non-judgmental questions to help the client dig deeper so the client can understand their deeper truth and needs.

WHAT COACHING IS NOT

Coaching is not therapy: Coaching assumes the client is whole and has all the answers within; the job of the coach is to help the client see their truth so the client can move ahead. Also, coaching focuses on the future: In contrast, therapy focuses on what happened in the past.

Coaching is not mentoring: The coach's job is to help the client uncover what is best for the client. The coach assumes each individual has a unique purpose within our global community. While mentoring is typically a mentor helping another individual follow the same path that the mentor has walked, coaching is helping the client find the client's unique truth and path. The mentor explains the mentor's truth so that the mentee can copy or mirror the path of the mentor in order to be successful.

In contrast, the coach asks powerful questions so the client can determine the client's own course of action: The client travels their own path toward fulfilling their goals.

THE FOCUS OF COACHING SESSIONS

Career coaching sessions do not all take the same path. There is no written formula because each path is unique and determined by the client. Some clients want feedback on written business documents such as resumes or cover letters. Others seek to understand how to move ahead at their current employer. Others are not sure which way to proceed next and are looking to define what career success really means to them before deciding on next steps.

As an example, one client contacted a coach looking for coaching on their resume. After a few sessions, it became apparent to the client that they actually preferred staying at their current employer but felt stuck, not knowing what they wanted to do next. The coaching sessions helped the client determine their truth, which was the need to better their team dynamic skills, become more comfortable speaking up at meetings, and prepare for their next desired career move. Over the span of several coaching sessions, role-playing helped the client increase their confidence speaking up at meetings, while deeper reflection into the client's passion about their profession helped guide specific career move preparations and next steps.

Other clients have already accepted a new job and are looking for coaching to help them exude confidence from day one and forward. They want to start on the right foot to ensure the first impression was the best impression they could make. Still others want coaching on how to work with their boss or colleagues so they can move ahead toward their goals.

In the end: The focus is on whatever the client needs.

BENEFITS OF COACHING

The focus is on what is right for you and no one else. Coaching sessions initiate a path of personal discovery tailor made for the client. A coach will make no judgments, which frees up the client to explore and challenge norms, unwritten rules, and assumptions. These sometimes hold clients back from developing their aspirations.

The 3 hours of coaching time is sliced and pulled out of the 24-hour pie of the day. Both the client and coach solely dedicate the coaching time to concentrate on the client and develop a tactical plan. The coach's attention and effort for that hour is dedicated on what the client needs so the client can move closer to the client's aspirations. So much of our time is spent on taking care of work for others: Coaching sessions focus on doing the work that benefits the client.

A leader once said, "You don't know what you don't know because you can't see it." He believed that in order to facilitate positive change, he needed others to provide honest, respectful, direct feedback so he could grasp through their eyes what he could not observe. The world is waiting for and needs the client to travel the journey toward his aspiration(s) because by doing so, the client fulfills himself by giving back to the global community in the form of his skills, talents, and expertise unique to him and no one else. We have no one else but each other: Each distinctively gifted member of the human society is all that the world has, and we all need every ability and talent to make our world the best place.

OPPORTUNITIES COACHING BRINGS

Utilize a coaching relationship to dig deep into what is preventing you from being successful. Understand what is really standing in your way, what you have control over, and what you can take responsibility for changing. Just like the baseball coach who asks questions and works with the pitcher to help the pitcher learn how to pitch to left-handed batters, coaches ask a lot of questions to help the client dig deep into what surrounds the client to keep the client from taking action. It usually takes a few coaching sessions to obtain clarity on your decision of what to move ahead on. Don't be afraid to challenge your preconceived notions about assumptions: Coaching is the safe time to explore why your assumptions exist as they do today.

Be accountable to yourself by using a coach to focus on yourself and what is best for you. In the mad-dash craziness of life, take time with a coach to be sure you are focused not only on what you need to do now to maintain your situation, but also what to do in the future to plan your success. One client asked to focus on work-life balance. She wanted a coach to help her dig deep into why her life seemed out of balance and help her plan to be more successful. She asked for a quarterly coaching session to help her keep digging into her challenges as well as ensure she was steadily progressing. Quarter by quarter she kept herself true to the balance and came to realize boundary setting was a skill she was working on in order to maintain that balance.

The coaching session is all about your agenda, so ask for the help you need. Don't be surprised if you go into a coaching session believing the focus of your discussion will be on one topic, and after a few minutes, you decide it would greatly benefit you to concentrate work in a different area. As we peel back the layers of the onion of who we are, our unique talents, attributes, and skills are better revealed. Just like the ball player who concentrates his efforts to better his pitching skills may find skills in other areas, the client may find he possesses other talents and skills which were beforehand hidden to his perception. Similarly, as a client explores his long-term career plans, he may find that other jobs may interest him that he had not considered before the coaching.

HOW TO KNOW IF A COACHING SESSION WAS SUCCESSFUL

After a few sessions, ask yourself if through the coaching you have learned anything new about yourself, changed the way you approach a situation(s), better defined your future, become more comfortable in a situation(s), or taken an active role in moving toward your definition of career success. Since the coaching sessions focus on what you want to accomplish, what it really boils down to is did you learn more about yourself, your path, and your responsibility to see that journey through?

HOW DO I FIND A COACH?

As stated before, some companies fund professional coaches for employees. Ask your colleagues and friends to recommend a coach they have used. The International Coach Federation, https://www.coachfederation.org/ [3], has a list of coaches. Additionally, many have attended coaching training given by professional coaches at Blue Mesa, who in addition provide coaching services: http://bluemesagroup.com/ [4].

HOW TO SELECT A PROFESSIONAL COACH THAT IS RIGHT FOR YOU

References from other people are a great place to start. But, to make sure you select the right coach for you, the President of Blue Mesa, Professional Coaching Company provides these tips [4]:

- The coach offers a complimentary introductory session and does not pressure you to work with them and clearly cares that you find the right coach.
- You have clear agreements with your coach regarding cost, logistics, and how you will best work together.
- It is a partnership of equals; the work together is a co-creation (the coach is not directing your actions or giving advice).
- The coach creates a trusting environment where it feels comfortable to reveal a full range of feelings.
- The coach attends to your agenda (i.e., the things that are important to you).
- The coach does not judge you or recriminate you for choices you have made.
- You feel that the time spent with your coach is well spent.
- You are encouraged to articulate and achieve your desired outcomes.
- The coach is comfortable giving you direct feedback when it is appropriate. [4]

CONCLUSION

In conclusion, life is your journey: Find a coach to help when you are stuck so that you fulfill your full potential!

REFERENCES

1. Anderson, M. (2014). Leadership Coaching Return on Investment (ROI). Available at http://www.findyourcoach.com/roi-study.htm
2. McMillan, M. (2010). Blue Mesa Group, Micki McMillan, MCC, "Mental Models: Why a Straight Line Isn't Always the shortest Distance between Two Points" 2010.
3. International Coaching Federation. (2021). https://www.coachfederation.org/, The International Coach Federation (ICF) is the largest worldwide resource for professional coaches, and the source for those who are seeking a coach. We are a nonprofit organization formed by individual members-professionals who practice coaching, including Executive Coaches, Leadership Coaches, Life Coaches and many more, from around the world. Formed in 1995, today ICF is the leading global organization, with over 20,000 members, dedicated to advancing the coaching profession by setting high professional standards, providing independent certification, and building a network of credentialed coaches.
4. Barlow, P. (August 2016) from Blue Mesa Group; Personal Interview.

Section IV

The Aspiring Leader

16 Developing as a Leader

Christopher B. Harris
FHIMSS

CONTENTS

INTRODUCTION

Leadership is fundamentally about setting the vision and goals that drive value for the enterprise AND enabling the workforce to deliver on that vision. This requires leadership that is flexible and dynamic with regard to *how and where* the work gets done but remains always consistent in describing the desired outcome. In the healthcare information systems world, this means understanding and leading in two critically important areas:

1. Anticipating and capitalizing on the changing nature work.
2. Engaging and empowering the changing nature of the workforce.

ANTICIPATING AND CAPITALIZING ON THE CHANGING NATURE WORK

There are several macro-economic trends that are influencing the future of work:

Public Health

The COVID-19 pandemic has and will continue to have far-reaching impacts on governmental policy priorities such as increased focus on interoperability, supply chain management practices, and capacity to scale response rapidly. Healthcare leaders will need to adapt and evolve their organizations to new ways of dynamically operating in these uncertain times.

DOI: 10.4324/9780429398377-20

Public health is not just local; indeed, the increasing connectedness of our world populations—coupled with continuing international expansion of large healthcare systems, the emergence of personalized medicine, exponential technologies, disruptive competitors, expanded delivery sites, and revamped payment models—is injecting uncertainty into the global health economy.

Global health care expenditures continue to increase, driving the need to reduce costs and increase efficiency. Spending is projected to increase at an annual rate of 5.4% in 2017–2022, from USD $7.724 trillion to USD $10.059 trillion, although cost-containment efforts combined with faster economic growth should maintain the share of GDP devoted to health care at around 10.4% over the five-year period to 2022. In addition, the trend toward universal health care is expected to continue, with more countries expanding or deepening their public health care systems to reduce out-of-pocket (OOP) expenses (*World Industry Outlook, Healthcare and Pharmaceuticals,* 2018).

Automation and the Arrival of Data as Currency

Emerging technologies across the world will make it possible to automate tasks traditionally performed by a human workforce. It is estimated that in five years, 95% of all customer interactions will be driven or enabled by artificial intelligence (Friedman, 2016). This shift, coupled with increasing sophistication of predictive analytics, enables the transformation of data into information and into action, at the right time and right place. Market dominance and success will go to those organizations that understand how to harness this power and drive business and clinical outcomes. The healthcare technology leader must be able to develop competency and capability in the application of these tools and techniques. In a recent Deloitte 2020 survey of Chief Financial Officers of health systems and health plans, 78% expect to increase spending on digital technologies while 53% expect to reduce capital spending on new building assets (Burril et al., 2020).

ENGAGING AND EMPOWERING THE CHANGING NATURE OF THE WORKFORCE

Leadership in these challenging global and technical conditions requires understanding how the workforce is shifting (*Time to Care: Securing a Future for the Hospital Workforce in Europe,* 2018):

- Changing demographics of the talent pool are due to aging of the current workforce, combined with an increasingly competitive market for people with the required skills and talent.
- Millennials currently make up almost 50% of the work mix and are expected to account for nearly 75% of the overall U.S. workforce by 2025 (Betts & Korenda, 2018). Millennials will bring different expectations around work-life balance, flexible careers, rewards and incentives, and relationships with their employer.
- Over the past five years, freelancers, gig workers, and contractors made up 94% of net new job growth (Schwartz, 2018). The proliferation of gig, virtual contract, and other new talent models requires new skillsets and change where work is performed.
- There is increasing use of artificial intelligence, robotics, automation, and advanced digital and cognitive technologies.

Developing yourself as a leader and managing your career development in these dynamic and changing times also means reflecting on your own capabilities, interpersonal dynamics, and emotional maturity. Perhaps, the first place to start is by asking yourself these questions:

1. How well do I know myself?
2. How do I develop performance potential in others?
3. How do I create the opportunities to grow my leadership?

This chapter will provide perspective and suggestions on these questions as you consider your development as a leader. An important note before proceeding: There is no right or wrong set of answers to these questions. You will find literature on leadership replete with examples about all kinds of different people, management styles, personality traits, and career paths to leadership. What matters is what you do with the information, knowledge, and passion you have.

HOW WELL DO YOU KNOW YOURSELF?

There are a variety of different personality or business trait type tests that you can take to further understand key characteristics about how you process information, communicate, solve problems, and respond to external stress and/or ambiguous situations. This is important because people who become leaders use this information to navigate the opportunities they decide to pursue and to manage to their strengths; understand their own "blind spots"; and influence their teams to achieve the desired outcomes. These personality-type assessments will also provide insights and actionable considerations on how to identify and assess those you interact with in a similar manner. There will be insights and tips about how to adapt your management style to motivate and engage the teams and people you interact with. Some examples of these kinds of personality tests include:

- Myers-Briggs Type Indicator
- The Color Code
- Business Chemistry

These kinds of assessments should give insights into not only your management style and preferences, but also your strengths and weaknesses. The definitions of strength and weakness are, perhaps, different than traditionally understood. Strengths are understood to be natural capacities that we yearn to use, that enable authentic expression, and that energize us (Govindji & Linley, 2007).

Strengths
- Make you feel like you can do it over and over again without feeling tired
- Cause you to lose track of time
- Leave you feeling successful or fulfilling a need
- Are harder to not do than to do

A weakness, on the other hand, "is a shortage or misapplication of talent, skill, or knowledge that causes problems for you or others" (Brim, 2007).

Weaknesses
- Drain you
- Cause you to procrastinate because you dread doing them
- Take you longer to do than someone strengthened by those activities
- Feel like a weight until you do it and you do not feel relief

You are the best judge of your strengths. No one can tell you what is uniquely your own strength; however, through engaged dialogue with your co-workers or superiors you can learn how you might be able to apply your strengths each week. You define what strengths you will use and how you will utilize them to meet the goals and expectations of your work each day and each week. Leaders understand that they will get the greatest return on their investment by developing strengths, not weaknesses. However, you do need to address any fatal flaws and meet performance expectations, then from there, focus on growing your strengths. You will learn and grow the most in areas where you are already strong. Developing strengths will provide exponential improvement.

Action tips for identifying strengths:
  1. Consider the best day you had at work recently. What made it so good?

This question is intended to help you identify what defines accomplishment for you. When you have a strong feeling of accomplishment, is it related to personal interactions, solving technology issues, managing an activity such as requirements definition, or testing?

2. I loved doing what activity?

When you realize your accomplishments, what is the activity within those accomplishments that really excited you? For example, is the activity building relationships such as in sales? Is the activity focused on delivering a project? Is the activity interacting with a specific kind of technology?

3. Did you care about what the subject or topic of the activity was?

This question is trying to understand the role process plays within your accomplishments. It may not matter the specific subject, but solving complex problems with certain kinds of people may be key.

4. Did you care about who you did the activity with, to, or for?

Does the "who" matter in your most exciting accomplishments?

5. Did you care about the objective or desired outcome of the activity?

This question helps identify process importance versus being outcomes driven.

Answers to these questions starts to build a profile that indicates where you find your passion, energy, and drive. The challenge, as a leader, is to then make decisions about the kind of career opportunities you will pursue. Consider how you can best allocate your time each day or week to engage these strengths and recognize how to manage the teams and people around you to shore up your weaknesses.

Action tips for identifying weaknesses (Moran, 2016):

1. Notice what you are avoiding.

What are the things on which you are spending your time? And what are the things you are avoiding? If you are actively putting off the same important tasks on a regular basis and there is no compelling reason why, it could be a good indication that you have not mastered those activities.

2. Look for patterns in feedback.

Think back on your performance review history and other feedback from managers and colleagues. Does that information reveal patterns? If you have a history of different people telling you the same thing, it is worth investigating whether you need work in that area.

3. Find someone who doesn't hold back.

It is critical to find people in your professional and personal lives who will tell you the truth, even when it is difficult. They do not necessarily have to be your best friends—but they do need to be honest, trustworthy, and unafraid to tell you when your efforts just are not cutting it.

4. Get to the punch-line.

If you are often the focus of jokes about your disorganized approach or inability to be on time, it could be a clue that these are issues the people around you are trying to correct through humor. Listen to the people around you for clues about the things that really bug them, then analyze whether they are areas that could potentially hold you back.

5. Find past failures.

No path to success is all just wonderful steps forward in the sunshine. You cannot get better until you look honestly at your past failures and figure out why they happened. It is not pleasant. But if you can look at the situation honestly, you can assess the role you played. That gives important insight into areas that might need work. Then, you can reframe them from "weaknesses" or "shortcomings" to the next areas you want to build in your skillset.

Another important element to consider in developing as a leader is your emotional intelligence. Emotional intelligence is the capacity to be aware of, control, and express one's emotions and to handle interpersonal relationships judiciously and empathetically (Maignan, 2014). The ability to lead is critically dependent on ability to lead *people*. An obvious statement, perhaps, but one worthy of self-reflection is how well you deal with other people in a variety of business or even personal situations. Indicators of when you need to work on emotional intelligence (Maignan, 2014):

- You often feel like others do not get the point, and it makes you impatient and frustrated.
- You are surprised when others are sensitive to your comments or jokes, and you think they are overreacting.
- You think being liked at work is overrated.
- You weigh in early with your assertions and defend them with rigor.
- You hold others to the same high expectations you hold for yourself.
- You find others are to blame for most of the issues on your team.
- You find it annoying when others expect you to know how they feel.

According to Muriel Wilkins, there are several strategies for working on developing your emotional intelligence such as soliciting feedback from coaches and mentors, developing an awareness of the gap between intent and impact of your words, understanding when to pause in the moment and prevent negative behaviors, and engaging in active listening.

HOW DO YOU DEVELOP PERFORMANCE POTENTIAL IN OTHERS?

Gallup is well known for its surveys and research into defining the characteristics of high-performing organizations and teams. Over the course of many years, Gallup organization has surveyed 2.2+ million employees across 190+ organizations, 40+ industries, and 30+ countries (Gallup, 2013). One question accounted for 79% of engagement of high-performing teams: "At work, I have the opportunity to do what I do best every day." The results of team members who "strongly agree" they have the chance to play to their strengths every day:

- 38% higher productivity
- 44% higher client satisfaction scores
- 50% greater employee retention

Enabling your teams to play to their strengths every day is a critical success factor in driving high-performance teams. The key to developing this potential rests in the ability to listen, engage, and create clarity with your teams.

ACTIVELY LISTENING

The same exercise noted above to determine your strengths and weaknesses can be done with your team members. Each team member is asked to share their strength findings. Ask questions to clarify understanding but never make judgments. The key outcome of this is an understanding by you as a leader and your team regarding team member strengths. In fact, it may be very helpful to categorize or organize the strengths to create a Team Capability Map. This map consists of identifying the key capabilities that your department or team must provide to its customers, either internal or external. These capabilities may be grouped or organized as you clarify your thinking. These required capabilities are matched against the strengths that emerge from this exercise. At the intersection of each strength and capability is either an "x" or a team member name. This allows you to see where you have gaps based upon required capabilities. It is also helpful to guide your thinking about how best to delegate and manage your team based upon their strengths. Figure 16.1 illustrates this concept.

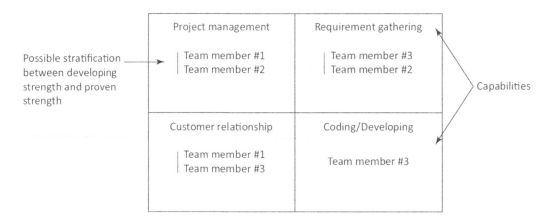

FIGURE 16.1 Sample team strengths to capabilities matrix.

As team members better understand the key strengths that each wants to "play" to each day, they can utilize this knowledge to help each other complete activities and tasks. You are seeking to create an understanding by each team member that enables a clear answer to: Do the people on my team know where they can rely on me the most?

It is also important to understand and document how the team prefers recognition. How will the team celebrate success, and how does each person like to be recognized when they do a great job? As a leader, you will need to follow through on celebrating key successes and milestones in a manner that your team values. This leads to reinforcing positive behavior and being actively engaged with your team.

ENGAGING

As a leader, you will enjoy much more success with your teams by accentuating the positive and recognizing the individual contributions that each team member makes. Engagement is created as a result of many things; however, being a leader that recognizes the specific, positive individual contributions that are made on a regular basis is far more motivating than constantly highlighting negative behaviors and focusing only on individual improvement needed. Gallup will refer to a survey question that asks: Has my supervisor or leader provided positive feedback to me in the past 7 days?

As a leader, you need to nurture and develop the team and team members each and every week through being consistent in the vision and objectives of the work to be done and working with your team members to establish expectations for individual work. This leads to creating clarity.

CREATING CLARITY

It is important to make sure your teams and team members understand what is expected of them at work. This means taking the time to discuss and document expectations. Expectations can include:

1. *Roles and responsibilities:* Defining and documenting a RACI matrix of Responsible, Accountable, Consulted, and Informed individuals for specific activities can help provide clarity between team members.
2. *Behavior and etiquette around such things as video meeting management, email responses, and virtual working hours:* Establish standards for meeting agendas, notes, timeliness to meetings, and engagement at meetings. It is important to provide your full engagement in a meeting and not show disrespect or lack of engagement. With increasing remote or virtual

work, ensuring you have an appropriate network connection and are able to communicate from a place safe from noise and secure for any confidential related matters is critically important. For more information on workplace manners, please see Section IV, The Aspiring Leader; Chapter 19, Minding Your Manners in the Workplace and Beyond.

3. *Work product or deliverable:* It is important to describe and document the expectations for the work output. A planning session is usually most helpful for driving to a level of common understanding and clarity. Ensure review and validation of a work product outline as a key quality step before the team commits significant effort.

4. *Identifying key metrics that will be tracked for a work activity:* Regardless of the metric, establishing a clear, shared understanding of how it is calculated and the source of data or information used is important for team member alignment.

5. *Communications between and among team members:* Defining expected work hours; work location; and responsiveness to emails, phone calls, and pages helps to clarify appropriate use of these tools and others for collaboration.

Making sure your team members understand what is expected of them, creating shared understanding of strengths and working consciously to utilize those strengths, and recognizing individual team members as well as teams for their positive contributions in ways that meet their needs will create the environment your teams need to drive high performance. As a leader, you establish the vision, the goals, and the expectations for success. Empower your team to generate the great ideas needed to realize success, and provide them the guidelines to take action. A great leader taps into this natural power and guides the team without needing to review and control every detail.

This brings us to the topic of creating the opportunities to develop your leadership.

HOW DO YOU CREATE THE OPPORTUNITIES TO GROW YOUR LEADERSHIP?

Creating the opportunities to grow your leadership skills is about how you take advantage of the role you currently perform and make it much more than was ever expected. New research shows that the jobs in highest demand today, and those with the fastest acceleration in wages, are so-called "hybrid jobs" that bring together technical skills, including technology operations and data analysis and interpretation, with "soft" skills in areas such as communication, service, and collaboration (Sigelman, 2017). As a leader, the ability to re-design jobs and work to combine the strengths of the human workforce with machines and platforms can result in significant improvements in customer service, output and productivity (Evans-Greenwood et al., 2017).

The keys to this are attitude, empathy, and action.

ATTITUDE

Attitude is a mindset and approach to how you interact with the work and people needed to execute your job. A key part of attitude for a leader is how you model it each and every day. Leaders establish principles concerning the way people (constituents, peers, colleagues, and customers alike) should be treated and the way goals should be pursued. They create standards of excellence and then set an example for others to follow. Because the prospect of complex change can overwhelm people and stifle action, they set interim goals so that people can achieve small wins as they work toward larger objectives. People unravel bureaucracy when it impedes action; they put up signposts when people are unsure of where to go or how to get there; and they create opportunities for victory (Kouzes & Posner, 2016). In short, demonstrating an "I own it" mentality in everything you do will create progressively more career growth and leadership opportunities.

EMPATHY

Empathy, the leader's ability to put others before themselves, to seek to understand and build rapport, and to show concern for direct reports impacts the ability to build an environment based on trust, enabling people to reach their full potential (Blanchard, n.d.). Your capacity to be empathic goes a long way in your ability to garner assistance and support from other people. Indeed, empathy is among the most human of all abilities, playing a profound role in being able to make meaningful connections and building quality relationships. Understanding and sharing the feelings of others enables you to interpret people's viewpoints effectively.

Recent research underscores just how valuable this is now and will be in the future. Since 1980, the labor market's growth in jobs requiring social skills outpaced the growth in jobs requiring routine skills, even routine analytical skills. Equally important, the jobs requiring good social skills are higher paying than those that don't require them. Although jobs requiring both high cognitive and high social skills are at the top of the earnings list, jobs requiring high cognitive skills but low social skills pay less than those requiring high social skills (Deming, 2015).

When your team members feel you understand their challenges, you gain credibility to engage the discussion on how to address the challenges at hand. Questions that help create that empathy should be open ended and can include things like:

- How is this affecting you?
- What have you tried?
- What is your desired outcome?
- What are the criteria for evaluating the solution?
- What did you learn or we learn?

The intent of the questions above is to create a deeper, more reflective discussion. It is in these situations that new or innovative solution ideas can emerge, empowering both the team member and the developing leader.

ACTION

The accelerant for attitude is action. As health IT professionals, we are inundated with data every day and yet are often challenged to find the right information and context to make informed decisions. Volume of email, ability to store ever-larger amounts of data, and the constant "on" access to the Internet are examples of the data stream that can cause lack of clarity and raise more questions than provide insights. This can create barriers to taking timely action. Leaders focus first on determining the right objective, then on understanding how the data and information inform approach and action. Data becomes information when you interpret and assess or provide context. Context can mean organizing and interpreting the data in terms of the overall objective of the plan currently in place. Further, analysis of risk, cost/benefit, options, and recommendations are helpful tools for the leader to divine the right thing. This can be confusing and, at times, overwhelming. The information becomes impactful when you choose what *action* to take with it. A quote may be illustrative of the point:

> *"I think Lee's army, and not Richmond, is your true objective point...Fight him when opportunity offers. If he stays where he is, fret him, and fret him."*—Abraham Lincoln's response to Gen. Joe Hooker, who'd asked for permission to advance on the Confederate capital rather than engage the enemy in combat—June 10, 1863 (Phillips, 1992)

The elements of attitude and action combined are powerful, but also need to be guided by several factors. These factors include organizational mission, project guiding principles, and business or clinical imperatives for the service being provided. Understanding the business or clinical mission of your organization, department, and work unit bound by guiding principles for the work is important. It is this framework that enables the ability to assess risks and barriers and mitigation strategies for the work that needs to be accomplished with your colleagues in support of the customers you serve. During the initiation of large projects, there are often guiding principles established that are used to inform project participants and stakeholders about how decisions will be made and the enterprise rational behind the project (i.e., the desired outcomes). Similarly, understanding and assessing risks and mitigation strategies associated with complex decisions helps frame the options for action and makes clearer what is acceptable to the management of the business enterprise.

BRINGING IT ALL TOGETHER

Growing your leadership skills and capabilities is about taking advantage of the opportunities to be proactive within your current role, modeling leadership behavior, and seeking counsel and advice from people with diverse skills and capabilities. Establishing trust and credibility with your team means demonstrating empathy, truly seeking to understand your team member's concerns, challenges, strengths, and passions. Developing those relationships provides valuable insights into the actions needed to meet and exceed expectations, solve problems, and influence the people around you.

As you begin to put this all together for yourself, there is no right or wrong or single formula; rather, it is about how you assemble these elements into a package that makes the most sense for who you are and where you want to go. Creating an action plan is a great next step in this process.

CONCLUSION

Our healthcare industry both here and abroad is changing at an ever more rapid pace, and this presents many leadership opportunities. Developing as a leader means developing an understanding of yourself, including assessing your management style, strengths, and weaknesses. Also important is recognizing how the nature of work and the workforce is changing and adapting to emerging technologies. As indicated in the beginning of this chapter, more and more healthcare organizations will be investing in technologies that drive intelligent automation as well as those that increase the ability to engage the customer and patient beyond the traditional brick and mortar of the institution. These initiatives will have unmistakeable impacts on the people within the organization as their definition and understanding of work changes; routine tasks become automated, and their role changes from task processor to knowledge manager. The opportunity for you to continue to develop as a leader will have significant challenges—ones you can address with the tools, tips, and approaches outlined in this chapter.

Your leadership will be defined by (Evans-Greenwood et al., 2017):

- The outputs and problems the workforce solves, not the activities and tasks they execute.
- The teams and relationships people engage and motivate, not the subordinates they supervise.
- The tools and technologies that both automate work and augment the workforce to increase productivity and enhance value to customers.
- The integration of development, learning, and new experiences into the day-to-day (often realtime) flow of work.

Developing performance in others through listening, engaging, and establishing clarity in expectations is critical not just to survive but to becoming an innovative leader. While working remote or virtually from home office locations has sky-rocketed during the COVID-19 pandemic, this trend is likely to continue. In the past, where meetings and various one-to-one interactions could easily take place in person, the ability to interact well with others takes on new significance as you must navigate virtual meetings, instant messaging, video chats, and emails. The ability to be empathetic, communicate effectively, and set the vision will require careful consideration on how and when best to utilize these tools, coupled with a plain old-fashioned phone call.

Listening and engaging others, as Gallup research identifies, is about tapping into the strengths of your team and harnessing those strengths every day and celebrating successes. Finally, we discussed approaches to finding opportunities to develop your own leadership through attitude, empathy, and action.

REFERENCES

Brian Brim, Debunking strengths myth #1. October 2007. www.gallup.com/businessjournal/101665/debunking-strengths-myths.aspx. Accessed on August 7, 2016.

David J. Deming, The growing importance of social skills in the Labor Market, National Bureau of Economic Research, Working paper # 21473, August 2015. http://www.nber.org/papers/w21473. Accessed on August 28, 2016.

Devaid Betts and Leslie Korenda, Inside the patient journey: Three key touch points for consumer engagement strategies. Findings from the Deloitte 2018 Health Care Consumer Survey, Deloitte Insights, September 25, 2018.

Donald T. Phillips, *Lincoln on Leadership, Executive Strategies for Tough Times*, New York: Warner Books, 1992.

Gallup, State of the Global Workplace 2013. http://www.securex.be/export/sites/default/xontent/down-load-gallery/nl/brochures/Gallup-state-of-the-GlobalWorkplaceReport_20131.pdf

Gwen Moran, The importance of finding (and facing) your weaknesses. www.fastcompany.com/3026105/dialed/the-importance-of-finding-and-facing-your-weaknesses. Accessed on August 7, 2016.

James M. Kouzes and Barry Z. Posner, *Learning Leadership: The Five Fundamentals of Becoming an Exemplary Leader*. San Francisco, CA: Wiley Books, May 2016.

Jeff Schwartz et al., The future is here, Deloitte, April 2018.

Karen Taylor, Mina Hinsch, and Amen Sanghera. Time to care: Securing a future for the hospital workforce in Europe, Deloitte UK Centre for Health Solutions, 2018. https://www2.deloitte.com/global/en/pages/life-sciences-and-healthcare/articles/time-to-care.html

Ken Blanchard, Critical leadership skills, key traits that can or break today's leaders, n.d. http://www.kenblanchard.com/img/pub/pdf_critical_leadership_skills.pdf. Accessed on August 28, 2016.

Steve Burril, Wendy Gerhardt, Maulesh Shukla, Deloitte 2020 Survey of Chief Financial Officers of Health Systems and Health Plans. Deloitte Insights. Retrieved August 27, 2021, from https://www2.deloitte.com/content/dam/insights/us/articles/6874_CHS-Health-care-CFO-survey/DI_CHS%20Health%20care%20.

Peter Evans-Greenwood, Harvey Lewis, and Jim Guszcza, Reconstructing work: Automation, artificial intelligence, and the essential role of humans. *Deloitte Review*, 21, July 31, 2017.

Thomas L. Friedman, Thank you for being late: An optimists guide to thriving in the age of acceleration, Farrar, Straus and Giroux, 2016.

Reena Govindji and P. Alex Linley, Strengths use, self-concordance and well-being: Implications for strengths coaching and coaching psychologists. *International Coaching Psychology Review*, Vol. 2, No. 2, 143–153, July 2007.

Matt Sigelman. By the numbers: The job market for data science and analytics. Burning Glass Technologies, February 10, 2017.

Muriel Maignan Wilkins, Signs that you lack emotional intelligence. *Harvard Business Review*, December 2014. https://hbr.org/2014/12/signs-that-you-lack-emotional-intelligence. Accessed on August 7, 2016.

World Industry Outlook, Healthcare and Pharmaceuticals. The Economic Intelligence Unit, September 2018.

17 Nurturing Inter-Personal Skills Development

John R. Zaleski
EMT, NREMT, CAP, CPHIMS, Ph.D., M.S. B.S.

CONTENTS

INTRODUCTION

The healthcare enterprise involves many individuals in many roles, both on the front lines of care, in the form of the physicians, nurses, and other allied healthcare providers, and those staff supporting the technology systems, facilities, housekeeping, and medical devices used in patient care. As with most large and complex enterprises, the hospital ecosystem is truly a system of systems, in which many individuals and technologies are brought together to achieve a common objective: caring for the patient. Each part of the whole interacts for a defined purpose within the ecosystem, wherein the patient and his or her care is the object. Each member of the team caring for the patient and providing various support services for those directly interacting with the patient should know that his or her actions are directly related to quality of patient care: this is not solely reserved for the clinicians operating on the front line.

The ability to work harmoniously and efficiently as a team and promote positive work environments was developed into a worldwide campaign, the Positive Practice Environments (PPE) Campaign, to "… introduce and maintain improved working conditions and environments within health systems."[1] A collaborative effort was initiated by the International Council of Nurses, The International Pharmaceutical Federation, the World Dental Federation, the World Medical Association, the International Hospital Federation, and the World Confederation for Physical Therapy. Among the various aims, some elements of positive practice environments are:[2]

1. Fair and manageable workloads
2. An organizational climate reflective of effective management and leadership practices
3. Safe staffing levels
4. Support, supervision, and mentorship
5. Open communication and transparency
6. Access to adequate equipment, supplies, and support staff

DOI: 10.4324/9780429398377-21

In this section, a review of the competencies needed to interact harmoniously and to succeed in this type of environment will be conducted.

HEALTH ECOSYSTEM TEAM

In a healthcare environment, the various roles of individuals comprise what can truly be identified as a team, with many competencies and roles participating according to functional or operational areas, education, and needs. One way to visualize the various roles and competencies is through a diagram that depicts the patient as the pinnacle of a triangle, as illustrated in Figure 17.1. The patient is identified at the top of the pyramid (here termed an "Eco-Pyramid" because the representation also comprises the healthcare ecosystem).

Each functional role is essential in the Eco-Pyramid. Clinical personnel, such as physicians, nurses, and allied health providers (including therapists, pre-hospital emergency medical technicians, paramedics, and in-hospital technicians) form the backbone of the healthcare operational environment, as they are the front line to the patient and meet their needs. Supporting allied health individuals, including administration, health information technology, facilities, housekeeping, network management personnel, buildings and grounds, food service personnel, security personnel, and others provides the necessary and supporting roles that are required to operate the ecosystem that is the healthcare enterprise.

Importance should be placed on those skills that are not only specific to unique functions, such as treating illness, managing data centers, food service, buildings and grounds, and facilities, but also to the soft skills necessary for human interaction.

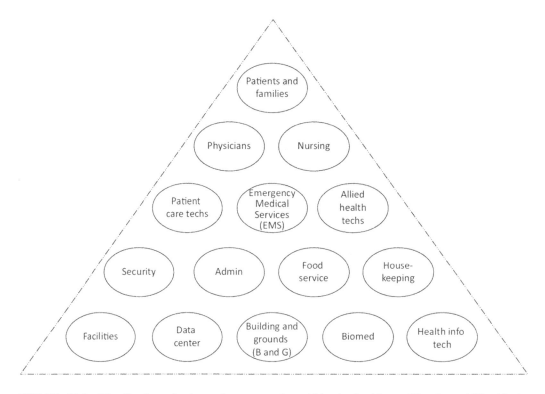

FIGURE 17.1 Visualization of roles and competencies within the healthcare "Eco-Pyramid," with the patient at the pinnacle. Each role or competency is an important component of the healthcare system in which individual members are part of the team.

KEY TEAM COMPETENCIES

Perhaps there are no more important key competencies than communication and listening skills. The skills of interpersonal communication (sometimes referred to as "soft skills") are as important as technical skills in terms of cooperating as team members to deliver efficient and effective care of a high-quality standard. The ability to communicate effectively is essential since without communication, technical skills will not be passed along, nor will they be understood.

Communicating and interacting with team members is a key interpersonal skill required in all aspects of our personal and work lives. They are equally as important for health information technology planning and deployment as they are for interaction with patients.

Communication is a key skill regardless of activity, whether communicating with a patient or communicating as part of a project team in the process of rolling out new hardware, new software, or new processes. As relates to health information technology: selecting or implementing departmental clinical information systems (CISs), electronic health record systems (EHRs), and medical device integration (MDI) are three examples where communication and organization are essential elements of success.

Any activity or project must be organized, focused, coordinated, and managed through project planning functions headed by a project manager who calls regular meetings, chronicles minutes, follows up on action items, and manages the project schedule. Furthermore, with regard to project meetings, a regular schedule should be established and adhered to. This is where focus on end-objectives is key to preventing disarray. To this end, managing group interaction through regularly planned and conducted meetings is an important competency.

Project meetings are an essential vehicle for communication. Yet, effective meetings require planning, identifying an objective while consuming the minimum amount of time.[3] An empirical timeframe for a project meeting of one-hour duration is a reasonable outside target, as meetings of longer duration are often difficult to schedule together with diminishing returns in terms of productivity, particularly with increased attendee participation. If more in-depth meetings are required, these should be taken offline and scheduled as individual deep-dives into particular topics, the results of which can then be reported at the regular project meetings.

All regular meetings within the scope of the project will undoubtedly create action items. These must be tracked and identified through a single responsible individual. Report-outs on actions should occur at every regular project meeting.

Project teams, and project meetings, need to be respectful gatherings that nurture positive, complete, and unrestrained communication. To this end, listening is a key skill that should be cultivated. All members of the project team should be treated as equal participants. This includes vendors who are invited to participate.

Organizational boundaries need to be removed to facilitate necessary communication. The points of view of all participants need to be respected in order to work together toward a successful solution. Toxic environments can and do result wherein there is political angling, repression of facts, or oppression of individuals or necessary communication. Such environments which foment conflict, judgment, and repressed communications are certain to result in failure and can result in wider-ranging negative impacts to the overall organization.

This observation leads to the next key attributes: mutual respect, honesty, and integrity. Communicate openly and directly with people, relaying all facts as they are pertinent to the topic at hand. Do not engage in rumor or unprofessional behavior, such as maligning individuals or talking behind people's backs. Integrity involves representing yourself and information honestly, without bias, and without participating in blame or "the search for the guilty." Avoid seeking blame. People make mistakes and should be encouraged to own up to them and make amends and corrections. Focus on the problem, and identify actions to measure improvement and performance. Respect for all individuals, their experiences, and their talents and gifts as individuals serves both the project as well as all individuals participating. Everyone has experiences that make them unique as individuals, and everyone has value to add. It is up to the talents of the facilitator or team leader to seek and nurture these talents.

Turn frustrations into group solutions—don't sit and stew on problems. Communicate frustrations in a calm and clear way, and solicit assistance in solving problems. Sometimes uniting two or more individuals in the cause of solving a technical or business issue can elicit new ideas or approaches. Hence, open communication often serves the purpose of initiating the finding of a solution—enunciating a problem openly serves to start the process of problem solution. Involve all stakeholders up frot, and communicate the importance of seeking their participation. Identify and delineate roles and intentions clearly.

Setting positive examples for staff with less overall experience, such as student interns or trainees, makes opportunities to mentor these less experienced staff. Sometimes taking the time to mentor can be perceived as an impediment because it can be seen as taking time away from problem solution. Yet, involving other people can enable one to view the problem less myopically, and it is always worthwhile to train and grow the next generation of individuals who will carry the organization forward. Taking time to mentor teach is never a wasted effort. Ensuring best practices are communicated forward is an essential aspect of mentoring.

Knowing how to separate one's own emotions from a problem or situation at hand is also a key skill. People can be defensive, particularly regarding their own ideas or projects. Although a natural response, defensiveness promotes boundary creation and closed-mindedness. It can be difficult to look objectively at challenges or situations if one is bound to them. Promote brainstorming of ideas and the creative process: encourage participants to suggest solutions or approaches for improvement. It can be difficult for the author or a creator of an idea to receive criticism of his or her idea. Yet, the key point must be communicated and reinforced that the object is improvement, and criticism or interrogation of an idea is not a personal reflection on the value of an individual.

Each participant should take responsibility for their tasks and action items. Oftentimes there are as many personalities present. Some people are natural leaders; others wish to be led. While some people are tolerant and considerate of others, still others are not. If problems or issues arise with certain individuals as part of the group dynamic, and these issues rise to the level of disruption, then discuss with those individuals privately offline and outside of group meetings. Never make "examples" of individuals inside of group meetings or otherwise identify targets for correction. This serves to make people defensive and further results in disruption. It is better to set clear rules for discussion and to table certain ideas or points that are controversial to be discussed offline prior to dissemination within the larger group.

FOSTERING THE CREATIVE PROCESS

One view of an approach to interdisciplinary thinking is expressed through the four-stage model of the creation process:[4]

1. Research
2. Concept
3. Evaluation
4. Implementation

This model, modified from the source and represented with a relative scale of number of collaborators, is illustrated in Figure 17.2. Number of collaborators corresponds to co-developers, co-inventors, or co-creators. Oftentimes at the beginning of the creative process, many are involved in the initial "birth" and creation or "ideation." That is, there are a larger number of collaborators present.

Ideas beget innovation resulting from the creative process, as everything that is created starts as a thought in someone's mind. The idea may be the brainchild of just one person, developed among

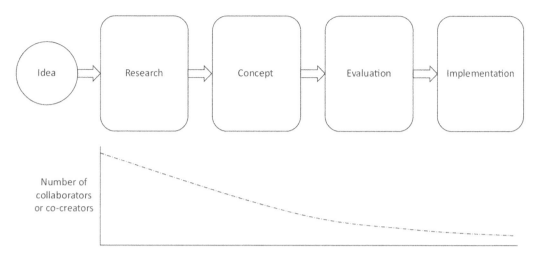

FIGURE 17.2 Suggested model of co-creation (project, implementation, offering, etc.) illustrating qualitatively how the number of collaborators in a multidisciplinary collaboration team may evolve over time: from many at the beginning of the process involved in defining the goals and framing the activity, to a relatively fewer number later on once the project has solidified and more specialization and logistics are needed to bring the project to fruition.

several people, a group, or a committee. The idea may be related to a business objective, improvement project, or cost-saving effort, or the result of a motivating event that has occurred within the larger organization. The idea may be born of external motivators, such as regulatory requirements or patient safety objectives, cost-saving initiatives, the need for acquiring new equipment, hospital realignments, etc.

The research process involves seeking as much information as possible related to the concept as can be found. Most general collaboration occurs up-front in the research and conceptualization stages (i.e., *"ideation"*). Conceptualization can involve creating a straw-form of the idea—a model, or test artifact or implementation, such as a pilot project or limited rollout of the objective.

The evaluation stage seeks to bring recommendations and conclusions together from the various collaborators and create an objective method for establishing a decision process that can be translated into a crisp implementation.

Implementation represents an actionable or operational phase which translates the creation into a real-world artifact. For example, if the enterprise is engaged in selecting a new electronic health record system (EHR), the decision-making process would consist of many participating disciplines up-front during the research and concept phases. The evaluation phase would be culled to a smaller number of specific and dedicated team members, and the implementation phase would consist of an even more specialized team.

GENERAL TEAMWORK OBSTACLES

> True collaboration...means a work culture where joint communication and decision making among all members of the healthcare team becomes the norm... [is] an ongoing process that grows over time.
>
> Ramon Lavandero[5]

The working dynamics among individuals vary almost as much as the number of people involved in a project. People can and will be passionate about ideas, and if not appropriately channeled, this passion can lead to arguments, lack of understanding, or the domination of the process by certain strong-willed individuals.

Listening can become difficult if you believe as a participant you have a better idea, or your ideas are not being heeded. Yet, listening can be more important at times than getting your ideas across, particularly if you can assimilate other ideas into your response so as to convey your interest in what others are saying as well as demonstrating that you are indeed listening to them.[6]

As such, a facilitator is oftentimes necessary to channel the energy of many individuals participating within the team ecosystem. As part of this, identifying and recognizing the value of member contributions is essential. All members of the team have talents, knowledge, wisdom, and agendas, and it is important to coordinate and clearly define the objective at each stage of the creative process to set the project objectives to guide and channel energies at the outset.

Individuals involved in a project have different capabilities ("gifts") that can be brought to bear and at different times during the project's evolution. Thus, at certain stages of project evolution, some individuals may have more to offer or more burden of responsibility. Human dynamics at each stage of a project need to be managed to ensure that all participants are equally valued for their individual contributions. As stated earlier, there may be some individuals who stand out more—who are more outgoing or gregarious than others. It is important to ensure that all voices are heard, and those individuals who have something important to offer but yet are, perhaps, shy, are made to understand that their contributions are just as important. Thus, part of the role of project management is to manage the organizational dynamic of many individuals having differing personalities. These differing personalities result in stylistic and interactive differences among individuals that need to be integrated to ensure the group is pulling together. A straightforward way of facilitating this is to ensure that each individual at a meeting is given an opportunity to speak his or her mind.

Furthermore, differences in "history and culture, coupled with historical [inter- and intra-professional] rivalries, complicate the establishment of effective collaborative care teams."[7]

Self-perception of contributions versus external perception is important for effective collaboration, as well. Hence, it is important for a facilitator or project lead to balance the objectives of the project with the talents and personalities of participants. While objective metrics for participation should be established up front by the facilitator—clearly identifying project objectives and boundaries—expectations of participation as "good citizens" of the project should also be set forth to establish guard rails for expected behavior in participation.

VIRTUAL TEAM-BUILDING IN SUPPORT OF COLLABORATIVE ENVIRONMENTS

In today's healthcare business environment, it has become more accepted to work remotely. The costs and impracticality of relocating individuals, as had been the norm years ago, are simply prohibitive for many smaller companies. But, even beyond the cost implications, many organizations are realizing that the nature of bringing in the best talent can be severely hindered by geography, and that individuals operate best when they are comfortable, happy, and motivated, particularly when they have interests outside of the office, such as being care providers for children or other family members. It has been estimated that savings in real estate costs alone by large companies such as Aetna has resulted in a saving of $78 million per year. Furthermore, Dell reports that it has saved $39.5 million in real estate costs in two years and anticipates having 50% of the "global company" work remotely by 2020.[8]

Teams that are distributed geographically and which must collaborate over media, via virtual presentation, video and audio (e.g., Skype, GoToMeeting, Zoom, etc.) can experience the disadvantage of the lack of collaborative benefit that face-to-face individuals enjoy, and face-to-face teams have been documented as being "more effective on all decision making behaviors."[9] The implication is that individuals who collaborate remotely need more organization and clear direction in order to be as effective. The ability to interact face-to-face brings with it physical and psychological cues that are not available through remote interaction. Yet, this handicap can be offset through improved organization and through team leadership ensuring unambiguous direction and roles assigned to remote participants. Hence, successful virtual collaboration means retaining as much of the power of a physical interaction as possible."[10]

Challenges associated with operating as a member of a virtual team have been documented and include:[11]

1. Managing technology
2. Handicap of infrequent face-to-face contact
3. Asynchronous communication (e.g., email)
4. Establishing norms
5. Collaborating cross-culturally

An anecdotal observation of individuals who have participated in virtual meetings with many participants is that the lack of social cues, time lags, and inability to observe facial expressions can serve to squelch some communication as asynchronous communicated can "restrict the frequency and wealth of relational messages," or can result in some members remaining silent due to feelings of uncertainty.[12]

Structurally, virtual teams are different in the following four ways:[13]

1. *Leadership vitals:* Teams require clearly defined direction with little ambiguity. Centralized coordination is seemingly the best approach taken. Roles need to be formalized and responsibilities clarified.
2. *Decision making:* Styles of decision making can vary broadly depending on the the the experiences of the individuals—particularly with global teams. Hence, adaptive approaches to a "one-size-fits-all" model are seemingly the optimal approach.
3. *Building trust:* Tactile and interpersonal interaction on a daily basis are ways in which collaborators get to know their peers. When a team is virtual, this component of interaction is missing. Hence, substitutes or proxies for increasing trust need to be established. One way in which trust can be attained is by fulfilling defined deliveries of work products.
4. *Communication:* An essential link among collaborators, communication is not merely the acknowledgement that various technologies need to be employed that allow for video teleconferencing or sharing of work products. The implication is that the members of the team are better served when they can see the various collaborators so as to associate the communication with the visual.

The bottom line is fuzzy in terms of which is judged to be better: virtual employees or in-office employees. Depending on the role and the individual, remote and virtual interactions are better for some people, and there are studies that have shown certain individuals to be more productive. Long-term, the facts are that organizations will be utilizing more people from wider diverse geographic locations, so remote collaboration is a cost-effective way of bringing talent to various tasks.[14] Perhaps the larger question is how best to attain the highest efficiencies and benefits to the organization and the employee. The answer seems to be through varied methods that are highly dependent on the organizational challenges, goals, and individuals.

COLLABORATION IN OPERATIONAL HEALTHCARE ENVIRONMENTS AND IMPROVED PATIENT OUTCOME

A suggested working definition of *collaboration* is to "function effectively within intra- and [interprofessional] teams, fostering open communication, mutual respect, and shared decision-making to achieve quality patient care."[15]

Of the key essential competencies for collaborative partnerships,[16] a suggested set of key competencies adapted from the source reference are as follows:

1. Know your capabilities, biases, strengths, weaknesses, and values.
2. Respect and value diverse opinions.
3. Resolve conflicts constructively and impersonally.
4. Seek to create resolutions and situations that allow everyone to win something in the end.
5. Recognize that collaboration requires integrating many different viewpoints, and this is akin to systems thinking. Contextualize the solution from the perspective of the integrated total of what the project objectives are in light of the participants and their talents.
6. Recognize that to be an effective contributor, you need not be correct 100% of the time. Mistakes are part of the process or journey of creation. Acknowledge errors and mistakes, and treat them as opportunities to learn, or improvement opportunities.
7. Take advantage of opportunities to seek multiple creative inputs and critiques.
8. Recognize that every collaborative effort need not require formal organizing and planning.
9. Provide people with enough flexibility to balance autonomous versus unified action as a group. People operate and function differently: some require strict direction and highly organized control. Others prefer to operate autonomously or individually and express themselves more effectively when unfettered by "groupthink." Respect all individual approaches, and seek to integrate their contributions into the overall effort.
10. All decisions need not be made as a group. Don't over-engineer decisions and mandate an over-developed solution that needs multiple tiers of decision makers when a solution with fewer individuals is appropriate.

Perhaps a good metric of interdisciplinary collaboration and communication in the healthcare environment can be reflected through the culture and behavior of its operational staff: in particular, the nursing staff. In one study of 100,000 nurses across nine countries, burnout, job dissatisfaction, and communication failures have been documented in large multiple-country studies as impacting more than 20% of nursing, and close to half of nursing lacked confidence that patients could care for themselves post discharge.[17]

In other studies[18,19], clinical staff members working in intensive care units (ICUs) with mortality rates lower than anticipated perceived their teams as functioning in better harmony and as being more trusting than did staff members of units with higher mortality rates. Finally, it is suggested that a positive link exists between healthy and positive clinical staff interaction and coordination (i.e., physicians and nurses) and improved patient status outcomes.

In an earlier study from 1986,[20] treatment and outcomes in 5,030 ICU patients at 13 tertiary care hospitals was performed. Patients were stratified by individual risk of death using diagnosis, indication for treatment, and APACHE II scores. Actual and predicted death rates were compared as the standard. One hospital had 69 predicted but 41 observed deaths, while another had 58% more deaths than expected. These differences occurred within specific and unique diagnostic categories and were related principally to the interaction and coordination of ICU staff, unit administrative structure, and treatment specializations.

EXAMPLE PROJECT TEAM: ROLLING OUT MEDICAL DEVICE INTEGRATION SOLUTIONS

Rolling out an enterprise medical device integration (MDI) solution requires a cooperative multi-disciplinary team involving the talents of staff from the data center and information technology, clinicians, clinical or biomedical engineering, telecommunications and networking, and facilities.[21] The MDI system facilitates charting patient care device (PCD) data in support of anesthesia information management systems, ICU documentation, sub-acute medical/surgical units, post-anesthesia care units, and others involving the real-time or near-real-time cardiorespiratory monitoring of patients. Medical device data are required for patient care management.

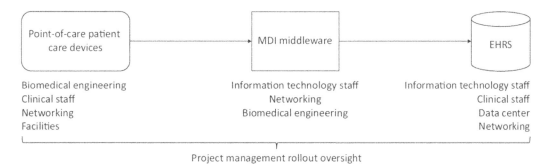

FIGURE 17.3 High-level view of point-of-care medical devices communicating to electronic health record systems using medical device integration middleware. Project management oversees the entire integration and members of various subgroups, from biomedical engineering to networking staff, participate at different stages across the enterprise implementation.

Figure 17.3 illustrates the high-level scope of an MDI rollout, with patient care medical devices transmitting data from the point of care (left-hand side); MDI middleware in the center; and EHR (right-hand side). Shown in this diagram are three separate components:

1. Point-of-care patient care devices (i.e., medical devices that collect patient care data from the patient bedside)
2. MDI middleware (i.e., the hardware and software that communicate data from the patient care devices to the her)
3. EHR that receives the data and provides the user-interface to the operational end user (i.e., clinician).

The implementation of an MDI solutions represents one example of a multi-member team comprising different stakeholders from the healthcare enterprise, each having varying (sometimes competing) interests, expertise, objectives, and motivations. A project manager who oversees the rollout of such an endeavor must be cognizant of the talent, training, and skills each member brings. The project manager must work with team members to effect the rollout within what can oftentimes be a tight schedule carried out in parallel with other projects, and may even fall within the implementation scheduling timeline of the EHR.

Implementing the MDI solution involves:

1. Assembling the project team
2. Facilitating an enterprise walk-through
3. Planning, defining scope, and setting weekly contact meetings
4. Deployment and system configuration
5. Unit testing the individual components, both hardware and software
6. Integrated system testing of the hardware and software, as well as evaluating within the context of clinical workflow
7. Establishing procedures for maintenance & support and clinical & technical training
8. Planning for the transition to live operations
9. Providing for post-live support

The project team includes the aforementioned staff members plus the EHR and MDI system vendors. Following team assembly, the project manager facilitates refinement of the configuration and deployment by scheduling an enterprise walk-through of the affected clinical spaces to determine specifics on configuration, facilities, networking, clinical workflow, and other environmental particulars. This serves to identify the target deployment environments and establish an understanding of the specific implementation, facilities modifications, and other impacts.

The walk-through, combined with an overall EHR deployment schedule, leads to the creation of a detailed project plan together with an organized and regular set of standing meetings to measure progress. During the rollout, hardware and software will be deployed by the MDI vendor in concert with hospital personnel. Progress on deployment is reported at regular standing meetings. Defining expectations for the team in terms of which hospitals and departments are to be deployed is a key goal of the project manager, as well as identifying specific tasks and dependencies together with measures by which successful completion is determined. Tasks need to be assigned to individuals by name and tracked regularly.

Implementation of MDI software (e.g., system and medical device drivers) together with hardware involves managing cross-functional tasks that impact both the information technology and biomedical/clinical engineering departments. It is important for the project manager to work with the information technology, data center, and networking teams to establish test environments in which to stage new software and upgrades prior to rolling into production settings. To this end, software component testing is followed by end-to-end integrated systems testing, from point-of-care data collection to EHR. This is the phase in which data mapping to the EHR needs to be validated and data posting to the chart is verified. This is an iterative process and can take some time. As such, it is essential that the project manager maintain tight reign over action item creation and closure, together with identification of individuals responsible for ensuring closure.

Similarly, staging, testing, and deploying hardware needs to be managed closely to ensure that access to environments, availability of power, and networking connectivity are all available in a timely manner. Deploying hardware in clinical environments necessitates planning around staff usage and patient occupancy. This can delay deployment and does introduce variability into the overall project plan that can be significant unless mitigation approaches can be determined (e.g., closing off certain units or sections of units for a period of time). Depending on the census, approaches for closing or restricting clinical units may not be possible, and schedules will need to be extended to accommodate this reality.

Training and support workflows are conducted by the MDI vendor with the hospital project team and all stakeholders. The project manager must ensure that all clinical and technical stakeholders are scheduled for training and that the MDI vendor provides a comprehensive training plan prior to go-live, with all operational staff clearly identified as to specific expectations for them together with clearly-delineated success criteria. If training certification is offered, it is imperative that the project manager work with clinical and affected technical staff to ensure requirements are met for certification, continuing education, and qualification on hardware and software before go-live.

Prior to go-live, a good practice is to conduct a "soft opening" or parallel charting, in which live charting occurs in parallel with a legacy system (e.g., other EHR or paper). The process can require as much time as is necessary depending on the complexity of the rollout, comfort level of clinicians, and findings requiring corrective action. During this stage, daily meetings may be necessary. Once all issues are resolved or a plan to resolve has been accepted by all and current issues do not represent a hindrance to live operations, transition to live operations takes place. The healthcare system, led by project management, should convene regular meetings with the EHR and MDI vendors to assess feedback on operations, report lessons learned, identify improvement needs, and facilitate a continuing and active relationship among all parties.

CONCLUSION

In this chapter, a review of key team collaboration competencies was conducted. These included:

1. Communication
2. Focus
3. Honesty
4. Integrity
5. Listening
6. Organization
7. Respect

All of these are essential elements of successful team collaboration. The facilitator or team leader will seek to nurture all elements in team members and understand that a better outcome will be achieved by enabling participants to express themselves appropriately and creatively while focusing the group efforts towards the objective or outcome.

NOTES

1 Global Health Workforce Alliance "Positive Practice Environments Campaign." URL: http://www.who.int/workforcealliance/about/initiatives/ppe/en/ Accessed July 4th, 2016.
2 Positive practice environments for health care professionals Fact Sheet. Copyright © 2008 International Council of Nurses, International Hospital Federation, International Pharmaceutical Federation, World Confederation for Physical Therapy, World Dental Federation, World Medical Association.
3 "Running Effective Meetings." https://www.mindtools.com/CommSkll/RunningMeetings.htm
4 Orviz, AF, "Effective Collaboration in Multi-Disciplinary Teams." © Copyright Angela Fernandex Orviz. MDes Design Innovation, Glasgow School of Art 2010. www.academia.edu, p. 10.
5 Debra Wood, Collaborative Healthcare Teams a Growing Success Story. *Healthcare News.* AMN Healthcare. April 25th, 2012. URL: http://www.amnhealthcare.com/latest-healthcare-news/collaborative-healthcare-teams-growing-success-story/
6 The Importance of Interpersonal Skills, © 2010–2016 Saylor Academy, p. 1: https://learn.saylor.org/course/ bus209
7 Canadian Medical Association (CMA) Working Group, Putting Patients First®: Patient-Centered Collaborative Care: A Discussion Paper. July 2007, p. 2.
8 John O'Duinn, *Distributed Teams: The Art and Practice of Working Together While Physically Apart.* September 2018. Located in Introduction By the Author.
9 T.A. O'Neill, S.E. Hancock, K. Zivkov, N.L. Larson, S.J. Law, "Team Decision Making in Virtual and Face-to-Face Environments." *Group Decision and Negotiation*, September 2016, Vol. 25(5), pp. 995–1020.
10 B Aklilu Taye, "The Contrinbution of Collaborative Tools and Technologies in FGacilitating Tacit Healthcare Knowledge Sharing amongst Clinicians In the Case of Akadamiska Hospital, Uppsala, Sweden." Masters Thesis. Uppsala Universitet. May 2014, p. 3.
11 J. Schulze, S. Krumm, "The "virtual team player": A review and initial model of knowledge, skills, abilities, and other characteristics for virtual collaboration." *Organizational Psychology Review*, 2017, Vol. 7(1), pp. 66–95.
12 Ibid.
13 Erin Meyer, "The Four Keys To Success With Virtual Teams." Aug 19, 2010. *Forbes.com*. URL: https://www.forbes.com/2010/08/19/virtual-teams-meetings-leadership-managing-cooperation.html#b7bebb330cc2. Accessed on May 13, 2019.
14 Larry Alton. "Are Remote Workers More Productive Than In-Office Workers?" March 7, 2018. Forbes.com. URL: https://www.forbes.com/sites/larryalton/2017/03/07/are-remote-workers-more-productive-than-in-office-workers/#2495982f31f6. Accessed on May 13, 2019.
15 Joanne Disch, Teamwork and Collaboration Competency Resource Paper. University of Minnesota School of Nursing. http://www.qsen.org (Quality and Safety Education in Nursing), p. 2.
16 Deborah B. Gardner, Ten Lessons in Collaboration. *The Online Journal of Issues in Nursing* 2010, Vol. 10(1).
17 Linda H. Aiken et al., Importance of Work Environments on Hospital Outcomes in Nine Countries. *International Journal for Quality in Health Care,* 2011, Vol. 23(4), pp. 357–364.
18 Susan A. Wheelan, et al., The Link Between Teamwork and Patients' Outcomes in Intensive Care Units. *American Journal of Critical Care.* November 2003, Vol. 12(6), pp. 527–534.

19 Joanne Disch, Teamwork and Collaboration Competency Resource Paper. University of Minnesota School of Nursing. http://www.qsen.org (Quality and Safety Education in Nursing), p. 4.

20 William A. Knaus, et al., An Evaluation of Outcome from Intensive Care in Major Medical Centers. *Annals of Internal Medicine* 1986, Vol. 104(3), pp. 410–418.

21 J.R. Zaleski, Connected Medical Devices: Integrating Patient Care Data in Healthcare Systems. Copyright © 2015 HIMSS, pp. 73–74.

18 Understanding the Multi-Generational Workplace

Laura Marks
Dr. PharmD, RPh, CPHIMS

CONTENTS

INTRODUCTION

Americans are facing a much longer work-life expectancy, which means our workplace often has five different generations working elbow-to-elbow. It has been common to identify the different workforce generations and to perhaps stereotype one another along age lines. As our workforce continues to evolve, this may be less appropriate, and we will need to put on a "post-generational" mindset that looks at philosophy and culture more than age. The premise of this chapter is that we cannot move beyond generationalism until we fully understand how the generations differ and, perhaps more importantly, how they are similar.

A "generation" is defined as a group of individuals born and living contemporaneously per Merriam-Webster dictionary.[1] Over a span of 15–25 years there are significant forces at work which develop similar experiences, expectations, and an outlook on life within that generation.

There are still individual differences in family life, personality, and temperament amongst a generational group. For example, I became interested in the different generations when I was quite young because my family is made up of a Traditionalist Matriarch (Grandma, my mother); 11 children (8 Baby Boomers, 3 GenX); 18 grandchildren (9 GenX, 9 Millennials); and 10 great-grandchildren (Generation Z). I am the tenth child out of the 11 and so was a GenX being raised by a Traditionalist Mother and Baby Boomer elder siblings. This promoted some attitudes and perspectives that differ from my generation such as valuing Self-Direction, Universalism, Benevolence, and Tradition that would be more common in my mother's generation. My sisters, Joyce and Barbara, were born within one year of the Baby Boomer cutoff of 1964, making them "cusp" children. Cusp children or cusp babies will show characteristics of both the generation before and after them. Using the generation groupings allows us to speak in terms of similarities and trends, while still respecting each person's particular story.

LEADERSHIP STYLE

To better understand how members of different generations are motivated, we need to understand leadership and power. There are three types of leadership styles as defined by Kurt Lewin (1939).[2]

- *Authoritarian:* This leader makes all decisions without necessarily taking input from others. They may give directions only for one step of a process, leaving members in the dark about future plans. This is more of the "do as I say" approach to leadership. This leader tends to be friendly to impersonal and uses very personal praise or criticism to motivate.

- *Democratic:* This leader uses team input and facilitates group discussion for decision making. This leader may give members a list of options and then encourage members to work with each other to determine the process needed to achieve the end result. This leader works freely with the group and uses objective praise or criticism to motivate.

- *Laissez-Faire:* This leader allows the group complete freedom to make decisions and achieve goals without participating unless requested. This leader does not offer praise or criticism unless directly asked.

POWER TYPES

Leaders, knowingly or unknowingly, combine their leadership style with one or more bases of power to achieve desired goals. Elias (1959)[3] define five types of power.

- *Legitimate or Positional Power:* This power is bestowed on the manager through a title or role. The team members understand this role/title and believe that this position gives the manager the right to give direction. This is typically demonstrated through some type of organizational hierarchy (manager, director, vice president). This type of power uses directing, delegating, and expectations of compliance to achieve goals.

- *Coercive Power:* Using this power the manager enforces compliance with an order through the threat of punishment. Punishment may be official (written warning) or non-official (disappointing the leader, group pressure).

- *Reward Power:* Using this power the manager gives some form of reward to the member to reinforce desired behavior. This can take the form of money or incentives, gifts, or other tangible compensation. It may also be intangible such as recognition, prestige, or a word of praise.

- *Referent or Personal Power:* This power is based on the member's respect for the manager and a desire to emulate them. Personal Power leads by example or empowerment, which leans heavily on trust between the individual and the manager. This leader uses motivation, persuasion, and cooperation to achieve goals.

- *Expert Power:* This power is based on a belief that the member has exceptional knowledge or skill which merits them authority, perhaps beyond what their organizational hierarchy warrants. This leader uses education, expert guidance, and expertise to achieve goals.

As we discuss the generations, we will discover which type of leadership style and power type work and which are not as successful. We will also find that different generations carry different types of values, so let's review the types of values and their definitions.

TYPES OF VALUES

- *Power:* Social status, control over people or resources; may include social power, authority, wealth, and public image
- *Achievement:* Success through demonstrating competence according to social standards
- *Hedonism:* Pleasure, sensuality, enjoyment of life
- *Stimulation:* Excitement, novelty, and challenge
- *Self-direction:* Independent thought and action
- *Universalism:* Tolerance, appreciation, protected welfare of all
- *Benevolence:* Preservation and enhancement of personal welfare
- *Tradition:* Respect and acceptance of long-standing customs and ideas
- *Conformity:* Restraint of actions and impulses likely to upset or harm others
- *Security:* Safety, harmony, stability of society or relationships and self

For this writing I will be using the AARP definitionof the generations as updated per the Pew Research Center (2018)[13]

- *Traditionalist Generation (born 1928–1945):* Also known as Silent, World War II, Builders, Matures, Industrialists, Depression Babies, GI Joes, Greatest Generation
- *Baby Boomer Generation (born 1946–1964)*: Also known as Boomers, Vietnam, or Me Generation
- *Generation X (born 1965–1980)*: Also known as GenX, Baby Busters, Thirteenth Generation (since the American Revolution), or Post-Boomer Generation
- *Millennial Generation (born 1980–1996)*: Also known as Generation Y, Echo Boomers, Boomlet, Generation Next, Nexters, or Internet/Nintendo/Sunshine/Digital Generation
- *Generation Z (born 1996 and after)*: Also known as the iGeneration or Post-Millennials

In 2016, Millennials became the largest generation in the workforce, making up about 35% of all workers.[14]

Millennials became the largest generation in the labor force in 2016

U.S. labor force, in millions

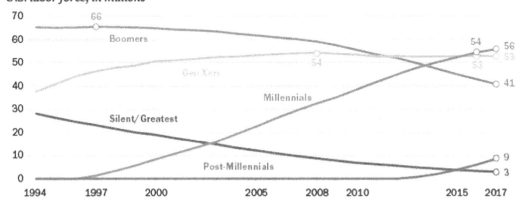

As of the 2019 U.S. Census, Millennials (aged 23–38) now have the title as largest generation surpassing the Baby Boomers (aged 55–73). It is important to note that the Millennial cohort is still growing due to immigrants to the United States within that age group. Generation-X has traditionally been much smaller than the Baby Boomer generation but will surpass them by the year 2028.[15]

Projected population by generation

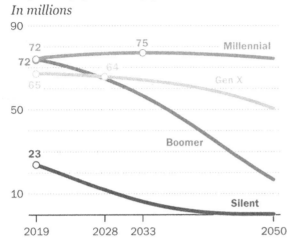

In millions

With concerns for retirement and Social Security funds compared to the rising cost of living, many workers are and will continue to remain in the work force past the traditional retirement age of 65. As of 2018, 34% of Boomer men and 25% of Boomer women remain in the workforce between the ages of 65–72.[16] This trend is expected to continue, which means there will be multiple generations with a wider age range in the workforce for the foreseeable future.

For each generation, there are seminal events that shape the basic fabric of that generation.

In previous generations, these events were country specific; a person born in 1955 in the United States had different shaping events than a person with the same birthdate from another country. Once we reach the Millennial Generation, we find that country and nationality does not have the same impact on the development of the generation. Due to worldwide media and cultural events, future generations will be referred to globally, and the demarcations of a generation's start and stop dates are less clear.

Let's now look at the important events that shaped each generation.[1]

TRADITIONALISTS (BORN 1928–1945)

- 1937: Hindenburg Tragedy; Disney's first animated feature (*Snow White*)
- 1941: Hitler invades Russia; Pearl Harbor; United States enters World War II
- 1945: World War II ends in Europe and Japan
- 1947: Jackie Robinson joins major league baseball; HUAC investigates film industry
- 1950: Korean War begins

Most influential technologies: the radio and record player
    Values: Benevolence, Tradition, Conformity, and Security
    Leadership style preferred: Authoritarian Leadership
    Power style most respected: Positional Power
    Best method to reward/recognize: Tangible symbols of loyalty, respect, and commitment such as plaques or certificates
    Best communication style: Slightly more formal language, avoiding slang or profanity. Use memos, letters, or personal notes.

This generation saw the beginning and end of World War II with all of its social, political, national, and personal tragedy. They endured rationing and other hardships while listening to their radios for an update on the war effort. They were much more likely to start and end their career for the same employer. They were given several compelling messages such as "Make do or do without"; "Stay in line"; "Sacrifice for the common good"; and "Be heroic."

Traditionalists are generalized as being "Old School" because they lean towards a conservative approach to traditional values and tend to prefer simplicity but demand excellence. This generation was taught how to do a thing and was then expected to do that thing *correctly* each time. This expectation comes with them into the workforce, where they expect processes to "make sense" and assume that everyone will naturally do what is best for the good of everyone else around them.

Using my mother's teachings as an example, you don't dare trim celery and throw away the yellow, leafy innards because they can be used to make soup stock, and you *never* throw away leftovers. My mother taught me how to pound a nail, stretch a fence, make a chocolate cake, and sew a dress. Each skill was taught with a minimum of fuss, and praise was a smile or "that will do." And there is no use for a fancy omelet for breakfast when a basic banana and peanut butter sandwich does just as well.

There are now only 3-million Traditionalists in the workplace, meaning they have less positional power than they used to. Their power comes today mainly from personal or expert power, which they may see as a vulnerable position.

In working with this generation, it is important to understand that they have been raised to not "brag" on themselves or to "bother" others. They are not as likely to express their feelings and are uncomfortable with conflict. If given a safe environment to express their thoughts, they will share their concerns and opinions in a positive way. If not, these feelings may "come out sideways" in the form of criticisms or judgments.

This generation will have adapted to technology at different rates depending on their personal abilities. Some may not even have a computer while others are on social media.

If you are communicating with a group of this generation, regardless of their job or educational level, be ready to send the communication both electronically and via traditional mail. Radio and newsletters are effective tools for this generation.

Following generations may see Traditionalist as too rigid or not welcoming of different approaches or styles. Traditionalists can have a positive influence in groups, volunteer organizations, and the workplace if they openly share their knowledge and experience while accepting that others may apply their knowledge in a non-traditional way.

BABY BOOMERS (BORN 1946–1964)

- 1954: First transistor (portable) radio
- 1960: Birth control pill introduced
- 1962: John Glenn circles the earth
- 1963: Martin Luther King, Jr. leads march on Washington; President Kennedy assassinated
- 1965: United States sends troops to Vietnam
- 1966: Cultural Revolution in China begins
- 1967: World's first heart transplant
- 1969: U.S. moon landing; Woodstock
- 1970: Women's liberation demonstrations

Most influential technology: Television
  Values: Hedonism, Stimulation, Universalism, and Benevolence
  Leadership style preferred: Democratic and Laissez-Faire
  Power style most respected: Personal and Reward
  Best method to reward/recognize: Personal appreciation, promotion, or recognition
  Best communication style: Personal communications by phone, one-on-one, or group meetings

This generation was witness to the medical, scientific, and social strides made in the post-World War era. This generation was taught that you *can* make a difference, and if you can, then you should. It was still common for workers to start and end a career working for one employer, but this started to change in the 1970s. American product loyalty was strong, although they watched this erode in the following decades. Baby Boomers heard the compelling messages of "Be anything you want"; "Change the world"; "Work well with others"; and "Duck and Cover." This was the generation referred to in such movies as *It* and *Stand by Me,* where children were given lunch sacks and a bicycle and told to come home by dark.

Boomers prefer to be led by consent and treated as equals whose opinions matter. When a leader sends the message to a Boomer that their input is not needed or wanted, the Boomers' natural reaction is to withdraw support from that leader or project.

Because Baby Boomers have previously outnumbered the generations before and after them, they have been accustomed to using their collective strength to influence the workplace, communities, and the social world around them. It is only with the coming of age of Millennials that there is now a generation that surpasses Baby Boomer numbers. Because of this we are witnessing a shift from a Boomer modeled workplace to one more heavily influenced by Millennials. This can cause Boomers to feel a vulnerability to ageism and job and power loss.

Boomers are relationship oriented and require an interpersonal warm-up before conducting business, such as "I saw your child in the newspaper; very impressive win" or "How is your spouse doing, did they get that new job they were looking for?" Boomers prefer to use personal phone calls and meetings to make decisions or solve issues; "we just need to get the right people around the table."

Other generations feel Boomers at times present a "know-it-all" attitude and lean towards being impatient or interrupt when others are working or expressing their views. Boomers may also need to be careful that the value they place on personal achievement doesn't come across to other generations as taking credit for the work of others.[8]

Boomers have a very valuable part to play in all organizations and groups when they use their democratic leadership style to gain buy-in on decisions and move the team forward. This generation brings a personal touch, social awareness, and a teamwork orientation that at times are be overlooked by other generations.

- 1972: Watergate Scandal
- 1973: Global energy crisis; abortion legalized
- 1976: Tandy and Apple market the first Personal Computers
- 1978: Mass suicide in Jonestown
- 1979: Three-Mile-Island accident; Margaret Thatcher first female British Prime Minister; massive corporate layoffs
- 1980: John Lennon killed
- 1981: AIDS identified
- 1986: Chernobyl disaster; Challenger disaster
- 1987: Stock market plummets
- 1989: Exxon Valdez oil spill; Berlin Wall falls; Tiananmen Square uprisings

Most influential technology: Personal Computers
   Values: Achievement, Benevolence, Stimulation, and Self-Direction
   Leadership style preferred: Laissez-Faire
   Power style most respected: Positional and Expert Power
   Best method to reward/recognize: Flexible or free time, upgraded resources, opportunities for growth and development
   Best communication style: Voice mail, email, text

When happily ever after fails and we've been poisoned by these fairy tales, the lawyers dwell on small details, since daddy had to fly.

Don Henley's End of the Innocence, 1989

With better methods of birth control and legal abortions, Boomer families were able to plan their children, which resulted in less children than had by their Traditionalist parents. With divorce rates doubling in the 1960s and 1970s, and the number of moms in the workplace doubling from 1969–1996, added to nuclear, religious, civil, and environmental disasters, this created a generation that clearly heard messages such as "Don't count on it"; "Heroes don't exist" or "Heroes are dead"; "Get Real"; and "Always ask why."

While Boomers might see computers and technology as learning a foreign language, X'ers tend to be technology savvy. Although X'ers were born in the analog world, they were there through the early years of computer development, AOL, and the World Wide Web. This provided this generation with the platform to start moving, and they haven't stopped since.

X'ers, as a whole, are skeptical, cautious, independent, practical, and adaptable. This generation tends to be "down to business," which can come across as blunt or proud. X'ers may need to soften their presentation style, at times, when dealing with others and remember to give a social warm-up or a supportive gesture.

X'ers are more likely to be drawn to entrepreneurial or non-traditional work opportunities and feel it is better to "work to live, than live to work." What might appear to be a lack of interest is a tendency of the X'er to focus on their own task and assume that someone equally as competent is managing the other tasks.

X'ers are strong advocates for community service, the betterment of society, their workplace, and friends. With their ability to drill down to what is important and make a focused plan to accomplish goals, they are a strong asset to any organization.

MILLENNIAL GENERATION (BORN 1980–1996)

- 1990: Nelson Mandela released; Hubble Telescope launched
- 1992: Collapse of Soviet Union; Bosnian Genocide begins; Rodney King riots
- 1993: Apartheid ends; compound in Waco Texas
- 1994: Channel opens between Britain and France; Rwandan Genocide
- 1995: Bombing of Federal building Oklahoma City; Sarin Gas Tokyo Subway; eBay founded
- 1997: Princess Diana dies
- 1998: Viagra marketed
- 1999: Y2K scare; Columbine school shooting
- 2001: World Trade Center attacks
- 2002: Enron, Worldcom and corporate scandal
- 2003: Iraq War begins
- 2004: Tsunami in Asian Ocean; Facebook founded
- 2005: Hurricane Katrina

Most influential technologies: Internet and Cell Phones
  Values: Power, Hedonism, Stimulation, and Security
  Leadership style preferred: Authoritarian and Democratic
  Power style most respected: Reward and Expert
  Best method to reward/recognize: Tangible items of achievement such as awards, certifications, and other markers of credibility
  Best communication style: Virtual (social media, video chat, messaging) and in-person

The events affecting the Millennials are more global, and natural disasters are much more a part of their social landscape. Older Millennials were raised by Baby Boomers, who are referred to as "helicopter parents" and took a keen interest in the life of their children. Younger Millennials were raised by GenX parents, known as "stealth fighter parents" due to their tendency to let minor issues go, but they responded enthusiastically when something important came to light. Both parenting styles worked to provide their children with the best possible opportunities for achievement while focusing on safety. The messages Millennials heard while growing up included "You are Special"; "No one gets left behind"; "Connect 24/7"; and "Achieve Now!"

This is the first generation to be fully Techno-Natives, meaning, computers, smartphones, and social media have always existed for them, and running multiple "gadgets" is a natural part of their daily lives. This means Millennials have the platform to act collectively, to be instantly famous, and to affect trends worldwide.

This generation really struggles with Laissez-Faire leadership style if they haven't previously had the opportunity to learn to self-govern and self-motivate. This generation will not tolerate Coercive Power and might struggle with Positional Power unless it offers educational opportunities with a positive coaching and collaborating approach.

As Millennials assume decision-making positions as leaders on the global stage, they will continue to push the boundaries of technology and connectivity policies. They will look for ways to work from remote locations and other non-traditional work settings.

Millennials have perhaps spent more time using social media and virtual or gaming environments than engaging in interpersonal relationships. This can leave them unready for the messy challenges of work life. They may expect their manager to protect them from angry customers or rude co-workers. So, it is very important for the manager to set clear expectations with the newly hired Millennial for which situations they should handle and then to give them the tools to successfully do so. This generation is used to constant feedback in the form of likes, views, and followers; therefore, a management style of "If you don't hear from me, you're doing okay" will not be successful with this generation. Managers will be challenged to find new mechanisms to stay in contact with these workers and learn to include IMs, blogs, text messages, email, and messengers.

In general, Millennials are better educated than the previous generations, but there is also a greater financial divide between those with a degree and those without. Millennials are more likely to delay getting married and starting a family and are more likely to live with parents for longer stretches. The Great Recession of 2007–2009 has presented Millennials with some interesting work and financial challenges.[17]

As Millennials climb the corporate ladder or start their own multimillion dollar company, they are bringing their environmental, social, and global concerns and passions with them. Millennials are just as likely to have worked for their employers for at least five years as GenX employees did at the same age.[17] [10] They are just as likely to leave an employer as a Baby Boomer for similar reasons although the Millennial is more likely to be looking for a job that pays more money.[16]

About 1/3 of Millennials and Baby Boomers reported feeling oppressed by or pushed out of the workplace by the other generation. This seems to be related to irritations over work practices regarding smartphone use and what is perceived as laziness or ego in the opposite generation.

When working with a Millennial, avoid sarcasm or telling them they are too young to contribute. If you pair a tech-savvy Millennial who lacks interpersonal inexperience with a mature Boomer who can accept assistance with technology while providing positive coaching on how to handle difficult interpersonal situations, you have a recipe for success.

GENERATION Z (BORN AFTER 1996)

- 2001: World Trade Center attacks
- 2002: Enron, Worldcom and corporate scandal

- 2003: Iraq War begins
- 2004: Tsunami in Asian Ocean; Facebook founded
- 2005: Hurricane Katrina
- 2006: Saddam Hussein executed
- 2007–2009: The Great Recession
- 2009: President Obama elected
- 2011: Osama Bin Laden killed
- 2015: NASA spacecraft New Horizons reaches Pluto
- 2017: Triple Hurricane—Harvey, Irma, Maria
- 2020: COVID-19, wildfires, 5 Hurricane/Tropical Storms—Paulette, Sally, Teddy, Vicky, Rene

Most influential technologies: Smartphones and Digitalized Electronics
    Values: Stimulation, Self-Determination, and Universalism
    Leadership style preferred: Authoritarian and Democratic
    Power style most respected: Reward and Personal
    Best method to reward/recognize: Authentic, pragmatic, functional signs of appreciation
    Best communication style: Digital and texting

Generation Z was raised primarily by GenX parents, which means they tend to be independent and able to figure things out for themselves. They are used to being given brief, timely instructions and then, after a moment for self-reflection, begin the necessary task. They have been part of structured activities since they were little and are used to working with a coach.[21]

About 10% of all eligible voters for the U.S. 2020 election are part of GenZ. This generation was set to inherit a strong economy, but that has been altered by the COVID-19 pandemic. These workers were vulnerable to job loss because they tend to be in high-risk work categories such as food or personal services. This is a more racially and ethnically diverse group than the generations before them.[18]

This generation is not just tech-native; they are digital-natives for whom smartphones, GPS, High-Definition (HD), and streaming services are all lifetime norms and the phone is an extension of the self.

When comparing the age-range 18- to 21-year-olds, GenZ are more likely to have completed high school, or it's equivalent, and are going to college but less likely to be working full-time jobs then either Millennials or GenX when they were that age.[18]

GenZ believes in being inclusive to different lifestyles, cultures, and customs. Expect this generation to be both entrepreneurial and financially cautious while focusing on how to sustain the environment.

The key to managing a GenZ is to provide them with multiple, brief, single topic, one-on-one moments of coaching. Authenticity is key to building relationships with GenZ since they have grown up streaming online "influencers" who are there 24/7 providing real-time personal advice.

We are just beginning to explore the amazing things this generation has to bring to the workplace, and if we listen and provide them the path, they will make every step count.

CONCLUSION

When we have a workplace with some individuals who want in-person communication but others who want text messages, it becomes clear that as managers we must use a combination of leadership and power styles while being flexible in how we communicate and measure success.

As we continue to build a workforce that is mobile and dynamic, we must make our systems flexible enough so that we don't crack under pressure but are strong enough to survive the rigors of this world. I would propose the following suggestions:

- Foster collaboration and avoid silos.
- Foster well-trained and highly accountable managers.
- When we don't know the answers, we look for wisdom.
- Reduce meetings to essentials, and avoid inefficient use of time.
- Allow flexibility in work and communications styles.
- Get comfortable with virtual and online workplaces and classes.
- Give feedback in real time, and communicate more than you think is enough.

To accommodate the diversity and basic humanness of our workplace, we must change our mindset. We must thoughtfully provide a work environment that has a clearly identified mission, vision, and goals. This workplace will use a combination of leadership and communication styles to accommodate all needs and will allow a certain amount of flexibility in the workplace to include off-site, virtual, global, as well as in-person staffing models. This workplace model would respect all persons and accept the different cultural influences by providing needed training in multiple formats to create accountable managers who will lead by example.

There will be many stubbed toes and pitfalls as we move through the evolving workplace. But, if we keep an open ear and value each other's needs, we will see remarkable growth and success in the years to come.

REFERENCES

1. Smyrl, Barbara J., "Leading a Multi-Generational Workforce: Understanding Generational Differences for Effective Communication" (2011). College of Professional Studies Professional Projects. Paper 28.
2. Planning for Success in the Multigenerational Workforce, Mark Taylor, 2015, www.taylorprograms.com
3. Tackling the Challenges of the Multigenerational Workforce, Nicole Fallon, *Business News Daily*, June 16, 2014.
4. Effectively Managing the Multigenerational Workforce, *Under30CEO*, August 25, 2011.
5. Leading a Multigenerational Nursing Workforce: Issues, Challenges and Strategies, Rose Sherman, *The Online Journal of Issues in Nursing*, 2006.
6. Why You Should Plan to Work Until Age 70, Emily Brandon, July 9, 2012.
7. Why can' t Generation X get ahead at work? Ronald Alsop, July 11, 2013.
8. Old School Management Tweaks for a New Generation, Ryan Mead, August 12, 2015.
9. Facts about the Millennial Generation, Fred Dews, June 2, 2014. http://www.brookings.edu/blogs/brookings-now/posts/2014/06/11-facts-about-the-millennial-generation
10. Leadership Styles and Bases of Power, David A. Victor, revised by Monica C. Turner. http://www.referenceforbusiness.com/management/Int-Loc/Leadership-Styles-and-Bases-of-Power.html
11. Types and Values over Generations, Vera Routamaa, Katri Heinasou, Psychological Type and Culture—East & West: A Multicultural Research Conference, Honolulu, Hawaii, January 6–8,2006. http://typeandculture.org/Pages/C_papers06/RoutamaaGenerations2.pdf
12. Employee Outlook: 2010–2020—Occupational employment projections to 2020, C. Bret Lockard and Michael Wolf, *Monthly Labor Review*, 2012.
13. New Guidelines Redefine Millennials, AARP, Shelley Emling, March 2, 2018. https://www.aarp.org/politics-society/history/info-2018/millennial-generation-defined-fd.html
14. 10 Facts about American Workers, Fact-Tank, Drew Desilver, August 19, 2019. https://www.pewresearchorg/fact-tank/2019/08/29/facts-about-american-workers/
15. Millennials Overtake Baby Boomers as America's Largest Generation, Fact-tank, Richard Fry, April 28, 2020. https://www.pewresearch.org/fact-tank/2020/04/28/millennials-overtake-baby-boomers-as-americas-largest-generation/
16. Baby Boomers Are Staying in the Labor Force at Rates Not Seen in Generations for People their Age, Fact-Tank, Richard Fry, July 24, 2019. https://www.pewresearch.org/fact-tank/2019/07/24/baby-boomers-us-labor-force/

17. Study Reveals Relationship Between Millennials and Baby Boomers in the Workplace, Olivet University, Survey Feb/March 2020. https://online.olivet.edu/news/study-boomers-millennials-working-together

18. Milliennial Life; How Young Adults Today Compares with Prior Generations, Pew Research Center, Kristen Bialik and Richard Fry, February 14, 2019. https://www.pewsocialtrends.org/essay/millennial-life-how-young-adulthood-today-compares-with-prior-generations/

19. On the Cusp or Adulthood and Facing and Uncertain Future: What We Know of About Gen Z So Far, Pew Research Center, Kim Parker and Ruth Igielnik, May 14, 2020. https://www.pewsocialtrends.org/essay/on-the-cusp-of-adulthood-and-facing-an-uncertain-future-what-we-know-about-gen-z-so-far/

20. Thriving in the Multi-Generational Workplace, AARP, Janice Holly-Booth, June 27, 2017. https://www.aarp.org/work/on-the-job/info-2017/succeed-in-multigenerational-workforce-lr.html

21. The Most Effective Way to Lead Generation Z, Inc, Ryan Jenkins, Sept 26, 2017. https://www.inc.com/ryan-jenkins/most-effective-way-to-lead-generation-z.html#:~:text=Coaching%20is%20the%20leadership%20style,to%20their%20DIY%20work%20mentality

22. Generation Z: Who Are They and What Events Influenced Them? Management is a Journey, Robert Tanner, June 25, 2020. https://managementisajourney.com/generation-z-who-are-they-and-what-events-influenced-them/

19 Minding Your Manners in the Workplace and Beyond

Michelle Cotton
CPA, CPHIMS, CIA, CFE, CCA

CONTENTS

INTRODUCTION

In this chapter, you will have the opportunity to recognize proper manners and etiquette in the workplace as we walk through five manners of the past and how to incorporate those prior learnings into your present and future. Please join us as we take a walk down memory lane and remember the importance of saying "please" and "thank you," being kind, paying attention, not interrupting, and holding the door for others.

SAY PLEASE AND THANK YOU

Did you ever wonder why adults told you to say "please" when you were younger? Is it not quicker to just say what you need and drop the "please"? Beginning a request with "please" is a sign of respect. Without the "please," your request can come across as an order. Do you ever find yourself saying, "Do this" or "I need that"? Statements beginning with those phrases can be perceived as orders and could immediately put others in a position where they are less willing or eager to do something for you. Regardless of whether the recipient of the request reports to you or is paid to perform the task, you should still treat him or her with respect. Would you not rather be politely asked to do something than told to do something?

And what about "thank you"? Most individuals enjoy gratitude in some form or fashion. Think about what a boost it was the last time someone thanked you for a job well done in front of your boss. Now, pay it forward and do that for someone else when that someone else is deserving. If someone does you a favor, and you are gracious, that will likely warrant the receipt of favors from that individual in the future.

BE KIND

Remember hearing the phrase "kill them with kindness"? Interestingly enough, this also applies in the professional setting. Think about a time when you were conversing with someone regarding a problem that needed to be solved and brainstorming potential solutions where you had conflicting opinions. How did you respond when the individual proposed a solution that was in direct conflict

DOI: 10.4324/9780429398377-23

with your opinion on how to solve the problem? Was your initial response, "I don't think that's right" or "I disagree with you"? If so, you may want to consider rethinking your word choice. Responses of that nature often put the other individual in the conversation in a defensive position and could lead him/her to perceive that you are closed-minded and not open to a discussion. Now, try this: "OK, I think I'm following you. I'm seeing it a little differently, but maybe you can help me better understand your thinking." That opens the door for healthy dialogue while still getting your point across.

And what about those times when you have had to provide constructive criticism? It is of course important to have those tough conversations as it is a disservice to others to not, but you can always lead with kindness and respect. Let us think about two different approaches to these types of discussions and which we might prefer.

> First, your boss sits you down and says, "I have significant concerns about your performance and fear you may not be able to do this job. You're going to have to make some changes." How would that make you feel? You might immediately engage from a defensive position into what one might consider a more hostile conversation. Now let us think about a second approach. In the same situation, your boss sits you down and says, "Thank you for the time and effort you put into this project. I'd like to chat about how we can improve the next time. We, myself included, always have opportunities to improve, and I'd like us to work through how we can make sure you have the necessary tools to do your job so we can be more successful in the future."

Safe to say, the majority of us would prefer this approach. While it may require a greater investment of time, the recipient of this message would likely be less defensive, and the boss would be able to get his or her point across while simultaneously preserving the relationship. So next time you have a tough conversation ahead of you, take a minute to think about how you can "kill them with kindness."

PAY ATTENTION

Remember your parents telling you to pay attention and listen to others? The same goes for the professional environment. If you are at a presentation, meeting, or something of the like where someone has taken the time to prepare for the event, show them respect and pay attention. In these situations, it is important to give your undivided attention to the presenter or meeting leader. While you may believe you are quite talented when it comes to multitasking (and you probably are), if you are working on your computer, consistently checking your phone, or taking calls in the room, you are sending a message to those engaged in the discussion that you do not value their time nor do you value their contributions to the discussion.

If you are unable to give your undivided attention, it is best to bow out gracefully and conduct your work outside of the presentation or meeting setting. Now, pay attention to this last thought: Everyone in the room notices your actions, and if you happen to be in a leadership position, what kind of example are you setting for others?

DON'T INTERRUPT OTHERS

It is important to remember to listen first and engage second. When you interrupt, you are likely losing out on valuable information you would have otherwise gained if you had just let the other individual complete his or her thought. You are also, albeit likely unintentionally, sending the message that what you have to say is more important than what others are attempting to contribute to the discussion. With that being said, we all know it happens from time to time. So when you do interrupt someone (again, hopefully unintentionally), simply apologize for the misstep (yes, another manner we learned as a child) and let the other individual complete his or her thought.

Now, let us consider technology interruptions. In this fast-paced world we live in of ever-evolving technology and social media (constant emails, instant messages, texts, scheduling meetings over meetings), patience is quickly becoming a lost virtue. What we may forget is that some may perceive these "need it now" forms of communication as interruptions. Be mindful when communicating via technology and scheduling meetings. Think about what it is you need before selecting your method of communication. Is it a quick question like "Can you remind me how many people will be attending the design session tomorrow?" Or is it a question or need where a more detailed discussion is likely warranted, such as "Would you please share your ideas as to how we can best plan and prepare for the upcoming design session?" While the former might best be accomplished via instant messaging, the latter may require a phone call or in-person discussion. For the latter, a nice marriage of two communication methods might serve you best in that you could instant message the individual asking, "Mind if I hop on your calendar for a quick discussion about the upcoming design session?" You can then follow up by scheduling a meeting when the individual is available. Incorporating other previously discussed manners of "please and thank you" and "be kind" will also serve you well in these situations.

HOLD THE DOOR

In its literal interpretation, we should of course still do this today (remember "be kind"), but how can we also apply this old-school learning in our professional environment? It is actually quite simple. Offer to help when help is needed. We often get bogged down in our own world and forget we have value to offer in other areas of the organization. By offering to help others, there are multiple benefits to be achieved. First, you are leading with kindness, and that will be respected. Second, you are showing you are willing to do anything and that you do not have the "that's not my job" mindsight. Lastly, you will likely become a better employee as you will learn more about the individual you are helping as well as the organization as a whole; you will be more educated as a result.

A wise approach is to always raise your hand, literally and figuratively, when given the opportunity and rarely say no. While you may feel overworked from time to time (as we all do), the value in raising your hand when volunteers are requested and not turning down opportunities that come your way will greatly outweigh the cost of performing the work.

CONCLUSION

To sum it up, surprise surprise, something you learned as a child is actually relevant in your adult life. Falling back on the manners outlined in this chapter will serve you well as you continue on your health information technology (IT) journey. So remember, say "please" and "thank you," be kind, pay attention, don't interrupt, and hold the door for others. And now, last but not least, thank you for your time!

20 Encouraging Diversity in the Workplace

John A. Mandujano
CPHIMS, PMP, CSM

CONTENTS

INTRODUCTION

The cultural and demographic character of the patient population is changing rapidly. To accept and prepare for this rapid change, the health information technology (IT) community, which is experiencing its own demographic changes, must embrace diversity to be successful in their initiative to deliver quality healthcare. In addition, as patients become more educated on medical procedures and risks, they also have more information regarding health grades among competing medical providers. If a provider organization intends to succeed in this competitive environment, it must leverage the best personnel with the best ideas, which may come from unfamiliar ethnic and cultural backgrounds.

ACCESS THE HEALTHCARE: A STATISTICAL REVIEW

Projections estimate that by 2050, there will be 2.3 billion additional people in the world.[1] In 2017, there were 19.9 million refugees, primarily leaving sub-Saharan African countries.[2] Poverty, civil disorder, extreme weather events, and war are fueling a refugee crisis. Addressing the refugee crisis without consideration of the causes creates slapdash, reactive government policies. This governmental reaction ignores the fact that refugees prefer to remain in their homeland. The United States is experiencing its own refugee crisis as displaced people from Guatemala and Mexico are creating immigration issues for similar reasons: poverty and civil unrest.

As agriculture requires fewer people to be productive and is less safe due to civil unrest, displaced migrants often seek refuge in urban environments. Increased urbanization in places like Lagos, Nigeria, and Central America often occurs without urban planning and without adequate infrastructure. Without sufficient sources of clean water and sewage treatment, these areas of urban sprawl become breeding grounds for infectious diseases.[3]

Prior to the enactment of the Patient Protection and Affordable Care Act (PPACA) of 2010, ethnic and minority groups did not have as much access to healthcare. Although there have been significant challenges to PPACA, the demand for healthcare coverage is not subsiding. Health sharing plans, short-term insurance, and limited benefit indemnity insurance programs are poised to replace PPACA[4]. Health coverage is recognized as being more important than ever. In 2009, 79% of African Americans, 68% of Hispanic Americans, and 88% of white Americans had health coverage. The resulting lack of health coverage is reflected in chronic health statistics. African Americans have higher rates of obesity, diabetes, hypertension, and heart disease than any other group. Hispanic women contract cervical cancer at twice the rate of white women. Hispanics are 50% more likely to die of diabetes as non-Hispanic whites [1]. In the United States, although the population is expected to grow more slowly, the mix of cultures, races, and nationalities will give that population a decidedly different content. In addition, changes within existing demographic groups will alter demands on healthcare delivery. An aging population creates new demands for different types of care. For example, Japan's aging population has created more demand for dementia care.[5] By 2030, one in five people in the United States will be 65 or older.

Due to the trend of people living longer, combined with lower birth rates, we see an increase in the number of multigenerational households. These multigenerational and shared households are less likely to be homogeneous as inter-racial relationships increase and, in the United States, are less likely to be Caucasian. In 1980, 12% of the population in the United States lived in a multigenerational household. By 2018, that percentage increased to 20%. In 2017, 32% of the U.S. adult population were part of a shared household.[6]

By 2044, more than half of all Americans are projected to belong to a minority group. And by 2060, nearly one in five of the United States' total population is expected to be foreign born. The Hispanic population in the United States is projected to increase from 55 million in 2014 to 119 million in 2060, an increase of 115% [2]. The number of Hispanic patients is increasing; yet, the number of Hispanic doctors is decreasing.[7] This disparity means healthcare workers will be more likely to treat patients with demographic characteristics different from their own. As more patients come from multigenerational and shared households, household members are more likely to participate in patient protocol decisions.

RESPECTING CULTURAL SENSITIVITIES

In most industries, customer service representatives must evaluate customers to determine their level of sensitivity. Healthcare workers are in a unique situation in that they are already aware, or should be aware, that all patients are especially sensitive. Patient families are also very sensitive. In many instances, this may be the patient's first exposure to a situation where their health is at risk. Healthcare workers are mindful that emotions are raw, and care must be taken to explain circumstances and protocols. Healthcare workers should carefully explain and describe the patient's problem and how it will be addressed. Healthcare workers also need to be certain that the patient and their family understand; this is a dialogue, not a lecture. This is a demanding situation where healthcare workers should avoid medical jargon. After all, the patient probably does not have a medical background. Prior to my working in a hospital, my ex-wife, who happened to be nurse, had a backache, and she asked me to get her something for the pain. I brought her acetaminophen. She yelled at me saying she needed an anti-inflammatory, not an analgesic. How was I to know? I am a reasonably intelligent person but, at the time, I lacked medical knowledge. Protocol explanations should be simple but not simplistic.

A new challenge for healthcare is that patients and their extended families are becoming more assertive in their treatments. There are reasonably well-educated patients that foolishly think their adherence to good food sources and careful attention will protect them against airborne viruses like measles. Patients are looking for alternative protocols that include substances like cannabidiol (CBD). We will see more involvement from extended and shared households.

We take into account a patient's cultural and religious background. For example, some patients may opt not to have a blood transfusion or an organ transplant for religious reasons. Being aware of a patient's culture is part of delivering quality care. That same courtesy should extend to fellow healthcare workers.

SHORTAGES OF HEALTHCARE WORKERS

The current shortage of healthcare workers, particularly among nurses, will increase the demand for alternatives like using more foreign-born healthcare workers. Healthcare workers with less than a bachelor's degree are racially and ethnically more diverse and overwhelming female. Men are the minority of all of these professions except for emergency medical technicians and paramedics [3]. Foreign-born or entry-level healthcare workers could perform specialized tasks like a Certified Nursing Assistant (CAN) or a phlebotomist, thereby easing the workload on staff.

The aforementioned shortage of healthcare workers will also increase pressure to utilize more technology to improve productivity and allow healthcare specialists to give more attention to patients. Some of these technologies might consist of telemedicine and advanced monitoring systems, including surgical implants. The health IT community, largely responsible for the implementation of these technologies, has also demographically changed dramatically in the past 20 years, largely due to the influx of H-1B non-immigrant workers [4] and the increasingly diverse population. Many students from South Korea, India, and China still arrive in the Unted States, and many choose to stay. The United States is considering a merit-based immigration policy, like Canada and Australia, and healthcare workers would have an advantage under that policy.[8] This is the situation: The landscape of the healthcare workplace is experiencing demographic changes in patient population, healthcare workers, and IT technicians. Healthcare organizations need to establish new structural policies and procedures, also known as cultural competence, to encourage and leverage diversity on all levels and to work effectively in this cross-cultural environment [5].

EQUAL EMPLOYMENT OPPORTUNITIES FOR ALL

In the United States, employers are required to provide equal employment opportunities (EEO) based on qualifications and related experience and not on the basis of extraneous factors such as race, color, religion, national origin, disability, age, gender, gender identity, sexual orientation, veteran status, or marital status. There are similar protections in other countries. It is incumbent on workers in any field to know the laws intended to protect them. Employers can also issue guidelines regarding conduct in the workplace and typically enforce zero tolerance toward discrimination or harassment. These policies are commendable, but one cannot judge a policy based on intentions. Large corporations satisfy many EEO goals by recruiting minorities at college job fairs, but similar opportunities for more experienced professionals are lacking. A better metric would track how minority employees advance within a corporation. If minority employees are not given high-profile assignments, their chances for advancement are impacted. This assignment of work favoring one group over another is an example of disparate discrimination and should not be tolerated. Eventually, this discrimination is reflected in the lack of minority representation on corporate boards of directors [6].

DIVERSITY PROGRAMS THAT RESPECT TIME AWAY FROM EMPLOYMENT

Diversity programs do not have to be a drudgery or stilted in regulation. It can be as simple of being more aware of holidays, including holidays we might take for granted. A foreign worker may not be aware that July 1 is Canadian Independence Day and July 4 is American Independence Day in the United States. Most cultures have a holiday that celebrates the annual harvest like

Thanksgiving, the fourth Thursday in November in the United States, but Canadian Thanksgiving is celebrated on the second Monday in October. Hindis in North America celebrate Diwali in autumn and often include elements of Thanksgiving. Inventive organizations incorporate Diwali with Thanksgiving for a celebration of food from all nationalities.

Some holidays are not actual holidays, but if the majority of employees do not come to work, it may seem like a holiday. For example, at some companies in upstate New York and Pennsylvania, so many people arrange personal time off on the first day of deer hunting season, it may seem like a holiday. In addition, someone originally from outside of the United States might be confused how Americans have appropriated St. Patrick's Day and Cinco de Mayo into unofficial holidays. The biggest unofficial holiday in the United States is the day after the American football championship game. Keeping everyone informed of respective holidays and non-holidays can be instructive and entertaining.

We can allow religion to divide us or unite us. Respecting each other's beliefs should direct us to concentrate on what we all have in common, like a belief in a higher power. A Muslim hijab is not very different than a veil or a habit a nun might wear or attire preferred by the Amish. Hindis might have a tilak on their forehead, much like Roman Catholics might have ashes on their forehead on Ash Wednesday. I believe the Camp David accord was successful because Jimmy Carter, Menachem Begin, and Anwar El Sadat respected each others' religious beliefs [7]. There are anomalies we can use as role models of people respecting religious beliefs, like when the Palestinians had a woman as their diplomatic spokesperson, or Dublin had a Jewish mayor and London now has a Muslim mayor.

LINGUISTIC RELATIVISM

Linguistic relativism hypothesizes that language affects cognition [8]. Imagine hearing a phrase where you know all the words but the words do not connect to your reality. To tell someone they are "out in left field" or "off base" or warned they already have "two strikes" is meaningless to someone unfamiliar with the sport of baseball. Or someone unfamiliar with American football may not realize a "Hail Mary", in this context, is a last-minute, desperate attempt at success. Even among Americans there can be misunderstanding. Someone recently told me they read me "five by five." Apparently, this is a military term meaning they understood me loud and clear. However, since I was never in the military, their message was unclear to me. In an environment where people accept each other's differences, there is no fear of asking for a definition of a colloquial phrase. One should not feel alienated if they ask for clarification if you use a term like "hunky-dory." A helpful phrase like "bindaas" can build bridges across cultures. "Bindaas" is Hindi slang for "cool."

MANAGEMENT AWARENESS AND SENSITIVITY

Being aware of current events in other cultures is also important. Current events that might affect foreign works include elections, changes in government policies, and extreme weather events. Personally, I have visited a hospital where the nurses were predominantly Filipino. Likewise, I also consulted at a pharmaceutical distribution corporation that used many contract IT workers from the Philippines. In either case, it is helpful to be aware when a typhoon impacts the Philippines. Understanding their concern for their families is completely understandable.

As some workers advance to middle management, many are now evaluated on how they have mentored others. Such mentoring initiatives can reap benefits throughout an entire organization. Like The Butterfly Effect in Chaos Theory [9] that says a butterfly flapping its wings at the right time and place in Africa could spur the creation of a hurricane in the Atlantic Ocean, encouragement at all levels to all employees has a ripple effect, encouraging advancement and productivity. Mentoring does not have to be a formal program, but it should recognize the importance of an encouraging environment. Identify talent and encourage it. The other side of that transaction is that we should all be open to accept mentoring and be willing to adapt. The extent to which you will improve is dependent upon your willingness to accept constructive guidance. If you are not comfortable with coaching or mentoring at work, seek out mentoring outside of the workplace. Mentors can be anyone you feel comfortable with.

When we think of role models, sometimes our first instinct is to look for someone who is like ourselves. I am a fan of the actor, comedian, writer John Leguizamo. He was born in Columbia, but he seems to be more aligned with people from Peurto Rico. When asked who he used as role models, he mentioned Lily Tomlin (a white woman), Whoopi Goldberg (a black woman), and Eric Bogosian (an American of Armenian descent).[9] Find a role model, and disregard their background. It is their creativity, motivation, and intelligence you should emulate.

You may not feel that you have achieved everything you want, but you can still be a mentor or a role model for someone else. Do not underestimate your experiences. If you see someone struggling, offer assistance. Sharing your understanding with someone with less experience will benefit both the mentor and mentee. How? The mentee has not had your experiences yet, and the mentor may look at obstacles with a new perspective as the mentee asks questions. In essence, a mentor is a more advanced student.

Organizationally, when a complaint is made, it is absolutely vital that an organization act quickly and decisively on complaints. Not acting quickly sends the message that the organization does not take complaints of discrimination or harassment seriously. Likewise, if we witness discriminatory behavior, it is our moral responsibility to speak up. We should know better. We should not have to cite respective codes of professional responsibility. Treating each other with respect should be the norm.

THE UNDER-REPRESENTED WORKFORCE

For those of us that are under-represented in the workforce, an honest self-examination is in order. What makes you different? Is it your race, heritage, religion, language, physical size, gender, sexual orientation, age, physical disability, political orientation, socio-economic status, occupational status, or geographical origin? There may be structural hindrances to diversity like caste systems, gender preferences, educational backgrounds, and politics. Your differences might be based on your experiences. For example, in an acute care setting, your opinion may be dismissed because you were never a healthcare worker like a doctor or a nurse.

Your self-appraisal should also recognize your strengths and weaknesses. If you are a technician, you may be more comfortable with statistics than you are presenting those statistics to a group of people. If this is the case, you should join a public speaking club to overcome those fears. If your weakness is more technical, take classes to shore up your technical skills. If you need strength for a group task, volunteer. If your team needs your guidance or leadership, it is your responsibility to provide what they lack. Too many people in the workforce want a job title but not the job. Take on the responsibility of leadership, and the title will come your way.

The truth is, if you are a member of a minority group, it is not enough to be competent. Everyone expects you to be competent. To advance, you should obtain certifications, pursue advanced education, and work harder. To stand out from your peers, you must take the initiative, like volunteering for leadership positions. If those opportunities are not forthcoming at work, volunteer outside of work, build your confidence, and bring that confidence back to your job. Your skills, both natural and acquired, will allow you to become an innovator, a contributor, and an early-adopter poised to make a big impression in your organization.

If access to support groups is limited, consider reaching out to a web-based community with similar interests. If you cannot find a community of like-minded people, start an organization. You will be surprised how people feel the same way you do.

Opportunities are not delivered to your doorstep. You have to pursue them and be prepared to act. When should you pursue opportunities? Recent studies have shown that male applicants typically do not possess 100% of the qualifications for a position, while female applicants will only apply for a position if they have all 100% of the qualifications [10]. Hiring organizations need to evaluate their judgment and recognize that males are being judged for their potential and females are being judged on their track record. They should be judged by the same criteria and be aware of gender bias. Part of the self-examination process should include identifying instances when you have held yourself back.

The Dalai Lama has said, "If every 8 year old in the world is taught meditation, we would eliminate violence from the world within one generation [11]." Consider how that same dynamic could be applied to educating under-represented children. Boosting diversity in the workplace, and thereby improving the competitive placement of healthcare organizations, begins with encouraging children to pursue their interests in the sciences and technology. A balanced education that includes science and the arts, to encourage creativity, would greatly improve all children. If a young girl or minority shows interest in science, we should all encourage that interest.

Initiatives like "Take Your Children to Work Day" are wonderful for showing children what adults do at work. Understandably, many that work at acute care facilities are unable to participate in such initiatives due to the nature of their work, liability insurance issues, and safety. In the absence of such participation, parents and guardians should teach their children about their careers, and they should also be involved in their children's education. I am most impressed with parents who take the time to work with their children on their home assignments. This degree of involvement is most admirable. Granted, due to circumstances beyond their control, not every guardian can meet this demand. A guardian's interest, any interest, in the progress of their progenies has a lasting impact.

RESPECTING OTHERS

In addition to learning subjects in school, a child's upbringing should also include lessons at home regarding teaching respect of other people. Respect for others is good parenting. Guardians need to communicate to their children the importance of courteous behavior or else children will consider other sources of information like the Internet, video games, or television programming as models of acceptable behavior. Learning respect for others begins with active parenting [12].

Patients and co-workers come from varied cultural backgrounds and experiences. Allow your good work ethic to guide your behavior. Concentrate on providing quality healthcare and excellent customer service and know that everyone around can contribute to that success.

Too often, we rely on what is legislated to guide our behavior. Too many unethically sanctioned legal policies like slavery, the Holocaust, and segregation are abhorrent in a civilized society. Even great thinkers like Aristotle and Thomas Aquinas relegated women to an inferior moral status. If we recognize everyone has equal moral status, it is more logical to accept an egalitarian society where differences are accepted. Indeed, we are different, but like two sides of a piece of currency, we are the same. We come from different backgrounds and have had different environmental factors that formed us. But together, we deliver healthcare to patients, like the seal of the United States declares, "E Pluribus Unum," which is Latin for "Out of many, one."

Many acute care facilities have interpreters on staff as well as post-operative care instructions in multiple languages. As a supplement to those efforts and to gain additional insight into the needs of a diverse and sometime unfamiliar patient population, I strongly suggest a tremendous resource on the Web from the U.S. Department of Health and Human Services, National Library of Medicine, and National Institute of Health: https://sis.nlm.nih.gov/outreach/multicultural.html. This web portal is specifically for healthcare professionals. Topics include guidelines for cultural competency in a healthcare setting, standards for interpreters, and information on many healthcare topics designed for different cultures.

NATIONAL LIBRARY OF MEDICINE'S OUTREACH AND SPECIAL POPULATIONS BRANCH

In 2000, the National Library of Medicine (NLM) created the Office of Outreach and Special Populations (OOSP) in the Division of Specialized Information Services (SIS) as a way to focus efforts to reach its objectives of improving access to quality and accurate health information in underserved and special populations. In 2008, the Office was elevated to the Outreach and Special Populations Branch (OSPB).

Outreach programs are developed in an effort to eliminate disparities in accessing health information by providing community outreach support, training health professionals on NLM's health information databases, and designing special population websites that address specific concerns in various racial and ethnic groups. SIS outreach programs reach health professionals, public health workers, and the general public, especially about health issues that disproportionately impact minorities such as environmental exposures and HIV/AIDS. OSPB collaborates with other components of NLM involved in similar activities, particularly the National Network of Libraries of Medicine and the Office of Health Information Programs Development.

OSPB is committed to improving access to toxicology and environmental health information to underserved communities, improving access to health-related disaster information in Central America, improving access to HIV/AIDS information resources by community-based organizations, and improving access to health information for all minorities and underserved populations.

SUMMARY

Patients, healthcare workers, and healthcare vendors are undergoing changes in their cultural, racial, and gender makeup. In order to compete and accept the challenge of providing quality healthcare in this changing environment, all players need to embrace diversity. Recognizing similarities, accepting each other's customs, and realizing our customs may seem unusual to others but helps to create an environment where we can all work together toward common goals.

NOTES

1 https://www.prb.org/2018-world-population-data-sheet-with-focus-on-changing-age-structures/
2 https://www.pewresearch.org/fact-tank/2018/07/05/for-the-first-time-u-s-resettles-fewer-refugees-than-the-rest-of-the-world/
3 https://www.sandoz.com/stories/system-capacity-building/changing-societies-and-healthcare-needs-three-demographic-trends
4 https://www.forbes.com/sites/johngoodman/2019/01/30/alternatives-to-obamacare/#59fcd64b61ff
5 https://www.sandoz.com/stories/system-capacity-building/changing-societies-and-healthcare-needs-three-demographic-trends
6 https://www.pewresearch.org/fact-tank/2018/04/25/7-demographic-trends-shaping-the-u-s-and-the-world-in-2018/
7 https://www.sandoz.com/stories/system-capacity-building/changing-societies-and-healthcare-needs-three-demographic-trends
8 https://www.pri.org/stories/2019-05-17/can-merit-based-immigration-system-modeled-canada-or-australia-work-us
9 http://nymag.com/nymetro/movies/features/10866/

REFERENCES

1. https://www.americanprogress.org/issues/healthcare/news/2010/12/16/8762/fact-sheet-health-disparities-by-race-and-ethnicity/
2. Colby, Sandra L. and Jennifer M. Ortman, Projections of the size and composition of the U.S. population: 2014 to 2060, Current Population Reports, P25–1143, U.S. Census Bureau, Washington, DC, 2014.
3. http://www.rand.org/news/press/2013/11/04/index1.html
4. http://www.judiciary.senate.gov/meetings/the-impact-of-high-skilled-immigration-on-us-workers
5. https://nccc.georgetown.edu/
6. http://www.nytimes.com/2014/06/01/business/not-walking-the-walk-on-board-diversity.html?_r=0
7. http://www.npr.org/2014/09/16/348903279/-13–days-in-september-examines-1978–camp-david-conference
8. http://www.linguisticsociety.org/resource/language-and-thought
9. http://fractalfoundation.org/resources/what-is-chaos-theory/
10. https://hbr.org/2014/08/why-women-dont-apply-for-jobs-unless-theyre-100–qualified
11. https://responsiveuniverse.me/2012/11/20/if-every-8-year-old-in-the-world-is-taught-meditation-we-will-eliminate-violence-from-the-world-within-one-generation-dalai-lama/
12. http://www.parents.com/toddlers-preschoolers/development/manners/the-return-of-respect/

21 The Aspiring Female Health IT Executive

Kristin Myers
MPH

CONTENTS

INTRODUCTION

As a female Chief Information Officer at Mount Sinai Health System, a $7 billion not-for-profit organization, I have been fortunate to have had supervisors, senior executives, colleagues, and my team be supportive of my career aspirations, and I have received the training and education needed to progress. I have been entrusted with many complex transformative programs exceeding $100 million which make a difference to our patient lives every day.

For the majority of the last 20 years in health information technology (IT), I have been very focused on my career development. My attitude has always been that I can achieve anything that I want to do or be, which was a common mantra from my parents since I was a child. My parents and brother always encouraged and supported me throughout my career and in all aspects of life.

However, in the last three years, after becoming a mother, I have had to change how I work, what I focus on and prioritize, and how I spend time with my son every single day. I have reflected on the many challenges, barriers, and opportunities that women face in the workplace and the many lessons learned in my career, which will be explored below. I recognize that not everyone has had a similar experience to me in their careers or the family support that I have had. I can only share what my experience has been to date in the workplace against the broader landscape of gender-related concerns.

WOMEN IN HEALTHCARE

While 78% of the healthcare workforce is comprised of women, women continue to lag in the executive ranks [1]. According to a 2015 Rock Health study [1], only 34% of executives at Top 100 hospitals were women, 27% of board members at Top 100 hospitals were women, 21% of board members at Fortune 500 healthcare companies were women, and only 6% of CEOs of funded digital health companies were women.

In a research study by Health Data Management about women and healthcare IT careers conducted in April 2016 [2], women still are facing challenges as they progress in their careers.

Career obstacles cited were the old boys' network, lack of mentoring programs, perceived lack of management experience/skills, lack of a peer support group, lack of diversity/inclusion initiatives, lack of flex time, and lost career momentum due to family leave. In addition, 29% of women in the survey stated that gender was a reason that they were not offered a promotion at some point in their healthcare career. Women are financially penalized for having a family. There is a 20% "motherhood penalty" on salary as women who are unmarried without children make 20% more than married mothers [1].

Research by the Healthcare Information and Management Systems Society (HIMSS) in the 2015 HIMSS Salary Calculator and Compensation Survey [3] has shown that first-year female health IT executives and senior managers receive 63% of the compensation of men in the same position. It takes a further 15 years to close the wage gap.

Gender pay differentials are unacceptable and must be acknowledged and addressed. Eliminating negotiations for pay and implementing salary transparency across organizations are two solutions that are frequently cited to end gender pay disparity. In the absence of these being implemented in the near future, women must add negotiating skills to their set of core competencies. This is an area that I have at times shied away from; however, after taking negotiation courses, and in some cases calling on a negotiation coach to work with, I recognize that it is an important skill to have.

Preparation is key to a successful negotiation by cataloguing your achievements and engaging in research about comparable salaries at other organizations similar to your own. This can be achieved informally by networking locally and at organizations that bring collective groups of health IT professionals together such as HIMSS. Practicing your negotiating skills with a mentor or a trusted advisor to refine your pitch is an important step in this process. According to Hannah Riley Bowles, a Harvard Law School course leader in negotiation, "use the pronoun 'we' instead of 'I' when making your pitch for a pay raise" [4]. Taking a communal approach to your salary negotiation as a woman "mitigates the negative reputational affects for women" [5]. Salary negotiations can be a difficult discussion to have with your supervisor; however, it is an important practice to develop and ultimately master for your economic well-being long term.

UNCONSCIOUS BIAS

There are some gender stereotypes that are deeply held in the workplace. An example is that women tend to be "nurturing and communal," and we expect men "to be ambitious and results-oriented." Studies have shown that in situations where identical help is given by both a man and a woman, "a man was significantly more likely to be recommended for promotions, important projects, raises, and bonuses. A woman had to help just to get the same rating as a man who didn't help" [6].

The tendency is for women to assist others and mentor others more privately, which can be time-consuming. Women (and men) achieve "the highest performance and experience the lowest burnout when they prioritize their own needs along with the needs of others [7]." One example cited by Adam Grant that resonated with me was instead of meeting one-on-one with junior colleagues or team members, have group lunches. I have adopted this practice by having lunch sessions on a leadership development book with 10–12 colleagues at a time, which saves me time and also provides a forum for support and learning [7].

According to the 2015 Rock Health Study [1], 50% of women have adopted male behaviors in order to advance their career, and 33% believe being female is disadvantageous to their career. It is hardly surprising that these views are held when many of the role models and mentors available to women have been men. Studies have shown that when "female executives spoke more than their peers, both men and women punished them with 14% lower ratings" [8].

Men and women at the workplace can counter the above narrative by creating a collaborative environment where ground rules are created and set by all members of the team at the beginning of the meeting, calling on women in meetings for their opinion and making sure that women sit at the table where the discussion is taking place. The more the workplace becomes accustomed to women speaking up, the more this bias. The longer-term solution is to increase the amount of women in leadership roles, which starts at the hiring process.

NETWORKING

One of the most important lessons I have learned over the years in my career is that time must be invested in networking every week. This was not an area that I focused on for most of my career as I was too busy and immersed in my day-to-day work. No matter how content you are in your current job, it is essential to network, as increasingly leadership is about "your ability to connect to others" [9]. Many women do not feel they have time for networking as they balance their careers, families, and other personal interests; however, this is a missed opportunity. Networking internally at your own organization creates that "space where professional boundaries are softened by personality, often paving the way for women to be more effective in driving initiatives forward in the workplace" [9].

I typically block my Friday calendar to be able to catch up on the week and to spend at least 1–2 hours networking, whether it be lunch with colleagues, responding to LinkedIn requests, reaching out to other executives/mentors and coaches to discuss healthcare IT trends, and giving/receiving advice. I also think it is important to join organizations/associations that align with your career aspirations, such as HIMSS, American College of Healthcare Executives (ACHE), American Medical Informatics Association (AMIA), College of Healthcare Information Management Executives (CHIME), and/or Project Management Institute (PMI). Joining your local chapter of these organizations can be a good first step.

MENTORING AND SPONSORSHIP

A critical component to career advancement is mentoring. Lack of access to mentors is still a barrier for women. Many women do not have a female mentor or do not have a mentor at all. In the Health Data Management Research Study: Most Powerful Women in Healthcare IT [2], lack of mentoring programs was cited as a top challenge. In my career, I have had different mentors for different time periods. Some of been formal; some have been more informal. The majority of the mentors that I have worked with have been men. More recently I have had the opportunity to meet other senior executive women outside of my workplace and have incorporated these women as part of my network to call upon when I need coaching and/or mentoring. It is important for women to take advantage of their network to identify mentors. I mentor both men and women; however, we have a special responsibility to coach, develop, and mentor other women.

One of my professors at Columbia University spoke about the concept of sponsorship in her career, which changed my viewpoint on mentoring in a fundamental way. While mentoring is important, securing sponsorship is more effective. Sponsoring is advocating for someone to receive a job or promotion, actively assisting that person to advance. Sponsorship can make a real and significant difference in women helping other women advance in their careers:

"A sponsor can lean in on a woman's behalf, apprising others of her exceptional performance and keeping her on the fast track. With such a person—male or female—in her corner, our data shows, a woman is more likely to ask for a big opportunity, to seek a raise and to be satisfied with her rate of advancement" [10].

MOVING UP THE CAREER LADDER

In terms of career advancement, the only person who can make that happen is you. I have always been interested in understanding what it is like to work in different roles within IT as well as hospital administration. Through my network, I have been fortunate enough to be able to reach out to contacts or referrals, people in positions of Chief Information Officer, Chief Operating Officer, or Chief of Staff to the Chief Executive Officer. In my discussions, I learned about their journey to the role, their education, why they were chosen, what key skills are important for the role, and what lessons learned would they advise someone considering the role. The knowledge imparted in these discussions has helped me refine my career goals. It also highlighted a gap in my education, as most of the people I spoke to had a master's degree (i.e., MBA or MPH). This led me to enroll and complete my master's of public health at Columbia University.

It is also important once your career goals are refined to share them with your manager. At Mount Sinai Health System we have an opportunity to do this via an Individual Development Plan, which focuses on your career goals, what training and education you need, or exposure in the organization to reach the next level. If there is not a process in place, having a career discussion with your manager is important so he or she can sponsor your career progression, provide feedback as to what competencies are required to progress, or just be aware that you would like to take on greater responsibilities, so when these opportunities come up, you are on the short list to be chosen.

I also recommend at key career points having an external coach. This person can be a trusted friend or professional who is paid and is willing to speak the truth about your strengths, weaknesses, and areas of value. Coaches have challenged my perspective in a positive way.

WHAT ARE THE OPPORTUNITIES FOR CHANGE?

In order for there to be gender parity in the workplace, we need men to be sponsors and advocates for the change. Frequently, organizations rely on women for gender and diversity initiatives. Men are untapped resources that need to be engaged and not alienated for the real and long-lasting organizational change. According to a study by the Catalyst group in 2009, "the higher men's awareness of gender bias, the more likely they were to feel that it was important to achieve gender equality" [11]. The study also demonstrated that "men who had been mentored by women were more aware of gender bias than men who had not had this experience" [11]. We need men to sponsor the organizational change around fairness, which starts with gender diversity in the hiring process and developing a culture that is based upon flexibility and is respectful of employee priorities. The organization environment needs to recognize the many ways that employees add value, such as informal mentoring and development of team members or volunteering. Each of us has had different life experiences that can be valuable to the team as a whole: "The overall goal in the workplace is to get to a point where you evaluate people by total contribution. But to get there, you have to be open to acknowledging biases. If men are willing to speak up for and advocate work that isn't being appreciated, it would improve equality for everyone" [12].

CONCLUSION

In conclusion, there are a number of opportunities for change in the workplace for women. As a female leader, I feel strongly that women supporting one another and sponsoring to create opportunities is a responsibility of leadership. It is critically important to career success to have a mentor and/or a sponsor. Seek out mentors, and accept opportunities to mentor other women. View networking as a key to developing strong professional relationships rather than seeing it as political or insincere. There are many organizations and publications that focus on change and gender parity, such as HIMSS [13], TechWomen [14], and Healthcare IT News [15] to name a few. Getting involved in these networks can be a good first step. Finally, be intentional about your career, and learn to negotiate.

REFERENCES

1. Rock Health. 2015. The State of Women in Healthcare. https://rockhealth.com/state-women-healthcare-update/
2. Health Data Management. 2016. Most Powerful Women in Healthcare IT: Research Study. http://www.healthdatamanagement.com/whitepaper/the-status-of-women-in-healthcare-it
3. HIMSS. 2015. HIMSS Salary Calculator and Compensation Survey. http://www.himss.org/compensationSurvey
4. Lutz, K. 2016. Salary Negotiation Skills Different for Men and Women. http://www.pon.harvard.edu/daily/salary-negotiations/salary-negotiation-skills-different-for-men-and-women/
5. Slavina, V. 2016. Why Women Must Ask (The Right Way). https://www.themuse.com/advice/why-women-must-ask-the-right-way-negotiation-advice-from-stanfords-margaret-a-neale
6. Heilman, M.E., and Parks-Stamm, E.J. 2007. Gender stereotypes in the workplace: Obstacles to women's career progress. In S.J. Correll (Ed.), *Social Psychology of Gender. Advances in Group Processes* (Volume 24) 47–78. Elsevier, JAI Press.
7. Sandberg, S., and Grant, A. 2015. Madam CEO., Get Me a Coffee. https://www.nytimes.com/2015/02/08/opinion/sunday/sheryl-sandberg-and-adam-grant-on-women-doing-office-housework.html
8. Sandberg, S., and Grant, A. 2015. Speaking While Female. http://www.nytimes.com/2015/01/11/opinion/sunday/speaking-while-female.html
9. Bartz, C., and Lambert, L. 2014. Why Women Should Do Less and Network More. http://fortune.com/2014/11/12/why-women-should-do-less-and-network-more/
10. Hewlett, S. 2013. Mentors are Good. Sponsors are Better. http://www.nytimes.com/2013/04/14/jobs/sponsors-seen-as-crucial-for-womens-career-advancement.html
11. Catalyst. 2009. Engaging Men in Gender Initiatives. http://www.catalyst.org/system/files/Engaging_Men_In_Gender_Initiatives_What_Change_Agents_Need_To_Know.pdf
12. Sandberg, S., and Grant, A. 2014. When talking about Bias Backfires. http://www.nytimes.com/2014/12/07/opinion/sunday/adam-grant-and-sheryl-sandberg-on-discrimination-at-work.html
13. http://www.himss.org/get-involved/roundtables/women-health-it
14. https://www.techwomen.org/
15. http://www.healthcareitnews.com/womeninhit

22 Joining the C-Suite

John P. Hoyt
FACHE, FHIMSS

CONTENTS

INTRODUCTION

The CIO is a member of the C-Suite, but what does that really mean for a new CIO? What skills and competencies are expected of C-Suite members that are different from the skills needed for the day-to-day interactions that the former health information technology (IT) professional, now turned CIO, would have used with their staff in the last few years?

Having the most senior person responsible for health IT becoming a member of the C-Suite was an idea championed by the College of Healthcare Information Management Executives (CHIME) in 1992, where the founding members defined the CIO as the "highest ranking IT executive of a provider organization and a member of the executive committee." That helped fuel the move of IT Directors into the C-Suite.

So quickly, what is the C-Suite? The C-Suite is generally also called the Executive Committee of the hospital or the health system. (This definition, of course, also applies to non-healthcare businesses as well). The C-Suite is the senior-most committee for strategy development and execution directing in the organization. Typically, in a hospital or an Integrated Delivery Network (IDN) the C-Suite would include, but not be limited to, the CEO, COO, CO, CFO, CMO, CMIO, CNIO, CTO, and CISO. Certainly there are variations in membership which will be a derivative of the size and complexity of the organization and its local market. No doubt, in highly competitive markets with a high managed care payer mix, we may likely see the senior-most person for contract management and also the senior-most person for marketing and public relations in the C-Suite. Large health systems with their own legal staff may also have the Chief Legal Counsel in the C-Suite.

So, why should the CIO be a member of the C-Suite? Today that question may seem superfluous, but in the 1990s that was an open question. This author clearly remembers conversations with a new CEO who wondered why the "IT guy" would need to be with executives. Doesn't the

"IT guy" belong in the basement printing green bar paper? Well, clearly the world of healthcare delivery was changing as those thoughts were articulated.

As we know, health IT is so pervasively integral to the success of healthcare delivery that the CIO needs to be involved in the leadership of the health system. Other C-Suite members see it that way as well. The success of the CIO and the projects they lead and the investments they make need the support of the other C-Suite members. Conversely, the other C-Suite members need the CIO to be successful for their programs to be successful. It is a symbiotic relationship. This recognition of the integral nature of health IT to virtually all of the current healthcare initiatives, beginning with early EMRs in the early 1990s to the role of health IT for population health, marketing with websites and patient portals, plus finance and supply chain has led to the unquestionable need for the CIO to be in the Executive Committee.

The C-Suite has core members who are deeply involved in patient care: the CNO, CMO, VP of Professional Services, a VP over ambulatory practices. Other members are peripheral to patient care: the Chief Marketing Officer, CFO, and the CIO. However, the CIO can have more of a positive or negative affect on patient care. It is imperative that the CIO understand the patient care processes throughout the continuum of care. The CIO should "walk the floors" with the fellow C-Suite members, VP of Nursing or the Chief Medical Officer, to really be familiar with the processes that the health IT function needs to support.

SO, WHAT SKILLS AND COMPETENCIES ARE NEEDED FOR THE C-SUITE?

The C-Suite are the leaders of the organization; the managers of the organization report up to them. Is leading different than managing? Certainly so, say numerous academics since the 1970s such as Warren Bennis, who was one of the first to write extensively on leaders versus managers. Managing is maintaining the base, dealing with the status quo, making sure that there is no serious upheaval so that business as we know it can continue.

So, how is that different from leading? Leading is about creating new realities, about looking at the horizon more than looking at the bottom line. Leaders define a vision and, just as importantly, articulate and communicate the vision. Leaders inspire trust and ask what and why instead of how and when.

Are CIOs prepared to do this after a career as a Health IT Director? Where a Health IT Director has been focusing inward to "run the business of health IT," the CIO will look outward and into the future to help define how IT will serve the enterprise in new future initiatives. To better understand how health IT investments can assist in patient care, the CIO will need a solid understanding of the patient care processes.

KEY COMPETENCIES FOR LEADERSHIP

The book, *Exceptional Leadership,* by authors Carson F. Dye and Andrew N. Garman, published by Health Administration Press, provides excellent guidance on the competencies needed for leadership by the CEO and members of the C-Suite. This book is a guide to this next portion of this chapter. There are certain skills, or competencies as the authors put it, that define exceptional leadership, which are needed to make the health system successful in achieving its goals and executing its strategy. The CIO, as an equal member of the C-Suite, needs to be equally skilled in these competencies to be successful as a contributing member of the leadership team. So what are these main competencies?

Positive Self-Concept

Why would this be the first competency to mention? Leaders with a positive self-concept are confident in their ability to achieve what they set out to do. Leaders need a transformational style to move the organization in a significantly different direction than it has been steadily heading in the recent past. Leaders need followers, and followers are intrigued by charismatic leadership, which fundamentally takes a positive self-concept. Leaders with a positive self-concept can certainly have failures; however, "failures and setbacks may bother them, but they do not tear them apart" [1].

Leaders with a positive self-concept are very capable of successfully working with others. As stated, leaders need followers. Executives who are very poor at working with others will simply have fewer followers, and thus a significantly diminished success rate: "Leaders with a positive self-concept do not have to tear down others to bring themselves up" [1].

CIOs need a positive self-concept as much as any other executive in the C-Suite. Is this different than they needed as a Health IT Director? Probably not, except their audience and "followership" is much broader now that the entire enterprise is involved, so the skill may need to be stronger and more pronounced in the CIO's persona.

A positive self-concept enables the leader to live by their personal convictions. These personal convictions suggest to them how the world should be, according to Dye and Garman. That enables clarification of their vision, which we will address later.

There are boundaries to this competency as well. Being overly moralistic, or ascribing to "my way or the highway" because there is over-conviction, so to speak, will work against the CIO if they are perceived as being too self-righteous in their personal convictions.

Possessing Emotional Intelligence

"Long-term effectiveness depends on the quality of the leader's working relationships, which are in turn a function of the leader's capacity to understand and work effectively with emotions—of others as well as themselves" [2]. Emotional intelligence is a concept that emerged in business academic writings in the early 1990s. Emotional intelligence pertains to the concept of understanding other people's emotions while understanding and managing your own emotions and responses to others. Emotions play a major role in leadership. There are discussions and planning sessions where emotions can get very "heated." The CIO is in a position to take blame for every fault that IT brings to the users. Angry medical staff members who feel that patient care is jeopardized will test the emotional intelligence of any CIO. Successful CIOs, like any successful C-Suite member, will have a strong emotional intelligence to help them map their way through the tumultuous waters of health IT deployment.

Emotional intelligence enables leaders to confidently engage in dialogue and planning with others, both internally and externally. Truthfully and selfishly engaging with others to work on common goals and strategies engenders trust, and trust enables followers to follow. Remember, a leader is not a leader without followers.

The lack of sufficient emotional intelligence can appear as not trusting others. One major symptom of this is not delegating to staff, which, in turn, does not enable staff to develop. This creates a long-term problem for the entire organization, especially since so many health IT projects require successful cross-functional teams to work together for several years. CIOs need to be cognizant of their emotional intelligence and hone the skill to enable successful leadership and comradery with fellow C-Suite members.

The Vision

It's all about the vision right? This is clearly a significant competency for the CEO who wants to lead the organization in a different direction than it has been in its recent past. The same can be said about the CIO who needs to define a vision and future state with the use of health IT. The CIO will be in a position to articulate the vision to board members and fellow executive committee members, as well as rank and file workers as investments in healthcare IT ramp up. Being a visionary means that the CIO needs to have a broad awareness of industry trends and needs to articulate the value of those trends to the enterprise stakeholder groups.

There are several key skills within this very important category. The first is knowing which of the broader trends in the industry are appropriate for the enterprise at this point in time. Some CIOs have been rightly accused of seeking "technology for technology's sake." This can be an extremely strong "turn-off" for other members of the executive committee. Is the organization a cautious, conservative organization that takes change slowly? If that is the case, then some technologies, such as RFID employee badges for logging hand-washing time, may be totally inappropriate. The CIO must be able to appropriately judge the value of the technology, the current enterprise strategy, and the role that health IT is expected to play in that strategy, as well as the organization's current ability to absorb and utilize technology.

Second, the CIO needs to define which evolving technologies best align with the organization's strategic plan. If the organization is intent on building an integrated delivery system (IDS) and a clinically integrated network (CIN), then the CIO must have the skillset to lead the organization in adopting the technologies that are most likely to serve accomplishing the strategic intent of the organization. Furthermore, the CIO must be able to resist those who may push for "the latest coolest thing" if it does not clearly serve the strategic needs of the organization. In the IT department, and even in the medical staff, there will be those who push for the adoption of cutting-edge technologies because they are new and "cool." The CIO must convincingly resist this as a distraction if it clearly does not meet the strategic needs of the organization. Failure to do so if it is not appropriate for the organization will certainly be a negative impression for the CIO among the C-Suite.

Third, articulating the vision. What good is a vision if it cannot be explained? The vision of health IT must be clearly explained to several audiences with widely different perspectives. The idea of articulating a vision is to teach its value and to engender support. Few Americans who were born before the late 1960s can forget hearing President John F. Kennedy articulate the vision of landing an astronaut on the moon before the end of the decade of the 1960s. The articulation of the vision achieved two purposes: explain the vision and engender support for it.

CIOs must be able to do the very same thing, explain the vision and engender support for it. But, do CIOs have any particular issues in this competency to address that other members of the C-Suite may not have? This author believes that yes, they do. For many CIOs who have "come up through the ranks," their strength is in understanding and using technology. For those people who have used IT in a development mode for years have spent much "one-on-one" time with a keyboard and a monitor. This author thinks it is fair to say that this could lead to less developed verbal and social interaction skills than other members of the C-Suite. The CIO can quickly lose support with "techy talk," and too many CIOs often fall into that trap. So, this author thinks it is fair to say that the skill of articulating the vision may be more important, and possibly more of a challenge, for the CIO than other members of the executive committee. Thus, it could be a notable failure point that shortens CIOs' careers.

Overreliance on the vision compared to other competencies can lead followers to lose faith in the vision. Too often overreliance can lead to multiple "visioning exercises," and thus followers may "wait this one out until we re-vision next year." An overreliance on the vision can also lead to an inadequate focus on operations. Of course, operational failures in the IT department can have an extremely detrimental effect on clinical and financial operations.

The CIO will be called upon to conduct visioning exercises where ideas are percolated for potential health IT investments and operational improvements. These exercises will be performed in executive committee and board retreats as well as with directors, mid-level managers, and day-to-day users of systems. To manage these exercises effectively, the CIO will need to have excellent social skills, group dynamics understanding, and the ability to hear negative news without a defensive reaction. The first attribute that we mentioned, a healthy self-concept, is a key ingredient to manage visioning exercises where negative information may be a frequent subject.

The vision and the articulating of the vision are often cited as the major skillset that separate leaders from managers. This obviously is a skill for which the CIO will need to have an excellent grasp to be a successful member of the C-Suite.

Earning Loyalty and Trust

It was previously stated that leaders are not leaders without followers. Loyalty and trust makes followers stay with the leader "through thick and thin." But trust takes years to develop. Clearly, a leader has to earn trust, not demand it.

Well, how do you earn trust? Trust can be earned through openness of conversation by encouraging dissenting opinions, being accessible, and being a role model inside the workplace as well as outside the workplace. Many organizations ask their leadership to conduct charitable activities outside the workplace not only to assist in the value of the charitable activity, but to also engender trust of the organization's leadership.

So, how do you turn trust into loyalty? With success over time and with serving the self-interest of the followers, trusted leaders develop a loyal following: "Exceptional leaders are capable of taking these individual interests and finding ways to bring them into alignment with the organization's goals" [3].

So how would a CIO who has gained trust and loyalty lose it? By not "walking the walk and talking the talk." Failing to lead by example and not taking ownership of the problems is a fast way that CIOs can lose trust and loyalty. How often can the CIO say, "it's the vendor's fault," or "the end user made mistakes," etc.? While there certainly are times when that will be the case, a CIO who consistently fails to lead by acknowledging their leadership responsibility will quickly lose trust and loyalty, and that is the beginning of the end for many CIOs.

Mentoring Others, Developing Teams, and Being an Active Listener

So many tasks that IT leaders need to direct, manage, and see to fruition involve team efforts. Implementing clinical systems requires health IT leadership to work closely with clinicians to make certain that the software and workflow processes work together to serve clinicians and to improve patient care. The CIO is responsible for building a sense of "we," of building self-supporting teams.

Mentoring is also a leadership skill that eventually serves individual mentees as well as the teams of which they are a member. Mentoring is the activity of providing advice to and guiding an individual to help them meet their potential to achieve their career goals. The art of mentoring and developing individuals is to enable them to not need as much guidance. In other words, one could say that a successful mentoring manager "should work themselves out of a job."

A very key skill that enables successful mentoring is active listening. CIOs need to be active listeners. Active listening involves demonstrating that you are listening and not just waiting for your turn to speak. An active listening technique is repeating back to the speaker "what I heard you say is…". Active listening helps the CIO understand the person and their aspirations and goals, thus enabling the CIO to staff project teams with a deeper level of interpersonal trust. Active listeners take the time to focus on the individual and their opinions. Active listeners do not make the speaker feel rushed or make the speaker feel like they have to avoid a volatile reaction.

So why are mentoring, team building, and active listening so important for an executive committee member such as the CIO? The CIO's direct reports as well as the project team members must be convinced that their individual interests are served by listening to and following the CIO. The CIO needs to build strong relationships with all direct reports and team members, not just those who obviously need assistance. That strong relationship is built upon a solid understanding of the individual's personal goals and a perception of a clear opportunity to personally grow to achieve those goals. It is the exceptional leader who enables the alignment of personal goals with organizational goals and staffs the project teams accordingly.

The delicate balancing of the interdependence of team members, each with their own goals, must result in an alignment of these goals with a common purpose. Exceptional leadership involves the skills of mentoring, team building through trust development, team member selection, active listening, developing a spirit of seeking a common goal, and helping teams work through inevitable internal conflicts that teams will have.

Generating Informal Power

What exactly is "informal power"? Informal power is defined as the ability to influence others. It is the ability to influence; attain cooperation from; and most probably gain access to resources, funds, and opportunities inside the organization. A CIO will need to use both formal and informal power to achieve the goals to meet the intent of the strategic plan.

But how do you use power that is not "formal" as displayed on an organization chart? Dye and Garman tell us that it requires the knowledge and sensitivities of people's relationships and the ability to use that knowledge creatively. Politicians speak of "political capital" that is expended as needed to influence others. The exceptional leader CIO will generate such influence and will use it sparingly and appropriately. And such expending of informal power will not necessarily be with the names that always appear at the top of the organization chart. The CIO will need to know who may wield the most power and influence within a division or department.

Let us not be blind to the fact that informal power can be used too frequently to the detriment of the leader. Playing power politics, getting back at people who did not support you, and focusing too much on your own agenda could turn informal power against the CIO. So, it is clear that informal power can take time to gain and not much time to lose.

Building Consensus and Making Decisions

For sure, not all decisions that executives make are consensus-backed decisions. First, the CIO leader needs census building skills. This relates so tightly with competencies that we have mentioned before:

* Creating and articulating a vision
* Building trust and loyalty
* Building teamwork

These competencies lay the groundwork for potential consensus, but only the potential. It is great if a CIO can have consensus for decisions without "blind yes man loyalty" as in a dictatorship. But if the consensus is not there, then decision-making skills will be needed.

Dye and Garman tell us that decision-making skills are learned skills that can be refined. Exceptional leaders "decide how to decide" and use a defined, predictable decision-making process. The authors suggest that exceptional leaders keep a log of their decisions so that they can study the log carefully over the years to determine if patterns emerge. CIOs need to show evidence that there is a strong degree of transparency in their decision-making process and that they act with consistency and integrity.

Failure to have a known decision-making process can wreak havoc on the organization. We are all familiar with the concept of analysis paralysis, which is often an indication of a fear of making a wrong decision or being extremely risk adverse. Good decision makers have an excellent sense of timing. Analysis paralysis is the antithesis to timely decision making.

Driving Results to a Higher Level

Exceptional leaders from the C-Suite drive the organization to achieve a higher level of goals. But that gap between the leader's expectations and the mid-level managers needs to be addressed flexibly with the skills that still engender support and loyalty. Defining goals is not the same thing as driving results. CIOs need to establish a series of performance behaviors or performance habits. CIOs need to ensure that goals are clarified, that progress is regularly tracked, and, importantly, that success is acknowledged. This latter point cannot be underestimated for CIOs because of the nature of system design, implementation, and go-live support. These are tremendously stressful times for health IT project teams, and we must ensure they are supported with recognition for their hard work. This certainly can be extended to vendor partners as well. The CIO's responsibility is to build a solid relationship with the vendor side of the health IT projects and investment. There is no reason that celebrations of success should routinely exclude the vendor personnel as well.

CONCLUSION

When a CIO makes the move from a Health IT Director or an Associate CIO to a position in the C-Suite, significantly different competencies are needed to work successfully with other, more experienced, members of the executive committee. There are numerous competencies that others may think of, but these should be considered the key competencies that the CIO must embrace and exhibit in day-to-day life. Developing and honing these skills is a lifetime effort. We always can improve them, but clearly, a new member of the C-Suite needs to focus on these competencies defined here. A CIO can find a mentor in the C-Suite to help them begin this self-development process. And certainly, other CIOs who have been successful members of C-Suite can also serve as a mentor.

REFERENCES

1. Carson F. Dye and Andrew N. Garman, *Exceptional Leadership: 16 Critical Competencies for Healthcare Executives* (Chicago: Health Administration Press, 2006), xxvii.
2. Carson F. Dye and Andrew N. Garman, *Exceptional Leadership: 16 Critical Competencies for Healthcare Executives* (Chicago: Health Administration Press, 2006), 17.
3. Carson F. Dye and Andrew N. Garman, *Exceptional Leadership: 16 Critical Competencies for Healthcare Executives* (Chicago: Health Administration Press, 2006), 57.

Section V

The Importance of Lifelong Learning

23 Earning an Advanced Degree

Tiffany Champagne-Langabeer
PhD, MBA

CONTENTS

INTRODUCTION

This book illustrates the many facets of lifelong learning and its positive impact on the health informatics professional. In this chapter, the focus will build upon several concepts already discussed earlier, such as identifying your professional potential, diversifying your skillset, and developing your career roadmap. We will concentrate specifically, however, on the process of considering and earning an advanced degree.

This chapter is organized in five sections (or steps) that systematically move lifelong learning from a casual thought process to a concrete set of activities that culminate in earning a graduate degree. The first of these (Step 1) takes readers through the process of considering all options, which helps to explore the decision process for ensuring that you really can and should pursue a degree now. Step 2 describes the admission process and identifying the right program and university. Step 3 describes the process of gaining admission for that program and the types of activities necessary to complete before a university can accept you. Step 4 describes briefly what happens when you have been admitted and now must work your way through the 30- to 60-hour academic program. Finally, Step 5 provides some guidance on what learners should do when they graduate. Figure 23.1 summarizes the major stages of earning an advanced degree.

DOI: 10.4324/9780429398377-28

FIGURE 23.1 Stages of earning a graduate degree.

CONSIDERING THE GRADUATE DEGREE OPTION (STEP 1)

The decision to earn an advanced degree is both exciting and intimidating: exciting because it can open up new opportunities, but intimidating if one has not been in an academic setting for some time. Returning to school for advanced study will alter the quality of one's life, not only for the short term but for the long term as well. The choice to earn an advanced degree must be carefully considered. Seeking another degree will take a significant amount of time and resources and, depending on the degree, can impact up to six years of a person's life.

The rewards, however, are significant, including the potential for increased salary, advancement in one's career, and a substantial boost to personal confidence and efficacy. According to the career website Monster.com and the U.S. Bureau of Labor Statistics data, candidates with a bachelor's degree working as a health informatics specialist could expect to earn a median salary of $60,000, while one with a master's degree working in an information management position could earn as much as $90,000 (Bureau of Labor Statistics, 2016; Monster.com, 2016). The field of health informatics has exploded as a result of the Health Information Technology for Economic and Clinical Health (HITECH) Act of 2009 and the resultant mandates for electronic medical records implementations and interoperability, not to mention the flourishing entrepreneurial mobile health (mHealth) field. There is a growing demand for those trained in health informatics. The opportunities are abundant for more and more highly skilled workers in the field.

In larger healthcare organizations, there are often hundreds and even thousands of information technology (IT) professionals. Some examples of potential positions, which often require a graduate degree in the health IT field, include the following: Director of Medical Informatics, Assistant Vice President of Information Management, Clinical Data Analyst, Lead Developer or Data Manager of EHR Applications, Compliance Officer (especially for those with a legal background), Chief Medical Information Officer (physician informaticist), Chief Nursing Information Officer (nurse informaticist), Research and Development, Systems Analyst, Clinical Informatician, and Senior Consultant. These are just a few examples among many possibilities depending on the professional's background, area of interest, and desired career path. This does not take into account the myriad of fascinating options in the entrepreneurial field, where health informatics professionals can develop new software, solutions, and companies. For many professionals, earning an advanced degree affords the chance to not only grow in their careers but to embark upon something new and exciting.

Before committing to a life-altering decision, there are several questions to consider:

- What type of degree will I earn and in what type of organization?
- What modality works for my schedule, such as online or in person?
- If in person, are there evening classes?
- Should I consider a weekend only or executive program?
- What university is best for me to attend?
- How will I finance my education?
- What is the process for applying to graduate school?
- How will I balance work, family, and social life?
- Can I manage the additional stress of being a student…again?
- Where do I see myself after this degree?

The next sections of this chapter will focus in detail on addressing these questions. This will later culminate in a decision matrix, which learners can adapt to their own needs to determine the best path forward. This practical tool can be used to assist professionals considering several programs to weigh the best options in an objective manner.

FINDING THE RIGHT PROGRAM (STEP 2)

Once a learner has determined they are ready to pursue a graduate degree, the second major step involves identifying the right degree program, campus, and university to apply for admission. This is more complicated than it seems. There are literally thousands of graduate programs and degree concentrations throughout the country. Some are online; some are accredited (or officially recognized by a governing body); some are low-cost; and some focus on healthcare primarily, while others offer only a few courses in health IT. In order to identify the right program for you, it is necessary to think through a number of areas, such as "which degree should I earn?"

Choosing a Degree Program

There are several types of graduate degrees a health IT professional can consider when seeking an advanced degree. After obtaining a bachelor's degree, the next obvious step is to seek either a graduate certificate or master's level degree. In this chapter, we will focus on a master's degree program. Most professionals currently working in health IT likely have a degree related to the field either in some type of technology or in a healthcare-related area. However, there are also many cases where successful professionals with liberal arts degrees are working in the field. In either case, the option to pursue an advanced degree for professional advancement should follow the desired and future career path. Someone with a bachelor's of history or English should consider a master's level degree in the health IT field, given they would like to advance in health IT, as opposed to the fields of history or English.

One of the first questions is to decide which specific degree to obtain. Although not an exhaustive list, Table 23.1 lists several of the degrees a student may encounter and consider for either a master's or doctorate level degree.

Although a few students may opt to directly seek a doctoral degree following their bachelor's programs, these students tend to be those who wish to pursue a research or academic profession, to become professors. For most working professionals, the master's level degree is the logical next step for those seeking an applied, professional path. For those who already have a master's degree and are considering a doctoral degree, this is a lengthy path and most often requires a full-time commitment to education. Traditionally, there are fewer program options for doctoral degrees in health IT, and they tend to be more technically focused. These intense programs prepare students to become thought leaders, researchers, and university faculty. The finale of this path characteristically requires the student move locations for a faculty position, so additional consideration is required for making the doctoral leap. In recent months due to the increased demand for an applied doctorate of health informatics, an innovative university in Texas has developed a Doctorate of Health Informatics (D.H.I.). This program is designed for professionals with experience in the field of health IT at the supervisory or managerial level and who also hold a degree in a related field. Other options for working professionals who wish to attain a doctoral degree but not strictly for research include those with a focus on healthcare administration or another applied health field such as nursing (D.N.P. or D.N.) or public health (Dr. P.H.). Many D.N.P., D.N., and Dr.P.H. programs offer concentrations in health IT as an optional area of focus. Most programs with this level of specialization will be located in urban areas with major academic medical centers.

The total number of credit hours required for a master's degree ranges from 36 to 60 hours, and similar to undergraduate courses, most classes are 3 hours per course. The time it takes to graduate will depend on a number of factors, including: full-time versus part-time attendance; how many

TABLE 23.1

Listing of Degrees with Potential Health IT Concentration or Minor

M.S.	Master of Science in Bioinformatics, Project Management, Computer Science, Health Informatics, Clinical Informatics, Healthcare Information and Information Management	Primary degree focus and coursework in information sciences and management
M.S.M.I.	Master of Science in Medical Informatics	
M.Sc.	Master of Science	Courses and concentrations available in computer science, IT, or information sciences
M.S.I. or M.S.A.	Master of Science in Information; Master of Science in Analytics	
M.I.S.	Master of Information Systems	
M.S.I.M.	Master of Science in Information Management	
P.S.M.	Professional Science Masters also H.I. P.S.M. (Health Informatics)	
M.H.A	Master in Health Administration	Courses and concentrations available in information sciences and management
M.S.P.H.	Master of Science in Public Health	
M.P.H.	Master of Public Health	
M.B.A	Master of Business Administration	
Ph.D.	Doctor of Philosophy	
Dr. P.H.	Doctor of Public Health	
D.H.A	Doctor of Health Administration	

courses are taken per semester; if summer coursework is available; and if a culminating thesis (or research project) is required. It is reasonable for a dedicated, full-time student to complete an advanced degree in two years, while a part-time student might take an additional year or two, depending on the course load. Seeking a doctoral degree from a master's degree will typically require an additional 48 hours of coursework plus research and an undetermined number of dissertation hours. Doctoral degrees vary largely in scope, breadth, and length and should be evaluated on a case-by-case basis. Universities establish reasonable limits on the estimated time they allow students to matriculate through their programs; this provides a good approximation of the time it takes doctoral students to graduate. Another excellent question all doctoral students should ask is, "How many students who begin actually complete the doctoral degree?" It is estimated over half of all doctoral students never finish the complex dissertation stage of a doctoral program, so those considering a doctorate need to carefully evaluate their options before casually deciding on this path forward. Figure 23.2 shows the approximate number of hours it will take to earn an advanced degree, starting with the bachelor's degree for reference.

FIGURE 23.2 Approximate hours required for earning a degree.

In 2019, the annual Healthcare Information and Management Systems Society (HIMSS) HIMSS19 Global Health Conference & Exhibition featured over 30 universities and colleges with greater than 300 education sessions, many from university researchers. It is worthwhile to speak to these institutions while attending professional events. Universities typically have their senior student affairs staff and professors in the program at the convention. They are eager to speak to potential students and are competitively seeking the best candidates. The HIMSS Global Health Conference & Exhibition offers a more relaxed format to get information from the top programs in the health IT field, and potential students can ask honest questions about the program such as the number of hours, coursework, part-time options, and the modality (in person versus online) offered. Students should ask about the profile of other similar students in the program, their backgrounds, and the length of time the programs are taking to evaluate the "fit." It is also helpful to follow up with a contact at the university in case there are more specific questions after the event.

Graduate schools can be a much more personal experience than undergraduate programs, as the class sizes and cohort are typically smaller. It is worth the effort to get to know the university staff and administration. Several top programs in health IT admit only graduate students, so the student body, coursework, and research exist as the combined focus of the campus.

CHOOSING A PROGRAM FORMAT/MODALITY

Students are not limited to their local university when seeking a degree in the health IT field, and there are many national options to evaluate and consider. Most advanced degrees in health IT will have some portion of their coursework delivered in an online medium. Many master's degrees are offered entirely online, meaning the student does not need to leave their home to take classes. Classes may be delivered through an online Learning Management System (LMS), which serves as an online classroom, convening students from various locations. As demand for health IT professionals increases, online programs are guaranteed to exist and even dominate the landscape of available degree plans. The most prestigious programs continue to evolve from traditional universities where courses are also available on a physical campus. A student may have the option to enroll in a hybrid program, whereby classes meet some of the time in person and the remainder of the coursework is completed remotely. The third option commonly offered is an executive-style program and is commonly offered for healthcare management degrees. Executive programs are condensed classes offered less frequently (e.g., on Fridays and Saturdays) and may be offered similar to a working schedule of 8:00 a.m. to 6:00 p.m., instead of in 3–hour blocks. This format also offers less disruption and a more desirable schedule for students who do not live near the campus. The fourth option is the traditional program, where all courses are in person or face-to-face.

Each of these program modalities has benefits and disadvantages. For instance, traditional courses offer the ability to network and interact with professionals from other organizations, providing direct contact and exposure to potential contacts and job opportunities. Yet, traditional classes require students to adapt to a specific course schedule. Online learning offers complete flexibility as to scheduling, and students can complete coursework on their own timetables, at midnight if they wish. But, online programs provide little exposure to a campus, professors, or fellow students for networking. Table 23.2 lists the four primary types of degree program options available.

CHOOSING A UNIVERSITY OR COLLEGE

When selecting the institution (university or college), there are a few things to keep in mind. First and foremost should be the quality of education you will receive, and this is typically reflected in the accrediting agencies that recognize the program and the overall integrity of the program. Accreditation is a means of ensuring adherence to standards of quality. The university should be "institutionally accredited," and the specific degree program should also be recognized as well.

TABLE 23.2

Classroom Formats for Graduate Degree Programs

Online	All coursework is completed via the Internet, through an online Learning Management System
Hybrid	Online coursework is combined with face-to-face classes
Executive/Professional	Condensed classes offered all day for select days
Traditional	All courses are offered in-person

Some of the best healthcare-focused programs are connected with external partners such as hospitals and academic medical centers, industry leaders in biotechnology or precision medicine, and entrepreneurs in health IT. The prospective student can find the links to these partners by searching the university's website. The website should be flawless in execution, engaging, and transparent. Those that are not might indicate problems with transparency of the program or quality of the education. Especially if you are considering an online degree program, the website needs to be even better. The student should be able to discover most of the desired information about the program, tuition, coursework, faculty, and other contacts a student would want to learn about the school. A description of each class is especially helpful for those seeking specialized interests such as entrepreneurship or advanced technical skills.

When exploring programs, identify the courses required in the degree plan. The degree plan is the assortment of courses necessary for successful completion of the degree. On school websites a sample degree plan should be available, but the university should also have courses in more esoteric subject matter areas such as natural language processing (NLP), cognitive science, leadership and entrepreneurship, healthcare delivery, strategic decision making, or data mining. In addition to the required coursework, there should be alternate courses which are appealing to the student as electives and will serve as enhancements to one's career portfolio and skillset. Notice if the degree plan includes a capstone course, a thesis, or a culminating project. Depending on your skills and interests, one of these final options might make a difference. Table 23.3 provides a sample degree plan for a master's program in health informatics.

When researching the university website, a good graduate program will have a link on their website for "Current Students" and "Prospective Students." The first category should describe coursework, student events, and resources for students. There may be alumni statements, or some universities have videos of their current students stating why they chose the program. This is a great way to hear directly from real students who are actually engaged in coursework. The prospective student can gain an idea of the culture of the program and the expectations of the students, as well as any student activities or networking events. This is a perfect place to see if the university

TABLE 23.3

Sample Master's Degree Plan (39 hours Coursework + 3–6 hours Thesis)

Introduction to Health Informatics	Legal and Ethical Aspects of Health IT
The U.S. Healthcare System	Security in Health IT
Introduction to Electronic Health Records	Quality and Outcome Improvement in Healthcare
Standards and Standards Development in Applied Health IT	System Analysis and Project Management
Technology Assessment and Evaluation	Clinical Decision Support System
Health Information Visualization and Visual Analytics	Health Information Exchange
Technical and Scientific Writing	Practicum or Thesis in Applied Health IT

has recruiting events and any other resources a prospective student would need to consider in order to make a decision. Many reputable programs have alumni groups or events where graduates of the program can network or attend continuing education events throughout the year. These events and resources offer invaluable opportunities for the graduate to remain connected to the university and stay abreast of the latest developments in the field.

The reputation of a university is important, so the student should speak to influential colleagues in the health IT environment. Colleagues may be current employers or trusted peers who hold mid- to senior-level positions in health IT. Although this may weigh less in the final decision, it is a good decision point to gather information. For this reason, a student needs to consider the peers who will be joining them as classmates. Peer learning plays a larger role in a graduate degree when compared with an undergraduate degree. The student body may be more diverse and will have more experience in the workforce. Students are encouraged to work in teams on large projects and writing assignments in graduate school, as this mirrors the working environment of a professional. While students are enrolled as classmates, outside hierarchy is left out of the classroom. Physicians will work equally with IT technicians, and nurses work seamlessly with software engineers and researchers. Classmates form important friendships and connections for networking in health IT after earning their degrees. Classmates get to know each other's competencies, weaknesses, and desired career paths. They make great references for future positions!

An excellent program has excellent professors. The people who teach the students are an essential and obvious component to the program; however, many students do not take advantage of the opportunity to engage with the faculty before applying to the program. All graduate programs should list their faculty along with the faculty's interests, degrees, and current research on the university website. Most questions can be answered through student affairs; however, students also have the option to contact the faculty directly.

FINANCING GRADUATE EDUCATION

Graduate school can be financially evaluated as a single purchase, in the same way one might buy a luxury vehicle or a home, depending on the institution. Since the total cost of earning a graduate degree can easily get into six figures, it is best to carefully examine how one will finance their degree. Some choices include student loans, scholarships, grants, or paying as you go.

Although in general, there are fewer subsidies such as grant opportunities offered to graduate students when compared with undergraduates, there are other factors which simplify the process. For example, graduate students receive the benefit of independence. No longer does one need to request tax documents from their parents to complete financial aid forms. The process is greatly simplified in this regard, as the Free Application for Federal Student Aid (FAFSA) only requires the student's tax return information. The calculation is made based upon the university's estimate of what it will cost students to attend and live reasonably while attending the program, then estimates the resources the student has to contribute to the cost of the enrolling. According to the U.S. Department of Education in 2016, current graduate students who meet the qualifications for aid and are entering their first semester of study can borrow up to $20,500 of unsubsidized federal loan money (Federal Student Aid Overview, 2016). Students should check with their program of interest to determine exact amounts, as schools establish their own cost of attendance. The interest on an unsubsidized loan accrues immediately, giving the student further incentive to finish on time.

Another option for financing graduate education is to seek company reimbursement or let someone else pay for it. Many large organizations offer generous tuition reimbursement programs for employees seeking to advance in their current position. The company considers this an investment in their human resources, and most will pay from 75% to 100% of the total tuition and fees for state universities and colleges.

As many of the programs are offered online, and this is undoubtedly a benefit; the downside is the student may face unexpected out-of-state tuition fees. Check the institution's in-state tuition

TABLE 23.4

Affordable Graduate Programs with Master's Degrees in Health IT

University Program	Location	Degree	Approximate Cost of Attendance
The University of Texas Health Science Center in Houston School of Biomedical Informatics	Houston, TX	M.S. Health Informatics	$6,500 per year
University of North Carolina at Charlotte	Charlotte, NC	H.I. P.S.M.	$9,000 per year
University of Utah	Salt Lake City, UT	M.S. Biomedical Informatics	$9,500 per year

Source: University's individual websites.

policy versus out-of-state policy. Some state universities offer a waiver for out-of-state students or there may be a scholarship threshold, which qualifies the student for in-state tuition. For private institutions, the tuition is typically a set fee without negotiation. In this case, the best option is to seek financial aid or merit-based scholarship funds.

Based on available data from the Institute of Educational Sciences, the research and statistics section of the U.S. Department of Education, there are several excellent and affordable graduate programs across the country designed to meet the needs of working professionals. Table 23.4 lists a sample of a few of the more "affordable" programs, with the location, degree, and average annual cost.

Lifelong Learner Case Study: Examples

A student's individual background and experiences help determine which programs are better suited for their needs. To provide an example, below are four of the more common "types" of students.

Student A: Dual Degree Option, Early Career

A student is currently in an MPH program focusing on Health Promotion and Behavioral Sciences. She has a background in psychology and volunteer experience working at a clinic with electronic health records. She would like to pursue a program that utilizes her interests, bachelor's degree, and volunteer experience. Since she lives in a small town, she does not have a local program, so she pursues an online dual MPH/MSHI program. In order to finance her education, she applies to be a graduate research assistant. She also has the option to work in a clinic, complete a FAFSA and apply for an unsubsidized loan, or self-finance her education as she attends school part-time.

Student B: Entrepreneur with Broad Qualifications

A student with a liberal arts education and a medical degree has always been interested in technology. He is currently trying to build a start-up but does not have all the technical skills and industry connections necessary. He seeks a specialized program with an emphasis on mobile development and entrepreneurship. As part of his research, he checks the faculty profiles and industry connections of the university. He also researches the graduates of the program. He is results oriented, so he asks questions about the number of hours in the program and flexibility of the class schedule. He is employed by a hospital with a tuition reimbursement program and has also worked out a small stipend to work with a professor on a part-time basis.

Student C: Business Degree, Executive Experience, Career Change

A student with a business degree and executive management experience in the health insurance industry is considering an MBA. After further research, looking through the schedule of classes, and meeting with professors, the student finds a program which utilizes her business background. She learns from former students this program will add new skills in integrated delivery systems, data management, and predictive analytics. She is fortunate to live near an academic medical center and negotiates time off from work to attend the executive MBA with a focus on health informatics. Her organization has an existing relationship with the university and receives a discount for the program. She also takes advantage of her company's tuition reimbursement program.

Student D: Registered Nurse, Looking for Advancement

A student has worked his way up in healthcare from a staff-level register nurse (RN) to supervisor over the past 15 years and for the past five years has worked in the IT department. He has substantial knowledge of patient workflow, electronic medical record (EMR) systems, and the healthcare system in general, but lacks certain technical skills to advance into management. Although the student is an excellent employee, advancing to the manager of the department will require more than experience. It will require a master's degree in an health IT-related field. The student considers online programs in MSIS, MIS, and MS in various fields to strengthen the specific areas of expertise needed. He learns there are many programs specific for nurses, including nursing informatics and program management degrees. He speaks with trusted colleagues and mentors, then considers programs which are taught at the local nursing school. Knowing informatics professionals with clinical backgrounds are in high demand, he works out a contract with his employer to commit two years of service for two years of tuition and returns to school full time.

Decision Matrix: Putting the Pieces Together

Once you have identified all of the information necessary to compare and evaluate the various degree program choices, one of the best ways to make a decision is through a structured decision matrix. A decision matrix helps to turn an otherwise qualitative decision into a quantitative one, where you place values and weights on the importance of key criteria to you. For example, if living in Denver was the most important factor in your decision and a program was based in Denver, that criteria would receive higher scores and weighting. If online learning was your top priority, that should receive a higher weighting, and any program that offers online degrees should receive higher scores. A sample decision matrix is shown in Table 23.5 below. Feel free to add or edit the criteria and weighting to fit your personal situation.

GAINING ADMISSIONS AND GETTING IN (STEP 3)

Once the learner has made the selection of the right degree program to pursue, the start of any new adventure requires planning to gain admission, which requires practical preparation. During the previous two steps for identifying and selecting the desired degree program and university, the admission criteria should have been closely examined. In this step, students should now begin preparing to meet those criteria.

Typically, admissions criteria takes into consideration work experience and background, but there are also standard expectations for minimum grade point average (GPA) based on the student's undergraduate work, as well as scores on standardized graduate admissions exams. Those seriously considering graduate school should begin studying for the required admissions exam. Most graduate programs in the United States will require students to take the Graduate Record Examination (GRE). The GRE consists of three general sections: verbal, quantitative, and writing skills. It may seem intimidating for someone who has not taken an exam in years; however, solid training and practice is the key to success for this exam. Many universities will make the average scores of their current

TABLE 23.5
Program Selection Decision Matrix

Criteria	Weight (Importance)	Program 1	Program 2	Program 3
Course Format/Modality Aligned with Learner Preferences (e.g., Online, Traditional, Hybrid)	25%	9	5	
Institution Prestige, Rank, or Brand	20%	8	5	
Region/Location	5%	2	10	
Length of Program	5%	2	10	
Cost of Program/Financial Aid	20%	9	2	
Thesis versus No Thesis	5%	4	10	
Work/Life Balance	10%	7	2	
Probability of Success	10%	10	10	
Total Score	100%	7.75[a]	5.35	

Note

a   When interpreting the matrix, based on the weighted importance of each criterion and the score you gave the program, the total can be found in the bottom row. In this example, Program 1 would be a more attractive option (7.75 versus 5.35).

students available, so applicants are aware of the range of scores expected. Some programs will focus more on quantitative reasoning, while other schools will want a high verbal score. The exam typical takes just under 4 hours and can be taken on a paper or computer-based format. More detailed information about the GRE is available at http://www.ets.org/gre/. There are many excellent study guides and courses you may take to help potential students prepare. These include:

- Kaplan Test Prep (https://www.kaptest.com/gre)
- The Princeton Review (http://www.princetonreview.com/grad/gre-test-prep)
- The Manhattan Review (http://www.manhattanreview.com/gre/)

The GRE was theoretically created to approximate the student's aptitude and ability to achieve in graduate school. GRE scores are valid and acceptable by most universities for five years; after five years, a student will need to retake the exam again.

In addition to excellent scores on the GRE, prospective students will be asked to submit former transcripts verifying a conferred undergraduate degree, as well as a resume of work accomplishments and a goal statement. The professors who will instruct the graduate students are the ones reading the goal statements, and these are taken as seriously as the scores on the GRE. Professors want to know students are serious about their educational goals, focused on their future, and have taken the time to research their specific degree program. Goal statements should be tailored for the university and degree program. The ideal statement should convey depth and passion while deferring from overly dramatic prose. Significant and relevant work or life experiences are worth noting, as are any major educational or health IT-related accomplishments, honors, or awards. It is always a good idea to have several trusted friends or colleagues proofread a goal statement. Ideally this statement should convey one's passion for advancement, interests in that university and degree programs, preferences for working with specific faculty, as well as being a writing sample in which the student feels a sense of pride.

Once an application is made to a program, it often takes weeks or even months to find out if a student is admitted or denied. It is worth mentioning, some universities may allow students to take graduate-level coursework prior to admission to a masters level program. The amount of coursework allowed will be limited, as will the conferred status as an admitted graduate student; however, this may be an efficient way to begin the journey. Otherwise, many schools work on admissions cycles, and these cycles dictate the communication timing. It is best to apply for multiple degree programs (based on your ranked preferences from the decision matrix), to ensure you get positive news from at least one.

DEGREE COMPLETION: STAYING IN (STEP 4)

When a prospective student receives their acceptance letter to graduate school, no matter the prior accomplishments, one should celebrate! Students should respond within the required deadlines and adhere to any guidelines established in the acceptance letter. This may include prerequisite coursework, forms, meetings, or mandatory orientation. Plan to spend at least 6–8 additional hours per week per course, especially in the first semester to get acclimated to graduate school. Depending on the timeline the student has established for completion, it is customary for students to take between one and two classes each semester, including summer terms. This creates a rhythm and inertia to coursework and the life of a graduate student. The suggested schedule, however, is highly dependent on the degree plan, workload, and individual capacity of the student.

Once you are admitted, there will be a registration process for the semester in which you are admitted. During registration, it is important that you follow the degree plan and select your first courses based on the timing of the degree plan (fundamental and introduction courses must be taken prior to advanced courses, for instance). Take note of any courses that require prerequisites, as these must be taken first.

A key concern in the first (and subsequent) semesters should be around balancing work, family, and social life with the new educational endeavors. It is important to maintain a healthy position in all of these areas. Consider this when determining whether to enroll for one course (3 hours) or more. Obviously an individual who works full time should think carefully before enrolling for more than one to two courses per semester.

Lifelong learners will need to balance and manage the additional stress of being a student, again. Writing reports, developing presentations, analyzing data, developing computer scripts, and reading multiple chapters of textbooks require significant time and effort. The ability to manage time and coursework effectively in graduate school is as important as learning new concepts.

For students who work while attending school part-time, this is especially important. It is customary for professors to provide students with a schedule of assignments for the entire semester. This provides an opportunity for students to plan ahead and break larger assignments into smaller segments. Just as with projects at work, deadlines are serious, and missing an assignment carries serious consequences, including making a zero and possibly failing the course. Professors expect the same work product of all students, regardless of the outside demands. The assumption is even greater for full-time students: the majority of time is to be devoted to graduate work. While this may seem daunting, especially at first, many students find their creativity, effectiveness, and confidence soar as they get more immersed in graduate work. Recent studies have also shown that diligent scheduling actually produces a more productive life and can increase happiness overall (Hobson et al., 2001).

During your first semester, in addition to managing your course load, there are other considerations. Whether you are in an online or traditional format, it is important to connect and network with your colleagues and faculty. This provides significant opportunities for learning about new people, organizations, and positions. In many programs, there will likely be 'team' projects, which require you and fellow classmates to get along and produce a collaborative report or project.

Work your way through the degree plan, semester by semester, with grades that are typically A or B level. Keep in mind that a 36-hour program is usually only 12 courses, so completion of the degree will be upon you before you know it!

GRADUATION AND NEXT STEPS: WHERE AM I GOING? (STEP 5)

Assuming the student was able to learn discipline and patience during the program, and continued to stay on top of all assignments, a few years later the graduate degree will be completed. This is a time to celebrate, as now new initials can be placed behind the name on email signatures and on resumes. These few letters can make all the difference for future earning power and job opportunities.

Now the question remains: What should you do next? This is the challenging part of earning a graduate degree. Obviously there were factors that stimulated your interest in pursuing the degree, and now might be the opportunity to make those happen. If you were unhappy being a staff nurse, then the new master's degree in informatics might allow you to apply for a new position as a Senior Clinical Informatician. Some others might be comfortable staying where they are, but earning more money, or there is the option to relocate to a different region with a new position. Some even change to the healthcare industry from a different industry. Whatever your goals and desires, the graduate degree is now completed, and the lifelong learner must decide what to do next.

CONCLUSION

Whichever path is chosen, this author hopes you strive for excellence! Graduate degrees provide credentials, but the career strategy should now be the focus. Aiming high for a position that balances career goals, new educational platform, and personal interests will help ensure lifelong success. Subsequent chapters will describe this in even greater detail.

REFERENCES

Bureau of Labor Statistics. (2016). Occupational Outlook Handbook. Available at www.bls.gov/ooh
Federal Student Aid Overview. (2016). U.S. Department of Education. Available at https://studentaid.ed.gov
Hobson, C., DeLunas, L., and Kesic, D. (2001). Compelling Evidence of the Need for Corporate Work/Life Balance Initiatives: Results from a National Survey of Stressful Life-Events. *Journal of Employment Counseling*, 38(1), 38–44.
Monster.com. (2016). 5 Healthcare Informatics Jobs and Salaries. Available at https://www.monster.com/career-advice/article/health-informatics-jobs

24 The Many Facets of Continuing Education

Christine Hudak
Ph.D, RN-BC, CPHIMS, FHIMSS

CONTENTS

INTRODUCTION

Continuing professional development (CPD) has been defined in various ways. Wylie (2015) defines CPD as the "…means by which people maintain their knowledge and skills related to their professional lives…" The Chartered Institute of Personnel and Development (CIPD) defines CPD as "… the need for individuals to keep up to date with rapidly changing knowledge" (retrieved from http://www.cipd.co.uk/). The Institute of Hospitality defines CPD as: "a framework of learning and development activities which is seen as contributing to an individual's continued effectiveness as a professional" (retrieved from https://www.instituteofhospitality.org/Careers/cpd). In previous iterations, this term was known as Continuing Education, with each profession inserting their name between the two words; thus, we had Continuing Nursing Education, Continuing Medical Education, and the like. Regardless of what it is called, the activity shows a personal commitment to professionalism, personal responsibility for skill/knowledge enhancement, and a desire to challenge the expectations of a volatile, ever-changing business environment (Schambach and Blanton, 2002). The same applies to the healthcare sector.

DOI: 10.4324/9780429398377-29

Health IT professionals engage in CPD for a number of reasons. Whether it is to obtain or retain certification, obtain a promotion, maintain competence in their chosen area, learn and apply new knowledge, to improve job performance, or simply seeking out new learning for its own sake, (Mizell, 2010; Schambach and Blanton, 2002), health IT professionals have multiple opportunities to engage in this activity. Whether it is a class for college credit, a webinar for CPHIMS/CAHIMS hours, a journal club for sharing and discussing new advancements, or even a vendor presentation to learn about new technology, the health IT professional has myriad ways to obtain the knowledge and skills to meet their individual goals.

GOAL OF THE CHAPTER

In this chapter, we will define the many opportunities available to the health IT professional for professional development. We will define ways to meet the requirements for obtaining and retaining certification, methods to obtain new knowledge and expand professional practice, and paths to building and maintaining professional competence in health informatics. Through it we hope to assist the newly minted, mid-career, and seasoned professional to find the balance between personal and job-related responsibilities while finding time to accomplish professional goals.

SCHAMBACH AND BLANTON'S PREMISE AND HOW TO ACCOMPLISH

Schambach and Blanton state that "IT professionals who want to maintain an appropriate degree of professional competence need effective professional development… But because participation is generally voluntary, they have to be personally motivated before they are willing to participate" (2002, p. 84). The same can be said for health IT professionals: they may be motivated, but if the available opportunities do not allow for a work-life balance, they may be willing to forgo the benefits that CPD can offer. So how do we offer CPD while maintaining the motivation of the employee? The next sections of this chapter will outline traditional and not so traditional methods and some new methods to reap the benefits of CPD. They will also classify these offerings as formal or informal.

TRADITIONAL METHODS OF CPD: EXEMPLAR HIMSS GLOBAL CONFERENCE

Many in health IT have probably attended a sponsored one-day or two-day workshop in their professional life. Indeed, if you have attended a Healthcare Information and Management Systems Society (HIMSS) Global Health Conference & Exhibition, you have experienced at least three traditional and formal types of CPD.

STAND-UP, IN-PERSON PRESENTATIONS

Myriad in-person, stand-up, educational presentations abound at the annual conference. Multiple tracks reflecting current content in health informatics allow participants to attend those sessions that are of interest to them as well as sampling some not so familiar topics. Presentations are vetted by peer reviewers (the Global Health Conference Education Committee, or GHCEC) for criteria such as originality, timeliness, relevance, data accuracy, and freedom from vendor bias. CAHIMS/CPHIMS holders can obtain credit for recertification. Nurses can receive Continuing Nursing Education (CNE) hours. Physicians can receive Category 1 Continuing Medical Education units. Pharmacists can receive Continuing Education Units, as can Board Certified Informaticists, Information Security Professionals, ACHE and AHIMA members, and Certified CIOs (CHCIO). Project Managers can receive Professional Development Units (PDUs). This is a very traditional way of CPD in a compact, prevetted format that allows attendees to accumulate numerous hours in a short period of time.

Select stand-up presentations are recorded and made available in the HIMSS Learning Center so that additional hours can be earned by listening to the recordings of the sessions. Attendees can listen to extra sessions in the comfort of their home, office, or car. The extension of the stand-up presentations to the mobile/home platform reflects the changing needs and the time constraints of the health IT professional. Those who cannot attend the in-person event due to financial, time, organizational, or personal constraints still have the opportunity to benefit from the conference through the recordings.

Similar types of presentations can also be found at the individual HIMSS chapter level through smaller, more targeted conferences in a specific geographic area. Chapter programming as well as programming by other organizations rely primarily on these stand-up presentations to disseminate knowledge to the professional. Stand-up, formal presentations are also offered in individual healthcare organizations, though cost prohibitions see them decreasing over time.

ROUNDTABLES

Getting multiple experts in a single room to discuss a single topic in depth is a benefit of roundtable sessions at the annual conference as well as smaller HIMSS chapter events. The opportunity to attend a session where CIOs or other hospital leaders discuss a singular topic provides a broader perspective to a problem and allows a deeper understanding of current issues in healthcare informatics. Panel discussion also falls into this category in their deep discussion, with varied viewpoints of a single topic.

VENDOR PRESENTATIONS/DEMONSTRATIONS

Though not usually a way to obtain credits toward continuing education requirement, vendor presentations are another form of CPD. Software and hardware demonstrations are the standard way to tout features of a product or service to decision makers as well as staff persons. If the idea of keeping up to date with rapidly changing knowledge in hardware and software is integral to the job being done, then these vendor presentations are invaluable to this group. These same (or similar) presentations may also be seen in individual hospitals or other healthcare venues, where they are typically called in-service presentations or vendor demonstrations. They are frequently held when an organization is considering a new system, an updated system, or a replacement system. At the HIMSS global health conference, these demonstrations are readily accessible and cover the majority of hardware and software vendors for healthcare venues.

INTEROPERABILITY SHOWCASE

A not so traditional method of CPD held in a traditional in-person conference is the HIMSS Interoperability Showcase. Here the attendee can become the patient through a clinical use case scenario and will be able to see how their patient information can move from system to system. This method of using a clinical use case (a formal way of representing how a clinical system interacts with the environment) to demonstrate what can be accomplished if a system is interoperable is a powerful method to learn about this specific topic in the annual conference setting.

MORE TRADITIONAL AND FORMAL CPD: PURSUING A FIRST OR ADVANCED DEGREE

Pursuit of a first degree, an advanced degree, or a different credential is a step that many health IT professionals decide is right for them. Demands of a current position, the pursuit of an advanced or different position, or simple enhancement of current knowledge and skills lead many health IT professionals back to school. However, "One problem for adults is the constant, competing tension between life obligations and educational obligations" (Pelletier, 2010, p. 3). What this means for the health informatics professional is that educational programs leading to a first, advanced, or new area of study must be congruent with the lifestyle and working situation of the potential student. Evening and weekend programs, accelerated programs, independent study programs, online degree programs with synchronous or asynchronous discussion (Internet only), distance-learning programs (real-time classes in remote locations), and hybrid programs (classroom and Internet) offer the first or advanced degree student multiple options for learning that fit into professional and personal life.

Academic transfer programs that allow completion of up to three years of work toward a baccalaureate degree at a community college with guaranteed transfer of credits assist those obtaining a first degree to meet their goal. The College Level Examination Program (https://clep.collegeboard.org/exam) allows the working professional to obtain college credit for those general education courses required of all baccalaureate degree programs (history and social sciences, composition and literature, science and mathematics, business and world languages).

MORE TRADITIONAL AND FORMAL CPD: NON-CREDIT COURSES (MOOCS AND SPOCS)

Massive Online Open Courses (MOOC) as well as Small Private Online Courses (SPOC) have been touted as revolutionizing the academic and corporate education landscape (Kaplan and Haenlein, 2016, p. 441). These MOOC and SPOC are offered by leading universities and provide the health informatics professional an alternative to traditional non-credit workshops and in-person courses. One or many courses can be taken at a single time, and specializations can be obtained by completing sequences of recommended courses. With the completion of a capstone project, the student can receive a certificate of completion or a diploma.

MOOCs are accessible to anyone (massive enrollment), while SPOCs are designed for a small group targeting a specific subject. Participation in both of these methods of learning requires a high degree of "…intrinsic motivation and self-discipline. Successful graduates tend to be older… (… 25–30 years) and already hold a first degree (80%), which they obtained through more traditional means. For most participants, a MOOC is primarily a way to build new skills in order to strengthen an existing professional career" (Kaplan and Haenlein, 2016, p. 444).

Both MOOCs and SPOCs can be synchronous or asynchronous, with the asynchronous mode dominating MOOCs and synchronous mode dominating SPOCs (Kaplan and Haenlein, 2016). Testing of course material is conducted either online or in person at test centers. Multiple online providers offer these educational options through leading universities such as Duke University, University of Michigan, Rice University, The Pennsylvania State University (Penn State), and Stanford University. Costs are variable, and discounts are applied if a student takes a series of courses leading to a specialization. Courses can be taken in such diverse areas as: Hospital and Health System Preparedness (Penn State Homeland Security Portfolio); Data Science (Johns Hopkins University); a multi-course statistics specialization (Duke University); and Bioinformatics Methods (University of Toronto).

SOME LESS TRADITIONAL AND INFORMAL MEANS OF CPD: THE INTERNET AND WEB 2.0

E-learning, or E-CE, is an all-encompassing term that can describe a number of informal options made possible by the Internet (Lam-Antoniades et al., 2009). Included in this designation are webinars, online journal clubs, mailing lists, blogs, evidence-based tweeting, LinkedIn™ discussion groups, podcasts, personal learning projects, and multiple Web 2.0 tools such as forums, bulletin boards, wikis, tagging, and aggregators (Orok and Usoro, 2015). Web 2.0 refers to services on the Internet that allow users to share data and interact with each other, (Constantinides and Fountain,

2007). Though the tools were initially thought of as a new generation of Internet services (Cosh et al., 2008; Dotsika and Patrick, 2007), they have become ubiquitous in social communication and shown great promise in CPD and the acquisition of knowledge through virtual learning environments (Chen et al., 2015; Minocha, 2009). They have also shown great promise in the workplace for both in-place and mobile learning. The Web 2.0 technologies and the other entities included in E-learning, or E-CE, are appropriate additions to the more traditional methods of CPD.

The next section of this chapter will focus on these entities with brief descriptions of each.

TOOLS OF THE INTERNET

Webinars are one of the most prolific Internet tools for CPD by the working professional. Webinars are live meetings that take place over the Internet using tools such as Adobe Connect™, GoToMeeting™, WebEx™, or any other proprietary products that allow audio and video sharing of information (https://www.minitex.umn.edu/Training/Webinars.aspx). These meetings can be a discussion, a PowerPoint presentation for instruction, a demonstration of software or hardware, a panel presentation, or any other educational offering. They are generally 30–90 minutes in length and require nothing more than a web browser and/or a telephone line. The webinars can accommodate large or small numbers of participants and can be found through professional organizations, the Federal government (https://www.healthit.gov/news/2015/5/12/2015-edition-webinars), universities and colleges (http://northerno-hio.himsschapter.org/event/ksu-nohimss-webinar-series), and vendors of health IT hardware and software, as examples. Organizations such as HIMSS offer access into annual conference presentations either during or after the conference through a webinar client. Continuing education credits can be obtained through many of the webinars, making it an effective and efficient method of CPD for the health informatics professional.

ONLINE JOURNAL CLUBS

Online journal clubs are a relatively new entry into the CPD arena. With a history dating back to the time of Sir William Osler at McGill University in 1875, journal clubs provide a way for peers within and outside of individual institutions to meet and discuss knowledge and translate that knowledge into practice (Chan et al., 2015). The traditional journal club was usually found within a single medical specialty and was an in-person gathering either at a hospital, a clinician's home, or a remote location. A journal article or articles were distributed to the participants ahead of the meeting with explicit instructions to read and be ready to discuss. Despite the usefulness of this approach to knowledge sharing, traditional journal clubs have had low attendance, and their value has been disputed among practitioners (Lizarondo et al., 2010).

Fast forward to the development of online journal clubs. These Internet-based entities offer distinct advantages over their face-to-face equivalent. First is the ability of the journal club to reach a wider audience of participants on a regular basis. It is possible to include colleagues outside of local borders, including international colleagues. Next is the convenience of the online version. With the use of webinar format, synchronous communication is possible. Since the journal club can be recorded, it is possible for those unable to attend in real time to listen to the discussion and contribute in an asynchronous fashion. Members can participate where and when they choose.

An asynchronous-only version of the online journal club is possible with the use of a facilitator or moderator who may use any number of tools at their disposal: tutorials, research question development, discussion and appraisal of multiple literature sources, and evaluation of the journal club itself (Lizarondo et al., 2010). The availability of full text services through the Internet, as well as the use of newsfeeds and improved search functions, extends the reach of the journal club to a larger number of practitioner views and opinions from a larger number of research and practice articles.

Originally designed as a way to promote better patient care and evidence-based practice, the online journal club allows this knowledge-sharing tool to be used by allied health professionals and health IT professionals. It allows them to keep pace with current literature, share use cases with each other, compare best practices in health information technology (IT), and solve problems of implementation and analytics using academic research.

To date, the online journal club format has been primarily used by medical informaticians, nursing informaticians, and bioinformatics practitioners. The use of this format by health informaticians should be explored to a greater degree. Not only will it increase the CPD of the professional, but it will also bring to the forefront a more academic focus for the health informatics practitioner. The two articles noted in the reference list provide excellent tools for setting up an online journal club.

LISTSERVS

Listservs are one of the earliest inventions on the Internet, but they are still relevant to the health informatics professional pursuing CPD. Though the Listserv was a program primarily created to manage email discussion lists (Manjoo, 2010), it has become much more in this age of burgeoning information. Further, if you want to have a real discussion about a topic, the Listserv is the most reliable tool available that will allow you to do this. While Facebook™, Tumblr, and Twitter™ allow an idea to be popularized, criticized, and widely disseminated, a Listserv allows you to really discuss an idea, in either a negative or positive way (Manjoo, 2010). In addition to the opportunity to really discuss an idea, a Listserv allows for longer and more meaningful messages.

Another advantage of the Listserv over Twitter™ or Facebook™ is that Listservs are closed. You must subscribe to be a part of them, and that allows for more honest discussion when an individual is sharing with a group invested in the topic of the Listserv.

So, how does one find a Listserv of interest? The best place to start is on health informatics websites. Many of the popular websites used by health IT professionals allow subscription on the first page. Type in your email address; perhaps send an email to the list with the command "Subscribe," and you will start receiving information about discussions of interest. For instance, if you want the latest information on meaningful use, the Office of the National Coordinator of Health Information Technology allows subscriptions to various Listservs on the front page. Colleges and universities frequently have Listservs for their students but may allow outsiders if they apply. Another way to find health informatics Listservs is to go to http://www.lsoft.com/lists/list_q.html. This is a website that allows a user to search for Listservs related to their particular interest. You do not have to read all the discussion immediately; most Listservs archive the discussion activity, so you can return to it when you have the time.

While Listserv activity cannot be used to obtain recertification hours, it does provide an effective method of having a discussion of various sides of an issue with like-minded colleagues.

LINKEDIN™ DISCUSSION GROUPS (COMMUNITIES OF PRACTICE)

Related to Listservs are the communities of practice built on a social media platform, such as LinkedIn. As defined by Trayner and Wenger-Trayner, "Communities of practice are groups of people who share a concern or a passion for something they do and learn how to do it better as they interact regularly" (2015, p. 1). The use of social media has been shown to be an effective tool in creating communities of practice as well as pursuing continuous professional development (Grajales et al., 2014; Moore, 1973). Communities of practice allow the participants to share and compare knowledge, but also to develop an identity as a member of that community. As an example, Dong et al. (2015) describe a LinkedIn group formed by hand surgeons called Hand Surgery International. This group develops, shares, and maintains specific knowledge about the practice of hand surgery, with a goal of members interacting with peers in the online community of practice to share knowledge about hand surgery and to develop their professional identity as hand surgeons.

Communities of practice have not been frequently used in health informatics, though a cursory review of LinkedIn groups indicates multiple groups that relate to health informatics and could become communities of practice. Among these are: Healthcare IT and Electronic Medical Records, Health-IT/EHR/HIS, Health Information Technology, Healthcare Analytics and Informatics, HIEWatch, Healthcare Informatics Knowledge Network, Health Informatics Forum, CPHIMS, Clinical Informatics Leadership, HIMSS, American Nursing Informatics Association, American Medical Informatics Association, and many, many more. While there is a plethora of groups relating to healthcare informatics, few of them have more than three or four messages posted, and none of them act as a community of practice. In order for this to occur, moderators and members of these groups need to take an active role in the group and assign value to what is being written and discussed. Because the concept of communities of practice is not well known in the healthcare informatics community, there are no shared domains of interest, there are few interactions or opportunities to learn together, and many of the participants are not practitioners, but merely persons whose interests lie in health informatics. Unless and until all elements (Domain, Community, and Practice) are combined and developed, these LinkedIn groups will not become communities of practice and will not contribute to CPD for health IT professionals (Trayner and Wenger-Trayner, 2015).

It is important that the concept of communities of practice be developed among health IT professionals to take advantage of the sharing and learning opportunities that can be realized.

Evidence-Based Tweeting and Tweeting the Meeting

There are a growing number of healthcare professionals using Twitter™ for professional purposes. In 2010, it was estimated that there were 19,100 nurses on Twitter™ (Moorley and Chinn, 2014b). In 2014, there were 3,800 health communities, with 6.6 million healthcare Twitter profiles and 10,000 provider profiles (Moorley and Chinn, 2014b). There are multiple health IT-related hashtags (http://www.symplur.com/healthcare-hashtags/regular/page/1/I) that handle thousands of health IT-related tweets per day.

With the use of Twitter by health IT professionals in general, and health IT professionals in particular, increasing, it is safe to infer that this social media platform can be a useful mechanism for CPD. Evidence-based tweeting and tweeting the meeting show the most promise.

Evidence-based tweeting uses URL links in the tweets to Pub Med articles about a particular topic (Djuricich, 2014). The information in the tweet allows those following the feed the opportunity to access evidence about the topic as well as peer-reviewed publications. Followers can join in on a live or asynchronous discussion using the URL provided by the tweet. Evidence has shown (Moorley and Chinn, 2014a) that either formal or informal use of Twitter through a formal community denoted by a hashtag contributes to CPD through the sharing of information, ideas, and opinions.

Tweeting the meeting, that is, setting up a hashtag prior to a local or national educational conference and using that hashtag as a filter, has seen increased use in the past five years (Chaudhry et al., 2012; Djuricich, 2014). Participants at the meeting are asked to tweet about the meeting itself or the content of the meeting such as research findings and treatment options, or to set up "tweet chats," prearranged synchronous online conversations with tweets posted to the same hashtag (Chaudhry et al., 2012).

Both evidence-based tweeting and tweeting the meeting can be useful tools for the health informatics professional to learn and disseminate information about important topics. Those in a meeting and outside of the meeting can potentially benefit from the live tweeting and the subsequent "conversations" that can take place. The use of live tweeting, especially at a conference where groundbreaking findings are being released, can outpace the normal rate of dissemination of either print or online information and can be used as a powerful tool for CPD.

PODCASTS

Audio and video podcasts have been used in health professionals' education for multiple years. These podcasts consist of digital media made available on the Internet for download to a computer, a portable device, or a smartphone. Many podcasts are available by subscribing to a site and may be comprised of a series of presentations around a particular topic.

While audio podcasts are the predominant form of the tool, video podcasts have become increasingly popular. Video podcasts usually consist of a set of PowerPoint slides and an audio track that captures the narration. They can be used to augment or even replace a live lecture by removing geographic and time restrictions. Parts of the podcasts can be repeated at will.

The use of both audio and video podcasting could create relationships between professionals that allow them to engage in active discussions and seek out additional resources for learning. However, as useful and convenient as these tools are, many seeking out CPD view them as less stimulating than a live lecture and tend to use them only sporadically (Schreiber et al., 2010).

BLOGS

The use of blogs in CPD can be a way to store opinions, thoughts, ideas, and reflections about a topic. As open access, personal web pages for a health informatics professional, a blog can be a way to share insights and encourage open and honest discussion through comments on the blog. While blogs are not peer reviewed, the discussion that occurs on them can be seen as a form of peer review as individuals react to postings (Moorley and Chinn, 2014b).

The reflective component of a blog can be used as a personal log of CPD and a method to review the thought processes that were at work in the individual postings. A user can put themselves in the shoes of any number of people to reflect on the various aspects of a situation and gather information that will enhance their own learning. Reflection on a topic and receiving feedback from like-minded individuals help the blogger to develop thinking in a structured manner and become more analytic (Moorley and Chinn, 2014b). While not used by many health IT professionals, this is a tool than can help an individual pursue CPD while recording their work experiences, their reflections, and their disappointments.

WIKIS

While blogging is primarily a solitary exercise unless connected to other blogs, true collaboration for CPD can come from the use of wikis, long considered true social networking tools (Minocha, 2009). As a collaborative writing tool, the development of a wiki can aggregate the information from many professionals into a single document that reflects the totality of the users' knowledge.

Because of the collaborative nature of a wiki, it has occasionally been suggested that letting anyone edit allows for misinformation to be perpetuated (Kohs, 2015). Indeed, the recent experiment by Kohs (2015) indicates that even while trying to correct the misinformation, he was blocked from continuing and the old information was being restored. While that may be a potential problem in Wikipedia, the control exerted by a group of like-minded professionals collaborating on an article for publication, developing a knowledge base, and/or building community among themselves is a deterrent to deliberate misinformation in that wiki. The very nature of a collaborative effort supposes that there will be some mistakes made, or perhaps some biased statements made. But collaboration is an activity that can assist in correcting these items, and contributions made by the members of the wiki can be vetted by them. Wikipedia and a wiki for CPD by a group of like-minded professionals are two different entities and, as such, cannot be compared. It is a disservice to the concept of wiki to regard all wikis as clones of Wikipedia.

As a tool for collaboration and sharing among health IT professionals, a wiki can be a useful tool to build a knowledge base and share information.

CONCLUSION

CPD by health IT professionals can take a variety of forms and be pursued for various reasons. Whether it is a formal workshop to obtain certification renewal credits, the pursuit of a first or advanced degree, or an informal gathering of like-minded professionals sharing information through a blog, a wiki, or a podcast, the pursuit of CPD is a necessity for obtaining and maintaining knowledge and skills.

Health IT professionals work in a complex and volatile environment as a result of changes in healthcare brought about by legislative, financial, and philosophical issues. Thus, CPD is no longer a solitary activity of an individual seeking further continuing education credits. It is, instead, a complex issue that resides at the organizational, departmental, and unit level. Changing the behavior of an individual is a reasonably difficult activity if the individual does not desire change. Changing that same behavior but in an organizational context, is more difficult due to the complexity of the situation and the number of individuals involved (Olson, 2012).

If we wish to change the practice of health informatics professionals, we must focus on the collaboration among professional teams and not on the individual professionals. Interprofessional education must become more commonplace, and health IT professionals must emerge from their silos along with their physician and nurse counterparts and pursue CPD as a group.

There are multiple reasons to pursue CPD as an individual; there are more reasons to work in a collaborative and interprofessional way to achieve the goals of CPD.

REFERENCES

Chan, T.M., Thoma, B., Radecki, R., Topf, J., Woo, H.H., Kao, L.S., Cochran, A., Hiremath, S., and Lin, M. (2015). Ten steps for setting up an online journal club. *Journal of Continuing Education in the Health Professions*, 35(2), 148–154.

Chaudhry, A., Glode, M., Gillman, M., and Miller, R.S. (2012). Trends in twitter use by physicians at the American society of clinical oncology annual meeting, 2010 and 2011. *Journal of Oncology Practice,* 8(3), 173–178.

Chen, Z.S.C., Yang, S.J.H., and Huang, J.J.S. (2015). Constructing an e-portfolio-based integrated learning environment supported by library resources. *The Electronic Library*, 33(2), 273–291.

Constantinides, E., and Fountain, S. (2007). Special issue papers. Web 2.0: Conceptual foundations and marketing Issues. *Journal of Direct, Data and Digital Marketing Practice*, 9(3), 231–244.

Cosh, K.J., Burns, R., and Daniel, T. (2008). Content clouds: Classifying content in Web 2.0. *Library Review*, 57(9), 722–729.

Djuricich, A.M. (2014). Social media, evidence-based tweeting, and JCEHP. *Journal of Continuing Education in the Health Professions*, 34(4), 202–204.

Dong, C., Cheema, M., Samarasekera, D., and Rajaratnam, V. (2015). Using LinkedIn for continuing community of practice among hand surgeons worldwide. *Journal of Continuing Education in the Health Professions*, 35(3), 185–191.

Dotsika, G., and Patrick, K. (2007). Knowledge sharing: Development from within. *The Learning Organization*, 14(5), 395–406.

Grajales, F.J., Sheps, S., Ho, K., Novak-Lauscher, H., and Eysenbach, G. (2014). Social media: A review and tutorial of applications in medicine and health care. *Journal of Medical Internet Research*, 16(2), e13.

Kaplan, A.M., and Haenlein, M. (2016). Higher education and the digital revolution: About MOOCs, SPOCS, social media and the cookie monster. *Business Horizons*, 59(4), 441–450.

Kohs, G. (2015). Experiment concludes: Most misinformation inserted into Wikipedia may persist. Retrieved from: http://wikipediocracy.com/2015/04/13/experiment-concludes-most-misinformation-inserted-into-wikipedia-may-persist/

Lam-Antoniades, M., Ratnapalan, S., and Tait, G. (2009). Electronic continuing education in the health professions: An update on evidence from RCTs. *Journal of Continuing Education in the Health Professions*, 29(1), 44–51.

Lizarondo, L., Kumar, S., and Grimmer-Somers, K. (2010). Online journal clubs: An innovative approach to evidence-based practice. *Journal of Allied Health*, 39(1), E17–E22.

Manjoo, F. (2010). The joy of listservs. *Slate*. Retrieved from: http://www.slate.com/articles/technology/technology/2010/08/the_joy_of_listservs.html

Minocha, S. (2009). Role of social software tools in education: A literature review. *Education and Training*, 51(5 & 6), 369–553.

Mizell, H. (2010). Why professional development matters. Retrieved from: https://learningforward.org/docs/pdf/why_pd_matters_web.pdf?sfvrsn=0

Moore, M.G. (1973). Towards a theory of independent learning and teaching. *Journal of Higher Education*, 44(9), 661–679.

Moorley, C., and Chinn, T. (2014a). Nursing and Twitter: Creating an online community using hashtags. *Collegian*, 21(2), 103–109.

Moorley, C., and Chinn, T. (2014b). Using social media for continuous professional development. *Journal of Advanced Nursing*, 71(4), 713–717.

Olson, C.A. (2012). Twenty predictions for the future of CPD: Implications of the shift from the update model to improving clinical practice. *Journal of Continuing Education in the Health Professions*, 32(3), 151–152.

Orok, B., and Usoro, A. (2015). Factors affecting the effectiveness of web 2.0 as a mobile learning tool in the workplace: A conceptual view. *Computing & Information Systems*, 19(1), 6–14.

Pelletier, S.G. (2010). Success for adult students. *Public Purpose*, 1–6. Retrieved from: http://www.aascu.org/uploadedFiles/AASCU/Content/Root/MediaAndPublications/PublicPurposeMagazines/Issue/10fall_adultstudents.pdf

Schambach, T.S., and Blanton, J.E. (2002). The professional development challenge for IT professionals. *Communications of the ACM*, 45(4), 83–87.

Schreiber, B.E., Fukuta, J., and Gordon, F. (2010). Live lecture versus video podcasts in undergraduate medical education: A randomized controlled trial. *BioMedCentral Medical Education*, 10(68), 1–6.

Trayner, E., and Wenger-Trayner, B. (2015). *Communities of Practice: A Brief Introduction*. Retrieved from: https://wenger-trayner.com/wp-content/uploads/2015/04/07-Brief-introduction-to-communities-of-practice.pdf

Wenger. (1998). Communities of practice: Learning as a Social System. https://participativelearning.org/pluginfile.php/636/mod_resource/conte nt/3/Learningasasocialsystem.pdf.

Wylie, J. (2015). *10 Reason for Continuous Professional Development (CPD)*. Retrieved from: https://www.linkedin.com/pulse/10-reasons-continuous-professional-development-cpd-jordan-wylie

Bibliography

Al-Badi, A. M., Al Roobaea, R., and Mayhew, P. (2013). Improving usability of social networking systems: A case study of LinkedIn. *Journal of Internet, Society, Networks and Virtual Communities*, 1–23.

Harris, H., and Park, S. (2008). Educational uses of podcasting. *British Journal of Educational Technology*, 39(3), 548–551.

25 Engaging Socially to Expand Professional Competency

Kevin P. Seeley
Colonel USAF, MSC, B.S.CIS, MBA, CPHIMS, FHIMSS

CONTENTS

socialize verb *so·cial·ize\ ˈsō-shə-ˌlīz*
to talk to and do things with other people in a friendly way
to teach (someone) to behave in a way that is acceptable in society
intransitive verb
to participate actively in a social group
—Merriam-Webster.com

INTRODUCTION

As health informatics professionals working in a constantly changing healthcare system, it has become imperative to network and engage socially with other health information technology (IT) colleagues, peers, and thought leaders to ensure professional growth, development, and reciprocal mentorship. Regardless of whether you're a health IT executive (Chief Information Officer [CIO], Chief Medical Information Officer [CMIO], Chief Nursing Information Officer [CNIO], Chief Information Security Officer [CISO], Chief Technology Officer [CTO], Chief Digital/Data Officer [CDO]); physician, nurse, or pharmacist in a health informatics-related position; informaticist; health data scientist, analyst, or researcher; vendor salesperson; health systems architect, administrator,

DOI: 10.4324/9780429398377-30

application developer; front-line IT support technician; or IM/IT director; connecting with other health IT professionals will help you learn and gain outside expertise that you could not otherwise obtain on your own within your current organizational environment. As you commit to engaging socially, you not only improve and enrich the careers of others, but you also fill the roles of teacher, influencer, and student in a continuous learning cycle, advancing our health IT profession together as citizens of a community. Sharing information with other health informatics professionals, both online and in person, helps create a personal learning environment that stimulates constructive dialogue and promotes the exchange of innovative ideas, insights, and experiences across the health informatics and healthcare industry.

To develop and grow your health informatics professional competencies, you should understand and embrace the role social engagement and social media play in supplementing your knowledge and expertise. As healthcare becomes increasingly connected, interoperable, and regulated, health informatics professionals cannot limit themselves solely to local social networks. Career success now depends on using social media tools to establish a professional online presence and expand professional net- work connections. Without social media to maintain professional relationships and share the latest industry information, one risks being left behind (Arora 2014). So whether you're just starting out, or already have an extensive professional network and are fully connected online, this chapter will help guide your social engagement journey by (1) discovering "*why*" you need a personal vision and social engagement plan to get the most out of professional interactions, (2) exploring the different "*ways*" health informatics professionals socialize online and in person, (3) discussing social media platforms as a primary "*means*" of discovering professional health IT learning and growth opportunities, and (4) distilling information on "*how*" to leverage LinkedIn, Facebook, Twitter, YouTube, Pinterest, and other social media tools to boost the value of your engagement across the health IT community.

THE WHY

An important early step in your social engagement journey should be to establish a vision and goals for your future. Take a moment to inventory where you want to be in your health IT career in two, five, and ten years and consider how engaging socially, both online and in person, could help you get there, as well as what mutual benefits you can offer others across the profession. Ask yourself, "Why should I expend my time and energy to engage with other professionals, either online or in person, and what can I contribute back to the health IT community?" Examples of items to consider when answering could be your desires for: learning; career advancement; job transition(s); professional reputation branding and marketing; special interest problem solving, collaboration and contribution; benefit(s) to patients, clinicians, customers, and your organization; academic pursuits; human capital networking, exposure and growth; sharing specialized expertise; and local, regional or national thought leadership.

If you have trouble narrowing your career vision and goals, you can try the Warren Buffet method… that is, according to Angela Duckworth, author of *Grit: The Power of Passion and Perseverance*, there is a famous story about Warren Buffett telling his pilot to make a list of all the things he wanted to get done in life. As it turned out, like many of us, Buffet's pilot had a long list. Mr Buffet then tells him to circle his top five things and separate the rest of the items onto another list. He subsequently advises him to avoid at all costs anything that was not circled and to only focus on his five things. As it turns out, by identifying his top five things, Buffet helped his pilot discover his own personal theme, the "why" that motivated him to do the things that matter most, and ultimately the criteria upon which to base all his future decisions and priorities about where to expend time and energy. His lesson … you cannot get everything done in life that you want to, so prioritize, then deprioritize the rest (Duckworth 2016).

Another method to assess your vision is proffered in the book *Start With Why* by author and speaker Simon Sinek. In the book, he gives sage advice about identifying personal, professional, and organizational purpose. As the title states, Sinek encourages everyone to start by answering a core question, "Why do you do the things you do?" rather than "What things do you do?" or "How you do things?" Sinek claims that too often most of us start with the "what" and "how" and do not spend enough time digging into the "why," which he emphasizes is the most powerful influence on our actions. The "why" reveals our core purpose, beliefs, and values that create our identity and drive our behaviors. The profound simplicity is that "what" and "how" we do the things we do outwardly serves "why" we do them. He goes on to explain that since our brains are separated into feeling and logic functions, it is easier for us to articulate our "what" and "how" logic, versus our "why" feelings, and only through conscious effort can we trace our "what" and "how" to our "why" (Sinek 2009). Regardless of how you get there, at the heart of every individual quest is a reason and purpose for expending valuable time and energy to act. Discovering why you identify with certain shared common values and beliefs should drive your personal health IT career vision and help you evaluate and establish goals upon which to plan your social engagements.

There are many different personal and professional reasons why you should expend time and energy to engage socially. Writing down your reasons through a process of self-reflection and introspection will help you shape, guide, and understand your personal motives and goals, as well as create your own professional social engagement plan. As an example, a self-assessment may read something like this:

"As a current Electronic Health Record (EHR) Senior Database Administrator I believe that technology and data will continue to transform and improve the future of healthcare delivery to benefit patients in my community and around the world. I can contribute to that future throughout my career by optimizing health technology and data in my organization and helping others do the same. I see myself advancing from my current position to a Director of IT Operations in two to five years, then to a CIO position within ten years. To help achieve this I will establish a professional digital presence on social media platforms where I will connect with colleagues directly, as well as join, subscribe, and follow applicable online health IT groups and opinion leader forums. There I will specifically share my work and expertise in partnering with clinicians, CMIOs, and local Directors of Laboratory Services to solve community-wide COVID-19 lab test resulting and reporting to the Centers for Disease Control (CDC). I can also share my involvement in establishing contact tracing capabilities through regional Health Information Exchange (HIE) HER interfaces, and showcase my recent innovative solution to population health data hosting challenges. This will showcase my unique and relevant technical problem-solving skills and allow me to connect and learn from health IT peers, colleagues, and senior professionals about how they solved similar issues. I will also seek their mentoring and advice about obtaining an advanced degree in my field of interest. Furthermore, I will follow through with my social engagement by joining and participating in my local chapter and interest groups and attending key events in-person that allow me to engage with directors of health IT departments and healthcare CIOs face-to-face. My stretch goal would be to start a YouTube channel, Twitter feed, or LinkedIn forum to post and share 'how-to' videos and advice to aid other health IT professionals."

Taking the time to write a similar paragraph in a statement tailored to your own circumstances and desires will give you a starting point of reference and personal social engagement strategic plan. This will help you focus and integrate your efforts with your health IT career goals and learning endeavors.

THE WAYS

Now that you have embraced your purpose for social engagement and developed a personal strategy, review the definition of "socialize" at the beginning of this chapter, and consider the different ways you can interact, teach, and participate in social groups across the health IT landscape. Social engagements can happen between you and others in *one-to-one*, *one-to-many*, *many-to-many*, or *many-to-one* relationships. When these quantitative relationships are cross-referenced with the three basic

TABLE 25.1

Ways to Socially Engage

	Direct In-Person Examples	Direct Virtual Examples	Indirect Third-Person Examples
One-to-One (you)	Face-to-face, formal and informal events, mixers mentor/protégé coffee, work lunches, outside work socials, post seminar Q&A discussion line	Online forums, social media, phone calls, media, blogs, vlogs, chat rooms, individual email, peer-to-peer gaming, file sharing, email, YouTube video tutorials, computer-based training modules, instant message, avatar to avatar	Online or in-person word-of mouth, shared gossip, facial/name/ brand/ reputation recognition, grapevine, re-tweets, my profile views, profiles I viewed, content/interest group recommendations/ sharing, forwarded email
One-to-Many (you)	Speaker to audience, keynote address, teacher to students, professional affiliation chapter board member, local special interest group leader	Host live-stream or recorded webinars, Twitter (other) feed host, blog host, online LinkedIn, Facebook (other) special interest group facilitator/moderator, mobile SMS, author professional publication/articles	Interested listener, bystander, loiterer, watcher; monitor/share online activity with others, but do not subscribe, join, commit; para-social interaction; forwarded email to group; retweet, re-share, or re-post to larger groups
Many-to-Many (you)	Roundtable participant, working group member, conference attendee, think tanks, special interest groups, active local chapter participant, flash mob	Shared posts, chat rooms, online collaboration tools, LinkedIn, Facebook special interest group discussion contributor, online gaming, avatar worlds, crowd-sourcing, Google Hangouts	Rumors, likes, dislikes, subscribers, voting, shared opinions, comment threads, retrospective analysis, shared group email with larger group, social media sharing/interest groups, re-post, re-pin, re-tweet
Many-to-One (you)	Audience to speaker, attendee at keynote address, conference plenary and breakout sessions, conference keynote	Twitter/RSS feed subscriber, blog/vlog subscriber, personal learning network, webinar attendee, e-Mentoring, live-stream webinar attendee, avatar attendance	Reference another's work, pass along referrals, gossip, rumors, reputation to friend/colleague, hearsay, likes, dislikes, para-social interaction, retweet, re-share, re-post, email blast recipient, Pinterest followers

ways we professionally socialize and interact: (1) *Direct in person* (i.e., face-to-face), (2) *Direct virtual* (i.e., digital persona), (3) *Indirect third person* (i.e., word of mouth in-person or online), it renders practical examples of the different ways we engage and communicate socially. Table 25.1 provides examples of ways health informatics professionals can interact and engage socially to expand their professional networks; remain visible; and learn, teach, and contribute across the health IT community.

Looking back to the earliest days of computing, we saw a desire to leverage social digital engagement from the start. Long before Facebook or Twitter, or even MySpace, users would connect to bulletin board systems, or BBSs, where they exchanged some of the first instant messages and peer-to-peer files with other like-minded BBS users. BBSs were effectively the first widespread online digital chat rooms, and arguably the first digital "social media" tools prior to the introduction of the term. In the 1980s, BBSs were primarily used by computer enthusiasts because it took special knowledge and tech savvy to navigate command lines to push and retrieve messages and files. Back then, in order to message different people on different BBSs, you had to hang-up your telephone modem and dial another BBS to connect with different social or interest groups, and if you received a busy signal you'd have to try back later. Avid BBS users had multiple phone lines installed so that they could be on multiple BBSs with multiple modems and computers at the same time.

Fast forward to today. In slightly less than one generation, social media has become one of the most powerful and influential tools in our world. As shown in Table 25.1, the common thread in the "direct virtual" and "indirect third person" columns is the prevalent use of online interactive, virtual, and social media tools. Because social media is available 24 hours a day, seven days a week, 365 days a year, individuals can now maintain a digital presence anytime and anywhere to engage at their convenience without constraints of physical presence at specific times or places. Capitalizing on a no-cost or low-cost (depending on the social media services you choose) professional digital persona that is always on duty should entice you to set up and manage, or improve upon, your current social media profile(s). Doing so can amplify your reputation, name, and face recognition across the health IT community at in-person organizational events, regional or chapter professional affiliation gatherings, and national conferences. It also provides you with a way to invite, track, and maintain the connections you make in person with other professionals. Your social media profile is now the 21st century equivalent to a business card ... health IT professionals should not be caught without one.

Table 25.1 again highlights the expanding role and growing number of ways to engage socially online. Virtual/digital social media engagement and networking can be initiated via blogs, fan pages, RSS (really simple syndication) feeds, interest groups, forums, podcasts, video/picture-sharing, vlogs, wall-postings, email, instant messaging, peer-to-peer content sharing, and unified communications tools. With the limitless reach of social media, individuals, businesses, academia, governments, and healthcare organizations can conduct more effective information sharing, promotion, and outreach to target audiences and like-minded people.

There are hundreds of social media platforms and applications, as well as an ever-growing number of social media management and aggregation tools to help holistically manage your digital presence. Depending on your personal goals and limited time, health IT professionals must carefully choose the ways to engage and which social media tools to leverage as a means of generating the best learning opportunities. Thoughtfully utilizing the right social media tools as a primary means to exchange information and make connections that focus on your goals will create the greatest value to you as a health IT professional.

THE MEANS

Health informatics professionals serious about social media engagement will immediately encounter an overwhelming number of social media platforms from which to choose. To highlight just how many platforms exist, Table 25.2 lists 20 social media platform categories and over 250 social media tools, applications, and utilities. Many social media applications often cross multiple categories and functions, making clear alignment of applications to categories difficult at best.

The lists are not exhaustive, and you will notice the more familiar mainstream social media applications are comingled with less recognizable applications. These lesser-known applications sometimes offer niche capabilities and may come and go as usage fads are often driven by hype or narrow use functionality. It is easy to get caught up in constant hype, suggestions, and referrals from friends and colleagues; however, the large mainstream applications can provide stable, far-reaching platforms upon which to start and establish a solid social media presence.

One of the first recommendations to maximize your limited social media engagement time and energy is to initially focus on the most popular market-share leaders like LinkedIn, Facebook, Twitter, YouTube, and Pinterest. These are the familiar mainstream applications that you consistently see on the primary "Share This" buttons located on nearly every corporate and social media webpage today. As you progress and advance your social media skills you can investigate and potentially leverage other tools, like those designed to be exclusively for healthcare professionals (Ventola 2014). According to Debra Beck, author of "Social Media Vital to Professional Development," these mainstream tools offer the best immediate access to authors, educators, and opinion leaders and will most amplify your online presence and exposure to professional and career development resources.

TABLE 25.2

Social Media Categories, Tools, Platforms, Applications, and Services

Social Media Categories: (20)

- Conversation Apps - Social networking - Micro-blogging - Publishing-Wikis - Photo Sharing
- Aggregators - Audio - Video - Live Casting - RSS - Mobile - Crowd Sourcing - Virtual Worlds
- Gaming - Search - Engagement - Marketing - Management - Analytics - Influencer

Social Media tools, Platforms, Applications, and Services: (250+) alphabetical compilation

- 100zakladok - Adfty - Adifni - Adobe/Omniture - ADV QR - Agorapulse - Amazon - Amen Me!
- AngiesList - AOL Lifestream - AOL Mail - Appinions - APSense - Argyle Social - Arto - Attensity
- AvatarsUnited - Awareness - Awasu - Baidu - Balatarin - Beat100 - Bebo - Bit.ly - BizSugar - Blab
- Bland takkinn - Blogger - Blogkeen - Blogmarks - Bobrdobr - BonzoBox - Bookmarky.cz - Bookmerken - Box - Buddy Media - Buffer - Camyoo - Care2 - CSS Based - Cherry Share - CiteULike—ClassMates - CleanPrint - CleanSave - Cloob - Communicate - Copy Link - COSMiQ—CoTweet - Crimson Hexagon - Crowd Booster - Dashburst - Delicious - Diary.ru - Digg - Diggita—Diigo - Doc2Doc - Docphin - Douban - Doximity - Draugiem.lv - EdCast - EFactor - eHost - EngageSciences - EventBrite - Evernote - Exchangle - FabDesign - Fabulously40—Facebook - Facebook Messenger - Facenama - Fai Informazione - Fancy - Fashiolista - FAVable—Fave - Favorites - Favoritus - Feedly - Financial Juice - Flickr - Flipboard - Folkd - FourSquare - FreeDictionary - FriendFeed - GG - G-mail—G-Suite - Go.vn - Google Analytics - Google Bookmark - Google Classroom—Google Currents - Google Reader - Google Translate - GroupHigh - Hacker News - Hatena - Hearsay Social - Hedgehogs - historious - HootSuite - HTML Validator - Hyper—IFTTT Indexor—InstaChat - Instagram - Instapaper - Involver - iOrbix - Jappy Ticker - Jugnoo - Kaixin RepasteKakao - Ketnooi - Kik - Kindle It - Kledy - Klout - Kred - LiDAR Online - LINE - LinkedIn - Linkuj.cz - Lithium - LiveJournal - Mail.ru - mar.gar.in—Marco-Polo - Markme - Medworm - meinVZ - Meltwater BuzzMemonic - Memori.ru - Mendeley - Meneame - Mindomo - Mixi - Moemesto.ru—MouthShut - mRcNEtwORK - MS Lync - MS Outlook - MS Skype for Business—MS Teams - Myspace - myVidster - N4G - Nasza-klasa - Netvibes - Netvouz - NewsNetWire - NewsMeBack - Newsvine—NextDoor - Ning—Nujij - Nurses Lounge - Odnoklassniki - OKNOtizie - OpenTheDoor - Ovid - Oyyla - PageLever - pafnet. de - Path - PDFmyURL - Peach - Peek Analytics - People Browsr - Periscope - Pinboard—Pinterest - Plaxo - Plexus Engine - Plurk - Pocket - Posteezy - Postling - PrintFriendly - Pusha - QRSrc.com - Quantcast - QuantiaMD - Quora - Qzone - Radian6 - Reddit - Rediff MyPage - Renren - ResearchGate - Retellity - Safelinking - SAS - Scoop.it - Second Life - Sermo - Sharpreader—Shots - ShortStack - Shoutlet - Simply Measured - Sina Weibo - Skyrock Blog - Slack - Sloodle—SMI - SnapChat - Social - Bakers - Shots - SocialBro - SocialEngage - SocialFlow—SocialMention - SocialOomph - SodaHead - SpinSnap - Spredfast - Sprinklr - Sprout Social - Startaid—Startlap—Steam - studiVZ - Stuffpit - StumbleUpon - Stumpedia - SUP BRO - Surfingbird - Svejo - Swix—Symbaloo - Syncapse - Sysomos - Taringa! - TED - TEDMED - Telegram - Tencent QQ - Tencent Weibo - ThisNext—TikTok - Tinder - TinyPulse - TinyURL - Trackur - Trello - TrustedID Reppler - Tuenti - Tumblr—Tweepi - TweetDeck - Twitter - Typepad - Urlaubswerk - Viadeo - Viber - Vimeo - Vine - ViralHeat—Virb - Visible Technologies - Visitez Mon Site - Vitrue - Vkontakte - vKruguDruzei - Vocus - VoiceThread - VOXopolis - vybrali SME - Wanelo - Wayz - Wayback Machine - Web.com - WebMoney - WeChat - Weebly - WhatsApp - Whois Lookup - Wiggio - Wikipedia—Wildfire - WishMindr - Within3 - Wix - WordPress - Wykop - XING - Yahoo Mail - Yammer - Yelp—YikYak - Yo - Yookos - Yoolink - Yorumcuyum - YouMob - YouTube - Yummly - Yuuby - Zakladok.net - ZicZac - Zimbra - ZingMe - Zoho

Source: Compiled from web search results and Bard (2010), Baer (2015), and King (2011).

They present legitimate opportunities to not only share information and resources, but also frequently enable individuals to initiate and invite direct engagement with industry leaders (Beck 2014).

LinkedIn is consistently recommended as a premier networking site for professionals and business people. Its primary focus is connecting professionals and sharing ideas and important information about work in a business-like atmosphere. Although Facebook was originally rooted in personal networking, it is now firmly established in the professional networking space, too. An important factor to consider when using Facebook is the crossover potential between personal and professional profiles. It is important that a conscious effort is made to ensure your professional digital persona stays professional. Similarly, Twitter, YouTube, and Pinterest can be used as both personal and professional sharing platforms; yet, all of these mainstream tools provide the means to establish your digital persona and connect with and learn from health IT professionals across town and around the globe.

A recurring theme and recommendation for professionals who desire to fully leverage the benefits of the mainstream social media giants is to adhere to a disciplined approach and commit to certain platforms for personal use while keeping others strictly professional. You may want to consider an "all professional content" approach with the mainstream social media applications and use the niche tools for sharing of personal life items. Whichever applications you choose to use, you must study and clearly understand how to use and maintain the often-changing privacy and security settings on each social media platform to help keep your data and digital persona safe.

A good way to review your digital persona is to search for yourself, or watch a friend search for you, on the primary search engines such as Google, Yahoo, and Bing so you can see what other professionals see when they search for you. If you do not like what you find, you should clean up and update your profile(s) content, privacy, and security settings. Advanced users of multiple social media tools may want to consider aggregation and online image monitoring tools to manage all profiles.

THE HOW

Although you may not recognize it, you already have what is described as an informal personal learning network (Arora 2014) made up of your relationships with the people you know and interact with frequently. These existing relationships are the foundation upon which to build and expand social media network connections and link to further professional development opportunities. To begin or advance your social engagement journey your next step should be to establish or improve online profile(s) on one or more mainstream social media tools.

A closer look at what LinkedIn, Facebook, Twitter, YouTube, Pinterest, and other tools can offer will help you choose which ones best fit your health IT professional learning needs. By summarizing the basics of mainstream social media platforms and how to establish a professional digital profile on each, you will be able to quickly start leveraging their networking, content-sharing, and functional capabilities for your personal learning network. In every case you should reference and apply the repeatable generic social media "Do's and Don'ts Checklist" in Table 25.3. It summarizes important tips and reminders on configuring and maintaining social media profiles, privacy, and security settings.

As you step through setting up your social media profiles, be sure to refer back to your "why" social engagement strategy to ensure your desired outcomes stay at the forefront. Specifically search each social media tool to find, bookmark, and connect with target health IT groups and individuals who match your career goals and personal objectives. Since LinkedIn has a professional focus and search results indicate 54,000+ individuals, groups, jobs, and posts related to health IT, and, more specifically, 1,784 groups related to health information practices, it is a great place to start connecting.

LinkedIn

LinkedIn claims to be the world's largest professional network with more than 300 million members in 200+ countries. About 61% of LinkedIn's members are located outside of the United States; members did nearly 4.2 billion professionally oriented searches on the platform in 2011. It offers a large database of other people's job titles, professions, career paths, companies, and career opportunities from which to mine, study, and learn. Similar to other mainstream social media applications, LinkedIn has a powerful mobile app for Android and iOS, which allows you to remotely manage your profile and connections on the go (Prodromou 2015). For more on LinkedIn stats visit https://omnicoreagency.com/linkedin-statistics.

TABLE 25.3

Checklist of Social Media Do's and Don'ts for Health IT Professionals

DO	DON'T
• Search for yourself to see what others see	• Add unprofessional content (personal pix)
• Remove unprofessional and personal content	• Post sexual, religious, political, or cute content
• Develop a professional profile	• Comingle personal and professional content
• Business-like email address only	• Completely replace in-person interaction
• Professional photos only	• Accept invites to vague groups or evident solicitors; keep your network pure to you
• Consistent across platforms	• Ignore your profile or set-it and forget it
• Update every 2–3 months	• Include phone numbers, just email or social media handle for contact
• Add professional sig block	• Post where you live; the postal code of your place of employment is enough
• Make a great first digital impression	• Create different profiles for different social media platforms; all should be consistent
• Add health IT key words/tags/current and future interest areas to profile so others can search and find you	• Ignore or relax privacy and security settings
• Join health IT interest groups/areas	• Compromise your network by friending or allowing connections that tarnish your image
• Only accept/seek professionals in your area(s) of interest that you want to learn from	• Make negative, insulting, or petty posts
• Contribute to your online forums ...ratings are good value to your career	• Discuss controversial hot topics
• Consider paying for premium services at strategic times in your career	• Forget to add at least one attention-getter picture to posts ... still worth 1,000 words
• Create a professional signature on your email	• Forget that the information you put online benefits the company through aggregation and sale of information to other companies that use it to target audiences for products and services; refer to last item in "Do" list
• Consider aggregators to monitor multiple social sites in one place if advanced user	
• Answer visitor messages	
• Post, tweet, share, and contribute twice a week	
• Unfriend or disconnect with those acting unprofessionally	
• Keep messages short and succinct	
• Reduce/filter/delete irrelevant clutter/noise	

Source: Adapted from Murray (2016) and Pollak (2012).

Set up a LinkedIn account and complete your profile as thoroughly as possible using the automated interview. Be sure to include your current and two prior positions, skills, education, a professional photo, and a professional career summary. Treat your profile as if it were your digital resume. The site provides you with a "profile completeness" metric from 0% to 100%. The higher your completeness, the more likely you are to appear higher up in LinkedIn's search results. Search health IT-related terms in your specific areas of interest to find and join one or more groups. Immediately connect with those already in your personal learning network sphere that also have a profile. To get your first "50 connections" in LinkedIn, make use of its many algorithms and data-mining features on the "People You May Know" page. Generously give and request endorsements and recommendations. To learn more about LinkedIn, you can read *Ultimate Guide To: LinkedIn for Business*, by Ted Prodromou.

FACEBOOK

Facebook has more than 1.28 billion active monthly users, which is roughly one-sixth of the entire world population. The social networking giant has introduced an extensive array of tools throughout its evolution that can be used effectively for professional growth. Whether it is Facebook groups, Business pages, or Events, each of these functions is a great way of communicating with experts, spreading new ideas, building relationships and contacts, and trying new things (Arora 2014).

Create a professional Facebook page by adding the same information to your profile that you did on LinkedIn, then search for and take advantage of online communities to which you are already affiliated. This might include your organization's page, your university's wall, the Facebook fan page of a nonprofit you support, or an industry association Listserv. Once you are a member use the Facebook search tool to find and join health IT interest groups and friend-related companies. Connect with people and groups who share common interests. Comment on and participate in discussion threads. The Events feature will keep you informed about the latest learning opportunities happening in and around your city and update you on professional activities that you can attend for further networking. The search engine combines the job databases of USjobs, Monster, Jobvite, BranchOut, and WORK4LABS, enabling discovery of exclusive job opportunities. Be sure to "Like" and "Share" professional interest pages, company and organizational pages, and content with others. Add descriptions titles and tags in the "About" section of your profile that reflect your health IT professional interests. Again, try to avoid personal likes and dislikes, hobbies, opinions, and descriptions. Use your "Status" to discuss your accomplishments and future goals. Become an active contributor to your connected group pages to build and enhance your professional network.

TWITTER

According to the company's latest reports, Twitter has over 250 million active users. Since Twitter accounts, tweets, and pages are indexed by Google, Twitter can be a powerful online presence for users. Foremost it allows users to connect with like-minded learning professionals who follow shared interests, news stories, and industry trends. Twitter is also a powerful tool to research and connect with recruiters, industry experts, and colleagues. Even if you primarily "monitor" content more than you tweet, you'll value the information because it is customized to your professional interests.

After setting up a Twitter account, you will need to learn Twitter jargon. This social media tool has a small learning curve, but as you become familiar with terminology such as hashtags, tweets, promoted tweets, RT (retweet), RLRT (real-life retweet), IRL (in real life), MT (modified tweet), OH (overheard), Timestamp, and Activities, you'll become a mature participant in no time. Actively sending and relaying informative/instructional tweets and participating in Twitter chats around a particular subject area can bolster career development by increasing your professional exposure and reputation. Additionally, companies are increasingly tweeting job postings so you can be the first to hear about and share career opportunities with others.

Twitter can set you apart in the health IT community not only by enabling you to stay current within the industry and your field of interest, but also by helping you prepare for interviews and keeping you engaged in real-time opportunities. Once on Twitter, consider following your university, health IT professional organizations, respected health IT professionals, companies of interest, and your current organization of employment. Use a short professional "handle" (username on Twitter) that people can refer to you by if your real name is long, and "hashtag" using words that are career related such as #HITjobs, #HITemployment, and #healthIT. Your tweets should include your career interests, goals, experience, and training. Use your profile to showcase your skills and capabilities to other professionals. Avid users may want to consider organizing followed Twitter pages into lists and grouping them by related topics. This will enable you to view grouped tweets separately so that you are not overwhelmed by other users' tweets.

YouTube

This ubiquitous video-sharing site has more than 1 billion unique monthly users. Created in 2007, the YouTube Partner program has 30,000+ partners from 27 countries around the world (Arora 2014). With estimates from 60 to multiple 100 s of hours of video uploaded every minute, users can find video resources on almost any topic imaginable. The large variety of instructional videos available and the fact that its hosted content is linked to more sites across the web than any other makes YouTube one of the top interactive social media tools for professional development. Professionals can even start their own YouTube channel to produce and post educational and instructional videos and vlogs (video blogs) on topics of interest. It is a great means to demonstrate your individual personal strengths and professional public speaking and communication skills.

Pinterest

Pinterest is used to create an online visual identity for networking purposes and build a profile that displays you as a health IT professional. Professionals will "Pin" resumes, events, organizations, academic institutions, volunteer and charity work, former employers, inspirational quotes, and general things that they have created. The content that you display on Pinterest is important, so keep your content consistent. You can "Like," "Pin," and "Repin" images that reflect your interests, as well as cross-link your other social media profiles.

When using Pinterest, be sure to choose images that represent you, your past accomplishments, your future goals, and website links that are educational and meaningful to your health IT colleagues. Consider how the content you choose will showcase you. What you choose to share on your "Board" is the most important part of your profile. Everything that you "Pin" should lead to something that represents you as a health IT professional. Make your Pinterest Board interesting and visually pleasing with eye-catching pictures to attract and gain more followers.

Blogs

Blogging allows you to demonstrate your professional expertise or knowledge of a specific subject by writing about it. A few popular blogging sites are Wordpress, Tumblr, WorkBuzz, One Day, One Job, and Blogger. Your blogs have the potential to be shared widely across the Web and can lead to vast networking opportunities. Blog posts should be between 500 and 1,000 words and include an enticing heading and a catchy summation title. This signals to potential readers that they can learn a lot for a small investment of time.

Professional bloggers keep blogs relevant and current and often include references to further materials, books, articles, and research. Like other social media posts, the success of your blog can also be easily increased by adding pictures, videos, and music. Check to see if a health informatics professional that you like has a blog and "Follow" the blogs of those that share your interests. Be cautious of how you comment on other's blogs. Constructive and suggestive comments can be uplifting, while harsh comments reflect negativity and can be discouraging.

Aggregators

Social media aggregation tools such as Ning, Tumblr, TrustedID Reppler, TweetDeck, and Hootsuite are applications that automate the management of multiple social media platforms or profiles at once. These tools can help professionals manage information overload in an era where social media, email, and 24-hour news cycles can inundate the savviest users. An increasing number of dashboards and platforms are available to bring accounts, services, and content together on a single central location for ease of use. Social media developers have consolidated applications such as RSS feeds, Facebook, LinkedIn, Wikipedia, and Twitter so they work together from within one account and user environment.

For social media power users, aggregation allows for one-stop updating and information-monitoring in real time. It also enables busy professionals to monitor and view syndicated content from multiple sources simultaneously in one tool on the go using mobile devices and helps sift and filter real-time content across networks rather than searching the Web or individual social media tools.

In addition, aggregation tools allow their users to add/remove content quickly; easily monitor streams; filter and create sub-streams; and respond, comment, and chat with people instantly. It powerfully schedules information retrieval using tracking tools and adapts content accordingly in one space. Some aggregators even aid in automated monitoring of your professional image, providing users with an "image score" using feedback algorithms that assess overall factors of having good social media pages such as language, phrases, activity, likes, dislikes, and types of individuals tied to your social media pages. This lets professionals know how their social media image comes across to others. Some can even alert you to privacy and security risks and provide you an activity summary of how information on your pages could negatively affect your online image.

Corporate, Asynchronous, Community, and Neighborhood-Centric Apps

Socializing and mentoring should not be just a footnote in your mainstream social media toolbox. Recent online and micro-social media and internal use applications such as CultureAmp, Energage Jive, Google Currents, Lattice, MS Teams, OfficeVibe, Tiny Pulse; asynchronous video and chat applications like InstaGram, Marco Polo, Snapchat, Slack, and TikTok; and neighborhood platforms such as Amazon's Neighbors, Citizen, Front Porch, and NextDoor make real-time communications easy, convenient, and personalized. They leverage spritz messages, video clip sharing, and short message strings to ask and share "near-orbit" knowledge and advice between colleagues, professionals, and neighbors. The curated content and near-field communication flows are specifically tailored to your workplaces and the neighborhoods where you live.

Engaging in the places where you live and work is relevant to extending your personal and professional network to colleagues, friends, and neighbors. Do not ignore these tools in your social engagement strategy. Wherever you are, there are tools that make it easy to find professionals and engage socially. In a COVID-19 punctuated world as developers integrate more virtual social interaction features and functions into their platforms, we can anticipate an ever-increasing emphasis and number of ways to leverage online and virtual social engagement. Investigate these tools to see which ones work best for your lifestyle and personal communication rhythms. Join your colleagues or neighbors for a backyard bar-b-que or cup of coffee, and be open to engaging them about your interests to gain knowledge and develop yourself and others.

HIMSS Resources

A great way to learn and socialize as you determine your interests across the healthcare technology landscape is to consult with the Healthcare Information and Management Systems Society (HIMSS). Ask a HIMSS staff member about how to connect with one or more of its associated special interest or advocacy groups, professional communities, network forums, national committees, or local chapters. Review HIMSS.org as a tremendous professional learning and development resource tool with a "Members-In-Action Feed" and "Career Services" where you will find hundreds of health informatics professionals and thought leaders to connect with one another. The "HIMSS Learning Center" enables health IT career-oriented professionals to join webinars and briefings, view online courses, and interact with speakers and user communities. The "HIMSS eMentor" initiative helps connect nurses, pharmacists, and executives via LinkedIn and Twitter. From informatics to medical devices, or from data interoperability standards to HIEs, there is bound to be something at HIMSS for you to participate in. Once you are connected, take it a step further and volunteer some time to engage socially with your peers in person.

As a long-time HIMSS member, Certified Professional in Healthcare Information and Management Systems (CPHIMS), Fellow, Health Information Management Systems Society (FHIMSS), past chapter president, and prior Chair of the HIMSS Federal Health Community, I can attest that social engagement for career development works. I have met health IT professionals through online social media and in-person engagements who have influenced the course of my career and opened doors for me across our community. I've personally and professionally bene-fited by learning and sharing ideas with these colleagues and thought leaders. Specifically, my health IT social connections helped me learn about the operational impacts of legislation such as the Health Insurance Portability and Accountability Act (HIPAA); Health Information Technology for Economic and Clinical Health (HITECH) Act; Food and Drug Administration Safety and Innovation Act (FDASIA); Affordable Care Act (ACA); Federal Information Technology Acquisition Reform Act (FITARA); and more recently the Coronavirus Aid, Relief, and Economic Security (CARES) Act upon my healthcare organization. Professional colleagues introduced me to other professionals and enabled my participation in the Health and Human Services Office of the National Coordinator (ONC) for Health Information Technology-first Meaningful Use request for information (RFI) analysis and certification criteria development. Colleagues inspired me to ad-vocate for grants supporting health IT training and education, engaged me in HL7® FHIR® standard working groups, and invited me to moderate the HIMSS16 Annual Conference & Exhibition session with the White House Chief of Science and Technology. The people I've met have helped advance my career and provided professional engagement and learning opportunities that I would not have experienced solely within my own organization. The knowledge I gained and shared has helped the health IT community progress forward. For that I am sincerely grateful. And to all those engaged health IT professionals who helped me advance over the years (you know who you are), you were there with me as I received the HIMSS National 2018 Federal Health IT Leadership award. I owe you all a debt of gratitude for sharing yourselves with me and keeping me engaged, challenged, and encouraged. Sincere thanks!

CONCLUSION

In closing, how we decide to engage socially, network professionally, or share of ourselves and how others decide to share with us, both online and in person, can change the healthcare industry one health IT professional at a time. With the growing number of ways to engage using social media and digital tools, I encourage you to proactively start your social engagement journey today and stay open to learning from your health IT colleagues and the broader professional community. Do not wait for someone to invite you, but if you are the type of person who needs an invite to explore and engage socially, I extend that invitation to you now. Try it. Set up a profile on at least one of the aforementioned tools and turn the page to the next chapter in your career by putting your digital presence to work for you. And if the flow of information becomes overwhelming, return to your "why," narrow your focus, stay engaged in-person, and remember that although information is available 24 hours a day, seven days a week, 365 days a year, you decide when to access it and for how long. Leverage the valuable information in this book to keep learning continuously. Respect your inevitable learning curve, and know that persistence will yield rich learning rewards (Beck 2014).

REFERENCES

Arora, D. 2014. How to Use Social Media for Professional Development. SocialMediaToday.com. http://www.socialmediatoday.com/content/how-use-social-media-professional-development

Baer, J. 2015. Clearing Clouds of Confusion: The 5 Categories of Social Media Software. Convinceand Convert.com. http://www.convinceandconvert.com/social-media-tools/clearing-clouds-of-confusion-the-5-categories-of-social-media-software/

Bard, M. 2010. 15 Categories of Social Media. "The Social Web" graphic. http://www.mirnabard.com/2010/02/15-categories-of-social-media/

Beck, D. 2014. *Social Media Vital to Professional Development*, University of Wyoming. http://evolllution.com/opinions/social-media-vital-professional-development/

Duckworth, A. 2016. Warren Buffet's Famous Advice for Leading a Fulfilling Life is Simple. Business Insider Video. https://www.youtube.com/watch?v=Lf5ii3Q9AKs

King, C. 2011. 22 Hot New Social Media Tools Worth Exploring. http://www.socialmediaexaminer.com/22-hot-new-social-media-tools-worth-exploring/

Murray, J. 2016. Using Social Media for Professional Development. TeachHub.com. http://insight.cumbria ac.uk/id/eprint/3422/1/Ward_AttitudesToSocial.pdf

Pollak, L. 2012. 10 Tips for Using Social Media in Your Job Search. Job Choices. https://www.roanestate.edu/webfolders/HARRISKB/placement/articles/students/10_Tips_for_Using_Social_Media_in_ Your_Job_Search.pdf

Prodromou, T. 2015. *Ultimate Guide To: LinkedIn for Business*, 2nd Edition. Irvine, CA: Entrepreneur Press. https://books.google.com/books/about/Ultimate_Guide_to_LinkedIn_for_Business.html?id=Zlv_BgAAQBAJ&source=kp_cover&hl=en

Sinek, S. 2009. *Start With Why: How Great Leaders Inspire Everyone to Take Action*. New York: Penguin Group (USA) Inc.

Ventola, C. L. 2014. Social Media and Health Care Professionals: Benefits, Risks, and Best Practices. MediMedia USA, Inc. http://www.ncbi.nlm.nih.gov/pmc/articles/PMC4103576/

26 Viewing the Workplace for On-the-Job Training

Dennis Winsten
MS

CONTENTS

INTRODUCTION

Health information technology (IT) professionals who have an interest in expanding their knowledge of the many opportunities in the healthcare setting should look to on-the-job training (OJT) as a source of continuing professional development (CPD). OJT will equip the professional with additional skills, with greater depth of understanding of the role that he or she is in, and with increased potential for advancement in the field. The IT profession offers one of the most dynamic careers an individual can enjoy. OJT presents learning opportunities that offer the ability to stay abreast of the increasing demands and depth and breadth of skills that are required to succeed in this exciting field.

This chapter will:

- Provide alternative definitions of OJT consistent with today's health IT work environment
- Recommend questions that the reader should ask himself or herself to help in making appropriate decisions about the types, scope, and focus of OJT opportunities in which to engage as an avenue for professional growth and advancement
- Describe some of the types of OJT programs being offered by healthcare institutions and healthcare systems vendors
- Challenge the reader to think about OJT opportunities in a broader sense and to consider how to leverage/utilize OJT to meet current and future professional goals

WHAT IS OJT?

Some common definitions of OJT are:

> On-the Job Training (OJT) means training in the public or private sector that is given to a paid employee while he or she is engaged in productive work and that provides knowledge and skills essential to the full and adequate performance on the job.[1]
>
> On-the-job training is a form of training taking place in a normal working situation, sometimes called direct instruction, it is one of the earliest forms of training (observational learning is probably the

DOI: 10.4324/9780429398377-31

earliest). It is a one-on-one training located at the job site, where someone who knows how to do a task shows another how to perform it.[2]

On-the-job training focuses on the acquisition of skills within the work environment generally under normal working conditions. Through on-the-job training, workers acquire general skills that they can transfer from one job to another and specific skills that are unique to a particular job.[3]

A definition that is broader and reflects today's expansion of OJT might be more relevant for the reader. In that context, an alternate definition could be:

> OJT means training and/or education by employers in the public or private sector that is given to a paid employee, or self-financed by the employee, while he or she is engaged in productive work. OJT provides the knowledge and skills essential to the full and adequate performance of the employee's present job as well as opportunities for future job advancements and professional growth.

OJT programs are offered for different reasons. They benefit the employer by helping staff perform better on their job rather than learning new skills. To the employer, OJT is a way to develop a custom-trained workforce, and the investment that the employer makes in the employee reflects confidence in the employee's potential for growth and productivity, improves morale, and can generate the mutual loyalty of employee to employer, and vice versa. To the employee, OJT is a "free" opportunity for learning, growth, and job security, particularly in the fast-paced world of health IT. It uses the workplace and paid work hours to the benefit of both employee and employer, and it is a learning opportunity that helps to prepare the employee for a fulfilling and productive future.

How can someone enhance his or her professional development using experiences gained while working in a health IT position? OJT doesn't necessarily have to be training offered by the employer. A broader view of OJT can include any education, learning experience, or training that the employee undertakes while working at the job. This could include after work hours opportunities paid for by your employer such as community college or university courses or webinars by professional organizations (e.g., Healthcare Information and Management Systems Society [HIMSS]) or vendors. Some, but not all, of these options may provide continuing education units applicable towards the renewal of a credential. Regardless, the opportunity will add to your knowledge base. Some employers may offer tuition reimbursement and/or paid time off for studies.

Organization-sponsored or required OJT as a concept is not without issues. Often employees anticipate the training to be boring, disruptive to their project timetables, and not beneficial to them personally, and OJT may trigger concern for their career future should they not perform well during the training.

However, the fields of IT and healthcare have been and continue to evolve very rapidly. Keeping abreast of changes in computer technologies, networking, mobile applications, regulatory issues, medical advancements, etc., is a formidable task. OJT and education in the health IT domain are critical to maintain and/or obtain the necessary job skills to be successful in such a dynamic environment.

TYPES AND SCOPE OF OJT OFFERINGS

What are the types and scope of on-the-job training offered today? It's useful to look at what a number of organizations are doing to get an idea of what you might look for in a current position or in seeing a future career opportunity. OJT offered by various healthcare institutions, health IT systems vendors, and professional organizations include:

Health Systems/Medical Centers/Hospitals

- A large Michigan health system offers extensive professional development opportunities for both those in IT as well as departmental (e.g., laboratory, radiology, pharmacy) informatics staff. Most of this is done though either "leadership academies," which are face-to-face courses, or online education that uses the health system's online, self-paced learning management system (LMS) where access to thousands of hours of IT courses are available. Health IT staff are required to participate in at least one course per year. Many employees with a commitment to continuous learning take more courses. They know this is required for their best chance of success. In addition, annually, all staff attend an initial full two-day or one-day refresher Lean Six Sigma course. Group managers identify the most appropriate courses that will benefit an employee. Not all the course work is technical; other topics like project management and communications are offered to employees for OJT.
- A major university medical center in Maryland is engaged in a contract with Skillsoft for a broad range of online courses on IT and non-IT-related subjects available to its staff. To access this content, staff log onto the Skillsoft site with their institutional ID and password to access the training materials. A very broad range of IT and business-related content is available. Additionally, staff at the medical center receive tuition reimbursement for taking internal courses from the university's Computer Science Department, its Business School, and its School of Public Health, all of which offer advanced degree graduate programs via evening and summer courses.
- A major California cancer center provides support for its health IT staff, allowing them to participate in various certification programs. Certification programs include the Project Management Institute's PMP (Project Management Professional) to help employees learn the competencies needed to lead and direct projects as well as the ITIL (Information Technology Infrastructure Library) practices and processes credential for ITT service management that aligns IT with the needs of the medical center. The PMP and ITIL programs are conducted externally by one of the certification organizations. Annually, on a quarterly basis, there are sessions for IT teams on high performance training. There is also an organizational leadership program offered to senior health IT staff at the director level and above. This "Leadership Academy" is an offsite one-week program administered by an external firm. All of these OJT programs are provided at no cost to the employee and are funded out of the IT budget.

IT Vendors

- Microsoft Innovation Centers are offered by local government organizations, universities, industry organizations, and software or hardware vendors who partner with Microsoft and share a common goal to foster the growth of local software economies. These are state-of-the-art technology facilities that are open to students, developers, IT professionals, entrepreneurs, startups, and academic researchers. The e-Learning library includes a broad array of classes, including basic computer skills, Microsoft Office software, and advanced technical courses, ensuring that there is something for everyone regardless of current computer skill level.
- One large electronic health record (EHR) vendor reimburses its staff for additional ongoing training, which includes classes, conferences, or webinars. In addition, staff members can access a "professional development fund" each year to purchase books related to their professions or work assignments, or to learn more about a topic in healthcare.
- A long-time healthcare IT company in the Northeast provides a comprehensive training program for new hires. These training programs are conducted in classrooms as well as by webinars and through e-Learning modules that allow for self-paced learning. The training

programs can last anywhere from two months to six to eight months depending on the participant's role. Employees also have the option to register for any number of continuing education offerings. Staff are permitted to attend classes on more specific or focused topics to further enhance their job training. The company provides all internal training, creates e-Learning modules and training materials, and offers access to educational websites free of charge to the staff member. The company also provides a tuition reimbursement program for staff who wish to pursue outside education opportunities provided it is with an accredited institution and is related to their specific role or to healthcare in general.

- Another major health IT/EHR vendor offers its staff a performance support tool with the sole purpose of OJT-related learning. The tool is intended to assist staff involved in sales, support, or consulting to clients by providing pertinent information, guidance, and training. Additionally, as part of an OJT experience, instructor-led training is provided to prepare staff members for client engagements.

PROFESSIONAL ORGANIZATIONS

- HIMSS offers many opportunities for professional learning and growth while working on-the-job. HIMSS Virtual Events provide insights into a number of industry important topics presented by health IT experts. HIMSS webinar events are offered on a complimentary basis. Many of the events provide credits for continuing education requirements for the Certified Professional in Healthcare Information and Management Systems (CPHIMS) or Certified Associate in Healthcare Information and Management Systems (CAHIMS). The HIMSS Global Health Conference & Exhibition provides a forum to interact with other health IT stakeholders, hear presentations on current health IT issues of importance, and see the latest in technological advancements at vendor exhibitions.
- The American College of Healthcare Executives (ACHE) similarly provides learning opportunities for its members. Face-to-face offerings include educational seminars for professional development with topics integral to healthcare management, customized ACHE on-location programs held on-site at an organization, or specialized executive programs. Distance education is provided via webinars and multi-week online seminars, both of which provide ACHE Qualified Education credits.

The type and scope of OJT offered by healthcare institutions, health IT vendors, and professional organizations varies, but some form of OJT and educational support is almost always available to health IT staff who have an interest in furthering their professional development while attaining career goals.

THINGS TO THINK ABOUT

There are many questions that you need to ask yourself... and answer as you consider job preparedness and advancement, career goals, and future opportunities in the health IT profession. Questions you may want to ask are: Is the cumulative experience gained in a single health IT position sufficient or is it better to gain knowledge from the perspectives of several, perhaps radically different, health IT jobs? Would experience gained in jobs outside of health IT be an advantage to broaden professional expertise and value to prospective employers? Can professional development be planned or simply based on opportunities that arise? Can you select OJT opportunities that will further your goals so that OJT could also mean "Objectives Job Training," where the training is intended to meet your personal professional objectives?

Any new job should require sufficient prior experience yet offer a considerable amount of new learning. The extent of new learning in a new job that one is willing to undertake depends on a person's tolerance for risk. "What if I can't do this? What if I fail?" Nelson Mandela once said: "I never lose. I win or I learn." Learning is not meant to be comfortable undertaking. Learning means change, and while change is inevitable, it can be very uncomfortable and incurs some level of risk. One advantage of OJT, as with any well-designed learning environment, is that the student is allowed to make mistakes—they are part of the learning process, in other words the risk is minimized.

Accepting a new position that requires basically the same skill levels and expertise that one already has is not a way to grow professionally. Employees need to add "layers" of new expertise and skills over the years. Consider how much of a "stretch" you are willing to make in a new job or new position in the same company.

Continuing professional development through OJT can help you make that stretch and can often be achieved from a plan based on your interests and aspirations. Do you wish to always be highly technical in your endeavors or would you prefer to move into progressive levels of management? The OJT steps that you take depend on your ultimate professional goal.

Suppose your long-term goal is to continue to be a technical "guru" and lead a technical project team or systems technical department. If so, your goal should be to obtain OJT that will further that objective. Steps that you could take are:

- Attend technical training courses offered by your employer, by universities, or by vendors. HIMSS offers various webinars that can provide learning while on the job. Attending national and regional health IT-related conferences (e.g., HIMSS Global Health Conference & Exhibition) can provide an excellent source of useful job-related information both from the presentations offered and the technologies displayed in the Exhibit Hall. Even if you can't attend in person, you can obtain session recordings via the HIMSS Learning Center.
- Study and consider the direction in which health IT will progress, then google and read all that you can on related subjects.
- Volunteer for projects that will utilize advanced technologies.
- Consider working in a different technical area (e.g., networking, mobile technologies, imaging), perhaps even outside the healthcare domain.

Suppose you envision your long-term goal as that of a top-level manager in health IT. If so, your goal should be to obtain OJT that will further your objectives. Steps that you could take are:

- Work to develop communications and "people" skills.
- Attend project management training courses offered by your employer, by universities, or by vendors.
- Consider earning a degree in a non-technical subject (e.g., business, human relations, psychology). You may be surprised at how much these non-technical disciplines will broaden your perspective and help you become a better manager.

Opportunities for OJT may not "knock on your door"; rather, you may need to seek them out. Be alert to opportunities in your workplace that may identify roles that you can play in addition to your current job responsibilities. Volunteering to take on some new functions and learn new skillsets, even on a limited basis, can prepare you for a more advanced position in your organization. Case in point, a non-health IT individual who started out as a laboratory technician began helping the Health IT Department with some data entry and validation issues. Today, he is the Director of the Health IT Department in his hospital.

CONCLUSION

Most healthcare institutions and health IT vendors offer a varied range of OJT opportunities, many at no cost to the employee.

OJT opportunities can be either "passive" or "active." Passive OJT derives from employer-sponsored training programs whose emphasis is usually on benefits to the company, that is, helping employees do a better job in their work capacity and lesser on the employees' professional career. Active OJT results from individual choices based on their career objectives, such as technical or management. These opportunities may be taken at the employee's expense or underwritten and supported by the employee's company.

For health IT professionals, there is a bright future in your industry. Technology has and will continue to expand in new and exciting ways. Rapid change is the "watchword," and professional advancement requires continuous learning and evolving practical experience. OJT, whether sponsored by employers or undertaken as an individual initiative, will be a key factor in successfully meeting professional goals.

NOTES

1 West Virginia Dept. of Health and Human Resources.
2 Wikipedia.
3 *Encyclopedia of Business*, 2nd Edition.

27 Talent Management for the Health IT Professional

Richard E. Biehl
PhD, CSQE, CSSBB

CONTENTS

INTRODUCTION

An organization conducts operations that consume skills and knowledge. It *demands* talent. As professionals, we use our skills and knowledge to work with, and for, operational organizations. We *supply* talent. That supply–demand relationship regarding talent is the centerpiece of our employment relationships as professionals (Figure 27.1). The mechanisms by which that

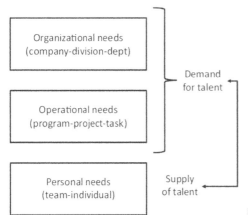

FIGURE 27.1   Talent supply-demand perspectives.

relationship is maintained have changed in our economy over a period of decades in ways that have altered how we actually perceive employment as a social institution.

Establishing an employment relationship (e.g., getting a job) requires demonstrating some minimum requirement for having the talent necessary to perform required duties. In some organizations, that demonstration is in the form of a credential earned through education. Most relationships in healthcare that we would classify as professional positions use the basic four-year college degree as a minimum credential. Some professional positions require a much higher minimum.

Achieving that level of required credential has always been a self-managed process. While society as a whole might provide or even insist on everyone going through primary and secondary education, the notion of continuing education to achieve college-level credentials is left to individual choice. Until the minimum requirements have been met to achieve employment in a desired field, talent management is dominated by self-management of one's education.

Once employed, that situation undergoes a shift. A generation ago, a person entering a position in an organization expected her or his employer to take over responsibility for talent management. The employer saw the shift in the same way, usually putting significant human resource processes in place to make sure that everyone in the organization was being continuously trained to promote and enhance their talents for current and future positions and operations. The line between the talent you needed to demonstrate prior to gaining employment and the levels of talent you were expected to achieve throughout your career in employment was very clear. Your employer would take it from there.

Today, a person entering an organization holds few, if any, such expectations. The shift is largely the result of bigger and broader changes in the social relationship represented by employment generally. Few people think in terms of lifetime employment when they enter an organization anymore. Organizations are not enthusiastic to develop extensive new or additional talents in people who they now perceive as highly mobile in their employment. Indeed, people in organizations are less likely to be employees in a formal or legal sense anymore. Organizations are reluctant to make talent management investments in people with whom their relationship is only contingent. Under these circumstances, lifetime talent management has become self-managed.

The line between pre-employment talent management that was largely focused on going to college has shifted forward into one's career as a professional. For a few, talent management has become a permanent exercise in self-management. For most, talent management has become part of a portfolio that is shared with one's employer. If the ratio is dominated by the employer, less change is perceived or needed. If the ratio is dominated by self-development, either because of working for an employer that doesn't see talent management as a core responsibility anymore or because entrepreneurial interests might drive a career with many employment changes, the need to develop and manage one's own talents can become of paramount concern.

Many of the lines described here can be quite fuzzy. Employers might invest in certain types of talents, but not others. Developing talents for one's current or next position can be viewed differently from developing those involved in a career change. Talents that support licensure or accreditation might be managed very differently than others. Many talent categories aren't measured in clearly demarcated levels such as bachelor's, master's, or doctoral degrees. Realistically, most talents needed to perform a professional function aren't covered directly by any such degrees. The pool of talents being managed for an individual can be diverse and evolving as career interests and opportunities change or emerge.

The bottom line out of all of this is that self-managing one's own talent development has become a critical skill for professionals throughout the economy, particularly in the fast-changing and dynamic healthcare and information technology (IT) sectors. The one talent this requires us all to have, therefore, is a talent for managing our own lifelong learning.

ADAPTING STANDARDS INTO A SYSTEMIC PROCESS

Since adopting and adapting industry standards is part of the set of recommendations for talent management offered later in this chapter, it's only fitting that this chapter uses that approach. When we adopt existing standards, we accelerate the development of key talents called for in those standards, and we avoid the need to identify and characterize specific skills and knowledge. Letting a published standard do most of the work for us is a core competency if we're to effectively self-manage our personal talent pool.

To make effective use of a set of standards, whatever type and category of standards you ultimately choose as representing the domains against which you want to self-manage your talents, it helps to organize them into a framework that makes them easier to order and integrate in your planning. As process engineers, we are usually trying to build a system that converts inputs into outputs through an effective system design. As we build our talent management process, we want to identify standards that will define the outcomes we want to achieve through talent management (typically denoted as Fs). We also want to define input standards that can help identify the requirements that our talent management process must satisfy to be effective (typically denoted as *Xs*) (Figure 27.2).

Bridging our inputs to outputs is our talent management process or system. Its design and controls convert the input standard process guidelines into effective talent management outcomes (typically denoted by the transfer function $F_1 = f(X_1, x_2, \ldots x_N)$ for any desired outcomes defined by our output standards. Since most published standards target organization or industry applications and scope, their use in this context typically requires refocusing both their scale and language to the individual personal management process that we're aiming for. That translation is made easier by the notion that we're developing a personal process for something that historically was the responsibility of the organization within which we worked. We're now trying to do the same thing for ourselves over the span of our careers, but the same effective functionality must be present for the process of managing talent to work at the individual level.

SELF-GUIDING TALENT MANAGEMENT

One output standard against which the quality of a talent management process can be measured is the *Baldrige Excellence Framework* of the Baldrige Performance Excellence Program in the United States. The fifth of the seven criteria categories evaluates *Workforce* outcomes. The core concern in this category is how the organization builds an effective and supportive workforce environment, and this is the area in which talent management processes would have an impact. Among the areas of concern are the capability and capacity of the workforce in terms of skills, competencies, and staffing levels. The criteria include maintaining a diversity of ideas and thinking, as well as ensuring that core competencies are capitalized upon in accomplishing work.

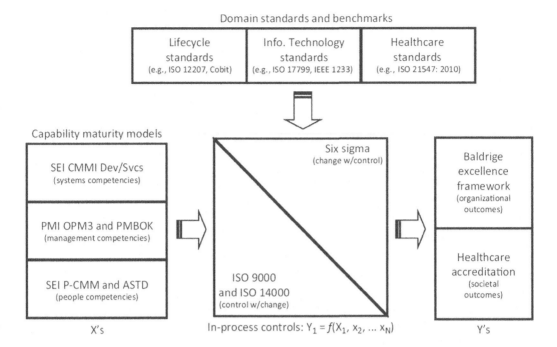

FIGURE 27.2   Standards integration framework.

The criteria also emphasize a continuing focus on customers and stakeholders working to exceed their performance expectations. As we implement a process to self-manage our talents throughout our lifelong careers, we must be accountable to ourselves to meet these requirements just as an organization for which we might work might be held accountable for meeting them with regard to their contributions to talent management in our career.

In order to define a process for talent self-management that will be capable of delivering the desired outcomes, we can turn, again, to an organizational standard that can be adapted for our own individual use. One such standard is the *People Capability Maturity Model* (P-CMM) from the Software Engineering Institute. The process area of interest in the P-CMM is *Training and Development,* and it covers those aspects of an organization's processes that must be in place to effectively ensure that individuals in the organization have the appropriate knowledge and skills to carry out their duties and that appropriate development opportunities are presented to each individual. Table 27.1 outlines the eight key practices that need to be present to satisfy the P-CMM Training & Development capability goals. These are precisely the focus of talent self-management, looking at ourselves as one-member organizations.

To the extent that the Baldrige framework provides the justification for focusing on talent management (the "why"), and the P-CMM provides a rationale for assessing whether a training management process is capable of meeting outcome expectations (the "what"), what we still need is a procedure for ensuring that the practices modeled in the P-CMM actually get carried out (the "how"). Continuing the notion of adapting organizational standards to our individual efforts, we can turn to the quality management field for guidance on developing sound and systematic procedures; and one of the dominant models in quality management today is Six Sigma.

PERSONAL SIX SIGMA FRAMEWORK

As a quality movement, Six Sigma is about process capability. It emphasizes reducing the variation in a process, and increasing our control over a process, such that we can predict with considerable

TABLE 27.1

P-CMM Training & Development Practices

Practice	Emphasis
1	Critical skills for assigned tasks are identified.
2	Training needed in critical skills is identified.
3	Plan is maintained for meeting training needs.
4	Timely training is received for assigned tasks.
5	Training progress is tracked and monitored.
6	Development options are discussed periodically.
7	Development opportunities are made available.
8	Development activities are pursued by individuals.

accuracy exactly how the process will behave. This level of capability can be used to implement improvements in the process where we set targets for future behaviors and achieve those targets within the levels of quality control that we choose to design into the improvements. This perspective on Six Sigma applies equally well in both individual and organizational settings; yet, the history of the Six Sigma movement is almost exclusively a history of organizational adoption and change. That history, as it applies to individuals, includes obtaining certification as a Green Belt or a Black Belt, always within the context of an organizational Six Sigma program.

A Six Sigma methodology can be adopted and adapted by individuals to personal self-management settings. In particular, it can be adapted to the development of job and career goals in order to create a regular periodic cycle of review, planning, and learning. Many large organizations have adopted Six Sigma practices as part of organizational quality initiatives. Working professionals in these organizations can sometimes find it difficult to adapt Six Sigma techniques to their own professional practice because the emphasis of the organizational initiative is on organization-wide and project-level implementation. Individuals working in organizations that are not adopting Six Sigma can feel completely overlooked by the Six Sigma movement. You can adopt the Six Sigma thought process to enhance or improve an operational process that you are involved with, regardless of whether or not the organization in which you work has adopted Six Sigma as an improvement model.

You can focus on learning and adapting Six Sigma techniques at a personal level, incorporating these techniques and tools into your professional practice even if you work in an organization that is not adopting Six Sigma. Readers involved in human development or leadership disciplines can consider expanding this approach to other individuals within their organizations.

Six Sigma DMAIC

Large organizational initiatives and projects tend to get the most attention in the Six Sigma literature. The intent of most organizations adopting Six Sigma is that the tools and thought processes of Six Sigma will eventually become so embedded throughout the organization that Six Sigma simply becomes the normal way of conducting business for everyone in the organization. Using this perspective, the idea of defining and conducting Six Sigma projects targeted at improving certain processes or products—the current dominant model in the Six Sigma world—can be viewed as an immature application of Six Sigma. As Six Sigma programs mature, the specific improvement project increasingly gives way to a continuous improvement of processes and products while they are being used (Figure 27.3).

Whether as a distinct project or an embedded activity, the Define-Measure-Analyze-Improve-Control (DMAIC) lifecycle of Six Sigma is applicable to a large variety of situations. Its application

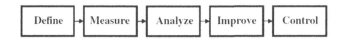

FIGURE 27.3   Six Sigma DMAIC lifecycle.

as an implicit embedded tool is not without precedent. For example, when a project manager or systems engineer tailors a standard organizational lifecycle into a project lifecycle, the tailoring act is an improvement activity preceded by a definition of the project, measurement of risks and opportunities, and an analysis of options for mitigating and managing scope and risk. The resulting tailored project lifecycle is then used to control the effort. The tailoring process is an implicit DMAIC cycle.

The DMAIC thought process can, and should, be used to improve and control virtually any process, whether or not the organization in which that process occurs is aware of its use. When added to existing practices, such as project tailoring, additional benefits and improvements will quickly materialize. The benefits are immediate and substantial when introduced into processes that do not already contain any implicit improvement capability. This is the basis for Personal Six Sigma.

TALENT SELF-MANAGEMENT

When personally adopting Six Sigma to a professional practice, an obvious starting point is in the application of Six Sigma thinking, and the DMAIC lifecycle model, to the management of your professional career. The DMAIC lifecycle can be used to understand the elements of a human resource management system that affect your personal career choices and opportunities (Figure 27.4).

The resulting model involves the process of improving personal competencies, where the key inputs are your current personal competencies, and the key outputs are your improved personal competencies. Each of the Six Sigma phases offers opportunities to continuously recognize and improve talent needs through assessment, training, education, reviews, and continuous reflection. As a lifecycle, this process can be carried out as often as seems necessary. Initially, an arbitrary plan of conducting such an analysis annually might make sense. As the process matures, the aspects of the DMAIC Control Phase will determine how frequently you need to repeat the lifecycle (Table 27.2).

DEFINE PHASE

The Define Phase of Personal Six Sigma requires that your job competencies that are to be addressed be clearly and accurately defined so they can later be measured and improved. The inputs

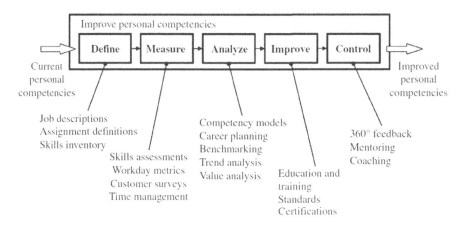

FIGURE 27.4   Personal Six Sigma lifecycle.

TABLE 27.2
Personal Six Sigma Lifecycle

Phase	Emphasis
DEFINE	Understand positions, assignments, and skills for current and future jobs.
MEASURE	Assess actual skills use and how time is really spent.
ANALYZE	Identify gaps and opportunities in skills and behaviors.
IMPROVE	Enhance skills and develop adopted behaviors.
CONTROL	Use feedback to monitor and initiate further improvements.

that drive this definition process are job descriptions, assignment descriptions, and a skills inventory. Define Phase activities are the most difficult to complete the first time Personal Six Sigma is put into practice. Subsequent passes through the lifecycle need only update materials created on previous iterations.

Job Descriptions

The first definitional activity requires establishing a detailed definition and model for your job and career path. This involves collecting or creating a job description for your current job, as well as detailing descriptions of any anticipated or desired jobs for the future. If you work in an organization that is good at creating and maintaining accurate and detailed job descriptions, this activity is much easier than if you work in an organization that only offers vague or superficial job descriptions.

It is critically important that a clear and detailed description of your current and future jobs be defined as the baseline model for the DMAIC improvement cycle. Future job descriptions can be especially challenging because there may be multiple career paths that you consider possibilities, including the potential for future jobs that do not yet exist in the current job market. Your definition need not be clairvoyant to be useful; a best estimate of the future is all that is needed since this DMAIC cycle will be repeated over and over throughout the course of the unfolding of those jobs. Your current view of the talent requirements that will materialize in the future need only be accurate enough to guide effective plans or decisions in the current cycle.

Assignment Descriptions

Job descriptions tend to provide a relatively static definition of your professional responsibilities. An additional layer of definition is provided by systematically defining your actual job assignments. The assignments you carry out in your job provide a more dynamic view of your professional practice. For many, assignments will be dominated by project work. However, even when project work constitutes the bulk of your assignments, there are typically still many aspects of your job that would be omitted if only project work was included. For some professionals, project work may even constitute only a small percentage of their responsibilities.

Where feasible, assignment descriptions should be projected into the future. Being able to forecast the assignments that you plan to undertake in the future can be a key element in career and competency planning. The level of difficulty of these descriptions will depend upon the level of detail and breadth of the job descriptions captured initially. Some job descriptions also describe assignments in a fair amount of detail; however, many do not. Even with detailed job descriptions it can be difficult to get an accurate picture of how a working professional will actually spend her or his days. A complete combination of job and assignment descriptions provides that picture and, to the extent that it projects into the future, will enable more effective measurement activities in the next phase.

Skills Inventory

The third definition activity in the Define Phase involves cataloging an inventory of all of the talents that are implied by the current and future jobs and assignments defined previously. Depending on how they were written, the job and assignment descriptions might already explicitly lay out the skills required. Even so, there are likely to be additional skills that should be included in the skills inventory beyond those explicitly identified. This inventory should be as complete as possible. It is important to capture all of the skills associated with your job, not just those that might be listed in an official job description or assignment.

MEASURE PHASE

The Measure Phase of Personal Six Sigma requires that an accurate and quantified picture of actual job, assignment, and skills performance be collected so improvement opportunities that are well-grounded in the data can be identified. The inputs that drive this quantification process are skills assessments, workday metrics, customer surveys, and time management data.

Skills Assessment

A critical input to an understanding of professional talents is an honest and thorough skills assessment. A skills assessment involves reviewing each skill in the skills inventory created in the Define Phase and assessing whether or not you possess the required levels of skill. This measurement activity depends on establishing a scale for measuring competency levels and for determining the likelihood that you will need certain levels of skills in the future.

For example, you might use a five-point scale, where 0 indicates that you have no knowledge of the skill; 1 indicates a general familiarity with the skills but no current real capability; 2 indicates some knowledge or capability, usually as the result of some training; 3 indicates sufficient competency to practice the skill; 4 indicates experienced competency to the point of being able to help others with the skill; and 5 indicates that you have mastered the skill to the point where you can teach, adapt, or extend the skill.

If an item in the skills inventory requires a 4 but your current capability is a 3, then action might be needed to improve the competency. However, if future job assignments might only require the skill at level 3, then the need for immediate capability enhancement might be mitigated. The use of current and future job and assignment descriptions, coupled with the ever-changing profile of job skills across the industry, makes a skills model rather complex. Here in the Measure Phase, the emphasis is on building accurate skill assessments, not making decisions about improvements. Improvement decisions need to be made based on an entire picture of your capabilities and plans, and will be the subject of the later Analysis Phase.

Workday Metrics

Each combination of job and assignment descriptions will have a unique profile of actual work activities that are conducted on a typical workday. Within this variation, however, it is important to be able to measure the actual activities performed. If you work in an organization that already collects time-reporting data, these metrics will be easier to identify and collect. However, since the objective here is competency development, it will be important to collect data beyond traditional time-recording mechanisms. In particular, while job and assignment activities and time should be tracked, so should actual utilization of your competencies in the skills inventory.

Depending upon the specifics of your professional practice, you will count different things. Typical metrics might include information about the timings and quality of the many different work products that you are responsible for in your position, including how and when you verified or validated those work products with peers or managers. Metrics should include the relative size of each artifact, time or effort expended, defect and issue data, rework time and scale, and skills actually used. In collecting workday metrics, try to think of yourself as a production line turning out products and services. The idea is to collect metrics regarding everything going on across your production line. Particular note should be made of any skills that you need to immediately improve in order to complete some activity.

Customer Surveys

A critical set of data needed for Personal Six Sigma is customer feedback. A challenge the first time through the cycle is to accurately identify all of the customers of your professional practice. We are often more accustomed to identifying our company's customers or even the customers of our projects, but the customers of our professional practice are sometimes less visible to us. The customers of interest are the individuals or work groups that directly receive our work products. The list will vary depending on job assignments. Think in terms of identifying the level of your customer's satisfaction with everything you produce, including the major work products that you are responsible for on a regular basis, as well as the many ad hoc or periodic work products or services that you provide as part of your job. Note that the customers of interest here are your direct and immediate customers.

Once your customers are identified, seek methods or occasions where direct customer feedback can be obtained. While this can be as formal as a feedback survey given to these individuals periodically, it need not be. Effective feedback can be obtained using less formal methods, including simple feedback discussions or a shared coffee break. Many such opportunities might already be available if an effective peer review program is in place in your organization.

Time Management

The fourth category of data to be collected during the Measure Phase is time data. How do you spend your time? Useful categorizations include value-added versus non-value-added time, as well as time on or off task. Time spent off task might include a variety of meeting types, training, or other administrative activities.

This type of data most closely aligns with data that might already be collected for time reporting in your organization. Depending upon the level of project management maturity in the organization, much of the data required might already be available. However, such data is less likely to be available for non-project work. If sufficiently detailed, this data will identify the aspects of your job assignments that are being completed on time and on budget, or late and over budget.

Do not limit your time data to on-the-job time. Pay particular attention to how you spend time outside of work hours. How much personal time are you spending for learning? How many professional journal articles are you reading per week? How much time are you devoting to professional society memberships? These time investments are strong enablers of career and talent growth that remain hidden if your measurement effort is limited to at-work activities.

ANALYZE PHASE

The Analyze Phase of Personal Six Sigma requires that the metrics collected be reviewed objectively in order to identify trends and opportunities that can be addressed for improvement or growth. The inputs that drive this analysis process are competency models, career planning, benchmarking, trend analysis, and value analysis.

Competency Models

A comparison of your actual job description and assignments (from the Define Phase) to how often you actually use your competencies (from the Measure Phase) can serve as an indication of whether or not your talents are being developed and used in ways that are consistent with your career plans and goals. If not, then analyzing the gaps between your plan and actual competency use can help identify places where your talents might need to be realigned with real job opportunities, or job opportunities might need to be rethought in light of how your competency development is actually unfolding.

Career Planning

While your organization often has a career planning model available, it is typically limited to career options within the organization. Depending upon your personal goals, you might need to develop a career plan that extends beyond your current organization. If the workday metrics, customer data, and time management data point toward career change opportunities or needs, then potential career improvement might entail a rethinking of the job and assignment descriptions that currently form the basis of this DMAIC cycle. Be particularly alert to new career opportunities that might be emerging that were not available or considered during the Define Phase.

Benchmarking

Envisioning a change is always easier when the target change can be visualized or observed. You should continually look for opportunities to measure or observe other professionals as they progress through similar career paths. Professional publications and conferences are excellent sources of benchmark data: many trade publications provide periodic salary surveys, and many professional societies provide detailed body of knowledge materials to members. All of these sources provide a clear picture of what a might-be career target can include. This view can be used to help define a working path from your current basis model to some future to-be model.

Trend Analysis

Pay particular attention to trends in the data, even if they are small. Picturing your job five years ago can highlight how much can change over the course of time, and yet those changes rarely stand out during very short-term discussions or observations. The influence of technologies, organizational changes, and skill models are constantly changing the way your organization functions and the ways you experience being a part of your organization. By noting trends in the data you can spot areas that need improvement long before your supervisors or peers do. Such trends might include the frequency with which your skills are used or shifts in performance data related to certain types of artifacts meeting specifications. By planning for improvements in these areas, it is possible to prevent anyone else from ever observing slippages in your skillsets or performance.

Value Analysis

A particular form of analysis, perhaps viewable as a subset of trend analysis, is value analysis. What value are you providing to your customers over time? Ideally, there should be significant upward trends in the conducting of value-added activities that directly impact customers. On-time performance and skills utilization should continuously improve over time. As a Personal Six Sigma goal, these value measures should be improving notably faster than corresponding value measures for your entire organization. If not, you should work to identify reasons why not, and think about ways to improve such situations.

Improve Phase

The Improve Phase of Personal Six Sigma takes the information gleaned from analysis to directly implement improvements. The inputs that drive this improvement process are education and training, standards, and certification.

Education and Training

The most obvious improvement opportunities will involve forms of education and training. These might vary from focused training opportunities to improve specific skills, to full academic degree programs. Long-term planning will often involve both extremes. Professional conferences or professional society involvement can also provide for skills enablement or expansion. Simply reading publications from the many professional societies that cover aspects of your job can be an excellent improvement strategy.

Many other educational opportunities are likely to be available all around you in your current position. The many committees, task forces, or special assignments available in your workplace offer excellent opportunities to develop skills that might otherwise not be needed or practiced in the day-to-day activities of your job. The question shifts from whether or not you have the talents to participate, to whether or not participating will help you develop needed or desired talents. Very often these activities present opportunities to develop specific skills or relationships that would rarely be developed through your normal work assignments.

Standards

Standards are an important part of planning improvements. Standards have become an increasingly important aspect of most work or knowledge domains, so there are likely at least a few standards that provide guidance in the working of the tasks within your areas of responsibility. Identifying and adopting standards is the easiest way to improve the direction of your skills and career without needing to "reinvent the wheel." Adopting a standard can help even if the organization in which you work is not moving in the direction of that standard. (This chapter is an example of an adoption of Six Sigma if your organization isn't pursuing Six Sigma as an organizational strategy.) Many standards and guidelines are available through the Healthcare Information and Management Systems Society (HIMSS), the International Standards Organization (ISO), the Society for Human Resource Management (SHRM), the Project Management Institute (PMI), and many other related organizations. Don't overlook the myriad organizations that also promulgate technical standards that might be relevant to your position, now or in the future.

Certifications

As an extension of education and training, obtaining professional certification can be an important component of any competency improvement program. The body of knowledge for a certification program serves as a standard for the purposes of defining what needs to be learned. The examination process for the certification serves as an important benchmark for the level of competency that should be developed and how it should be measured. Because most certification programs also require some form of periodic recertification, they also serve as good initial components for the Control Phase.

Control Phase

The Control Phase of Personal Six Sigma works to institutionalize the improvements made, and assure that new cycles of DMAIC activity are driven by the data generated through the improved processes. The inputs that drive this improvement process are 360° feedback, mentoring, and coaching.

360° Feedback

Just as the Measure Phase includes soliciting customer input, the Control Phase also ties actual performance to stakeholder feedback. Data should be continuously collected from customers, suppliers, peers, and managers. Shifts in this feedback over time might represent signals that something has changed in the work environment, or your performance has shifted. In either event, such feedback can serve as an early warning that problems might be occurring that can be addressed through another iteration of this DMAIC lifecycle.

Mentoring

To obtain more future-oriented feedback, it is important to identify one or more mentors and to enter into mentoring relationships with those individuals. A mentor can often help you identify trends or opportunities that affect your future plans long before the details behind those trends become evident. In the most extreme case, such information might trigger a replanning of your job or career options that would necessitate a complete redefinition of future job, assignment, or skill opportunities.

Coaching

Try to identify individuals in your organization who can serve as coaches on a day-to-day basis. Coaching provides an additional control over whether things occurring in the environment are being properly interpreted and used to influence your plans over time. Again, the emphasis is on using the coaching relationship to identify data or thought shifts that would necessitate a recycling through this DMAIC lifecycle.

Personal Six Sigma offers a framework for you as an individual practitioner to adapt Six Sigma techniques and tools to your personal professional practice and talent management. Applications include using Six Sigma to model and improve your personal career path and opportunities, including an improvement cycle that can be repeated over time to help assure that your career is unfolding in the way you desire.

In addition to improving your personal career competencies, major opportunities exist for improving your technical performance in your job through understanding the mapping of Six Sigma processes and techniques against the processes and techniques of your work domain. Whether or not you ever actually create any of the common Six Sigma tools, you'll benefit from adapting Six Sigma thinking to the domain-specific tools you already use. As your knowledge of Six Sigma increases, you will increasingly use Six Sigma tools and techniques to supplement your domain-specific tools. The complementary nature of these tools will boost both your productivity and effectiveness. You will probably not spend as much time using Six Sigma tools as you typically spend using your domain-specific tools. That path is best reserved for individuals who choose the Six Sigma Black Belt career path. As a self-managing talent development practitioner, your roots will remain in your chosen disciplinary specialty while you develop additional Six Sigma skills to assist you in continuous improvement.

CONCLUSION

Managing one's own talent development, including assuring that current talents meet the needs of current positions while also developing new talents for desired positions in the future, is a critical competency for working professionals. To make that self-management more effective and efficient, systemically adapting industry and professional standards is a means to short-cut what would otherwise be a long and tedious process of identifying and defining individual needed talents and skills. Every individual might end up with a slightly different portfolio of standards around which talent management might develop.

Figure 27.2 presented one such framework that includes many of the standards that are relevant to managing talents in the health IT field. Your personal framework might include these components, as well as a variety of others to suit your needs. In fact, the process development outlined in this chapter included three components of the Figure 27.2 framework: the Baldrige Excellence Framework defining outcomes (the "why"), the People CMM defining inputs (the "what"), and the adaptation of Six Sigma for personal use as the transformative process (the "how").

By adapting standards, we take advantage of a lot of other people doing much of the development work for us, and we ensure that the talents and skills we target for ourselves are both relevant and timely to our career needs. We want the process to be effective while consuming little of our resources, because the journey of lifelong learning is both continuous and never-ending.

Section VI

Industry Influences Critical to Your Career

28 Driving Digital Health Transformation: Achieving a Person-Enabled Health System

Anne Snowdon
RN, PhD, FAAN

CONTENTS

DOI: 10.4324/9780429398377-34

LEARNING OBJECTIVES

1. Identify the importance of personalized health care on achieving value and impact as it relates to what matters to people, their quality of life, health and wellness, and the role of the healthcare provider in a digital health ecosystem.
2. Examine the importance of the empowered consumer as a motivating factor in the use of technology and the ways in which health systems and consumers can learn from each other.

INTRODUCTION

Health systems have experienced unprecedented change in the last several decades, resulting in new ways for consumers to seek and engage health services and revolutionary technologies that have completely transformed how health challenges are managed. Consumers can connect virtually to global experts to access information about health. Discoveries in genetics are providing a mechanism for consumers to evaluate their risk for disease. Pacemakers and smart devices are able to wirelessly transmit heart rhythms, enabling individuals with cardiac arrhythmia to connect to a cardiologist. Yet, these impressive advances may not have realized their potential in the populations they serve. Why? Health systems around the world are challenged by increasing demands for healthcare services in the face of diminishing economic resources. Every developed country in the world expends substantial economic resources on healthcare which has driven health system priorities to focus on cost containment and sustainability. Yet, as health system costs continue to increase over time, the value health systems are able to achieve for the population they serve remains unclear. Health systems have long been focused on delivering services to treat, manage, or cure disease, illness, or injury; they are not so much "healthcare" systems, but rather, "disease management" systems. Health services focus primarily on assessing and diagnosing patients, prescribing care and treatments based on standardized protocols or best evidence available for a particular disease or condition. Traditionally, health teams have been the key decision makers in most health systems and consumers are the "patient" who is viewed largely as the recipient of care. Although many health systems aspire to deliver "patient-centered care", health professionals primarily focus on making decisions for, and occasionally, with the patient. In recent decades, the desire to improve the quality of care while reducing health costs has led to a focus on standardizing services to ensure every patient has access to high quality health services. To achieve this, health teams have embraced clinical practice guidelines and evidence-based care planning to direct their day to day practice. Although this has achieved great value for health systems in terms of quality outcomes, the scope of most health systems has remained narrowly focused on the safe and effective management of disease, illness and injury and a top-down style of decision-making whereby health professionals are deemed the experts, and the focus on managing disease has remained virtually unchanged even in light of the new resources available. In addition, there has been little attention placed on whether health systems are delivering value to the populations they are mandated to serve, both in terms of the nature of what they are delivering and also in terms of the fact that people want to be treated as people and not the substrate for diseases. This traditional structure worked very well over the last 50 years for two primary reasons: health providers were the primary (and often sole) source of health information; and, the pace of scientific discovery was steady but not revolutionary. Health provider teams—led by physicians—had more or less exclusive access to all health information, serving as brokers of what information was shared with their patients and when, based on their assessment of what they felt was needed. Exclusive access to, and control of, a patient's health information gave physicians positions of power over the patients they cared for. However, advancements in communications technologies have shifted this power dynamic. Entire populations are now connected through the World Wide Web, which is accessible through an expanding set of technologies including mobile phones, computers, tablets, and wearables.

These two drivers of change, unprecedented access to health information and revolutionary medical discoveries, are working together to generate demand for personalized healthcare. However, given the very dominant focus of most every health system on standardized pathways for disease management, most health systems are not designed to respond to consumer demand for personalization. Health systems are under substantial pressure to deliver value to the populations they serve within limited fiscal resources, while at the same time, the role of the consumer is evolving as they begin taking steps to engage and manage their health and wellness in a manner that is personalized to meet their unique needs and life circumstances. What is critically important about the rapid evolution of information technologies is that they enable the engagement of entire populations of consumers, who now use online tools to access the health information needed to manage their health and wellness, and connect to health system experts, clinicians, and services globally. Essentially, the boom of information and communication technologies is a major influence in driving the emerging personalization of healthcare globally.

To more fully examine the growing consumer demands on health systems, we consider the following key questions:

- What matters to individuals in regard to personalization of health care?
- What are the emerging trends in technology and consumer behavior that are contributing to and influencing the personalization of health systems?
- What are the key personalization strategies that have been successfully used by industries and organizations outside of healthcare?
- What could a personalized health system look like?
- What are the necessary steps health systems must undertake to achieve personalization?

PERSONALIZATION: WHAT MATTERS TO PEOPLE

Personalization in healthcare is not a new concept. Over 2000 years ago, the Greek physician Hippocrates emphasized the importance of individualizing medical care proclaiming, "*it is more important to know what sort of person has a disease than to know what sort of disease a person has*".[1] Personalization in this traditional sense means that individuals are able to seek healthcare services and treatment tailored to meet the unique challenges of a particular disease or condition they are experiencing. Advances in both "omics" sciences and information and communication technologies, offer health systems a new way forward to "personalize", by engaging these technologies to focus on achieving value in terms of what matters to people—quality of life and wellness. As a result, a very new perspective on personalization is now emerging which is very distinct from Hippocrates' vision. Health systems have the opportunity to leverage these emerging trends, to achieve sustainable personalized health systems that deliver value to the populations they serve.

WHAT IS PERSONALIZATION?

The concept of salutogenesis[2] provides a strong theoretical basis for defining personalization. Salutogenesis, first described by Antonovsky in the 1980s,[3] defines health relative to what matters to people, where the ultimate goal of healthcare is to enable or facilitate health, which is viewed as a key determinant of quality of life. Lindstrom and Eriksson [4] use the analogy of the "river of life" as a potential vision for personalized health systems. Downstream, healthcare systems offer disease management, which can be likened to trying to save people from drowning in the river. Upstream, healthcare is more closely aligned with people's values of health and wellness to achieve quality of life, and is designed to prevent or mitigate risk of disease which compromises health and wellness. In this vision, healthcare systems offer a balanced portfolio of services to populations, both supporting people so that they can experience a good life where they are well and healthy, and providing supports when disease or illness occurs so that individuals can be rehabilitated and returned, where possible, to good health.

In this chapter, personalization is considered through a population-based lens, where health systems strive to achieve value in terms of health, wellness, and quality of life—factors that vary across population health sub-groups. Before personalization can be contemplated, it is important to first understand the key philosophical dimensions of healthcare that matter to people and therefore reflect value.

PERSONALIZATION BASED ON VALUE

If health systems are to deliver value to the populations they serve, it would require that value be defined in terms of quality of life, health, and wellness, as an alternative to a narrower focus of value relative to disease and illness. Value-based outcomes, beyond those that are purely economic in their construction, are not currently defined or measured by health systems. Indeed, one of the greatest challenges health systems face is delivering value to the populations they serve in a way that is meaningful to health consumers, and sustainable from a cost perspective. A first step to achieving a personalized strategy towards health and wellness is a greater understanding and consideration of the values and needs of people, and the ways in which they want to engage in health services. If population health and wellness is at the core of what health systems are mandated to address, then system priorities and measures of performance must be directly aligned to measuring outcomes based on articulated value. Only then can the existing gap be addressed between health-related values held by a population and how the healthcare system is currently designed, organized, funded, and evaluated.

As exciting as the advances are in genomics and in technology that enables access to health information, it is important to recognize how these elements may shift how individuals and populations consider and access healthcare services. Bioethics examines questions related to the impact healthcare decisions have on people, to ensure that health services and technologies are not used in ways that violate human interests. Bioethics informs policy making as decisions are considered through the lens of how to achieve the best health outcomes that maximize human interests while minimizing harm. As noted by Arnason, "the benefits or damage that might result from personalizing medicine will depend no less on political and policy decisions than on pharmacogenomics developments…moral issues must not be restricted to an evaluation of risk for individuals".[5] Bioethicists are on the whole in favor of personalized healthcare, but just as with any new healthcare technology, procedure, or policy, a philosophical examination of personalized healthcare has revealed a number of important criteria against which it must be measured including: achieving benefit and preventing harm; the importance of self-determination; and, justice and fairness in distribution of health services.

1. Achieve benefit and prevent harm

Health systems must determine whether the new technologies and services achieve benefit and prevent harm. To do so, those controlling the access to expensive healthcare technologies must consider the socio-political-economic impact of the technology including "privacy and consent, risk of harm or discrimination".[5] For example, new genomic-based technologies have substantial implications for health systems. How do health systems personalize their services to the segment of the population who need particular types of preventive, or risk mitigation therapies? Does the entire population receive genetic screening? How would individuals who do not want genetic screening "opt out"? How does the outcome of genetic screening observe privacy needs of individuals? At what cost, meaning what resources, have to be made available to pay for population-wide genetic screening? What is the value proposition that genetic screening offers to populations? And what social-political- and economic impact would genetic screening have for individuals and their families (i.e., impact on seeking insurance, impact on workplace and employment). These questions must be addressed through active dialogue between the population and the social and political structures that make decisions, to create a personalized health system.

2. Self-determination (Agency)

The issue of self-determination discussed in the bioethical literature raises the question, "Who decides?" Self-determination, the right to decide on what is best or most valued, suggests that personalized health systems must be structured to engage ordinary citizens to determine policy through public deliberation, with the help of experts to provide information and other feedback. In a personalized healthcare system, policy decisions must involve serious public dialogue involving demographically representative members of the public who negotiate with each other using good (consistent and with empirically accurate claims) moral reasoning.[5] Personalization at the level of the health system means a movement away from the paternalistic "doctor (or health provider) knows best" approach, towards a collaborative "what will best serve the personalized goals of quality of life and wellness of the population" model that is deeply embedded throughout the entire healthcare system. This collaborative model of personalization should be structured beyond the level of the individual-provider context to include the community-health organization context, and the regional/sub-population context in order to achieve meaningful outcomes for the population served by the health system. The shift in decision-making requires that individuals, communities, and populations collaborate on how health systems are structured so that they are meaningful and achieve value for the populations they serve.

3. Justice and fairness

A significant lens through which the field of bioethics considers the distribution of healthcare resources is justice and fairness. In many health systems, fairness and justice is related to access to care. Accordingly, this principle of justice as fairness, that "unequal distribution of social goods is justifiable only insofar as it benefits the worst-off" [6] forms part of the historical foundation of modern thinking in bioethics. Fairness must necessarily involve the creation of healthcare policy based on what decisions would be made when stakeholders from all relevant demographics are consulted and their recommendations are considered when establishing policy. Values of fairness and equity require that every citizen has the same access to health services. In many countries, universal access to healthcare is ensured for all citizens by legislation. While equity in access to care does not necessarily "personalize" a health system, it is a necessary condition that matters to most populations around the world given the central importance of healthcare to the quality of people's lives. Given that personalized medicine has the potential to divert health system resources to expensive and high-technology strategies for curing disease and illness which, in socialized health systems, limits the funding available for other services and procedures, the concept of justice will continue to important.

ROLE OF RESEARCH IN A PERSONALIZED HEALTHCARE SYSTEM

Healthcare is a knowledge intensive sector that relies on complex models of research to discover, test, and implement new approaches for achieving health outcomes among populations. A personalized health system makes use of the translational research model in order to understand best evidence for the impact of strategies to achieve personalized approaches. Importantly, research will continue to shift from a dependence on clinical trials research that is typically disease focused, to a more values-based translational model that examines the impact of personalized health system approaches designed to fit with population values. Translational research focused on value-based outcomes will need to bring a new perspective on evidence to guide and support policy structures for a personalized healthcare system. What is required to accomplish this shift is a process of rational deliberation, where the best evidence and most reliable methods are used to shape and inform public understanding and judgment, rather than self-interest of influential stakeholders in health systems.[5] The public needs to engage in a transparent and impartial dialogue to better understand the ethical and economic challenges of delivering healthcare services that create value within limited fiscal resources. It is only through this public dialogue that communities and countries will be able to accelerate the transformational shift required to move from the traditional, top-down healthcare model, to one that introduces personalization in a rational and considered way that protects ethical boundaries, treats populations fairly, and delivers individual and population goals.

THE EMERGENCE OF THE EMPOWERED CONSUMER

Patients are increasingly ready and able to manage their own health and wellness. Patients actively seek out strategies and tools (e.g., mobile health apps) to take charge of their health and to change the way they access health services. Factors that contribute to this ability for patients to be active participants in their own healthcare include:

1. Global access to information and online tools. These tools are more widely available than ever, which has allowed a complete shift in the flow of information and ability to engage in health and wellness
2. The availability of digital tools and online resources that are often external to the formalized healthcare system (e.g., virtual patient forums, mobile health applications, self-help programs, health tracking devices).

These resources now offer a virtual library of health information for consumers to independently learn and study conditions, procedures, or treatment options. The use of these online tools and resources are allowing entire populations to create their own personalized model to self-manage their health and wellness, usually independently of formalized health systems. This emergence of the empowered consumer has significantly changed healthcare, re-framing the traditional 'top-down' model, to a consumer-led model where patients are equipped with information and prepared to engage with their healthcare providers, informed by available information and becoming partners in their own healthcare. The same rapid evolution of information and communication technologies that has enabled the empowered consumer, has also been identified as one of the most significant enablers of health system innovation.[7]

However, there are two primary reasons why there continues to be a disconnect between what the health consumer is seeking and what the health system provides. The first reason is that health systems remain primarily focused on managing illness and disease, rather than a focus on health, wellness, and quality of life.[8] There is a poor fit between what formal health systems have to offer (i.e., disease management) and what empowered consumers value and are seeking to achieve (i.e., health and wellness). The second reason is that the majority of the digital tools and online platforms used by consumers are not connected or interfaced with the formalized health system. There is little opportunity for consumers to link their personalized health tools to the formalized patient health data embedded in health systems. Essentially, what has now emerged are two, almost completely distinct and separate healthcare systems. One is the traditional healthcare system, which is often institution-centric and provides services to manage illness and disease. The other is the consumer-based system within which people select and engage online tools, virtual care services, and resources to personalize their own system of health and wellness that is custom-made to the needs, values, and goals of the individual.

WHAT MOTIVATES CONSUMERS TO PERSONALIZE HEALTH AND WELLNESS?

In order for a health system to transform toward a person-enabled system, it is essential to understand what drives consumers towards these personalized approaches to health and wellness care. These key motivations and expectations of users must be leveraged by health systems and be foundational to the design of care delivery that enables health systems to achieve value for the populations they serve. There are a number of motivators that influence the desire for consumers to take control of their health and find tools that allow them to manage their own health and wellness.

1. The desire to better understand their own health and wellness

In today's society, consumers are empowered to pursue value in decisions about their health and healthcare, more broadly.[9] Why? Because consumers do not want to wait to get sick before they are able to seek healthcare services, they are driven to achieve health and wellness. This is a major value proposition for consumers worldwide, which is supported by recent research. A 2018 report found that 73% of Americans search for health information on the internet,[10] up from 59% in 2013.[11] Within the online channel, mobile phones are becoming an increasingly important delivery mechanism for health information. With 81% of Americans owning a smartphone,[12] it is not surprising that of all cell phone users, more than half (62%) of those with a smartphone have used it to gather health information online.[13] There is clearly an increasing trend on the part of consumers to use mobile technologies to access health information. The increase in online mechanisms to access health information is only fueling this demand, and the explosion over the past five years in the use of health applications on mobile technologies is a clear indication that this desire is only growing as individuals discover the tools available to them to increase their health literacy.

2. The drive to engage and connect socially

People are actively engaging others by creating online "communities" composed of people who are experiencing similar health challenges. This type of online peer to peer support is offering consumers the opportunity to learn from "people like me", which assists them in managing or achieving the health goals they all have in common. Although there is limited evidence, the use of peer communities may also be a strategy for validating an individual's personal experience with health treatments, therapies or procedures, to ensure they are reaping the same benefits others have experienced. Online communities of peers focused on supporting each other to achieve health goals may also offer people the confidence of comparing their progress with that of others, which will further inspire them to work towards their goals. Individuals are also engaging broader groups through mechanisms such as crowdsourcing, where information is solicited from the mass population in response to healthcare questions, especially for diagnosis or second opinions. While the validity of the medical information provided through these methods may not be considered "evidence based", people often consider the experience of others as important evidence to consider when making their own health decisions. This ability to create or join online communities or request information and advice through crowdsourcing are especially valuable for people who have geographical barriers or financial barriers to accessing health services or specialized practitioners.

3. The drive to "take control"

People naturally strive for self-determination, and are driven to make their own decisions to achieve their personal goals according to their own values. In the traditional 'top-down' structure of health systems, care and treatment decisions are prescribed by care pathways, or directed by health professionals and are prescribed to patients who are to 'comply' with these decisions, which are often determined based on best evidence and are limited to prescriptive disease management services. Yet, people strive to make decisions based on what is important and valuable for their own health and wellness journey. The explosion of sophisticated information technologies has enabled people to take control of their own personal health goals and seek ways to become active participants in their own healthcare. Patients are no longer waiting for information to be given to them by their care provider; they are now taking initiative, to look for and use information pertinent to their individual health circumstances to assist them in understanding what is currently happening to them, and what is likely to happen in the future. This quest for information is being supported by private sector health ventures operating outside the traditional health system paradigm. There are numerous digital tools and online services that have now clearly engage and enable consumers to take control, define health and wellness in their own way, and set out to achieve their personal health goals. People are increasingly using these tools to gather information, track their health and health conditions, and use this data to make healthcare-related decisions.[14] This emerging trend will undoubtedly influence health systems and the life sciences market. Frist suggests that if only 10% of the population begins to seek value in the care it receives, the health sector will have to respond positively to the benefit of the other 90%.[9] Through their desire to become more educated, enlightened consumers will drive physicians, hospitals, clinics, and health organizations to restructure, focusing on providing quality care that is personalized to the needs and values of the population they serve.

4. The drive to "self-manage" health information

There is no question that consumers today are seeking access to information that is relevant to their personal values and needs which links directly to health outcomes that are both valued and meaningful. Consumers want to fully understand all of the possible treatment or health program options, the associated risks and benefits for each, so that they can make informed decisions about their health and wellness. The challenge is that health systems have always been structured to ensure providers have access to patient information and records, with little opportunity for individuals to have access to their own health information. The drive of consumers to acquire and manage their own personal health information is starting to emerge. This trend has grown exponentially in recent years as information technologies have revolutionized the automation, connectivity, decision support, and mining of health information and data that are expected to radically transform health service delivery.[9] There is an emerging trend towards using technologies to provide people personalized health information through online access to their health records and lab results that also connect with physicians or healthcare teams. This access to medical data increases health literacy and at the same time enables consumers to better understand their health status as it changes over time. People who have access to their health information prior to appointments with health providers have the ability to shift the patient-health practitioner dialogue to a conversation that is more informed. Patients often bring a list of questions to their appointments, to ensure they are asking all the necessary questions to make informed decisions. In some cases, providers have now limited office or clinic visits to "three questions only" to manage time pressures that demands for information are creating, a symptom that health systems are ill-prepared for actively engaging empowered consumers.

5. The drive to ensure accuracy

People who have access to, and manage, their own health information are more likely to recognize changes or error in health data. Given the self-interest demonstrated by patients in their personal health information, any anomalies in diagnostic tests may be discovered more quickly; this can be important given that 7% of abnormal lab results are not communicated to the patient and improper follow-up can result in inappropriate or delayed diagnoses.[15] Being able to access doctor's notes when a patient finishes an appointment helps minimize the possibility that a person might forget or misunderstand instructions when they rely solely on a single interaction with health providers. Online tools and platforms available could help individuals manage their personal health information more easily, potentially creating the ability to more effectively manage choices that will directly impact health and wellness. This is particularly important given that the most influential driver of health status is individual lifestyle behavior.[9] Currently, the most significant challenges health systems face globally is the growing prevalence of chronic illness due to lifestyle behaviors (i.e., obesity, smoking, alcohol). By making it easy to track personal data, patients can witness firsthand what triggers their adverse health effects, making the link between actions and health outcomes more tangible, inspiring them to actively monitor and track their progress.

6. The drive to collaborate with health providers, not be simply recipients of care

Empowered with access to information, consumers are striving to create a new dialogue with health providers. Communications strategies that link people to their care team are being built into new technology platforms, enabling the potential for information sharing from both the patient and the provider in ways that were unthinkable 25 years ago. These technologies create an opportunity for consumers to achieve greater connectivity for ongoing engagement with health providers, creating the conditions for shared decision-making.[16] Consumers are increasingly making use of technology, such as fitness and health monitoring devices, and are becoming increasingly willing to share this data with their healthcare providers.[14] In the United States, almost half of healthcare consumers are open to receiving medical care between visits via email, while 85% felt that emails, text messages and voicemails are as helpful, if not more so, as an in-person or phone conversation with health providers.[17] Many providers are now employing online tools and virtual care visits to more readily connect with people. Online tools are being used by a growing number of physicians to reach out and connect more efficiently with patients, including widespread use of virtual care, telehealth, home health programs, videoconferencing with specialists for referrals, and even an online model that provides remote intensive care specialists to rural hospitals.[17] From 2019 to 2020, the amount of consumers using virtual visits increased from 15% to 19%.[14] The recent COVID-19 pandemic further accelerated the use of virtual visits across many global health systems. These trends demonstrate that healthcare providers and consumers are making more using of digital technologies to engage more efficiently and effectively. This trend is likely to continue to grow as much more informed health consumers will continue to strive for a deeper engagement with the healthcare team of their choice.

7. Drive towards consumer engagement

Health systems are being challenged to respond to the rise of discriminating healthcare consumers, who are demanding to be involved in decisions about treatment, and empowered with choice in flexible, responsive and patient-centered healthcare services. The desire for greater personalization is evident in the desire to take control of one's health and wellness using mobile technologies, driving the explosion of health applications for mobile phones and computer tablets. The desire for greater personalization was also evidenced in a 2012 Deloitte Survey of US Health Consumers which found that a majority of respondents (57%) were interested in creating plans that were specific to their needs rather than relying on pre-defined options.[18] Responding to the trend of the empowered consumer is challenging for health systems as it has the potential to undermine the hegemony of the medical model of health, where there are established traditions of professional dominance and the requirement that professional judgments of clinical 'need' be considered above the 'wants', 'preferences' or 'choices' of patients. However, healthcare consumerism is much less about what some may view as responding to limitless consumer demands for services and technology and the preponderance of an entitlement mentality, and much more about enabling patients to make informed treatment choices and set priorities for their own healthcare agenda, providing the public with information about health and healthcare quality, respecting rights to privacy, enhancing health literacy, and, with expert guidance from healthcare professionals, helping people understand what is necessary versus what may be discretionary.

Consumer Use of Health Apps to Achieve Personalization

There is no question that the rapid evolution of the mobile application market, dominated by Apple (iPhone) and Google Play (Android), has become one of the most influential drivers of personalization of healthcare for consumers. There are currently more than three billion smartphone users worldwide; a number that is forecast to increase by hundreds of millions in just the next few years.[19] Over one hundred million smartphone users reside in the United States, with a reported 81% of Americans owning smartphones, and more than half of Americans owning a tablet computer.[12] Globally, there are now over 318,000 health apps available, with more than 200 added daily to this number. There are also 340 consumer wearable devices (e.g., Fitbit) worldwide, with over 55% of the most popular health apps making use of sensor data.[20] The number and range of health apps keeps growing, from fitness tracking apps, to medication-related apps. The most popular apps, with highest download rates continue to be primarily fitness and diet apps,[20] which are un-regulated, consumer-facing apps that allow personal management and tracking of health in terms of fitness and diet. The exponential increase in availability of health apps and wearable devices, that are accessed easily and efficiently using mobile technologies, provides important insights for health systems into the ways in which consumers are driving personalization of health services. The rapid growth in the use of these technologies may offer important trending and insights into how consumers are using these apps and what the purpose and intent the app is designed to achieve, in order to consider how health systems may engage or leverage consumers' personalization of health services.

Major Categories of Consumer Health Apps

The widespread use of apps by consumers is focused on self-management of personal health and wellness. The two broad categories that make use of these personalized programs, and self-management tools are health and wellness management (including fitness), and medical condition management (e.g., diabetes, mental health). Many apps make use of wearables and biosensors. For example, personal health and wellness wearables such as Fitbit, which monitor physical activity and basic biometrics; or specific disease-management biosensors such as blood glucose monitors connected to apps that send out reminders. Over 55% of the most popular health apps use sensor data.[20]

In the health and wellness management category, 30% of digital health apps are exercise and fitness apps, 19% lifestyle and stress, and 12% diet and nutrition. While wellness management apps still make up the majority of health apps, disease management apps now make up 40% of medical apps.[21] When it comes to these apps that are designed for health condition management, 16% of these are disease specific, 9% women's health and pregnancy, 11% medication-related, and 4% healthcare providers or insurance apps.[21] In addition, health and fitness devices that track biometrics have gained popularity, with the most popular devices being fitness trackers and heart rate monitors.[21] Health and wellness apps (specifically diet and fitness apps) are also those that are most often prescribed to patients by their healthcare providers.[21]

The Benefits of Health Apps

There are a number of immediate benefits to health apps beyond just their convenience, ease of access and often low cost for the consumer. Health apps and mobile technologies empower people to self-manage their personal health and wellness to achieve what matters to them - quality of life. Health apps also enable a more personalized or tailored approach to health and wellness which may result in better health outcomes at the population level. The majority of health apps are still created for consumers, which is likely due to the desire for people to take control of their healthcare.[22] However, apps designed for consumers are almost exclusively focused on health and wellness behaviors, primarily for the purpose of self management. However, there is significant potential for health apps to reach beyond patient self-management of health and wellness behaviors, to be integrated into healthcare systems, enabling personalized, integrated healthcare for each and every consumer. For example, integration of applications into electronic health records.[22] Further, the integration of novel biosensors and wearables provides the opportunity to improve patient care by supporting personalized care and remote monitoring.

Health apps provide a way for people to engage in their health that is consistent with social norms. The average smartphone user checks their phone 96 times a day;[23] given the norm associated with cellphone use, it becomes more discreet for people to use mobile health technologies to monitor health behavior as it is easily integrated into the routines of day to day life. Imagine the formalized health system and the inconvenience of arranging an appointment, waiting to see a health provider and having to leave work, or day to day routines in order to access care. Mobile health offers the impressive opportunity to engage healthcare services, in real time, at the convenience of the individual person, rather than at the convenience of health providers as is currently the routine in many global health systems.

The benefits in terms of cost savings are also a significant advantage of integrating mHealth into healthcare systems. An analysis of digital health apps found that if these apps were used in five groups of patients (diabetes prevention, diabetes, asthma, cardiac rehabilitation, pulmonary rehabilitation), that not only could acute care utilization be reduced, but that there could be an estimated $7 billion in savings per year for the healthcare system in the US.[20] Extrapolated to all disease areas, the estimated cost savings was $46 billion.[20]

Why Aren't Health Systems Engaging and Adopting Health Apps?

The wide availability and popularity of health apps offers a golden opportunity for health systems to engage consumers, using tools they are already familiar with and accessing on their own. These tools can facilitate a personalized, consumer-driven healthcare system. The tools feature social networking platforms, allowing engagement of peers, experts, and health services worldwide, which could provide value in terms of diagnoses, personalized treatment plans, patient education, and access to care models that engage applications that offer tracking and traceability of outcomes.[24]

Even though the availability of mobile health apps and personal use by consumers has significantly increased, the integration and use of apps in health systems remains low, with only 56% of physicians in the US have reported discussing mHealth with patients.[24] Further, only 26% of clinicians reported that they had recommended these patient engagement platforms, while only 13% reported the use of remote patient monitoring.[20]

Significant barriers still exist that prohibit the widespread integration and use of healthcare apps in health systems; these include,

1. *Privacy, security, and liability concerns*

A major barrier to the use of these platforms in healthcare is the concerns surrounding privacy, security, and liability related to accessing health data that is uploaded or stored in health apps. The highly sensitive and private nature of health information validates these concerns regarding liability should inappropriate access to information take place, or if health information is inadvertently released due to technical issues.

2. *Lack of empirical evidence to support their use*

Health systems are knowledge intensive and rely heavily on empirical evidence before the adoption of new technologies and innovations are even considered. The rapid development of millions health apps in recent years is unprecedented. Thus, it is difficult to get evidence on the impact of an app when it has been available for such a short period of time, and it is challenging to measure the impact of apps on health outcomes when the technology used is constantly evolving. Although there has been an increase in clinical evidence for health apps in various therapeutic categories, only a relatively small number of clinical conditions have strong clinical evidence to support the use of health apps.[24] Due to this lack of evidence, health providers are less likely to recommend health apps for their patients,[25] leaving the use of health apps as primarily patient driven.

3. *Lack of regulation & evaluation*

One of the greatest challenges to the use of health apps is the limited regulatory requirements in place to help make sure health apps reach certain quality and performance standards,[26] which would likely promote their use, particularly by health providers and health systems through the validation of clinical safety and value. Privacy and security of data that is stored or collected by health apps remains a significant challenge for health systems, that precludes the adoption of health application tools and technologies at the health system level.

4. *Limited integration into health systems and clinical practice*

The enormous number of health apps available, limited regulation and testing to prove effectiveness and cost-efficiency, significantly inhibits the integration of health apps into clinical care.[27] To date, there are few apps that are available to manage health conditions that have been integrated into clinical workflow to support widespread adoption by provider teams.[20]

Critically there is a mismatch between the apps that are being created and their applicability and/or utility for patients and healthcare organizations.[28] Further, the evidence to identify the best apps and the evidence supporting their use is insufficient,[27] leaving a significant need to both create and identify apps that provide value.[29] Further, these apps will then need to be integrated into clinical practice in order to realize their true value.[27]

While the challenges surrounding health apps and the use of mobile technologies as healthcare enablers must be addressed, it is clear that the advent of these tools in the health sector has the opportunity to revolutionize healthcare globally. Health systems need to find ways to meaningfully engage consumers through the use of apps to ensure that the convenience, the "real time" nature of app based tools, are built into the system to achieve the same value that apps have achieved – to expand access health services and resources at the convenience of the person, not at the convenience or schedule of the provider or health system. Apps offer an impressive range of health and wellness tools that are designed to be easily accessible and understandable, providing global health systems with important, low cost tools for delivering health services more effectively in a consumer-centric model. These app technologies cannot only change how healthcare is delivered, they hold the potential for the rapid dissemination of health innovation with the goal of improving patient outcomes, and delivering on the value proposition to the populations that health systems are designed to serve.

PERSONALIZATION IN INDUSTRY: WHAT CAN HEALTH SYSTEMS LEARN?

Healthcare is predominately designed and implemented at the system level with a "one size fits all" perspective, with little thought given to patient preferences and values. There are few opportunities for patient choice and input into clinical, service, and operational decisions. Health services are not tailored to a patient's individual needs or preferences, sometimes creating a disparity between patients. Designing strategies to better understand consumer preferences or decisions related to health and wellness, would allow health systems to move beyond the traditional disease-diagnostic approach, and enable the provision of healthcare that is value-based. Designing a personalized system that achieves value is based on an understanding of what consumers appreciate and desire and the choices they make regarding their healthcare. Given the lack of healthcare innovation on this front, there is an opportunity to look to other industry sectors and examine successes in fostering consumer choice while not adding to system costs, and determine whether there is an ability to adapt and translate these successes into healthcare contexts. Contained in the following section are three "lessons" that healthcare systems can learn from industry when it comes to personalization, providing examples from various industry sectors and organizations of successful application and implementation.

LESSON 1: USE CONSUMER PREFERENCE TO ACHIEVE PERSONALIZATION

Personalization is a common strategy used in many industry sectors to achieve a competitive advantage and increase market share. The populations that are served by industry sectors such as banking, travel, automotive, and retail shopping, are the very same populations that health systems serve. However, health systems have only embraced personalization strategies in a limited way. The successful customization practices that have been employed for decades by industries outside of healthcare can offer important insights into the way forward for the personalization of global health systems.

There are three strategies that industry uses to understand consumer preferences and values that inform industry's strategy to "personalize" and strengthen customer experience. These include: active, passive, and progressive personalization.

1. *Active personalization*

Active personalization is a strategy that enables consumers to make choices to meet their needs, such as placing a specific order for a product or service. In this strategy, consumer choice is used to understand consumer preferences and values, enabling an industry to "personalize" their products and services. The analysis of mobile applications to support self-management of health and wellness is an example of how consumers are personalizing their healthcare to achieve health and wellness goals based on what matters most to them. Active personalization using mobile apps has occurred largely outside of formalized health systems. Health systems have the opportunity to engage active personalization by creating ways for consumers to link these personalized programs and tools (i.e., mobile health tools) to formalized health systems. This would allow health providers and teams to collaborate and partner with consumers in achieving their health goals, and provides health teams with valuable information.

2. *Passive personalization*

Passive personalization is the second type of strategy that industry uses to personalize experiences for their customers. Industry gathers information about customer patterns (i.e., their purchases) to better understand what customers want, how they want to engage or be served, and to link or match a product with a user demographic or typology. Software analytic programs are used to monitor user preferences, analyze them and then industry uses this "passive" market intelligence in targeted marketing campaigns that are "personalized" to particular sectors of the population. Health systems do not use passive personalization tools although they do track utilization of health services to understand patient volumes, frequency and prevalence of health services utilization. However, most utilization data is acute care centric, given that health services in communities are not as well documented or tracked using utilization approaches.

3. *Progressive personalization*

Progressive personalization in industry seeks or obtains consumer feedback in order to improve products as the consumer uses them, or as consumer feedback is obtained. Examples include consumer surveys or telemarketing strategies, which are used by a variety of industries to better understand the value proposition for consumers. Healthcare has not embraced these methods nearly to the extent evident in other industries. A possible application for health is patient satisfaction or patient experience survey tools. While health systems globally have identified patient experience as a system priority, patient satisfaction tools are limited to obtaining feedback on specific care transactions, most often in hospitals. There are few, if any, examples of progressive personalization strategies that seek feedback relative to consumer choice, preference, values, and health and wellness goals, even at the level of a health organization. Yet, if health systems were to learn from industry's use of progressive personalization, health systems would be informed much more directly about what people value, and what matters to them, so that health services and approaches to care can be tailored to offer real value to the populations they serve.

How can these three types of industry strategies inform health systems to achieve personalization? In many publicly funded health systems, consumers have few choices in terms of where they seek health services or who they can access in terms of care providers. One of the few opportunities to gain insights into consumer preference and value may be the use of active or progressive personalization tools to better understand the values and needs of the population. This knowledge can then be used to personalize how health services are organized, structured, and delivered to achieve value based on first-hand information from the people who will be accessing the services. With current technology, the ability of online tools to provide customization and personalization for web-based products and services is unprecedented. Tools such as data mining, statistics, artificial intelligence, and rule-based matching are popular for building recommendation systems.[30] The analogues for healthcare may include using online tools such as search engines and algorithms to increase access to health systems by helping people locate nearby practitioners, healthcare facilities, specialized services, and drug stores/pharmacies, or give patients and their families/caregivers information that is tailored to their personalized needs (i.e., using artificial intelligence modeling). A better understanding of population values and preferences enables the designing of health products, services or procedures to achieve greater relevance and meaning (i.e., "what matters") for people. This could transform healthcare services to focus on an individual's personal health and wellness outcomes rather than the limited focus on an illness or disease. Personalization that strengthens a person's experience and links care services directly with consumer health and wellness goals, would offer health systems an important way forward to achieving a personalized health system, capable of delivering value to populations. The following are industry examples of personalization from diverse industry sectors that may offer important insights into strategies health systems may consider.

ORGANIZATION EXAMPLE: DISNEY'S PERSONALIZATION OF CONSUMER EXPERIENCE

Disney's MagicBand bracelets with RFID technology is an example of how the corporation has customized their theme park experience for visitors. The band allows Disney guests to make purchases (it is linked to a credit card), it also serves as a hotel key, acts as a ticket for theme park admission, allows admission to VIP experiences, and stores 'Fast Passes' for priority access to rides. The band also allows for personalized interaction with Disney characters; for example, robot characters greet guests with personalized greetings such as, "Happy birthday, Alexander". The band is linked to an app called My Disney Experiences, where users can book hotels, make dining reservations, buy park tickets, and pre-select ride times. For Disney, there are multiple benefits. Not only does it put decisions in the hands of consumers, freeing up the need for staff resources, it provides customers with a variety of choices so they can customize their experiences and through minimal points of contact – they just have to swipe their band. In addition, all of the information is aggregated and placed into databases used by Disney to monitor customer behaviors to understand preferences, experiences, and opportunities for personalization allowing, them to tweak their service offerings to more accurately reflect consumer demand. The data gathered through their MyMagic+ database will be used to create wait areas that can increase guest purchases and reduce the frustration caused by the inevitable lineup-related gridlock.[31]

Consider the use of Disney's MagicBand concept in hospital settings. Hospital bracelets enabled with "smart" sensors or RFID tags may enable hospitals or health facilities to identify a person's routines or preferences (such as activity patterns or hygiene) so that care processes could be more easily personalized to meet an individual's needs. Just like Disney uses the band to identify and track customer behavior in theme parks, hospitals or clinics could track patient activity during waiting periods. This could allow the hospital to design more preferable waiting areas that offer additional services, which could be revenue generators for the organization. Linking a band to a credit card could allow patients to purchase books in the gift shop or a coffee in the hospital cafeteria. General patient information could be contained on the band, which could be swiped upon entering the facility, reducing the requirement to repeat information to each individual provider along the care chain. Organizations could also use this tracking data to better understand waiting routines and patterns to optimize appointment systems to better utilize health services and reduce wait times. Use of advanced information technologies could also be used to offer people the opportunity to book or cancel appointments online, receive notices of delays, cancellations, or changes in appointment times digitally, or access diagnostic tests remotely.

ORGANIZATION EXAMPLE: AMAZON RECOMMENDATION SYSTEM

Amazon has successfully focused on personalizing the consumer experience.[32] Amazon gathers customer information from previous purchases or browsing histories from which to provide personalized services. Examples of this personalization implemented by Amazon include greetings by name, personalized recommendations, bestseller lists, and personal notification services, as well as purchase pattern filtering. Amazon believes that customization and creating the perception of a one-on-one relationship with the consumer is essential to their value proposition, and the company continues to invest in ways that improve their personalization services. Adding to the personalized shopping experience is the one-click technology used to save user payment information, reducing customer checkout time.

ORGANIZATION EXAMPLE: TESCO PERSONALIZATION BASED ON CULTURE

An example of personalization based on culture is Tesco, a British multinational grocery and general merchandise retailer. This retailer has successfully expanded to include stores all over Europe, Asia, and North America. Attributed to the international success of this company is that it remains sensitive to the local culture of the countries in which it is expanding to.[33] A significant strategy used by Tesco is partnerships, mergers, and acquisitions, which allow the company to more readily meet the culturally-specific needs in order to succeed in international markets.[33] Healthcare systems serve populations which often represent highly diverse cultures, particularly in countries such as Canada, France, and the United Kingdom. Personalizing health systems using culture is an opportunity for health systems to achieve value for populations they serve. For example, considering ways employees can be engaged to align cultural values with specialize health services is a strategy that has been very successful in industry, however, has had little uptake in health systems. There are ways to tailor meals in hospitals and long-term care facilities to recognize cultural preferences and traditions, and personalize care experiences by providing choices in service delivery to respect cultural values.

LESSON 2: USE SEGMENTATION TO ACHIEVE A "ONE SIZE FITS ONE" STRATEGY

Segmentation is a strategy that acknowledges that one size does not fit all; it is used by industry to categorize the consumer population into groups that define their preferences, values, needs, or even demographic. In this way, companies are able to drive sales by personalizing products to meet the specialized needs of each consumer segment. Typically, health systems tend to use standardized approaches to programs or services based on best evidence, and services are designed to achieve specific health or disease outcomes, rather than meeting personalized approaches to care tailored to fit with the needs and values of specific populations. For health systems, segmentation may offer important opportunities to design and organize services to meet the personalized needs of specific segments of the population they serve. Despite the significant complexity of health systems—unlike other sectors such as retail banking, travel, grocery, or retail—segmentation tools focused on understanding value associated with experiences in health systems may offer in important strategy for health systems to achieve value.

INDUSTRY EXAMPLE: INSURANCE INDUSTRY SEGMENTATION USING HEALTH STATUS AND LIFESTYLE

The insurance industry uses a strategy called gerontographics to segment the population by physiological, psychological, and social characteristics, in order to develop specific insurance practices based on personal preferences. Consumers are divided into groups based on their health and lifestyle preferences and socialization habits. Consumers over the age of 55 are divided into four groups: "healthy indulgers"; "healthy hermits"; "ailing outgoers"; and, "frail recluses". These typologies segment seniors based on their health (healthy or ailing) and based on their need for socialization (i.e., hermits, recluses, indulgers) to provide insights into the health and lifestyle preferences of seniors. Segmentation of consumer groups in this way is a useful tool for industry to develop products and services based on the desires of each group. For example, healthy hermits and frail recluses would be attracted to products that enable them to remain independent at home, while healthy indulgers and ailing outgoers may want programs and services that engage them socially outside the home. Gerontographics has demonstrated that the most important factors for the aging population is the freedom of the individual to choose their place and type of health and personal care.[34]

Segmentation of the population provides an opportunity for healthcare systems to design service delivery models tailored to specific populations, providing choice in healthcare services; where healthcare services are personalized to effectively meet the needs of each sub-group (e.g., 'healthy hermit', 'ailing outgoer'). The most valuable lesson health systems can learn from insurance may be to recognize that one size will never fit all, and a more personalized approach can be successfully achieved by recognizing that groups within the population vary widely and health services need to be structured using a variety of approaches in order to meet the unique needs and values of all segments within a population.

INDUSTRY EXAMPLE: RETAIL BANKING SEGMENTATION BASED ON RISK TAKING, EXPERIENCE, AND EXPECTATION

In the banking industry, consumers are able to access services online, 24 hours a day, tailored to individual preferences.[35] Consumers are also able to develop customized investment packages through the selection of investments based on their risk tolerance, time horizon, and investment goals.[34] In essence, these customers are each creating a personalized investment fund. However, unlike the insurance industry, segmentation methods based on demographic information are not as successful.[35] The additional requirement of taking personality differences, which relate to behavior, is an essential part of segmentation decisions in this sector. In retail banking, psychographic models have been used to identify investor motivations, resulting in segmentation based on risk tolerance; this has created "risk-taking" classifications such as conservative, moderate, and aggressive.[35] Other segmentation methods in this sector include classification according to experience[35] (e.g., "financially confused", "cautious investor"), or investor expectation (e.g., "idealist", "pragmatist"). A combination of these modes has been used in banking to segment consumers into broad groups based on investor types, which include "cautious", "confident", "optimist", "careful"," realist", "individualist", "integrator", and "well-balanced." Segmentation along these metrics allows for personalized services that work with the person's strengths and weaknesses, but still allow for economies of scale in the development of marketing products or mutual funds based on these typologies. Not unlike the insurance sector, banking has identified the importance of recognizing the individual personality traits relative to risk tolerance matter in terms of the value consumers aspire to achieve when accessing banking services.

Segmentation based on risk may offer important insights for health systems. Banking focuses on the individual's comfort level for taking on the risk of losing money when investing. Risk in healthcare might be viewed in terms of risk of becoming ill, particularly the risk of becoming chronically ill. For example, prevention programs focused on healthy eating and exercise have yielded little evidence of impact despite the risk of chronic illness associated with lifestyle. To date, health systems (i.e., public health programs in particular) have tended to use a "one size fits all" approach to educating populations about health behaviors such as diet, exercise, smoking, and the use of alcohol. Applying lessons learned from the retail banking sector by segmenting populations based on personality types or risk of chronic illness, and tailoring prevention programs to fit with the unique values of population segments may achieve greater impact. Using segmentation strategies to identify specific needs, values, and preferences of sub-groups of the population with specific risks or challenges enables the design of more effective prevention programs.

Given the increasing demand for health services which is raising health expenditures almost exponentially, the use of segmentation may also provide a solution to help manage health costs. There is an economic incentive to assess individual risk of chronic health conditions, as chronic health conditions cost companies 10.7% of their total labor costs.[36] To assess risk, companies appraise employees' physical and mental health, healthy behaviors, work environment, basic access, and life evaluation.[37] These metrics are measured as they impact presenteeism and job performance. After these areas are measured, employers then decide on the proper intervention required. Evidence has demonstrated that workplace intervention may improve mental health, disability and employee turnover.[36] By measuring quality of life before taking action, interventions will be more effective as preventative care programs offered only to those at risk of developing chronic conditions may very well increase the benefit-to-cost ratio of healthcare systems in a number of countries.

INDUSTRY EXAMPLE: AUTOMOTIVE AND RETAIL SEGMENTATION BASED ON WILLINGNESS TO PAY

The automotive industry demonstrates segmentation based on willingness to pay. Companies such as General Motors have created a number of brands to appeal to different income levels. Car market segments include basic, small, lower-medium, upper-medium, executive, luxury, sports, minivan, and SUV.[38] Different offerings within brands allow customers to evaluate the specific product based on whether it is best suited to their needs,[30] which allows the company to fulfill an entire population's quality and price demands by offering a variety of products or services. Brand extension can be used to either step up or step down in terms of the types of customers targeted. For example, Purina ONE, a pet food supplier now offers' luxury cat and dog food with a price premium as well as its lower priced, mid-level Purina brand.

Willingness to pay is a strategy that has a varying degree of utility in health systems. Funding models for health systems determine the level of choice consumers have in deciding which health services they will access based on, directly or indirectly (depending on the country), a person's "willingness to pay". Health systems have, and may continue to design strategies to personalize their services using "luxury" features that segments of the population value and choose to access. Currently, one could argue that hospitals offer private rooms at a premium price to the consumer. Health systems may benefit by considering ways to segment additional "luxury" services that may be valued by consumers in order to strengthen experience and enhance personalization for populations. Health systems may benefit from taking a broader perspective and considering how "willingness to pay" offers a strategy to more effectively personalize health systems to fi t with the values across income sectors of the population they serve. Segmenting the consumer base may be done in a variety of different ways. However, all methods have in common the primary goal of grouping the population into segments based on key features that could be used to personalize health services to achieve value. Segmentation of populations based on experience, value of time, knowledge of health, and expectations offer ways that health systems could personalize care and tailor approaches to achieve value.

LESSON 3: USE CUSTOMIZATION AS A STRATEGY FOR PERSONALIZATION

Customization is another strategy for achieving personalization. It differs from segmentation in that some of the responsibility of personalization lies with the consumer rather than the supplier. Rather than guessing or studying customer desires, customization involves strategies that enable the consumer to instruct the company or organization (i.e., health system) on how best to engage them to achieve their goals. Customization eliminates possible misinterpretation of what consumers want and value, and reduces the costs related to delivering services or products that are not used by the consumer or are not valued by them. The most important feature of customization may be the ability of the health system to actively engage consumers in tailoring services to achieve value. Traditionally, the manufacturing industry has focused on maximized efficiency through standardization, but has more recently experienced a shift in production strategies with customers now demanding greater input into the design and quality of products and services without paying the full cost currently associated with customization.[39] Manufacturers are moving towards mass customization, a system that combines the low unit costs of mass production processes with the flexibility of individual customization,[40] as a way to offer personalized products at a lower cost, attracting a greater diversity of customers. In the healthcare industry, there could be an opportunity to better understand "mass customization" due to the increasing volume of patients as a result of factors including increased life expectancy and growing prevalence of chronic illness. This growing demand for care puts pressure on health systems and has been managed by attempting to increase efficiencies in time or quality, using techniques such as Lean, a concept that originated from the automotive industry (Toyota Inc.). While processes designed to achieve efficiency in hospital-based services may decrease time and increase productivity, these approaches will do little to decrease volume due to growing demands over time, particularly for aging populations and the growing population sector with chronic illness. Customization strategies that focus on prevention and self-management of health and wellness may more effectively strengthen quality of care through mass customization, while at the same time reducing demands for expensive hospital care. In healthcare, two technological advances are making customization possible: personalized medicine, whereby therapies are customized to the genetic make-up of individuals; and advances in information technologies, which enable direct communication between populations and their health systems. These advances offer health systems opportunities to engage consumers directly to "customize" health services and approaches to care, while at the same time allowing innovative communication strategies to engage consumers more directly in achieving value relative to health, wellness, and quality of life. Examples of the use of mass customization in other sectors provide further insights into how health systems may engage this strategy to achieve personalization of health systems.

INDUSTRY EXAMPLE: MASS CUSTOMIZATION IN THE APPAREL INDUSTRY

Though individual customers are unique, the apparel industry is increasingly using mass customization strategies to respond to consumer trends and customer input in clothing design.[41] Companies such as Nike and Kate Spade allow individuals to take a standard product such as shoes or handbags and customize them based on limited selection of designs, colors, and materials. New technologies including fully-body scanning, computerized routing and made-to-measure pattern development are achieving personalized fit which has been shown to be the most important issue for consumers. The comparator in health systems is the emerging technology that creates "made to measure" therapies based on genomic technologies to offer a personalized fit with consumers. Although this technology is emerging rapidly, genomic therapies have not been mobilized across health systems to date, largely due to their excessive cost.

INDUSTRY EXAMPLE: MASS CUSTOMIZATION IN THE AUTOMOTIVE INDUSTRY

The automotive industry uses four ways to achieve mass customization: product design; process design; information system; and, process management. The auto industry uses a virtual "build to order" (VBTO) approach to engage consumers directly in the product design. Using a standard vehicle design, consumers can select different features such as automatic transmission, type of interior, heated seats and steering wheels, GPS systems, and sound systems. To make it easy on the consumer, car companies offer "product packages" which offer, at a discounted price, a grouping of the most popular options.

This type of consumer choice could be adopted by health systems to allow for customization within largely standardized health systems system. Consider a health region that serves a wide range of communities, some of which are rural and remote, others which are urban, and populations within each community that vary in terms of age and healthcare needs. Customization to create "product packages" could be used to design how community-based care and services are offered to elderly citizens in each community. Home visiting in rural and remote communities would very likely need to look different from services in urban communities, which have close proximity to health professionals and health organizations. Customization of health services could be designed with the input of individuals they are designed to serve. This way they would be far more likely to achieve seamless service models to deliver value to each community.

Health systems have much to learn from industry in terms of how to personalize products and services to achieve value for "customers". Personalization strategies that identify and then tailor services to the unique needs and expectations of consumers offer health systems a way to move beyond the "one size fits all" approach to healthcare to begin to transform the system to a "one size fits one" philosophy. To accomplish this, healthcare needs to develop tools, services, programs, and organizational approaches that make the individual feel like an individual, rather than just an anonymous number in a system. Industry has demonstrated countless successful approaches and examples of how to personalize services for entire populations to drive market share and revenues. Personalization of health systems can achieve the same value proposition for populations they serve, simply by learning by example of other industry sectors.

Ten Steps to Achieve the Personalization of Health Systems

Health systems around the world have achieved somewhat limited progress in personalizing health services to achieve value for the populations they serve. How can health systems personalize their structures, services, and care delivery models to achieve a personalized system that achieves value for the populations they serve? We suggest ten steps to achieve a personalized health system, which can be tailored to the unique cultural and population values of any population a health system serves.

Step 1: Reframe the Conversation from "What is the Matter" to "What Matters to You"

People judge the experience in healthcare by the way they are treated as a person, not by the way their disease is treated or by a provider's assessment of their "clinical outcome".[42] In our current healthcare system, conversations focus on the illness or injury, not on the person. This has the unintended consequence of dehumanizing individuals and identifying them by their disease. Patients are often described or identified by their diagnosis, such as a "cancer patient" or a "cancer survivor", "a COPD patient", "she is autistic", "he is bipolar". They become defined by their illness, not by who they are as a person. A personalized health system begins with the person, not the illness or treatment or disease.[42] Making a personal connection with the individual—as an individual—sets the appropriate tone from the beginning of the interaction at a level and context that focuses the dialogue on the person, not on their disease or illness. In every subsequent conversation or transaction, the health and wellness goals are the focus of the conversation and the treatment plan is specifically designed in collaboration with the individual to achieve personal goals and outcomes. While it sounds simple, considering people to be individuals rather than elements of a system, and determining what matters to them rather than what is the matter, reframes the conversation and the experience in the healthcare system to focus on the person rather than the disease, disability, or injury and the treatment protocols they are undergoing. It is a critical first step to create personalized health systems.

Step 2: Redefine Success in Terms of Health and Wellness Outcomes that are Valued by a Population

Every health system in the world measures health system performance outcomes such as quality, safety, access, and satisfaction; these indicators have been the dominant focus of health system quality and performance for decades. These measures focus on the transactions and the services health systems provide related to diagnosing, treating, managing, or curing disease or injury. Success of most health systems is defined as achieving the best possible quality outcomes for the patients the system serves. Yet, these clinical outcomes are of limited value from the perspective of the individual person, family, or community. What people really value is their wellness and quality of life.[8] In order to achieve a personalized health system, we need to define success by mapping health and wellness outcomes/goals onto the important work of clinical quality and performance outcomes throughout the health system.[9] As an example of the disconnect between clinical and system indicators, and personal wellness goals, consider the elderly man who goes to his primary care physician about having to get up at night several times to go to the bathroom causing him frustration and exhaustion day after day. The man is referred to a specialist and receives a diagnosis of early bladder cancer. The treatment plan is to eradicate the cancerous cells in the bladder. He undergoes treatment which deemed highly successful by all measures of quality and clinical outcomes in the healthcare system; the cells are gone and there is a low risk of their return. When you ask the patient if he achieved his health goals, he passionately states, "No, it was a big waste of time and I am not going back!" When asked why he feels it was a waste of time, he states, "Because I still have to get up at night four or five times and that was why I went to see the doctor in the first place". The clinical outcomes for this man were highly successful from the health systems viewpoint; yet achieving his personal health goals of getting a good sleep at night without waking up were a failure and he now refuses to continue the recommended follow up prescribed by the specialist. A personalized health system would build a treatment plan for this man that includes a strategy or support for managing his nightly urinary issue, which is eroding his quality of life as he is chronically feeling fatigued and frustrated.

Step Two in personalizing a health system requires building the customized outcomes identified in Step One into measures of health system achievement that reflect what people view as success—the health and wellness goals of the person, family, and community. Personalizing success means that every region and each sector of the population will have different measures or outcomes that reflect the uniqueness of the community or population. This step does not suggest ignoring or moving away from clinical outcomes of quality, safety, and performance based on best evidence; rather, it suggests building a personalized wellness focus into existing measures of success in a way that incorporates the individual or community's unique objectives.

Step 3: Put People in Charge—Shift the Decision-Making Process from the "Provider as Expert" to the "Person as Expert"

In current healthcare systems, the health professional or health team assesses the patient and makes decisions on the most optimal treatment plan. The patient consents to proceeding with the care strategy and then implementation of the care strategy begins. Decisions are by and large determined by the health provider (or team), personal health information is managed by the health system organization or practitioner, and patients are primarily in the role of "recipient" of care and are expected to follow the protocol that is prescribed. In the current system, the power balance is clearly in favor of the health system, which determines resource allocation to support service delivery in the communities the system serves. By design, health professionals offer those services to individuals/communities within the constraints the system places upon them. Consider the example of an elderly woman with Alzheimer's disease who always told her family, "Don't ever put me in one of those places (Nursing home). I would rather die than be in a place like that". When the primary care physician meets with the family to discuss strategies for keeping the woman safe from wandering at night, he suggests "Long-Term Care is really the best available option for your mother. It is a home-like environment and is a locked facility so that she will always be safe, and her safety is the most important priority for her". When the family identifies the woman's wishes, the physician defends his recommendation stating, "If it were me, I would have my parents in this facility in order for them to be well cared for". Inherent in this dialogue is the assumption that the physician "knows best". In this case, the priority goal from the physician's perspective was to ensure the woman's safety by putting her in a locked facility. The limitation of this approach is that the provider as expert identifies the goals for the person or for a family; there is no discussion of all potential options to determine the best fit with the needs and values of either the individual or the family.

Putting the person in charge, or, in the case of community organizations, putting the community in charge, means changing the power balance in the healthcare system from the dominant provider focus to a dominant person/community focus. A personalized system shifts this imbalance to one that supports individuals, families, or communities in making decisions about their own health, and designs care strategies or approaches that are tailor made to fit with the individual's personal values and health and wellness goals. The role of the health provider shifts from being the decision-maker to being the facilitator of the decision-making process. Once an individual defines what success looks like with and for the health provider, the conversation moves to examining all possible treatment options against how well they achieve the health and wellness goals of the individual, family and community they live in. In a personalized system, the focus on nurturing the individual based on their goals and values creates the conditions for the person to identify what success looks like, and then work with the health team to design the healthcare strategy that achieves that success.

Step 4: Shift Care Processes from "One Size Fits All" to "One Size Fits One"

Step Four requires health systems to turn the current person-health system interface "inside out", so that care delivery teams connect meaningfully to patients to support their progress towards health and wellness, whenever and wherever care is needed. Consider the example of the middle-aged man who is experiencing irregular heart rhythms and requires a pacemaker to restore heart health. He lives in a small rural community which has no access to specialist cardiology care within a 300 km. radius. Once the pacemaker is installed, best practice models for restoring cardiac arrhythmias include (evidence-based) follow-up care for monitoring the effectiveness of the pacemaker, educating the patient on heart health, consulting with the cardiologist on changes in the patient's condition, and following cardiac wellness protocols that re-build and strengthen heart health through exercise and lifestyle changes. To follow these best practice guidelines, our patient would have to travel regularly to access this type of care, which would require a loss of time at work, expense, and inconvenience. While the clinical goal of restoring heart health has been met with the pacemaker and care pathways, the system has not adapted strategies to meet to the individual's personal circumstances and goals. In short, the person has to fit into the model of care, as the traditional care model is not tailored to fit with the personal needs, values, and life circumstances of the individual.

Step Four focuses on how care happens in personalized health systems to ensure that it is linked to a person's health and wellness goals. It is one thing to suggest that the conversation needs to be reframed to "what matters to the person"; it is quite another to implement the care, therapy, or protocol in a manner that is personalized to what individuals value. Personalization of health systems will require embedding a personalized strategy into every service delivery model, which requires practitioners to really understand what matters to their patients. This is not to suggest that current evidence-based protocols or care processes are no longer appropriate; a shift to a personalized health system will require that current protocols/processes be implemented in a manner that is aligned with the person's goals, and values. To achieve this transformation, providers will require education programs to socialize them towards a collaborative partnership model, rather than a dominant decision-maker role. A focus on "one size fits one" will also require health professionals to be educated as members of an interprofessional healthcare team, who collaborate with colleagues across the continuum of care, collectively driving to achieve health and wellness goals of an individual or population. In a personalized health model, the territorial "scope of practice" debates of yesterday must shift so that health teams—who incorporate all elements of the care continuum - debate and dialogue on how best to work together with people in achieving their health and wellness goals. Step Four builds on shifting the dialogue towards the whole person, delivering the best practice protocol or care pathway in new and different ways in collaboration with the patient and the entire care team. Personalizing health systems means tailoring best practice protocols and programs of services to be accessible, equitable and achievable to all who need it, personalized in a way that achieves health and wellness goals within the unique circumstances in which they live.

Step 5: Stop Competing and Start Collaborating

In so many health systems, organizations, and health professional groups, communities and jurisdictions compete for "market share" of the resources spent on healthcare. In publicly funded systems, they compete for finite resources to fund their particular agency, organization, health profession, or service delivery model. In privatized health systems, they compete on market share directly and aspire to attract consumers to their organizations to drive revenue. Health systems compete most commonly on their achievement of clinical outcomes (disease focused outcomes, performance metrics such as safety and quality) to make the case that they are offering the "best care available". Yet, using the current measures of clinical outcomes, populations achieve little in terms of meeting their health and wellness goals. Simply put, key stakeholders within health systems compete with each other for resources and funding. In order to achieve personalization of a health system, stakeholders and organizations across the health system have to collaborate, not compete, in order to achieve value for populations they serve. Consider the situation of an elderly woman who is experiencing severe pain and limitations to mobility due to osteoarthritis in her knees. The most likely solution to improve her wellness and quality of life is to undergo a knee replacement to remove the severe pain and restore her mobility to regain her independence. In a personalized health system, she receives an overall wellness score that will not only depend on the hospital experience and clinical outcome of the knee surgery, it will also depend heavily on the supportive services she receives at home during her recovery and the access to physiotherapy to ensure she is able to regain her mobility effectively. The wellness score will be the cumulative sum of the efforts of organizations across the continuum of care, the hospital, the primary care follow up, the community rehabilitation, and the community level supportive services necessary for her to restore and improve her quality of life, health and wellness. In the current, competitive health system environment, there is very little interaction or collaboration across the continuum of care as each agency or health provider is focused solely on their individual contribution to the woman's recovery. In a personalized health system, each of the contributors to this woman's recovery would be integrated and would collaborate as a team to efficiently and effectively restore this woman's quality of life, while focusing on her unique and personal health and wellness goals—to remain independent at home, to continue to care for her pets and eventually re-join her bridge club when she regains her mobility. In order to achieve this type of team synergy, funding models (such as Accountable Care, or bundled payment models in publicly funded systems) must incentivize the collaboration. Currently, fee for service or pay for quality models incentivize competition among health organizations and provider teams, where the group with the largest volume of services delivered, achieves the greatest revenue. To personalize health systems, this antiquated model of funding service transactions needs to shift to funding outcomes that are targeted for specific populations and aligned with value and the personalized needs of population segments. In this model, health providers, teams, and organizations only receive funding when both the short-term and long-term priority outcomes are achieved; how they are achieved by the various provider groups is of little consequence. When outcomes are funded, rather than services delivered, health professionals or health organizations will have to collaborate to figure out the most efficient and effective process for achieving population targets. Step Five must incentivize collaboration across care teams (e.g., specialists in the hospital, community-based organizations, primary care, and work-place health programs) to collaborate to personalize service delivery to achieve wellness at the community level and the achievement of individual health goals at the personal level.

Step 6: Join the 21st Century, and Get Connected

People are "connected" to the world around them, in digital societies, using digital tools, apps, and platforms to conduct their banking, to arrange travel, to purchase retail goods, and to engage their social networks to learn and participate in day to day interactions. The only sector to which people cannot connect using digital technologies at a system level is healthcare. The analysis of mobile apps in this chapter revealed that people extensively use online tools and technologies to self-manage their personal health and wellness. The challenge is that they do so independently and have limited ability to connect their personalized goals and wellness activities to their interactions with their health providers. Essentially, consumers are designing and engaging in self-management of their health and wellness, yet they do not have the advantage or benefit of engaging in self-management with the support and expertise of their health provider or health team. In order to personalize health systems, the key stakeholders in these systems need to connect more directly, and differently, to the populations they serve, using digital tools and platforms. Health systems need to connect to consumers where they are online, rather than continuing to expect and require that consumers "come to the health system", in order to seek the support and expertise of health providers. In a personalized health system, health teams would transform their practice structure to directly engage people using digital tools that connect to the tools the individuals are already using to support self-management of health and wellness. As an example, in a personalized health system, the 38-year-old woman who has been just been diagnosed with Type II diabetes has downloaded three apps on her smart phone: one to track insulin doses and A1C levels; another to access personal training to achieve personal fitness goals through exercise; and, an app that offers calorie counts and menus to manage her diet. Periodic visits with her care provider (physician or diabetes educator) are supplemented or replaced by regular online monitoring of progress in real time using the tracking outcome data on the apps. Interactions between the person and provider are conducted virtually through email, virtual care visits, and secure texting when the person needs input into their health and wellness program and when the provider is "flagged" or alerted by the system when biophysical outcome measures are indicating a decline in the person's health status. Imagine how diabetes care might change into a personalized system whereby providers have online access and meaningful engagement with their patient's health and wellness program, and use digital technologies to reach out to support, encourage, and support decisions to proactively intervene when it is needed, where it is needed, to support individuals to achieve their health and wellness goals. There is a huge opportunity to augment and personalize care plans by taking advantage of data being gathered by people on their own. Digital tools put into the hands of care providers, with all of the security and privacy features used in other sectors (i.e., banking), connecting the care and services (re-designed to achieve connectivity to people) present an enormous opportunity to create personalized programs of health and wellness. It does not mean that digital strategies should be added on as another layer over top of the existing antiquated system. Personalization simply means that healthcare systems are connected to the population they serve more directly by leveraging digital tools technologies to understand and support the health and wellness goals of individuals, and designed in a way that offers seamless engagement of health teams to support people in achieving health and wellness goals. As health teams take advantage of technologies to assist in designing strategies for connecting to their patients in a more personalized manner, the practice structures and digital environments of health systems will adapt and shift towards a more "connected" healthcare system that is meaningful to the personalized needs of the population they serve.

Step 7: Democratize Information to Empower People to Take Charge of Their Health and Wellness

Many health systems work within information structures where the personal health information of individuals is held in "secure" information vaults managed by health system organizations or stakeholders. For example, it is common that all hospital visits/interactions are recorded in a patient record in which information is collected using a combination of paper-based and digital information systems, housed and securely stored in hospital databases. Primary care teams use either paper or digital health records to document patient visits and test outcomes which are then saved in health information systems. Similarly, community organizations house and store patient health information within their clinical information systems to capture utilization outcomes, and service delivery quality outcomes. In many health systems, all personal health information is managed autonomously by each of the health organizations in the system, with little or no ability to cross-reference their information with the other players in the health system. This not only creates unnecessary duplication, it does not allow for all of the pieces of an individual's health profile and progress to be considered in tandem. In the majority of current healthcare systems, personal health information (i.e., lab results, diagnostic testing outcomes, clinical assessment measures, and medication management) are the responsibility and purview of the health system stakeholders; they are not available to the very people the information is about, who require the information to make informed decisions about health, wellness, and quality of life. In a personalized health system, information about the health of individuals, communities, and populations is made readily available, easily and effectively accessed for the primary purpose of equipping the individual/community/ population with the information they need to make informed decisions and choices about their health in real time. Consider the 48-year-old woman who is the primary caregiver and decision maker for her elderly mother with Alzheimer's disease. In a personalized health system, the daughter and her mother would access their personal health information when required on their mobile device or computer, allowing them to share data and insights with all care partners in their healthcare team. This creates the condition for informed discussions by all parties as well as an ability to directly monitor progress over time to determine whether previously defined health and wellness goals are being met. This personalized approach empowers the woman to directly engage other health providers when necessary, share accurate and up to date information with them about her mother's health status and wellness goals, and make informed decisions based on accurate and detailed health information, available on an accessible digital app or platform.

Step 8: Learn From Industry and Customize Healthcare to the Needs, Expectations, and Values of the Population

Health systems have been delivering health services using a "one size fits all" approach, with little or no choice in how patients access health services or how those services are delivered where options are typically limited to clinic visits, the primary care office, and emergency department. However, growing numbers of people are designing and customizing their own healthcare using online tools, programs, and digital platforms. Why? Because health systems are not structured to achieve what matters to people. Health systems need to learn from other industry sectors to customize their services to the needs and expectations of the people they serve. The first lesson that can be adapted from industry is to use market segmentation to identify the desires and commonalities of sub-sectors within populations. Programs and services can then be tailored in a way that reflects these insights. The second lesson is to design new ways of accessing health services (i.e., "distribution channels") that offer individuals and their caregivers' choices and options to select the best care delivery strategy for their unique life circumstances. The current pandemic has witnessed a rapid implementation of virtual care approaches, while also limiting access to in person care delivery. Despite the access to virtual care, evidence suggests health systems determine the care delivery model, rather than offering consumers the choice of care options that best fit with their unique values and needs. IN addition, virtual care visits remain digital versions of traditional care appointments with provider teams, rather than new care models that are personalized to the unique needs and values of patients. Strategies to achieve personalization of care that responds to the unique needs and preferences of each population segment include the following:

a. Patients choose how and when they will engage with care providers, offering flexibility to choose in-person clinics or MD visit, virtual consultations, online or home visits
b. The use of digital tools (e.g., smart phone, tablets, online programs) designed for consumers that enable self management of their health and wellness, including health goals established by the patient, in consultation with the provider team to ensure health goals are meaningful and relevant to every patient
c. Health literacy tools that are culturally competent, respecting the unique cultures and life circumstances of all consumers, supporting health literacy to support progress towards health and wellness goals
d. Advanced analytics embedded in digital tools focused on keeping people well, by identifying risks to health to inform proactive health interventions to reduce risks to support health and wellness.

A personalized health system would be customized to fit each segment in the population and offer choices in terms of how people can access these services. For example, segmenting the population by demographics (i.e., age, gender, geography, or employment) is a simple way to categorize and then customize access to services. In a personalized health system, access to "in person visits" or home visits may be the most likely preference of seniors, whereas online appointments and secure messaging would be the most convenient access strategy for busy, working mothers. Offering choice and customization of health services and health system delivery mechanisms enables people to design the care strategy that best suits their needs, values and lifestyles.

Consider the health system which is challenged to meet the needs of aging populations, predominantly rural, with growing numbers of elderly citizens who are experiencing a range of chronic illnesses which are challenging to manage. In a personalized health system, the population could be segmented based on age and geographic setting in order to better respond to the values and expectations these seniors have for their health system. The segmentation is also cross-referenced with health utilization and clinical outcome data, and social determinants of health data in order to profile typologies or groups within the senior population to identify unique priorities and values. Health services would then be designed based on goals for health, wellness, and quality of life, including wellness targets such as "living independently in my home", "engaging in community social activities on a day to day basis", and "remaining within the home community" to be a part of family and friends social networks they have grown up with. The health team would provide a menu of choices for how services could be accessed and delivered in order to customize care to meet the needs of the senior, their family, and community. Seniors who prefer to remain at home and access virtual visits with their doctor would have the choice to do so and would be provided with technology support if required. The care team in the rural community would use digitally connected health to track and monitor medications, appointments, activity, and socialization with the seniors to help them remain independent and achieve their wellness goals. Personalized health systems are mandated to deliver value to the populations they serve; to achieve that mandate they need to recognize that there are wide variation across population sub-groups who have different needs, expectations and values which all require different approaches to how health services are structured and accessed. In a personalized system, customization and segmentation are enabled by accountable care funding models through which health teams are funded to achieve outcomes for defined populations and to meet priority health outcomes using a coordinated, customized approach to health service delivery that recognize what matters to people.

Step 9: Put the Population in Charge of Defining Value

Every health system in the world is struggling with the increasing demands for health services and managing the growing costs of delivering services where and when they are needed. Funding resources required to sustain health systems are rapidly outpacing the GDP growth in most countries, placing health systems in the challenging position of making decisions to fund, or not to fund, certain types of healthcare services. This is exacerbated by the rapid advancement of science and technology which offer new and innovative therapies, devices and treatment options, including genomic-based therapies for disease management or cure. These therapies come at an extraordinary cost and will lead to very difficult conversations and decisions about how and where health systems allocate their resources. Elected officials who oversee health systems walk a fine line to ensure they offer services populations need and desire, while at the same time managing fixed budgets within which they must be able to deliver said services. In the current health system, health leaders and decision makers focus primarily on cost cutting initiatives to achieve the maximum possible productivity, efficiency, and quality within limited fiscal resources.

In a personalized health system the population is actively engaged, using citizen dialogue to advance discussions around how to achieve value for the population. The personalized health system essentially puts the population in the role of a decision-maker-collaborator in making the difficult decisions about what services are provided and what services are not provided, what outcomes the funding models will pay for, and what population outcomes are abandoned when they do not achieve value. Citizen dialogue structures are embedded deeply within a personalized healthcare system and are used to achieve the following:

a. Fully understand and maintain a clear focus on population value for all decisions
b. Inform and debate decision options with citizens to ensure the population understands what is possible and what options are viable when making difficult decisions on what services to offer and what services/programs can no longer be offered

c. Engage citizens in determining the best way forward when making difficult decisions so that the population has a voice; and

d. Build health system literacy across the population, and across health system key stakeholders (including hospitals, community organizations, health professionals, private industry, policy makers/government, communities/regions/citizens) to engage in healthy debate and decision making that is informed, and reflective of the values of populations, which is centrally important in any decision made at the health system level.

Citizen engagement in health system level dialogue and decision-making is a necessary and foundational feature of a personalized health system that supports the transformation of health systems from one that is rather narcissistic (e.g., focused on the system, its processes, providers and clinical outcomes), to a personalized system that focuses on outcomes tied to the value it delivers to the population it is mandated to serve. Consider the example of the health system that deems "healthy aging" as the priority the health system will achieve over the course of a five-year mandate. The health system leader in most jurisdictions defines "health aging" as the priority health challenge to address, based on evidence in the literature and population demographics. Health system leaders then design the implementation strategy across the entire healthcare system, allocating the necessary resources to achieve their defined objectives. In a personalized health system, citizen engagement processes would enable and support dialogue between key citizen groups and health system leaders. Services are then personalized to fit with the needs and priorities of the target population that achieve wellness outcomes deemed important and worthy through citizen engagement. Thus, a personalized system determines population priorities and strategies to support achieving wellness outcomes by engaging the impacted citizens directly in designing the strategy, focused on using a values-based approach to determine what support is needed, how it should be delivered, and what it is designed to achieve in terms of wellness and quality of life.

Step 10: Measure What Matters

Health systems today focus on measuring performance and quality largely in terms of measuring the performance of the health system, rather than measuring whether the system is achieving value for the populations they serve. Personalizing a health system means that the current system-level metrics need to be augmented and strengthened to include metrics that reflect the values of individuals, communities, and populations served by the system. This will require creating new metrics to measure progress on a health system's ability to achieve value through personalization. A personalized system will reflect the idea that people and populations are the key to ensuring success. The metrics for a personalized health system are as follows:

1. Person-level metrics: Person-specific metrics would include what health systems measure now (i.e., biophysical measures such as A1c levels for diabetes care, blood pressure for cardiovascular health), but also add on health and wellness goals established by the person. This is the route to get people engaged in defining their treatment plans, as the metrics would be theirs rather than those purely of the clinician. For example, when considering the pre-offered range of treatment options, the person with COPD would decide on a plan with a level of exercise tolerance most closely aligned with their personal values. Including person-level metrics will personalize treatment plans, making it much more likely for people to take ownership of their care, as they have decided on the goals they feel are achievable and offer value to their lives

2. Population health metrics: These are key indicators of health and wellness of a population that reflect values such as quality of life. System-level utilization metrics mapped onto the population level outcomes can be used to determine the allocation of health system resources and patterns of utilization that achieve outcomes. These metrics act as a suite of currencies and more directly engage the providers of care to working with the populations they serve.

This is achieved by focusing on big system changes over populations where the expectation is that certain standards need to be met by all, and payment to system partners and providers is directly linked to achieving priority population health outcomes. For example, immunization for flu is a major predictor of hospitalization and illness in seniors. Population health outcomes would be identified through community engagement to define realistic immunization targets that are valued by the population. Groups within the population have varying health priorities; thus, health systems would define key population health metrics using segmentation to define value within each to achieve value. System-wide utilization metrics are the most dominant type of metrics in global health systems; however, they need to map onto the population health metrics to define the value health systems are achieving for populations. The economic metrics for the health system would provide evidence of cost versus value relative to population outcomes. For example, looking at emergency admissions on a practice by practice basis would enable provider teams to more effectively manage health outcomes at the population level to understand change over time.

Currently, health systems measure and manage clinical outcomes and system performance (i.e., safety, quality, access), but do so in isolation of whether the health system is achieving value for the people and populations they serve, in terms of wellness and quality of life. Consider the situation where the health system is achieving the highest quality of best practice management of disease and illness, yet the population they are mandated to serve report declining levels of self-reported levels of wellness. Despite well documented wellness measures in many global health systems, wellness is generally not linked to health system performance. Health systems at local and regional levels are not integrating measures of wellness in regional or community levels to inform and support personalization of health system services and outcomes. To achieve personalization of health systems, measures of wellness must be integrated into health system performance outcomes to allow for the direct comparison of health system performance relative to wellness of the population they are serving.

CONCLUSION

There is no doubt that digital health connects and empowers people and populations to manage their health and wellness. The person-enabled health system will be augmented by accessible and supportive provider teams working within flexible, integrated, interoperable, and digital-enabled care environments. To better align the growing consumer demands on health systems, health systems must articulate what a personalized health system should look like by taking into account what matters to individuals. Only when health systems identify and implement emerging trends in technology and consumer behavior will we achieve a person-enabled health system.

REFERENCES

1. Yurkiewicz S. The prospects for personalized medicine. *Hastings Center Report*. 2010;40(5). doi:1 0.1353/hcr.2010.0002
2. Eriksson M, Lindström B. A salutogenic interpretation of the Ottawa Charter. *Health Promotion International*. 2008;23(2). doi:10.1093/heapro/dan014
3. Antonovsky A. Unraveling the Mystery of Health: How People Manage Stress and Stay Well. In: *The Health Psychology Reader*; 2012. doi:10.4135/9781446221129.n9.
4. Lindström B, Eriksson M. From health education to healthy learning: Implementing salutogenesis in educational science. *Scandinavian Journal of Public Health*. 2011;39(1). doi:10.1177/14034948103 93560
5. Árnason V. The personal is political: Ethics and personalized medicine. *Ethical Perspectives*. 2012;19(1). doi:10.2143/EP.19.1.2152681
6. Rawls J. *A Theory of Justice, Revised Edition*. Harvard University Press; 1999.

7. Mcclellan M, Kent J, Beales S, et al. *Focusing Accountability on the Outcomes That Matter. Report of the Accountable Care Working Group. Doha.*; 2013. Accessed October 18, 2020. https://www.wish.org. qa/wp-content/uploads/2018/01/27425_WISH_Accountable_care_Report_AW-Web.pdf

8. Snowdon A, Schnarr K, Hussein A, Alessi C. Measuring What Matters: The Cost vs. Values of Health Care. Published online 2012. Accessed October 18, 2020. https://www.ivey.uwo.ca/cmsmedia/ 3467948/white-paper-measuring-what-matters.pdf

9. Frist WH. Connected health and the rise of the patient-consumer. *Health Affairs.* 2014;33(2). doi:1 0.1377/hlthaff.2013.1464

10. Polansky A, Leslie J, Heimann G, et al. *The Great American Search for Healthcare Information*; 2018. Accessed October 18, 2020. https://www.webershandwick.com/wp-content/uploads/2018/11/Healthcare-Info-Search-Report.pdf

11. Health Online 2013 | Pew Research Center. Published 2013. Accessed October 18, 2020. https://www. pewresearch.org/internet/2013/01/15/health-online-2013/

12. Demographics of Mobile Device Ownership and Adoption in the United States | Pew Research Center. Accessed October 18, 2020. https://www.pewresearch.org/internet/fact-sheet/mobile/#mobile-phone-ownership-over-time

13. More than Half of Smartphone Owners Have Used Their Phone to get Health Information, do Online Banking | Pew Research Center. Published 2014. Accessed October 18, 2020. https://www.pewresearch.org/ internet/2015/04/01/us-smartphone-use-in-2015/pi_2015-04-01_smartphones_03/

14. 2020 Health care consumer survey: consumer health trends | Deloitte Insights. Published 2020. Accessed October 19, 2020. https://www2.deloitte.com/us/en/insights/industry/health-care/consumer-health-trends.html

15. Oldenburg J, Chase D, Christensen KT, Tritle B, eds. *Engage! Transforming Healthcare Through Digital Patient Engagement.* Healthcare Information and Management Systems Society; 2012.

16. Zhou YY, Kanter MH, Wang JJ, Garrido T. Improved quality at Kaiser permanente through e-mail between physicians and patients. *Health Affairs.* 2010;29(7). doi:10.1377/hlthaff.2010.0048

17. Kvedar J, Coye MJ, Everett W. Connected health: A review of technologies and strategies to improve patient care with telemedicine and telehealth. *Health Affairs.* 2014;33(2). doi:10.1377/hlthaff.2 013.0992

18. Keckley P, Coughlin S. Deloitte 2012 Survey of U.S. Health Care Consumers. Published 2012. Accessed October 19, 2020. https://www2.deloitte.com/content/dam/Deloitte/us/Documents/life-sciences-health-care/us-lshc-2012-survey-of-us-consumers-health-care.pdf

19. Smartphone users worldwide 2020 | Statista. Accessed October 18, 2020. https://www.statista.com/ statistics/330695/number-of-smartphone-users-worldwide/

20. *The Growing Value of Digital Health Evidence and Impact on Human Health and the Healthcare System.*; 2017. Accessed October 18, 2020. https://www.iqvia.com/insights/the-iqvia-institute/reports/ the-growing-value-of-digital-health

21. *Use, Evidence and Remaining Barriers to Mainstream Acceptance Patient Adoption of MHealth.*; 2015. Accessed October 18, 2020. www.theimsinstitute.org

22. Kao C-K, Liebovitz DM. Consumer mobile health apps: Current state, barriers, and future directions. *PM&R.* 2017;9:S106–S115. doi:10.1016/j.pmrj.2017.02.018

23. Americans Check Their Phones 96 Times a Day - Asurion. Accessed October 18, 2020. https://www. asurion.com/about/press-releases/americans-check-their-phones-96-times-a-day/

24. Rowland SP, Fitzgerald JE, Holme T, Powell J, Mcgregor A. Perspective What is the clinical value of mHealth for patients?. npj Digital Medicine. 2012; 3 doi: 10.1038/s41746-019-0206-x.

25. Eric Wicklund. Doctors Still Don't Trust mHealth Apps. Published 2016. Accessed October 18, 2020. https://mhealthintelligence.com/news/doctors-still-dont-trust-mhealth-apps

26. Powell AC, Landman AB, Bates DW. In search of a few good apps. *JAMA May.* 2014;14:1851. doi:1 0.1001/jama.2014.2564

27. Gordon WJ, Landman A, Zhang H, Bates DW. Beyond validation: getting health apps into clinical practice. *npj Digital Medicine.* 2020;3(1):14. doi:10.1038/s41746-019-0212-z

28. Bates DW, Landman A, Levine DM. Health apps and health policy. *JAMA.* 2018;320(19):1975. doi:1 0.1001/jama.2018.14378

29. Mathews SC, McShea MJ, Hanley CL, Ravitz A, Labrique AB, Cohen AB. Digital health: A path to validation. *npj Digital Medicine.* 2019;2(1):38. doi:10.1038/s41746-019-0111-3

30. Kim JW, Lee BH, Shaw MJ, Chang HL, Nelson M. Application of decision-tree induction techniques to personalized advertisements on internet storefronts. *International Journal of Electronic Commerce.* 2001;5(3). doi:10.1080/10864415.2001.11044215

31. Barnes B. At Disney Parks, a Bracelet Meant to Build Loyalty (and Sales) - The New York Times. Published 2013. Accessed October 19, 2020. https://www.nytimes.com/2013/01/07/business/media/at-disney-parks-a-bracelet-meant-to-build-loyalty-and-sales.html?pagewanted=all&_r=1&

32. Perspective: The Definition of Consumer Personalization Varies | First Data. Published 2013. Accessed October 19, 2020. https://www.firstdata.com/en_ie/insights/Perspectives-UCIE-Personalization-Definition.html

33. The International Strategy of TESCO PLC – The WritePass Journal: The WritePass Journal. Published 2017. Accessed October 19, 2020. https://writepass.com/journal/2017/01/the-international-strategy-of-tesco-plc/

34. Kotler P, Haider D, Rein I. Marketing places: Attracting investment and tourism to cities, states and nations. The Free Press. Published online; 1993.

35. Chau PYK, Ho CKY. Developing consumer-based service brand equity via the internet: The role of personalization and trialability. *Journal of Organizational Computing and Electronic Commerce.* 2008;18(3). doi:10.1080/10919390802198956

36. Collins JJ, Baase CM, Sharda CE, et al. The assessment of chronic health conditions on work performance, absence, and total economic impact for employers. *Journal of Occupational and Environmental Medicine.* 2005;47(6). doi:10.1097/01.jom.0000166864.58664.29

37. Shi Y, Sears LE, Coberley CR, Pope JE. Classification of individual well-being scores for the determination of adverse health and productivity outcomes in employee populations. *Population Health Management.* 2013;16(2). doi:10.1089/pop.2012.0039

38. Reinecke K, Bernstein A. Knowing what a user likes: A design science approach to interfaces that automatically adapt to culture. *MIS Quarterly: Management Information Systems.* 2013;37(2). doi:10.25300/MISQ/2013/37.2.06

39. Bi ZM, Lang SYT, Verner M, Orban P. Development of reconfigurable machines. *International Journal of Advanced Manufacturing Technology.* 2008;39(11-12). doi:10.1007/s00170-007-1288-1

40. Adam S. A model of web use in direct and online marketing strategy. *Electronic Markets.* 2002;12(4). doi:10.1080/101967802762553521

41. Anderson-Connell LJ, Ulrich PV, Brannon EL. A consumer-driven model for mass customization in the apparel market. *Journal of Fashion Marketing and Management.* 2002;6(3). doi:10.1108/13612020210441346

42. Lee F. *If Disney Ran Your Hospital.* Health Administration Press; 2008.

29 Accelerating Health and Innovation: Improving Health for All

Kerry Amato
BA

Robert Havasy
MS

CONTENTS

LEARNING OBJECTIVES

1. Identify the role of culture in fostering innovation and the traits needed for an innovative workforce.
2. Evaluate the role of processes and governance in identifying and remaining focused on critical innovation.
3. Discover best practices for fostering persistent innovation in complex organizations.

INTRODUCTION

Introducing something new or disrupting the status quo is never easy, particularly in healthcare, where organizations tend to be more risk-averse than similar organizations outside of healthcare. Every chapter about information technology (IT) governance in a graduate textbook advocates closely linking governance principles to organizational strategy. In practice, it is common to see a tightly constrained budget result in a stifling set of governance rules that make innovation all but

DOI: 10.4324/9780429398377-35

impossible. Yet, health IT can create not only a competitive business advantage for hospitals but also a necessary foundation for providing the highest-quality patient care (Wager, Lee, & Glaser, 2009). Therefore, the health IT asset and associated processes must change, adapt, and develop to keep pace with changes to the business environment and support innovations in process, policy, and procedures across the entire healthcare enterprise. In a world where more and more everyday transactional services are being "Uberised," and consumers place more of a premium on convenience, healthcare innovation is no longer an option but rather a necessity.

For example, a 2020 research study by HIMSS shows that remote technologies such as telehealth services are the preferred way for younger generations to interact with healthcare organizations. The potential impact of this shift in care on primary care businesses is profound. Adapting to this change as a new generation of patients replace the current generation can ensure both the survival of some practices and deliver high-quality care via the preferred virtual channels. If fostered and implemented correctly, innovation provides the opportunity for healthcare to evolve to meet consumer expectations better, provide the best patient care possible, and ultimately survive in a changing world.

This chapter explores a culture's role in fostering innovation, examines the traits needed for an innovative workforce, and highlights best practices for fostering persistent innovation in complex organizations.

THE GOAL OF HEALTHCARE INNOVATION

Activist Iveta Cherneva wrote, "Technology innovation for the sake of innovation is an empty shell if we focus on what people don't need but would buy anyways." As global healthcare spending approaches $8 trillion and increases faster than global GDP, this warning becomes even more critical (World Health Organization, 2019). Healthcare innovation must have a purpose, and given the intensely personal nature of health, it must be more than simply to make money.

For more than a decade, the so-called Triple Aim promoted by the Institute for Healthcare Improvement (IHI) has been a guiding principle for innovation. The Triple Aim proposes three dimensions to measure the performance of the health system (Institute for Healthcare Improvement, 2020):

- The experience of care (for patients)
- The health of populations
- The per-capita cost of care

Seven years after IHI introduced the Triple Aim, physicians Thomas Bodenheimer and Christine Sinsky proposed a fourth dimension in an article in the *Annals of Family Medicine*: improving clinicians' and staff's work-life (Bodenheimer & Sinsky, 2014). Since that time, clinical burden and clinician burnout reside at the forefront of every leader's mind. Reducing their effects is an essential task for every healthcare leader (Figure 29.1).

Combining these dimensions into something now often called the Quadruple Aim is a good starting point for healthcare innovation leaders considering their role and plans. We firmly support these four dimensions as an anchor point when considering projects, whether inside a hospital or health system or as a market supplier looking to bring new ideas to the healthcare market. Several frameworks exist for measuring whether projects achieve the Quadruple Aim's goals, and dissecting those lies beyond this chapter's scope. However, one such framework for applying the Quadruple Aim to primary care practice innovation, *Core Principles to Improve Primary Care Quality Management,* makes two critical points worthy of highlight.

First, the Quadruple Aim must be considered whole and not just as "the sum of its parts" or dimensions. It is critical to look at innovation from a sufficiently high-level view to judge its overall impact, not just to score and measure it. And that measurements are "tools for quality, not

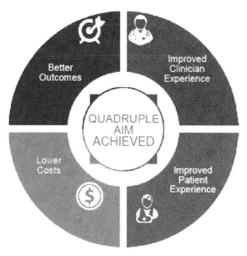

FIGURE 29.1 Reprinted from the Agency for Healthcare Research and Quality, https://digital.ahrq.gov/acts/quadruple-aim (public domain).

outcomes of quality" by themselves (Mutter et al., 2018). Modern management theory has become obsessed with measuring everything, but healthcare remains a uniquely personal product that must support and sustain the human interaction that we all value so dearly. Improved experiences are subjective goals, differing from individual to individual. A holistic view of innovation can help leaders determine if their efforts are at least directionally correct, even if the measurement of individual clinical parameters might not capture the impact on a personal scale.

The goal for innovation leaders then might be summarized thus: to create a culture and environment within an organization that encourages people to identify and think about problems in new ways to improve the caregiving experience for patients and providers, improve health outcomes, and lower costs.

CULTURE EATS STRATEGY FOR BREAKFAST

"Culture eats strategy for breakfast" is an oft-quoted management expression of uncertain origin (Quote Investigator, 2017). "Culture trumps strategy," declared the *Harvard Business Review* in 2011 (Merchant, 2011). Regardless of who proclaims it, the truth is difficult to escape. Innovation does not magically happen within organizations. It springs forth from a culture that values independent thinking and doesn't punish those who identify and raise problems. Innovative cultures often require employee behaviors that fly in the face of cultures focused on efficiency (Walker & Soule, 2017).

The typical adjectives used to describe innovative cultures include: nimble, agile, and customer-centered. Innovation-focused Silicon Valley companies like Facebook adopt mottos like, "Move fast and break things," at least until they mature and decide that careful planning and efficient use of their infrastructure investments matters after all (Murphy, 2014). The core idea is that innovation happens best when people aren't afraid of making a mistake and can view a problem from various perspectives. And here, many hospital cultures create the first friction to effective innovation: the nature of patient care, coupled with the traditionally tight profit margins in care delivery, creates limited tolerance for disruption.

Striking the right balance is the central challenge of innovation leadership. Lofty goals and slogans about tolerance for failure and the need to "think outside the box" don't change the organizational challenges of meeting care quality metrics and margin targets. Leaders who champion projects which lose sight of organizational objectives, key focus areas, and other priorities will not remain leaders for long. The key is an innovative culture with some guardrails that quickly whittles down proposals to the practical ones that align with critical organizational objectives. In short, while there may be "no bad ideas" in a brainstorming session, culture is the key to assuring that hair-brained ideas don't sap scarce resources and waste time and money by progressing too far before being judged impractical or superfluous. Rather than reams of formal process documents, hours of committee meetings, and dozens of difficult conversations, it is the people who sustain the culture that should put these guardrails in place themselves. And it is on those people that innovation leaders should focus most of their time and energy. As one innovation leader with more than 40 years of experience says,

> *Obsessing too much about budget and deadlines will kill ideas before they get off the ground. Once your scientists understand that they are ultimately accountable for delivering practical products and processes that can be manufactured affordably, you can trust them to not embarrass you by wasting a lot of money and effort. This trust helps forge an innovation culture. (Ishak, 2017)*

FOSTERING AN INNOVATIVE CULTURE

Fostering an innovative culture and workforce requires more than a few lofty slogans and constant admonishment to "think differently." Here, we run headfirst into one of the major roadblocks to building the right team: traditional Human Resources talent management strategies. As a practical matter, "thinking outside the box" requires people who have life experience "outside the box." Creative problem solving is one of the main benefits of a diverse workforce, allowing teams to bring varied perspectives to a problem as early as possible in the cycle, rather than anchoring an idea and then consulting different communities. For some leaders, it's not the specific experience an employee has that matters, but rather the desire to have new experiences in the first place. Jessica Stillman writes in *Inc.* magazine, "Repeated studies show a close link between the personality trait psychologists call openness and truly great brains." She goes on to quote Steve Jobs from a talk he gave to the Academy of Achievement:

> *"You have to not have the same bag of experiences as everyone else does, or else you're gonna make the same connections and you won't be innovative. [...] You might want to think about going to Paris and being a poet for a few years. Or you might want to go to a third-world country--I'd highly advise that. Falling in love with two people at once. Walt Disney took LSD," he says. (Stillman, 2020)*

Diverse organizations and the tolerant cultures that support them don't just happen. Innovation leaders must carefully construct the environment for them to flourish. In chapter three of his bestselling book, *Good to Great,* author Jim Collins described a consistent trait of organizations that had outperformed their peers over time regarding hiring people:

> *The executives who ignited transformations from good to great did not first figure out where to drive the bus and then get people to take it there. No, they first got the right people on the bus (and the wrong people off the bus) and then figured out where to drive it. (Collins, 2001)*

Numerous books and studies point out that employees stay at a job because of the people they work with and for, rather than the organization's mission or goals. When an organization or department is staffed by people who genuinely like working with each other and, therefore, challenge each other without succumbing to petty infighting, only then can you achieve the nimble, not-afraid-to-fail culture that an innovation organization prizes. This kind of diversity doesn't happen by luck, or at least not by luck alone. It springs forth from a carefully crafted plan to locate, identify, attract, retain, and value the kind of employees with the diverse experiences that leaders like Steve Jobs value so highly. Modern human resource managers know that implicit and explicit biases exist in all leaders and can help design recruitment strategies to overcome "cultural matching," or managers' tendency to hire people with similar cultural traits as their own (Rivera, 2012). The first step to creating the culture needed for successful innovation is explicitly stating that diversity of experience is a goal and then pursue a strategy to fulfill it.

ADDITIONAL CULTURAL SPEEDBUMPS

Healthcare creates unique difficulties for creative cultures, however, and innovation leaders must walk a fine line to find success. Healthcare is rooted in science and dominated by physicians, which creates a world where empirical evidence is often weighted more than in other industries. Evidence suggests that healthcare outcomes are improved and that healthcare organizations perform better overall when doctors and other clinical professionals occupy management roles (Clay-Williams, Ludlow, Testa, Li, & Braithwaite, 2017). This historical deference to physicians, highly educated and often with dominating personalities, can create a difficult environment for non "healthcare people" to be heard and respected. Applying even more cultural pressure, the often high stakes and deeply personal nature associated with clinical care can create an intimidating environment that naturally resists change. Finally, adding in the traditionally challenging business environment and financial sensitivities to any cost or pricing disruptions for most healthcare businesses, one finds the reasons that healthcare tends to innovate more slowly than other industries. The learning curve for new employees entering a healthcare environment can be daunting.

Like any industry, healthcare uses its own language. We talk about physicians and clinicians and often abbreviate everything with a TLA or three-letter abbreviation. Clinical staff have legal scopes of practice bounding what is and isn't possible for them to do in any given situation, along with SOPs (standard operating procedures) and standing orders that aren't SOPs. And don't forget the laws, rules, and regulations like HIPAA and GDPR and the agencies that make or enforce most of them like CMS, ONC, FDA, HHS, WHO, EC, NHS and others. These things can increase the time it takes for someone with a diverse but not healthcare-related background to gain sufficient knowledge to feel comfortable and become truly productive. This steep learning curve also makes healthcare innovation employees less elastic—they can be hard to find, expensive to train, and cause disruptions when they leave, increasing the value of a welcoming and sustaining culture.

One final paradox confronts healthcare innovation leaders buried in the preceding paragraphs: balancing healthcare business with the cultural expectations for the healthcare system. Suppose one looks at the part of the Quadruple Aim focused on reducing the cost of care. In that case, many healthcare innovations focus on gaining process efficiencies or reducing the variable costs of care, of which the labor of caregivers is a primary component. Stated more clearly, it can be difficult for organizations to think "outside the box" not only when the people in charge are firmly "inside the box," but when one of the aims of innovation is to reduce the amount of money spent on their colleagues. Therefore, to be successful, a cultural commitment to achieving goals through innovation must be anchored at the organization's top. More than finding executive sponsorship or buy-in, senior leadership must support the traits necessary through actions and recognition. Does the claim to allow people to fail but routinely pass over people who may have unsuccessfully pursued a project for inclusion in special teams or for promotions? Does the organization show preference to managers who bury failures underneath changing goals and creative language rather than celebrating those who share the lessons learned from failure via clear and direct communication? For well over ten years, medical professionals have heard that clearly and directly apologizing for mistakes to patients and their families is a critical part of the healing and learning process (Robbenholt, 2009; Sattinger, 2006). Employees deserve the same deference and support when they make mistakes or their ideas don't turn out as expected.

Finally, trust and respect often run headfirst into the most dreaded of human resource talent management tasks: the annual review. If your innovation team is subject to these torturous exercises, we strongly suggest you re-think the nature of these interactions. In the book, "*It's the Manager*," authors Jim Clifton and Jim Harter lay out a plan for building effective teams and cultures based around fulfilling a contract for providing "a good job," or one based around constant development, learning, and communication. Gone are the days of reviewing the attainment of annual goals and key performance indicators. They state bluntly in their introduction:

> One large global professional services company estimated that it was wasting $1 billion of leadership time per year on managers filling out ratings forms rather than developing employees and having ongoing coaching conversations with them. Like so many CEOs and CHROs are discovering, **there's no evidence anywhere in the world, in any institution of management science, that existing massive employee evaluation and rating processes are effective.** (Clifton & Harter, 2019)

IT'S WHAT YOU DON'T DO THAT COUNTS

Innovation, like photography, is the art of exclusion. The projects that an organization does not attempt may have far more impact on its success than the projects that it completes. Warren Buffet said of success, "The difference between successful people and really successful people is that really successful people say no to almost everything" (Haden, 2018). The same is true of innovative organizations. Saying no causes friction, and modern enterprises abhor friction. A leader can make more people happier, at least initially, by green-lighting every project. But such a leader may also soon find herself with an overwhelmed staff, a depleted budget, and angry colleagues.

Waguih Ishak talks of organizations dying not from starvation or a lack of good ideas, but instead of indigestion, too many ideas to execute effectively.

> Conventional wisdom holds that organizations die of starvation from a shortage of good ideas and projects. In reality, they are much more likely to die of indigestion. A surfeit of projects with inadequate staffing makes delivering on anything less likely. (Ishak, 2017)

He recommends that staff members commit to no more than two projects at once—more than one to alleviate boredom, but less than three to avoid dilution. Adding staff for every new idea is, of course, impractical for almost everyone, so the only hope of maintaining a delivery capacity begins with limiting the input to the system with a rigorous process of vetting ideas against organizational needs and capacity.

The battle between control and trust often tears organizations apart. The right mix of freedom to explore versus rigorously controlled processes for your organization is beyond the scope of any book. But we can assure you it lies neither in laissez-faire anarchy nor in dictatorial centralization and control of every idea. It likely moves back and forth on that spectrum as internal and external forces dictate.

STRIKING THE RIGHT BALANCE

The unique challenges that the COVID-19 pandemic created for healthcare have brought resiliency to the forefront of every manager's mind. Whether for IT asset management or innovation processes, governance models must also be resilient enough to adapt to changing circumstances. In a recent article, HIMSS proposed replacing the reactive planning that dominates many organizations with an adaptive environment that uses possible future scenarios as a basis for a new paradigm (Havasy & Piechowski, 2020). If COVID-19 taught us anything, it is that events can quickly overtake even the best static planning. So the second important characteristic of innovation governance is to know when execution on an idea needs to be paused or abandoned if externally-driven needs overcome an organization's execution capacity. Incorporating formal exercises to envision potential future states, alongside identifying current problems, is a possible basis for settling on which projects to begin and setting criteria to know what environmental changes may require abandoning them to free up capacity for more critical needs.

To resolve the paradox of fostering creativity for new ideas while maintaining execution capacity, healthcare leaders must separate the functions of idea development and project execution to the extent possible. While we all have encountered that rare unicorn who can focus like a laser when necessary while also seeing the 50,000-foot view of a problem, people with both of these characteristics are rare enough that one cannot expect to assemble a full department of them. In the most effective organizations the authors identified, professional project managers are available to run active projects, with input from the idea originators. Never is one person expected to simultaneously explore problems, identify solutions, then manage their implementation. An essential part of a solid innovative culture is mutual respect between individuals with different talents and abilities.

MEASURE THE RIGHT THINGS BUT TRUST YOUR GUT

When measuring an innovation program's success, it is important to look beyond the traditional key performance indicators (KPI) metrics like Return on Investment (ROI) or Customer Lifetime Value (CLV) and instead identify KPIs specific to the development of innovation. Examples might include the number of projects in the innovation pipeline or the engagement from the whole organizational staff with the innovation team's idea generation program. These are often non-traditional measures but add value to the ideation process and help predict the program's long-term success.

A strong innovation program considers the personal experience we each have with healthcare when measuring where we might add value, incorporating feedback on what patients think of our waiting rooms, valet experiences, welcome desk perceptions, and other parts of their experience. When patients rank their experiences with a healthcare organization, they often have little to say about IT and much more to say about other areas of their experience that aren't yet digitized. There can be a significant opportunity for innovation in these areas, leading to a more well-rounded customer experience and sometimes a fraction of the cost.

MAKING IT STICK

To ensure the development of a persistent innovation program, organizations need to invest in generalist leaders, share successes, and prioritize dreamers and doers.

INVEST IN GENERALIST LEADERS

Some of the best leaders are not necessarily experts in one or two things but rather generalists in many aspects of an industry or a technology and can create a viable vision around a set of ideas from different areas. Innovation is not about the depth of knowledge on a subject but instead continually demonstrating professional curiosity in all areas. That includes looking to other industries, models, and other ways of thinking. Just as individual contributors with diverse life experiences are valuable on innovation teams, organizations are best served by elevating leaders who bring an open mind to creativity and out-of-the-box thinking that inspires the same in their teams.

SHARE SUCCESSES

There is room for aspirational goals, long-term vision, and room for creativity in any innovation program. However, actively and consistently sharing goals, visions, and the outcomes of previous innovation efforts lay the foundation for the success of future innovation efforts. Nothing is more demotivating than not understanding the bigger picture or understanding the impact you have already experienced. An innovation feedback loop that shares both the goals and the outcomes creates a stronger affinity with staff and amplifies the chances of selecting successful solutions.

EQUALLY PRIORITIZE DREAMERS AND DOERS

In addition to setting goals, organizations need to close the gap between those goals and the end result. As Judy Estrin states:

> "Closing the innovation gap between goals and reality often comes down to a single idea: doing, not talking." (Estrin, 2009)

Successful innovation programs yield solutions that positively impact the organization/industry, not just a list of ideas. As such, organizations need to ensure a balance of dreamers and doers in their workforce.

CONCLUSION

There is a term in finance, a "black swan event," that denotes something unpredictable that disrupts business and has a severe and lasting impact. The onset of COVID-19 in the spring of 2020 led to worldwide stress on an ageing healthcare system. In many ways, COVID-19 seemed to shine a spotlight on the areas where technology was either lacking or inefficiently utilized. COVID-19 may indeed be the black swan event that creates a window for healthcare innovation explosions.

While implementing change is never easy, doing it during a crisis does afford an organization the ability to make room for those "crazy ideas" they may have overlooked in the past. The invisible boxes that we tend to put around the ideation process are often removed during a crisis, and suddenly, all options are on the table. We may even find ourselves looking at the problem or situation all together differently than we did before the crisis. History shows us that some of the most significant innovations were developed during a crisis: zippers, blood banks, and super-markets, among them. This may be the very moment awaiting healthcare.

A crisis such as COVID-19 also allows organizations to capitalize on the human desire to "want to help" during a crisis, which can mean bringing new people to the innovation process who have out-of-the-box ideas. It may also mean breaking down walls between different industries to share/ transfer ideas and even allow employees to bring their personal experiences into the ideation process to dive harder and faster on innovation.

All of this ultimately leads to an acceleration of the innovation lifecycle and an overall refocus on where an organization can make the most changes but where it must address the needs high-lighted by a crisis. This often means adopting a "fail fast" mentality where there is no wrong answer but rather a culture that is encouraged to take calculated risks.

REFERENCES

Bodenheimer, T., & Sinsky, C. (2014). From Triple to Quadruple Aim: Care of the Patient Requires Care of the Provider. *Annals of Family Medicine*, *12*(6), 573–576. doi: 10.1370/afm.1713.

Clay-Williams, R., Ludlow, K., Testa, L., Li, Z., & Braithwaite, J. (2017). Medical leadership, a systematic narrative review: do hospitals and healthcare organisations perform better when led by doctors? *BMJ Open*, 7, e014474. doi: 10.1136/bmjopen-2016-014474.

Clifton, J., & Harter, J. (2019). *It's the Manager*. New York: Gallup Press.

Collins, J. (2001). *Good to Great*. New York: Harper Collins.

Estrin, J. (2009). *Closing the Innovation Gap*. McGraw Hill.

Haden, J. (2018, December 11). *Warren Buffett Says 1 Thing Separates Successful People From All the Rest (and Leads to Living a Fulfilling and Rewarding Life)*. Retrieved from Inc.: https://www.inc.com/jeff-haden/warren-buffet-says-1-thing-separates-successful-people-from-all-rest-and-leads-to-living-a-fulfilling-rewarding-life.html

Havasy, R., & Piechowski, R. (2020). *The Impact of COVID-19 on Healthcare Business and IT*. Retrieved from HIMSS.org: https://www.himss.org/resources/impact-covid-19-healthcare-business-and-it

Institute for Healthcare Improvement. (2020). *IHI Triple Aim Initiative*. Retrieved from Institute for Healthcare Improvement: http://www.ihi.org/Engage/Initiatives/TripleAim/Pages/default.aspx

Ishak, W. (2017, September 28). *Creating an Innovation Culture*. Retrieved from McKinsey & Company: https://www.mckinsey.com/business-functions/strategy-and-corporate-finance/our-insights/creating-an-innovation-culture#

Merchant, N. (2011, March 22). *Culture Trumps Strategy, Every Time*. Retrieved from Harvard Business Review: https://hbr.org/2011/03/culture-trumps-strategy-every

Murphy, S. (2014, April 30). *Facebook Changes Its 'Move Fast and Break Things' Motto*. Retrieved from Mashable: https://mashable.com/2014/04/30/facebooks-new-mantra-move-fast-with-stability/

Mutter, J. B., Liaw, W., Moore, M. A., Etz, R. S., Howe, A., & Bazemore, A. (2018). Core Principles to Improve Primary Care Quality Management. *Journal of the American Board of Family Medicine, 31*(6), 931–940. doi:10.3122/jabfm.2018.06.170172.

Quote Investigator. (2017, May 23). Retrieved from Quote Investigator: https://quoteinvestigator.com/2017/05/23/culture-eats/

Rivera, L. A. (2012). Hiring as cultural matching: The case of elite professional service firms. *American Sociological Review, 77*(6), 999–1022. doi: 10.1177/0003122412463213

Robbenholt, J. K. (2009, February). Apologies and medical error. *Clinical Orthopaedics and Related Research, 476*, 376–382. doi:10.1007/s11999-008-0580-1.

Sattinger, A. M. (2006, June). I'm Sorry. *The Hospitalist*. Retrieved from https://www.the-hospitalist.org/hospitalist/article/123154/im-sorry

Stillman, J. (2020, September 16). All Highly Intelligent People Share This Trait, According to Steve Jobs. *Inc.* Retrieved from https://www.inc.com/jessica-stillman/this-is-number-1-sign-of-high-intelligence-according-to-steve-jobs.html

Wager, K. A., Lee, F. W., & Glaser, J. P. (2009). *Health Care Information Systems: A Practical Approach for Health Care Management*. San Francisco: Josey-Bass.

Walker, B., & Soule, A. S. (2017, June 20). *Changing Company Culture Requires a Movement, Not a Mandate*. Retrieved from Harvard Business Review: https://hbr.org/2017/06/changing-company-culture-requires-a-movement-not-a-mandate?registration=success

World Health Organization. (2019). *Global Spending on Health: A World in Transition*. Geneva: World Health Organization. Retrieved from https://www.who.int/health_financing/documents/health-expenditure-report-2019.pdf

30 The Healthcare Workforce of the Future: Preparing Today for the Opportunities Ahead

Nanne M. Finis
RN, MS

Kathryn Owen
MS, RN-BC

CONTENTS

LEARNING OBJECTIVES

1. Identify the ways the field of informatics will continue to make a significant impact on the future of healthcare delivery.
2. Recognize the various types of technology that will digitally transform the delivery of care for those engaged in the healthcare workforce of the future.

INTRODUCTION

Digital transformation has been slow in healthcare, but recent events are starting to speed up the process. Response to the COVID-19 pandemic has proven that global health systems, providers, and staff can rapidly adopt and harness technology in times of crisis, especially when governments remove regulatory barriers. Forcing a swift migration to telehealth, remote collaboration, and innovative supply chain solutions, the COVID-19 crisis has highlighted the increasingly crucial role technology will play in the future of work in healthcare.

This pandemic-driven momentum is expected to accelerate healthcare organizations' adoption and innovation of digital tools and technologies moving forward. As a result, digital-enabled health systems will increasingly rely on professionals with expertise in healthcare informatics to guide strategic alignment of technology with clinical workflows and best practices. Therefore, the industry

DOI: 10.4324/9780429398377-36

will see heightened emphasis on the role of the healthcare informaticist, whose skills are needed to most effectively manage healthcare information, drive efficiencies, and improve patient care.

As a hospital or health system broadens its strategic deployment of information technology (IT) in response to rapidly changing business models and patient needs, healthcare informaticists will be the ones to help ensure its practical use in clinical settings, its connection to mainstream processes, and its adoption by intended users. At the same time, the future of work will require that *all* healthcare professionals possess some level of digital fluency to keep pace with innovation and make data-driven decisions. This chapter discusses why now is the time to prepare the entire workforce to embrace digital advancements, and how one can develop informatics competencies to tackle new challenges and thrive in the future world of work.

THE COVID-19 EFFECT ON TECHNOLOGY ADOPTION

There is no question that the COVID-19 pandemic has been a force for change in healthcare, accelerating innovation and adoption of technology that had been slow to take off in the industry. For example, utilization of telemedicine services has surged since the outbreak, creating greater demand for platforms like Teladoc, MDLive, and Doctor on Demand. When COVID-19 put an abrupt end to most elective visits, many hospital systems and private practices implemented telehealth or videoconferencing platforms, such as Zoom and Microsoft Teams, to care for patients remotely. Industry and government regulators helped move the process along by temporarily reducing barriers to telehealth access and reimbursement.

Concerned about risk of exposure to COVID-19, healthcare consumers were broadly receptive to adopting telehealth for obtaining safe access to care. As a result, health systems, independent practices, and other providers had to rapidly implement telehealth technologies and scale them to meet the needs of the community they serve. According to an April 2020 McKinsey survey, providers reported seeing 50–175 times the number of patients via telehealth than they did pre-COVID-19 (Bestsennyy, Gilbert, Harris & Rost 2020).

Having gained strong traction during the pandemic, telemedicine offers tremendous promise for healthcare delivery moving forward. Telehealth, especially when used in combination with remote patient monitoring, has the potential to expand access to healthcare across rural and remote communities, and to better ensure continuity of care for the most vulnerable populations.

GOVERNANCE IS KEY AS TECHNOLOGY USE EXPANDS

Not since the widespread implementation of electronic medical records (EMR) has the industry seen such a major push to take digital transformation to the next level. Now that the healthcare industry has demonstrated the ability to integrate health IT solutions into clinical practice with expediency, organizations see that they can build on this momentum to apply technology to streamline work processes across the enterprise—from optimizing staffing and scheduling to improving supply chain resiliency, facilitating clinical collaboration, and extending patient monitoring beyond the walls of the hospital.

Organizations need support from the top, however, to make this happen. The seamless integration of technology into mainstream workflows across an organization must be guided by appropriate leaders who embrace a systematic, enterprise-wide approach that eliminates silos, facilitates interoperability, enforces the application of consistent data definitions, improves usability for increased workforce productivity, and drives enterprise goals. Depending on where one works, this leader might be the Chief Information Officer (CIO), the Chief Technology Officer (CTO), or the Chief Nursing Information Officer (CNIO). Right from the start, it is imperative that leaders bring the right people to the table to implement the new technology and help ensure it delivers its intended value. As health systems embrace this "big picture" approach, the industry will observe more informaticists involved in key advisory roles, lending their expertise to the practical application of technology.

With proper governance of technology integration, health systems can break down silos and other barriers that were obviated during the COVID-19 crisis, including those that hampered response efforts. At Northwell Health, which served 20% of COVID-19 patients in New York State, medical staff were collaborating in new multidisciplinary ways, which brought fresh perspectives and greater efficiencies to care and treatment (Robeznieks 2020). According to Mark Jarrett, MD, Northwell's senior vice president and deputy chief medical officer, breaking down silos is a key objective in health care quality improvement (Robeznieks 2020).

INTEROPERABILITY MATTERS MORE THAN EVER

The push for interoperability was already underway before COVID-19 renewed the industry's sense of urgency. In 2018, major tech companies, including Google, Amazon, Microsoft, IBM, Oracle, and Salesforce, jointly committed to removing barriers to the adoption of technologies for healthcare interoperability. As part of this commitment, they pledged to support open standards, such as the Fast Healthcare Interoperability Resources (FHIR®) standard developed by the Health Level Seven International (HL7®) organization as a common data standard to promote interoperability (Donovan 2020).

The COVID-19 crisis has also highlighted the need for enterprise agility to support fast, effective adaptation to a changing landscape. Healthcare leaders are placing greater emphasis on innovation to speed and facilitate data-driven decision making and support agile processes in both front-end clinical care and back-end administrative functions. Data analytics and artificial intelligence have played a key role in the industry's response to COVID-19, helping researchers track hospital capacity and identify high-risk patients (Kent 2020). Going forward, the industry needs to work toward achieving a truly interoperable digital ecosystem to facilitate data sharing and unleash the full potential of analytics. By involving health informaticists in these key technology decisions, organizations can better ensure that analytics use the right data to provide the right insights at the right time to achieve new efficiencies and improve patient care.

APPLYING LESSONS LEARNED DURING COVID-19

The COVID-19 crisis has been a wake-up call for industry leaders, illuminating disproportionate levels of organizational preparedness, including the ability to predict and accommodate surges in patient volumes. The future of healthcare will focus on population health and wellness, which will require providers to meet patients where they are—providing access to care and resources whenever and wherever the need may arise. But to make this happen, providers need visibility into the patient's entire wellness journey or illness trajectory—a capability that requires integrated technology and seamless access to data across the care continuum.

In addition to data visibility, the future of work will emphasize efficiency driven by automation and greater workforce productivity to improve employee engagement and, in turn, patient outcomes (Kronos Incorporated 2019). This creates more opportunities for healthcare informaticists to guide effective integration of technology into clinical and administrative workflows. During the COVID-19 pandemic, for example, Zoom, WebEx, Microsoft Teams, GoToMeeting, and other videoconferencing platforms have enabled specialists to collaborate on challenging patient cases—a practice that is expected to continue to improve care and treatment plans based on collective expertise.

Virtual collaboration and communication tools have also allowed many health system employees in human resources (HR), IT, and other administrative areas, as well as some practitioners, to work remotely. Doing so has not only lowered the risk of transmission in hospital and private practice settings amidst the crisis, but also offers value in the future. Looking ahead to what may be the post-pandemic normal, healthcare organizations with a robust, secure technology infrastructure that allows them to support remote work may be better positioned to recruit and retain employees who prioritize flexibility and work-life balance.

SHAPING MODERN HEALTHCARE TECHNOLOGY

As technology becomes even more integral to modern healthcare, leading hospitals and health systems are partnering with technology companies to take innovation to the next level. Developing successful partnerships with technology companies can help healthcare organizations boost efficiency, expand their reach, enhance their reputation, and better serve their communities. During the COVID-19 pandemic, the industry has witnessed the kinds of innovation these partnerships can achieve—and how quickly they can produce results.

Providence St. Joseph Health System in Seattle, which served some of the nation's first COVID-19 patients in early March, collaborated with Microsoft to develop online screening and triage tools that could rapidly differentiate between patients who might be sick with COVID-19 and those suffering from less threatening illnesses (Caroll et al. 2020). At both Brigham and Women's Hospital and Massachusetts General Hospital in Boston, physician researchers started exploring the potential use of smart robots developed at Boston Dynamics and MIT to perform medical tasks such as checking vital signs or delivering medication, which would otherwise require human contact, as a means of mitigating disease transmission (Caroll et al. 2020). Furthermore, Google Cloud AI partnered with the Harvard Global Health Institute to design and build the COVID-19 Public Forecasts, a dashboard that provides 13-day projections for hospitalizations and death rates across all states (Drees 2020).

These healthcare-technology partnerships are expected to expand, in many cases creating additional opportunities for informaticists to help shape the future of work in healthcare. Becker's Healthcare annually recognizes hospitals and health systems with dedicated departments, institutes, and organizations to promote research, development, and innovation. Of the more than 40 healthcare institutions recognized in 2019, several were engaged in process redesign, care delivery, and coordination improvement initiatives, while others were incubating innovative ideas for better integrating IT into healthcare delivery (Becker's Hospital Review 2019).

As the pace of innovation accelerates, use of new technology must be thoughtfully integrated into clinical practice to avoid losing focus on the human element of care. Clinicians need proper, ongoing training to ensure that emerging technologies, including virtual communication tools, are used to enhance—not detract from—empathetic, patient-centered care. With their valuable blend of clinical experience and technical expertise, nurse informaticists are uniquely qualified to guide compassionate care in a digital context to improve the patient experience and drive positive health outcomes.

USING TECHNOLOGY TO ENGAGE HEALTHCARE EMPLOYEES

Healthcare organizations are in a position to establish themselves as an employer of choice by leveraging technology to improve the employee experience. A study by The Workforce Institute and Regina Corso Consulting found an overwhelming majority of HR executives (93%), hospital IT staff (92%), and nurses (89%) expect the healthcare industry will go through significant changes in how it is staffed in the coming decade (The Workforce Institute at Kronos Incorporated 2019, 3)—a shift that could have a major impact on the future of work. This finding suggests a growing need for visibility into the entire workforce, even across locations, to support labor flexing and deploy resources where they are needed most.

According to the study, almost all HR executives (97%), hospital IT staff (96%), and nurses (95%) say it is important for healthcare organizations to actively think about the digital experience they offer employees, and half (50%) believe employee experience is directly impacted by an organization's investment in new technology (Kronos Incorporated 2019). Using technology for improving the employee experience may be good for ratings and profits as well. According to Harvard Business School research, hospitals that improve over time in distinct HCAHPS (Hospital Consumer Assessment of Healthcare Providers and Systems) survey measures of patient experience or employee engagement also see improvement in patients' global ratings of their care. Furthermore, there can be a compounding effect when organizations improve in both patient experience and employee engagement measures at the same time (Buhlman and Lee 2019).

Research suggests, however, that there is more work to be done in leveraging technology's potential for employee engagement. Only 41% of hospital HR executives, 37% of hospital staff, and 34% of nurses felt strongly that their organizations provide tools and resources that empower them to perform to their fullest potential (The Workforce Institute at Kronos Incorporated 2019, 4). Among organizations that have yet to take action, one-third of HR executives (32%) say their organization is actively talking about implementing future-of-work initiatives, but only 20% of nurses are aware of these discussions (The Workforce Institute at Kronos Incorporated 2019, 3). This highlights an important opportunity for healthcare leaders to involve informaticists in planning for the future of work, not only to strategically advise on the use and practicality of technology, but also to communicate its benefits to target users.

THE TIME TO EXPAND INFORMATICS COMPETENCIES IS NOW

As organizations prepare for the future of work, building informatics competencies across the healthcare workforce must be a top priority. The future of work in healthcare involves connecting people, technology, and data to improve patient outcomes—and this cannot be done effectively without developing informatics expertise within your workforce.

Clinical informaticists, including nurse informaticists, combine patient care experience and health IT skills to help ensure that new technology aligns with clinical workflows in the healthcare setting. They are uniquely qualified to evaluate potential efficiency gains by determining whether technology eliminates wasteful steps to simplify tasks, so nurses and caregivers can focus more time on the sharp end of care. They offer insight into how technology fits within the health ecosystem and how it interacts with other systems to achieve interoperability and inform decision making. Perhaps most importantly, informaticists understand the people who will utilize the technology every day, enabling them to make practical recommendations for optimizing usability and driving adoption.

Introducing new technology often prompts a mix of emotions from healthcare staff. Research reveals that while one third of nurses believe new technology helps them better serve their patients, 1 in 4 (24%) say that implementation of new technology can be stressful (The Workforce Institute at Kronos Incorporated 2019, 9). Nurse informaticists can facilitate change management within healthcare organizations by acting as a translator between clinicians and those who design and develop clinical technologies. Developing a base competency in informatics among all healthcare staff—not just those with an informaticist title—can further alleviate the stress associated with technology transition. This, in turn, will enhance your workforce's ability to adapt to change, embrace innovation, and identify opportunities where technology can add value in various disciplines.

Growing recognition of the value informaticists bring to the future of work is giving rise to new executive roles in healthcare, such as Chief Nursing Informatics Officer (CNIO). The 2020 Nursing Informatics Workforce Survey published by the Healthcare Information and Management Systems Society (HIMSS) shows that the CNIO/Senior Nursing Informatics Officer title continues to advance, with 41% of respondents reporting that their organization had the formal role (HIMSS 2020, 50). As informatics gains greater standing within health systems and hospitals, there is an opportunity to expand these competencies across the workforce through continuing professional development.

HOW TO ADVANCE YOUR CAREER WITH INFORMATICS

Keeping up with innovation in healthcare requires a commitment to lifelong learning. As use of health IT continues to expand, all prospective and current healthcare professionals need a foundation of informatics knowledge and skills to more effectively leverage systems and data for patient care and documentation. The Institute of Medicine (IOM) included the utilization of informatics as one of five core competencies that all health clinicians should have, regardless of their discipline, in order to meet the needs of the 21st-century health system (Institute of Medicine 2003).

Many nursing programs and medical schools have built health informatics courses into their curriculum; other universities now offer bachelor's or master's programs in nursing, health, clinical, or other informatics specialties. If you wish to pursue a career in nurse informatics, a bachelor's degree in nursing is the minimum educational requirement. Advanced degrees, such as a master of science in nursing (MSN) or a doctorate of nursing practice (DNP), are typically needed to climb into leadership positions.

A certification in nursing informatics is not always needed to work in the field but is a valuable credential for demonstrating a high level of competency and readiness to employers. If you possess a natural aptitude for or keen interest in technology, this might be a route worth considering. According to the HIMSS Nursing Informatics Workforce Survey, respondents noted credibility or marketability (49%), personal satisfaction (45%), and validation of knowledge (43%) as the top reasons to pursue informatics certification (HIMSS 2020, 38). There appear to be clear career benefits as well. According to the survey findings, 47% of respondents report that achieving certification has been highly impactful on their career and 41% have moved to a new role since becoming certified (HIMSS 2020, 33–34).

Within the healthcare field, there are a number of independent organizations that offer certification programs in informatics. For example, you can obtain certification in nursing informatics from the American Nurses Credentialing Center (ANCC). In addition, HIMSS offers healthcare informatics certification programs for both entry-level/early careerists and more experienced professionals in nursing or healthcare IT. Informatics certification opportunities also extend beyond nursing and IT to other professions in healthcare. Professionals in primary care, pharmacy, mental health, dentistry, and other specialties have opportunities to pursue post-graduate certification in informatics in order to enhance their digital fluency and take full advantage of available data and emerging tools to achieve positive patient outcomes.

By encouraging and facilitating professional development in informatics, hospitals and health systems can enhance employee engagement and improve patient care in the technology-powered, data-driven future of work. At the same time, growing informatics competencies can help healthcare organizations achieve prestigious distinctions, such as Magnet® Recognition Program designation, Joint Commission accreditation, or the Malcolm Baldrige National Quality Award, all of which are respected achievements and benchmarks for safe, high-quality patient care.

CONCLUSION

Looking ahead, digital technology must continue to support the work and workforce of the future in order to increase efficiency, improve effectiveness, and achieve desired outcomes in healthcare. As a hospital or health system shifts its digital transformation into high gear, future-of-work initiatives open up career opportunities for health informaticists who can bridge the gap between technical and clinical perspectives to streamline workflows and enable evidence-based decision making. At the same time, emerging technologies are driving the need for core informatics competency across the workforce—a growing requirement that is becoming a top priority for healthcare employers. Whether you are looking to advance your career or take it in a different direction, the field of informatics will continue to make a significant impact on healthcare delivery moving forward.

REFERENCES

Becker's Hospital Review. 2019. "40+ Hospitals and Health Systems with Great Innovation Programs." September 19, 2019. https://www.beckershospitalreview.com/lists/innovation-centers-to-know-2019.html.

Bestsennyy, Oleg, Greg Gilbert, Adam Harris and Jennifer Rost. 2020. "Telehealth: A Quarter-Trillion-Dollar Post-COVID-19 Reality?" *McKinsey & Company*, May 29, 2020. https://www.mckinsey.com/industries/healthcare-systems-and-services/our-insights/telehealth-a-quarter-trillion-dollar-post-covid-19-reality.

Buhlman, Nell W., and Thomas H. Lee. 2019. "When Patient Experience and Employee Engagement Both Improve, Hospital Ratings and Profits Climb." *Harvard Business Review*, May 8, 2019. https://hbr.org/2019/05/when-patient-experience-and-employee-engagement-both-improve-hospitals-ratings-and-profits-climb

Caroll, Colleen, Marco Iansiti, Adam B. Landman, Kelly A. Wittbold and Haipeng Mark Zhang. 2020. "How Hospitals are Using AI to Battle COVID-19." *Harvard Business Review*, April 3, 2020. https://hbr.org/2020/04/how-hospitals-are-using-ai-to-battle-covid-19.

Donovan, Fred. 2020. "Major Tech Firms Partner to Boost Healthcare IT Interoperability." *HIT Infrastructure*, November 18, 2018. https://hitinfrastructure.com/news/major-tech-firms-partner-to-boost-healthcare-it-interoperability.

Drees, Jackie. 2020. "7 Recent Big Tech Partnerships in Healthcare: Amazon, Google & More." *Becker's Health IT*, August 24, 2020. https://www.beckershospitalreview.com/digital-transformation/7-recent-big-tech-partnerships-in-healthcare-amazon-google-more.html.

Healthcare Information and Management Systems Society (HIMSS). 2020. "2020 Nursing Informatics Survey". https://www.himss.org/sites/hde/files/media/file/2020/05/15/himss_nursinginformaticssurvey2020_v4.pdf.

Institute of Medicine. 2003. *Health Professions Education: A Bridge to Quality*. Washington, DC: National Academies Press.

Kent, Jessica. 2020. "Could COVID-19 Help Refine AI, Data Analytics in Healthcare?" *HeatlhITAnalytics*, April 24, 2020. https://healthitanalytics.com/features/could-covid-19-help-refine-ai-data-analytics-in-healthcare.

Kronos Incorporated. 2019. "Healthcare Organizations Preparing for Big Staffing Changes by 2025, According to Workforce institute at Kronos Survey." October 16, 2019. https://www.kronos.com/about-us/newsroom/healthcare-organizations-preparing-big-staffing-changes-2025-according-work-force-institute-kronos-survey.

Robeznieks, Andis. 2020. "In COVID-19 Epicenter, Breaking Silos Led to Better Teamwork." *American Medical Association*, May 6, 2020. https://www.ama-assn.org/practice-management/sustainability/covid-19-epicenter-breaking-silos-led-better-teamwork.

The Workforce Institute at Kronos Incorporated. 2019. "2020 Vision: Working in the Future of Healthcare." Kronos Incorporated. https://workforceinstitute.org/wp-content/uploads/2019/12/2020-Vision-Working-in-the-Future-of-Healthcare.pdf.

31 HIMSS TIGER™: A Global Interprofessional Community of Development and Growth

Toria Shaw Morawski
MSW

Man Qing Liang
PharmD

Avni Doshi
PharmD candidate

CONTENTS

LEARNING OBJECTIVES

- Share about the TIGER (Technology Informatics Guiding Educator Reform) Initiative's evolution from a grassroots initiative focused on nursing to embracing an interprofessional approach.
- Describe the role TIGER is playing—from developing core health informatics competencies and resources—to enhance global workforce development.
- Highlight TIGER's work over the last six years with an emphasis on the tools, resources, and projects focused on helping the health informatics workforce expand their skillset and knowledge base.

DOI: 10.4324/9780429398377-37

INTRODUCTION

According to the U.S. National Library of Medicine, health informatics is the interdisciplinary study of the design, development, adoption, and application of information technology (IT)–based innovations in healthcare services delivery, management, and planning (National Library of Medicine 2020).

This multidisciplinary field serves as the perfect backdrop to the TIGER (*Technology Informatics Guiding Education Reform*) Initiative's focus on competency and curricula development in the benefit of education reform, fostering interprofessional community development, and gaining workforce development inroads (HIMSS 2020b). As a global community represented by 29 countries and growing, TIGER has worked to prepare the next generation of the healthcare workforce since the initiative formalized in 2006.

The TIGER Initiative's foundational mission was to engage and prepare the nursing workforce in using technology and informatics to improve the delivery of patient care. In recent years, TIGER has adopted and embraced an interprofessional approach, which has resulted in the development of projects, resources, and tools designed to equip students, educators (academic and clinical), adult learners and early careerists with an expanded skillset and knowledge base relevant to the multi-interdisciplinary field of health informatics.

In the rapidly evolving field of health informatics, upskilling and micro-learning have emerged as strategic approaches to ensure that the global health informatics workforce is able to advance their career trajectories as desired, within or outside of their current places of employment. Upskilling focuses on improving skillsets through practices such as virtual or in-person training and/or courses, mentoring, shadowing, "lunch and learn" sessions, and micro-learning (Rouse 2020). Micro-learning is a bite-sized learning approach that aims to keep learning simple and brief. This approach may be presented as small learning units or short-term learning activities (Andriotis 2018). Both upskilling and micro-learning are extremely important as the desire to learn, grow, and be promoted while on the job resonates for many. Upskilling and micro-learning offer an easy solution to learners who find themselves short on time but want to move beyond their current roles.

This chapter aims to acquaint those learning about health informatics and TIGER with a direct conduit on where to locate the tools and resources created through recent projects and international collaborations. We hope you will find this information to be of value as you seek to learn and advance your career.

This chapter will cover:
- TIGER's evolution from grassroots nursing informatics efforts to global interprofessional initiative and community
- Tools and resources targeted towards three sides of the TIGER coin:
  - *Student/adult learners:* Providing tools and resources to upskill knowledge base and understanding of health informatics
  - *Educators (Academic and clinical):* Curating open-source content and resources that can be leveraged to create supplemental and health informatics focused curricula and more
  - *Volunteers:* Leveraging a global network and contributing to the body of knowledge and identification of best practices

SECTION 1. EVOLUTION OF TIGER

TIGER's History

In 2004, President Bush established a goal that every American would have an Electronic Health Record (EHR) by 2014 (Executive Office of the President 2004). In July 2004, a national conference titled *Cornerstones for the Electronic Health Record* brought together healthcare leaders to discuss the plan to establish a national health IT infrastructure. This meeting included representatives from medicine, government, IT, hospitals, and the insurance industry whose thoughts and input were reflected throughout the program; yet, there was a severe lack of nurse representation. With the nursing profession largely invisible from the decision-making table, in the Fall of 2004, a group of nurses who connected at the conference initiated a working collaboration to ensure that the nursing professions' voice and expertise were woven into the national agenda as the health IT infrastructure was created (Shaw, Sensmeier, and Anderson 2017). In January 2005, a group of prominent and dedicated nurses called the "TIGER Team" for *Technology Informatics Guiding Educational Reform* agreed that informatics would become a core competency of all professionals in healthcare in the 21st century as the IOM acknowledged in *Health Professions Education: A Bridge to Quality* (Institute of Medicine (US) Committee on the Institute of Medicine US Committee on the Health Professions Education Summit, 2003). At that time, the nurses were also in agreement that the majority of U.S. nurses lacked basic computer and IT skills and struggled to integrate informatics competencies into their varying roles (American Association of Colleges of Nursing (AACN) 2019). The TIGER Initiative formalized as a grassroots effort in 2006 in response to largely being left out of the national health IT infrastructure decision-making process. The formation of TIGER was critical as nurses represent "the nation's largest healthcare profession with more than 3.8 million registered nurses (RNs) nationwide" (American Association of Colleges of Nursing (AACN) 2019).

In 2014, TIGER transitioned from a standalone foundation into the Healthcare Information and Management Systems Society (HIMSS) enterprise. As previously shared, TIGER's initial goal was to engage and prepare the nursing workforce in using technology and informatics to improve the delivery of patient care. As TIGER prepared its transition into HIMSS, pioneers of the initiative had the foresight to embrace an interdisciplinary approach to informatics as the work TIGER began in the nursing realm was applicable to all regardless of discipline. Today, TIGER embraces an interdisciplinary approach with a global perspective woven into every project, resource, and tool created. "Focused on education reform, interprofessional community development and global workforce development, TIGER offers tools and resources for learners to advance their (informatics) skills and for educators to develop valuable curricula" (HIMSS 2020b). The guiding spirit of TIGER continues to support a learning health system that maximizes the integration of technology and informatics into seamless practice, education, research, and resource development.

TIGER's targeted audiences are:
1. **Academic professionals:** Seek to find and easily integrate resources and modules to create supplemental and classroom curricula.
2. **Students:** Seek to expand their knowledge base and skillset as they prepare to graduate, secure an internship, etc.
3. **Early careerists/adult learners:** Also seek to expand knowledge and skillset to advance their career trajectories or gain inroad into the health IT/informatics fields.
4. **Clinical educators:** Like academic professionals, they also seek resources to support their staff in evolving their informatics knowledge base and skillset.
5. **Hybrid of two or more core audience types:** they may be working while studying to advance their careers. We know they are short on time when it comes to finding tools and resources to leverage for knowledge expansion.

Resources to leverage:

- HIMSS TIGER™ Initiative main landing page: www.himss.org/tiger
- *The Evolution of the TIGER Initiative* publication in Computers Informatics Nursing (CIN), June 2017 – Volume 35 – Issue 6 – p 278–280: https://journals.lww.com/cinjournal/Citation/2017/06000/The_Evolution_of_the_TIGER_Initiative.2.aspx

TIGER INTERNATIONAL TASK FORCE

The TIGER Interprofessional Community at HIMSS is led by the TIGER International Taskforce (TITF), charged with providing domain expertise, leadership, and guidance to activities, projects, and collaborations.

In 2012, the vision of expanding TIGER globally to support academic professionals, students, adult learners, and clinical educators was realized with the establishment of the TIGER International Committee. Today, the TITF is represented by 29 countries (and growing) with over 90 volunteers who are dedicated to advancing the TIGER cause globally (Figure 31.1).

The 29 countries represented by the TITF are: Australia, Brazil, Canada, Chile, China, Denmark, Finland, Germany, India, Iran, Ireland, Japan, Mexico, New Zealand, Nigeria, Panama, Peru, Philippines, Portugal, Qatar, Saudi Arabia, Singapore, South Korea, Spain, Switzerland, Taiwan, United Kingdom (UK-England), United Arab Emirates (UAE), and the United States (U.S.).

The TITF is aligned to work streams (WS) devoted to helping the initiative actualize goals that are created and/or refined on an annual basis. All help to co-create resources, tools, and publications that showcase best practices and competency attainment.

Beginning in 2021, a few of the core upcoming TITF goals include:
- Co-develop a global health informatics course with the University of Texas at Arlington's Multi-Interprofessional Center for Health Informatics (UTA-MICHI). This marks the first time TIGER is venturing into curriculum development.
- Populate and launch of an Informatics Educators Resource Navigator (IERN). IERN strives to curate a thoughtful collection of documents, best practices, case studies, tutorials, etc., to assist informatics educators with curricula development. IERN also seeks to serve as a framework to help measure current competency levels to ensure student achievement before graduation.
- Continue to build out the Global TIGER Network (GTN) by recruiting new country representatives to serve on the TITF. As volunteer terms expire, TITF members will be invited to remain aligned to the GTN and will be called upon for special projects, local presentations and other opportunities to serve on a limited basis.

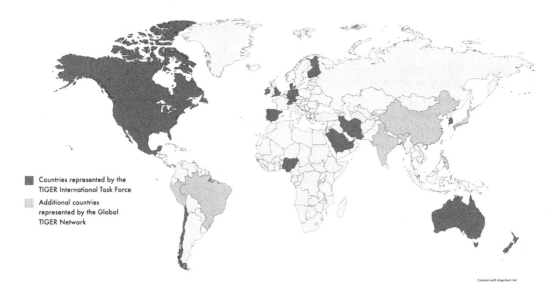

Countries represented by the TIGER International Task Force

Additional countries represented by the Global TIGER Network

Created with mapchart.net

FIGURE 31.1 The TITF is comprised of 96 members representing 29 different countries — and counting! (As of December 2020).

- Continue to refine the TIGER Virtual Learning Environment (VLE) Resource Library to ensure all offerings are up to date and globally relevant. Find more information about the TIGER VLE in this chapter under Section 4.1.

Resource to leverage:

- TIGER International Task Force landing page: https://www.himss.org/tiger-international-task-force

---

TIGER Scholars Informatics Internship Program Launch

In Spring 2019, TIGER launched the Scholars Informatics Internship Program. This is a unique internship program working to advance the spirit of TIGER as an interprofessional initiative by contributing to the development of the future informatics-focused workforce while also positively impacting the initiative's enduring legacy. Supported by the HIMSS Foundation, each year TIGER selects two interns (one domestic, one international) who are seeking a healthcare master's or doctorate degree to be mentored and coached for a full academic year (starting in the Fall and concluding at the end of the Spring semester).

The program's goal is to help students grow their informatics knowledge base as they prepare to graduate and seek career opportunities. The program provides the following opportunities to:

- Enhance their understanding of health informatics education and practice
- Grow their professional network with the global HIMSS TIGER™ community
- Develop mentoring relationships with informatics subject matter experts
- Participate as a member of the global TIGER interprofessional community through conferences, webinars, meetings, etc.
- Engage in activities that promote the informatics profession through education and advocacy
- Learn about the services and opportunities offered through HIMSS and TIGER for continuing professional development, certification, and career advancement

---

Resource to leverage:

For a complete overview of the program objectives and benefits, please visit: https://www.himss.org/tiger-scholars-informatics-internship. The annual application process opens in the spring of each year.

Program Components Include:
- Mentorship by HIMSS staff and the global TIGER volunteer network
- Opportunity to serve as a Program Assistant at the HIMSS Global Health Conference & Exhibition
- Complimentary HIMSS student membership
- TIGER VLE access to complete the courses tied to certificates of completion
- Program participation is remote only

GETTING INVOLVED WITH **TIGER**

Interested in getting involved with this dynamic global community?

- Sign up for the TIGER newsletter to ensure you receive this open call to serve directly in your email inbox via email at tiger@himss.org. Early careerists are strongly encouraged to apply. HIMSS members can opt in by logging into their membership profile at https://sso. himss.org/login.aspx
- Subscribe to the TIGER VLE.
- Opt-in to the TIGER Interprofessional community at HIMSS.

Every fall, TIGER recruits new members to serve on the TITF. The newsletter is how TIGER communicates out opportunities to become involved firsthand.

Resources to leverage:

- TIGER VLE landing page: https://www.himss.org/tiger-virtual-learning-environment
- TIGER Interprofessional Community landing page with opt-in instructions for HIMSS members: https://www.himss.org/membership-participation/technology-informatics-guiding-education-reform-tiger-interprofessional-community
- Follow TIGER on Twitter at @AboutTIGER; you can also find us under hashtags #TIGERInitiative and #TIGERVLE

SECTION 2. COMPILATION OF CORE INFORMATICS COMPETENCY RECOMMENDATIONS

TIGER's INTERNATIONAL COMPETENCY SYNTHESIS PROJECT (ICSP)

In 2015, TIGER began compiling recommended core informatics competencies reflective of many countries, scientific societies, and research projects. This project endeavor, known as the International Competency Synthesis Project (ICSP), comprised three components:

1. Deployment of a survey composed of 24 areas of core competencies in clinical informatics within five domains:
   i. Clinical nursing
   ii. Nursing management
   iii. Quality management
   iv. IT management in nursing
   v. Coordination of interprofessional care
      The questionnaire was sent to 21 countries yielding participation from 43 experts to capture a true global perspective.

2. Compilation of national case studies submitted by TIGER's global Committee members from Australia, Brazil, China/Taiwan, Finland, Germany (inclusive of Austria and Switzerland), Ireland, New Zealand, the Philippines, Portugal, Scotland, and the United States

3. Finally, publication of the *Recommendation Framework 1.0* derived from the national case studies, survey results, and stakeholder input. These recommendations focus on cognitive competencies in nursing aiming to provide knowledge about informatics competencies, professional roles, priorities, and practical experience.

TABLE 31.1

Top 10 Health Informatics Core Competency Areas for Health Professionals and Other Roles as Identified by TIGER International Competency Synthesis Project (ICSP) (HIMSS 2020e)

	Nurses, Physicians and Other Patient Care Providers	Health Information Management	Executives (Clinical and Administrative)	Chief Information Officers (CIO) (Clinical and Technical)	Engineering or Health IT Specialist	Science and Education
1	Communication	Communication	Leadership	Leadership	Communication	Communication
2	Documentation	Documentation	Communication	Communication	Care processes & IT integration	Teaching, training & education in health care
3	Information & knowledge management in patient care	Data analytics	Quality & safety management	Care processes & IT integration	Information & communication technology (applications)	Leadership
4	Quality & safety management	Leadership	Information & knowledge management in patient care	Principles of management	Leadership	Learning techniques
5	Leadership	Data protection & security	Strategic management	Quality & safety management	Project management	Ethics in health IT
6	Learning techniques	Information & knowledge management in patient care	Principles of management	Strategic management	Data protection & security	Documentation
7	Teaching, training & education in healthcare	Ethics in health IT	Legal issues in health IT	Process management	Ethics in health IT	Information & knowledge management in patient care
8	Ethics in health IT	Principles of health informatics	Process management	Change & stakeholder management	Interoperability & integration	Principles of health informatics
9	Information & communication technology (applications)	Care processes & IT integration	Resource planning & management	Ethics in health IT	Documentation	Quality & safety management
10	Care processes & IT integration	Learning techniques	Ethics in health IT	Resource planning & management	Process management	Data analytics

TIGER took a unique approach with this project as it believed to be the first to collect various competencies across countries to identify global commonalities and differences. Finally, these project findings and case studies were leveraged as a foundation upon which the EU*US eHealth Work Project began. *See Section 2.2 for additional information about the EU*US eHealth Work Project.*

Subsequently, the TIGER ICSP and the EU*US eHealth Work Project joined forces to describe and validate *Recommendation Framework 2.0* (Table 31.1). This Framework is meant to augment the focus from nursing towards a series of other professional roles, that is, healthcare providers, health information management professionals, executives, chief information officers, health IT specialists, researchers, and educators (HIMSS 2020c).

Resources to leverage:

- Both recommendation frameworks (1.0 & 2.0), as well as additional project information, can be found and downloaded at: https://www.himss.org/tiger-initiative-international-competency-synthesis-project
- TIGER VLE landing page: https://www.himss.org/tiger-virtual-learning-environment
- TIGER Interprofessional Community landing page with opt-in instructions for HIMSS members: https://www.himss.org/membership-participation/technology-informatics-guiding-education-reform-tiger-interprofessional-community

---

EU*US eHealth Work Project

In September 2016, TIGER was co-awarded funding to address the need, development, and deployment of workforce IT skills, competencies, and training programs via the European Commission's Horizon 2020 research and innovation grant program (Figure 31.2). The EU*US eHealth Work Project, spanning from September 2016 through spring 2019, worked to measure, inform, educate, and advance development of a skilled eHealth workforce throughout the European Union (EU), United States (U.S.), and globally.

A Timeline of TIGER's Work in Competency Development
*From TIGER's International Competency Synthesis Project (ICSP) to the EU*US Work Project and beyond*

TIGER's International Competency Synthesis Project (ICSP)	The EU*US Work Project
In 2015, TIGER began compiling core recommended international informatics competencies reflective of many countries, scientific societies and research projects.	TIGER was co-awarded funding from the European Commission's Horizon 2020 to measure, inform, educate and advance development of a skilled eHealth workforce throughout the EU, US and globally.

2015 – current   **2016 - 2019**

National Case Studies	*Survey deployment*	*Recommendation Framework 1.0 – nursing centric*	*Survey & gap analysis*	*Global case studies*	*Foundational course*	*Recommendation Frameworks 2.0 - interdisciplinary*
Compiled national studies from the global TIGER community	Deployed a survey composed of 24 core competencies within five domains	Creation derived from case studies, survey results and global stakeholder input.	1,080 professionals participated from 51 countries; 10 gap areas identified	22 studies compiled to highlight and enrich the survey and gap analysis findings	Global introductory online course in eHealth	TIGER joined forces with the EU*US eHealth Work Project to describe and validate the framework.

*The EU*US Work Project has since been featured in book chapters, publications, online guide, presentations and more!*

FIGURE 31.2 Milestones in TIGER's Work in Competency Development – From TIGER's International Competency Synthesis Project (ICSP) to the EU*US Work Project.

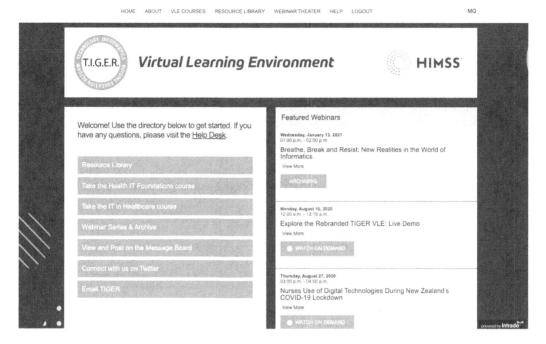

FIGURE 31.3 The TIGER VLE's lobby/home page.

Consortium member organizations include:
- Omni Micro Systems/Omni Med Solutions of Germany; served as the project coordinator.
- European Health Telemedics Association (ETHEL) of Belgium
- Tampere University of Technology of Finland
- Steinbeis Europa Zentrum of Germany
- HIMSS Foundation of the United States (U.S.) with project fulfillment by the global HIMSS TIGER™ Initiative
- University of Applied Sciences Osnabruck Germany

The Consortium's mission was to map skills and competencies, provide access to knowledge tools and platforms, and strengthen, disseminate, and exploit success outcomes for a skilled transatlantic eHealth workforce (Figure 31.3). The overall project goal was to create a legacy of digitally empowered health care professionals now and into the future (HIMSS 2020d).

Under the project scope of work, TIGER executed project deliverables on behalf of the HIMSS Foundation (Table 31.2). The project was an opportunity for HIMSS *and* TIGER to collaborate with European partners to enable a highly skilled workforce regionally, across borders and on a global scale. It also enabled TIGER to capitalize and build upon the ICSP work. As a Consortium member, TIGER worked to transform healthcare through information and technology in global workforce development.

Additional project resources to leverage:

o. Health IT Competencies Tool & Repository (known as HITComp) (http://www. hitcomp.org/): A searchable database that can be leveraged to compile information on skills and competencies needed for a variety of healthcare roles and areas of knowledge; HITComp's competency categories mirror the TIGER ICSP's

o. Skills Knowledge Assessment and Development Framework (SKAD) (http://ehealthwork.org/tools_resources.html): A question-based self-assessment that helps learners better understand their digital literacy skills

o. Global case studies report (https://www.himss.org/resources/developing-skilled-transatlantic-ehealth-workforce-case-studies-report): Reporting detailing the global case studies compilation as shared above

o. Interactive website platform (IWP) (http://ehealthwork.org/IWP/index.html): One-stop location for tools, resources, education, and information (TRIE) for eHealth

o. Interactive education demonstrator modules (IEDM): Video instruction related to the following areas of focus:

- Cybersecurity (http://ehealthwork.org/Cybersecurity_FINAL_020617.mp4)
- Foundational Curriculum Tutorial (http://ehealthwork.org/Foundational_curricula_video.mp4)
- HITComp Tutorial (http://ehealthwork.org/hitcomp.mp4)

TABLE 31.2
Description of the EU*US Project Milestones

Project Survey	Served as the flagship of the project with the goal of capturing information to identify workforce development needs, trends, gaps, and core competency insights. The survey yielded 1,080 participants from 51 countries.
Gap Analysis	In addition to the survey, the project also conducted an extensive Gap Analysis on the survey results, with findings demonstrating ten major gaps in skills, training, funding, and other area of eHealth workforce preparation, development, and advancement.
Global Case Studies Compilation	Next, 22 global case studies were compiled to capture examples from institutions and organizations to showcase and demonstrate real-world successes, best practices but also issues, challenges, and/or gaps to further underscore the findings of both the survey and gap analysis.
Foundational Curriculum	A global introductory online course in eHealth that provides baseline and basic eHealth skills (digital competency in healthcare) upon completion.

SECTION 3. ALIGNING CORE HEALTH INFORMATICS COMPETENCIES ACROSS HEALTH INFORMATICS PROFESSIONS

HIMSS HEALTH INFORMATICS GUIDE

Inspired by TIGER's work over the last six years, the *HIMSS Health Informatics Guide* was created to provide learners with an easy way to explore the Initiative's tools, projects, and resources (HIMSS 2020a). This guide also synthesizes TIGER's work focused on the development of global informatics competencies across multiple disciplines tied to:

- **Understanding basic health informatics competency terminology:** This section outlines the core competencies identified in the TIGER ICSP and describes how "core competencies can be understood as a broadly specialized system of skills, abilities or knowledge necessary to achieve a specific goal" (Thye 2020). Healthcare organizations, health informatics educators and students are encouraged to use the recommendation framework as a compass to identify core competency areas relevant to their local setting (Hübner et al. 2019)

- **Aligning core health informatics competencies:** Numerous health professional associations have identified proficiency with informatics solutions as an essential competency to develop as a health professional. Due to the rapidly changing and evolving informatics landscape, informatics educators are having a hard time keeping up with the required skills necessary to not only understand informatics but teach it to their target audiences. This section of the guide expands upon the core competencies required in nursing, medicine, and pharmacy; addresses gaps in education and training; and shares possible solutions and resources.
- **Workforce development needs tied to health informatics branches:** Health informatics is a multidisciplinary field that weaves together technology, healthcare, computer science, research, and information. By leveraging the informatics competencies showcased throughout the guide, professionals can pursue a career in one of the many branches of health informatics, which include:

1. Clinical Informatics
2. Consumer Health Informatics
3. Nursing Informatics
4. Pharmacy Informatics
5. Public Health Informatics

With an ever-increasing amount of data generated in healthcare, the last decade has created many new exciting career opportunities at the intersection of healthcare and informatics. Aspiring health informatics professionals are encouraged to develop a mix of competencies in diverse domains, such as technology, computer science, management, ethics, communication, and patient care, to meet the increasing demand for a competent informatics healthcare workforce in the years to come (HIMSS 2020a).

Resources to leverage:

- HIMSS Health Informatics Guide: https://www.himss.org/resources/health-informatics
- Developing a Skilled Transatlantic eHealth Workforce Case Studies Report and Gap Analysis Findings Report: https://www.himss.org/resources/developing-skilled-transatlantic-ehealth-workforce-case-studies-report

---

SECTION 4. VIRTUAL LEARNING AND INFORMATICS RESOURCES

TIGER's VIRTUAL LEARNING ENVIRONMENT

Rooted in the early activities of setting up a virtual demonstration center, the TIGER Virtual Learning Environment (VLE) emerged as a web-based education portal in 2009.

Powered by HIMSS, the TIGER VLE is an interactive, online learning platform for academic professionals, students, adult learners, and clinical educators. This personalized learning experience—containing courses and webinars—expands knowledge and skillset in a self-paced format.

The VLE has moved through several iterations over the last 11 years, with the latest relaunch taking place in summer 2020. Guided by HIMSS TIGER™ staff and volunteer subject matter experts (SME), the re-conceptualized VLE offers a streamlined and intuitive education portal for those seeking to expand their health informatics knowledge and skillset (Figure 31.3).

Highlights of the VLE include:
- Courses tied to certificates of completion
- Robust resource library with content tied to 18 categories such as AI/ML, innovation, interoperability, privacy and security, etc.
- Webinar archive featuring recording aligned to 11 content categories.

By highlighting the work of open-source collaborators, TIGER does the work of sifting through information from around the world to curate content for VLE subscribers. Educators can then easily integrate resources and modules into classroom curricula and more.

Resource to leverage:

- What is the TIGER VLE? https://www.himss.org/tiger-virtual-learning-environment

---

ILLUMINATING INFORMATICS TERMINOLOGY

Driven by the purpose of providing context to the global, interdisciplinary community it represents, the HIMSS TIGER™ Initiative published its first informatics definitions document in 2016 (HIMSS 2020f). The goal of this document was to leverage existing terminology from leading global institutions and subject matter experts to serve as a helpful tool for those learning about the field of informatics and informatics competencies. As part of its mission to integrate technology and informatics seamlessly into practice, education, and research, the HIMSS TIGER™ Initiative has committed itself to curate the most relevant terms and graphics into one easy, centralized document biannually.

The fourth iteration of the document was published in July 2020. In addition to terminology from various disciplines, for the first time, TIGER features terminology that could be applied at local, regional, national, and global levels. As the informatics field continues to grow and evolve, it is important to lead with a global perspective. Post COVID-19, more than ever before, we are connected virtually, sharing data, information, and knowledge with a click of a button or the start of a Zoom meeting. It is important to ensure that the terminology showcased be effortlessly applied regardless of where one is located. In addition, the fourth iteration of the document features a refined statement of purpose, showcases an informatics timeline that reflects the past and future trajectory of the field, and includes new and updated infographics.

Informatics Timeline

This newly created timeline provides a visual representation of the field's development and growth. This enables learners to see the evolution of informatics and integration into clinical, biomedical, nursing, medicine, and today, artificial intelligence and machine learning (Figure 31.4).

Resource to leverage:

- Download the full document from https://www.himss.org/resources/tiger-informatics-definitions and begin leveraging the terminology and resources in benefit of yourself and target audiences.

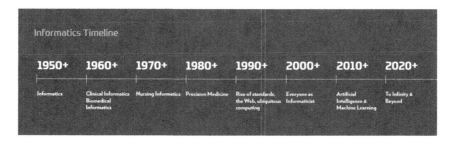

FIGURE 31.4 Version 4 of the *TIGER Global Informatics Definitions Document's* **Informatics Timeline**; Figure from: HIMSS TIGER™ Informatics Definitions (HIMSS 2020f).

CONCLUSION

Since its inception in 2006, the TIGER Initiative has evolved from a grassroots movement to a multidisciplinary, international effort to provide resources focused on curricula development and competency standards for the health informatics community. With the dynamic and expanding pace of health informatics, it is important for the global modern-day students, educators, and adult learners to have opportunities to expand skillsets in a feasible and holistic manner. The TIGER Initiative offers upskilling and microlearning avenues to guide health informatics professionals and learners through a variety of resources. Through its growing collection of enriched resources, TIGER offers a unique global perspective to learners across all healthcare informatics learners at any point in their career. By continuing to expand its resource collection, partnerships, and curriculum offerings, the work conducted by the TIGER Initiative continues to impact the delivery of healthcare services and patient care.

REFERENCES

American Association of Colleges of Nursing (AACN). 2019. "AACN Fact Sheet - Nursing." April 1, 2019. https://www.aacnnursing.org/news-Information/fact-sheets/nursing-fact-sheet.

Andriotis, Nikos. 2018. "What Is Microlearning: A Complete Guide For Beginners." ELearning Industry. December 10, 2018. https://elearningindustry.com/what-is-microlearning-benefits-best-practices.

Executive Office of the President. 2004. "Incentives for the Use of Health Information Technology and Establishing the Position of the National Health Information Technology Coordinator." Federal Register. April 30, 2004. https://www.federalregister.gov/documents/2004/04/30/04–10024/incentives-for-the-use-of-health-information-technology-and-establishing-the-position-of-the.

HIMSS. 2020a. "Health Informatics." 2020. https://www.himss.org/resources/health-informatics.

HIMSS. 2020b. "Technology Informatics Guiding Education Reform (TIGER)." 2020. https://www.himss.org/tiger.

HIMSS. 2020c. "TIGER International Competency Synthesis Project." 2020. https://www.himss.org/tiger-initiative-international-competency-synthesis-project.

HIMSS. 2020d. "TIGER's Horizon 2020 Work Project via the European Commission." 2020. https://www.himss.org/tigers-horizon-2020-work-project-european-commission.

HIMSS. 2020e. "Global Health Informatics Competency Recommendation Frameworks." May 22, 2020. https://www.himss.org/resources/global-health-informatics-competency-recommendation-frameworks.

HIMSS. 2020f. "HIMSS TIGER Global Informatics Definitions." July 23, 2020. https://www.himss.org/resources/tiger-informatics-definitions.

Hübner, Ursula, Johannes Thye, Toria Shaw, Beth Elias, Nicole Egbert, Kaija Saranto, Birgit Babitsch, Paula Procter, and Marion J. Ball. 2019. "Towards the TIGER International Framework for Recommendations of Core Competencies in Health Informatics 2.0: Extending the Scope and the Roles." *Studies in Health Technology and Informatics* 264 (August): 1218–1222. https://doi.org/10.3233/SHTI190420.

Institute of Medicine (US) Committee on the Health Professions Education Summit. 2003. *Health Professions*

Education: A Bridge to Quality. Edited by Ann C. Greiner and Elisa Knebel. Washington (DC): National Academies Press (US). http://www.ncbi.nlm.nih.gov/books/NBK221528/.

National Library of Medicine. 2020. "Health Informatics." 2020. https://hsric.nlm.nih.gov/hsric_public/topic/informatics/.

Rouse, Margaret. 2020. "What Is Upskilling and Why Is It Important?" WhatIs.Com. 2020. https://whatis.techtarget.com/definition/upskilling.

Shaw, Toria, Joyce Sensmeier, and Christel Anderson. 2017. "The Evolution of the TIGER Initiative." *CIN: Computers, Informatics, Nursing* 35 (6): 278–280. https://doi.org/10.1097/CIN.0000000000000369.

Thye, Johannes. 2020. "Understanding Health Informatics Core Competencies." September 9, 2020. https://www.himss.org/resources/health-informatics.

32 Disruptive Technology: It's About People, Culture, and Technology

Fran Ayalasomayajula
MPH, MSMIS

Amir Ismail
MPharm

CONTENTS

LEARNING OBJECTIVES

- Describe the influence of data on the performance culture of healthcare systems.
- Recall the dynamics that either hinder or promote the application of technology for the purpose of system optimization.
- Distinguish between the data needs of administrators, providers, and patients and how such data is used to support the healthcare journey of patients.

INTRODUCTION

Does data generated within a healthcare ecosystem benefit each constituent? It is an essential question to answer as active participants in the digital health realm.

Data directly influences all groups within a healthcare organization, from administrators and clinicians to patients. Health informatics professionals need to consider all these groups to understand the wide impact of data and the need for specificity. Generated data directly influences processes in place, whether it is a protocol or a standard, a department, or patient care. Over time, data can affect the culture and behavior of these environments in ways that may inform or justify the continuation and modification of processes, protocols, and standards. Depending on the outcomes, data integration could result in the adoption, adaptation, or even abortion of technology.

If we can agree for a moment that people, cultures, and technologies constitute a system then what we're aiming toward as health informatics professionals is to optimize those environments. It is our job to take our roles as health informatics leaders as the opportunity to improve those systems.

DOI: 10.4324/9780429398377-38

In a recent 2020 study, Reach, a nonprofit organization that supports the role of public health professionals in shaping conversations related to care, explored the role of system optimization and the role of technology—digital health technology in particular. A diverse population of executive administrators in healthcare, including practicing physicians and pharmacists, answered a series of questions on the topic. The goal was to understand the perception of technology and unearth the possibilities of technology and its ability to reform and refine the practice of care.

Findings indicated that the volume of data in the healthcare setting is predicted to grow exponentially as organizations operate in the digital health arena. Use of chatbots, virtual assistants, and other smart tools will add to that volume. Even though information flow has become a reality, using data optimally and fostering a data-driven culture has been challenging. Data on its own has limited value.

For the most part, we are currently amassing more data into the healthcare system, creating larger and larger pools of information. However, we are not leveraging and interpreting the data to provide comprehensive direction to patients and other groups within healthcare.

Healthcare organizations tend to operate in silos, struggle with basic data access, and find it difficult to create ways to use analytics to help all of the groups within healthcare. Organizations are continually seeking ways to better support their people and cultivate high-performing teams.

Current research suggests that the healthcare industry has a productivity level of approximately 43% (Howe 2017). The demand for care is increasing and budgets are being strained. Systems performance optimization can help address this modern-day challenge by improving care, accountability, and resource management at both individual and institutional levels.

A significant opportunity lies in leveraging individual patient data and using that data in the context of a larger population to develop and refine patient care plans, and healthcare planning as a whole. However, as with any cultural shift, building an environment where big data and analytics become everyday thinking starts at the top. Analytics needs a seat at the executive table (Mircoff 2018). As the results of the Reach Study suggest, employees using and generating data will thrive when findings are addressed and are in line with organizational values, moving beyond the confines of an information technology (IT) department. In other words, an entire organization must embrace the ability of data and analytics to improve processes, standards, and delivery of patient care.

SECTION 1. LEVERAGING THE INTELLIGENCE OF DATA WITHIN CULTURES

Healthcare organizations around the globe aim to use data, analytics, and artificial intelligence to lower costs and become more efficient (Meskó, Drobni, Bényei, Gergely, and Győrffy 2017). Often, these goals lie within IT departments and may not go very far without leadership support. Accelerating change through technology demands a systemwide cultural shift.

The understanding that data is an asset is pervasive. However, comprehending its value and putting it to good use remains a mystery at most organizations. Even with the best of tools and the most meaningful data, organizations can struggle to undergo a transformation toward the use of data. Without the proper expertise to provide context for data, education, training, and placing information in the right hands, discovering the value of data can prove to be unsurmountable.

Data literacy is one of the biggest roadblocks for healthcare IT professionals (Waller 2020). An organization that lacks a data-driven culture can make it even harder for professionals to gain acceptance and support when promoting smart tools such as artificial intelligence, for example, or the need to mine other information resources.

Defining data-driven goals and aligning organizations to abide by those priorities is not an easy task. However, clarity and purpose at the leadership level, when it comes to data, can introduce changes from basic standards to bold programs that achieve missions. As the Reach study identified, proper preparation, assessment, planning, action, measurement, and communication can nurture successful outcomes.

Building a data-driven culture, where data is viewed as a strategic asset, requires changing conversations surrounding information. If one's organization claims to be data-driven, does it demonstrate the business value of data in everything it does? Does data influence decisions? Is leadership engaged with health informatics professionals and inquiring of impact all the through to the front line?

Unless we examine all the aspects of a data-driven culture—from business value to ethical implications—as healthcare organizations, we will be unable to make that change and reinforce behaviors and attitudes toward information analytics (Napier et al 2020). This change in behavior also impacts data literacy, moving it beyond the domain of certain business units and IT departments. Just as much as data is pervasive, the language and conversations surrounding data need to be inclusive across departments and inspire collaborations to fully realize systems performance optimization.

SECTION 2. EXAMINING DATA-POWERED TECHNOLOGY FOR PERFORMANCE OPTIMIZATION

Organizations can turn to performance optimization to provide better access, improve clinical effectiveness, and achieve operational efficiencies. In modern day medicine, the need for, and expectations centered around, care delivery and the quality of care are extremely high, which is why performance optimization is necessary at any healthcare facility or anywhere care is being delivered.

While specific hurdles in performance optimization for individual healthcare organizations can vary from hospital to hospital and from organization to organization, the Reach study identified that the problems may be grouped into four main categories: technology adoption, accessibility, education, and optimizing the patient experience.

- Technology adoption
  The adoption of new technology is often slow, even though the technology may create some operational efficiencies. New technologies challenge existing modes of care. Technologies will need to integrate with the current system's chaos. This is compounded by IT professionals believing that their organizations are not accepting of change, resulting in sluggish adoption. Three-fifths, or 60%, of practitioners interviewed by Reach believe that the role of technology is under-emphasized in assisting with achieving performance optimization.

"Integration of APIs from other devices such as wearables is a challenge in my organization."
—Physician, Internal Medicine

- Limited access
  Providing access for patients and their families in an environment of financial constraint and increased demand creates hurdles for healthcare organizations. Patients would like access to a number of services, such as social services, transportation, and respite services, that enable them to maintain or improve their health. Eventually, organizations would need to provide and preemptively offer such services.

"We need to integrate social care into healthcare to provide more access for patients to control their health." —Chief Medical Officer

- Training and education
  Inadequate education and training stymies performance optimization, resulting in time wasted completing administrative tasks. Proper training and staff education can help reduce administrative incompetencies. Ninety percent of practitioners in the Reach study thought there was a lack of training when attempting performance optimization.

"Education can reduce duplication and waste of resources." —General Practitioner

* Patient care
  Patient care is central to systems optimization. Making the healthcare experience uneventful for patients by removing complications, such as simplifying the billing processes, co-ordinating healthcare teams, and establishing communications between the physician and the patient, can have a significant impact on the patient experience.

"There is the challenge of complex and often unclear billing processes for patients and physicians."
—Cardiologist

Four practitioners in the Reach survey thought cost pressures and working to improve margins at an institutional level were key hurdles to performance optimization, while three leaders pointed to the ability to maintain quality care, personalized care, communication, digital health proficiency and lack of training. Others commented that providing access for patients in an environment of increasing demands requires attention as does demonstrating value in terms of patient outcomes.

SECTION 3. CREATING PERFORMANCE OPTIMIZATION ACROSS ORGANIZATIONS

Obstacles in performance optimization are often centered around cost pressures which in turn impacts quality of care, the adoption of digital health, and the training provided. As healthcare professionals must streamline care, introduce new revenue models and automate processes wherever possible to tackle the challenge of cost pressures, and to at least contain, if not reduce, costs.

Making smart investments in digital technology and reducing reliance on expensive care delivery methods with minimal benefits, will aid performance, education, and data sharing with patients. Providing training and education on behavioral economics, communication and empathy, as well as sharing data freely with patients, could overcome obstacles. Offering physicians more support, through additional training and strategically appointed auxiliary staff, are ways to help an organization use data to its advantage and prioritize patient care.

In the Reach study, respondents indicated that, in order to meet the needs of patients, maximizing the use of staff, incorporating telehealth where possible, and augmenting evidence-based practice and systems optimization across organizations are necessary steps.

Care coordination teams are a key component of the healthcare organization. Practitioners believe that patients need empathy, respect, and trust from care coordination teams. They also pointed to the value of shared decision making. To facilitate shared decision making and achieve optimization of the healthcare system, integration of data is essential. Digital decision support tools, with acceptance continuing to grow, significantly helps in the data-integration process. However, it is worth noting that integration depends on how that tool was trained and what the tool was used for. And it is even further noted that such tools should not be limited to aiding providers, but patients as well.

As depicted in Figure 32.1, the Reach study identified four (4) key components in building and sustaining performance optimization (Reach 2020).

Digital tools: Embracing digital technology and demonstrating the ability to deploy innovations in digital health technology can drive efficiencies and sustainable improvements within an organization. Healthcare organizations must seamlessly connect across the entire patient pathway to enable access to all involved in coordinating care. Organizations can do this by using digital tools like telemedicine.

Collaboration: This requires a drive to change the culture and behavior of an organization which can streamline care and reduce variations in the quality and efficiency of care. At the same

Creating performance optimization in an organization

Education and Training
Continuous training and education of physicians on new models of care

Digital tools
The use of digital tools and telemedicine

Value based care
Focus on outcomes to bring high value care and learn to lose the fear of change

Collaboration
Create a collaborative culture to streamline care

FIGURE 32.1 Creating data-driven performance optimization.

time, organizations need to keep measuring performance and benchmarking against others to improve and optimize performance overall. When an organization coalesces around the same mission of performance optimization, it can reap significant rewards.

Education and training: Continuous training and education of physicians and patients will sustain performance optimization, enhancing the delivering high-quality care.

Value-based care: Connecting patient health outcomes and clinician performance is integral to system improvement. The benefit of value-based care is derived from measuring health outcomes against the cost of delivering those outcomes. Organizations must recognize that value-based care can create performance optimization. There are many benefits to value-based care for patients, including lower costs and better outcomes. For providers, it translates into higher patient satisfaction scores, efficiencies, and lower costs. If optimally employed, it may even boost morale and reduce clinician burnout.

"Measure performance and outcomes of clinical staff openly, not to punish but to compare and learn. Everyone can improve." —General Practitioner

SECTION 4. THE POSSIBILITIES OF DATA-DRIVEN SYSTEMS OPTIMIZATION

What may be inferred from the research is that system optimization can be achieved by discerning data, curated data gathered and analyzed to more comprehensively and impartially address organizational needs, and digital footprints. Consider the use of a wearable such as a step tracker. If a patient achieves 16,000 steps on a given day and the action is recorded by the digital platform, it can reinforce the behavior by saying, "Good job!"

But what does that reinforcement mean? At an individual level, the patient has a sense of accomplishment. At an organizational level, using that data in the context of a pool of individuals might uncover conditions which "super walkers" may be prone to experiencing, such as foot muscle fatigue. An optimized system, one that would mine and harness the value of such data, would then say to the patient "Good job! Let's massage those feet." Or "Good job! Don't forget the importance of good insoles in your shoes." So now, the individual knows foot care is important or that it might be useful to pay attention to aches and pains.

Such a system could go one step further by inquiring not only about any aches or pains but also assessing for any potential injury. It would subsequently use that information to alert the individual's care provider of the person's activity, health state and, if deemed appropriate, make suggestions on the course of action to be taken by the clinical team—not just in an acute care scenario, but also in preventative ones. This would further lead to the opportunity to create the much-needed relationship-building and improved communication between providers and patients as noted in Reach's study.

Let's explore this concept of patient-centered, intelligent, system optimization further. Consider whether the system was able to detect a patient's location and their type of activity (e.g., walking, running, or doing errands). Does it learn how individual feels? Whether the person feels calm or whether person remembered to rest? With data points like these, the system would have the possibility of promoting whole-person health and well-being.

As health informatics professionals, need to consider leveraging data in a holistic manner. Simply collecting data, whether it is blood pressure statistics or patient weight, is ineffective. Data is only as effective as the appropriateness of the systems from which it is collected and integrated, the questions that are posed, and the analysis that is undertaken. Practitioners in the Reach study preferred artificial intelligence (AI) applications that over time are integrated into healthcare information systems. Some digital tools, such as highly sensitive registrations, may need to remain separate from the overall system. These factors need to be considered when trying to achieve a performance-optimized culture.

When ranking the most important outcomes for practitioners (see Graph 32.1), Reach practitioners thought the most important outcomes were improved quality of care, increased patient safety, and reduced medical errors (2020). Eighty percent had improved quality of care and patient safety in their top five outcomes, and 70% had reduced medical errors in their top five. In contrast, for the overall system, patient safety, decreased re-admission, and improved quality of care were at the top of the list as shown in Graph 32.2 (Reach 2020).

Based on the results of the Reach study, leadership style, empathy, and innovation can have impacts on system optimization and organizational performance (Graph 32.3) (Reach 2020). Leadership is an important factor in making a data-driven organization successful and ultimately in the delivery of care. Organizational leaders will use both their skills and knowledge, as well as data

GRAPH 32.1 Most important outcomes for practitioners.

Most important outcomes for your organization/care delivery site

% Practitioner rating outcomes in Top 5

Increased patient safety	80%
Decrease in re-admissions	70%
Improved quality of care	70%
Better standardization of care	40%
Better staff satisfaction	40%

GRAPH 32.2 Most important outcomes for systems.

supported discernment, to manage and strengthen the various components of an organization, thus having an overall impact on the optimization of a system.

As Elena Mircoff describes in Leadership in Healthcare and Public Health, "building an organizational culture that elevates analytics can be achieved through distributed leadership roles" (2018), and everyone has the opportunity to gain. The organizations that will lead the industry in the end are those that learn to extract insightful inferences from the data and use those insights to foster the introduction and adoption of innovative solutions. Achieving successful adoption is the key, as innovative solutions in the context of organizational culture and performance optimization require that the data reflects a high regard for the opinions of the people within the organization. "This again relates to building a culture with empowered employees that have access to quality and true data" (2018).

SECTION 5. EXTENDED SYSTEM OPTIMIZATION TO PATIENTS

It is evident that building, sustaining, and improving systems performance optimization across the healthcare system cannot be successful without keeping the patient at its core. Using the power of data to enable patients to meet their individual needs is critical. Healthcare systems must not overlook the ultimate beneficiary of healthcare data, patients. Whether it is communication data through patient portals or remote monitoring and telehealth, the empowered patient has an expectation today. They turn to information beyond hospital stays and temporary visits.

> "We need to tear down the current system and start over with the patient really at the center."
> —Cardiologist

Optimizing data within healthcare systems to empower patients is paramount to meeting the needs at an individual patient level. We can empower patients by providing incentives. Gamification, for example, encourages patient engagement in such programs as remote patient monitoring and may promote better value care for patients. As healthcare informatics professionals, the presentation and delivery of data to patients and caregivers—to ensure they remain actively engaged in their

 Impact on system optimization

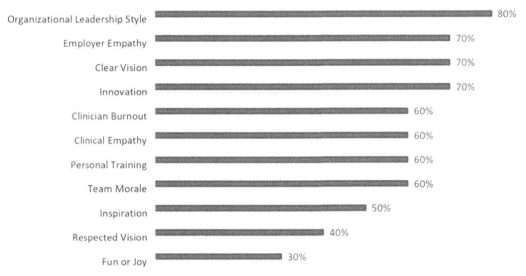

GRAPH 32.3 Impact on system optimization.

wellness—will lead to better health outcomes. We can encourage the gathering of patient-generated data through the establishment of interoperable systems that enable to collection of data from a variety of sources and formats, and presents the data in a manner most relevant to the who care team, including the patient and the patient's personal caregiver.

Patients are beginning to recognize that knowledge is power, whether it is through access to biometric information, online portals, the use of wearables, or even conventional devices such as blood pressure monitors. Access to information allows patients to begin to actively participate in shared decision making, and in some cases, initiating self-directed care. Systems performance optimization can encourage and simulate that behavior with the use of digital tools and data.

> *"Patients should have more control of their data. Health systems should encourage patient ownership of data." —Surgeon*

Patients who have more control of their data are better informed and are more likely to establish stronger connections with clinicians. As health informatics professionals develop new analytical tools, such products need to be optimally designed and drive value across the organization.

CONCLUSION

Digitization of healthcare is here. Disruptive technologies can enhance the quality of care, improve health outcomes, and introduce efficiencies within healthcare organizations.

Becoming an organization that enables data capture and integration requires a culture that empowers, trusts, and encourages inquiry. In doing so, organizations can commit to analytics, using data to solve problems, and increase patient satisfaction. A simple way to encourage the use and collection of data is by offering executive positions to informatics professionals and the creation of new, more defined roles that directly reflect the rise of emerging digital health technology platforms (Hermes 2020). Leaders in these roles cement the commitment to driving value from data, instilling a theme throughout the organization's processes, standards, and controls.

There is also the opportunity to recognize the value in empowering every level within the organization with data—from patient-centric information to clinician performance. As we are rapidly witnessing the digital evolution of the healthcare delivery system and the transition of care responsibilities to the patient, health informatics professionals are charged with developing paths for and access to resources that promote the newly-charted emphasis on the active participation of patients in their care management. It further puts pressure onto healthcare organizations to use data in a manner that raises the performance level of the organization and satiates the requirements of those care plans that are instrumental in the digital transformation of care such as telehealth, remote patient monitoring, and continuous health monitoring (de Langhem and Puntoni 2020).

Perhaps the loudest call for optimized, data-efficient healthcare models has been the COVID-19 pandemic. It not only prompted the proliferation of telemedicine, symptom checkers, and remote monitoring, but it also enabled big-data analytics to forecast hospital capacity and resources (Kent 2020).

The value and efficacy of remote patient monitoring systems has been proven across a variety of therapeutic areas. These positive results have driven institutions and governments to deploy such programs on a national scale. The deployment of telehealth programs, as an example, has been deemed a key strategy in containing and preventing the spread of COVID-19 (CDC 2020). Healthcare providers were able to keep tabs on attitudes, behaviors, and concerns of patients.

Additionally, analytics were able to offer a glimpse into the possibilities for population health management (Kent 2020). Connecting those dots with physicians and healthcare organizations to identify and reduce disparities could lead to better patient outcomes.

It is vital for healthcare organizations to direct data initiatives with approaches that result in action and create value across the entire enterprise, enhancing performance, enriching the culture of the organization as well as shifting, sustaining, and supporting patients at the center of care (Gartner Report: 10 Ways CDOs Can Succeed in Forging a Data-Driven Organization 2019). These approaches might challenge an institution to think differently and provide support to teams collecting data or designing tools to gather information to feed the organization. However, therein lies the opportunity for healthcare informatics professionals to adapt, understand, and leverage culture and technology to deliver quality, cost-effective care for all.

REFERENCES

CDC. (2020). Using Telehealth to Expand Access to Essential Health Services during the COVID-19 Pandemic. CDC: COVID-19 Healthcare Workers. https://www.cdc.gov/coronavirus/2019-ncov/hcp/telehealth.html

de Langhem B. and Puntoni, S. (2020). Leading With Decision-Driven Data Analytics. Sloan Review. https://sloanreview.mit.edu/article/leading-with-decision-driven-data-analytics/

Howe, G. (2017). How Performance Optimization Can Improve Healthcare. Ernest and Young. https://www.ey.com/en_gl/health/how-performance-optimization-can-improve-health-care

Gartner Report: 10 Ways CDOs Can Succeed in Forging a Data-Driven Organization. (2019). Gartner. https://www.gartner.com/doc/reprints?id=1-1ZM4VXMV&ct=200804&st=sb

Hermes, S., Iasanow, T., Clemons, E.K. et al. (2020). The digital transformation of the healthcare industry: exploring the rise of emerging platform ecosystems and their influence on the role of patients. Bus Res 13, 1033–1069. https://doi.org/10.1007/s40685-020-00125-x

Kent, J. (2020). How Big Data Analytics Models Can Impact Healthcare Decision-Making. Health IT Analytics. https://healthitanalytics.com/news/how-big-data-analytics-models-can-impact-healthcare-decision-making

Meskó, B., Drobni, Z., Bényei, É., Gergely, B., and Győrffy, Z. (2017). Digital health is a cultural transformation of traditional healthcare. mHealth, 3, 38. https://doi.org/10.21037/mhealth.2017.08.07 https://www.ncbi.nlm.nih.gov/pmc/articles/PMC5682364/

Mircoff, Elena. (2018). Leadership in healthcare and public health: Leaders role to create organizational culture that embraces big-data and data analytics. Ohio State University. https://ohiostate.pressbooks.pub/pubhhmp6615/chapter/leaders-role-to-create-organizational-culture-that-embraces-big-data-and-data-analytics/

Napier, L., Libert, B. and de Vries, K.D. (2020). Changing Culture Is Central to Changing Business Models. https://sloanreview.mit.edu/article/changing-culture-is-central-to-changing-business-models/

Reach. (2020). Understanding System Optimization to Create Better Efficiency in Care Delivery. https://reachtl.org/resources

Waller, D. (2020). 10 Steps to Creating a Data-Driven Culture. Harvard Business Review. https://hbr.org/2020/02/10-steps-to-creating-a-data-driven-culture

33 Caring for the Underserved: Both a Professional and a Personal Responsibility

Leslie Evans
BA

CONTENTS

In my role as the Director of the HIMSS Innovation Center, I was introduced early on to a true champion of health equity and a passionate community trust broker in Cleveland, Ohio—Silas Buchanan, CEO of The Institute for eHealth Equity. Much of what I have assembled in this chapter was first brought to my attention by Silas. I dedicate this chapter to my friend Silas with much gratitude for allowing me to walk alongside him and for opening my eyes to the truth of health disparities and instilling me with hope that we can do better and ultimately improve health outcomes for everyone.

    I. Setting the Stage
        a. Defining Health Equity
        b. Staggering statistics

    II. Understanding Implicit Bias
        a. How can bias undermine health outcomes
        b. How does bias skew data

    III. Barriers to equal outcomes
        a. Digital Divide
        b. Health Literacy

DOI: 10.4324/9780429398377-39

INTRODUCTION

Health information technology has the power to be deployed to improve health outcomes for everyone, everywhere. To achieve that goal, healthcare leaders must acknowledge the prevalence of health disparities across the globe and be intentional about developing an understanding of the factors and history at the root of these inequities. Powerful and complex relationships exist between health and socioeconomic status, the physical environment, discrimination, racism, literacy levels, and legislative policies. Factors which are not directly related to healthcare delivery but which influence an individual's or population's health are known as determinants of health. These factors are often far more influential than the quality of acute or specialty care and improving health equity will require ongoing societal efforts to provide equal access to health and wellness services regardless of a person's geographic location, ethnicity, social-economic status, gender, and other demographic factors.

DEFINING THE PROBLEM

Health equity is defined as reducing—and, ultimately, eliminating—disparities in health and in its determinants, including social components and contributors. Pursuing health equity means striving for the highest possible standard of health for all people and giving special attention to the needs of those at greatest risk of poor health, based on social, economic, and other circumstances.

Health equity and health disparities are intertwined. Health equity means no one is denied the possibility to be healthy for belonging to a group that has historically been economically/socially disadvantaged. Health disparities are the metric we use to measure progress toward achieving health equity. A reduction in health disparities is evidence that we are moving toward greater health equity.

Margaret Whitehead of the United Kingdom defined *health inequalities* as "health differences that are avoidable, unnecessary, and unjust". The Whitehead definition concisely captures the essence of what health disparities are, and why we are committed to eliminating them. Health disparities, on the other hand, are differences and /or gaps in the quality of health and healthcare across racial, ethnic, geographic and socio-economic groups. It can also be understood as population-specific differences in the presence of disease, mortality rates, health outcomes or access to healthcare.[1]

Consider, for example, not everyone in the United States enjoys the same health opportunities. Studies show that minority Americans experience poorer than average health outcomes from cradle to the grave. They are much more likely to die as infants, have higher rates of diseases and disabilities, and have shorter life spans.

While this has been true for generations, the focus on health disparities originated quite recently. It was initially documented the 1985 Report of the Secretary's Task Force on Black & Minority Health issued by U.S. Health and Human Services Secretary Margaret M. Heckler. The poor health status, poor outcomes, and limited access to medical care for more than 300 years, anecdotally well known by many African Americans, and in some cases by academicians and public health officials, gained greater awareness with the "Heckler Report." The report objectively detailed the wide disparity in the excess burden of death and illness experienced by blacks and other minority Americans as compared with the nation's population as a whole. It also put forth that such disparities had been in existence for as long as federal health statistics were routinely collected. The report further emphasized the fact that six medical conditions between blacks and whites accounted for 86% of excess black mortality and the fact that close to 45% of deaths up to the age of 70 years (58,000 of 138,000) in the black population would have been avoidable if better evaluation, detection, and treatment had been available. The six conditions were: cancer (3.8%), heart disease and stroke (14.4%), diabetes (1.0%), infant mortality (26.9%), cirrhosis (4.9%), and homicide and accidents (35.1%).

Although generally well received, the work and initial analysis detailed in the Heckler-Malone Report was not followed up until 2003, when the Institute of Medicine published its groundbreaking report "Unequal Treatment: Confronting Racial and Ethnic Disparities in Healthcare". This report brought the imperative of addressing health disparities to the forefront of the public consciousness.[2]

The IOM report contributed further to a more robust dialogue on health disparities by offering an integrated model of health disparities that places in context the complex causes of disparate treatment decisions and outcomes (Figure 33.1).

In the years since the release of the Heckler Report, significant efforts have been organized to address health disparities. The report served as a catalyst for the coordination of federal and state responses to address disparities and the establishment of the Office of Minority Health within the U.S. Department of Health and Human Services. However, despite such progress, it is clear that much work remains to be done to fully address health inequities. Many barriers still exist in the healthcare, social, and policy domains, including:

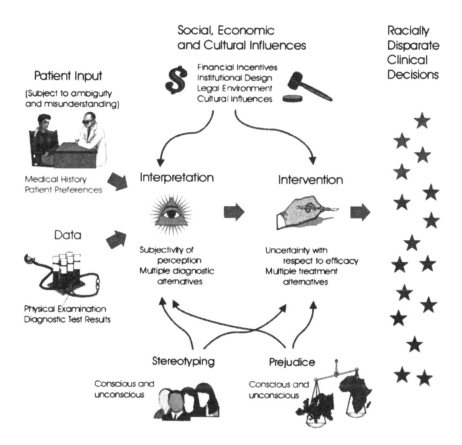

FIGURE 33.1 Integrated model of health disparities from the Institute of Medicine (IOM).

- Unconscious and Implicit Bias
- A Digital Divide
- Disparate Health Literacy
- A Lack of User-Centered Design

UNDERSTANDING UNCONSCIOUS AND IMPLICIT BIAS

Common to groups that experience health disparities—such as poor or marginalized persons, racial and ethnic minorities, and women—is lack of political, social, or economic power. These groups have systematically experienced greater social or economic obstacles to health historically linked to discrimination or exclusion. Thus, to be effective and sustainable, interventions that aim to reduce inequities must typically go beyond addressing a particular health inequality and address both the social and delivery system factors driving inequity. We must solve for unconscious bias as well as limit the impact of social and economic factors on health to fully address disparities and better serve vulnerable populations.

Clinical care teams are comprised of individuals who hold personal beliefs and social constructs, both positive and negative. Bias and prejudice are as much a part of healthcare workers as in the general population and because healthcare workers are in positions of influence with regards to a patient's health, the impact of their individual bias on health outcomes can be significant and long lasting.

Implicit bias, a phrase that is not unique to healthcare, refers to the unconscious prejudice individuals might feel about another thing, group, or person. According to the Kirwan Institute for the Study of Race and Ethnicity at the Ohio State University, implicit bias is involuntary, can refer to positive or negative attitudes and stereotypes, and can affect actions without an individual knowing it:

"Also known as implicit social cognition, implicit bias refers to the attitudes or stereotypes that affect our understanding, actions, and decisions in an unconscious manner. These biases, which encompass both favorable and unfavorable assessments, are activated involuntarily and without an individual's awareness or intentional control. Residing deep in the subconscious, these biases are different from known biases that individuals may choose to conceal for the purposes of social and/or political correctness. Rather, implicit biases are not accessible through introspection."[3]

To be clear, implicit bias is unconscious, but implicit bias does have consequences, not least of which are strained patient–provider relationships and clinical outcomes. In many situations, patients are able to pick up on a provider's implicit bias, and patients often report a poor experience as a result. A patient who picks up on a provider's implicit bias may feel less inclined to adhere to the recommended care plan. Implicit bias could limit how well a patient understands her own health or is invited to engage in her care. For example, some providers may limit the depth of shared decision making or explanations of medical concepts because their implicit bias tells them a patient does not have the health literacy to fully engage with her care. This, coupled with some implicit biases that tell providers a patient may not be able to afford specialty care, can decrease the odds a patient gets the depth of medical care she might need.

One example of how this plays out in North America is disparities in maternal and child health that have led to persistent and devastating outcomes for black women and babies. Recent media coverage has uncovered the impact of bias, racism, and discrimination in and out of the healthcare system, noting for example that black women in the highest education, income, and wealth groups have worse maternity outcomes than white women on the lowest end of the socioeconomic strata.[4]

Research also demonstrates that racial and ethnic minorities and women are subject to less accurate diagnoses, curtailed treatment options, less pain management, and worse clinical outcomes. This is true even within the four walls of the healthcare system, when external factors would not be expected to play a major role.

The Harvard Implicit personality test (https://implicit.harvard.edu/implicit/takeatest.html), developed 20 years ago, allows you to assess your own biases with tests measuring biases on skin-tone, race, weight, gender, sexuality, disability, and age. Taking this time to open your eyes to your own unconscious bias will go a long way to building empathy for those you hope to serve.

HOW DOES BIAS SKEW DATA?

Healthcare systems use algorithms to guide clinical decision making processes. These machine learning algorithms look at data about how decisions were made in the past and use that data to make future decisions. Unfortunately, this can have the unintentional consequence of perpetuating health disparities because the data used to develop the algorithm reflects historic biases.

AI algorithms that were trained with data that do not represent the whole population often perform worse for underrepresented groups. For example, algorithms trained with gender-imbalanced data do worse at reading chest x-rays for an underrepresented gender, and researchers are concerned that skin-cancer detection algorithms, many of which are trained primarily on light-skinned individuals, do worse at detecting skin cancer affecting darker skin.[5]

A study published in *Science Magazine* found that a healthcare risk-prediction algorithm, a tool used on more than 200 million people in the United States, demonstrated racial bias because it relied on health costs for determining need. Historically, less money is spent on black patients who have the same level of need, and the algorithm made the faulty conclusion that black patients are healthier than equally sick white patients. This resulted in black patients with high-risk health needs not receiving the additional specialized care which white patients at the same risk level were recommended to receive.[6]

Given the consequences of an incorrect treatment recommendation or withholding necessary treatment, eliminating bias in high-stakes medical AI algorithms needs to be a priority. This is a complex issue requiring a holistic approach to train algorithms with data sets drawn from diverse populations, frame questions which include the perspectives of minority populations, and build an inclusive workforce of developers and data analysts to work with the algorithms.

DIGITAL DIVIDE

The gap between those with Internet access and those without is called the Digital Divide. It's a serious roadblock for the healthcare industry as it leaves rural and portions of urban communities and poor populations behind.

Although a majority of underserved communities do have access to mobile phones, they still lack consistent access to Internet service. Sometimes Internet service providers won't cover those regions; other times the access is there, but residents can't afford the necessary data plans to use it.

According to bankmycell.com website, it is estimated that more than 5 billion people across the globe have mobile devices, and approximately 3 billion of these connections are smartphones—44.87% of the world's population. But the benefits of smartphones hinge on reliable Internet connection, and Nielsen Online reports 43.2% of the world's population doesn't use the Internet due to connectivity issues and a lack of modern technology. In the United States, the Federal Communications Commission (FCC) reports that 31% of American rural households still lack access to broadband Internet an according to the National Digital Inclusion Alliance website, about one-fourth of the large and medium-sized cities in the United States, more than a third of all households still don't have a wireline broadband Internet connection.

Digital health solutions such as telehealth and remote patient monitoring are dependent on reliable broadband access to extend access to care. Yet, patients without Internet access are also likely to lack specialist care and medical expertise in their community—making them the ones who need telemedicine the most. Hence, a technology solution that may reduce inequity is hindered by a lack of necessary infrastructure.

HEALTH LITERACY AND CULTURAL COMPETENCY

Along with geographic location and income level, health literacy plays a significant role when it comes to explaining the digital divide and differences in technological use in most countries.

The U.S. Department of Health and Human Services (HHS) defines health literacy as "the degree to which individuals have the capacity to obtain, process, and understand basic health information needed to make appropriate health decisions."

Underserved populations require assistance navigating complex health systems in order to make informed healthcare decisions. Some patients may struggle to provide accurate medical histories or complete complex medical forms without assistance. Low health literacy intensifies communication barriers between patients and healthcare providers which may lead to a variety of negative health outcomes. The impact of poor health literacy may affect adherence to treatments or medication dosing and has been shown to cause an increase in the use of emergency departments.

A number of factors may influence an individual's health literacy, including living in poverty, education, race/ethnicity, age, and disability. Some of the greatest disparities in health literacy occur among racial and ethnic minority groups from different cultural backgrounds and those who do not speak English as a first language. Results from the National Assessment of Adult Literacy demonstrated that Hispanic adults have the lowest average health literacy scores of all racial/ethnic groups, followed by black and then American Indian/Alaska Native adults. People with low health literacy and limited English proficiency are twice as likely as individuals without these barriers to report poor health status.[7]

To address poor health literacy, healthcare teams must adjust their communication style and incorporate language which is more broadly understood. Healthcare systems should ensure translators are accessible and work to attract culturally competent providers who speak the patient's native language and are knowledgeable of cultural norms which are pertinent to care. Other supplemental resources such as videos and pictures can be utilized to increase understanding and educate patients to ensure they comprehend their diagnosis, understand medication directions, and know how to locate providers and services.

EMPATHY AND USER-CENTERED DESIGN

Taking the time to understand the root causes of health inequities and the challenges underserved populations experience is a good first step in building empathy. Practicing empathy, "the ability to understand and share the feelings of another", can help healthcare providers become more aware of their own implicit bias and play a valuable role in building trust with underrepresented communities resulting in more accurate and informed clinical assessments and improved health outcomes.

Empathy is a core component of user-centered design which involves the end-user of a product in every stage of the design process and has been identified as essential in creating accessible products which meet the needs of a diverse, cross-cultural audience. Employing user-centered design processes in the design of digital health solutions for underserved communities is a significant step forward in addressing health disparities. At its core, the purpose of healthcare technology is to improve clinical decision making, remove barriers to access, and improve health outcomes. In order to successfully achieve this aspirational goal, user-centered design needs to become a best practice.

When technology is designed to meet the needs of the most vulnerable populations, there are major benefits upstream. Today, unfortunately, the inverse is true. We have primarily designed solutions to address the needs of our least vulnerable patients and have left a vast percentage of the world's population behind.

Engaging underserved communities in the user-centered design of digital health solutions and leading with empathy provides safeguards to ensure development teams address unconscious bias, health literacy, the digital divide, and social determinants of health to create solutions which truly reduce barriers to health and healthcare (Figure 33.2). Figure 33.2

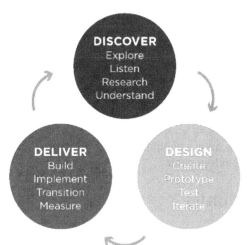

FIGURE 33.2   Human-centered design process (University of Vermont Medical Center).

Source: https://medium.com/design-uvmmc/bringing-human-centered-design-to-healthcare-5d8ede2aee3b.

VULNERABLE POPULATION: SENIORS

One specific vulnerable population are seniors. It is estimated that by 2050, people over 65 will represent more than 20% of the population; those who are 85 and older are the fastest growing segment. For the first time in history, people over 85 will outnumber children younger than five years of age[8]. This "silver tsunami" is expected to put tremendous stress on the healthcare system and workforce as they have a large number of chronic conditions which accumulate with age.

As we approach the "silver tsunami", there are focused efforts to improve healthy aging and mitigate the stress on systems and caregivers with digital health solutions designed to care for seniors and aimed at providing options for "ageing in place".

As government payers and providers quickly understood the challenges associated with caring for the aging population, the industry looked for ways to address challenges with technology. Unfortunately, too few employed user-design best practices and simply attempted to use technology which already existed to meet the needs of a population for whom technology isn't intuitive. This generation did not grow up with technology and the impact of ageing on vision, hearing, dexterity, and digital literacy were not originally considered in the design of solutions.

User-design is now more commonly utilized in creating innovative solutions to address the specific needs of caregivers and seniors, including the use of voice-activated technology which has been demonstrated as a preferred method of engagement by seniors and a good solution for families to engage with their loved ones.

WORKFORCE

Building a culturally competent, inclusive workforce will help to expand healthcare access for underserved communities and enrich the pool of leaders and policymakers to meet the needs of a diverse population. Acknowledging the importance of cultural competence in improving health outcomes, technology companies and medical schools are employing efforts to attract a more diverse workforce.

Unfortunately, according to the Association of American Medical Colleges, entrance to professional schools by racial minorities has stagnated or in some cases dropped at a time when more diverse physicians and leaders are needed. In an effort to combat this unsettling statistic, tech companies and medical schools are finding private-public partnerships to be instrumental in supporting efforts to engage students from diverse backgrounds in STEM-related fields by establishing relationships with high schools, community colleges, and historically black colleges and universities (HBCUs) and funding scholarships, STEM focused-camps, internships, and the development of curriculum.

CONCLUSION

Innovative approaches to foster multi-sector and cross-cultural collaboration are needed to successfully reduce health disparities and improve health equity. The root causes have existed for centuries and will take time to overcome in order to establish understanding and trust. The path forward will require humility, empathy, honesty, and education and ultimately a desire to see every human, everywhere receive equal access to the best health possible.

STAGGERING STATISTICS ON HEALTH INEQUITIES

Appendix CHART

The figures below have been taken from World Health Organization reports and reports published by the United Nations and can be found at https://www.who.int/sdhconference/background/news/facts/en/

1. Today, there is a 36-year gap in life expectancy between countries. A child born in Malawi can expect to live for only 47 years while a child born in Japan could live for as long as 83 years. In Chad, every fifth child dies before they reach the age of 5, while in the WHO European Region, the under-five mortality rate is 13 out of 1,000. There is no biological or genetic reason for these alarming differences in health and life opportunity.

2. There are significant gaps in health outcomes within countries, too—rooted in differences in social status, income, ethnicity, gender, disability, or sexual orientation. For example in the United States, infants born to African-American women are 1.5 to 3 times more likely to die than infants born to women of other races/ethnicities. American men of all ages and race/ethnicities are approximately four times more likely to die by suicide than females. African-American men in the United States are the most likely, among all ethnic groups in the United States, to develop cancer—a rate of 598.5 per 100,000.

3. Every single day, 21,000 children die before their fifth birthday of pneumonia, malaria, diarrhea, and other diseases. Despite substantial progress in reducing under-five mortality around the world, children from rural and poorer households remain disproportionately affected. Children from the poorest 20% of households are nearly twice as likely to die before their fifth birthday as children in the richest 20%.

4. According to the latest estimates, the number of people living in hunger in the world is over a billion, the highest on record. Half of the world's workers—nearly 1.53 billion people—are in vulnerable employment. These workers do not tend to have formal work arrangements or receive social security and health benefits.

5. Worldwide, about 150 million people a year face catastrophic healthcare costs because of direct payments such as user fees, while 100 million are driven below the poverty line. Even if they could pay, access to doctors would be a challenge. Low-income countries have ten times fewer physicians than high-income countries. Nigeria and Myanmar have about 4 physicians per 10,000, while Norway and Switzerland have 40 per 10,000.

6. In Afghanistan, Somalia, and Chad, the maternal mortality ratio is over 1,000 (out of 100,000 live births) while the same average figure for the WHO European Region is 21. Developing countries account for 99% of annual maternal deaths in the world, with the decline being the slowest in WHO's Eastern Mediterranean and African Regions.

7. About 16 million girls aged 15 to 19 years give birth every year—roughly 11% of all births worldwide. The vast majority of adolescents' births occur in developing countries. Young people, 15 to 24 years old, accounted for 40% of all new HIV infections among adults in

2009. In any given year, about 20% of adolescents will experience a mental health problem, most commonly depression or anxiety.

8. Women in the richest 20% of the global population are up to 20 times more likely to have a birth attended by a skilled health worker than a poor woman. Closing this coverage gap between rich and poor in 49 low-income countries could save the lives of more than 700,000 women between now and 2015.

9. The European Parliament has estimated that losses linked to health inequalities cost around 1.4% of GDP within the European Union—a figure almost as high as the EU's defense spending (1.6% of GDP).

REFERENCES

1. Braveman, Paula MD, MPH. 2014. "What Are Health Disparities and Health Equity? We Need to Be Clear". Public Health Report. https://www.ncbi.nlm.nih.gov/pmc/articles/PMC3863701/

2. Riley, Wayne J. MD, MPH, MBA, MACP. 2012. "Health Disparities: Gaps in Access, Quality and Affordability of Medical Care". US National Library of Medicine National Institutes of Health. https://www.ncbi.nlm.nih.gov/pmc/articles/PMC3540621/

3. Heath, Sara. 2020. "What is Implicit Bias, How does it affect healthcare?" Patient Satisfaction News. Xtelligent Healthcare Media. 10/16. https://patientengagementhit.com/news/what-is-implicit-bias-how-does-it-affect-healthcare

4. Villarosa, Linda. 2018. "Why America's Black Mothers and Babies are in a Life of Death Crisis". New York Times. 4/11. https://www.nytimes.com/2018/04/11/magazine/black-mothers-babies-death-maternal-mortality.html

5. Kaushal, Amit, Altman, Russ, Langlotz, Curt. 2020. "Health Care Ai Systems Are Biased". Scientific American. 11/17. https://www.scientificamerican.com/article/health-care-ai-systems-are-biased/

6. Obermeyer, Ziad, Powers, Brian, Vogeli, Christine. 2019. "Dissecting racial bias in an algorithm used to manage the health of populations". Science Magazine. 10/25. https://science.sciencemag.org/content/366/6464/447

7. U.S. Department of Health and Human Services, Office of Disease Prevention and Health Promotion. National action plan to improve health literacy. Washington (DC): Author; 2010. https://www.healthypeople.gov/2020/topics-objectives/topic/social-determinants-health/interventions-resources/health-literacy

8. Das, Reenita. 2015. "A Silver Tsunami Invades the Health of Nations". Forbes. 8/11. https://www.forbes.com/sites/reenitadas/2015/08/11/a-silver-tsunami-invades-the-health-of-nations

34 Applied Artificial Intelligence and Machine Learning: The Impact on the Health Informatics Workforce

Tom Lawry

CONTENTS

LEARNING OBJECTIVES

1. Explore the rise of intelligent health systems and the rise of intelligent health systems.
2. Identify the expanding role of informatics and technology leaders with technologies like applied artificial intelligence and machine learning.
3. Examine the skills and competencies needed to thrive in the world of intelligent health.

INTRODUCTION

Artificial intelligence (AI) is pervasive in our daily lives and will disrupt the world of health and medicine in ways not thought possible even a few years ago. In a world of "intelligent everything" there will be no room in the future for unintelligent health.

DOI: 10.4324/9780429398377-40

What if we could detect heart disease in a single heartbeat? How about unlimited, AI-assisted virtual health consults for one dollar a visit? Sound like AI hype? It's not. Transformative health services are happening now.[1,2] They're driven by restless individuals and organizations unwilling to accept the status quo in health.

Such change could not come at a better time. Clinical and health leaders today are faced with an unrelenting set of challenges: Ever-expanding medical capabilities. Constrained resources and staff shortages. An increasingly diverse mix of patients and consumers whose needs only grow. Merely getting better with the tools we have is not going to deliver the results we need.

The COVID-19 pandemic unexpectedly challenged many aspects of the health delivery system. It also demonstrated two important points. It showed us that the healthcare industry is capable of agile transformation when needed and that AI can be deployed in ways that are very real and impactful in a short period of time.

It is against this backdrop that a different model is emerging with AI that will eclipse current systems in delivering on the promises we make every day: to improve health while delivering greater value. To provide highly personalized experiences to health consumers. To restore clinicians to be the caregivers they want to be rather than the data entry clerks we're turning them into by forcing them to use systems and processes conceived decades ago.

Along with this change comes a new set of challenges and opportunities for informatics and technology professionals. Going forward, AI will require them to expand not only their technical knowledge of AI but also develop new skills to understand and manage a host AI-related change ranging from process improvement to workforce transformation.

AI gives us the ability to harness the power of healthcare's data tsunami to make us better at virtually everything we strive to better at. In this regard, AI will augment much of what we do but will not replace us…Everything about AI in health starts with humans using it to do good.

Today, the move towards AI is starting to take hold within traditional health organizations. Early adopters of AI in health are already seeing benefits. These include increases in informed decision making (46%), cost savings (42%), automating processes (41%), and revenue generation (41%).[3]

A study by Frost and Sullivan reports that AI has the potential to improve healthcare outcomes by 30% to 40% and reduce the cost of treatment by as much as 50% in the next 7 to 10 years.[4]

A key market dynamic that traditional providers of health services must recognize is that AI is also changing the competitive landscape of the industry itself. Ever-expanding AI capabilities and the rise of the intelligent consumer is bringing a new breed of entrants into the health market. They are born as "digital-first" organizations and focus on demolishing historical market boundaries. They move quickly. They are leveraging AI and adopting disruptive strategies with the goal of delivering better consumer experiences at lower costs.

THE RISE OF INTELLIGENT HEALTH SYSTEMS AND THE EXPANDING ROLE OF INFORMATICS AND TECHNOLOGY LEADERS

Looking ahead the use of AI within health systems to improve clinical and operational performance will become pervasive. At the same time, the demands and expectations of health consumers to make their experiences fully digital will continue. The combination of these and other forces will give rise to Intelligent Health Systems.

Unlike traditional health systems that may make sporadic use of AI, Intelligent Health Systems will emerge by making better use of data and a growing array of AI-powered tools and apps to redefine how services are delivered across *all touchpoints, experiences and channels*.

Intelligent Health Systems will take new approaches to overcoming the age-old challenges of improving access, quality, effectiveness, and costs of health services. They will do this by being faster and smarter than similar organizations in making use of AI-enabling technologies, ubiquitous connectivity, and smart devices and systems. The end results will be designed to not only benefit patients and health consumers, but also focus on improving clinical and operational performance.

Critical to the success of Intelligent Health Systems will be a new breed of informatics professionals and technology leaders. Their skills and experiences will be critical to success in planning, deploying, and managing AI-driven solutions and processes that serve as the backbone for Intelligent Health.

Future roles will require not only an expanded knowledge of the technical side of AI systems, but also a broader understanding and skillsets in leading organizational change efforts on which the success of AI systems is dependent. These include developing expertise and experience in leading or influencing clinical and operational automation, workforce skilling, data governance, managing modern, cloud-based data estates, and a new set of evolving regulatory and ethical issues.

Today most informatics and technology leaders understand and are excited about the opportunities to use AI and smart systems to drive systemic change in keeping with the mission and goals of their organization. At the same time there is a growing recognition that most organizations, and their staffs, are not adequately prepared for the industry disruptions that lie ahead.

AI will not only change the way in which healthcare works, it will require informatics and technology leaders to reevaluate skills and experiences as well as redefine the roles they play in guiding their organizations in areas that are not typically found in an informatics leader's job description.

As you consider your own career path, planning for the future starts with understanding these broad trends.

RECOGNIZE THAT AI IS DIFFERENT THAN ANY OTHER TECH TREND YOU HAVE SEEN OR MANAGED

The first thing to recognize about AI is that it creates a true paradigm shift in how data and IT systems add value. Up until now, information technology has mainly served as static data repositories that tell us something about the past and possibly the present.

Historically we have created value with these systems by dipping our "data ladle" into many pools of information. Once we "retrieve" data we then use our human capacities to evaluate the data and make decisions on everything from diagnoses and treatment recommendations to a range of decisions affecting operational and financial performance.

AI upends this model. As technology that mimics human functions like vision, speech, and cognition comes into play, it is moving us to a future state where machines act more like humans. It also means that humans act less like machines in performing lower value, repetitive tasks. This blurring of the lines between humans and computers to perform tasks and predict things serves as the basis for dramatic transformation. As this happens, it requires informatics processionals and technology leaders to understand and help health organizations address a variety of issues.

The core value of AI is in how it allows us to rethink and automate virtually all clinical, operational, and financial processes and activities. When done right, the use of AI removes the shackles of repetitive activities to empower knowledge workers to perform at their highest value. It also creates new opportunities to serve health consumers in ways that are more personalized and efficient. It is this single dynamic that sets AI apart from other technology breakthroughs and requires leaders to reexamine all aspects of how services are provided.

Another critical factor driving AI and intelligent health forward is what is happening in the rest of the world. The rise of intelligent consumers and their expectations is a reality. The question is not whether intelligent systems are becoming the norm, but rather how the health industry will adapt and keep up with the revolution that is already occurring.

Consumers and businesses expect smart systems to make their lives better. According to data from Accenture, consumers and patients are already six times more likely to view AI as having a positive impact in the delivery of health services. This makes AI a competitive differentiator when it comes to acquiring patients and building loyalty.[5]

A tectonic shift in how health services are delivered is coming as AI allows technology to mimic human functions. As the roles between machines and humans begins to blur, it gives us the opportunity to reimagine the health consumer and patient experience while rethinking and re-working most aspects of clinical and operational workflows.

HEALTHCARE'S 'DATA TSUNAMI' IS THE NEW CURRENCY FOR AI AND INTELLIGENT HEALTH

AI needs, feeds, and thrives on data. From clinical records, diagnostic images, to the "digital exhaust" produced by consumers as they complete others digital activities, data from all sources are valuable assets to be used in creating intelligent health services.

In the emerging world of intelligent health systems, data is the new currency by which health organizations will rise or fall. How your organization curates and manages a modern data estate will be as strategically important as how it manages its financial and operational assets.

In many regards, creating and managing a modern data estate that supports enterprise-wide AI is different than traditional information management.

For example, Electronic Health Records (EHRs) were a major breakthrough in the past few decades in how data is curated, stored, and used. They ushered in a new approach to making better use of information collected in the care process. The value proposition, however, has historically been in making data more accessible. Data was no longer tethered to a single, physical master copy of a medical record. Instead, it became available in digital form to all with access privileges.

While the benefit of EHRs shifting information from paper to a digital format was important, this move was akin to freezing water. When frozen, water takes on a different form, but its underlying elements remain the same.

Today massive amounts of data are available and growing at an exponential rate in healthcare. This includes all the data you manage today plus a growing array of data that greatly expands the capabilities of AI systems to help clinicians be better at all aspects of health and medicine. These new data include Social Determinants of Health (SDOH), cloud-based disease registries, genomics, environmental, and a variety of structured and unstructured data that, when combined, greatly expand the capabilities and impact AI has on improving virtually all aspects of the health and medicine.

For example, the magnitude and explosive growth of medical knowledge and patient information is outpacing the human capacity to keep up and assimilate this intelligence into meaningful form in the daily practices of a clinician. In 1950, a newly minted physician going into practice would go 50 years before seeing the body of medical knowledge double. By 2010, medical knowledge was doubling every 3.5 years. Today it is likely doubling every 73 days.[6]

Despite the torrents of valuable data available, many organizations remain behind the curve in harnessing its use. Cross-industry studies show that on average, less than half of an organization's structured data is actively used in making decisions. Even worse is that less than 1% of its unstructured data is analyzed or used at all. More than 70% of employees have access to data they should not. Data breaches are common. Rogue data sets propagate in silos. As the complexity of security and compliance grows, many organization's data technology or cloud strategies are not up to the demands put on them.[7]

A contributing factor to these issues is that data has traditionally been perceived as just one aspect of technology projects rather than being treated as organizational assets. As a result, the belief has been that traditional application and database planning efforts were sufficient to address ongoing data issues. In the world of AI and Intelligent Health, they are not.

For AI to create the value necessary to move health organizations forward there must be a recognition and actions that treats all data as a strategic asset. Historically, health organizations have used analytics to optimize existing sources of value, rather than leveraging data and analytics to innovate and create new value. Creating new value is what AI is all about. This requires treating data as an asset, just like capital and human resources.

AI IS THE NEW UI FOR HEALTH

In the world of software and digital solutions the term *User Interface,* or UI, describes the way or manner in which a user engages or interacts with a system. Think about the apps on your phone or computer that do this well. Now think about apps and websites that increase your blood pressure as you try and get something done with a UI that is neither intuitive, convenient nor personalized. With this concept in mind, consider how easy or difficult your organizational interfaces make it for today's consumers to utilize your services.

For example, in a recent survey of health consumers by Change Healthcare and the Harris polling organization, over half reported that finding, accessing, and paying for healthcare requires so much work that they avoid seeking care. Nearly all said they want shopping for healthcare to be as easy as shopping for other common services—including making it a fully connected digital experience.[8]

It is a useful exercise to apply the UI concept to how patients and consumers interact with your organization today. How might the application of AI plus intelligent processes and systems be used to improve your organization's "UI" for patients, clinicians, and staff?

In the world today, products, services, and surroundings are increasingly customized with data and AI to cater to the individual. The challenge and opportunity in healthcare is to reimagine the existing processes and touchpoints we run consumers, clinicians, and staff through every day.

SKILLS AND COMPETENCIES TO THRIVE IN THE WORLD OF INTELLIGENT HEALTH

Beyond understanding the impact of the broad trends noted above, your career development plan should take into account the role you will play in the transformation of healthcare itself. Beyond the honing of your technical and managerial expertise should also be a recognition that Intelligent Health Systems will be built by those who are prepared to think differently about how AI will drive changes to clinical and operational processes along with a laser focus on improving the experience for consumers, clinicians and staff.

With this in mind, career success will require the following skills and characteristics:

DEVELOP YOUR AI ACUMEN BY RECOGNIZING THAT AI IS ONE THING AND MANY THINGS

The terms *artificial intelligence* and *AI* are often bandied about as if there is a singular definition that is universally understood. In reality, AI is not one technology. A simple Google search of "What is AI?" turns up 4.3 billion results.

AI is an umbrella term that includes multiple concepts and technologies used individually and in combination to add intelligence to computers and machines. It is important to broadly understand AI and the various components used to develop applications and solutions. Recognize though that it is virtually impossible to develop deep expertise in all aspects of AI as the breadth of the subject is broad and constantly evolving.

To effectively plan and lead your organization's AI strategy it's important to have a general understanding of what it is. This includes having a framework for how the "components" and "capabilities" that exist that can be used in defining, building, and managing intelligent systems and how to put them to work in service of your organization's mission and goals.

BECOME A PLANNING VISIONARY

Effectively managing the introduction and pursuit of AI-driven transformation starts with defining a vision and then backing it up with razor-sharp clarity about the new market demands, future operating models, the rationale for why change is needed, and how successful systems will be developed and deployed. While this overall charter is the responsibility of a larger team, your skillset for understanding things like market trends plus your technical expertise are an important combination to ensure you have a seat at the table.

Planning visionaries do well when they focus on the end results. Move your focus to the end. As organizations begin to understand the many options for AI-driven transformation, they quickly realize that have more opportunities than they can pursue. Success means you have planning skills to carefully choose the specific opportunities your organization will want to target. Just as important is helping your organization decide which opportunities not to target. With these things in mind your planning process will work backwards to determine how to get started.

STRATEGICALLY AMBIDEXTROUS

Large-scale change and disruption are on the horizon as you move people and the organization into the next phase of intelligent health. Successful informatics and technology leaders understand this, and lead organizations to pursue a dual strategy. This includes supporting core service technology and data that exist today while actively investing in AI solutions that seed new growth opportunities in keeping with market and consumer demands. This pursuit of "two journeys" sets an organization in a new direction while recognizing that a transition period is needed accommodate the move to new processes and ways of doing business.

CUSTOMER OBSESSED

Shifting expectations are pushing health organizations to improve the consumer experience across all touch points. Excellence in one area is not sufficient as consumers expect the same frictionless experience across all interactions and touch points.

An obsession with improving the consumer experience is foundational to the success in creating an intelligent health system. Informatics and technology leaders should aspire to evaluating and fixing every error or bad experience. Customers in this case include your existing patients, consumers in the markets you serve, your clinicians, employees, and referral sources.

INTERNAL EVANGELIST

An important determinant in early success for enterprise-wide AI and intelligent health is how effectively you bring everyone along in the move to reinvent the organization.

An important factor for driving cultural change and stimulating new growth is having all employees and constituents understand what is happening and why it is their interest as well as the organizations to embrace the change that is occurring through AI. In this regard, an important role of informatics leaders is to be effective storytellers. While professional communications staff (HR, PR, marketing) can support the packaging and positioning of change, informatics and technology leaders must be on the frontlines to effectively communicate the "what and why" messages surrounding AI transformation.

AGILE ADAPTABILITY

Informatics and technology leaders must be prepared to think differently about how AI and intelligent systems change clinical, operational processes and be prepared to drive change.

If you work in a traditional health system, your role in part will be to help lead efforts that challenge the status quo rather than accepting historical norms. Assume there is an unknown company looking to enter the health space asking the exact same question as it plots to disrupt your organization's business or referral patterns. It is no coincidence that many textbook cases of companies redefining themselves come from Silicon Valley, the epicenter of digital disruption.

TECH AND DATA ENABLED

AI done right will impact the organization's entire value chain. It will do this by taking different shapes and forms in different areas. Informatics and technology leaders will need to invest in the right talent and a full set of AI tools and solutions. Additionally, leaders must understand that the technologies and the market are changing and should be prepared to keep up with rapid advancements.

CHARTING YOUR CAREER COURSE

Preparing for and navigating through the change brought about by AI is a key element in charting out your career progression. While some take a narrow a view of AI by relegating it to being just another technical improvement to be managed, the difference of intelligence being imbued into smart systems and its ability to help move towards becoming an Intelligent Health System requires informatics professionals and technology professionals to think and act differently. Successful leaders will leverage AI to create new approaches in which an organization's activities, people, culture, and structure are aligned with the new expectations of the market.

Whether you are a new grad, a "midcareer" millennial, or in "wind-down" mode, it is a sure bet that AI will impact your work and career. The question is not whether AI will reshape the workplace and your role as an IT professional. Instead the most important question for informatics and technology leaders to consider is how to successfully transition your skills and experience to help lead the change that is coming.

From global health organizations to clinical divisions within a hospital and new entrants to the health sector, intelligent health systems will come in all sizes and shapes. The glue binding them together will be informatics and technology leaders who understand and successfully leverage AI to address changing market and consumer demands.

While no one has a crystal ball to predict exactly what will happen, one thing is certain. As health organizations are increasingly AI-enabled, your value to your employer and profession will increase was you become a pivotal role in the transformation of healthcare.

Paul Daugherty is Chief Technology and Innovation Officer at Accenture and author of a great book about the interplay and impact of AI and humans, aptly called *Humans + Machines*. Based on research drawn from how AI can strengthen productivity, enable innovation, and increase efficiency, Daugherty thinks that one of the biggest problems with AI today is the belief that AI will make human jobs redundant, while missing the key point that when done right AI will make our working life better.

Smart informatics and technology leaders in health recognize that the goal of AI is not to replace people with machines but rather how to bring the two together in an effective collaboration that drives success. Or as Daugherty sums up the opportunity: *"Humans plus machines equals superpowers."*

CONCLUSION

As applied AI and machine learning revolutionize the way healthcare data is analyzed and delivered, health informatics professionals must engage in lifelong learning to continually develop professionally by maintaining a passion for leveraging the power of reasoning, knowledge representation, planning, learning, natural language process, and other methods. By doing so, health informatics professionals can positively affect the health informatics workforce by enhancing efficiencies, reducing risk, increasing value, improving outcomes, and reducing clinical variation through the use of technologies such as applied AI and machine learning.

NOTES

1 Mihaela Porumb, Ernesto Iadanza, Sebastiano Massaro, Leandro Pecchia, A convolutional neural network approach to detect congestive heart failure, Biomedical Signal Processing and Control Journal, 2019.
2 ANNE D'INNOCENZIO and TOM MURPHY, Walmart's Sam's Club Launches Health Care Pilot to Members, AP Business Writers, 2019, https://www.usnews.com/news/us/articles/2019-09-26/walmarts-sams-club-launches-health-care-pilot-to-members
3 https://www.infosys.com/smart-automation/Documents/ai-healthcare.pdf
4 Artificial Intelligence—Top 10 Applications in Healthcare, Global, 2018–2022, Frost and Sullivan, April 2019.
5 Weber Shandwick, "AI-Ready or Not: Artificial Intelligence Here We Come!," https://www.webershandwick.com/news/article/ai-ready-or-not-artificial-intelligence-here-we-come
6 Densen, Peter MD, "Challenges and Opportunities Facing Medical Education." Trans Am Clin Climatol Assoc. 2011: 122: 48–58.
7 Leandro DalleMule, Thomas H. Davenport, What's Your Data Strategy?, Harvard Business Review, 2017, https://hbr.org/2017/05/whats-your-data-strategy
8 2020 Change Healthcare – Harris Poll Consumer Experience Index, July 2020, https://analyze.change healthcare.com/healthcare-consumer-experience-research

35 Establishing and Practicing Ethical Standards: Both a Professional and Personal Responsibility

Craig M. Klugman
Ph.D.

CONTENTS

INTRODUCTION

Siena Health Care Systems is a large midwestern hospital corporation with 4,000 healthcare workers, 12 hospitals, and 200 outpatient clinics that has entered a partnership with Bailey Informatics, a startup company in precision health. Under the terms of the agreement, Bailey makes an annual payment to Siena Health for full access to its patient records. Bailey will use the data to train its proprietary algorithms to better diagnose disease and to make more precise treatment recommendations. Siena hopes to be able to use any resulting artificial intelligence to improve patient outcomes in the future.

This scenario describes collaborations between healthcare institutions and health data companies that have become common over the last decade (Kayyali, Knott, and Kuiken 2013). Patient records include valuable information that can feed the growth of big data initiatives, precision medicine, and artificial intelligence in healthcare. For the healthcare system, the opportunity represents potential revenue as well as the possibility of improving patient outcomes and satisfaction. For informatics companies, the size and depth of the record repository would be impossible to get any other way. While working together would seem to be a win-win from a financial standpoint, these collaborations raise a host of ethical, moral, and legal issues that can affect patient privacy, trust, and autonomy.

Consider that when entering the clinic Siena's patients sign consent forms that say their health information can be used to diagnose and treat them. Did the patients know that their information would also be used for research and product development? Does a broad consent form cover sending personal health information to an outside company? Siena's patients share their private information because the hospital and physicians have a fiduciary responsibility of confidentiality. Bailey is not a covered health entity and therefore has no such legal requirement. If a discovery is made from a patient's record, does that patient get a share of any profits?

DOI: 10.4324/9780429398377-41

This chapter explores ethical issues that arise in health informatics including definitions, explaining why protections in research and patient care exist, and examining codes of ethics and what values they embody. Lastly, this chapter will offer guideposts for holding people in the health informatics field to the highest professional standards.

DEFINITIONS

Good ethics begins with (a) good facts and (b) shared definitions. This chapter begins by defining common terms that are important when working in healthcare: ethics, morality, and law.

Ethics is a branch of moral philosophy that explores how people make decisions regarding right and wrong. Ethics is both (a) the science of morality and (b) the principles and values that guide the behavior of a group of people. More specifically, *bioethics* is the study of moral issues in the life sciences (Reich 1978).

One problem with the term ethics is that even when applied to issues of right behavior, it is used differently in different settings. For example, in government, "ethics" refers to a set of laws that guide action. A lawyer or a politician who violates ethics has actually committed a criminal act because the ethics of that group is ensconced in the civil law. For example, a pharmaceutical company provides a gift of a $15 burrito meal to a judge who is hearing a case to which the company is a party. This is a violation of law (bribery), and the company as well as a judge accepting such an offer may face criminal prosecution.

A physician who violates ethics has violated a standard norm for a group to which they have chosen to belong. Thus, in medicine and health, ethics is not necessarily a legal requirement but a question of what this group of professionals has decided is proper conduct for its members. This standard is often encapsulated in an aspirational set of principles, the code of ethics. A physician who accepts the same burrito from a pharmaceutical company is not violating a law but may be violating ethics. Professional organizations have determined a dollar amount of what is an acceptable gift from companies to doctors that is unlikely to influence their prescribing habits. Some medical schools and hospitals have policies that their faculty, staff, and students cannot accept pharmaceutical company gifts because any amount could compromise their objectivity. The burrito is not a legal matter, but rather an ethical one as determined by the standards of their professional peers.

Morality, on the other hand, is one's personal belief about what is right and what is wrong. This belief system is shared and learned among a group of people. One's notion of right and wrong might be learned from one's family, school, religious leaders, sacred texts, pop culture, and formal study. Morality may not be based in logic and may be part of a larger belief system (e.g., Catholicism, Hinduism, or Islam). Some believe that morality is culturally bound (applies only to a select group of people who share historical beliefs in common), and others hold that morality is universal (what I believe is right applies to everyone, even if they believe differently).

Law is the set of rules that a society establishes for itself to determine what behaviors are permissible and what are not. For almost any possible behavior or action there are people who would find it moral and immoral. In a pluralistic society, it is necessary to develop rules of permissible behavior that recognize varied moral beliefs but provide guidance for all people who live under that government. Some groups and nations believe that law should reflect morality (in the form of say religious belief). Islamic countries that follow Sharia law have agreed to allow their religious morality to form the basis of their laws. Heterogeneous societies, however, often value individual choice and try to allow a wider set of laws as long as they do not harm others. In terms of health, the law represents the minimum that one is required to do.

Consider that some people find HIPAA (a law) to be ethical (in that it meets a professional standard of protecting health information) but others find it morally problematic (many clergy like to visit their congregants in the hospital but HIPAA means that they cannot see who is a patient in a hospital unless that particular patient gives information for that specific clergy to know of their admission). Laws are compromises between the various morals of the citizens.

HISTORY OF ETHICS IN MEDICINE AND RESEARCH

The history of medicine and medical research is replete with violations of patient and subject trust. Bioethics, medical ethics, and research ethics were born out of this abusive history and have led to the regulations and ethical standards that exist today. In 1946, the world witnessed the first trial for crimes against humanity in Nuremberg, Germany. In the Doctor's Trials, 23 German physicians and administrators were accused of performing medical experiments on prisoners without their consent as well as for torturing and abusing them, and of committing mass murder of those the state found "unworthy of life". Sixteen of the doctors were found guilty and sentenced to imprisonment. Seven of them were executed (Leaning 1996). The defendants were charged under the Nuremberg Code, a set of ten principles drawn up by the United States (Shuster 1997).

The first principle says "the voluntary consent of the human subject is absolutely essential" (Shuster 1997). The other nine principles say that the experiment should have an expectation of producing useful results, there should be no other ways of gathering the information, subjects should be protected from physical and mental harm, the benefit should outweigh the risk, staff should be properly trained and credentialed, and the experiment can be ended at any time if the subject withdraws or the researcher believes continuing could harm the subject. These principles have become the worldwide basis of both human subjects research and delivering medical treatment, leading to the development of professional codes of ethics under the World Medical Association's Declaration Of Helsinki (1964) that governs medical research (WMA 2013).

Even though authorship of the Nuremberg Code is American, U.S. researchers have not always abided by them. In 1932, the U.S. Public Health Service began the Tuskegee Study of Untreated Syphilis in the African American Male (a.k.a. Tuskegee Study). This experiment sought to observe the natural progression of syphilis in Tuskegee, Alabama—a poor, mostly Black community. Over 600 men were enrolled in the study (399 with syphilis; 201 without the disease). The men were told that they had "bad blood"—a local folk category of blood-born illnesses that included a number of conditions and infections. The men received a modest death benefit for participation to pay for their burial and received regular check-ups that included spinal taps, which they were told was "treatment". Syphilis is cured by penicillin, which was discovered in 1928 and was standard treatment for this infection by 1947. The subjects were not told about this cure and were actively prevented from getting access to it (Jones 1981). The study ended in 1972 when it was splashed on the front page of most major newspapers after Jean Heller, an Associated Press writer, broke the story (Heller 1972).

The story of Tuskegee led to a Congressional investigation and establishment of the National Commission for the Protection of Human Subjects of Biomedical and Behavioral Research. The Commission's 1978 report—known as the Belmont Report after the name of the conference center in Maryland where members met—established three ethical principles for the conduct of human subjects research in the United States:

- *Respect for persons*—Research subjects have autonomy (the power of self-governance) that must be protected by securing their informed consent. Such agreement requires that potential subjects be told the risks, benefits, alternatives, and the procedures they will undergo. The researcher must be honest and transparent in this informational process. A potential subject/ patient must have the volition to make a choice free of coercion. They must be able to say no without any repercussions to their ability to get or receive healthcare.
- *Beneficence*—Experiments should be designed to minimize harm to subjects and to maximize benefits. Projects should function to provide a benefit to society and individuals. This altruistic perspective means that a project solely focused on profit is ethically problematic. Protecting the potential subject/patient from mental, physical, and data harm is also essential. The health informatics specialist has a positive obligation to take steps to ensure the protection of records and record holders.

- *Justice*—fair distribution of benefits and burdens within a research protocol. This includes not using a population simply because it is convenient. In later interpretations, the idea has come to mean being inclusive in recruiting research subjects (U.S. Department of Health Education and Welfare 1979).

Consider the opening scenario to this chapter that lays out a bioinformatics study using patient medical records. How would Belmont view such a study?

- *Respect for persons*—Have the subject-patients given informed consent to participate in the research? Were they told the risks, benefits, alternatives, what procedures their data would undergo, and been given the opportunity to withdraw from participation? The answer, of course, is no. The subject pool are all patients of Siena Health System and if this fictional study follows the real-life examples on which it was based, the patients were never even informed that their data was being used. Under the federal Common Rule (45 CFR part 46) that regulates human subjects protection, such a study would have had to undergo an institutional review board (IRB or human subjects review committee) to collect new data. However, recent edits to this law allow for the secondary use of anonymized data without getting consent and undergoing IRB review. The revisions also permit the use of broad consent where a patient signs an agreement at the hospital giving permission not only for diagnosis and treatment but often to have any records or specimens used in research (and they likely will not be told about such studies). While the law allows broad consent, such action violates the ethics and standards that patients and subjects expect. Namely, data collected for purposes of diagnosis and treatment is expected to be kept confidential (only shared with people involved in the patient's care).
- The hospital system has a legal and ethical obligation to maintain confidentiality of patient data, but Bailey Informatics is not a "covered entity" (i.e., not a healthcare provider) and thus does not have a legal duty of confidentiality. However, this author holds that they have an ethical duty in order preserve trust with the community and as a partner in the research enterprise. Thus, ethically, using patient data for research purposes should require re-consenting all potential subjects for the use of their data, though such an act could be burdensome. The least that Siena and Bailey can do is to inform their patient-subject population of the project and establish a method for people to withdraw their data from the study.
- *Beneficence*—Can patients be harmed by the transfer of their data to Bailey Informatics? Technically, the data transmitted should be anonymized, but accidents can happen where unintended information is shared. Also hacking is a real possibility when information exists in electronic form. The ethics of beneficence asks what protocols and procedures exist to protect patient identity and information from falling into the wrong hands or being used in untoward ways. Medical information is sensitive information, and many patients do not want others to know of their health conditions. Beneficence also holds that the project needs to have a likelihood of benefit to the community. Thus, a project that merely seeks to produce a marketable product and profit. The goal must be to improve patient outcomes because that may also include a potential benefit to the subjects.
- *Justice*—As originally conceived, justice as an attempt to ensure a sharing of benefits and burdens. For example, if a drug was tested on an impoverished population but the drug will only be affordable by the wealthy, then all of the risk is being taken by a group that will not benefit. More modern interpretations hold that the subject population must be diverse in terms of sex, age, ethnicity, and socioeconomic status. One of the problems that has haunted most informatic projects is that the work is based on limited datasets that do not represent the population at large (O'Neil 2016). In terms of informatics, data is often taken from the people who are easily available (i.e., those who work in tech). That workforce is

overwhelmingly male and Caucasian or Asian (Harrison 2019). An unjust dataset will lead to conclusions and algorithms that are not generally accurate. The data from Siena Health is partially a corrective to this problem since its information is likely broader and more diverse than a convenience sample. But such diversity is not guaranteed since communities of color and impoverished neighborhoods can be near the hospital (Gaskin et al. 2012). Thus, only gaining the records from a single hospital system or even in a single geographic location will not necessarily eliminate bias. The informatics professional needs to be aware of the bias in selecting data sources.

PROFESSIONALISM AND CODES OF CONDUCT

In the sphere of medicine and health, ethics may seem more stringent than in other areas of human endeavor. The reasons are twofold: (1) The potential for harm (morbidity and mortality) is high and (2) healthcare workers are professionals who have extraordinary moral obligations. A profession is "an occupation that regulates itself through systematic, required training and collegial discipline; that has a base in technical, specialized knowledge; and that has a service rather than profit orientation enshrined in its code of ethics" (Starr 1982, 15) The original professions (medicine, law, and clergy) grew out of the medieval guilds whose purpose was to protect their practitioners and their livelihood. Professions have a monopoly on working in a specific area or providing certain services. For example, only a lawyer who has passed the bar and holds a license may practice law. Only a physician who has passed a series of exams and holds a medical license may cut into a human being (if someone else did this they would be arrested for committing a battery or a murder if things did not go well). The state offers this monopoly in exchange for the profession setting standards of excellence and self-policing its members.

Professions exist to benefit patients and clients, not the practitioner. Thus, professions are often considered to be a calling (rather than a job) and require a substantial amount of adult education, passing exams, and licensure that is controlled by the profession (e.g., a state board of medicine that grants licenses is staffed by doctors) and has a code of ethics. The reason for this high level of accountability and responsibility is the necessity of gaining and keeping the public's trust. In 1847, the very first act of the newly founded American Medical Association was to pass an ethics code. Since then, other trades that have aspired to be professions have passed similar codes of ethical conduct for its members. Such codes bind members to particular conduct and to accept investigation and punishment by their peers if the code is violated.

In the field of health informatics, two professional organizations have crafted codes of ethics to guide behavior. The goal of both of these codes is (a) to establish the profession of health informatics and (b) to engender trust with the public. The American Health Informatics Management Association code of ethics begins:

> *The ethical obligations of the health information management (HIM) professional include the safeguarding of privacy and security of health information; appropriate disclosure of health information; development, use, and maintenance of health information systems and health information; and ensuring the accessibility and integrity of health information (AHIMA 2019).*

The specific principles of the code include putting the customer first, putting the interest of others first, preserving confidentiality, mentoring, using technology and information wisely, and honesty. One of the goals is to work for the good reputation of the profession, ensuring trust and that health informatics is seen as a benefit rather than as a danger.

The International Medical Informatics Association also has a code of ethics which focuses on the field's obligations to society. The IMIA code includes principles of ethics such as autonomy, equality/justice, beneficence, non-malfeasance, impossibility, integrity, privacy, openness, security, access, accountability, and the least intrusive alternative principle (Kluge 2016). This code protects the record holders and healthcare workers by ensuring that they know how, where, and by whom their information is being used. The emphasis is on protecting the data and furthering social interests.

Is Bailey Informatics following these codes of ethics? Is the point of this project to provide a benefit to the community and patients or is it solely to make money for the company and the hospital? Have all safeguards been taken to protect privacy and security? Have patients been informed about the use of their records, and what actions have been taken to ensure data security? Is there built-in accountability such as a plan to inform patients if the system is hacked, or to let them know if new information that affects their health is found? Have patients been informed about who owns the records and the data? Have patients been asked for informed consent or is that covered under any broad consent they previously signed? Do patients have opportunity to withdraw their record from participation? Have the credentials and history of Bailey Informatics been shared with patients? Considering that not all companies succeed, what is the plan for the records if Bailey Informatics goes out of business? The brief scenario does not allow us to answer these questions, but the codes of ethics require they be answered before the project commences.

PROFESSIONAL VIRTUES

Beyond a code of ethics, professions are guided by virtues—traits or characteristics associated with being a good person, or in this case, with being a good health informatics professional. The virtues are aspirational and as we practice them, they come a habit and part of our character. For instance, *confidentiality* is a fiduciary responsibility to keep a person's secrets private. In medicine, private details are shared to help the healthcare worker to diagnose and treat the patient. In research, private details are shared to contribute to data and someday improve people's lives. In both cases, this virtue requires protecting a person's identity as well as health details that if released could cause negative consequences to their life.

Health informatics professional should uphold *accountability* and *security*. The professional is expected to use the highest standards of data protection to thwart hacking and to prevent accidental releases of private information. These virtues also demand *transparency*. Ideally, there should be a record of where records are stored, how and when they are used, and who has accessed them. The patient or subject should be able to know their record is being used.

Health informatics professionals must be *truthful* and *transparent*. They should be able to show how the data led to conclusions (instead of simply saying the data is crunched in a "black box" and no one know how it works). Although many big data-dependent systems use proprietary algorithms that are not released to the public (or even necessarily understood by the programmers), the profession should aspire to make these processes transparent and understandable to the people whose records contributed to the project.

Health informatics professionals much recognize data justice. *Data justice* is "fairness in the way people are made visible, represented and treated as a result of their production of digital data" (Taylor 2017). This concept is essential to minimize potential biases in conclusions made from health information. Given that health data reflects structural biases in society, science, healthcare institutions, and individual biases held by healthcare workers and health information professions, information systems may inadvertently reflect and further such biases. Health information is always biased—what information is collected, what questions are asked of whom, what recommendations are made, what tests are run can differ with each person or population. Thus, it is important to actively look for and minimize such biases in data.

Health informatics professionals must be *competent* and honest in representing their credentials to create trust. This requires a dedication to continuing education and gaining skills necessary to do needed work. Additionally, it means representing oneself truthfully to potential employers and to clients.

Health informatics depends on people and institutions trusting them with their data. Society has to trust that the information, algorithms, and advise generated by looking at these big data sets. Without *trust*, the enterprise will cease to exist. Principles outlined in codes of ethics and virtues of practice are essential to creating such trust.

CONCLUSION

Virtues and codes of ethics can be aspirations, or they can be part of the professional and personal character of those who choose a profession. Aristotle says that to know the good and the right is not enough, one must practice it until it becomes a habit and part of their character. To achieve this aim requires deliberative action to understand and practice the ethical behaviors of the profession. This can be achieved through education by making ethics a required part of training programs, certificates, and continuing education. Professionals should practice upholding the values—be an asset and model of the profession—including transparency, supporting autonomy, and promoting diversity and justice. In addition, professions self-monitor; thus, professional organizations must establish mechanisms for enforcement—reporting ethical violations and repercussions for violations. And because the future is unknown and technology and needs change, a professional ethics needs to have a system for revision to respond to new opportunities and challenges.

REFERENCES

AHIMA. 2019. "AHIMA Code of Ethics." The American Health Information Management Association, accessed October11. https://bok.ahima.org/doc?oid=105098#.X4SSyy9h2qA.

Gaskin, Darrell J., Gniesha Y. Dinwiddie, Kitty S. Chan, and Rachel R. McCleary. 2012. "Residential Segregation and the Availability of Primary Care Physicians." *Health Serv Res* 47 (6):2353–2376. doi: 10.1111/j.1475-6773.2012.01417.x.

Harrison, Sara. 2019. Five Years of Tech Diversity Reports—and Little Progress. *Wired*. Accessed October 12, 2020. https://www.wired.com/story/five-years-tech-diversity-reports-little-progress/.

Heller, Jean. 1972. "Syphilis Victims in U.S. Study Went Untreated for 40 Years." *The New York Times*, 1.

Jones, James H. 1981. *Bad Blood*. New York: Free Press.

Kayyali, Basel, David Knott, and Steve Van Kuiken. 2013. *The Big-Data Revolution in U.S. Health Care: Accelerating Value and Innovation*. New York: McKinsey & Co.

Kluge, Eike-Henner W. 2016. Ethics for Health Informations Professionals: The IMIA Code, Its Meaning and Implications. Accessed October 11, 2020. https://imia-medinfo.org/wp/wp-content/uploads/2015/07/Handbook-for-revised-Code-of-Ethics.pdf.

Leaning, Jennifer. 1996. "War Crimes and Medical Science." *BMJ* 313 (7070):1413–1415. doi: 10.1136/bmj.313.7070.1413.

O'Neil, Cathy. 2016. *Weapons of Math Destruction*. New York: Crown.

Reich, Warren T. 1978. Bioethics. In *Encyclopedia of Bioethics*, edited by Warren T. Reich. New York: Free Press.

Shuster, Evelyne. 1997. "Fifty Years Later: The Significance of the Nuremberg Code." *N Engl J Med* 337 (20):1436–1440. doi: 10.1056/NEJM199711133372006.

Starr, Paul. 1982. *The Social Transformation of American Medicine*. New York: Basic Books.

Taylor, Linnet. 2017. "What is Data Justice? The Case for Connecting Digital Rights and Freedoms Globally." *Big Data Soc* 4 (2):6-10. doi: https://doi.org/10.1177/2053951717736335.

U. S. Department of Health Education and Welfare. 1979. "Protection of Human Subjects; Notice of Report for Public Comment." *Fed Regist* 44 (76):23191–23197.

WMA. 2013. Declaration Of Helsinki – Ethical Principles for Medical Research Involving Human Subjects. 2020 (October 12). Accessed August 29, 2021. https://www.wma.net/policies-post/wma-declaration-of-helsinki-ethical-principles-for-medical-research-involving-human-subjects/.

36 Global Workforce Trends of Today: A Health Informatics Perspective

Anne L. Drabczyk
Ph.D.

CONTENTS

LEARNING OBJECTIVES

After reading this chapter the learner will be able to:

- Define global health informatics trends.
- Describe how emergent global health informatics trends inform planning priorities.

INTRODUCTION

You never know where innovation will spark as you move through your professional career. Shortly after publishing a doctoral dissertation, a healthcare professional was asked to speak at an

DOI: 10.4324/9780429398377-42

international symposium in Edinburgh, Scotland. During a meet and greet with colleagues at the conference social, the shoptalk demonstrated a shared vision for the discipline. The passion and commitment to be the best was paramount, even if the policies or procedures differed culturally.

Our collective experience of the Novel Coronavirus underscores the benefits of learning from one another. During the pandemic some countries performed well and others not, but there were lessons learned from both. New abilities were required of essential health workers like securing limited personal protective equipment or navigating restrictive visitation policies. These fresh capabilities had to be incorporated into well-established roles of seasoned professionals. The steep learning curve was met, but what knowledge gained in the midst of the crisis could have been anticipated?

This chapter will explore a day in the life of a health informatics specialist anywhere in the world and how their ambition to excel in their chosen field can be informed by associates. Building awareness of global trends can serve as catalysts for creativity and source ideas from best practices that have been successfully applied in affinity settings, despite the geography. In the rapidly evolving world of technology, analytics, and new devices, health informaticists must envision next steps in order to achieve excellence. Being aware of global trends will enable us to posit and meet the steep learning curves that are ahead for health informatics professionals.

GLOBAL SNAPSHOT: LESSONS LEARNED

An analysis of literature regarding global health informatics trends yields a recurrence of several themes: collaboration, evidence-based outcomes, interoperability, infrastructure cybersecurity, and equity. Selection of the representative cases in this chapter are presented simply as a sample of what individual health informatics specialist might encounter daily. Examining both promising practices and underdeveloped areas within these trends produces insights into lessons learned along the spectrum of the discipline.

COLLABORATION

Focus on health informatics collaborative networks appears frequently across the globe. Given the breadth, depth, and complexity of health informatics, individual practitioners would likely feel limited in trying to solve complex challenges in isolation. Formation of networks that serve as a repository of ideas and an avenue to exchange them was inevitable to offset the seclusion. Being a member of such a community of practice would be an asset in navigating daily tasks; knowing colleagues are facing similar challenges with comparable resources. Collaborative networks can arise from an organization, a region, a country, multiple-countries, or within sub-specialties of health informatics. Having an awareness of existing networks can serve as a resource for any professional striving to meet daily competencies and expand personal capabilities.

eHealth Ireland Ecosystems

One example of an in-country collaborative network is the eHealth Ireland Ecosystems. The term *ecosystem* sounds very organic, like it is a living breathing and evolving entity. Given the moving target that healthcare is today, it seems logical that a system that supports optimization of service would also have to be as fluid. The purpose of the ecosystem is breaking down silos, fostering innovation, creating better patient care, driving economic growth, and of course developing lasting collaborations.

The eHealth Ireland Ecosystem encourages stakeholders to use a common platform to access health information and communicate as a collaborative. Aspects of the eHealth Ireland Ecosystems include a virtual health team that enables access to specialist with a click, case studies that profile promising practices and solutions, and a division called Access to Information and Health Identifiers (A2I-HID). An Information Health identifier (IHI) is a unique number for each patient that can assist with maximizing care of the patient in several ways. Any one of the patient's practitioners or specialist can access the medical record. It is easier to gauge trends in diagnosis and prognosis for that patient, with each interaction in the health system, and a profile is generated. The IHIs are also beneficial to researchers who can access real-time health data in aggregate. The common denominator across all the eIreland Health Ireland platforms is collaboration, and access to the very specialist or information a professional needs to fulfill their daily tasks.

European Union Connected Health Alliance

The eHealthIreland Ecosystem is a member of an even larger collaborative; the European Union Connected Health Alliance (ECHAlliance). The European Union Connected Health Alliance (2019) operates on a global scale targeting 78 countries and 4.4 billion people globally with over 700 member organizations from America, Canada, China, Latin America, Europe the Commonwealth, and Australia. At the heart of the European Union (EU) collaborative opportunity exists several avenues for participation. An assortment of ecosystems on the ECHAlliance website are portrayed as an at-a-glance wheel with resource links that include start-ups, subject matter experts, policy-makers, funders, health and social care communities, insurance companies, higher education, and research outlets. There is even a "pop-up ecosystem" dedicated to COVID-19, so the system is agile and responsive. Another interesting feature of the website is a global map displaying connector sites, and so no matter where a healthcare informatics practitioner is in the world, they can access a regional partner.

Primary Care Practice-Based Research Networks

Much like our colleagues in Ireland and the EU, the United States has a robust collaborative with emphasis on research, through the U.S. Department of Health and Human Service Agency for Healthcare Research and Quality (AHRQ). The AHRQ brings together eight Primary Care Practice-Based Research Networks (PBRN) to share big data sets and make sense of information for real-world health challenges.

It is interesting to note that formation of PBRNs was a bottom-up process in response to the needs of independent practitioners anxious to translate research findings into solutions for their patients. The need was evident because according to Agency for Healthcare Research and Quality (2019) as of August 2020, there are "185 PBRNs representing practices from all 50 states and over 25 countries". PBRNs focus on varied issues from pediatrics, women's health, rural communities, and vulnerable populations. Responding to emergent health needs, new non-traditional partnerships have also been established with dentistry, mental health, and alternative medicine.

Entrée into a collaborative network can be job specific as with PBRNs, country-focused similar to eHealth Ireland, or regional and global like the ECHAlliance, and each holds merit. Meeting multi-stakeholder and sector partners, accessing the latest information and trends, and gaining awareness of innovative projects and business opportunities are just a few of the benefits. Readers will take note that even though the ECHAlliance has origins in the EU, it has branched out globally and is filling a niche. Ecosystems are a trend worth considering and becoming a member of such communities of practice should be a component of one's professional portfolio.

EVIDENCE-BASED OUTCOMES

Another trend that appears globally is evidence-based outcomes. All the data in the world will not mean a thing unless it is applied toward achieving specific objectives and a larger goal. The outcomes help to justify technology, talent, resource, and remain a moral obligation for health informatics professionals. Referred to as real-world data, evidence-based data, or evidence-generated data, gathering evidence from the most basic level of patient care and translating it onto population health will maximize health outcomes. In daily roles as health informaticists generate and gather real-world data. These professionals know that information becomes just one component of the bigger picture connected to the ultimate outcome of a broader view of world health. Real-world data becomes real-world evidence, and we are engaged in evidence-based practice.

National Health System Scotland: Outcomes-Focused Approach

One example of a countrywide approach to maximizing health informatics derives from the National Health System (NHS) Scotland. Launched in 2017, NHS Scotland invested in an outcomes-focused approach rather than simply concentrating on technology. They fixed sights on the practitioner and patient because both would benefit most from a comprehensive approach. The appeal of this tactic translates to "participatory design with stakeholders to understand users' stories and identify the pressure points in care processes where decision support will have maximum effect" (Wales, 2020, 1). Human stories help to frame the data in context and meaning. One of the key tenants of the system is a "shared, open repository of quality assured decision support models, algorithms and content. This will provide a 'once for Scotland' single source of truth for decision support" (Wales, 2020, 3).

Canadian Medical Association: Real-World Data

In contrast to the NHS Scotland approach to harness big data toward improved health outcomes, Canada is still trying to input the data. The Canadian Medical Association held a summit in 2019 to explore findings of a survey on Canadians' perspective of the healthcare system, and online connectedness was an acknowledged weak link. According to the Canadian Medical Association (2019), the nation's online health presence resembled "a puzzle with missing pieces where you can't make out what the picture is". Adding to the truant bits of data were findings that "only about 1% of Canadians report using virtual care or online patient portals... 66% of Canadians over 55 are very concerned about who owns the data". Clearly, these are just a few hurdles to overcome before practitioners can even start gathering real-world health data.

The good news is that the potential for real-world data as a vital component of evidence-based health outcomes is not a hopeless. Encouraging statistics from the survey included that "77% of Canadians felt likely that in 10 years they will have access to and contribute to their complete medical history and be able to share it with their doctor at any time, and 83% felt this would make their life better". With core sentiments that health data will improve health and well-being, the journey toward evidence-based practice is well underway.

The overarching lesson learned about evidence-based outcomes from our colleagues in Scotland and Canada is that data matters, and health information specialist play a vital role in the collection, management, and meaning making of that data. Humanizing the story the data tells, owning the data, like "once for Scotland", and being optimistic about the role health data contributes to overall well-being in the life of those we serve, should inspire us all.

INFRASTRUCTURE AND INTEROPERABILITY

Global attention to infrastructure and interoperability trends are as old as the discipline because they are foundational. When we think of infrastructure, we picture hardware, software, routers, servers, and the very physical plant or facility that houses the mechanics and logistics that enable IT processes. When we think of interoperability, we imagine these systems successfully interfacing and handing off data to be applied to a particular objective or case. Considering these basic assumptions and connections, it is difficult to examine infrastructure and interoperability as separate entities.

The Office of the National Coordinator for Health Information Technology (ONC) is located within the Office of the Secretary for the U.S. Department of Health and Human Services, and is responsible for health information technology (IT) initiatives nationwide. The ONC defines interoperability as being meaningful to the recipients by getting the right data to the right people at the right time. Currently, health information is "not sufficiently standardized to allow seamless interoperability, and it is still inconsistently expressed with vocabulary, structure, and format" (Office of the National Coordinator for Health Information Technology, 2018, 4). As part of a

10 Year Vision to Achieve an Interoperable Health IT Infrastructure ONC offers a number of guiding principles and building blocks to remedy the status.

Surprisingly, one guiding principle is to simplify. Rather than build something new and shiny, work with what is available, within the range of end-user needs and capabilities. Consider the solo rural practitioner versus a metropolitan medical center and how each interfaces with electronic medical records. Both need interoperable systems, but at varied scales. ONC also recommends that the system have built-in "modularity" to be able to adapt as medicine and technology advances. In other words, when we think of interoperability, flexibility should be the watchword with both the starting point and the end goal. Simplicity and suppleness support the concept that is interoperability.

The ONC offers five building blocks that must be meet to assure the nationwide demand for interoperability, and core technical standards and functions is one block. If we reflect on the rural versus urban healthcare provider, finding a way to harmonize the standard and function of an electronic medical record would boost interoperability. Exploring a process of certification for emergent health information products and services is another building block. Supportive regulatory environments provides yet another piece that would lift our current infrastructure standing. Finally, fostering "rules of engagement" regarding authenticating data input and data access, along with privacy and security protections, provides another wedge of building.

As we become aware of the work being done in the United States to advance infrastructure and interoperability, it is helpful to observe global trends. Are concerns around standards, function, language, and meaningful use an independent phenomena or a universal one?

Swiss Personalized Health Network Initiative

An example of a meaningful use approach to interoperability comes from Switzerland in the form of two separate but intertwined initiatives, the Swiss Personalized Health Network Initiative (SPHN), and BioMedIT. The SPHN manages the myriad of health data and patient files stored across the nation's hospitals, and BioMedIT works with researchers and institutes of higher education. The premise of the partnership is that interoperability is a prerequisite for data exchange. According to the Swiss Institute of Bioinformatics (2019) both areas of specialization have the shared objective to "move from fragmented heterogeneous data to a harmonized pool of quality health information, with a range of common standards, and processes".

One way the Swiss have met the objective is through a continuous gap analysis to be sure SPHN and BioMedIT are talking to one another through a single national infrastructure with universal standards. Needs analysis is accomplished through workgroups who identify "driver projects" that fit the national health initiative. Through a rigorous beta-testing process, the focus is kept on top tier health issues that can yield "best-practice toolboxes".

As hospitals gather data, it can be de-identified, encoded, and encrypted to protect the identity of the patient, and then seamlessly transferred to researchers through a BioMedIT node. This connectivity maximizes the profile of healthcare for the country. Each specialty profits from this arrangement. Researchers have tangible data sets of health trends within the country with which to meet their directive. Practitioner's transfer findings onto care of their patients and can make informed diagnosis and treatment recommendations based on innovative science. Arriving at a national standard comes about by reviewing all possible options and then adapting those that will best serve the shared vision. This process has a familiar ring, sounding similar to the ONC premise of simplicity, flexibility, and scalability.

Health Information Exchanges in China

Similar to the SPHN and BioMedIT infrastructure and interoperable scheme in Switzerland, the Chinese are exploring a government-driven approach, Health Information Exchanges (HIE). Working with a pilot project in Xinjin County, the intent is to construct an HIE architecture that could handle basics, such as medical records, referral, telemedicine, public health, and prescription renewals. At face value, this task may not seem too impressive until you realize that the county where the pilot study was launched, Xinjin County, has "198 types of medical and health institution, including eight medical and health institutions at the county level, 11 township public health centers, two community health service centers, 135 village-level medical and health institutions, five private hospitals, and 37 clinics...with 2213 medical staff, many of whom lack advanced computer skills" (Lei et al., 2017, 2). The key to the successful achievement of the first round of basic goals, was government support and leadership at the county level. The teams building and testing the systems met weekly and honestly discussed challenges and potential solutions. The project was faced with the reality that there was insufficient trained health informatics professionals, necessitating ongoing trainings to bolster personnel.

A benefit of the county level or regional HIE was a shared data warehouses, and collecting similar data that is then advanced to the national system. The authors recommended incentivizing healthcare stakeholders that have not yet contributed to the HIE arrangement, especially non-public service providers. For example, medical records are a standard data set exchange, but other records would broaden the data warehouse and enrich analysis capabilities. The next steps include more digitalization and centralization of public health records, lab tests, EKGs, and similar imaging results. Finally, as more provincial HIEs come online, a stronger delineation of roles and responsibilities will be needed to offset the potential for duplication of effort.

As we become aware of how divergent nations manage infrastructure and interoperability challenges, we learn that both components must be considered in tandem. Without solid infrastructure, systems will not be able to interface, even if they speak the same data-language. Our Swiss colleague's foster synergy by melding patient data and research, and our Eastern contemporaries focus on provincial systems feeding into the national system. As health informatics practitioners navigate their roles, regardless of what aspect along the continuum the function, they are connected to a bigger picture.

CYBERSECURITY

A focus on health informatics cybersecurity is another trend that is persistent globally. Cyber vulnerabilities can take many forms including e-mail phishing, hacking of personal medical devices, identity theft, insurance theft, malware and ransomware attacks, and data breach or loss. The cost associated with cyberattacks is high for any business, but it is unacceptable for healthcare because it can put patient's lives at risk. Hacks into university systems, credit card institutions, social networks, and even hospitals have been reported on the news intermittently, and with more frequency. These events likely lead to heightened awareness by cautious consumers, and the health institutions that serve them have to be cyber-vigilant.

Cybersecurity Breaches in Australia

A glimpse into healthcare cybersecurity in Australia revealed, "No community healthcare providers had a dedicated budget for cybersecurity, and only 16% of public hospitals allocate funds specifically to cybersecurity" (Offner et al. 2020, 569). Currently notifiable data breaches across Australia pertain to private providers only and not public health systems, so it is difficult to get an accurate picture of the cybersecurity challenge. Further analysis of cybersecurity in Australia revealed a lack of mandatory reporting of breaches, leaving the system defenseless to remedy for victims, and repercussions for hackers. Policy shifts in the system will be needed to include mandatory reporting laws and consequences. The U.S. Health Insurance Portability and Accountability Act of 1996 (HIPAA) law, for example, dictates mandatory reporting of breaches and penalties are commensurate with negligence. There is also a need to foster a cyber-savvy culture in the healthcare industry and increase funding to improve systems and mitigate breach incidents.

As health information specialist process data throughout their day, awareness of cybersecurity has to be uppermost on mind. We learn from Australia that introduction of policy and laws that are working in other countries could change the trajectory of their current cybersecurity profile.

Knowing that large hospitals are as vulnerable as individuals demonstrates that cyber breaches are not particular about targets, but professionals in the health information field have to be fastidious about deterrents.

EQUITY

The final global trend to be aware of is equity. When we think of equity, or something being equitable, we think of basic human rights such as food, shelter, employment, education, and access to healthcare, as being a fair assumption for all humans. These basic socio-economic markers have to be addressed before individuals have an opportunity to exist, let alone thrive. In this chapter, we have been exploring global trends in digital health, and a common understanding is that patient-centered health information can lead to better outcomes. Health informatics play a vital role in examining equity and the potential for improved health outcomes, but systems have to be in place to enable access and management of the core data necessary for such progress.

Capacity and Training in Latin America

Readers will not be surprised to learn that "Latin America is still recognized as the most unequal region in the world. According to the 2019 Global Multidimensional Poverty Index report by the United Nations Development Programme and the Oxford Poverty and Human Development Initiative, 39 million people in Latin America experience multidimensional poverty" (Curioso, 2019, 1). The economy is fragile, and every socio-economic marker such as housing, adult literacy, and access to healthcare, renders a good portion of the population marginalized. Infrastructure disparities exists with electricity and technology limited or non-existent in rural areas. If ever there was a profile of a region that would benefit from the promise that digital health offers, it is Latin America. However, in addition to the socio-economic and cultural challenges facing Latin America, the World Health Organization (WHO) has identified the shortage of training opportunities for health informatics specialist as an obstacle hindering progress toward the digital health mission. For training to have a positive impact, it has to be accessible, affordable, and meaningful.

Accessibility means being able to obtain that which is desired, and in order to meet the informatics training objective, it has to be within reach. The Pan American Health Organization (PAHO) offers a variety of workshops through a virtual campus format. The basics are covered such as how to access the Internet for research, establish knowledge networks, and manage electronic health records. Several partnerships have been forged to coordinate and fill the training void, including the Open University of Catalonia, Spain, WHO, PAHO, Doctors Without Borders, and the University of Washington in Seattle.

Affordability of training programs in a region with such economic despair seems insurmountable if it were not for outside assistance. The American Medical Informatics Association receives funds from the Gates Foundation to support capacity-building initiatives. The mHealth Alliance, is supported by the Rockefeller Foundation, and is a collaborative to strengthen the digital health objective,

In order for a Latin American health informatics platform to have meaning, it has to be culturally relevant. The region serves an intercultural and multilingual population with diverse socio-economic markers, infrastructures, and needs. Because a one-size-fits-all approach will not have impact, training should include guidance on how to be innovative, flexible, and scalable. For example, one of the PAHO virtual training programs trains on how to fill out a death certificate; both a universal need and one that adds to the dataset for the region. Keeping uniform death records augments morbidity and mortality data, and contributes to the overall health profile in the region.

Bias Potential in Africa

Similar to the socio-economics and cultural sensitivities experienced by Latin American, Africa faces comparable equity challenges toward strengthening its health informatics mission. According to Owouemi et al. (2020) Africa is resource poor with just 39% Internet penetration and less than 30% of facilities on the continent having access to reliable electricity. Given the limited assets to work with, the lesson learned is to work with what is available. One example the authors provide is use of smartphones to track some of the top health issues in country such as recurrent disease outbreaks, maternal and child health challenges, and immunization distributions. Artificial intelligence (AI) algorithms could provide solutions to medical concerns when applied through low-tech and easy to use digital devices, such as smartphones. Smartphone ownership prevalence and low cost make for a feasible foray into AI on the continent.

A cautionary aspect to development of AI-driven systems is awareness of bias potential. When algorithms are designed without being vetted by end-users, bias is possible. Use of datasets that do not represent the population will also lead to biased results. A counter measure to this potential defect is to engage more representatives from the community. Healthcare workers, students, NGOs, and patients themselves could lend voice and vetting to algorithm design and deployment.

Equity is a complex global trend, and manifest in shared realities for marginalized countries, such as Latin America and Africa. As health informatics practitioners, it is edifying to note that progress is being made to level the playing field. Lessons learned from our global colleagues include the power of innovation, such as using phones as mobile platforms, and the possibility of partnerships to enhance training opportunities.

EMERGENT TRENDS INFORMING PLANNING PRIORITIES

It is apparent that the emergent global trends highlighted in this chapter are interconnected. If we visualize health informatics as a blanket and tug on one corner, the opposite corner also shifts. What does this interconnectedness mean to the practitioner as they hold themselves accountable to their daily tasks? It means that we are all under the same blanket, and working together will learn how to prioritize our planning with input from associates, ecosystems, and promising practices. We can adapt, adopt, and scale an innovative idea up or down to meet the customized needs of our constituents.

COLLABORATIVE NETWORKS AND DATA-DRIVEN PATIENT-CENTRIC OUTCOMES

We gained awareness of the power of collaboration, whether the network is a sub-specialty like PBRNs, a single country like eHealth Ireland Ecosystems, or a multi-country alliance such as the EU. Through these supportive networks, we can gain access to subject matter experts anywhere in the world, be inspired, and even secure funding. Such rich resources enable us to focus on our end-users and tailor data to meet the needs of clients. Regardless if the outcomes are for patients in Scotland, or Canada, there is potential in what a data-driven, and network supported system can yield. The next time a health information specialist is tasked with a planning assignment, they know there are vast resources available to them.

INFRASTRUCTURE, INTEROPERABILITY, AND CYBERSECURITY

We learned lessons from Switzerland, China, and Australia regarding the need to pay attention to how systems are built, interact, and can be protected. It is difficult to isolate the life force of data as it is generated and released on its journey, but as professionals, we must be aware of the impact of our actions at every step of the excursion. When prioritizing a plan for infrastructure upgrades, informaticists know to build in failsafe and integration points, otherwise, the architecture will be meaningless.

EQUITY AND SCALABILITY

Equity is present in all the global trends reviewed in this chapter. Without fair and accessible opportunities for collaboration, evidence-based outcomes, functional infrastructure and interoperability, and cyber-vigilance, health informatics risks being inconsequential. It is essential therefore for health informaticists to keep scalability in mind as they prioritize planning objectives for their respective projects, departments, or systems. Start where you are, learn from colleagues, and adapt a best practice to expand to your situation, or render down a larger initiative to one element that suits your needs. Scale your ecosystem to that of just one stakeholder in your sphere, or work toward a full-blown overhaul of how you conduct business. With an equitable playing field, the potential, and possibilities are endless.

CONCLUSION

Readers began this chapter with a nod to the unexpected benefits of keeping an open mind and finding career enhancers in sometimes unlikely places. Awareness of global trends in our discipline inform us of a shared vision for the possibilities that health information contributes to improving health and well-being. Rather than having to learn under pressure in a crisis situation, it makes sense to be proactive in gaining the requisite knowledge to excel in ones' role before calamity strikes.

REFERENCES

Agency for Healthcare Research and Quality. 2019. Practice Based Research Networks: Research in Everyday Practice. https://pbrn.ahrq.gov/ (accessed August 22, 2020)

Canadian Medical Association. 2019. The Future of Connected Health Care Reporting Canadians' Perspective on the Health Care System. https://www.cma.ca/sites/default/files/pdf/Media-Releases/The-Future-of-Connected- Healthcare-e.pdf (accessed August 30, 2020)

Curioso, W.H. 2019. Building capacity and training for digital health: Challenges and opportunities in Latin America. *Journal of Medical Internet Research* 21(12): e16513 https://www.jmir.org/2019/12/e16513/?utm_source=feedburner&utm_medium=feed&utm_campaign=Feed%3A+JMedInternetRes+%28Journal+of+Medical+Internet+Research+%28atom%29%29#Copyright

European Union Connected Health Alliance. 2019. https://echalliance.com/ (accessed September 5, 2020)

Lei, J. et al. 2017. Enabling Health Reform through Regional Health Information Exchange: A Model Study from China. *Journal of Healthcare Engineering*. https://www.hindawi.com/journals/jhe/2017/1053403/

Office of the National Coordinator for Health Information Technology. 2018. Connecting Health and Care for the Nation: A 10-Year Vision to Achieve an Interoperable Health IT Infrastructure. https://www.healthit.gov/sites/default/files/ONC10yearInteroperability ConceptPaper.pdf (accessed September 5, 2020)

Offner, K. L., Sitnikova, E., Joiner, K., and MacIntyre, C.R. 2020. Toward understanding cybersecurity capability in Australian healthcare organisations: A systematic review of recent trends, threats and mitigation. *Intelligence and National Security* 36(4): 556–585 https://www.tandfonline.com/doi/full/10.1080/02684527.2020.1752459

Owouemi, A., Owoyemi, J., Osiyemi, A., and Boyd, A. 2020. Artificial Intelligence for Healthcare in Africa. *Frontier Digital Health.* (July 7) https://www.frontiersin.org/articles/10.3389/fdgth.2020.00006/full

Swiss Institute of Bioinformatics. 2019. Bringing Swiss Health Data to Biomedical Research: An Interoperability Journey. https://www.sib.swiss/about-sib/news/news-2019/10524- bringing-swiss-health-data-to-biomedical-research-an-interoperability-journey (accessed September 20, 2020)

Wales A. 2020. Decision Support for Scotland's Health and Social Care: Learning from an Outcomes-Focused Approach. *British Medical Journal of Health Care Information* 27(August 17):e100124. https://informatics.bmj.com/content/bmjhci/27/2/e100124.full.pdf

PERMISSION VERIFICATION FORM (PVF)

Author Information

Anne L. Drabczyk October 7, 2020

☐ **Option A/No permission Required** – The entirety of my Work, text/figure(s), table(s), is original, has not been published before, is in the public domain, or I am the sole copyright holder.

☑ **Option B/Written Permission is Required** - Portions of my Work, text/figure(s), table(s), are taken from other sources, and I, the author, will obtain written permission from the copyright owner for the content. Please note quotes from these sources were kept under 50 words, and therefore did not require permission. The majority of sources were also Open Source, such as Creative Commons.

Source	Status Notes and/orPermission Granted
Agency for Healthcare Research and Quality. 2019. Practice Based Research Networks: Research in everyday practice. https://pbrn.ahrq.gov	✓N/ALess than 50 word quote/paraphrased material
Canadian Medical Association. 2019, August. The future of connected health care reporting Canadians' perspective on the health care system. https://www.cma.ca/sites/default/files/pdf/Media-Releases/The-Future-of-Connected-Healthcare-e.pdf	✓N/ALess than 50 word quote/paraphrased material
Curioso, W.H. 2019. Building capacity and training for digital health: Challenges and opportunities in Latin America. *Journal of Medical Internet Research:* 21(12): e16513https://www.jmir.org/2019/12/e16513/?utm_source=feedburner&utm_medium=feed&utm_campaign=Feed%3A+JMedInternetRes+%28Journal+of+Medical+Internet+Research+%28atom%29%29#Copyright	✓N/ALess than 50 word quote/paraphrased material [Creative Commons} Walter H H Curioso. Originally published in the Journal of Medical Internet Research (http://www.jmir.org), 18.12.2019. This is an open-access article distributed under the terms of the Creative Commons Attribution License(https://creativecommons.org/licenses/by/4.0/), which permits unrestricted use, distribution, and reproduction in any medium, provided the original work, first published in the Journal of Medical Internet Research, is properly cited.
European Union Connected Health Alliancehttps://echalliance.com/	✓N/ALess than 50 word quote/paraphrased material
Healthcare Informatics Society of Ireland (2020) eHealth Ireland Ecosystemhttps://www.hisi.ie/ecosystem/	✓N/ALess than 50 word quote/paraphrased material
Lei, J. et al. 2017. Enabling Health Reform through Regional Health Information Exchange: A Model Study from China. *Journal of Healthcare Engineering*https://www.hindawi.com/journals/jhe/2017/1053403/	✓N/ALess than 50 word quote/paraphrased material. Copyright © 2017 Jianbo Lei et al. This is an open access article distributed under the Creative Commons Attribution License, which permits unrestricted use, distribution, and reproduction in any medium, provided the original work is properly cited.
Office of the National Coordinator for Health Information TechnologyConnecting Health and Care for the Nation: A 10-Year Vision to Achieve an Interoperable Health IT Infrastructure https://www.healthit.gov/sites/default/files/ONC10yearInteroperabilityConceptPaper.pdf	✓N/ALess than 50 word quote/paraphrased material

Source	Status Notes and/orPermission Granted
Offner, K. L., Sitnikova, E., Joiner, K. and MacIntyre, C.R.Towards understanding cybersecurity capability in Australian healthcare organisations: A systematic review of recent trends, threats and mitigation. Intelligence and National Security 36(4) (2020):556–585 https://www.tandfonline.com/doi/full/10.1080/02684527.2020.1752459	✓N/ALess than 50 word quote/paraphrased material. This is an Open Access article distributed under the terms of the Creative Commons Attribution-NonCommercial-NoDerivatives License (http://creativecommons.org/licenses/by-nc-nd/4.0/), which permits non-commercial re-use, distribution, and reproduction in any medium, provided the original work is properly cited, and is not altered, transformed, or built upon in any way.
Owouemi, A., Owoyemi, J., Osiyemi, A., and Boyd, A. 2020. Artificial Intelligence for Healthcare in Africa. *Frontier Digital Health.* (July 7) https://www.frontiersin.org/articles/10.3389/fdgth.2020.00006/full	✓N/ALess than 50 word quote/paraphrased material. Copyright © 2020 Owoyemi, Owoyemi, Osiyemi and Boyd. This is an open-access article distributed under the terms of the Creative Commons Attribution License (CC BY). The use, distribution or reproduction in other forums is permitted, provided the original author(s) and the copyright owner(s) are credited and that the original publication in this journal is cited, in accordance with accepted academic practice. No use, distribution or reproduction is permitted which does not comply with these terms.
Swiss Institute of Bioinformatics. 2019. Bringing Swiss health data to biomedical research: an interoperability journey. https://www.sib.swiss/about-sib/news/news-2019/10524-bringing-swiss-health-data-to-biomedical-research-an-interoperability-journey	✓N/ALess than 50 word quote/paraphrased material
Wales A. 2020. Decision support for Scotland's health and social care: Learning from an outcomes-focused approach. *British Medical Journal of Health Care Information;* (August 17);27:e100124. https://informatics.bmj.com/content/bmjhci/27/2/e100124.full.pdf	✓N/ALess than 50 word quote/paraphrased material. Open access This is an open access article distributed in accordance with the Creative Commons Attribution Non Commercial (CC BY-NC 4.0) license, which permits others to distribute, remix, adapt, build upon this work noncommercially, and license their derivative works on different terms, provided the original work is properly cited, appropriate credit is given, any changes made indicated, and the use is non-commercial. See: http://creativecommons.org/licenses/by-nc/4.0/

37 The Clinically-Integrated Supply Chain: A Critical Component of Healthcare Delivery

Anne W. Snowdon
RN, Ph.D, FAAN

CONTENTS

INTRODUCTION

While quality and safety have been the fundamental goals of all global healthcare systems from both a patient and a provider perspective, performance of North American healthcare systems remains far behind that of other OECD countries, ranking 10th for Canada and 11th for the United States (Davis et al., 2014). Despite many well-funded initiatives to strengthen quality and safety, healthcare systems worldwide have not experienced significant improvement in these core areas. Patient safety is a particular challenge despite decades of research and safety initiatives to define the problem, at both a country and the global level. Medical error, a core element of patient safety, has now become the third leading cause of death in North America, behind heart disease and cancer (Makary and Daniel, 2016; Statcan, 2016). Although there is growing awareness of the challenge of patient safety, there has been little evidence of improvement in the rates of deaths and serious injury related to error and adverse events in recent years. Moreover, although the prevalence of adverse events and safety challenges has been widely reported related to hospital care, it is not well documented in community and long-term care settings.

DOI: 10.4324/9780429398377-43

This chapter focuses on how clinically integrated supply chain processes could transform the care delivery environment of healthcare settings to ensure that adverse events are substantially reduced resulting in safer healthcare systems for global citizens. Supply chain infrastructure and processes are profoundly underdeveloped compared to virtually every other business sector. Just one example is the automotive industry, which has created vehicle environments that alert the driver and vehicle occupants to proactively manage risk. Warning sounds that encourage use of seatbelts, and warning lights and signals that alert drivers of potential collisions, have dramatically reduced the rate of accidents and severity of injuries due to vehicle crashes. These examples demonstrate the importance of the environment identifying risk, and creating signals to individuals to identify risk proactively to encourage, or require, preventive behaviors to reduce risk of harm. When compared to other industry sectors, healthcare environments lack the sophistication of supply chain infrastructure to proactively reduce risks to patients by accurately identifying the products and care processes to ensure patients receive the right care, and then link patient outcomes to determine value of care delivery to ensure that care processes are as safe as possible and protect patients from harm at all times. Healthcare has much to learn from other business sectors, described in the following section.

WHAT THE HEALTHCARE SECTOR CAN LEARN FROM OTHER INDUSTRY SECTORS

Many other industries (e.g., grocery, automotive, airline) have achieved tremendous impact in terms of safety, efficiency, and performance through supply chain transformation. These business sectors have well-developed supply chain management processes, which are viewed as strategic assets that contribute directly to ensuring the safety of their products and services. From these other industries, we can learn what a highly effective supply chain infrastructure can achieve towards safe environments for health systems.

In the airline industry, every passenger carries a barcoded boarding pass, which identifies both the passenger and the flight, ensuring that travellers board the correct flight, sit in the correct seat, and arrive at their destination safely. When airline staff scan the passenger's boarding pass, they are immediately informed by visual monitors (e.g., green check mark if information is correct, red "X" if information is incorrect). These cues are a proactive monitoring system that enable an important "doublecheck" for gate agents to overcome the risk of misreading the boarding pass and alerting agents to intervene and prevent the passenger from boarding the plane. The key features of the system are the tools embedded in the working environment to automatically scan and display information to alert staff to potential adverse events before they happen, significantly reducing the frequency of error. In healthcare, there are few such systems that proactively identifies a potential risk for patients. Imagine the scenario if the airline tools were applied to healthcare systems: the nurse would scan a patient's identification band as the patient is wheeled into the operating room to ensure that the right patient is entering the correct operating room with the right surgical team ready to conduct the correctly planned surgical procedure. The patient's identification and surgical procedure would appear on an overhead monitor so that the entire medical team could see the information and validate the exact surgical procedure to be conducted on the exact surgical site (e.g., left hip versus right hip) before the procedure begins. This dynamic system of proactively double-checking for clinical teams, using visual cues on a monitor, could be a key feature of healthcare environments to reduce the risk of preventable errors, such as administering the wrong medication, conducting the wrong surgery, or administering the wrong tissue or implant during a procedure, all of which are events that should never happen in health systems. One of the most critical limitations of clinical environments in healthcare systems today is the absence of tools that track and trace patients, products, and procedures land outcomes to create a system-wide visibility of care processes and product use (e.g., medications, devices, and implants) in patient care (Rising et al., 2012; Sedrakyan, 2012). Unlike many other sectors, there are very few such systems in healthcare environments that identify the potential risk of an adverse event at the operational level.

Most other industries or sectors have the infrastructure in place to reduce the occurrence of errors. For example, banking has automated tracking of all transactions whereby unusual transactions are flagged immediately and all future transactions are stopped to mitigate the risk of theft or counterfeit activities as quickly as possible. This system relies on evidence-informed algorithms to alert banking officials to high-risk situations of fraud or theft. Yet, in healthcare, these tracking tools do not exist in most clinical settings, leaving clinical environments to rely on staff and health professionals to remember to manually check and double-check to reduce the risk of adverse events. This reliance on human behavior to check and double-check each step in healthcare delivery has been the primary strategy of patient safety efforts to date, focused on educating provider teams to raise awareness of safety risks and build a safety culture. However, these efforts have not been effective in reducing the growing rates of adverse events, particularly given the increasing complexity of health system environments. Just as other industry sectors have already demonstrated, there is a need for system infrastructure tools that enable and empower providers to deliver the safest care possible, with automated checks and double-checks in the clinical environment to make the occurrence of adverse events far less likely. Comparisons with other business sectors that have successfully integrated supply chain management in complex environments illustrate how profoundly underdeveloped the supply chain processes are in healthcare.

CHALLENGES OF HEALTH SECTOR SUPPLY CHAIN

A number of key challenges exist in current health system environments that limit the ability of healthcare environments to prevent risks to patient safety. The following will discuss the key supply chain characteristics challenging current systems. There are five challenges that must be overcome in order to advance supply chain infrastructure in health systems to advance patient safety.

   1. *Lack of automated alerts at the point of care for clinicians to identify risks and proactively intervene to protect patients from harm.*

There is very little "line of sight"—visibility—in the key conditions that contribute to adverse events in healthcare systems. Take for example, joint replacement surgery. Most patients in the world have no ability to identify the hip or knee implant that was used during their surgery. In the event of a recall or a failure of the joint implant or product, there is almost no way to identify, at the level of the individual product and patient, which patients received the defective device or implant. Few tools are currently available in healthcare environments to track and trace what products are used in individual patient care processes, where a product was manufactured and when, or how different products link to individual patient outcomes. In countries such as Canada and, to a large degree, the United States, there is no national-level infrastructure that evaluates adverse event outcomes related to products such as joint implants, nor is there a way to alert health system leaders to risk when these products enter the market and demonstrate adverse outcomes for patients. Although there are many organizations that track use of products in patient care, they most often use proprietary information technology (IT) infrastructure barcoding, which is not standardized. Therefore, these products can only be tracked internally to individual organizations; there is no ability to track and trace individual patients and product use across organizations, regions, or jurisdictions and thus no ability to disseminate information broadly in the event of product failure. In many health systems, supply chain is not viewed as a strategic asset and has not been leveraged to strengthen health system safety.

   2. *Manual supply chain processes with limited digital infrastructure.*

A lack of digital infrastructure in health supply chain results in a lack of transparency making it impossible for health system leaders to make decisions informed by accurate supply chain data

(Snowdon and Alessi, 2016). Leaders must make decisions without any data to accurately track products and supplies on hand and the location of supplies and product utilization rates (e.g., burn rate), or to accurately forecast demand.

There are few tools currently available in healthcare to track and trace the products used in patient care processes, at the individual level, including where a product was manufactured and how it is linked with patient outcomes. Should there be a failure or recall of the implant, there is almost no way of identifying—at the individual product or patient level—which patients received the recalled implant. In countries such as Canada and, to a large degree, the United States, there is no national-level infrastructure that evaluates adverse event outcomes related to products such as joint implants, nor is there a way to alert health system leaders to risk when these products enter the market and demonstrate adverse outcomes for patients (Sedrakyan, 2012).

Health organizations do not have the digital tools and infrastructure required to enable clinicians with automated "double-checks" and alerts to proactively manage risks and protect patients from harm. Few healthcare providers have access to reports or searchable data to analyze patterns and root causes of adverse events (e.g., error rates, product failure, recall) in real time, or outcomes and trends across organizations and health systems that could prevent error or redesign processes to mitigate risk. The tracking and tracing of products, processes, and people creates visibility in these highly effective systems. This visibility creates strategic value that enables the entire system to measure the effectiveness, efficiency, performance, and value of every step of the business process.

3. Lack of standardization of products and product data.

Current health systems lack the standardization of products and product data to enable accurate identification of product attributes or product specifications. Supply chain processes manage the movement of products from manufacturers and distributors to clinical settings in every organization that delivers healthcare. Not only is the healthcare system complex, but it relies on the availability of a very large number of products that are needed by clinicians when and where they are required to deliver care. Without product data, there is no way to track and trace products from manufacturer to patient care and patient outcomes. Improving safety—for example, in the event of a recall—requires all product details to be linked from supplier to the individual patient and patient outcomes. Further, for supply chain teams to evaluate new sources of products, or alternative products, to determine whether alternative types of products could be substituted for critical products in short supply (e.g., in the event of a disaster or product shortage), these details are required. The lack of global standards for product identification makes it impossible for supply chain teams to compare products or distinguish suppliers selling counterfeit or inferior products.

4. Inability to manage surge in demand or disruptions to supply of critical products.

Healthcare supply chain is typically characterized by a lack of redundancy within supply chain models that favor "leanness" over resiliency and domestic manufacturing. In an effort to keep costs down, products are typically sourced from a single, typically international, source. This can also be exacerbated by a "just-in-time" supply chain model, where there are not large quantities of supply on hand at any one time.

These challenges were exemplified during the first wave of the COVID-19 pandemic, where health systems were unable to rapidly respond to the massive surge in demand for personal protective equipment (PPE). The sudden surge in demand for PPE and other essential supplies overwhelmed healthcare supply chains (Snowdon et al., 2021, in press). Health systems struggled to provide the PPE and supplies necessary to deliver safe and effective patient care. Multiple jurisdictions were unable to meet the surge in demand for products and equipment, which led to the prioritizing of PPE and equipment (e.g., ventilators) (Truog et al., 2020; Snowdon et al., 2021, in press). The first wave of the COVID-19 pandemic was characterized by a limited ability to manage the surge in demand for the products critically needed by health teams to safely deliver care and support preventive efforts to contain or reduce the spread of the virus. A significant factor contributing to this inability to meet demand was the reliance on a single geographic source for critical products. Approximately 90% of products (e.g., face masks, gowns, N95 masks) in North America are sourced from manufacturers in China (Snowdon et al., 2021, in press), the first country to be shut down in an effort to contain the spread of the SARS-CoV-2 virus. This worldwide shortage created intense competition, where companies sold products to the highest bidder. Supply chain teams were forced to procure products from unfamiliar—and sometimes fraudulent—suppliers, at exorbitant costs, or miss the chance to secure the products needed for health systems to manage the demands of care for patients with COVID-19. Reliance on single jurisdiction sourcing, or single supplier sourcing, poses a great risk for supply chain failure because of the limited capacity to compete globally to find alternative sources during supply shortages.

KEY FEATURES OF CLINICALLY INTEGRATED SUPPLY CHAIN

It has only recently become very clear that health supply chain infrastructure and processes require rapid transformation, given the very significant challenges and lessons learned during the COVID-19 pandemic. The integration of supply chain and clinical care is becoming essential in a safe and quality driven healthcare system. The following are key steps to achieve a clinically integrated supply chain.

1. *Adoption of GS1 standards as the global language of supply chain in healthcare systems.*

The first crucial step towards a clinically integrated supply chain is creating the policy framework to support the tracking and tracing of healthcare products. This requires the adoption of global identification standards that link the products used in care delivery to each patient and provider. Over 20 industry sectors globally have adopted these standards, developed and implemented by a worldwide network of GS1 organizations, currently operating in 114 countries. GS1 standards are currently used for every retail and pharmaceutical product, to accurately identify and track product movement from manufacturer to supplier to the organization that purchases them. The GS1 standards are the only standard that are globally accepted, operating in over 114 countries world wide. These standards create a common language that every health system can adopt to enable accurate identification of products, to order and ship products to ensure they are available when and where they are needed, and then to track products and their use at the point of patient care. Adoption of GS1 standards enables the use of barcodes, RFID, or other standardized identification, allowing for a rich set of data (e.g., lot number, expiry date) to be encoded and then tracked in any health organization in the world, linked to unique identification of patients and individual providers who are assigned a Global Service Relationship Number (GSRN). For example, when a doctor prescribes a medication to a patient, the medication is dispensed by a pharmacist; a GSRN identifies the doctor and another GSRN identifies the pharmacist who filled the prescription, which is then linked to the patient, who has their own unique GSRN. The medication has a global trade identification number (GTIN) that identifies the key attributes of the product to inform and ensure clinical teams and providers that they have the correct product information they need to make decisions. A number of retail organizations, such as pharmacies, have already adopted GS1 standards and already use fully automated systems for traceability of pharmaceutical products to individual consumers. However, the same capability has not been achieved in hospital pharmacies due to the lack of policy mandates governing health systems. Once policy makers establish this requirement, healthcare organizations can leverage the many GS1-compliant barcodes to encode critical supply chain and clinical information, standardized to be read in any healthcare setting worldwide, to establish transparency in healthcare systems.

2. *Integrate ERP digital infrastructure with EMR platforms to enable traceability and risk management at the point of care.*

Electronic medical record (EMR) platforms enabling clinical documentation in EMRs during care delivery are an important tool to advance digital capture of patient data. This data, however, is not always integrated or interoperable with other data platforms across health systems. For example, EMRs capture the progress notes, lab results, diagnostic imaging reports, and clinical assessment data for every patient, to enable clinicians to track patient health status. Advanced analytics tools (e.g., algorithms) have the ability to be used for decision support or to enhance inventory software to manage demand for products and supplies. These tools provide detailed product attribute data (e.g., expiry date, lot number, batch number), which are required data points in the event of a recall. Typically, hospitals have a wide range of diverse software platforms operating at any given moment, estimated to be as many as 30–40 tools or applications across the organization. The EMR platform is able to collect and store patient data, but insufficient to advance quality and safety due to the limited interoperability of EMR data and other datasets such as product data, finance data, and inventory software, which are typically housed in the ERP (Enterprise Resource Management) platform. To achieve a clinically integrated supply chain with the infrastructure able to support safety and quality for patients, there must be a fully integrated digital infrastructure. This infrastructure must be capable of traceability of every patient, the care processes they receive, the products used in care, linked to patient outcomes, to determine what care models and processes work best for individual patients, and under what conditions best outcomes are achieved. Clinically integrated supply chain infrastructure ensures all of the data platforms are interoperable and include embedded analytics able to support point of care capture of data, to serve as a "double-check" that the correct care processes are provided to patients. It allows data platforms to identify that the products used in care are safe (e.g., check expiry date and recalls), alerting clinicians in the event of risk to enable clinicians to intervene proactively to prevent adverse events and support the best possible outcomes for patients. Clinically integrated supply chain infrastructure offers the ability to track and trace progress over the patient's journey of care (e.g., primary care, long-term care, hospital care, etc.) so that all provider teams can access data on care processes and decisions that all of the other clinicians have implemented. This data infrastructure creates the opportunity to overcome the greatest risk and prevalence of error; during care transitions one provider team has no way to access the documentation of care across various clinician teams providing care to patients in different care settings. Perhaps the most important opportunity in a highly transparent system is the implementation of clinical safety tools to track and report the processes, procedures, and products allocated to each individual patient to evaluate safety and effectiveness of care outcomes. Point of care capture of patient data (e.g., barcode or RFID scanning) generates alerts at the point of care for clinicians, and generates analytics profiled on dashboards for program teams to track quality and safety, in near real time. The adoption of global standards enables traceability of outcomes across organizations, regions, and geographies to inform all health organizations of trending analyses for specific patient population segments, automated recalls of products with evidence of adverse outcomes, and segmentation of patient populations to reveal best outcomes linked to unique health needs and outcomes of individual consumers. Clinically integrated supply chain infrastructure integrates all data sources across the organization, links data to patient outcomes to determine value, and enables traceability of patient care across the continuum of care to inform decisions of patients and clinician teams to ensure best outcomes are achieved, personalized to every individual.

3. *Traceability of product performance, product notification, and recall.*

The opportunity to identify and manage potential risks for patients is one of the most important features of a clinically integrated supply chain in healthcare. Product manufacturers are estimated to send out approximately 3,500 notifications annually worldwide, reporting product failures or product warnings that require health organizations to locate and remove products, mitigating the risk of harm for patients. For every recall notification, health system stakeholders must identify the patients who received the product and the outcomes patients may have experienced by manually reviewing patient records to locate use of recalled products. In an automated system, the identification of patients who received the product in question could be conducted in a matter of a few hours using the data infrastructure that cross references product attributes and recall information with patient care data that identifies which patients may be at risk due to exposure. Standardized and automated traceability offers a further opportunity that is critically important for achieving a highly transparent health system. Automated traceability creates transparency for healthcare systems by enabling safety information to be reported and made available to system stakeholders and the public for analysis and learning. When adverse events occur, disseminating what happened and, more importantly, how the event can be averted or prevented, is a key outcome transparency achieves in healthcare systems. Automated reporting of events and recalls, linked to patient outcomes, is a key feature of a highly transparent health system with a well-developed clinically integrated supply chain infrastructure. Such systems not only advise the public of progress towards safer healthcare, but also inform and enable clinicians, teams, and organizations to quickly identify patterns and prevent adverse events. Additionally, they proactively protect patients from harm and effectively disseminate information across healthcare systems to further mitigate risk. An automated recall and tracking system not only provide system-wide analysis of adverse events; it also provides automated feedback for clinical teams, who can use the information to inform their practice and streamline processes to reduce the risk of error that causes harm to patients.

4. Measurement strategy that captures strategic supply chain outcomes in healthcare.

Measurement in health systems, although established for decades, has focused primarily on patterns of illness of diagnoses, health system utilization, cost and performance (e.g., quality and safety). Unlike other business sectors, health system measures do not capture supply chain outcomes for both patients and for health systems. A robust measurement framework to track the capacity and effectiveness of supply chain strategies offers a tool for health leaders to better understand the progress and maturity of supply chain infrastructure and the outcomes that can be achieved. Key metrics that reflect supply chain transformation must include patient care outcomes, such as the prevalence and type of adverse events. For example, medication errors measured using automated reporting from digital infrastructure, product outcome measures such as frequency of shortages, product performance outcomes such as infection rates related to product use, product failures identified across clinical settings, recalls, and stockouts. Health system measures that reflect advanced supply chain management processes would include inventory cost savings, labor costs/case that contribute to the economic impact of adverse events, patient health and recovery time linked to product use, and procedure quality and safety. Additionally, the ability to rate shortages and stock-outs, conduct accurate case costing, and adverse event reporting can inform strategies to reduce the rate and severity of adverse events in healthcare. Measurement tools that leverage supply chain data assets could inform and support accountability for health services delivery as it enables leaders to use automated reporting systems, generated in near real-time, to understand quality, safety, and operational outcomes in each care setting. Robust measurement frameworks enable clinical teams to design and evaluate risk mitigation and prevention strategies to further strengthen the quality and safety of care delivery. A highly transparent system leads to best evidence strategies that achieve the greatest impact for patients, families, and populations.

REAL-WORLD EXAMPLES OF CLINICALLY INTEGRATED SUPPLY CHAIN

The following are a series of case studies that examine real-world evidence of impact of supply chain transformation in health systems that achieves improved health system outcomes such as safety, quality, and operational performance.

CASE 1: MERCY HEALTH SYSTEMS—UNITED STATES

This case examines the implementation of a transformational supply chain strategy across Mercy Health (Mercy), headquartered in St. Louis, Missouri. The following case examines the leadership strategy, outcomes, and impacts of supply chain transformation on Mercy's financial and operational performance.

In the early 2000s, Mercy leadership believed there was a better approach to overcoming the challenges of the business model of the American healthcare system, characterized by rapidly changing funding models, as well as misaligned and inefficient supply chain operations.

Mercy's strategy focused on three key objectives: (1) high-value care delivered by clinical programs, (2) sustainable change in operational performance, and (3) strengthened financial outcomes across the system.

LEADERSHIP STRATEGY

Leaders had the vision of transforming supply chain as a strategic asset across the Mercy organization to unify the system and to strengthen its performance and fiscal sustainability. The leadership vision was to transform clinical, operational, and financial performance of the health system by creating an integrated supply chain strategy that consisted of four strategic goals:

1. *Engage Clinicians:* Give clinicians a voice, engaging them in making unified strategic purchasing decisions.
2. *System Alignment of "One Mercy":* Align organizational stakeholders to empower leaders to focus on the entire organization, particularly its broader, mutually established goals.
3. *Minimize Waste:* Overhaul and optimize the ordering, packaging, and delivery of products.
4. *Release Provider Time for Patient Care:* Enable providers to spend more time on patient care by introducing efficient, seamless supply chain processes.

To operationalize their vision of supply chain transformation, Mercy's strategy focused on creating a consolidated supply chain infrastructure across the system. This infrastructure functioned as a strategic asset to optimize supply chain processes and create a new revenue stream by leveraging their supply chain expertise and services to serve other health systems. Optimizing and advancing supply chain infrastructure and processes across Mercy, served as a system "integrator" to bring the many Mercy hospitals together under one operational infrastructure model. Supply chain teams worked with each hospital to optimize supply chain and streamline supply chain processes, eliminating all costs of outsourcing to external commercial companies for contracts, transportation, and distribution of products.

The strategy focused on three pillars:

Connecting supplychain to operational strategy: Gaining control over operations began with a program analysis that revealed a trend in the perioperative program towards declining revenue, largely due to changes in bundled care reimbursement models. Projected revenues identified a risk of this program becoming a cost center rather than a source of revenue. Supply chain optimization, including introducing point of care scanning in the perioperative program, created the critical connectivity between supply chain and clinical teams. Clinicians demonstrated a better understanding of the value of inventory management, while supply chain staff learned firsthand of the challenges that clinicians experience in managing products and processes when delivering patient care.

Establishing control over information and data: This was a key priority in order to create visibility of care processes and outcomes, and to overcome variation. The value of seamless data captured across Mercy's programs created the opportunity for informing decisions on standardization of care, accurately capturing case costs, and leveraging traceability data for comparative effectiveness analysis and post-market surveillance. Automation of product inventory linked to financial and clinical information systems enabled clinical teams to capture the necessary data, informing decisions to strengthen safety, quality of care, and operational efficiency.

Gaining control over relationships—achieving clinician engagement: A robust clinician engagement strategy brought together clinicians from all Mercy hospitals to inform product procurement decisions, standardize products and care practices, and analyze data to strengthen quality of care. Building relationships of trust between supply chain and clinician teams was a key goal of Mercy's strategy. Point of care scanning and inventory management infrastructure created real-time data to support problem-solving and overcome challenges in clinical settings. Physicians worked collaboratively across the system as a team to strengthen operational, financial, and patient care quality.

OUTCOMES

Operational Impacts: The operational effects included increased efficiency and productivity in the perioperative program, which has since increased both surgical case volumes and revenue. Point of care scanning strengthened clinician workflow and preference card standardization improved frequency of preference card optimization by 284%.

Financial Outcomes: A 29.5% decline in labor cost per case over the four years the strategy was achieved, reduced from $799/case in 2014 to $523/case in 2017. Supply cost per case has declined 33.3%, reduced from $2,055/case in 2014 to $1,371/case in 2017. Mercy has achieved a growth in revenue of $81,242,551 over this four-year period, approximately $20 million per year, since introducing the supply chain strategy in the perioperative program.

Quality of Care: The outcomes included a 71% reduction in serious reportable adverse events, the introduction of automated safety alerts for product expiry and recall for clinicians, and tracking and traceability of product UDI to inform quality-of-care outcomes.

CONCLUSION

In this case, Mercy implemented a robust and comprehensive supply chain strategy with a key focus on financial, operational, and quality performance outcomes, leveraging supply chain infrastructure as a key asset. The outcomes of this case demonstrate the value and impact of a highly integrated supply chain strategy. Mercy has transformed the notion of supply chain from being a cost centre to becoming a strategic asset—able to drive quality and operational excellence while strengthening financial outcomes and creating new revenue. Mercy's integrated leadership and decision-making strategy mobilized clinician leadership to support and inform strategic decision-making focused on quality and safety of care delivery. As a result, Mercy has a high-performing system that is informed and driven by real-world evidence of value.

CASE 2: ALBERTA HEALTH SERVICES—CANADA

This case examines the supply chain strategy for Alberta Health Services (AHS), the first province-wide, fully integrated health system in Canada. In 2008, all health regions in the province of Alberta were amalgamated into a single, publicly funded health system, now known as Alberta Health Services, to improve efficiency and streamline the health system for both patients and

professionals. A key strategy to support and enable a high-performing system was the con-
solidation of all support services centrally, including finance, information technology, data integration and management, capital management, and contracting and procurement services. A
priority goal was to achieve a "clinically relevant" supply chain strategy across the province,
leveraging the province-wide infrastructure supporting the "one system" mandate.

Supply Chain Implementation Strategy

Implementation of the supply chain strategy began with a decision in 2010 to implement enterprise
resource planning (ERP) technology to support province-wide governance.

Implementation of ERP Across the Province: Stakeholders experienced many challenges during
this process, resulting in a new recognition and appreciation of the contribution of supply chain in
the delivery of patient care. Senior leadership and program teams became aware of the risks
associated with supply chain challenges and the interruptions to clinical care in priority programs,
such as surgery. The provincial ERP system was a challenge to implement, but has now become an
important platform and a key strategic asset.

Price Harmonization and a New (Centralized) Procurement: The price harmonization phase of
the strategy was designed to ensure consistency in pricing and supplier contracts across the province. The harmonization process included creating a standardized item master of products to be
used for all procurement and contracting. Price harmonization and product category analysis were
two key initiatives undertaken that resulted in standardization of supply costs across the entire
province resulting in substantial cost savings particularly for specialty programs.

Province-wide Item Master and Data Infrastructure: As the ERP implementation was completed, a master product item list, containing a comprehensive registry of products was identified
and tracked using global standards, consolidated with item-level data. Each item in the item master
was identified using GS1 standards to support the global trade identification number (GTIN),
obtained through the Global Data Synchronization Network (GDSN). The AHS team partnered
with industry to support use of global standards, and worked with vendors to agree on product
attributes and product information required by AHS teams, which are key enablers of an integrated
supply chain strategy able to track and trace every product to individual patient outcomes to
determine value.

Centralized Warehouse Strategy for the Province: Alberta leaders identified warehousing as one
of the key strategies to advance their supply chain infrastructure, creating a system to stock and
distribute supplies to all the sites across the province. The centralized warehouse and distribution
strategy offered the strategic advantage of greater visibility of product inventory, reduced duplication of products, and reduced surplus that contributed to substantial waste reduction.

Clinician Engagement: Clinician engagement was identified by the CPSM team as an integral
part of a successful supply chain strategy. The clinician engagement strategy focused on clinician
input and decision-making accountability for procurement of new products, and evaluation of the
value of existing products, to inform procurement decisions. This strategy ensured that clinicians
and stakeholder perspectives were deeply embedded in supply chain processes and decisions as a
key feature of AHS strategy, supporting a collaborative approach to identifying new innovations
and technologies that would bring value to programs.

Integration of Supply Chain Processes with Adverse Event Reporting: Safety and quality were
identified as key priorities for the Alberta supply chain strategy, informed by the six dimensions of
quality of the Health Quality Council of Alberta. A comprehensive digital adverse event reporting
system was created to offer a dashboard able to track and report adverse events to enable patient
safety and medical device teams to follow up on all actionable events across the province. The
patient safety team analyzes data and outcomes to identify trends across all health organizations in
the province to achieve a truly system-wide, adverse event reporting system that enables and
informs risk mitigation strategies. A performance summary (e.g., analysis of actions and orders) is

reported to executive leadership to inform strategic decisions focused on quality and safety across the Alberta health system.

OUTCOMES

Return on Investment (ROI) and Impact of the AHS Supply Chain Strategy: The opportunity for supply chain transformation to contribute to the reduction in health system costs across the province continues as a key strategy by AHS leaders. Key programs are actively engaged by the supply chain team to find program savings and standardize inventory costs. The harmonization of contracts for all the cardiology programs across the province achieved cost savings of $18.56 million, approximately 25% greater than was estimated by the CPSM team. A cost analysis for the 15 most commonly purchased drugs in one region revealed savings of more than $676,000. From 2010 to 2014, the CPSM team demonstrated a 7:1 return on investment, capturing $261,000,000 in total savings as of 2013. The supply chain strategy investment included $26,000,000 for the ERP implementation and $3,000,000 annually in operational costs to support the supply chain team, for a total investment of $36,000,000. This significant return on investment is impressive, given that the savings do not account for inventory optimization in patient care programs, and that integration of point of care scanning into clinical programs has not yet been completed.

CONCLUSION

The Alberta supply chain infrastructure and strategy have had impressive impacts and outcomes, demonstrating achievement of annual cost savings and cost reduction targets year over year since implementation. The digital online adverse event reporting system is among the most comprehensive among global health systems, and is a significant asset as Alberta continues their supply chain integration strategy. The consolidated health system strategy, coupled with the province-wide, integrated supply chain strategy, positions Alberta to make significant progress towards a high-performing, sustainable, and safe health system.

CASE 3: NATIONAL HEALTH SERVICES—ENGLAND

This case study examines the implementation of a transformational supply chain strategy across the National Health Service (NHS) in England. The strategy was established by Secretary of State Jeremy Hunt to transform the NHS into the world's largest learning organization, focused on transparency by reporting safety and quality outcomes across the continuum of care, from primary to acute care trusts and the community.

In April 2014, the Department of Health published the NHS eProcurement Strategy (later renamed Scan4Safety), mandating all trusts to adopt GS1 global standards to automate and standardize supply chain processes, as well as Pan European Public Procurement On-Line (PEPPOL) standards to enable digitizing transactions, such as the machine-to-machine exchange of data between trusts and their suppliers.

Six demonstrator trusts were selected, with £2 million provided to each trust to implement the Scan4Safety program. The program began by identifying every room location with a GS1 barcode and every product in inventory with a global trade item number (GTIN) and introducing GS1 barcodes on patient identification bands. These core enablers created the infrastructure in clinical settings to demonstrate three prescribed-use cases: (1) tracking and traceability of all products from manufacturer to patient, (2) automated purchase-to-pay transactions for product procurement between the trust and its suppliers, and (3) an automated capacity to remove products from inventory in the event of a recall. The majority of trusts initiated point of care scanning in high-cost and high-risk clinical settings, such as surgical theatres, cardiac catheterization labs, diagnostic imaging, and interventional radiology.

Outcomes

The Scan4Safety program has established the infrastructure necessary to automate traceability of each product, patient, staff member, care procedure, and location of care. Trust teams have achieved greater efficiency and productivity, automation of inventory and product recall processes, and full integration of supply chain processes in clinical care settings in the NHS Trusts participating in the Scan4Safety program. Integration of tracking and traceability has enabled full transparency in documenting which patients receive care, from which provider teams, and when and where care is provided throughout the patient journey, linked to outcomes for quality, safety, and value for patients.

Leadership Strategy—the Driver of System Transparency: The leadership strategy underpinning this case reflects the mandate of publicly funded healthcare systems. Political leaders are accountable to the public for ensuring the delivery of safe, accessible, and high-performing health services that achieve value for citizens. In this case, the strategy focused on creating transparency in the NHS system. Transparency is envisioned to enable learning from medical error or adverse events to strengthen quality, safety, and accountability in the health system. There is also ample evidence of the Scan4Safety program's capacity to enable a data-driven, evidence-informed health system that links product performance and clinician practice to safety and patient outcomes.

System Transparency—the Foundation for Accountability: The key leadership motivation was the government's accountability to British citizens for safe, high-quality care and confidence in their health system. The transparency generated by the Scan4Safety infrastructure created a platform to support clinician accountability for safe practice and quality, health system accountability for supply chain efficiency and safety, and supplier accountability for accurately identified products enabling traceability from manufacturer to patient outcomes. The integration of the supply chain data infrastructure with clinical information systems enabled a highly cohesive digital infrastructure that generates transparency of every patient, every product used in care processes, and accurate case costing, all linked to patient outcomes. This infrastructure produces objective data that, when analyzed, becomes knowledge and evidence to inform clinician practice, operational decisions, supply chain management forecasting, and accountability of suppliers to provide trusts with product information that supports safe and effective patient care.

Clinician Accountability: Transparency arises from system infrastructure that creates objective data and evidence of the care that is delivered, by whom, for which patients and under what conditions. Data emerges in clinical settings, in near "real-time," to enable clinical programs, such as the surgical theatre, to objectively measure variation in surgeon preference, surgical practice (operating time), and cost. In each of the trusts, the data is leveraged to identify opportunities to reduce variation, eliminate waste from products that are discarded or never used, and inform best-practice standardization. The data is also used by program and supply chain teams to inform staff and clinicians with evidence of outcomes. The transparency of data-informed strategies enables clinicians to streamline clinical processes, reduce product and preference tray costs by removing waste, and standardize high-cost products informed by value outcomes for patients.

Supply Chain Team Accountability—Return on Investment (ROI): Supply chain teams across the trusts are able to account for which products are purchased and at what price, informed by utilization and care demands to ensure that products are available when and where needed for patient care. The return on investment that emerged is an outcome of inventory savings from managing product waste and minimizing variation. Inventory savings achieved a 4:1 ROI, exceeding the Department of Health's projected outcomes. Each trust demonstrated an average savings of £2.4 million, realized from operational efficiencies and clinician time savings, redirected from managing supply chain processes to patient care—on average, the equivalent of 16 full-time equivalent (FTE) staff per trust. If and when the Scan4Safety program is scaled to all 154 trusts, it was projected to yield £30 million/year.

Conclusion

Implementation of the three core enablers resulted in significant reduction in product waste, and clinician time was released and redirected to patient care. Transparency may be the new currency that achieves an accountable, continuously learning, safe, and sustainable health systems—whereby decisions are informed by real-world evidence that is foundational to accountability of clinical teams working with supply chain teams to support the delivery of the best patient care. Clinically integrated supply chain cases, as described, demonstrates the value of transparency in creating system accountability informed by data and evidence. The data and evidence contribute to enhancing system efficiency, improving safety and quality of clinical care and real-world evidence of product and process performance linked to patient outcomes.

REFERENCES

Davis K, Stremikis K, Squires D, Schoen C. (2014). Mirror, Mirror on the Wall, 2014 Update: How the U.S. Health Care System Compares Internationally. Accessed January 15, 2021. www.commonwealthfund.org/sites/default/files/documents/___media_files_publications_fund_report_2014_jun_1755_davis_mirror_mirror_2014.pdf

Makary MA, Daniel M. (2016). Medical error—the third leading cause of death in the US. *British Medical Journal.* 353:i2139.

Rising, J.P., Reynolds, I.S., Sedrakyan, A. (2012). Delays and difficulties in assessing metal-on-metal hip 61 implants. *New England Journal of Medicine* 367(1):e1. doi:10.1056/NEJMp1206794

Sedrakyan, A. (2012). Metal-on-metal failures—in science, regulation, and policy. *Lancet (London, England).* 379(9822):1174–1176. doi:10.1016/S0140-6736(12)60372-9.

Snowdon, A. and Alessi, C. (2016). *Visibility: The New Value Proposition for Health Systems.* Retrieved January, 2021. World Health Innovation Network. https://issuu.com/worldhealthinnovationnetwork/docs/full_paper_-_win_visibility_thought/1?e=25657717/39177387.

Snowdon, A.W. (2018). Clinically Integrated Supply Chain Infrastructure in Health Systems: The Opportunity to Improve Quality and Safety. *Healthcare quarterly (Toronto, Ont.)* 21(3):19–23. https://doi.org/10.12927/hcq.2018.25706.

Snowdon, A.W., & Rocchio, B.J. (2018). Case Study: Supply Chain Transformation in the Mercy Health System. *Healthcare quarterly (Toronto, Ont.)* 21(3):28–33. https://doi.org/10.12927/hcq.2018.25704.

Snowdon, A.W., Saunders, M., & Wright, A. (2021). Key Characteristics of a Fragile Healthcare Supply Chain: Learning from a Pandemic. *Healthcare Quarterly* 24(1):36–43. doi10.12927/hcq.2021.26467.

Snowdon, A.W., Wright, A. (2018). Case Study: Supply Chain Transformation in the UK National Health Service. *Healthcare quarterly (Toronto, Ont.)* 21(3):24–27. https://doi.org/10.12927/hcq.2018.25705.

Statcan. Leading causes of death, by sex (both sexes). http://www.statcan.gc.ca/tables-tableaux/sumsom/l01/cst01/hlth36a-eng.htm. Accessed August 17, 2016.

Truog, R.D., Mitchell, C., & Daley, G.Q. (2020). The Toughest Triage — Allocating Ventilators in a Pandemic. *New England Journal of Medicine* 382(21):1973–1975. doi:10.1056/NEJMp2005689.

38 Protecting the Privacy and Security of Health Information: A Shared Responsibility

Rod Piechowski
MA, MS

CONTENTS

LEARNING OBJECTIVES

1. Discover the important relationship between informatics, security, and patient safety.
2. Describe fundamental privacy and security concepts.
3. Apply these concepts in daily work, career decisions, and leadership roles.

INTRODUCTION

The healthcare sector has come a long way when it comes to the use of information technology. In just ten years, the use of electronic health records and associated technologies rose dramatically. Information technology offers many advantages when implemented properly, and it offers benefits to patients, organizations, and in the larger picture, to our quest for medical insights and innovation. Prior to the ubiquitous presence of digital technology, records were stored in paper files that were not very portable, not conveniently searchable, and not available for research without a

DOI: 10.4324/9780429398377-44

great investment in time and resources. While information technology offers the promise of moving beyond the limits of paper, it comes with new challenges.

Today, data can be copied, moved, viewed, updated, and stored again much faster than could ever happen in a paper-based world. However, what is convenient for the user is also convenient for criminals, who can now steal or manipulate data in dangerous ways that pose a threat to privacy, operations, and patient safety. The transition to a digital environment is not a one-time investment, as many organizations are learning; devices and processes implemented even a few years ago pose a threat if not continuously evaluated for security issues. In a tradeoff few people foresaw, everyone in healthcare must now play a much more active role in protecting the information upon which medical care depends.

SECTION 1: PRIVACY VERSUS SECURITY

Privacy and security have a special relationship to each other. *Privacy* refers to how your data is shared and how much control you have over that sharing. This includes who gets to see the information the data reveals, why the data is shared, and for what purpose. *Security* refers to the controls put in place to help protect the privacy that an individual expects. Without security, you cannot have much of an expectation of privacy if the systems that hold your private information are easily attacked and breached. Security can be further broken down into other big buckets: *Physical security* involves the controls put in place to protect people, objects, and spaces. Fences, walls, lighting, guards, locks, and alarms are common examples of physical security controls. Physical controls protect our facilities as well as the information collected and stored within them, and they serve as the first line of defense. But what about the information itself, and the systems that are in place to protect that information? *Information security* and *cybersecurity* are common terms used to describe efforts to secure information and systems respectively. Most often, you will just hear about cybersecurity. For this discussion, the umbrella term *security* will suffice because, as you will see, we're all responsible for a bit of "physical," "information," and "cyber" security.

SECTION 2: ROLE OF PRIVACY AND SECURITY IN HEALTHCARE

Privacy and security are central to the healthcare system. Under the surface, healthcare is similar to many other types of services. People share information that can identify them every day. Hundreds of organizations know our names, addresses, identifiers, purchasing histories, credit information, tax records, and more. We trust these organizations with our data, whether it is a bank or an online vendor. Healthcare is similar, but very different: there is a special, much more personal relationship between patients and the care system. In order to receive proper care, people must share very personal details about their lives and health situation. The healthcare system has data related to people's work, what kind of insurance they have, their financial information, and health details, all in one place. Patients enter a relationship with that system with an expectation of privacy, and that includes the expectation that the people who need to see and work with that information will ensure its protection. Health information in the wrong hands leads to identity theft, or theft of services. In only a few years, criminals have attacked the healthcare system using more sophisticated techniques and with growing confidence. They rapidly evolved beyond individual identity theft to much more selective targeting of health systems. Healthcare faces a very real threat to medical knowledge, organizational stability, and lives. Around the world, healthcare and public health are part of a country's critical infrastructure, every bit as important as power, transportation, finance, and others (CISA 2020; Australian Government 2020; Cabinet Office (Cabinet Office United Kingdom, 2017). Security then, is foundational to the healthcare system.

SECTION 3: BASIC SECURITY CONCEPTS

PEOPLE, PROCESS, TECHNOLOGY

Security is not just about technology. Securing an organization against attack, be it physical or through cyber channels, involves people, process, and technology. This is one of the fundamental concepts behind successful security management for individuals and organizations. Many people incorrectly assume that cybersecurity is strictly the responsibility of technical teams, and the software and hardware they manage. Technology is only part of the picture. People are often the weakest link in the security chain. People can be manipulated to perform attacks on behalf of criminals, or they can act maliciously on their own. Solving the "insider" part of the puzzle is a big part of making an organization more secure. It involves education and awareness, along with the realization that everyone who works at an organization is responsible for security too. The third component is processes, which help people manage the technology and the flow of information. Process is extremely important in a highly technical world; without process, an organization would have no way to tell what vulnerabilities exist, have been patched, who has access to what information, etc. These three concepts form one of two "triads" that help manage privacy and security in any environment.

CONFIDENTIALITY, INTEGRITY, AVAILABILITY

Confidentiality, Integrity, and Availability are known as the CIA triad. *Confidentiality* involves ensuring that data is only seen by those with proper authorization. Confidentiality is closely related to the concept of privacy and are often used interchangeably. Confidentiality ensures that the information stays with those who have a right to know in order to provide treatment or services. Privacy deals with the amount of control an individual has relative to how the information is shared, or if it is shared, beyond that relationship. Maintaining confidentiality is a part of the job, and respecting that component crosses over into ethics territory. It is unethical to violate the confidentiality that patients expect. Breaking that confidentiality damages the trustworthiness of the institution and its reputation in the community.

Integrity refers to the data reliability. This is an extremely important concept as you can imagine. If an attacker alters the data is some way, it cannot be trusted; in a hospital environment, there are many forms of data collected and stored in a wide variety of systems. Data is everywhere, and it is part of keeping the underlying applications and networks running behind the scenes. It is used for payment and communications systems. And of course, clinical data is collected during every encounter with a patient; data volume continues to grow, so there is not only more to collect, but more to protect.

Availability refers to ensuring that the data required to provide services and quality care is there when needed. As we will see shortly, ransomware primarily attacks the availability of data. If all clinical and administrative systems are shut down due to a ransomware attack, a hospital cannot provide care. As with data integrity, data availability is intertwined with patient safety. The most dangerous threat to data is posed by attacks that somehow alter the original data. As you can imagine, this creates trouble across the data lifecycle, from its front-line use in a clinical setting to its later use in research.

Significant loss, damage to, or unavailability of data can have serious consequences for an organization. Hospital systems have had to shut down for days and sometimes weeks due to attacks on their networks and data. During that time, few if any services are available to the public. Trust is lost. Patients must go elsewhere to obtain care services. Even if an organization did everything right, there are ways that attacks can still occur. Reputational damage is extremely expensive to reverse. Trust takes time to establish but is lost in a moment; therefore, how an organization handles a data breach or cybersecurity event is critical. Trying to keep the event a secret is rarely the best path; depending on the number of records affected, the organization may be obligated to report the incident, which becomes part of the public record. When reviewing incidents, regulators have little tolerance for organizations that have not followed the most basic recommended privacy and security practices, especially if it is a continued pattern. Fines can and have put organizations into bankruptcy. Many current examples of violations and the resulting fines are published at the enforcement page at the U.S. Department of Health and Human Services website (HHS.gov 2020).

COMMON THREATS, VULNERABILITIES, AND ATTACKS

A threat can be almost anything or anyone. A threat is a potential harm to an organization, like a ransomware attack. A vulnerability is a weakness in the system that provides a threat actor to launch an attack. Vulnerabilities can be physical, like a hole in a fence; they can be technical, like an unpatched operating system with known weaknesses.

Threats can be internal or external. Internal threats could be something physical like fire, but could also be an employee. Malicious insiders have an advantage in that they have access to networks and data. According to the 2020 HIMSS Cybersecurity Survey, malicious insiders were responsible for 10% of reported security incidents over the previous 12 months. Negligent insiders were responsible for 13% of incidents; even if an employee meant no harm, insiders are still a threat, which is why awareness and education are so important in maintaining a secure environment (HIMSS 2020).

Information technology is complex by nature, and when organizations must maintain hundreds of servers, medical devices, switches, routers, personal computers, mobile devices, wired and wireless networks to maintain and secure, the complexity can be overwhelming. Complexity itself can pose a threat to an organization. Remember that each device probably has some sort of an operating system and some type of software that provides the human interface and expected functionality. Each device, whether it is a phone, or a laptop, or a scanner, employs several layers of technology to turn it on, record data, connect to other devices, and transmit data. At each layer, there may be vulnerabilities; devices can be vulnerable out of the box, or they may become vulnerable as weaknesses are identified in one or more layer. Keeping up with fixes through patching is time consuming and complex too. Consider, too, the incredible growth of smart devices ranging from coffee makers to thermostats and infusion pumps. There are billions of these devices and the number grows continuously. Each is a vulnerability. This complexity worsens when older devices cannot be upgraded or patched. Since their vulnerabilities are well-known in the security world (and therefore to criminals as well), they become perfect targets for attack.

It is important to note that *defending* a digital environment is much more challenging than *attacking* one. Even if a perfectly secure environment could exist, the defender cannot fail once. The attacker on the other hand, only has to know about and exploit a single vulnerability to gain access. Note that there are entire toolkits available designed to exploit known vulnerabilities in systems. Defenders must stay one step ahead, but it is challenging to do so. Attackers have many methods at their disposal.

SOCIAL ENGINEERING, PHISHING, MALWARE, RANSOMWARE

Attackers will try to exploit any weakness in a system, and they have highly specialized tools at their disposal. But it is much easier to go around the technical attacks, and manipulate people into circumventing any controls that are in place. For example, instead of brute-forcing a password, an attacker might pose as someone with the authority to work on a network, or to investigate a security issue, and simply ask someone for their password. *Social engineering* can get much more sophisticated than that, but it actually works. Social engineering also includes *phishing*, which is a type of attack that often comes in the form of an email. The 2020 HIMSS Cybersecurity Survey revealed that phishing is the number one significant security incident, and email is the primary entry point for this type of attack. Fifty-seven percent of survey respondents with significant security incidents named phishing as the method, while 20% reported social engineering attacks other than phishing (HIMSS21).

Phishing emails are more convincing than ever, and attackers take advantage of a worker's need to process a lot of information, answer questions, and get things done. Phishing seeks action on the part of the recipient, and typically takes the form of asking someone to click on a link to verify information or provide some other type of data, which could help an attacker gain access to an account. *Spear-phishing* is a form of phishing in which the attacker specifically targets an individual, usually someone who holds the type of credentials that, if stolen, would provide an attacker with easy access to high-value information and financial systems. *Whaling* is a type of phishing in which the targeted individual could be the CEO, CFO, etc.

RANSOMWARE

One type of attack that has gained in popularity is ransomware. In a ransomware attack, a nefarious link in an email could activate the invisible installation of malware, which can perform multiple operations. Usually, ransomware begins by taking inventory of every file it can find across a network; it then quietly encrypts files before notifying the user that the files are compromised. The attacker then asks for payment in exchange for decrypting the files so that they are usable again. This type of attack is big business for the operators, who "franchise" their software to people who then send it on to potential victims. The software creators take a percentage of the profit earned from this activity.

Ransomware is dangerous for a number of reasons. First, it can completely disable an organization's ability to operate. Criminals may encrypt operational data as easily as they can cripple clinical data. Second, in some instances, data is deliberately corrupted before it is encrypted, so even if a hospital manages to decrypt the data, it still has a data integrity problem. Quality backups are a must in order to restore full operation. Third, attackers are patient. Their malware may sit unnoticed for weeks or months and, as a result, may be included in several iterations of backups. Fourth, the malware may steal data before it is encrypted, which means the organization will most likely have to report the attack as a breach. The U.S. Health and Human Services Department recommends that ransomware attacks be treated as data breaches since the attackers have taken control of the data in order to encrypt it (Health and Human Services). Fifth, ransomware is a patient safety issue since data may be corrupted and until digital operations are restored, normal workflows, safety checks, and decision support are unavailable. Finally, recall that ransomware operators are criminals. Just because a company pays for a decryption key does not mean the attackers will follow through with their promise. Ransomware is a tricky space to navigate; in the end, each organization must consider this type of attack in its risk profile and decide how to respond. If you do not pay, you may not have backups from which to restore operations.

PASSWORDS

Aside from the scenario in which someone shares a password through social engineering or a phishing attack, cracking weak passwords is the easiest way for a threat actor to gain unauthorized access to a network. Each year, researchers pore over stolen data and access credentials to analyze patterns in the passwords. Analysis of stolen passwords in 2019 revealed the most-used and weakest passwords; unsurprisingly, the top five are: "12345"; "123456"; "123456789"; "test1"; and "password" (Winder 2019). Attackers can figure out passwords by looking at the hash value of common words (or commonly used passwords). A hash is a one way encoding of data that creates a fixed-length unique value for the password. For example, using one popular encoding algorithm, the password "12345" becomes "5994471abb01112afcc18159f6cc74b4f511b99806da59b3ca-f5a9c173cacfc5" (MD5CALC.com 2020). If an attacker manages to steal a list of hashed passwords, they simply compare a pre-hashed list of popular passwords to find a match; in this example, they now know the password is "12345". Complex passwords and phrases are best when they use a mix of characters and contain no common words.

Good password hygiene is essential; change them regularly, and do not reuse. Increasingly, multi-factor authentication (MFA) will complement the use of passwords. As the name implies, MFA requires the use of multiple factors. The three main categories of factors are something you *know* (like a password), something you *have* (like a token or code), and biometrics, or something you *are* (like fingerprints, retinal scans, etc.). MFA will continue to gain in popularity since it offers more security than passwords alone.

TOP WAYS TO PROTECT YOUR DATA

Creating a secure environment starts with awareness. Many companies send simulated phishing emails to their employees to demonstrate the kind of techniques threat actors use to trick someone into opening a document, or clicking on a web address. If the employee clicks on a simulated phishing attack link, they are notified that they have done so; further education and examples are shared. Consequences for continued failure vary by company, but at some, it can lead to dismissal. Phishing emails often contain misspellings or poor grammar. They may contain links to websites or attachments the attacker wants the victim to open. Often, the message creates a sense of urgency, which works in the attacker's favor, since it gives the victim little time to think about the request. Watching for these clues and thinking first go a long way toward reducing this very effective method used by attackers.

Data should be encrypted. That way, if a computer or digital files fall into the wrong hands, the attacker must expend time and computing power to break the encryption. Most casual attackers do not have those kind of resources, nor do they want to spend the time it takes to break the encryption key. Keep in mind that privacy and security are not just about protecting access to networks and servers. There are many instances in which a lost, unencrypted laptop was loaded with patient data. The loss is considered a breach and must be reported.

Another security issue involves legacy devices. These are software and hardware systems that are no longer supported by the manufacturer. From a security standpoint, legacy devices are dangerous because they do not get regular security updates. The HIMSS20 Cybersecurity Survey bears this out. Eighty percent of the survey's respondents said their organization still uses legacy systems. These include long outdated products such as Windows Server 2008, Windows 7, Windows XP, and Windows Server 2003 R2. Support for Windows XP was discontinued in 2014, while support for Windows Server 2003 was dropped in 2015. Yet these systems live on in a fragile environment in which patient safety is a critical issue. Technology is expensive to replace, and thousands of healthcare providers simply don't have the resources to keep up with the rapid pace of information technology development. Legacy systems should be prioritized for replacement.

Even recent technologies require frequent updates and security patching. Organizations should have a process in place to update systems as soon as possible when updates are released. Security patches are a must. Word of new vulnerabilities spreads rapidly, and attackers know there will be many opportunities to exploit the weakness. In the United States, the Office of Civil Rights (OCR) within the U.S. Department of Health and Human Services (HHS) can and has imposed significant fines when organizations suffer a breach. When that breach is due to a known but unpatched security issue, the organization's entire security mitigation process becomes suspect.

SECTION 4: LEGAL/REGULATORY

HIPAA

Privacy and security are global issues, especially now that billions of people have access to networks that send and receive information instantaneously. For the most part, information travels without regard to political boundaries. People can bank, attend classes, shop, and stay in touch with friends and family around the world. Health information is not freely shared with everyone for obvious reasons. The way sharing is controlled varies by region, culture, and country.

In the United States, the Health Insurance Portability and Accountability Act (HIPAA) was enacted in 1996. Its aim was to push for more standardized approaches to codes, unique identifiers, privacy, and security. The privacy rule specifies how protected health information (PHI) must be handled and used by covered entities. Covered entities include healthcare providers, health plans, clearinghouses that process data, and business associates. The rule outlines when PHI may be disclosed without authorization by the individual. It includes disclosure for treatment, payment, and operations, as well as for 12 other reasons categorized as national priority purposes such as public health; law enforcement; health oversight; victims of abuse, neglect, or domestic violence; some research; and others.

HIPAA's security rule states that covered entities must ensure the confidentiality, integrity, and availability of PHI. The rule also obligates covered entities to detect and safeguard against security threats, protect against impermissible uses, and certify that their workforce is compliant. Any breach involving over 500 names must be reported within 60 days and without unreasonable delay. There are significant fines for violations, especially where organizations operate without regard to the HIPAA privacy and security rules.

GDPR

The General Data Protection Regulation (GDPR) applies to people based in Europe. While HIPAA focuses on PHI, and is therefore healthcare specific, GDPR offers a much broader scope of protection that covers all personally identifiable information (PII) collected by any entity. Organizations outside of Europe are still accountable if they hold data on European citizens. GDPR contains provisions regarding which data is collected and where that information flows, so it is as much about how data is processed as it is about how it is protected. GDPR includes the right of an individual to be forgotten. That is, a citizen may request that their data be deleted from the record and can revoke consent to process data. In addition, GDPR allows people to correct personal data. Under GDPR, breaches must be reported within 72 hours, compared to 60 days under HIPAA. There are many other provisions, but one that bears mentioning relates to penalties for violating GDPR provisions. Fines are divided into two tiers, which are based on severity of the infraction, not on the size of the organization. For less severe infringements, the law holds that up to 2% of a company's annual global revenue or €10 million, whichever is higher. For more severe compliance failures, fines may be as large as €20 million or 4% of annual revenue, whichever is higher (Wolford 2020).

SECTION 5: CAREER IMPACT

There is a huge shortage of security professionals around the world. A 2019 (ISC)[2] survey estimates a workforce gap of 561,000 in North America. Asia-Pacific and Latin American regions are worse still, with estimated shortages of 2.6 million and 600,000 respectively. Europe fares best with a shortage of only 291,000 skilled security workers (ISC2 2019).

The COVID-19 outbreaks of 2020 proved again that threat actors will take advantage of any situation they can. Attackers specifically targeting the healthcare system rose during the pandemic, and they will likely continue the trend. Phishing and ransomware were particularly prevalent. The HIMSS survey revealed that 70% of all respondents experienced a significant security event in the previous year. These attacks increasingly target the integrity and availability of data needed to provide care services, as well as maintain operations. For healthcare, security is about patient safety and sector sustainability.

The rapid changes in technology and society have created new work roles and job titles that continue to evolve as these factors merge. As healthcare's use and understanding of technology matures, previously separate disciplines will converge, as has technology itself. Convergence will accelerate and those with a broad range of skills from a variety of disciplines will discover opportunities to apply those skills in new combinations and situations. As demonstrated during the COVID-19 epidemic, telehealth became an important tool, both for clinicians and patients; the rapid adoption of this technology also opened up more exploitable cracks in the system. Suddenly, telehealth security rose to the top of many priority lists.

The education system is playing catch-up (as we are) with new technologies and the social, economic, and political changes in a world made smaller by information and communications technology. One example of educational convergence is the development of advanced programs like the graduate degrees in security informatics offered at schools like Johns Hopkins University, Indiana University, and others (Indiana University 2020; Johns Hopkins University 2020).

In the United States, the National Institute of Science and Technology (NIST) runs a cybersecurity educational program called the National Initiative for Cybersecurity Education (NICE). The NICE framework is a great resource for anyone involved in cybersecurity education. Students can learn more about typical roles in security, skill requirements, and more. Employers and educators can use the framework to help define roles, education tracks, job descriptions, and more. While designed by a U.S. agency, the framework has global relevance (National Institute of Standards and Technology 2020).

CONCLUSION

The digitization of healthcare is well into its next phase. The first phase was implementing the technologies that allowed electronic data capture, storage, retrieval, and movement. This phase involves analyzing and protecting the data. Knowledge of data's purpose, structure, and meaning will continue as core skills. As we become ever more dependent on data to guide decision-making, clinical care, and public health, understanding how to safeguard its confidentiality, integrity, and availability will prove integral to ensuring that data is trustworthy. Information and knowledge gleaned from trustworthy data can be confidently applied to better analysis, decision support, and better health for all.

REFERENCES

Australian Government. 2020. "Critical Infrastructure Resilience." Department of Home Affairs website. Last modified April 23, 2020. Accessed December 3, 2020. https://www.homeaffairs.gov.au/about-us/our-portfolios/national-security/security-coordination/critical-infrastructure-resilience

Cabinet Office (United Kingdom). 2017. "Public Summary of Sector Security and Resilience Plans 2017." December. Accessed October 26, 2020. https://assets.publishing.service.gov.uk/government/uploads/system/uploads/attachment_data/file/678927/Public_Summary_of_Sector_Security_and_Resilience_Plans_2017__FINAL_pdf___002_.pdf

CISA (Cybersecurity and Infrastructure Security Agency). 2020. "Critical Infrastructure Sectors." Last modified October 21, 2020. Accessed December 3, 2020. https://www.cisa.gov/critical-infrastructure-sectors

HIMSS20 Global Health Conference & Exhibition. https://www.himss.org/global-conference

ISC2. 2019. "Strategies for Building and Growing Strong Cybersecurity Teams". Accessed August 30, 2021, from https://www.isc2.org/Research/-/media/6573BE9062B64FC7B4B91F20ECC56299.ashx

Johns Hopkins University. 2020. "Master of Science in Security Informatics Program." Accessed December 1, 2020. https://www.cs.jhu.edu/mssi-program/

Md5calc.com. "Online MD5 Hash Calculator." Accessed October 29, 2020. https://md5calc.com/hash

National Institute of Standards and Technology. 2020. "National Initiative for Cybersecurity Education (NICE)." Accessed December 3, 2020. https://www.nist.gov/itl/applied-cybersecurity/nice

U.S. Department of Health and Human Services. 2020. "Enforcement Highlights." Last modified September 30, 2020. Accessed December 3, 2020. https://www.hhs.gov/hipaa/for-professionals/compliance-enforcement/data/enforcement-highlights/index.html

U.S. Department of Health and Human Services. "Ransomware Fact Sheet." Accessed December 3, 2020. https://www.hhs.gov/sites/default/files/RansomwareFactSheet.pdf

Winder, Davey. 2019. "Ranked: The World's Top 100 Worst Passwords." Forbes, December 14. Accessed October 27, 2020. https://www.forbes.com/sites/daveywinder/2019/12/14/ranked-the-worlds-100-worst-passwords/#45dcf4a069b4

Wolford, Ben. 2020. "What are the GDPR Fines?" GDPR.EU. Accessed December 3, 2020. https://gdpr.eu/fines/

39 Health Interoperability and Standards: An Overview

Mari Greenberger
MPPA

CONTENTS

LEARNING OBJECTIVES

1. Recognize the importance of health data standards and information exchange across the entire healthcare ecosystem.
2. Discover relevant standards development and profiling efforts which are directly aligned with information exchange initiatives impacting advanced care models, clinician workflow, and efficiency.
3. Describe the imperative of including non-traditional data sources which captures an individual's social determinants that can address systemic challenges around health equity and access to care.
4. Discuss how health IT plays a key role in supporting immunizations driven by both routine care and by public health crises.

INTRODUCTION

Interoperability and health data standards have a reciprocal and critical relationship—they work in concert and cannot reach their fullest potential if not used together. Interoperability is not a destination, but rather it is what enables the entire healthcare ecosystem to function properly across the care continuum and enables the actualization of the quadruple aim of healthcare—enhancing patient experience, improving population health, reducing costs and improving the work life of healthcare providers, including clinicians and staff[1]. Health data standards are the individual pieces that are

DOI: 10.4324/9780429398377-45

fundamental to allowing the entire puzzle come into clear view—whether it's for an individual patient or a broader population—standards are essential to realizing true interoperability.

Definitions for complex concepts like interoperability continue to evolve, but there are core competencies that must be included. Currently HIMSS defines interoperability as "the ability of different information systems, devices and applications (systems) to access, exchange, integrate and cooperatively use data in a coordinated manner, within and across organizational, regional and national boundaries, to provide timely and seamless portability of information and optimize the health of individuals and populations globally"[2]. Going beyond a concrete definition, it's important to capture the multi-dimensional aspects of interoperability, which is why HIMSS has gone further to define the "four levels"[3] of interoperability, which include:

- **Foundational (Level 1):** Establishes the inter-connectivity requirements needed for one system or application to securely communicate data to and receive data from another
- **Structural (Level 2):** Defines the format, syntax, and organization of data exchange including at the data field level for interpretation
- **Semantic (Level 3):** Provides for common underlying models and codification of the data including the use of data elements with standardized definitions from publicly available value sets and coding vocabularies, providing shared understanding and meaning to the user
- **Organizational (Level 4):** Includes governance, policy, social, legal, and organizational considerations to facilitate the secure, seamless, and timely communication and use of data both within and between organizations, entities, and individuals. These components enable shared consent, trust, and integrated end-user processes and workflows

Compared to the evolving nature of defining interoperability, health data standards are more concrete in terms of how they are defined, categorized, and utilized. In order to understand the types of health data standards available for use, informatics professionals organize these standards into the following five categories: vocabulary/terminology, content, transport, privacy and security, and identifiers. HIMSS defines these standards[4] as the following:

- **Vocabulary/Terminology:** They address the ability to represent concepts in an unambiguous manner between a sender and receiver of information, a fundamental requirement for effective communication. Health information systems that communicate with each other rely on structured vocabularies, terminologies, code sets and classification systems to represent health concepts. Logical Observation Identifiers Names and Codes (LOINC®) and International Statistical Classification of Diseases and Related Health Problems (ICD)-10 are examples currently used in the marketplace.
- **Content:** They relate to the data content within exchanges of information. They define the structure and organization of the electronic message or document's content. This standard category also includes the definition of common sets of data for specific message types. Consolidated-CDA and HL7's Version 2.x (V2) are examples currently used in the marketplace.
- **Transport**: They address the format of messages exchanged between computer systems, document architecture, clinical templates, user interface, and patient data linkage. Standards center on "push" and "pull" methods for exchanging health information. Digital Imaging and Communications in Medicine (DICOM), Fast Healthcare Interoperability Resources (FHIR®), and Direct Standard™ are some examples currently used in the marketplace.
- **Privacy and Security:** These standards aim to protect an individual's (or organization's) right to determine whether, what, when, by whom, and for what purpose their personal health information is collected, accessed, used, or disclosed. Security standards define a set of administrative, physical and technical actions to protect the confidentiality, availability, and integrity of health information. In the United States, the main example is the Health Insurance Portability and Accountability Act (HIPAA) Privacy Rule and the Security Rule.

Within the Europe Union (EU), General Data Protection Regulation (GDPR), outlines privacy and security regulations for all processing and storage of data relating to data subjects (including people).

- **Identifiers:** Enable entities to uniquely identify patients or providers. Current examples in the marketplace include Enterprise Master Patient Index (EMPI), Medical Record Number (MRN), or a National Provider ID (NPI).

Data analytics is a core competency for all healthcare delivery organizations, provider settings, community-based organizations, payers, and the broader healthcare ecosystem, interoperability among exchange partners is essential for all to succeed. Each stakeholder needs data to create information about their patient, community, and region that they can trust. Over the last several decades, there has been incremental change to increase the technical infrastructure and ability to efficiently and securely share information where and when it is most needed, but more recently two major events have truly catalyzed the healthcare industry's investment in interoperability forward: The finalization of new regulatory mandates implementing provisions of the 21st Century Cures Act and the COVID-19 Global Pandemic. These two events have really accelerated and created an even stronger sense of urgency to implement strategies to realize interoperable data exchange for all healthcare stakeholders world-wide.

SECTIONS 1: HEALTH DATA STANDARDS: THE PIECES TO A COMPLEX HEALTHCARE PUZZLE

Standards provide a common language and a common set of expectations that enable interoperability between systems and/or devices[5]. The ability to communicate in a way that ensures the message is received and the content is understood is dependent on the use of standards—this is true for any industry—and healthcare is no different. Health data standards enable a reduction of ambiguity in communication so that actions taken based on the data are consistent with the actual meaning of that data. In order to seamlessly digest information about an individual and improve the overall coordination and delivery of care, standards enable all members of the healthcare ecosystem to share data regardless of application or market supplier.

There are several kinds of standard organizations that have a mission which ultimately strives to develop or set standards. These organizations are focused on developing, coordinating, promulgating, revising, amending, reissuing, interpreting, or otherwise producing standards that are intended to address the needs of a broad stakeholder base of affected adopters.[6]

In order to be recognized as a standard development organization (SDO), an organization may be accredited by one of two entities: the American National Standards Institute (ANSI) or the International Organization for Standardization (ISO). These Health data standards can also be developed by other groups such as trade unions or associations. To-date, the development and adoption of open, consensus-based standards has shown that it can be a complex process, as it involves many different stakeholders and subject matter experts, and takes time. These standards organization have varying processes, although generally follow shared rules of working through a multi-stakeholder and consensus-based process, to adequately respond to a specific market and industry use case.

Standards are created by several methods[7]:

- A group of interested parties comes together and agrees upon a standard.
- The government sanctions a process for standards to be developed.
- Marketplace competition and technology adoption introduces a de facto standard.
- A formal consensus process is used by a standards development organization (SDO) to publish standards.

As mentioned earlier, there are five different kinds of health data standards that are organized into the following categories: vocabulary/terminology (e.g., Current Procedural Terminology (CPT®)), content (e.g., Consolidated CDA (C-CDA)[8], transport (e.g., Direct Standard™[9]), privacy and security (e.g., HIPAA Rule[10]), and identifiers (e.g., Enterprise Master Patient Index, Medical Record Number). It's important to remember that standards are essential because they describe and constrain what data moves but implementation guides, including profiles, define how to implement these different kinds of standards.

A benefit to the use of implementation guides like Integrating the Healthcare Enterprise (IHE) Profiles is that they provide a common language for purchasers and market suppliers to discuss the integration needs of healthcare sites and the integration capabilities of health IT products.[11] They provide a clear process and definitions of how to implement standards to meet specific clinical needs. They offer developers a clear implementation path for standards that has been carefully documented, reviewed and tested as well as supported by industry partners. They give purchasers a tool that reduces the complexity, cost, and anxiety of implementing interoperable systems.

The next section will explore how these standards and implementation guides are being leveraged in the real-world to facilitate interoperable health information exchange and data sharing around the globe.

SECTION 2: WHERE THE RUBBER MEETS THE ROAD: REAL-WORLD EFFORTS DRIVING ACTION

Now that a baseline has been set around the fundamental components of interoperability and the kinds of health data standards that exist and how they come to fruition, this section will explore some of the ongoing initiatives happening around the world putting everything together to improve the health potential of every human, everywhere.

Public policy and government efforts have catalyzed so much of the real-world efforts driving interoperability into action. In order to achieve varying levels of interoperability differing levels of government involvement, guidance and regulation[12] have been required. The following highlights existing initiatives and key policies based on region.

United States focused:

- [United States] *21st Century Cures Act:* Among the health IT provisions outlined in 21st Century Cures Act, many sections provide directives to the ONC, Centers for Medicare and Medicaid Services (CMS), and other agencies related to improving interoperability[13]
- [United States] *Interoperability Standards Advisory (ISA):* The ISA process represents a single, public list of standards and implementation specifications published by ONC. ONC coordinates the identification, assessment and determination of these recommended standards and implementation specifications for industry use to fulfill specific clinical health IT interoperability needs. Stakeholders are encouraged to implement and use these recommended standards as applicable to their needs[14]
- [United States] *State-level initiatives:* In the United States, state public health agencies manage and track information for immunizations, infectious diseases, and vital statistics, however, they often lack adequate funding to ensure their information systems are updated and conform to national standards and profiles. Health information exchanges[15]—which are public or private entities, depending on the state and region—aim to ensure there is robust and standardized data exchange between and among public health entities and state and local health departments.

Internationally focused:

- Canada's Health Infoway manages an ePrescribing service, PrescribeIT[16], which electronically shares prescription information with clinicians from pharmacies for dispensing medications. Another Infoway initiative, ACCESS Health[17], aims to accelerate citizen access to personal health information and digital health services. The exchange initiative is expected to use a cloud-based infrastructure, a FHIR-based API service and a blockchain-enabled consent service

- The Global Digital Health Partnership (GDHP) is a collaboration of over 40 governments and territories, government agencies, and the World Health Organization, formed to support the effective implementation of digital health services[18]. Interoperability is one of the various work streams explored by GDHP. The proposed work stream activities focus on the evolving challenges of sharing patient data between care providers, organizations, caregivers, and patients. These challenges are partly a technical problem for health systems, clinicians and patients, however they also pose significant risks for patient safety, and detract from high-quality coordinated care and the efficient delivery of services. A GDHP report outlines a variety of government efforts from 15 participating countries
- The eHealth Digital Service Infrastructure (EHDSI) facilitates the two primary building blocks of cross-border digital health services in Europe: ePrescription and Patient Summary[19]. ePrescription (and eDispensation) allows EU citizens to obtain their medication in a pharmacy located in another EU country. Patient Summary provides information on important health related aspects such as allergies, current medication, previous illness, surgeries, etc. The digital Patient Summary is meant to provide doctors with essential information in their own language concerning the patient, when the patient comes from another EU country and there may be a linguistic barrier
- Australia's My Health Record is an opt-out, Clinical Document Architecture (CDA)-based document repository used to store shared health summaries, eReferrals, specialist letters, discharge summaries, event summaries, prescription records, diagnostic imaging, and pathology reports[20]. Once patients have their record, they are able to manage access and permissions
- Hong Kong's Electronic Health Record Sharing System (eHRSS) is the country's equivalent to a regional HIE, managing patient data on care episodes, lab results, radiology studies, and drug items[21]. The Hong Kong Hospital Authority launched eHRSS to public and private health sectors using an opt-in patient consent model.

While this list is not comprehensive, it highlights the comprehensive data sharing efforts occurring around the world.

SECTION 3: ADVANCE HEALTH EQUITY AND CHAMPION WELLNESS BY CAPTURING SOCIAL DETERMINANTS DATA

The social determinants of health (SDOH), or the conditions in which people are born, grow, live, work and age[22], have gained immense recognition across the health ecosystem for the broad ranging impact these conditions have on health equity and an individual's overall well-being. SDOH includes data points such as level of food security, socioeconomic status (inclusive of income, educational attainment and subjective perception of social status), access to care, reliable transportation, safe housing, neighborhood characteristics, and the composition of a person's social support network[23]. These conditions are shaped by a wider set of socioeconomic and political forces known as the structural determinants of health, including public and social policies, governance, macroeconomics, and societal and cultural values (Figure 39.1). These structural determinants can perpetuate inequities associated with race, sexual orientation, class, and other markers of human difference that produce systematic disadvantages, which lead to inequitable experiences of the social determinants of health and ultimately dictate health outcomes.

As the main driver of health inequities, or the differences regarding the access individuals have to achieve optimal health, the social determinants of health have shown a greater impact on

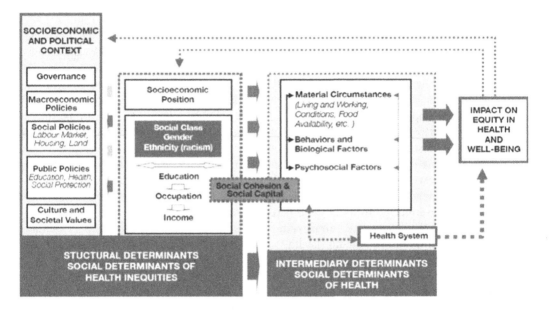

FIGURE 39.1

Source: World Health Organization (2010). *A conceptual framework for action on the social determinants of health: social determinants of health discussion Paper 2*. Geneva: World Health Organization.

population health and individual well-being than factors such as biology, behavior, and health-care[24]. Socioeconomic status, when compared to other health risk factors such as physical in-activity, diabetes, smoking, obesity, high blood pressure, and high alcohol intake is found to be one of the strongest predictors of illness and death worldwide[25]. Healthcare, although essential for health, has shown to be a relatively weak influencer of health in that it has been estimated to account for only 10–20% of the modifiable contributors to healthy outcomes for a population[26]. The other 80–90% have been attributed to the social, economic and environmental factors referred to as SDOH[27].

ADVANCING EQUITABLE ACCESS FOR HEALTH INFORMATION AND TECHNOLOGY

As healthcare continues to become increasingly digitized, the technological advances that pose the same promise of improved care has also posed the potential for unintended consequences related to the social determinants of health and health equity. The proclivity of technological advances in healthcare to produce or exacerbate health inequities is increasingly being highlighted as a concern for public health. Socio-demographic characteristics and social determinants of health—particularly age, education, income, geographic location, and perceived social isolation—can also predict internet access and use proficiency[28]. Rural populations, racial or ethnic minority groups, those of low-socioeconomic status, and older adults are less likely to have the digital health literacy skills, or the knowledge to use emerging information and communications technologies to improve or enable health and healthcare, and the access to Internet-capable digital devices needed to engage in and benefit from virtual health services[29].

   To avoid duplicating the social stratification that exists in society-at-large within healthcare, these "digital determinants of health" have rightfully become an area of heavy focus. Currently there is a push to advance equitable access to health information and technology as telehealth, remote patient monitoring, artificial intelligence, big data analytics and the use of mobile health apps have proven potential to enhance health outcomes by improving medical diagnosis, data-based treatment decisions, digital therapeutics, self-management of care, and person-centered care[30]. The COVID-19 pandemic, given its devastating consequences on the elderly, those with chronic comorbidities and racial or ethnic minority groups[31], has added significant urgency to the mission of using technology as the great equalizer in healthcare. The World Health Organization (WHO) recently released the "Draft global strategy on digital health 2020–2025" with the vision to improve global health by "accelerating the development and adoption of appropriate, accessible, affordable, scalable, and sustainable person-centric digital health solutions to prevent, detect, and respond to epidemics and pandemics, and developing infrastructure and applications that enable countries to use health data to promote health and well-being"[32]. Perhaps the most vital health data in the effort to sustainably and equitably address and improve population health while optimizing the use of health information and technology for all people, is data reflective of a person's SDOH.

INCORPORATING SDOH DATA INTO HEALTHCARE SETTINGS

The need to integrate SDOH data into care delivery settings to improve individual and population health outcomes is widely known and is accompanied by a set of technical, organizational, and operational considerations that require examination of current infrastructure, workflows, necessary cross-sector stakeholder relationships, and the return on investment (ROI) for health systems which are experiencing the shift to value-based care.

Health entities considering SDOH technology solutions and assessment tools will want to consider how the solution or tool integrates into the EHR, how it demonstrates ROI (i.e., emergency department readmissions or medication adherence) and how it engages with social services or community-based organizations (CBOs) on which many SDOH interventions rely. Regarding EHR integration, health IT projects are requiring expanded infrastructure components to either incorporate the SDOH data into EHR systems or to create federated enterprise information systems that access SDOH data and aggregate it to support both treatment and public policy formation.

Additionally, to integrate SDOH data into the EHR, workflows and intake processes will need to be addressed to determine at which point in patient care this type of data is collected, and by who. Currently there is a lack of well-established training methods for clinical staff on the use of available health IT tools (including screening tools, assessment tools and technologies such as AI and NLP) used to collect SDOH data. Largely dependent on the EHR, the manual transfer of SDOH data from patient questionnaires to EHRs can negatively affect clinical efficiency and add burden to workflow. Furthermore, SDOH data means little if the information can't be assembled in such a way that it can be shared with organizations that can implement an intervention for social care needs such as low food security or homelessness. For this reason, it is also important to consider whether the health system is the most appropriate or accurate place to collect this type of information.

Cross-sector stakeholder relationships between health systems, CBOs, public health entities and others are critical in the integration and meaningful use of SDOH data in care delivery settings. For example, large CBOs, when compared to health systems, are often better positioned to collect data on social needs as they have a greater ability to collect more nuanced, ongoing, and up-to-date information about individuals that present with social care gaps and needs[33]. Although CBOs often can lack the technical infrastructure and staff to participate in data sharing arrangements with health systems, these organizations, along with public health entities often maintain a multifaceted understanding of the communities in which they work and can offer health systems valuable insights as to how certain social services affect a community's health. In order to most effectively do this, universally accepted and utilized data exchange standards are needed to facilitate the bi-directional flow of information between health systems, CBOs, public health entities, and other stakeholders such as social care programs, public safety, and education.

Finally, long term investment in SDOH is difficult for healthcare providers and payers whose experience in ROI is more directly tied to fee-for-service care. This presents a need for bi-directional education on tangible value propositions for the stakeholders involved, including the community partners, government entities, providers, and payers in order to support long term investments that will measure and demonstrate valuable impact. While CBOs, public health entities, and other relevant stakeholders may allow health systems to determine which SDOH to prioritize via community health assessments, systematically implementing SDOH interventions in a fragmented social and healthcare ecosystem can prove difficult where financial incentives for health systems, CBOs, government entities, and other stakeholders may be misaligned.

SECTION 4: THE IMPERATIVE OF PUBLIC HEALTH INTEROPERABILITY

PUBLIC HEALTH INTEROPERABILITY

Public health interoperability can be defined as a system to "support the ability of different information technology (IT) systems and applications to communicate, as well as exchange and use of information, would ensure that the right information can be shared between public health agencies and healthcare providers in a timely manner to address public health crises and epidemics"[34].

IMMUNIZATION ROAD BLOCKS TO INTEROPERABILITY

The United States and its territories manage and operate 62 independent immunization information systems (IISs) located within state and city health departments and governed by the Centers for Disease Control and Prevention's (CDC) National Center for Immunization and Respiratory Diseases (NCIRD), Immunization Services Division (ISD). While a national immunization registry is currently not feasible for several factors, mainly political, IISs have developed solutions for local issues and operate independently. Consequently, EHR market suppliers are currently required to customize products to accommodate for the large variability of interoperability and information sharing needs from the 62 independent IISs. In an ideal situation, immunization interoperability involves inputting patient-level data into the EHR, the IIS receiving the information and then IIS staff gathering and using the data for population-level decision making (CDC, 2020) to support the inventory management, distribution, administration tracking and reporting of vaccines. Figure 39.2 represents the ideal process and use of information in immunization data sharing (CDC, 2020).

While the potential for positive impact is evident, state and city health departments and healthcare providers do not use the same information systems, data formats, or data standards[35], resulting in incomplete and inaccurate data, under- and over-vaccinating patients, and increasing the risk of vaccine-preventable diseases in a population[36].

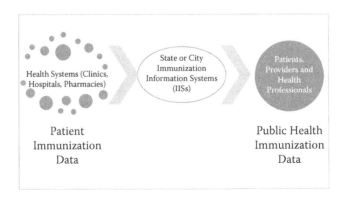

FIGURE 39.2   Immunization integration.

Furthermore, Indian Health Services that serve the American Indian/Alaska Native population of the United States, the U.S. territories, and rural areas have their own varying sets of issues to interoperability in the communities they support resulting in the lack of a comprehensive view of the health needs of a population. The American Indian/Alaska Native population primarily relies on regional Indian Health Services (IHS) for their primary and urgent care needs where their IISs are managed and operated[37]. The IHS IISs are not typically mature enough to have the technical capability to interoperate with most EHRs, resulting in gaps to preventative care and illness treatment. The U.S. territories independently manage their IISs, similar to state IISs, but present unique challenges including issues to basic network connectivity, hardware and system updates required to achieve interoperability with EHRs. Rural areas of the United States historically have lower rates[38] of immunization and are exacerbated by the outdated IISs that lack the technology for EHRs to share information that is complete and accurate.

OPPORTUNITIES FOR IMPROVEMENT

Although complex obstacles to achieving public health interoperability remain, strides are being made from different groups, associations and federal agencies that have recognized the gaps to achieving public health interoperability. These organizations are investing in initiatives that support the improvement and advancement of immunization interoperability. Outlined below in Figure 39.3, highlights of public health interoperability initiatives including sources of funding, purpose, and key stakeholders are represented.

UNIQUE CHALLENGES FOR SPECIAL POPULATIONS

In response to preparing for a new vaccine to address the COVID-19 pandemic, an incredible amount of decisions are needed to be made in a very short period of time. Some of the technical and programmatic issues include: coordinating the distribution of vaccines from the manufacturer to health systems; identifying the order of which patients will receive the first available vaccines; reporting and tracking vaccinations given throughout jurisdictions; and, organizing health education campaigns on the safety and effectiveness of the vaccine. Essential workers are not all defined equally across states and will need to be further defined and identified to be appropriately vaccinated in a timely manner. Since public health reporting requirements is currently centralized through IISs for vaccine inventory, distribution, and administration will present as particularly difficult as they continue to operate with conflicting data standards, information systems, and data formats—making public health interoperability near impossible in some regions.

Special populations face unique challenges, specifically for the American Indians/Alaskan Natives, U.S. territories and rural areas when preparing for a new vaccine. American Indians/ Alaskan Natives include just over 2% of the U.S. population but are 5.3 times more likely to be hospitalized due to COVID-19 then their white counterparts, as reported in U.S. News[39], the largest disparity for all other ethnic and racial groups represented in the U.S. Rural areas are confronted with distribution and storage issues since most state and local health departments in rural settings are often smaller in size and cannot accommodate supplies for mass vaccination. Therefore, these areas require a different vaccine administration plan before mass production begins. U.S. territories continue to present with different challenges, such as basic network connectivity issues, to ensure they have timely access to vaccines and population-level immunization data.

IMPERATIVE TO PUBLIC HEALTH INTEROPERABILITY

The issues to public health interoperability are complex but the problem and the solution encompass similar stakeholder groups including, but not limited to, clinicians, EHRs, HIEs, and IISs.

Public Health Interoperability Initiatives	Source of Funding	Purpose	Key Stakeholders
APHL'S Informatics Messaging Services (AIMS) Platform	Association of Public Health Laboratories (APHL)	▪ APHL promotes the role of state and local public health laboratories in the detection and surveillance of VPDs by improving knowledge, providing trainings and ensuring quality information exchange and offers, AIMS, a secure, cloud based platform that accelerates the implementati on of health messaging by p roviding shared services to aid in the visualization, interoperability, security and hosting of electronic data.	▪ Federal agencies ▪ United States Uniformed Services ▪ Regional commercial laboratories and hospitals ▪ State Health Information Exchanges ▪ State public health jurisdictions
Digital Bridge	Not Applicable	▪ Discussesthe challenges of information sharing and collaborate on ideas and solutions for a nationally consistent and sustainable approach to using electronic health data.	▪ Health care experts ▪ Public health professionals ▪ Industry partners
▪ Immunization Gateway (Vaccine Administration Management System (VAMS)	Department of Health & Human Services, Office of the Chief Technology Officer (OCTO)	▪ Increases the availability and volume of complete and accurate immunization data stored within IIS and available to providers and consumers regardless of their jurisdictional boundaries by providing a centralized technical infrastructure that facilitates the flow of immunization data through an intelligent message router between IISs, large multi-jurisdictional provider organizations to IIS, and from IIS to consumers.	▪ IISs ▪ Large multi-jurisdictional provider organizations ▪ Consumers
Immunization Integration Program (IIP): ▪ Collaborative ▪ Testing & Recognition	CDC's National Center for Immunization and Respiratory Diseases (NCIRD) Immunizati on Services Division (ISD)	▪ Brings key stakeholders to improveimmunization interoperability, information sharing and management with the goal of assuring clinicians and IISs have timely access to complete and accurate data to improve clinical decision-making and management, increase vaccination coverage and reduce vaccine-preventable diseases.	▪ Clinicians ▪ EHR Developers ▪ Health Information Exchanges (HIEs) ▪ IISs ▪ Public Health
Measurement & Improvement Initiative	CDC's National Center for Immunization and Respiratory Diseases (NCIRD) Immunization Services Division (ISD)	▪ Provides IIS with information and guidance to align with the IIS Functional Standards, a set of specifications which describe the operations, data quality, and technology needed by IIS to support immunization programs, vaccination providers, and other immunization stakeholders.	▪ IISs
Strategic Health Information Exchange Collaborative (SHIEC)	Not Applicable	▪ SHIEC strives to enable the secure exchange of patient information to improve the quality, coordination, and cost-effectiveness of healthcare locally, regionally and nationally.	▪ Governmental, business or legal entitiesprimarily engaged in providing health information exchange services in a multi-stakeholder environment; has an HIE regulatory, coordination, or standards development role, or the organization is a single entity (private) HIE

FIGURE 39.3   Opportunities to improve public health interoperability.

Sources: https://www.aphl.org/programs/informatics/Pages/aims_platform.aspx; https://digitalbridge.us/; https://www.hhs.gov/cto/initiatives/public-health-innovation/immunization-gateway/index.html; https://www.himss.org/what-we-do-initiatives/himss-immunization-integration-program; https://www.immregistries.org/measurement-improvement; https://strategichie.com.

Therefore, the issues to public health interoperability must be addressed collaboratively across sectors. AIRA has outlined IIS Policies to Support Pandemic and Routine Vaccination to "ensure that policies support complete and accurate data exchange"[40]. Immunization integration is one example of the imperative to public health interoperability but it signals an alarm to the need to reinvest in public health technology infrastructure and workforce development across the health ecosystem, as outlined in CDC'S Data Modernization Initiative[41]. Health information and technology advancements evolve at a rapid pace and public health interoperability should be viewed with the same level of urgency to advance infrastructures that support evidence-based decision-making to improve health outcomes for patients and communities.

CONCLUSION

As the global healthcare ecosystem continues to evolve and advance around critical areas, such as interoperability and health data exchange, the value and impact to all healthcare stakeholders should have a direct correlation of improved access to health information and care outcomes. Around the globe we are combatting the COVID-19 global pandemic, which has exposed many pain points and weaknesses that can lay the groundwork for systematic changes and solutions to drive improved health outcomes for every human around the world. More acutely, the COVID-19 global pandemic has shined a spotlight on the essential work that needs to continue around the inclusion of non-traditional data elements, such as those that encompass SDOH, along with all types of systems (IISs, EHRs, and HIEs) and devices interoperating seamlessly by managing public and social health needs.

This chapter was intended to provide a baseline understanding around the imperative to use health data standards to enable the highest level of interoperability across the industry. By doing so, this directly impacts our ability to fulfill the need for advanced care models, clinician workflow, and efficiency. It also highlights several pivotal policies and initiatives occurring worldwide to drive these standards forward and put them into action.

NOTES

1 https://www.ncbi.nlm.nih.gov/pmc/articles/PMC4226781/
2 https://www.himss.org/resources/interoperability-healthcare
3 https://www.himss.org/resources/interoperability-healthcare
4 https://www.himss.org/resources/interoperability-healthcare
5 https://www.himss.org/resources/interoperability-healthcare
6 https://www.himss.org/resources/interoperability-healthcare
7 Hammond, W. E. (2005). The making and adoption of health data standards. *Health Affairs, 23,* 1205–1213.
8 https://www.hl7.org/implement/standards/product_matrix.cfm
9 https://www.directtrust.org/standards#history
10 https://www.hhs.gov/hipaa/for-professionals/index.html
11 https://www.ihe.net/resources/profiles/
12 https://www.himss.org/himss-public-policy-center
13 https://www.himss.org/resources/21st-century-cures-key-interoperability-provisions
14 https://www.healthit.gov/isa/
15 https://strategichie.com/
16 https://prescribeit.ca/
17 https://www.infoway-inforoute.ca/en/solutions/access-health
18 https://www.gdhp.org/interoperability
19 https://ec.europa.eu/health/ehealth/home_en#:~:text=To%20facilitate%20greater%20cross%2Dborder,be %20exchanged%20between%20healthcare%20providers.
20 https://www.myhealthrecord.gov.au/
21 https://www.ehealth.gov.hk/en/home/index.html
22 World Health Organization. (2020). Social determinants of health. Retrieved October 10, 2020 from https://www.who.int/social_determinants/sdh_definition/en/

23 Healthy People 2030, U.S. Department of Health and Human Services, Office of Disease Prevention and Health Promotion. Retrieved October 10, 2020 from https://health.gov/healthypeople/objectives-and-data/social-determinants-health

24 American Academy of Family Physicians. (2019). Advancing Health Equity by Addressing the Social Determinants of Health in Family Medicine (Position Paper). Retrieved October 10, 2020 from https://www.aafp.org/about/policies/all/social-determinants-health-family-medicine.html

25 The Lancet. (2017). Low socioeconomic status reduces life expectancy and should be counted as a major risk factor in health policy, study says. ScienceDaily. Retrieved October 12, 2020 from www.sciencedaily.com/releases/2017/01/170131190102.htm

26 Hood, C. M., K. P. Gennuso, G. R. Swain, and B. B. Catlin. (2016). County health rankings: Relationships between determinant factors and health outcomes. American Journal of Preventive Medicine 50(2):129–135. https://doi.org/10.1016/j.amepre.2015.08.024

27 Magnan, S. (2017). Social Determinants of Health 101 for Health Care: Five Plus Five. NAM Perspectives. National Academy of Medicine, Washington, DC. https://doi.org/10.31478/201710c

28 Azzopardi-Muscat, N., Sørensen, K. (2019). Towards an equitable digital public health era: promoting equity through a health literacy perspective. European Journal of Public Health, 29(3): 13–17. https://doi.org/10.1093/eurpub/ckz166

29 Nouri, S., Khoong, E., Lyles, C., Karliner, L. (2020). Addressing Equity in Telemedicine for Chronic Disease Management During the COVID-19 Pandemic. NEJM Catalyst, Issue 3. https://catalyst.nejm.org/doi/pdf/10.1056/CAT.20.0123

30 World Health Organization. (2019). Draft global strategy on digital health 2020–2025. Retrieved October 10, 2020 from https://www.who.int/docs/default-source/documents/gs4dhdaa2a9f352b0445bafbc79ca799dce4d.pdf

31 Moore, J., Pilkington, W., Kumar, D. (2020). Disease with health disparities as drivers of COVID-19 outcome. Journal of Cellular and Molecular Medicine, 00: 1–8. https://doi.org/10.1111/jcmm.15599

32 World Health Organization. (2019). Draft global strategy on digital health 2020–2025. Retrieved October 10, 2020 from https://www.who.int/docs/default-source/documents/gs4dhdaa2a9f352b0445bafbc79ca799dce4d.pdf

33 O'Neil, S., Stagner, M. (2019). The Power of a Data-Informed Partnership: Working with Community-Based Organizations to Address Social Determinants of Health. Mathematica Blog. Retrieved October 10, 2020 from https://www.mathematica.org/commentary/the-power-of-a-data-informed-partnership-working-with-community-based-organizations-to-address-sdoh

34 https://www.astho.org/StatePublicHealth/Improving-Public-Health-Surveillance-Through-Interoperability-Data-Standards-Legislation/01-24-19/

35 https://www.astho.org/StatePublicHealth/Improving-Public-Health-Surveillance-Through-Interoperability-Data-Standards-Legislation/01-24-19/#:~:text=Interoperability%2C%20which%20supports%20the%20ability,timely%20manner%20to%20address%20public

36 https://repository.immregistries.org/files/resources/5c002cbde216d/aira_dq_guide_data_at_rest_-_final.pdf

37 https://www.ihs.gov/

38 https://www.cdc.gov/ruralhealth/vaccines/index.html

39 https://www.usnews.com/news/healthiest-communities/articles/2020-10-07/a-state-by-state-analysis-of-the-impact-of-covid-19-on-native-americans

40 https://repository.immregistries.org/files/resources/5ee9315f0930e/iis_policies_to_support_pandemic_and_routine_vax_6_18_20.pdf

41 https://www.cdc.gov/surveillance/surveillance-data-strategies/data-IT-transformation.html

40 Accelerating into the Future with Project Management

Al Kalman
BA

Shari Rathet
BA

CONTENTS

MAKING CHANGE

The world has entered uncharted waters: the COVID-19 pandemic has altered everything. We have witnessed the ways that high-impact events can affect our lives in profound ways. But when the pandemic ends, this constant change will only continue. There will be no "new normal." There is nothing new about change. The workplace has been undergoing disruption for many years, much of it driven by technology. It is reshaping the very nature of work—driving the growth of The Project Economy, where we have the flexibility to deliver value through projects, enabling people with the skills and capabilities they need to turn ideas into reality.

Improve Healthcare Outcomes

Project Management Institute's *Pulse of the Profession*® 2020 Healthcare Comparison found that healthcare organizations waste an average of US$113 million for every US$1 billion spent on projects and programs due to poor project performance (PMI, 2020). The survey also found that healthcare organizations lag the global average in making digital skills a high priority, as well as creating cultures that value project management. It identified the need for the healthcare industry to increase its organizational agility to be able to adapt to change and fully realize the benefits of its project work.

Organizations that undervalue project management as a strategic competency for driving change report an average of 67 percent more of their projects failing outright. At a time of extraordinary challenges, organizations can benefit from making investments to create a future-focused culture and hire people with the skills and mindset to deliver big, bold projects.

Why is project management so important? It's a capability that allows you to get things done: take an idea and make it into a reality. That is a really valuable skill set in this world of transformation and change. Case in point: when COVID-19 hit Mexico in March 2020, the National Institute of Medical Sciences and Nutrition Salvador Zubirán (INCMNSZ) was able to increase the country's supply of ventilators in record time. Collaborating with 15 companies, the team developed an innovative solution—retrofitting an experimental model from three decades ago and tailoring it for the pandemic. The VSZ-20-2's piston-based design does not require wall outlets, making it suitable for use in some of the more unusual emergency treatment facilities. With the help of the Mexican government, the team was able to make the idea of producing a low-cost ventilator a reality.

BE MORE THAN AGILE—BE GYMNASTIC

It's becoming increasingly clear that the future will belong to changemakers who are able to innovate and think creatively. The modern project management toolkit enables project managers to direct projects using multiple approaches—predictive, agile, and hybrid—in a range of environments. But project professionals need to continually upskill to maintain their relevance and position themselves to navigate this new ecosystem of work. As projects become more complex, new tools will be needed. Project professionals are evolving their way of working with tool kits like Disciplined Agile®, which guides you to select from a range of options and harness them to achieve the best outcomes. Everyone should be sharpening their creative problem-solving, collaboration, and other power skills, along with improving technical and business acumen—all while paying attention to global trends such as creating positive social impact and increasing diversity—to solve their everyday problems at work.

Many organizations are changing their core business models and growing more nimble and "gymnastic." This will require enterprises to go beyond agility in order to deliver financial, business, and societal value streams. The gymnastic organization combines structure, form, and governance with the ability to flex and pivot—wherever and whenever needed. Gymnastic enterprises focus more on outcomes than process, selecting the very best ways of working from a landscape of possibilities. And they aren't just good at reacting to change or even embracing it—they make change happen, starting with transforming their own organizations. Gymnastic enterprises focus on their people, knowing that organizational performance is a well-choreographed dance of individual performances.

PROJECT MANAGEMENT: DELIVERING OUTCOMES

Even before prehistoric peoples organized to drag enormous stones across Salisbury Plain to build Stonehenge, in what is now England, human beings were applying project management principles. Project management is the application of knowledge, skills, tools, and techniques to project activities to meet project requirements. However, formalized project management practices didn't truly evolve to meet the challenges of the modern world until the 1950s.

James R. Snyder, a founder of PMI, traces the emergence of modern project management back to a convergence of three events in 1958: (1) Peter Norden's paper on computer development at IBM; (2) James E. Kelly' and M. R. Walker's work on the critical path method (CPM), a modeling technique originated during their work at Remington Rand and DuPont, respectively; and (3) Willard Fazar's development of the Program Evaluation and Review Technique (PERT), a scheduling technique applied during the design of nuclear submarines in the U.S. Navy. "The easy answer is that it was the beginning of the age of the giant project," Snyder explains. "That point where the size, complexity, time span, resource requirements, and cost of projects demanded more than the Gantt chart."

WHAT IS A PROJECT?

According to the Project Management Institute, a project is defined as a "temporary endeavor undertaken to create a unique product, service, or result" (PMI, 2021, p. 245). The development of software for the storage of electronic health records, the construction of a hospital wing, and research to develop a new vaccine—all these are projects.

A project is temporary and has a clear beginning and ending. Predictive projects often have defined scope and resources, whereas adaptive projects may not at the start. Each project is unique and differs from routine operations—the ongoing activities of an organization—because projects reach a conclusion once the goal has been achieved. All projects must be expertly managed to deliver the on-time, on-budget results that organizations need.

The changing nature of work due to technological advances, globalization, and other factors means that, increasingly, work is organized around projects with teams being brought together based on the skills needed for specific tasks. Whether you work in healthcare, IT, production, construction, nonprofit, or any other sector, you are part of "The Project Economy," where work becomes "projectified," and workers will need to upskill as they move between functional areas and from project to project.

Project skills are essential to any industry. The need for adaptability means that, increasingly, change occurs through projects. And when people with the right skill sets work together as teams, the projects they work on—aligned to the strategic goals of their organizations—can transform and drive useful outcomes for their customers, other stakeholders, and the bottom line. The PMI Talent Triangle® is evolving and describes the balance of technical know-how; leadership; and other "power skills," such as problem-solving, communication, collaboration, and the business acumen needed for project leaders to be successful. It is this combination that enables organizations to maintain their competitive advantage and remain future focused.

It is now widely acknowledged that a basic knowledge of project management can provide value to people with a variety of titles in a vast range of endeavors. Project management skills can help a young student working on a science project to make expanding the use of solar energy a reality. They can help a coach trying to ensure their team peaks at just the right time to make winning a championship reality, or a director staging a theater production. These skills can help a nurse trying to streamline shift changes to improve patient response times on their ward a reality.

Research indicates that employers will need to fill nearly 2.2 million new project-oriented roles each year through 2027. Becoming a Project Management Professional (PMP)® certification holder is one way to fill the talent pipeline gap. By doing so, one demonstrates expertise and command of the vast body of knowledge for the project management discipline. But anyone involved in The Project Economy can improve outcomes through awareness of specific foundational concepts of project management, described as follows.

PROJECT VERSUS PRODUCT LIFE CYCLE

According to the Project Management Institute, the project life cycle is the basic framework for managing a project, often consisting of a series of phases or iterations that the project passes through between inception and completion (PMI, 2021). Projects may be undertaken to produce a product, but they differ in that the product life cycle may extend beyond completion of the project. Once the product—such as a new medical device, software tool, workflow, or vaccine is delivered—the project reaches its conclusion, and the project team can move on to other projects.

Project Charter

Projects vary in size and complexity, but generally consist of four generic phases—starting the project, organizing, and preparing, carrying out the work, and closing. The project charter is your opportunity to raise the flag and signal the intent of your project; it formally authorizes the existence of the project and allows you to apply organizational resources to achieve a business need or goal.

Project charters connect execution to strategy, often by establishing a defined scope; setting out roles and responsibilities; and including a budget, schedule, and key milestones. A project charter should also define the meaning of success. A healthcare project that proposes to apply artificial intelligence (AI) algorithms to improve outcomes in rural areas is not considered a success if it results in the implementation of a database of customer information but does not improve patient health.

Stakeholder Engagement

Equally important to realizing the desired outcome of a project is engaging the key stakeholders. Stakeholders include persons, groups, or organizations who have an interest in the project; they may be actively involved in the project, be end users of the product, or just be impacted by the outcomes of the project. Once stakeholders have been identified, communications should be established to understand and address their needs and expectations. Stakeholder engagement covers a complex set of relationships, and the communications should be tailored to address the intended audience.

Infinite Leap, a North Carolina healthcare-technology provider, took stakeholder management to the next level on a recent project. Infinite Leap engages users through extensive training that demonstrates both how to use the technology and the benefits it provides. Nurses who act as "super users" are the first to learn the new technology and then pass on that learning to their colleagues. When other nurses have questions about the technology, it will be easier for them to learn from someone in their own field.

Risk Management

All projects involve risk. Project risk is an unexpected event or condition that may have a positive or negative effect on project outcomes. The goal for a project manager, or indeed anyone trying to achieve a successful outcome, is to avoid or minimize negative risk while trying to realize the benefits of positive ones.

Project risk management involves identifying and analyzing possible risks and developing and implementing strategies to respond to them. A natural disaster, such as a hurricane or earthquake; a new law that may affect the regulatory environment; electrical failures; illness; contract disputes; or social upheaval are just a few examples.

The process of monitoring risk needs to be ongoing throughout a project, and the risk response plan should be adjusted to meet changing situations.

GE Healthcare recently partnered with Oregon Health & Science University (OHSU) on a six-month project to implement an AI-driven command center that manages patient logistics and treatment plans. The team identified a flaw as part of its risk identification process in the AI system-testing phase. None of the hospitals in the system was properly inputting patient-status data, limiting the impact of the AI command center. To mitigate the risk of such workflow problems on other projects, GE Healthcare teams now run simulation models of hospital processes on each project to uncover inefficiencies.

Benefits Realization Management

Benefits realization management (BRM) is an essential component of project management (Mossalam & Arafa, 2015). Organizations do projects—whether developing new products or improving existing technologies—for defined reasons, usually related to achieving or maintaining competitive advantage.

BRM is the collective set of processes and practices used for identifying and measuring those benefits derived from undertaking a project and aligning them with a formal strategy to ensure that the benefits are sustainable—and sustained—after project implementation is complete.

Incorporating risk management, BRM, and other project management practices can often make the difference between success and failure and should be embraced by those at the highest levels of an organization.

By establishing a project management office (PMO), organizations such as healthcare providers that manage multiple, complex projects ensure good governance, standardized project processes, and facilitated sharing of resources. This increases efficiency and provides cost savings.

The enterprise PMO (EPMO) is the highest-level PMO entity in an organization, responsible for alignment of initiatives to corporate strategy.

Kern Health Systems (KHS), a health plan serving members in Southern California, set up their EPMO in 2011 to facilitate rapid change due to regulatory shifts and the need to improve patient outcomes. The EPMO helped KHS, a 2020 finalist for PMI's PMO of the Year award, navigate several major transitions, including introduction of the Affordable Care Act and establishing access for a large population of low-income individuals. As a nonprofit organization, KHS must juggle limited resources, and the EPMO helps them find cost-effective ways to meet all members' healthcare needs (Jones, 2021).

THE IMPORTANCE OF PRIORITIZATION

Faced with the needs to adapt to new legislation, ensure the security and integrity of IT systems, improve the patient experience and outcomes, expand facilities and many other challenges, healthcare organizations will need to prioritize the projects in their portfolio. In this "do more with less" world, project prioritization helps win executive sponsorship and support and eliminates waste and misalignment.

At KHS, the EPMO partners with the organization's business intelligence unit to collect data that helps KHS decide which projects or programs will deliver the most business value, using analytics to solidify the business rationale behind each business case and clearly defining the anticipated benefits of their projects.

WORKING SMARTER

Gymnastic enterprises are leading the way in The Project Economy by empowering their employees to become changemakers—those who, regardless of their role, feel personally inspired and equipped to drive change and turn ideas into reality. This happens when people continuously get better at what they do by utilizing a variety of means to build a holistic portfolio of skills, from which they can choose the best ways to drive results and value.

Gymnastic enterprises are creating changemakers by enabling their people to work smarter in three key ways:

- Mastering different **ways of working**—whether that's agile, predictive, or hybrid approaches; or technology-enhanced tools like complex problem-solving techniques or microlearning apps.
- Elevating **power skills** to ensure effective leadership and communication—including collaborative leadership, empathy for customers and colleagues, innovative thinking, and the ability to build trusting relationships.

- Building **business acumen** to create well-rounded employees—those who not only have expertise in their specific roles and projects, but also understand how their efforts relate to the macro environment, strategic objectives, and other parts of the business.

FLEX TO THE FUTURE

While you can build your skills and plan for the unexpected, it's hard to plan for every possible outcome. Like a boxer in the ring, you need to be able to pivot and change as unanticipated challenges arise—you need to be agile. Former pro boxer Mike Tyson might have been talking about the COVID-19 pandemic when he famously said: "Everyone has a plan until they get punched in the face!"

When something surprising happens (and in boxing, it often does), you have to be ready to change your approach, pivot in a heartbeat, and quickly counter. If you don't, chances are you may not remember too much of what happens next.

Another boxer, Wladimir Klitschko, who holds a PhD in sports science, is a former world heavyweight boxing champion, Olympic Gold medalist, philanthropist, and entrepreneur, re-invented himself to tackle new challenges in the worlds of business and philanthropy.

After retiring from the ring, Dr. Klitschko began sharing his approach to "challenge management" with students from around the world and developed his own "F.A.C.E. the Challenge" method—a four-step process to develop willpower, with a focus on agility, coordination, and endurance. But what does this have to do with project management? There are some intersections you may not immediately expect (Prashara, 2021).

In April 2017, Klitschko faced Anthony Joshua, the undefeated British reigning heavyweight champion of the world on his home turf, Wembley Stadium, London, in front of 100,000 hostile and vocal fans. Klitschko and Joshua's buildup to the fight had probably begun six months earlier. As Klitschko later related, *he* was "the project." The Klitschko camp had trainers, physical therapists, nutritionists, doctors, cardiologists, strategists, sparring partners, hands specialists, dietitians, meditation gurus, mentors, and more—all working together to ensure that over the next six months their "project" reached maximum form at exactly the right time: the day of the fight.

To do this, they had the strictest of regimes to follow: too much weightlifting—you miss your target, too little food—you miss your target, and too much sparring in the ring—you miss your target! The training manager ("the project manager") coordinated all the preparation to the finest detail. The approach was structured and predefined. It followed a traditional methodology and had a defined outcome, at a specific time. In essence, his team used a "waterfall technique" to prepare for the biggest fight of Klitschko's life —a sequential and linear process, in which you know what specific outcome you want to reach and what you need to do to get there.

Then, the big day arrived. Klitschko had run a specific number of miles, performed specific workouts, sparred with some of the best, honed his skills, eaten specific foods, and researched his opponent's moves until he knew everything there was to know. Time is up. This is it. Klitschko "the project" was ready; bringing the full sum of his grit, knowledge, and training into the ring… but what if he encountered the unexpected?

Anthony Joshua hadn't been sitting idle; he also had his project team preparing him, in similar fashion, with a similar expected outcome and similar training regime. Each of them equally prepared and ready to fight for the coveted title of "undisputed heavyweight champion of the world."

Round one….

The boxers come together, sounding each other out… throwing leading punches, establishing positions, and laying their foundation and intent. At the same time, they observe their opponents' tactics, weaknesses, and unique styles. The months of training and strategy begin to pay off. After three minutes, the bell signifies the end of the round, and each boxer returns to his corner where his team awaits.

The next minute is filled with frenetic activity, as the team assesses what was learned and what may need to change. They ask themselves: Do we stick to the game plan? Do we change our strategy? The short one-minute break in the corner is akin to a "sprint retrospective" incorporated by agile teams. It is an evaluation of what just happened in that three-minute round, or sprint, and what to do in the next sprint. The next round may be the same… or it could be different… the bell rings and off we go again….

Round two….

The boxers are not boxing as anticipated, cautious of each other's approach. New tactics are needed and in real time. Another pivot in the strategy, a new angle, a new approach. We go into another retrospective. It's not easy, yet there are additional sprints to undertake before the project reaches its conclusion. Additional opportunities to get it right!

Each round/sprint is different—sometimes you are moving forward, sometimes you are covering up in defense. However, the desired outcome remains the same. The subtle changes in approach are those keeping both fighters in the game. In short, you become more agile.

Therein lies a couple of intersections between the world of the boxer and that of the project manager. Each uses the tools, resources, expertise, and methods available to get the job done. Yet, each must also be able to pivot and change when the need arises. However, to even embark and maintain such endeavors takes more than simple ability, ambition, and technique.

Klitschko did not win the fight, and the title went to the younger boxer he had mentored. Yet he was able to pivot from boxing to building a successful career helping others overcome personal challenges and make their dreams reality. He advocates that humanistic power skills truly make the difference. At PMI, we often talk about the importance of these capabilities—qualities such as collaborative leadership, empathy, and an innovative "can-do" mindset. Your superpowers.

While technology and innovation can automate more routine parts of work, humanistic skills—the stuff we might have called "soft skills" in the past—have become even more important.

As Wladimir Klitschko said: "I've learned that principles of focus, agility, coordination, and endurance are the same principles that any person needs in any field of activity" (Prashara, 2021).

WIN THE FUTURE

"What's next?" is a question many ask. As we continue to face uncertain times, how can we prepare our organizations for the next chapter?

Don't confuse process with outcomes

Too often executives can become overly fixated on following a specific set of practices as the end goal, when what they should *really* be after is business performance.

This can often happen as organizations transform and incorporate more agile practices. Agility itself is not the goal. Greater value and performance should be the goals. Agile can be a huge piece of the puzzle to maximize performance—but it's only one piece. Ask yourself: Is the end goal to become more agile or to maximize performance?

Your emotional intelligence (EI)—the ability to tap into the mental states of those around you—is arguably as important today as your IQ

Much of today's technology doesn't consider the natural ways in which humans connect when they are face-to-face. This trend is more relevant than ever in the virtual environment in which more people are working and learning online. Digital connections and communications must continue to strengthen. Improving one's ability to read nonverbal cues takes on increased importance in the healthcare field, as questions are raised about the effectiveness and limitations of telehealth or virtual care.

Empathy should be promoted as a value for all organizations. Empathy—the ability to put yourself in another person's place and see their perspective—also requires the ability to make decisions with both heart and mind. Leaders will need to strike the right balance between empathy and business outcomes on a range of challenging policy issues, including how to deliver on promises of diversity, equity, and inclusion (DEI).

UNLEARNING IS JUST AS IMPORTANT AS LEARNING

Knowledge can grow obsolete as conditions change over time. Recognizing this reality requires that leaders not only learn new knowledge but also let go of old practices that may have outlived their usefulness. Unlearning is not about forgetting, removing, or discarding knowledge or experience. It's about the conscious act of letting go of outdated information or approaches and actively engaging in taking in new information to inform effective decision-making.

Demands in the workplace change all the time. Many of the skills that once made us successful can ultimately go on to limit us in the future. COVID-19 was an accelerator for organizations to rapidly adjust to changing circumstances. Organizations that have thrived during the downturn share a commonality: they built systems that allow them to rapidly learn from customer behaviors and respond quickly.

With the best practices of the past as our foundation, we can build our skills and expand our conceptions of what's possible; better sense what is coming in the future; and find ways of working that continually enhance outcomes, put people first, and hopefully improve the world around us.

Project Management Institute Inc., *"Accelerating into the Future with Project Management,"* ©2021. Copyright and all rights reserved. This material has been published with the permission of PMI. Please visit https://www.pmi.org/permissions to request permission to use this chapter.

REFERENCES

Jones, T. (2021). The best medicine: Kern Health System's PMO is forging a change-ready framework and better patient access. *PM Network*, *35*, 60–65.

Mossalam, A., & Arafa, M. (2015). *The role of project manager in benefits realization management as a project constraint/driver. HBRC Journal*, *12*(3), 305–315.

Prashara, S. (2021). *Stepping into the ring: What do boxing and project management have in common?* The Official PMI Blog. Project Management Institute.

Project Management Institute (PMI). (2021). *A guide to the project management body of knowledge (PMBOK® guide)* – Seventh edition and *The standard for project management*. Author.

Project Management Institute (PMI). (2020). *Pulse of the profession® 2020: Research highlights by region and industry* (p. 34). Author.

41 HIMSS Maturity Models: An Overview

Reid Oakes
Chief Products Officer, HIMSS

CONTENTS

LEARNING OBJECTIVES

1. Describe the importance of using globally applicable standards to advance transformative digital health transformation change across the healthcare ecosystem.
2. Examine details of each of seven (7) maturity model available to global healthcare entities today.
3. Compare and contrast the four attributes of each maturity model while recognizing the differences among each.

INTRODUCTION

In this time of rapid change, hospitals, health systems and other healthcare provider organizations globally are building strategies to improve capacity. As demonstrated with COVID-19, there is a clear need to manage surges in demand for care, supply chain and logistics effectiveness, and building of new virtual care delivery models that ensure meaningful connectivity with patients when care is needed most. To meet these demands, HIMSS has created globally applicable frameworks, models and tools to build, measure and advance health system transformation.

WHAT ARE MATURITY MODELS?

The challenge facing health systems across the globe is to improve clinical outcomes for patients and populations, organizations' financial sustainability, and the operational efficiency that supports

DOI: 10.4324/9780429398377-47

their workforce. Without globally applicable standards to follow, it can be difficult to assess and improve an organization's progress. HIMSS offers a suite of healthcare maturity models, originating with the flagship model, the Electronic Medical Record Adoption Model (EMRAM), to provide prescriptive frameworks to healthcare organizations to build their digital health ecosystems. Each eight-stage (0-7) maturity model operates as a vendor-neutral roadmap for success and offers global benchmarking. HIMSS' healthcare models provide the standard to follow for measurable improvement across infrastructure implementation, EMR adoption, measuring what matters through analytics, digital imaging capabilities, and clinical supply chain technologies, chosen independently of an installed market supplier. (HIMSS, 2021a).

ADOPTION MODEL FOR ANALYTICS MATURITY (AMAM)

The HIMSS Adoption Model for Analytics Maturity (AMAM) measures the analytics capabilities that healthcare organizations have gained from having a strong analytics strategy and competency in place. By advancing one's organizational healthcare analytics regardless of the technologies installed, analytics serve to improve many facets of a healthcare business beyond clinical decision support, such as an organization's operational and financial aspects. Components of the AMAM that measure an organization's capabilities gained from analytics technologies and surrounding processes include:

- Growing data content to improve operational, clinical, and financial performance;
- Developing a data infrastructure and strategy for sourcing and collecting data;
- Building governance to manage your data assets;
- Aligning analytics efforts with the organization's overall organizational strategy (HIMSS, 2021b).

CONTINUITY OF CARE MATURITY MODEL (CCMM)

The HIMSS Continuity of Care Maturity Model (CCMM) helps healthcare leaders globally assess, implement, and scale the seamless coordination of patient care across a continuum of care sites and providers. Continuity of care is much more complex than implementing information and technology in a single care setting. Multiple stakeholders must act in concert to provide an environment that facilitates the best care and value. The CCMM assigns responsibility for critical aspects of coordinated care across administrators and governance leadership, clinical leadership, and IT/technology leadership. The CCMM measures an organization's capabilities gained from analytics technologies and surrounding processes by:

- Building and improving critical capabilities needed for coordinated patient care;
- Identifying and aligning actions from critical stakeholder groups;
- Helping organizations gauge performance across each setting in the care community and enhance coordinated care (HIMSS, 2021c).

CLINICALLY INTEGRATED SUPPLY OUTCOMES MODEL (CISOM)

The HIMSS Clinically Integrated Supply Outcomes Model (CISOM) assesses the supply chain maturity of health systems globally by providing a roadmap for outcomes improvement. An advanced and automated health system supply chain infrastructure, at the point of care, can proactively identify the risk of adverse events to strengthen quality and safety for patients. With the CISOM, organizations can build procurement best practices informed by real-world evidence emerging from data while identifying solutions and products that work best for patients. By mobilizing data to create real-world evidence of impact and outcomes for patient populations, organizations can

- Reduce supply cost informed by improved inventory management through product utilization tracking;
- Create traceability of care processes and products used in care to support patient safety;
- Drive the personalization of care for populations informed by best outcomes for patients (HIMSS, 2021d).

DIGITAL IMAGING ADOPTION MODEL (DIAM)

The HIMSS Digital Imaging Adoption Model (DIAM) helps healthcare organizations measure capabilities related to the secure delivery of medical imaging and its associated processes to improve quality of care, patient safety and organizational efficiency in both hospitals and diagnostic centers. The globally applicable DIAM facilitates enterprise imaging covering all areas of the health system, enabling management of digital imaging and multimedia content in a systematic, holistic, efficient, and effective manner by doing the following:

- Moving toward a fully digitized imaging IT environment based on a roadmap created by industry experts
- Identifying key opportunities to improve, drive and support your IT and business strategies
- Comparing imaging IT progress over time against peer organizations globally (HIMSS, 2021e).

INFRASTRUCTURE ADOPTION MODEL (INFRAM)

The HIMSS Infrastructure Adoption Model (INFRAM) helps healthcare leaders assess and map healthcare infrastructure and the associated technology capabilities required to reach their facility's infrastructure goals while meeting international benchmarks and standards set by this maturity model. A sound infrastructure is needed so that healthcare organizations may build upon other capabilities that will lead to the realization of digital health transformation strategies. The Infrastructure Adoption Model (INFRAM) assesses and maps the technology infrastructure capabilities required to reach clinical and operational goals while meeting international benchmarks and standards by achieving the following:

- Assessing and understanding where the healthcare organization's infrastructure stands compared to others;
- Evaluating the organization's mobility, security, collaboration, transport and data center, while understanding how they work together;
- Developing detailed strategic technology plans that define pathways to achieve clinical and operational goals;
- Acting on evidence to create compelling business cases for investments that link stakeholder experiences, outcomes, and technology (HIMSS, 2021f).

OUTPATIENT ELECTRONIC MEDICAL RECORD ADOPTION MODEL (O-EMRAM)

The HIMSS Outpatient Electronic Medical Record Adoption Model (O-EMRAM) is used to assess EMR implementation for outpatient facilities of hospitals and health systems globally, by guiding the data-driven advancement of facilities through EMR technology. With the O-EMRAM, organizations optimize the continuation of care for patients and populations external to the acute care setting while ensuring all care documentation is readily assessable to the clinical team when and where they need it by doing the following:

- Improving clinical-driven governance and decision support to assist the clinical workforce;
- Identifying and tracking gaps while improving clinical processes and health maintenance for patient populations;
- Ensuring clinician decision-making is driven by content, workflow, alerts received and standard tracking practices (HIMSS, 2021g).

ELECTRONIC MEDICAL RECORD ADOPTION MODEL (EMRAM)

The HIMSS Electronic Medical Record Adoption Model (EMRAM) is used to assess EMR implementation and adoption of the technology for hospitals and health systems globally by guiding the data-driven advancement of care in a health system's acute or inpatient care facilities through EMR technology. With the EMRAM, organizations optimize their EMR implementation to improve patient care and safety by leveraging information digitally, and, improving patient safety and satisfaction by reducing errors in care, length of stay for patients, duplicated care orders, and other benefits. Organizations achieve these benefits with the EMRAM by:

- Improving care delivery through better use of EMR technology;
- Measuring current EMR adoption and building a roadmap to achieve future goals;
- Tracking and monitoring care provided to patients, ensuring quality, safety and value;
- Appreciating how other healthcare providers across the globe are utilizing their EMR technologies (HIMSS, 2021h).

CONCLUSION

By appreciating how digital health transformation is measured with HIMSS Maturity Models, organizations can strive to ensure that the global ecosystem that connects clinicians and provider teams with people enables them to manage their health and wellness using digital tools in a secure and private environment. Delivering care whenever and wherever it is needed will truly transform care.

REFERENCES

HIMSS. (2021a). What are maturity models. Retrieved on October 11, 2021 from https://www.himss.org/what-we-do-solutions/digital-health-transformation/maturity-models.

HIMSS. (2021b). Adoption model for analytics maturity (AMAM). Retrieved on October 11, 2021 from https://www.himss.org/what-we-do-solutions/digital-health-transformation/maturity-models/adoption-model-analytics-maturity-amam.

HIMSS. (2021c). Continuity of Care Maturity Model (CCMM). Retrieved on October 11, 2021 from https://www.himss.org/what-we-do-solutions/digital-health-transformation/maturity-models/continuity-care-maturity-model-ccmm.

HIMSS. (2021d). Clinically-integrated Outcomes Supply Model (CISOM). Retrieved on October 11, 2021 from https://www.himss.org/what-we-do-solutions/digital-health-transformation/maturity-models/clinically-integrated-supply-outcomes-model-cisom.

HIMSS. (2021e). Digital Imaging Adoption Model (DIAM). Retrieved on October 11, 2021 from https://www.himss.org/what-we-do-solutions/digital-health-transformation/maturity-models/digital-imaging-adoption-model-diam.

HIMSS. (2021f). Infrastructure Adoption Model (INFRAM). Retrieved on October 11, 2021 from https://www.himss.org/what-we-do-solutions/digital-health-transformation/maturity-models/infrastructure-adoption-model-infram.

HIMSS. (2021g). Outpatient EMR Adoption Model (O-EMRAM). Retrieved on October 11, 2021 from https://www.himss.org/what-we-do-solutions/digital-health-transformation/maturity-models/outpatient-electronic-medical-record-adoption-model-o-emram.

HIMSS. (2021i). Electronic Medical Record Adoption Model (EMRAM). Retrieved on October 11, 2021 from https://www.himss.org/what-we-do-solutions/digital-health-transformation/maturity-models/electronic-medical-record-adoption-model-emram.

Appendix: Prioritize Your Career Development Plan

Joyce Zerkich
PMP, CPHIMS, ACC, MBA, MSBIT

CONTENTS

INTRODUCTION

Your plan will be a concrete list of actionable next steps of items you will do for yourself. We automatically and intentionally schedule everyday for the needs of our family, finances, health, living quarters, friends and more. With our fast-paced lives, we often forget to take time to plan our long term career goals based upon our aspirations. This approach guides you through a process that helps you to plan now (and into the future, too) for your career as well as remember to take time at least annually to reflect on your career goals and update your plan. Ben Franklin said "If you fail to prepare [plan], you are preparing [planning] to fail."

WHAT TO INCLUDE IN YOUR PLAN

The plan in this Appendix is ordered sequentially to match the chapters. However, your needs may dictate a different order with some chapters not applicable to your goals. First, carefully read and reflect on chapters one through four. Next, decide which of the remaining chapters to focus on that will provide many development roads that will enable your success.

HIGH LEVEL PLAN—GET STARTED!

Work (Tasks) To Be Accomtplished	Target Date to Complete the Tasks	Write Down Your Next Steps
My Development Plan		
1. Identifying Your Professional Potential		
Read the Chapter.		
Complete the HIT Evaluation.		
Update your resume.		
Practice interviewing with trusted friend who will give you feedback.		

(Continued)

Work (Tasks) To Be Accomtplished	Target Date to Complete the Tasks	Write Down Your Next Steps
My Development Plan		
Update at least annually with your successes and experience.		
2. Creating a Personal Brand		
Read the Chapter.		
Complete "Reach 1–2–3 Success" process to better understand your brand.		
Write or draw your brand.		
Reflect after one month to determine if your brand should be changed or updated.		
3. Diversifying Your Skillset		
Read the Chapter.		
Research and plan future education.		
Research and plan future certification(s).		
4. Developing a Career Roadmap		
Read the Chapter.		
Draw your roadmap.		
Identify two to three plausible future career goals.		
Identify and join a network.		
Reflect after one year to see what to change or update.		
5. Work-life Balance: Does it Exist? Can You Achieve it?		
Read the Chapter.		
Complete the values assessment in Appendix 5.1.		
Complete your mission statement.		
Map your key activities into the four quadrants so it is clear what you could eliminate.		
6. The Role of the Professional Association		
Read the Chapter.		
Research and find professional associations to help in achieving your career goals.		
Join the professional association(s).		
Get involved in the professional organization so you can network and learn.		
7. The Importance of Volunteering		
Read the Chapter.		
Reflect on organizations you are passionate about and choose one.		
Contact the organization.		
Commit to a time period to volunteer (even one day is good).		
8. Earning a Certificate to Demonstrate Competency		
Read the Chapter.		

Work (Tasks) To Be Accomtplished	Target Date to Complete the Tasks	Write Down Your Next Steps
My Development Plan		
Consider a health IT certificate. Research certificates that would align with your career roadmap. Sign up for one that interested you to help expand your knowledge.		
9. Differentiating Yourself with a Professional Certification		
Read the Chapter. Research whether professional certification would further your career. Research the available certifications and determine your eligibility. If eligible, sign up and plan your study time into your calendar. Set a target date to take for the exam and adjust your study schedule accordingly Take the exam.		
10. Seeking an Advanced Professional Designation		
Read the Chapter. Search for the institute that offers a professional designation which interests you. Target an exam date. Plan the pace of your studying into your long-term calendar. Solicit input from family and friends to support the extra study time you will require. Take for the exam.		
11. The Mentoring Process		
Read the Chapter. Decide if you would like to engage with a mentor. Check with your HR Department or local organizations for next steps to obtain a mentor. Consider a mentor outside of your employer. Assess the effectiveness of the time spent with your mentor and adjust as needed. Don't forget to become a mentor yourself later in your career to give back.		
12. Managing by Walking Around		
Read the Chapter. Make a plan to walk around your workplace to obtain input from others. Practice active listening.		

(Continued)

Work (Tasks) To Be Accomtplished	Target Date to Complete the Tasks	Write Down Your Next Steps
My Development Plan		
When walking around, take notes of action items, commitments, and communications.		
Reflect on your walk around notes.		
Prioritize next steps on the action items from your notes.		
Communicate changes to the team and the idea generator(s).		
13. Experiencing a Job Exchange		
Read the Chapter.		
Identify a job you'd like to exchange.		
Write a proposal detailing how this exchange will benefit you, others, and the company.		
Present your proposal to your manager.		
Record your lessons learned.		
14. The 360-Degree Assessment		
Read the Chapter.		
Contact HR to see which 360 degrees tool they recommend.		
Select a 360 degrees tool.		
Choose at least three to four current/recent former employees who will provide honest feedback.		
Receive and review the assessment.		
Review the feedback with your manager or professional coach to help you with next steps.		
15. Professional Coaching		
Read the Chapter.		
Make a list of issue(s) you have with someone or things holding you back in your career.		
Ask your HR department if a coach is offered through the company.		
Ask colleagues and friends for a referral to their favorite coach.		
Check with www.Coachfederation.org to locate a coach.		
In advance of the first meeting with the coach, plan what you'd like to accomplish.		
Commit to several coaching sessions (more than three).		
Commit you will finish the homework from each coaching session.		
16. Developing as a Leader		
Read the Chapter.		
Take an assessment to better understand yourself such as Myer-Briggs.		

Work (Tasks) To Be Accomtplished		Target Date to Complete the Tasks	Write Down Your Next Steps
My Development Plan			
	Ask your HR department if there is an assessment tool they recommend for employees.		
	Take the assessment.		
	Receive and read the results.		
	Reflect on what type of work gives you energy and what drains you.		
	Make note of your current emotional and social intelligence goals.		
	Offer assessment opportunities to your direct reports.		
	If you supervise others, work with your direct reports to help them improve in their weak areas.		
	Understand how each direct report's personality type affects you.		
17. Nurturing Inter-Personal Skills Development			
	Read the Chapter.		
	Understand the key competencies required to work in healthcare.		
	Reflect and record your biases, values, strengths, weaknesses, and capabilities.		
	Evaluate yourself on how you can contribute more positively and collaboratively.		
	Write down how you can build more collaboration into the coming week.		
	Evaluate at the end of the week your collaboration and plan future goals.		
18. Understanding the Multi-Generational Workplace			
	Read the Chapter.		
	Reflect on what leadership style tends to dominate each generation.		
	List each employee with their generation, leadership style, and power type.		
	Add to this list your generation, leadership style, and power type.		
	Reflect on your interactions with each other to understand your communication challenges.		
	Set an intention to change your communication style with certain employees.		
19. Minding Your Manners in the Workplace and Beyond			
	Read the Chapter.		

(Continued)

Work (Tasks) To Be Accomtplished	Target Date to Complete the Tasks	Write Down Your Next Steps

My Development Plan

Since the purpose of manners is to show respect, reflect on how you do so.

Rate yourself on the manners listed in the chapter.

Plan how and when you will improve your manners.

Research before traveling to understand local business manners.

20. Encouraging Diversity in the Workplace

Read the Chapter.

Reflect on the diversity in your staff and work teams.

Challenge yourself to improved diversity through hiring and/or development assignments.

Consider mentoring a new employee to help build the future workforce and challenge yourself to remain relevant.

Become an active supporter of a diversity program.

21. The Aspiring Female Health IT Executive

Read the Chapter.

Reflect to discover if you have an unconscious bias.

Take steps to change any biases.

Consider mentoring a rising female leader for six months to one year.

Ask your mentee for a 360-degree assessment so you can improve in the future.

22. Joining the C-Suite

Read the Chapter.

Rate your current progress to the key competencies.

Plan next steps such as certification, education, obtaining a mentor, etc.

Check in with this plan every six months to record your progression and update your plan.

23. Earning an Advanced Degree

Read the Chapter.

Decide if it will enable your career goals.

Research degree programs, and if applicable, register for one.

Work (Tasks) To Be Accomtplished		Target Date to Complete the Tasks	Write Down Your Next Steps
My Development Plan			
	Plan the studying rigor into your long-term calendar.		
24. The Many Facets of Continuing Education			
	Read the Chapter.		
	Decide if it will enable your career goals.		
	Plan which will help you in the short term.		
	Plan your next steps to participate.		
	Check in with this plan every six months and update the next six-month's plan.		
25. Engaging Socially to Expand Professional Competency			
	Read the Chapter.		
	Decide which will enable your career.		
	Plan which will help you in the short and long term.		
	Plan next steps to participate.		
	Check in with this plan every six months and update the next six-month's plan.		
26. Viewing the Workplace for On-the-Job Training			
	Read the Chapter.		
	Decide which will enable your career.		
	Plan which will help you in the short and long term.		
	Plan next steps to participate.		
	Check in with this plan every six months and update the next six-month's plan.		
27. Talent Management for the Health IT Professional			
	Read the Chapter.		
	Define the phases for yourself.		
	Define and review with each employee the phases for them.		
	Execute your plan (typically one to two years).		
	Check in with this plan every year and update the next year's plan.		
28. Driving Digital Health Transformation: Achieving a Person-Enabled Health System			
	Read the Chapter.		
	Write down ways in which within your current job personalized digital health could enable your customers.		

(Continued)

Work (Tasks) To Be Accomtplished	Target Date to Complete the Tasks	Write Down Your Next Steps

My Development Plan

If there is no application within your position, search within your company to find a committee you could serve on to enable digital health for your organization's customer(s).

Speak to your manager about your interest in digital health as a game changer for your organization and your desire to either serve on a committee, add this to your current role, or spearhead a new initiative at your company weaving personalized digital health for your customer base.

Update your resume with the digital health project you spearheaded to show your leadership skills and how you kept the needs of the customer at the forefront of your focus.

29. Accelerating Health and Innovation: Improving Health for All

Read the Chapter.

Write down what innovations you or your staff have developed and implemented within the past two years.

Honestly access if your management style encourages staff to innovate or whether you stifle it. Part of career development is broadening your span of control both formally and informally: How many employees from across the organization would want to be your employee because you encourage them to fail early and fast so that they are most successful?

Incorporate into you staff meetings and individual employee meetings questions about innovations they think could help your customers and their ideas to make the organization more productive.

Update your resume with the innovations you and/or your staff have developed (with words like "spearheaded...") to show your ability to adapt to change and lead a successful, cutting-edge team poising your organization for success.

30. The Health Workforce of the Future: Preparing Today for the Opportunities Ahead

Read the Chapter.

Work (Tasks) To Be Accomtplished		Target Date to Complete the Tasks	Write Down Your Next Steps
My Development Plan			
	If you don't already know, learn about how infomatics is currently utilized at your organization.		
	Consider a course in infomatics or an advanced degree to show your interest in leading future initiatives.		
	Review your interest with your manager along with your proposed next steps to obtain more information or education. Ask your manager for a stretch assignment to include the topic of informatics.		
	Update your resume with the infomatics courses and assignments you have completed.		
31. HIMSS TIGER™: A Global Interprofessional Community of Development and Growth			
	Read the Chapter.		
	Ask around your organization to learn of anyone's involvement in the TIGER Interprofessional Community.		
	Sign up for the TIGER newsletter: tiger@himss.org and join the TIGER Interprofessional Community at HIMSS.		
	Apply for mentorship by HIMSS staff or through the global TIGER volunteer network.		
	Download the TIGER Global infomatics definitions and Timeline (see link in the reading) and begin using the terminology with staff.		
	Update your resume with your mentorship.		
32. Disruptive Technology: It's About People, Culture, and Technology			
	Read the Chapter.		
	Understand to what extent your organization leverages data to provide better services or products to the customer (i.e., value).		
	Identify data in your area that could be utilized to develop a better service or product for your customer.		
	Review the findings with your staff to fine tune a proposal then present a plan to your manager asking for the resources to implement the change.		

(Continued)

Work (Tasks) To Be Accomtplished		Target Date to Complete the Tasks	Write Down Your Next Steps
My Development Plan			
	Update your resume indicating you and your staff found the need and implemented a game-changing service or product.		
33. Caring for the Underserved: Both a Professional and a Personal Responsibility			
	Read the Chapter.		
	Take the Harvard Implicit Personality test to discover your unconscious bias.		
	Review the different types of bias and make a plan of what you will change due to your unconscious bias.		
	Discover which type of disparities you are most passionate to help and research ways to help the group.		
	Review with your manager which group you'd like to help, ask for resources the company could provide, and encourage your staff to take the same Harvard test to begin their own journey.		
34. Applied Artificial Intelligence and Machine Learning: The Impact on the Health Informatics Workforce			
	Read the Chapter.		
	Understand how artificial intelligence (AI) and machine learning (ML) is used within your organization.		
	Become a planning visionary obsessed with the customer's experience to understand how AI and ML could be used.		
	Stay fresh on current AI and ML products at any upcoming HIMSS conferences or events.		
	Once you implement AI or ML, update your resume with the project and the value it provided the patient, payer, or provider.		
35. Establishing and Practicing Ethical Standards: Both a professional and Personal Responsibility			
	Read the Chapter.		
	Review the ethical standards and Codes of Conduct provided by your educational institution(s), certifications, or place of employment.		
	Research and read your organization's Code of Ethics governing the use of its customer's data.		

Work (Tasks) To Be Accomtplished	Target Date to Complete the Tasks	Write Down Your Next Steps
My Development Plan		
Reflect on how you have ensured your certification, education, or employer's ethical standards and Code of Conducts have been followed.		
Draft your own Ethical Standard or Code of Conduct so when issues arise, you have recorded your values and professional intentions. Review these with a close friend for feedback so you stay true to yourself.		
36. Global Workforce Trends of Today: A Health Informatics Perspective		
Read the Chapter.		
Make a list of how your organization is meeting the emergent global health informatics trends.		
Understand how cybersecurity protects your department's assets.		
Take a course on cybersecurity to better understand the risk and prevention.		
Consider an advanced degree and/or certification in cybersecurity.		
37. The Clinically Integrated Supply Chain: A Critical Component of Healthcare Delivery		
Read the Chapter.		
Research how your organization utilizes an integrated supply chain and how it increases patient safety.		
Take a course on supply chain management.		
Reflect on the strategy Mercy Health Systems used to understand the opportunities for improvement within your own department.		
Challenge your employees to be a part of the solution and brainstorm ways your department's work could produce a reduction in waste and/or increase time a clinician could provide care to a patient.		
Review the changes your department developed with your manager and include them in your resume to show the importance you place on customer needs along with your ability to add value to customer (i.e. clinician and patient).		
38. Protecting the Privacy and Security of Health Information: A Shared Responsibility		
Read the Chapter.		

(Continued)

Work (Tasks) To Be Accomtplished	Target Date to Complete the Tasks	Write Down Your Next Steps
My Development Plan		
Review confidentiality, integrity, and availability concepts with staff to ensure they understand its utmost importance. Ensure staff understand the threats, vulnerabilities, and attacks. Ensure staff understand HIPAA and GCPR. Involve your team in brainstorming on how they will better protect data in the future.		
39. Health Interoperability and Standards: An Overview		
Read the Chapter. Explain the Social Determinants of Health (SDOH) to staff so they understand how these could adversely affect the success of a future initiative. Challenge them to include efforts in future projects to ensure better success for patients. Keep updated on the information published by various public health interoperability initiatives to understand how they plan to better public health through public agencies. Understand which agency(s) your staff and organization are considered key stakeholders so can utilize the resources and information provided by the agency(s).		
40. Accelerating into the Future with Project Management		
Read the chapter. Define the components of project management.Identify ways to work smarter using project management principles.		
41. HIMSS Maturity Models: An Overview		
Read the chapter. Identify the importance of HIMSS Maturity Models for realizing digital health transformation.Identify the purpose of each HIMSS Maturity Model.		

CONCLUSION

In conclusion, even if your plan spans the next five to ten years, at least you are hoping to start at a point in time to plan for your future success and to meet your goals. Don't let the urgent in your life get in the way of the important (preparing for your future success).

Index

A

AACN. *See* American Association of Colleges of Nursing
ABP. *See* American Board of Pathology
ABPM. *See* American Board of Preventive Medicine
Academic transfer programs, 212
Accenture, 337, 341
ACCESS Health, 391
Accountability, 130, 348, 374
Accreditation, of university, 202
Accuracy, 261
Achievement, 159
Action, 142–143
Active listening, 139–140, 144, 191
Active parenting, 178
Active personalization, 265
Adaptability, 340
Administration leadership area, 110–111
Advanced Health Informatics Certification, 82
Advanced professional designation. *See* Professional designation
Adverse event reporting, 372–373
Afghanistan, 332
Africa, 357–358
Agency for Healthcare Research and Quality, 285, 353
Aggregators, 228–229
Aging population, 331
AHIC. *See* Advanced Health Informatics Certification
AHIMA. *See* American Health Informatics Management Association
AI. *See* Artificial intelligence
Alberta Health Services, 371–373
Amazon, 267
American Association of Colleges of Nursing, 303
American Board of Pathology, 80
American Board of Preventive Medicine, 80
American Express, 18
American Federation of Nurses, 67
American Health Information Management Association
    code of ethics, 347
    diversification, 28
    professional certifications offered by, 80
American Medical Informatics Association
    Advanced Health Informatics Certification from, 82
    electronic health record systems, 59
American National Standards Institute, 389
American Nurses Association, 67
American Nurses Credentialing Center, 80, 298
American Red Cross, 67
ANA. *See* American Nurses Association
Analyze Phase, of Personal Six Sigma, 247–248
ANCC. *See* American Nurses Credentialing Center
Anchoring, 20
Anderson, Merrill C., 127
ANSI. *See* American National Standards Institute
Apparel industry, 271

Apple, 15–16
Apps, health, 262–264
Arruda, William, 15, 18
Artificial intelligence
    in Africa, 357–358
    algorithms, 329, 358
    change brought by, 341
    core value of, 337
    data in, 338
    definition of, 339
    description of, 295, 320, 335–336
    healthcare outcomes affected by, 336
    in health organizations, 336
    health service delivery affected by, 337–338
    human function mimicked by, 337–338
    in intelligent health systems, 336–337
    user interface uses of, 339
Assignment descriptions, 245
Association of American Medical Colleges, 331
Associations. *See* Professional associations
Attention, 170
Attitude, 141–142
Audio podcasts, 216
Australia, 356–357, 391
Authenticity, 165
Authoritarian leadership, 158
Automation, 136
Automotive industry
    mass customization in, 271
    segmentation in, 269–270
Availability, 379

B

Baby Boomers, 159, 161–163
Baldridge Excellence Framework, 241
Banking segmentation, 268–269
Barton, Clara, 67
BBSs. *See* Bulletin board systems
Beck, Debra, 223
Belmont Report, 345
Benchmarking, 248
Beneficence, 345–346
Benevolence, 159
Bias, 328–329, 348, 357–358
Bioethics, 256, 344
BioMedIT, 355
Biometrics, 382
"Black swan event," 290
Blogs, 216, 228
Bodenheimer, Thomas, 284
Boston University, 75
Bowles, Hannah Riley, 182
Brainstorming, 286
Brand environment, 20–21
Branding, 8, 15–21

Printed in the United States
by Baker & Taylor Publisher Services